Fascist Voices

Fascist Voices

*An Intimate History of
Mussolini's Italy*

CHRISTOPHER DUGGAN

THE BODLEY HEAD
LONDON

Published by The Bodley Head 2012

2 4 6 8 10 9 7 5 3 1

Copyright © Christopher Duggan 2012

Christopher Duggan has asserted his right under the Copyright, Designs
and Patents Act 1988 to be identified as the author of this work

First published in Great Britain in 2012 by
The Bodley Head
Random House, 20 Vauxhall Bridge Road,
London SW1V 2SA

www.bodleyhead.co.uk
www.vintage-books.co.uk

Addresses for companies within The Random House Group Limited can be found at:
www.randomhouse.co.uk/offices.htm

The Random House Group Limited Reg. No. 954009

A CIP catalogue record for this book
is available from the British Library

ISBN 9781847921031

The Random House Group Limited supports The Forest Stewardship Council (FSC®),
the leading international forest certification organisation. Our books carrying the
FSC label are printed on FSC® certified paper. FSC is the only forest certification
scheme endorsed by the leading environmental organisations, including Greenpeace.
Our paper procurement policy can be found at
www.randomhouse.co.uk/environment

Typeset in Dante MT by Palimpsest Book Production Limited,
Falkirk, Stirlingshire

Printed and bound in Great Britain by
Clays Ltd, St Ives PLC

Contents

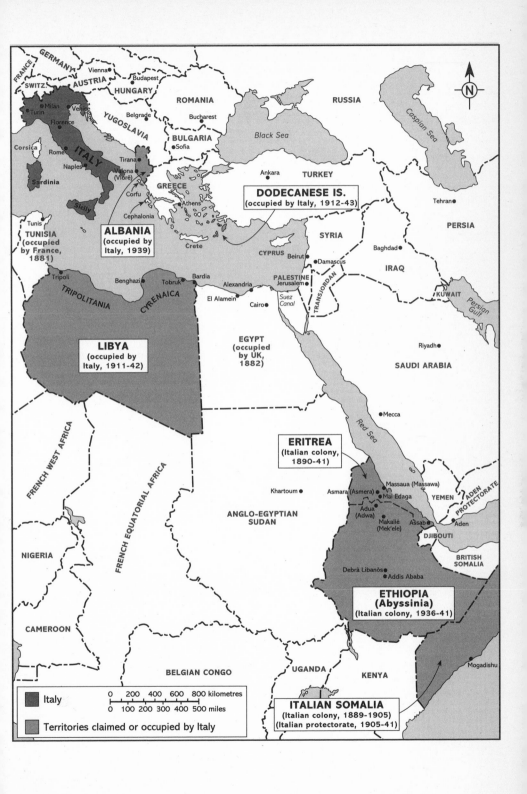

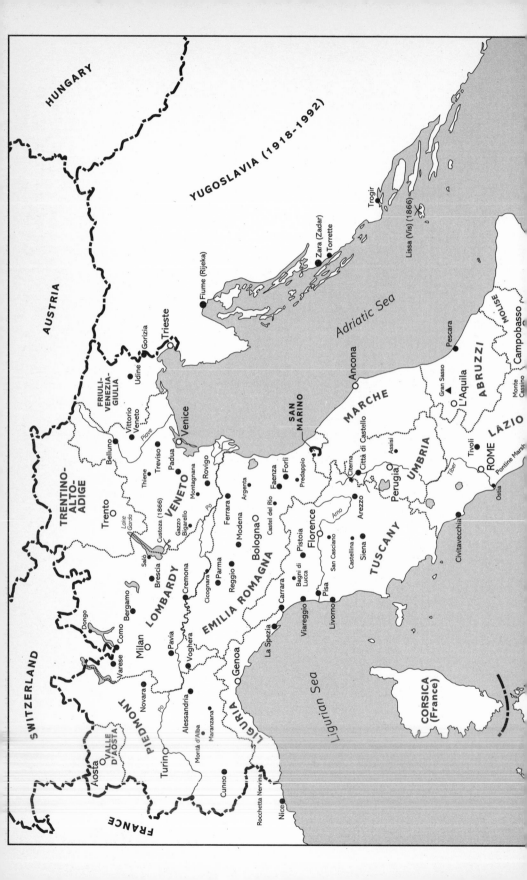

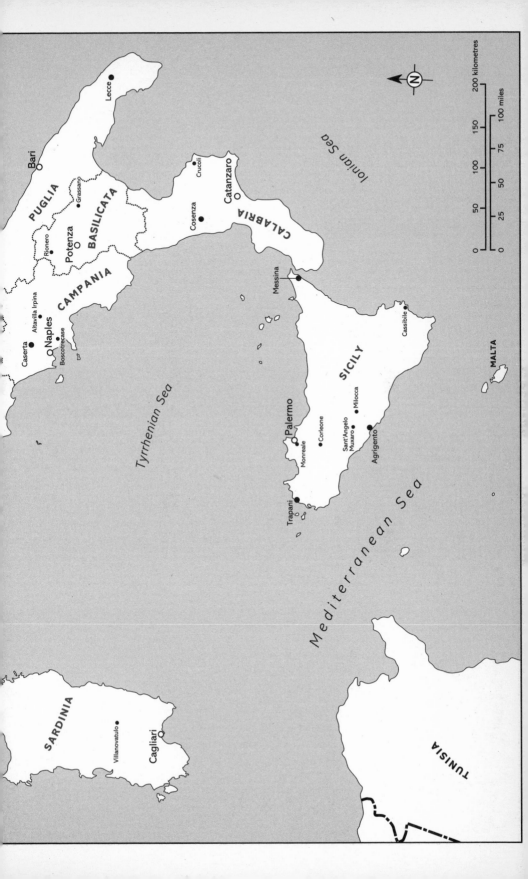

Preface

Carlo Ciseri is not a well-known Italian. For most of his long life he worked as a hotel manager in Florence. But to turn the pages of the diary that he kept from 1915 when, still in his teens, he attended military school in Modena, until his last years in a nursing home in the early 1980s, is to have a sense of something remarkable: what it felt like for an ordinary Italian to live through some of the most momentous events in the country's history. Here, in energetic handwriting, sometimes difficult to read, are the immediate thoughts of a proud ex-serviceman who has just found himself abused and taunted by socialists in a street in Milan in October 1919; a disaffected voter who, having sworn never to get involved in politics again, has heard Mussolini give a speech in March 1920 and been captivated; a confident young husband who has started to feel that the fascist government might restore to Italy 'the glories and honours of ancient Rome'; a patriotic middle-aged man who in December 1935 has donated his and his wife's wedding rings to the nation, 'with all my heart', in support of the conquest of Ethiopia; and a despondent prisoner of war in a British camp in Kenya who has almost fainted with incredulity upon learning of Mussolini's fall from power in July 1943.

A similar sense of immediacy emerges from the 122 boxes entitled 'sentimenti per il Duce' ('feelings for the Duce') that form part of the enormous archive – 4,227 boxes in total – of Mussolini's private secretariat, the Segreteria particolare del Duce. This office was created to deal with the constant flow of letters that were sent to the fascist leader in Rome – around 1,500 a day in the 1930s. The correspondence came from men, women and children of all social classes – though it should be remembered that there were still significant levels of illiteracy in Italy at this time, particularly among the poor (on the eve of the Second World War some 5 per cent of males and 7 per cent of females placed a cross rather than wrote their name in the marriage register). As with many of the government archives from the fascist period, what remains today of the secretariat is only a fraction of the original holdings, as much material was destroyed in the Second World War. But there is no reason to believe that it gives an unrepresentative picture of the relationship between Mussolini and members of the public.[1]

Inside the surviving boxes of 'feelings for the Duce', which date mostly from the later 1930s and early years of the war, are countless telegrams, letters, poems, drawings, paintings and photographs sent by ordinary Italians to Mussolini by way of congratulation, commiseration, thanks, encouragement or entreaty on a wide variety of occasions: following an attempt on his life or on his birthday and saint's day; when they wished to make an appointment to see him or after he had delivered an important speech; when a member of his family was ill or when they wanted him to stand as godfather to a new-born child; on a major fascist anniversary or during an international crisis; after they had had an interesting dream or when a husband or son had been killed in action. Partly, perhaps, because they make for somewhat unsettling reading, the contents have not attracted much attention from historians: the now rusty pins and paperclips that hold together the ageing sheets of paper have in most cases remained untouched since they were applied by fascist civil servants over seventy years ago.

The feelings that ordinary people articulated in Mussolini's Italy, and what these feelings might tell us about the appeal or otherwise of the regime, constitute the backbone of *Fascist Voices*. On one level the book is intended as a broad history of Italy between 1919 and 1945 – there is a general framing chronological narrative – but it does not set out to be a comprehensive survey of the period. There are many areas that receive little more than summary attention – the economy, welfare measures, cultural policies, and sport and leisure, to name but a few. The principal aim is rather to explore how men, women and children experienced and understood the regime in terms of their emotions, ideas, values, practices and expectations. The view from 'above', constructed largely with hindsight and free from the often disorientating fog of emotion and uncertainty that clouds the normal passage of time, is thus interspersed with perspectives from 'below' – making use of private diaries or letters to give a sense of how events were seen at the time. In some places memoirs have been employed, though these lack immediacy and pose questions about the reliability of authorial memory.

A number of the diaries used for this book are published. These include famous works by the likes of the constitutional lawyer and anti-fascist, Piero Calamandrei, the philosopher, Benedetto Croce and the fascist minister, Giuseppe Bottai, and also less well-known journals by such figures as the Padua student, Maria Teresa Rossetti, the Lombard priest, Don Primo Mazzolari, and the young Florentine blackshirt, Mario Piazzesi – the only diary of a rank-and-file member of an early fascist 'squad' to have come down to us. However, the great majority of the journals consulted are unpublished manuscripts or transcripts in the Archivio Diaristico Nazionale in the small town of Pieve Santo Stefano in eastern Tuscany and in the Archivio della Scrittura Popolare in Trento. Many of these two hundred or so diaries[2] were written during specific phases in the author's life, such as while serving in the army or being held in a prisoner of war camp, or, more briefly, when on a holiday or conducting a love affair, and contain only fleeting or indirect references to fascism – though these can often be revealing.

Yet, however immediate, the diaries – like other sources used in this book – present a number of major difficulties in assessing what ordinary people felt and thought under fascism. To begin with, there is the question of how 'representative' they are of Italian society of the time. There are two main problems here. The first is that the majority were written in the later years of the regime – particularly during the invasion of Ethiopia in 1935–6 and in the Second World War. For the 1920s the material is considerably less rich. The second relates to diary writing in general, which tends to be the preserve of the literate middle and upper classes. In the case of Italy this means a geographical bias in favour of the cities and larger towns over the countryside, and, to a certain extent, of the north over the south. However, one striking feature of the largest category of the unpublished diaries – those kept by soldiers – is the number that were written by men of modest (sometimes peasant) background and often rudimentary schooling. Spare time, a sense of adventure, and the proximity of death evidently acted as spurs to surmounting any feelings of educational inadequacy.

The letters filling the boxes of 'sentimenti per il Duce' in the Central State Archives in Rome raise similar issues. They, too, inevitably come predominantly from the literate sections of society. There is also the problem of knowing just what impelled so many Italians to seek direct contact with Mussolini – and therefore exactly how much these letters can tell us about popular opinion under fascism. In some cases the motives of those who wrote might have been at least in part mercenary: the hope that an expression of loyalty to the Duce would lead to material benefit of some kind. Since a majority of Italians lived in extreme hardship and the country as a whole was among the poorest in western Europe – average per capita income in Italy in 1934, measured in US dollars, was less than US$3,000, compared to US$4,239 in France and US$5,277 in Britain[3] – it is reasonable to assume that economic considerations motivated some writers and perhaps helped to shape the sentiments conveyed. But the effusive and seemingly spontaneous character of so much of the correspondence, and the fact that letters were not infrequently unsigned, suggest that more complex psychological and cultural forces were at work involving issues such as hope, reassurance, identity and trust.

Similar difficulties of interpretation relate to other sources used in this book to shed light on popular opinion under fascism. The reports sent by agents of the secret police service or by party and government officials to inform Rome about the political mood in the country cannot, as has often been pointed out, be taken entirely at face value.[4] Spies, for instance, had something of a vested interest in detecting and relaying negative comments about the regime: if they suggested that everything was well, they risked being seen as, at best, redundant, or at worst, incompetent or dishonest. A prefect who indicated that there were no grounds at all for concern in his province might equally be regarded by his superiors as out of touch or mendacious. At the same time, if he conveyed an extremely black and alarming picture, his superiors might be inclined to see him as the main cause of the problems – having given the impression that he was not in control. All official reports of what ordinary people were feeling or saying about fascism therefore need to be approached with a considerable element of caution.

Even if it is assumed, as historians are generally inclined to do, that reports of negative comments about fascism or Mussolini overheard in a bar, in a piazza or on a tram are for the most part likely to be accurate, there are further difficulties in assessing just what such statements might indicate about discontent or opposition. Irreverent jokes, for instance, which abounded under fascism as under all totalitarian systems, were part of the common currency of daily social intercourse. Grumbles and complaints about corrupt officials, administrative incompetence, food shortages, poor pay, inflation or unemployment were likewise staple features of everyday life in Mussolini's Italy. It is perfectly possible to imagine somebody finding it quite natural to be scathing about an aspect of the regime in a conversation with friends over a glass of wine or grappa, and yet on another occasion, in the privacy of the home, to feel inspired to write a letter of glowing and heartfelt praise to the Duce.

Even what would seem to be private sources for popular opinion under fascism need to be subject to certain caveats. The contents of a letter sent to a family member might be conditioned by an awareness that it could be read by censors; critical remarks about the regime were thus likely to be omitted. Conversely, it might have been calculated that an upbeat comment about Mussolini in a letter from a soldier to his wife could, as a result of being intercepted, earn the author the good will of the authorities. Diaries were also subject to a number of potential constraints on their contents. There was a risk the volume would fall into the hands of prying friends or relatives, or worse, of the police. More generally, there is the question of why the diary was being kept in the first place. Was it simply to provide an outlet for thoughts and feelings in the absence of a suitable person in whom to confide? Or was there an expectation that it would eventually be read by someone else? In the case of those serving in Ethiopia in 1935–6, for instance, a record of what they had been through might have been intended for family members after they got home (or if they were killed). Those with literary ambitions might even have been contemplating possible publication.[5]

These difficulties of interpretation posed by the sources are among the reasons why so little attention has been paid to the question of popular opinion in fascist Italy. Indeed, for a long time historians held the view that the machinery of oppression and propaganda in totalitarian regimes eliminated entirely the space for the expression of independent views and made any investigation of what ordinary people really thought impossible and meaningless. But in the case of Italy there have also been powerful ideological factors at work. The post-war Republic was built heavily on the idea that the inter-war regime had been a dictatorship from which the masses had been liberated by the Resistance movement (and the Allies) in 1943–5. Anything that suggested that fascism had enjoyed real support was unacceptable. When in 1974 the leading Italian historian of fascism, Renzo De Felice, claimed in the fourth volume of his exhaustive biography of Mussolini that by 1936 there was general 'consensus' for the regime, it caused an outcry – though De Felice had based his assertion not on any examination of what ordinary people thought as upon the absence of any visible or explicit opposition.

But even when investigations into popular opinion in totalitarian regimes such as Nazi Germany and the Soviet Union began to be undertaken more systematically from the 1980s, the picture in relation to fascist Italy did not change greatly. Politics again intruded. The end of the Cold War and the collapse of the two main parties on which the Republic had been built, the Christian Democrats and the Communists, opened the way in the 1990s for an assault on anti-fascism and the Resistance. It was now claimed by the new right of Silvio Berlusconi and his allies – including the neo-fascist (or 'post-fascist' as they chose to be styled) National Alliance party – that the fascist state had been unfairly demonised by the Communists. Mussolini had certainly made regrettable errors, they admitted – notably allying with the Nazis and passing racial laws – but overall his regime had been relatively benign. Emblematic in this respect was Berlusconi's claim in an interview with the *Spectator* in 2003 that 'Mussolini never killed anyone' and that the punishment of 'internal exile' (*confino*) had been a 'holiday'. In these circumstances evidence of the 'popularity' of fascism risked being exploited by the right as proof that the regime had in general been regarded as a force for good.

Bearing in mind their limitations, what can the sources used for this book tell us about popular opinion under fascism? The first point worth noting is how few of the diaries reveal any sense of serious antagonism to fascism and particularly to Mussolini. The fact that

most of the journals date from the 1930s and 1940s, after the regime
had brutally suppressed the opposition parties, eliminated space for
the articulation of serious dissidence and exposed the population to
years of blanket propaganda, helps to explain the generally uniform
tone of much of what was written. Nonetheless given that a common
motive for keeping a diary is to provide a forum in which to voice
feelings and thoughts that cannot be expressed openly, it is on the
whole surprising that there are not more signs of anger or disquiet,
particularly as the regime became drawn ever closer towards Nazi
Germany and war. The fact, too, that the diaries in Pieve Santo Stefano
have all been deposited by the authors or their families in the last
thirty or so years might, it would have been imagined, have favoured
the emergence into the public domain of inspiring records of political
protest or objection. There are some, and I have sought to give appropriate space to these in the book. But they are a small minority.

One powerful theme running through what people wrote in diaries
(and elsewhere) about fascism is the crucial importance of the figure
of Mussolini to emotional and political engagement with the regime.
There was certainly widespread discontent with many aspects of
everyday life – whether economic hardship, the incompetence and
corruption of state and party officials, or the apparent perverseness
of particular government measures – but it was very rare for grievances to spill over into criticism of Mussolini himself. Indeed the 'cult
of the Duce' harboured within it a mechanism (perhaps more psychological than ideological) whereby the notion of a blameless and benevolent leader, who would, if he had the information and the means,
intervene to rectify ills, was sustained in the face of often appalling
daily circumstances. When disasters occurred – and there were plenty
of them from 1940 – the tendency was to attribute blame not to the
Duce but to the corrupt, treacherous or incompetent ministers and
officials surrounding him. Mussolini became a victim rather than a
culprit, and in this way the trust that had been placed in him could
still appear justified (and continue).

The intensity of people's feelings towards Mussolini, evident in the
passionate letters that fill the boxes of the 'sentimenti per il Duce' as
well as in private diaries, makes it hard to discern the 'decline' of
fascism with any obvious clarity. The conventional view of the regime
is that it reached the apogee of its popularity with the conquest of

Ethiopia in 1935–6, and that thereafter its support began slipping steadily away as a result of the alliance with Germany, the racial laws, the so-called 'reform of customs', the hardship induced by economic autarky and the disastrous involvement in the Second World War. But certainly as far as the cult of the Duce is concerned, there was no simple link between disappointment and the withdrawal of support or trust. Indeed, the more people suffered the more they often seem to have looked towards Mussolini for hope. It was probably only in the course of the second half of 1942, as the inevitability of the disaster confronting Italy became almost impossible to deny, that the talismanic appeal of Mussolini began seriously to wane, at least on the home front.

Another reason why the regime's setbacks and failures did not automatically translate into an erosion of support for fascism lay in the absence of discernible alternatives. As many diaries indicate, a return to parliamentary democracy was for most people almost unthinkable. Liberalism was regarded as synonymous with weakness, division, licence and a betrayal of the dreams of national regeneration and greatness engendered by the patriotic movement of the Risorgimento in the nineteenth century. It was seen as having failed in Italy, and to go back to it would mean reverting to a political system that was widely considered to have been proved historically and cultur-ally unsuited to the needs of the country. Similarly communism and socialism appeared wholly unrealistic as potential substitutes for fascism. A few intellectuals inside Italy certainly began looking with interest at the Soviet Union in the 1930s; and there were residual sympathies still for socialism among sections of the working classes in the north and centre of the country. But the demonisation of the far left by fascism, and perhaps even more influentially by the Church, made it impossible to imagine how the introduction of socialism could do anything other than catastrophically split the nation.

In these circumstances disquiet and dissatisfaction found no clearly 'anti-fascist' channels into which to flow. Indeed the diaries of the late 1930s and early 1940s, particularly those kept by students, frequently confirm the suggestions made in some recent studies that the increased radicalism of the regime following the conquest of Ethiopia reflected a concern among intellectuals for Italian fascism to acquire a harder ideological edge.[6] The introduction of racial laws and the campaign against bourgeois values, while clearly very unpopular in many quarters, made sense to those who felt that the regime's goal of transforming Italy morally and spiritually had not been achieved – as the corruption, inefficiency and superficiality of so much of public life demonstrated. At the same time the dynamism of Nazi Germany indicated what might be accomplished with a more resolute fascist mindset. Many of the pulses of discontent in Italy were accordingly being directed into rather than against the regime. If things were not as they should be, the answer was to make fascism stronger and purer, not to jettison it. This remained a common view, it seems, well into the Second World War.

What some of the diaries and memoirs also reveal is the degree to which potential opposition was blunted by a central tenet of fascism: faith. The articulation of dissent was certainly fiercely curtailed by the repressive laws of 1925–6, the abolition of rival parties, the activities of the secret police, and various other measures designed to generate a 'totalitarian' society. But the barriers to protest were not simply the product of external constraints. As a number of the writers in this book indicate, 'rational' objections to particular policies of the regime – whether it was the introduction of the anti-semitic legislation or the alliance with Nazi Germany – could elicit anxieties in the minds of those entertaining critical thoughts about the status of their 'faith' and induce self-censorship. The enormous emphasis placed by the regime on belief, obedience and enthusiasm, and the constant assertion that the spiritual values of fascism were superior to the self-interested individualism of liberal cultures, acted as strong deterrents to entertaining seriously heterodox views and certainly to acting upon them. Indeed one of the definitions of faith was a capacity to survive the challenge of rational doubts.

It is certainly true that fascist Italy did not, unlike Stalin's Soviet Union, seek to open windows into the souls of men and women. In general it was content with external trappings of loyalty – manifestations of devotion to the Duce, wearing the appropriate uniform, making a Roman salute. Those who fell victim to the various purges of the party in the 1920s and early 1930s were usually expelled for allegations of impropriety or criminality, not for having heretical ideas: there were no show trials of the kind seen in Moscow in the later 1930s. It is also the case that Italy, in contrast to Russia, lacked a strong tradition among intellectuals of self-examination and a striving for personal improvement and connection with the forces of progress.[7] Nevertheless, a number of the diaries consulted for this book – for example those of Manlio La Sorsa, Giuseppe Caronia and Primo Boccaleri – indicate that the regime's obsession with forging 'new' Italians was internalised to the point of generating a desire to transcend old bourgeois and liberal habits and become attuned to the revolutionary mindset of fascism.

This raises the question of how much can be ascertained from diaries, letters and memoirs about the degree to which the ideology of fascism resonated with ordinary Italians and created an emotional and spontaneous – as opposed to formal and coerced – engagement with the regime. In the case of Nazi Germany it has been suggested that dissatisfaction with many aspects of everyday life was offset by widespread support for the visionary programme of national regeneration and greatness offered by Hitler – a programme that at least until 1942 seemed capable of realisation.[8] By contrast, it has been argued that in fascist Italy there was an absence of sufficiently 'big' (and credible) ideas to compensate for the relatively modest economic performance of the country in the 1920s and 1930s and the increasingly dispiriting picture of corruption, opportunism and incompetence presented by the party in many places. As a result, popular disgust with what was occurring at the grass-roots level was by the later 1930s, it is said, giving rise to disillusionment and apathy and a potentially terminal decline.[9]

The unpopularity of the party is beyond doubt: anger at the greed of provincial bosses is amply documented and was visible on the streets of many cities after Mussolini's fall on 25 July 1943 with targeted attacks on local officials. But this tier of discontent was just one part of the broad emotional framework surrounding fascism that this book seeks to chart. Against the grass-roots hostility towards the party needs to be set, for instance, the striking resilience of the cult of the Duce. As indicated above, this operated in a curious symbiosis with everyday grievances and often led people to imagine that when circumstances permitted Mussolini would descend like some latter-day Christ and drive the sordid money-changers from the temple. Such hopes were underpinned by an important component of the fascist leader's charisma: namely that he was in many key respects the antithesis of the average Italian – whose vices he was struggling to correct – not least in his probity and austere lifestyle.

Nor is it altogether clear that in the late 1930s there was a lack of 'big' ideas to counterbalance any growing sense of disillusionment with the regime. There was certainly much dislike of the alliance with Germany and a great deal of anxiety about the drift towards war. But as many diaries and letters indicate, the notion of a new European order, with the have-not nations replacing the old and selfish plutocratic democracies of Britain and France as the leading powers in the continent, reverberated widely. The enormous enthusiasm that surrounded the conquest of Ethiopia in 1935–6 and the sense of indignation that swept the country at what appeared to be the wholly unjust and hypocritical condemnation of the invasion by the League of Nations (led by Britain), underlined this point. A European conflict, it was commonly said after the Second World War had broken out, should result in 'peace with justice', with Italy finally gaining its fair share of the world's resources. The main concerns from 1940 were accordingly not so much with the justice of Italy's cause as with the lack of military preparation and the danger of Germany becoming too dominant and powerful.

What gave the idea of a new and fairer European order particular emotional resonance was that it connected with many highly charged themes in the country's collective memory. There was the resentment – which fascist propaganda never ceased to express – at the way Italy was felt to have been cheated out of its rightful share of territorial rewards at the Paris peace conference in 1919. There was the evocative concept of the 'proletarian nation' that the Nationalists had articulated in the years before the First World War to justify the pursuit of colonies, and which the poet Giovanni Pascoli had given currency to in a well-known patriotic speech at the time of the invasion of Libya in 1911. There were the traumatic memories of the humiliating defeat in Ethiopia at the Battle of Adua in 1896 and the sense of shame at the failure of liberal Italy to provide more support for the expansionist plans of the prime minister, Francesco Crispi, in the 1880s and 1890s. And further back still were the powerful hopes that had been generated by the Risorgimento and the rhetoric of the 'Third Rome'.

Other key aspects of fascism similarly acquired emotional force through the legacy of history. The idea of regenerating the Italian character, for instance, fed on a long tradition, which stretched back through the nineteenth century and beyond, of attributing the decline of the nation's fortunes since the Middle Ages to moral decay. Indeed, at the heart of the debates during the Risorgimento about how Italy could be resurrected and unification achieved had been discussions about the ways to overcome what were seen as the predominant vices of Italians. These included individualism, materialism, scepticism, indiscipline and indolence. A large part of the vitriol directed at liberalism in Italy from the 1870s arose from a belief that parliamentary government mirrored rather than corrected the weaknesses of the general population. A particular source of concern in the nineteenth century was the idea that Italians had lost the martial spirit that had once made them the masters of Europe. Again the obsession of the fascist regime with militarising the country resonated strongly against this backdrop.

In more general terms, as diaries and letters constantly indicate, many of the pivotal ideas and practices around which fascism was built derived enormous emotional charge from their intersection with the cultural landscape of the Church. The stress on faith and spirit; the emphasis on authority and hierarchy; the rejection of liberal individualism and socialist materialism; the glorification of martyrdom and self-sacrifice; the celebration of Rome and its universal mission; the extensive use of ritual and liturgy; the cult of the supreme leader – all these facets of the regime intertwined both morally and affectively with Catholicism. And the fact that the Church almost from the outset indicated its strong approval of Mussolini gave fascism a huge advantage over its liberal predecessor in terms of popular support. Of course, as was often pointed out, the doctrines of the Church and fascism were fundamentally at odds in key respects. But for most people it appears that the differences were obscured by the overlaps.

This raises the contentious question of whether fascism can be understood as a form of 'political religion'. Historians outside Italy have in recent years tended to shy away from this idea, preferring to view how people dealt with the gap between mundane reality and high-flown propaganda in more pragmatic terms. Ordinary Italians, it has been suggested, had little time for the grandiose rhetoric of fascism. Their principal concern was to survive in the face of economic hardship, the oppressive machinery of the police, the irksome demands of the party, and the corrupt behaviour of state and party officials. They did so through time-honoured practices such as evading unwelcome laws, string-pulling and clientelism, and by cynically going through the motions of consent in order to avoid trouble – being seen to cheer the Duce at a rally, donning a blackshirt or enrolling a son or daughter in the party youth organisations. The fact that enthusiasm for conventional religion and the Pope remained as strong as ever implies, it is argued, that Italians kept their spirituality in a separate box from fascism.[10]

This book does not seek to contribute directly to the debates about the validity of the concept of 'political religion' to the understanding of Italian fascism. Many of the often heated arguments on this score in the last twenty or so years have revolved around somewhat arid issues of definition.[11] However, in terms of how ordinary people related to fascism, it is hard, as the material presented here suggests, to ignore the dimension of religion – certainly in trying to understand what it was that gave the regime such a strong emotional impetus. And it was in terms of emotions that Mussolini's Italy was simultaneously so powerful and so insidious. In stressing the moral and political superiority of faith and obedience over rationality and criticism, the regime was able to mobilise huge swathes of previously untapped popular support. But at the same time, the ethos and institutions of fascism undermined constructive dissent at both individual and public level, fostered conformism and weakened the sense of personal responsibility. No less dangerously, the culture of enthusiasm promoted a pernicious disjuncture between words and reality. As crowds roared their support for the inflammatory rhetoric of Mussolini, the substance of what was being said – and the potential implications – easily became lost in the fog of collective euphoria. The consequences in terms of human suffering and death were to be incalculable.

The Fruits of Victory, 1919–20

Disillusion

Carlo Ciseri was born in Florence in 1896, into a family of distinguished artists. His grandfather, Antonio, had been one of the most successful painters of his generation, whose portraits of leading society figures and brilliantly coloured naturalistic canvases on religious themes – *Ecce Homo, The Incredulity of Saint Thomas, The Martyrdom of the Maccabees, The Apparition of the Sacred Heart of Jesus to the Blessed Alacoque, Our Lady of Lourdes* – can still be seen in many public and private collections and churches, especially in Tuscany. After Italy's entry into the First World War in May 1915, Carlo attended the prestigious Military Academy of Modena before being sent to serve as a junior officer on the front line that snaked north from the Gulf of Trieste across the Carso plateau, and around the Carnic Alps towards Trento, up to a height in some places of several thousand metres. More than half a million Italians perished on this brutally inhospitable front in three and a half years of fighting, most of them in the course of the eleven largely ineffective battles that were launched across the Isonzo river in an attempt to break through the Austrian lines and reach Ljubljana and Vienna. Carlo enrolled in the *bersaglieri*, a distinguished corps of mobile light infantry with proud patriotic traditions (and a highly distinctive uniform). Also serving in the *bersaglieri*, until he was wounded early in 1917, was a former socialist and journalist, Benito Mussolini.

Like many well-educated middle-class men, Carlo fought in the war hoping that a victory for Italy would finish the work of the Risorgimento, the movement for national independence and unity that had begun over a century earlier when the armies of Napoleon

Bonaparte had descended over the Alps and brought to the peninsula the revolutionary new concepts of liberty and popular sovereignty. The completion of the Risorgimento would not simply be territorial – the acquisition from Austria of the so-called 'unredeemed' lands of Trentino-Alto Adige and Trieste. More important was a desire to fulfil the frustrated moral ambitions of the patriots of the Risorgimento, of men such as Giuseppe Mazzini, who had wanted the unification of the country to inaugurate the 'Third Rome', with Italy resurrected once again as a leading political and cultural force in the world after centuries of decadence, internal divisions and humiliating domination by foreigners. And for such a regeneration to be achieved, it was vital, these patriots had argued, that unity should be the product of the will of 'the people', of ordinary men and women who felt sufficiently inspired by patriotic fervour to set aside centuries of municipal, regional and sectarian rivalry and discord, selflessly embrace the holy cause of the nation, and fight, and if need be die, for their fellow Italians.

As Mazzini and many other patriots ruefully acknowledged, such hopes had not been realised. Italy had not, in any meaningful sense, been created by 'the people'. The victories against Austria in 1859 that had resulted in Lombardy and subsequently Emilia-Romagna and Tuscany being united with Piedmont had been secured mainly by the French armies of Napoleon III, who had been looking to emulate his uncle and replace Austrian dominance in the peninsula with that of France. The defeat of the ruling Bourbon dynasty in Sicily and Naples the following year by Giuseppe Garibaldi and his volunteer followers had certainly owed much to local popular support; but the manner in which the southern provinces had then been annexed to northern Italy had been shaped more by the fears and ambitions of the king of Piedmont and his prime minister, Count Cavour, than by the will of 'the people'. Britain had also played a decisive part. Alarmed by Napoleon's expansionist goals, it had seen in Italian unification a means of restoring the 'balance of power' on the European continent. It had thus warned off the French emperor from intervening to stop Garibaldi and had been quick to sanction the blatant violations of international law that the events of 1860 entailed.

Nor had 1860 ushered in any glorious era of the 'Third Rome', and the gulf between the grandiloquent rhetoric of the Risorgimento and the prosaic reality of a country beset by grinding poverty, mass illiteracy and persistent internal divisions was glaring. As one of the most prominent patriots of the Risorgimento, Francesco Crispi, frequently remarked in the decades that followed unification, the crude stitching with which the different parts of the peninsula had been hurriedly sewn together in 1859–60 remained only too visible.[1] Old territorial rivalries, such as those between Lombardy and Piedmont, Naples and Sicily, Milan and Rome, and, above all, between the northern and southern halves of the peninsula, remained largely intact and undermined the workings of parliament and the bureaucracy. And onto these traditional regional and municipal rifts had been grafted new and in many ways more insidious divisions: such as that between the state and the Catholic Church – which from the outset had refused to acknowledge the legitimacy of the Kingdom of Italy and had urged the faithful (and nearly all Italians were Catholic and liked to consider themselves acceptably faithful) to boycott the political life of the country and work to restore the Pope's temporal power.

Perhaps even more damaging to the hopes of national greatness that the Risorgimento had inspired had been the yawning chasm that had separated the ruling classes from the mass of the population – a chasm commonly referred to as that between 'legal Italy' (the Italy of those who were entrusted with the vote – around 2 per cent of the population at the time of unification, rising to about 7 per cent towards the end of the century) and 'real Italy'. This gap had found expression in frequent revolts and insurrections, beginning in the early 1860s with what the government had euphemistically termed the 'great brig-andage', a smokescreen for a largely political and social revolt by huge swathes of the southern peasantry against a state whose imposition of high taxes and military service and confiscation of Church property rendered it odious if not illegitimate to the poor. The decades that followed had witnessed further widespread and violent manifestations of popular discontent; and from the 1880s this discontent had secured a potent political voice in a fast growing socialist movement, whose revolutionary character had shown little sign of abating in the years prior to the First World War.

The hopes of young intellectuals like Carlo that a solution to Italy's problems lay in a great war – that a collective national endeavour against a common enemy, crowned by the euphoria of victory and a sense of shared grief at the sacrifice of the fallen, would kindle those feelings of mass patriotism that Mazzini and the other protagonists of the Risorgimento had dreamed of generating – had a long pedigree. In the spring of 1866 Francesco Crispi had called in parliament for a 'baptism of blood' to consolidate the new kingdom. His words had been greeted with loud applause from his fellow deputies. Many other leading politicians, writers and journalists had invoked a similarly bellicose solution to Italy's problems in the years that followed. The sirens of war had grown especially loud in the late 1880s and 1890s as a collapse in the public finances, a corruption scandal that was threatening to engulf the entire political establishment (including the monarchy), and escalating social disorder and unrest, combined to produce a widespread fear that the country was heading towards disintegration.

But there was a fatal paradox in such desperate hopes that a 'baptism of blood' would cement the nation. As the crushing victories of the Prussian army against the French in 1870 had underlined, success in modern warfare required enormous resources, meticulous planning and coordination, and huge forces of fit, well-trained and highly motivated soldiers. Italy was still an economically backward country, with weak state structures and a population that was largely deficient in health, education and patriotism. In the summer of 1866 the new kingdom had decided to enter the Austro-Prussian conflict: it could have stayed neutral and still secured from Austria the territories that it claimed. 'We must win', an excited young student, Sidney Sonnino, had noted in his diary, 'for a new nation like ours cannot continue in a state of tension for so long without falling to pieces.'[2] (Nearly half a century afterwards, as the country's Foreign Minister, Sonnino was to take Italy into the First World War.) A fatal lack of preparation, and divisions among the commanders, had led to catastrophic defeats on land and sea at the battles of Custoza and Lissa. Thirty years later the country had suffered another humiliation, when a force of 17,700 Italian and native troops had been annihilated by more than 100,000 Ethiopians at the Battle of Adua – the worst defeat ever suffered by a colonial power in Africa. As in 1866, the government had been pressing for military success to bolster the beleaguered institutions and alleviate internal political tensions. And again inadequate planning and coordination (as well as insufficient resources) had been largely to blame for the disaster.

Italy's involvement in the First World War had been motivated in large measure by a similar desire to strengthen the prestige of the state and allay what had seemed a growing threat of revolution. In June 1914 hundreds of workers had been killed and wounded in pitched battles with the police and army in northern and central Italy as socialists, anarchists, and republicans had taken to the streets in protest at the shooting in Ancona of three young demonstrators. Public buildings had been burned, barricades erected, tax registers destroyed, trees of liberty planted, telegraph wires cut, railway stations seized and churches ransacked. A few weeks later, war had broken out in Europe. Italy had not been obliged to enter the conflict: although it was allied to Austria and Germany under the Triple Alliance of 1882, the terms of the treaty did not, as strictly interpreted, compel it to come to the aid of the central European powers. However, the prime minister, Antonio Salandra, and the Foreign Minister, Sonnino, had believed that neutrality posed a bigger threat politically to Italy than intervention, and on 24 May 1915, amid noisy demonstrations up and down the country of patriotic pro-war students like Carlo, Italy entered the conflict on the side of Britain and France.

Carlo's hopes that the war would unite the country proved unfounded. Italy began hostilities acrimoniously split between those who supported intervention and those who were opposed to it. In favour were members of the recently founded authoritarian and anti-parliamentary Nationalist Party, right-wing liberals, democrats (who thought mobilisation would encourage the state to open out to the masses), the Futurists – a flamboyant literary and artistic movement, whose 1909 manifesto had declared war to be 'the only cure for the world' – and, on the far left, various revolutionary syndicalists and dissident socialists (among them Mussolini), who believed that participation in the war might generate a more revolutionary environment than neutrality. Against them were ranged a majority of liberals in parliament, led by the four-times prime minister Giovanni Giolitti (who argued that Italy stood to gain a 'great deal' (*parecchio*) by negotiating with both sides the price of its abstention from the conflict), many Catholics and the Socialist Party. The latter was the only socialist party in the belligerent countries, with the exception of Russia, not to give its positive support to the government.

When Italy's war ended with the proclamation of victory on

4 November 1918, the country was still deeply split. The exertions
and sacrifices of three and a half years of bloody conflict had done
little to heal the divisions of 1914–15. If anything, the rifts had deep-
·ened. In October 1917 the Italian army had suffered a disastrous
reverse at Caporetto (present-day Kobarid in Slovenia), causing the
entire Isonzo army of around a million men to fall back in disarray
for over 100 kilometres to the Piave river, deep inside the Veneto,
with the loss of some 300,000 prisoners (and 400,000 deserters).
Violent recriminations had ensued. The supporters of intervention
had rounded on the socialists, accusing them of undermining the
·morale of the troops with subversive propaganda (the Bolshevik
seizure of power in Russia coincided almost exactly with Caporetto).
The Church had also been held responsible: in August 1917 Pope
Benedict XV had publicly described the conflict as a 'useless slaughter',
leading some senior figures in the army to call for his arrest and
hanging. There had also been widespread anger towards the liberal
government – and towards parliament in general, whose broadly
neutralist stance in 1914–15 had not been forgotten or forgiven, and
whose commitment to the war effort, and handling of it, were now
vociferously called into question.

It was thus to a deeply divided and unsettled country that Carlo
returned from the front in 1919. Emboldened by the success of the
Bolshevik revolution, and by a rapidly deteriorating economic situation, with manufacturers scaling down production from wartime levels,
unemployment mounting and inflation soaring, socialist leaders urged
Italian workers to militancy. Strikes, lockouts, factory occupations and
riots became commonplace. At its Bologna congress in October 1919
the Italian Socialist Party (PSI) proclaimed the Russian revolution to
be 'the most auspicious event in the history of the proletariat' and
demandèd that the 'instruments of oppression and exploitation of the
rule of the bourgeoisie – states, communes and public administrations',
be replaced with 'new proletarian organs'. It called on its followers
'to make use of violence, for defence against the violence of the
bourgeoisie, for the conquest of power, and for the consolidation of
revolutionary gains'.[3] In the streets of major towns and cities,
supporters of the socialists taunted officers in uniform as 'vile
warmongers' and 'capitalist lackeys', and even ejected them from trains
and trams.[4] As one returning officer, Emilio Lussu, himself of left-wing

inclinations – he was later to be a prominent anti-fascist – noted, it
was a bizarre and politically damaging situation. In the large factories
in particular, he said, the workers harboured 'the most passionate
hostility to the war':

> They had not taken part in it, but they continued to oppose it, almost
> as if it was still to break out rather than being over. In practice, this
> hostility expressed itself in scorn for all those who had fought, as if
> for the last four years the latter had been on some wild spree. This
> attitude was shortly to contribute greatly to the workers losing the
> sympathy of veterans and serving soldiers.[5]

Carlo was horrified by this situation. In October 1919 he was
stationed in Milan, and found himself abused by socialists, who jeered
at his *bersagliere* uniform and hurled insults at the army and the state.
On one occasion he felt in serious danger and had to get fellow soldiers
to come to his help. He was angry: angry at the socialists, but even
more angry at the government, which seemed incapable of keeping
order and defending the patriotic ideals for which he and so many
others had fought. His frustration boiled over into the diary that he
had kept intermittently since the start of the war. 'What desperate
disappointment!' he wrote, thinking back to the situation in May 1915
(with considerable disingenuousness). 'The great Italian family that
intervened, entirely united, at the right moment in the great war, is
today fragmented, horribly divided and horribly sick, feverish with a
dangerous illness: anarchy.' Even the women who had cheered the
returning troops a few months before were now in the piazzas singing
'Bandiera Rossa' ('Red Flag'). 'I feel at sea . . . I cannot begin to understand how, as a result of these vile political ideas, people can hate each
other so much that brother kills brother, when instead we ought all
to be united in restoring the nation, above all economically, and saving
it from the disastrous consequences of the war.' His hopes had been
shattered: 'I believe in nothing any longer.' He was almost ashamed
to be Italian. Above all, he hated politics and politicians, and confided to
his diary an oath, underlining the words heavily:

> In the most solemn manner: <u>I swear that I will never again concern
> myself with politics, that I will never belong to any party – my only</u>

<u>political party, my only big ideal, will be my family: my Father, my
Mother, my brothers, and one day my children.</u>

But he could not turn his back altogether on his beloved Italy, and he
prayed that somebody might yet arise to redeem it: 'Long live a new
Italy of peace and of grandeur! And it is with this great hope that I
direct a prayer to God and ask for an act of his mercy: that he will
grant to us a man who, overcoming everyone and everything, might
conquer and rule in true justice.'[6]

One slight consolation for Carlo came from reading *Il Popolo d'Italia*,
the newspaper that Mussolini had founded at the time he had broken
with the Socialist Party towards the end of 1914 in order to promote
the cause of intervention. Carlo was attracted by the passion of
Mussolini's articles in defence of those who had fought in the war
and by his support for the cause of the *bersaglieri* in particular. In
March 1920 he had an opportunity to hear Mussolini speak at a reception at the Grande Italia hotel in Milan. It was something of an
epiphany for him:

> I immediately felt drawn to him hugely. I liked his words, I liked his
> pride, his force, and the look in his eyes . . . I am not wrong. For some
> time I have seen something exceptional in this man. It gives me hope,
> real hope, that this man has put himself at the head of a movement
> that can fight back and founded what he calls the Fasci di combattimento.
> This movement could be the beginning of a return to good sense; the
> beginning of a new and better era than the present one. I had resolved
> never to talk of politics again – but how can you not feel a sense of
> joy when you see brightness on the horizon?[7]

In the months that followed, Carlo was still prey predominantly to
feelings of anger and disgust rather than of hope. In the spring of 1920
he was finally demobilised and returned to his native Florence. He found
the city 'a boiling cauldron', seething, like Milan, with militant strikers
and demonstrators. He was afraid at times to leave the house and
confessed in his diary that he was tempted to take out his pistol and use
it against the socialists. But that would be to kill fellow Italians, an unacceptable act of fratricide. He railed against the British and the French for
having deprived Italy of its just rewards at the peace conference in Paris

in 1919, and stripping the victory of its value; and he wrote of his murderous feelings towards the prime minister, Francesco Saverio Nitti ('that pig Nitti'), for failing to defend Italian interests and having humiliated the army by giving an amnesty to deserters.[8] To add to his sense of despondency there was his financial situation. Ideally, he wanted to be an artist or a musician (or perhaps a writer: he offloaded many of his strong feelings into his diary in romantic verse), but he needed in the meantime to secure remunerative work. However, like so many of the more than 2 million demobbed soldiers he struggled to find anything. Eventually he found a temporary job as a travelling salesman for a coal company. But this was not what he had dreamed of doing. By the autumn of 1922 he felt on the edge of nervous collapse.

'A voice of force . . . a man'

Carlo was far from alone in longing for 'a man' who might restore the fortunes of Italy. The notion of a providential figure who could bring peace and order to a troubled land derived powerful cultural sanction from two of Italy's most celebrated writers, Dante and Machiavelli. Both had seen discord and division as the besetting evils of Italian society, and both had linked the restoration of unity and harmony in the peninsula to the emergence of an exceptional individual. Popular millenarian traditions and Catholic ideas of sainthood offered further strands of validation for messianic and salvationist ideas. Intellectually the years before the First World War had witnessed growing interest in the nature of 'charismatic authority', with philosophers, political thinkers, sociologists and psychologists everywhere placing increased emphasis on the irrational, the subconscious and the mythic as determining elements in social behaviour. Friedrich Nietzsche had celebrated the heroic man of genius and the will to power, while Gustave Le Bon had analysed the emotional susceptibility of the masses to strong leaders. In Italy, Nietzsche's exaltation of the morally transgressive superman found self-conscious expression in the flamboyant lifestyle of the celebrated poet, playwright and novelist, Gabriele D'Annunzio. Le Bon's ideas about the psychology of crowds (which Mussolini admired) were developed by influential sociologists such as Scipio Sighele.

The calls for a strong and inspirational leader in Italy had gathered momentum from the 1890s. This decade was economically and politically the darkest since unification. A crisis in the banking sector brought the country to the verge of insolvency in 1893. The credibility of parliament was all but shattered by the Banca Romana scandal, when dozens of leading politicians were found to have taken loans from a bank that had been operating illegally. Riots in many parts of the country raised the spectre of a socialist revolution; martial law was declared in Sicily in 1894 and 40,000 troops dispatched to the island to restore order. The defeat in Ethiopia at Adua in 1896 led to further violence on the streets. It also brought an abrupt end to the political career of the prime minister Francesco Crispi, the one man whom many had for some time believed was sufficiently authoritative to hold the country together and onto whom almost messianic hopes had been projected.[9] The final years of the century witnessed yet more serious rioting, unruly scenes in the Chamber of Deputies, and a succession of weak governments. In July 1900 the king, Umberto I, was assassinated by an anarchist.

Amid the chaos there were repeated demands for an end to parliamentary government. The initial hopes of many conservatives were that the king might be persuaded to use the powers he had under the constitution (the Statuto) and ensure that the executive answered to the Crown and not the Chamber of Deputies. A former cabinet minister went so far as to warn Umberto publicly in 1893 that if he failed to take strong action, the common people might lose faith in the monarchy (which for them was necessarily 'an ideal') and the dynasty fall: 'They will see there the greatest impotence where fantasy had suggested to them the greatest power'.[10] A few years later, another former minister, Sidney Sonnino, pleaded with the king in a famous article to seize the initiative: 'Your Majesty . . . The executive power resides in You alone. You alone have the right to appoint and dismiss ministers . . . The Nation looks to You and trusts in You . . . Sire, beware!'[11] What Sonnino was hoping for was something akin to the German system of a strong chancellor who answered exclusively to the Crown. Crispi also openly favoured the German constitutional arrangement, and even suggested abolishing the Chamber altogether and replacing it with the purely consultative and non-elective Senate. 'The parliamentary system is not suited to the Latin peoples', he told

Queen Margherita in 1897, echoing fashionable views of contemporary sociologists about the tendency of assemblies and crowds to accentuate the excessive individualism and emotional volatility of southerners.[12]

But Umberto was a colourless and timid character, with little desire to take time away from his mistresses, horses and hunting by assuming an active political role. His son, Victor Emmanuel III, who succeeded him in 1900, was similarly lacking in political ambition (his great passion was coin collecting, for which he received an honorary degree from Oxford University). He was content to let the parliamentary system continue in much the same vein as before. The man who dominated government in the early years of the century, and gave his name to the entire pre-war era in Italy, was Giovanni Giolitti. Giolitti was a shrewd Piedmontese liberal, who in contrast to his predecessors believed that the socialists could be steered from the path of revolution and brought into the constitutional fold by economic, social and political reforms that would improve the condition of the working classes. But Giolitti's progressive programme was not matched by a change in the conduct or the image of parliament. Indeed, many commentators regarded Giolitti as the acme of immorality and corruption. In 1910 a well-known left-wing intellectual, Gaetano Salvemini, branded him 'the minister of the underworld' for his collusion with criminal elements in elections in southern Italy.

Giolitti's efforts to entice the socialists towards government were facilitated by an upturn in the economy, which led to the country's first industrial boom. Italy had been an overwhelmingly agricultural society at the time of unification, with some 70 per cent of the labour force employed on the land – perhaps three times the figure for Britain. In the absence of substantial deposits of coal and other minerals, the only manufacturing sector of importance had been that of textiles, silk especially, concentrated in the Alpine valleys of the far north. However, between 1896 and 1908 the industrial output of the country nearly doubled in value, with particularly notable increases in 'newer' areas such as engineering, chemicals, steel and rubber. Rural labourers moved from the countryside to find work in factories, and cities grew fast: net immigration into Milan stood at around 14,000 in these years and its population nearly doubled between 1880 and 1914 to 600,000. One striking indicator of Italy's first serious taste of economic modernity was its burgeoning automobile sector. In 1899 a young cavalry officer, Giovanni Agnelli, established the Fabbrica Italiana Automobili Torino (Fiat). His example was soon followed by a host of other entrepreneurs. By 1907 the country had 61 companies producing 18,000 vehicles a year, mostly in Turin and Milan.[13]

However, the modernisation of the first years of the century was confined principally to the 'industrial triangle' of the north-west (Turin–Milan–Genoa). Italy as a whole remained a predominantly agricultural and largely backward-looking society of landless labourers, smallholders and sharecroppers. Across the south in particular, methods of farming had scarcely altered in centuries, and here most peasants continued to scratch out a living on small plots of thin and stony soil, often leased from wealthy absentee owners whose attitudes to the rural workforce were feudal still in both spirit and practice. High population densities meant that wages remained low and under-employment widespread, especially in the wet autumn and winter months when there was very little to do in the fields. Malaria and other endemic diseases ensured that life expectancy was in most places scarcely more than forty. For the great majority of southerners the only avenue of escape from grinding poverty was emigration overseas. Between the 1890s and the First World War millions took advantage of cheaper fares on steamships to find employment in the booming industrial centres of North America.

The growth of manufacturing in the north-west of the peninsula in the first years of the century contributed to the development of a strong urban trade union movement. But the socialist party in Italy remained heavily rural in character, with the backbone of its support among the peasants of the Po valley and the central regions. In the small settlements of Lombardy, Emilia-Romagna, Tuscany and Umbria the PSI controlled large networks of cooperatives, mutual-aid societies, leagues and Chambers of Labour; and the atmosphere in many of these communities was confrontational, with clashes between local landowners and farm workers over pay and conditions often turning violent. Giolitti's guarantee of strict governmental neutrality in labour disputes – he maintained that the unfettered struggle between employers and employees would stimulate economic growth as well as result in better living standards for workers – encouraged the militancy. There were over 1,500 strikes, involving nearly 350,000 workers in agriculture and industry, in 1906–10.[14] The success of many of these strikes was an important factor in the continued growth of the socialist party at this time. In the elections of 1900 the PSI secured 216,000 votes and 32 deputies. By 1913 its tally had increased to 79 deputies and around a quarter of all the votes cast.

Among the fiercest critics of Giolitti's conciliatory approach to the working-class movement were the supporters of Nationalism, a movement that emerged at the turn of the century as a reaction against socialism and the perceived weakness of Italy's ruling class. The leading Nationalists were for the most part highly educated young men, often with strong literary ambitions. Enrico Corradini, for instance, who became spokesman for the dominant imperialist wing of the movement, trained as a priest before turning his hand (unsuccessfully) in the 1890s to writing novels and plays with *fin de siècle* titles such as *Virginity* and *After Death*; and throughout his career he continued to produce fiction and drama alongside political works and a vast amount of journalism. Many Nationalists were inspired by a crusading idealism born of sublimated Catholicism ('I have always sensed in the depths of my soul a religious and priestly mission', Giovanni Amendola confessed in 1904),[15] or a desire to reactivate the frustrated national hopes of Mazzini – whose reputation underwent a remarkable resurgence from the start of the century. As the writer Giovanni Papini said in 1906:

> I feel – like a Mazzinian of the old days – that I can have a mission in my country and that I must do everything to make Italy less deaf, less blind and less craven . . . Rome has always had a universal, dominating mission . . . [It] must become once again the centre of the world and a new form of universal power take its seat there . . . The Third Rome, the Rome of the ideal, must be the fruit of our will and our work.[16]

The Nationalists used journals such as *Il Regno* (1903) and (most famously) *La Voce* (1908) as the main vehicles for their ideas. The contributors included nearly all the most talented younger writers and thinkers in the country, who came together around a common platform of dislike of the status quo and a belief that a 'party of intellectuals' was needed to save Italy from its current degenerate ruling class. The Nationalists were convinced that the country was mediocre and morally impoverished, and they sought a 'spiritual' revolution: though precisely what form the revolution should take was unclear. In general, they had a sharper sense of what they hated than what they liked. They loathed parliament and the corruption of the capital: 'Rome is . . . the fundamental cause of all our economic, moral and intellectual backwardness . . . Fish begin to stink from their heads: Italy from Rome.'[17] They saw socialism as dangerous: its doctrines were materialistic, divisive, devoid of higher spiritual values, and intrinsically selfish. And they despised Giolitti, whom they regarded as sordidly pragmatic, lacking in idealism, and deeply misguided in thinking that the forces of the far left could in effect simply be bought off with piecemeal social, economic and political reforms.

The Nationalists became a highly influential political and cultural force in Italy in the years immediately prior to the First World War. They enjoyed widespread support among academics, students, army officers, diplomats, industrialists and landowners. In general terms they saw the solution to Italy's problems as lying in the mobilisation of all social classes around an idealised vision of the nation, with an aggressive foreign policy considered as a key instrument for whipping up popular enthusiasm. Visionary leadership was also required. As the writer Giuseppe Prezzolini explained in 1904, the trouble with Italy's middle classes was not their economic weakness, but the lack of someone to inspire them: 'What the Italian bourgeoisie has missed hitherto is an example and a voice of force . . . in other words a man.'[18] And the same year, looking back nostalgically to Francesco Crispi, who for a time had seemed to give the country the unity it needed, Papini described his ideal national leader:

> He is at one with the fatherland as the mystic is at one with God . . . [H]e is a guide and a chief . . . He must be like the pillar of fire that led the people of Jehovah through the desert. He must light the way and point out the goal . . . a lynx-eyed pilot with a fist of iron destined to take his people towards a higher destiny.[19]

Like most of his fellow Nationalists, Giovanni Papini was in due course to vest his hopes in Benito Mussolini as the man to drag the country out of the morass of weak and corrupt parliamentary government and lead it towards the spiritual heights of a glorious Third Rome.

By the time of Italy's entry into the First World War, the tension that existed in the minds of young men like Papini (and Carlo Ciseri) between a sense of despondency at the moral and political bankruptcy of the nation and a craving for Italy's spiritual renewal, was unresolved. And those who led the country from 1915 to 1918 did not seem to offer much prospect of change. They were for the most part uninspiring, conservative (and elderly) liberals. The generals, too, were lacking in flare and imagination. The one man who stood out from the crowd and succeeded in touching a popular chord was the writer Gabriele D'Annunzio. He had been among the most vocal supporters of Italy's intervention, and in May 1915 had incited a crowd in Rome, with characteristic extremism, to turn its anger on the neutralists and kill them as traitors ('should blood flow, that blood would be as blessed as any shed in the trenches').[20] During the war he served as a volunteer and led a series of daring and much publicised air and naval raids that earned him a string of medals for valour. His bald head, diminutive and wiry physique and distinctive oratory, laced with religious and mystical language, captivated crowds. A young middle-class officer, Attilio Frescura, heard him speak in the summer of 1916 and was mesmerised – not least by his singular appearance:

> [H]e took off his dark glasses and his cap. I could see his shining skull and translucent and emaciated face. He spoke. The Poet's eye did not look. When speaking, Gabriele D'Annunzio becomes an abstraction. He is not among the crowd. Even though he dominates it, he is above and beyond it. He did not talk to us, but to someone over his audience: to the race. The Poet was clearly improvising. And the exertion of finding the perfect form in which to express his ideas caused a large vein to stand out, thick and throbbing, from his neck up to his left temple and across his skull.[21]

The feeling that D'Annunzio somehow spoke for the superior interests of the nation or 'race' was widely shared by intellectuals like Attilio, and when the war ended, and chaos and disillusionment ensued, it was initially towards the poet-hero that many of those who had pressed for intervention turned to realise their hopes. The sense of expectation was great: 'We wait nervously . . . straining our eyes to the horizon whence a star might arise to bring us again the longed-for day', wrote the distinguished philosopher and future Minister of Education under fascism, Giovanni Gentile, in 1919.[22] The Nationalists, Futurists and others who had taken to the piazzas in May 1915 and pushed (as they saw it) a pusillanimous parliament into declaring war, regarded the conflict as having been primarily 'theirs'. The victory should be theirs too: they had little confidence in the country's liberal leaders to secure a settlement worthy of the nation's huge sacrifice. A few days before the armistice Gabriele D'Annunzio published a poem warning those who would soon be assembling to discuss the peace treaties not to 'mutilate' Italy's victory:

> Who would transform the greatness and beauty of this violence into
> a long debate between old men, in a senile council of trickery?
> The ink of scribes for the blood of martyrs? . . .
> Oh victory of ours: you will not be mutilated. Nobody will break your
> knees or clip your wings.[23]

The mutilated victory

Italy had negotiated its entry into the war in 1914–15 in a spirit of what the prime minister, Antonio Salandra, had rather cynically referred to in public as 'sacred egoism'. Salandra and the Foreign Minister, Sidney Sonnino, had sought the best possible territorial deal for the country, and had driven a hard bargain. On 26 April 1915 the Treaty of London had been signed secretly with Britain, France and Russia. Under this pact, Italy was to declare war on Austria and Germany within a month, and in the event of victory would receive Trentino, the South Tyrol and Trieste, Istria, much of Dalmatia, the islands of the upper Adriatic, the Dodecanese islands (which it had already occupied after invading Libya in 1911), a protectorate over central Albania, the port of Valona, and a share of Germany's African and Asian colonies. Italy did not in fact declare war on Germany until August 1916, a delay that helped to relegate the Alpine front in the imagination of the British and French to something of a sideshow to the principal theatre of operations against the Germans in eastern France. It also reinforced long-standing prejudices in Paris and London about the unreliability of Italy in international affairs. As far as Germany was concerned, Italy's defection from the Triple Alliance in 1915 left a residue of mistrust and resentment that was to cloud relations between the two countries for many years to come, and even after they became formal allies again in 1939.

By the time the war finished, and the delegates began to converge on Paris for the peace conference that opened there in January 1919, the Treaty of London had been made public by the Bolsheviks. The extent of the claims made by Italy sat uncomfortably with the spirit of idealism that the American president, Woodrow Wilson, was intending to inject into international relations. He wanted the 'principle of nationality' to be the touchstone of the new Europe. However, the mood in Italy was uncompromising. Whipped up by D'Annunzio and the interventionists, public opinion was calling for the maximum possible gains: not just the territories promised by the Treaty of London (which, apart from Trieste and Trentino, were not predominantly Italian speaking), but also the port of Fiume (Rijeka) on the Croatian coast, a town which from the mid-nineteenth century had developed a sizeable community of immigrant middle-class Italians. In demanding 'the Treaty of London plus Fiume', though, Italy risked muddying the ideological waters and creating an impression of blatant opportunism, for the Treaty of London had been premised on old-fashioned considerations of realpolitik (to ensure Italy's security in the Adriatic), while Fiume was being claimed on the basis of the 'principle of nationality'. However, it was in fact questionable whether a majority of the town's population was actually Italian, as the working-class suburbs were almost all Croat.

The Italian delegates thus found themselves in an awkward position in Paris. Their situation was made more difficult by the attitude of the three most powerful figures at the peace conference – Woodrow Wilson; the British prime minister, David Lloyd George; and the French prime minister, Georges Clemenceau – who all viewed Italy as something of a parvenu, and not quite deserving of full membership of the great power club. Such manifest condescension further inflamed nationalist feelings in Italy, forcing the prime minister, Vittorio Emanuele Orlando, and the Foreign Minister, Sonnino, to become more insistent in their demands in order to avoid being vilified back home as authors of what it was already widely feared would become 'the mutilated victory'. Orlando, a distinguished Sicilian law

professor, was generally well received in Paris – Lloyd George warmed
to his expansive Mediterranean manner (though Harold Nicolson
probably reflected more mainstream British opinion in describing
him, waspishly, as 'a white, weak, flabby man').[24] But Sonnino, with
his austere demeanour and rigid intellectual outlook, was the antithesis of the conventional Italian, and created a bad impression.
Moreover he was forced to do much of the talking as the British and
Americans found Orlando very hard to understand, despite his
frequent florid gestures.

The problem with Italy's demand for Fiume was that it ran up
against the French determination to create a strong Yugoslavia as one
of a chain of new states in central Europe that would pen Germany
in on its eastern flank: the port of Fiume was seen as economically
and strategically necessary for the future viability of Yugoslavia. There
was also another less easily voiced concern. Franco-Italian relations
had been volatile and often deeply strained since 1860. In the late 1880s,
for example, Francesco Crispi had striven to cajole his German allies
into launching a war against France in keeping with his long-held
ambition that Italy should replace its Latin neighbour as the dominant
power in the Mediterranean.[25] The elderly Clemenceau knew this, and
harboured few illusions. Thus, while the Italian government did all it
could to weaken Yugoslavia, sanctioning plans to foment civil war
there by sending in agents provocateurs and encouraging Italian
soldiers to heighten tensions by 'fraternising' with local women, the
French worked to keep the new state united as a way of holding an
unpredictable Italy in check. Orlando complained that it was galling
to have defeated Austria only to have another major power replace it
in the Adriatic. But he attracted little sympathy in Paris.[26]

A further difficulty facing the Italian delegation was that neither
France nor Britain believed that the contribution of Italy to the war
effort had been sufficient to merit the extensive territorial claims that
it was now making. It was pointed out that Italy had sustained far
fewer casualties than both France and Britain: the final military death
toll for Italy was around 650,000, a little less than half the figure for
France. There was much anger that the Italian commander, General
Diaz, had apparently only been willing to launch an offensive in the
autumn of 1918 when it was clear that the Austrians were on the brink
of collapse ('They all say that the signal for an armistice was the signal

for Italy to begin to fight', noted the British ambassador).[27] There was also irritation that the Italian navy had scarcely ventured out of port, despite promises to patrol the Mediterranean and the Adriatic, and considerable resentment at the huge sums that the hard-pressed allies had been obliged to lend to Italy (15 billion lire in the case of Britain), not all of which had then been spent on the war. The old idea that Italians were charming but unscrupulous played through the minds of many of the delegates in Paris. As Clemenceau put it: '[T]he Italians met [me] with a magnificent coup de chapeau of the seventeenth-century type, and then held out the hat for alms at the end of the bow.'[28]

With demonstrations and violent clashes escalating in Italy in the spring of 1919, particularly along the interventionist–neutralist fault line, Orlando and Sonnino felt in no position to compromise. Orlando claimed that a secret society had sworn to assassinate him if he returned home without having secured all Dalmatia, while Sonnino spoke grimly of how a 'mutilated victory' would tip the country over into anarchy. Orlando was desperate. On Easter Sunday, during a particularly difficult session with the British, French and Americans, he was reduced to tears, as Clemenceau looked on impassively and the British incredulously. (Sir Maurice Hankey, the conference secretary, said that he would have spanked his son for such a disgraceful show of emotion.) Four days later, with the talks deadlocked, Orlando left Paris in disgust. Crowds cheered his train as he travelled down through Italy, and when he reached Rome he was greeted with pealing church bells and enthusiastic cries of 'Viva Orlando! Viva Fiume! Viva l'Italia!' Everywhere walls were covered in slogans demanding the annexation of Fiume. In Turin students went along the Corso Wilson, so named in honour of a recent visit to the city by the president, changing all the signs into 'Corso Fiume'.[29]

Orlando secured a ringing endorsement from the Chamber of Deputies, by 382 votes to 40, for his firm stand in Paris. He declared that Italy's claims were based on 'such high and solemn reasons of right and justice' that they needed to be recognised by the allies in full. But he was painting himself into a corner, perhaps intentionally ('I am . . . a new Christ, and must suffer my passion for the salvation of my country', he announced a few days before).[30] When he returned to the conference table early in May, having aged, according to one observer, ten years, his negotiating hand was weaker than ever. In his absence the British and French had proceeded to carve up Germany's African colonies among themselves, while Wilson had lost any remaining semblance of patience with the Italian delegates, and now turned on them the full force of his chilly Protestant censoriousness. Orlando pleaded for his political life: 'I must have a solution. Otherwise I will have a crisis in parliament or in the streets in Italy', he told Lloyd George. 'And if not', the British prime minister asked, 'who do you see taking your place?' 'Perhaps D'Annunzio'.[31] But Orlando's pleas were in vain, and on 19 June he lost a vote of confidence in the Chamber and resigned, leaving his successor, Francesco Saverio Nitti, a radical economics professor from Basilicata, to concede Dalmatia to Yugoslavia and agree to Fiume becoming a neutral city under the newly formed League of Nations.

The seizure of Fiume

As demobilised troops exchanged the horror of the trenches for the harsh economic realities of civilian life, and as strikes, factory occupations, protests and riots increased, led by militant socialists preparing confidently for a revolution, 'as in Russia', it was to the florid language and images of romantic nationalism that young men like Carlo Ciseri readily turned to express their disenchantment. Such language had inspired Italians in the Risorgimento; and it perhaps seemed natural to those who had been brought up at school on the patriotic poetry of Ugo Foscolo and Giosuè Carducci to use similar language and imagery to describe the plight of the post-war nation. In July 1919 a sixteen-year-old schoolboy living in Florence, Mario Piazzesi, who the following year was to join Mussolini's fascist movement, recorded in his diary the passionate diatribe of an officer who felt 'crushed' by the insolence of the left-wing extremists and betrayed by the lack of support that he had received from the government:

> Our dreams, our fantasies, our sweet and rose-coloured vision of the fatherland, the mythic Italy with the crown of turrets on her forehead, the lion at her feet, the bundles of weapons and the stars of Savoy shooting out shafts of light like the cherubim of Fra Angelico – that

whole world has been shattered once and for all by the violent attacks [of the socialists].[32]

It was to men with a mindset such as this that D'Annunzio looked to appeal, with his patriotic, richly charged and intemperate rhetoric. Buoyed by the recent vote of an honorary doctorate by the university of Rome, he lambasted the treachery of the allies in a series of speeches to mass audiences in the late spring of 1919. He claimed that Italy, the poorest of the belligerent powers, had 'saved the world' through its heroism and generous sacrifice of blood in the war. He accused the 'triumvirs' of the three richest nations of working together to keep Italy impoverished and isolated, using the League of Nations as their tool. (Carlo Ciseri had a similar sense of conspiracy: 'they do not want Italy to become great and powerful', he confided in his diary.)[33] He denounced the historic perfidy of the French: had they not in effect looked to surround Italy in the Mediterranean by occupying Tunisia in 1881? And had they not been responsible for the defeat at Adua by supplying arms to the Ethiopian Emperor? He also caricatured Wilson, the 'Croatified Quaker', as a grotesque figurine with a 'long equine face' and false teeth.[34] The impact of these speeches on D'Annunzio's listeners was, as one not altogether sympathetic English eyewitness had to admit, extraordinary. His voice played on the emotions of the crowd, he said, 'as a supreme violinist does upon a Stradivarius'. 'The tones rose and fell in an unending stream, like the song of a minstrel, and they spread over the vast audience like olive oil on the surface of the sea.'[35]

D'Annunzio was a major threat to the authority (such of it that remained) of the government in Rome. He had a cult following in the army, particularly among the *arditi*, the specially trained units of assault troops that had been embedded at the front from the second half of 1917 in a bid to stiffen morale and breach the Austrian lines. Their celebration of ruthlessness and daring, and their crude language, mirrored well the poet's own feverish *Weltanschauung* (their motto, 'Me ne frego' – soon to be adopted by the fascists – was a slang expression meaning 'I don't give a damn', i.e. about death). In the course of the summer of 1919 D'Annunzio was heavily involved in negotiations with disaffected generals and officers, Nationalists, Futurists and other patriotic groups to seize Fiume by force. In Fiume itself the groundwork for a possible coup was laid by a society called Young Fiume (the name echoed Mazzini's famous Risorgimento association, Young Italy). Its activities helped fan a mood of ugly chauvinism in the city. In one incident Italian police opened fire on a party of children returning from a picnic who had failed to shout 'Viva Italia'. Nine were killed and twenty wounded.[36] The new prime minister looked to avert the gathering storm by buying off D'Annunzio with a government post. D'Annunzio declined it, and turned his abusive rhetoric against Nitti, dubbing him, in one of his most celebrated neologisms, 'Cagoia' ('Shit-itis').

D'Annunzio had a rival in the war of words in Mussolini, who on 23 March 1919 had founded a new movement, the Fasci di Combattimento ('Fighting Units'), in a rented hall overlooking Piazza San Sepolcro in central Milan. This was one of a number of initiatives launched at that time in the no-man's-land between liberalism and socialism, and the event had gone almost unnoticed in the press. A hundred or so people had turned up for the first meeting, most of them ex-combatants and interventionists of very different backgrounds and inclinations – Nationalists, Futurists (including their leader, the writer Filippo Tommaso Marinetti), anarchists, syndicalists, republicans, Catholics and *arditi*. The heterogeneous mix had been one important reason why Mussolini had not wanted to adopt a precise political programme.[37] The Fasci were to be a spiritual force, embracing all those who had believed in the war (an eclecticism underlined when ten people had been selected at random from the front row to sit on the executive committee). And the most powerful unifying bonds at this stage were feelings of anger, resentment and hatred. On the evening of the inaugural meeting a group of the most resolute new fascists, including the national spokesman of the *arditi*, Ferruccio Vecchi, had sworn a solemn oath, their hands stretched over an unsheathed dagger, 'to defend . . . Italy from the enemy within, and be willing to kill and to die!'[38] And a few weeks later Marinetti and Vecchi had organised the movement's first significant act of violence, ransacking the headquarters of the Socialist Party newspaper, *Avanti!*, and carrying off the captured signboard in triumph to the offices of Mussolini's newspaper, *Il Popolo d'Italia*.[39]

From his editorial office in Via Paolo da Cannobio in Milan (the 'lair' – 'covo' – as he liked to call it), sipping milk and surrounded by pistols, daggers, grenades and cartridges, Mussolini poured out a constant stream of journalism intended to outdo D'Annunzio in vehemence if not in literary inventiveness. He attacked the government for its feebleness at the peace conference: 'The Italy that deals and barters in Paris . . . is not the Italy of the Isonzo . . . It is the Italy of foreigners and storytellers, of beggars and lawyers, the Italy which sadly still survives on high, but which lower down among the people, who have a sense of its pride and glory, is dead and buried.' He dubbed Orlando a 'lachrymogen', an 'invertebrate who gets by propped up on strong zabagliones', and called on him to break with Wilson and the other 'bandits of international plutocracy'.[40] He denounced Britain as 'the fattest and most bourgeois nation in the world',[41] and vilified the Bolsheviks, 80 per cent of whose leaders, he said, were Jews operating in the service of Jewish bankers in London and New York: 'Race does not betray race.'[42] And following D'Annunzio, he mocked Nitti as 'His excrescency Cagoia' and 'Franz Joseph Cagoia' (for alleged Austrian sympathies).[43] Nothing, according to Mussolini, was sacrosanct other than the nation: 'We are loyal to Italy and to the fatherland alone.'[44]

During the summer of 1919 Mussolini and his fascist supporters were in close touch with D'Annunzio and those senior figures in the army who were toying with the idea of taking Fiume by force. They included the king's cousin, the Duke of Aosta. D'Annunzio himself was growing distracted by plans for a long-distance flight to the Far East (and by a new love affair), and when in August the Italian troops that had been stationed in the city since the end of the previous year were ordered out by allied commissioners eager to enforce Fiume's neutrality, it was to Mussolini and General Peppino Garibaldi (grandson of the great patriot) and to the Nationalist leaders Enrico Corradini and Luigi Federzoni that they initially turned for help with a coup. But it was D'Annunzio who enjoyed the greatest national cachet, and his involvement would cause most embarrassment to the government in Rome. Thus, early in September seven young officers who had sworn to defend the city on pain of death issued an appeal to him in the religiously charged allegorical language, laced with references to the Risorgimento, that had become almost instinctive in patriotic circles:

The Great Mother [Italy] does not know Fiume. She is not permitted to know the finest of her daughters, the purest and most holy of Italian women . . . We have sworn upon the memory of all who died for the unity of Italy: *Fiume or death!* . . . And you do nothing for Fiume? You who have all Italy in your hands – great, noble, generous Italy – will you not shake her out of the lethargy into which she has so long fallen?[45]

D'Annunzio was persuaded. On 12 September he set out from the small town of Ronchi to the south of Gorizia with around 200 Italian troops and 26 armoured trucks seized from a local depot. As he advanced along the road to Fiume, he was joined by patriotic veterans, mutineers (including many *arditi*), Futurists, students, adventurers and even schoolchildren, so that by the time the column reached the outskirts of the city it had swollen to more than 2,000. The commander in Fiume, General Vittorio Emanuele Pittaluga, had been given strict orders to halt this blatant act of rebellion. He parleyed with D'Annunzio at a roadblock, telling him that Italy would be severely discredited by his actions and face 'incalculable consequences'. 'It is you who will destroy Italy if you prevent her destiny being fulfilled,' retorted the poet. And in a scene reminiscent of Napoleon's famous gesture at Lake Laffrey in 1815, when the former emperor had bared his chest to the French troops sent to arrest him, D'Annunzio pulled back his coat and invited Pittaluga's men to aim at the medals pinned over his heart. Pittaluga hesitated, and then stepped forward and shook D'Annunzio's hand: 'I will not shed Italian blood nor be the cause of a fratricidal war . . . Long live Italian Fiume!'[46] D'Annunzio carried on into the city, without a shot being fired. Flags were waved, bells tolled, laurel leaves tumbled from the balconies, and the *arditi* sang their marching song, 'Giovinezza' ('Youth-time'), soon to be appropriated by the fascists as their official anthem.

When, the next day, Giovanni Bartoli, a twenty-year-old former *ardito* from a modest middle-class family in Rome, who had served on the Piave front in 1917–18, learned of what had happened in Fiume, he asked his old commanding officer what it meant. The officer reassured him that it was 'a great episode' that would 'save Italy from dishonour'. Giovanni, who was based in Naples at the time, decided to take a train north: evidently nobody was going to stop him. He

travelled through the war-torn Carso, with its still rudimentary cemeteries, abandoned trenches and dark red rocky landscape, that seemed
to his battle-scarred imagination like a 'massive drop of congealed
blood', and walked the last stage of the journey from Mattuglie,
avoiding the *carabinieri* who were ineffectually trying to stop people
arriving. The spectacle that confronted him when he entered Fiume
was breathtaking:

> When I reached piazza Regina Elena, there was no empty window.
> There were tricolour flags everywhere. I wondered how these people
> could have got hold of so many flags. There were flowers at every
> point, and posters saying: *Italy or death* or *Fiume or death* . . . I found
> soldiers of all kinds wandering around. Officers and groups of Fiume
> girls were singing patriotic songs.

In the weeks that followed the sense of excitement hardly diminished.
The account which he wrote of his experiences, probably in 1920,
reflected the charged language and feelings of the time:

> To describe the enthusiasm of the first month in this city would be an
> extremely difficult task. I will say simply that we seemed to be reliving
> an old page out of the history of the Risorgimento. Everywhere people
> were shouting 'death to the Croats', and the city was entirely green,
> white and red. Every evening there were conferences, demonstrations,
> parades and patriotic songs . . . Little by little the enthusiasm
> disappeared, leaving only the faith in the glorious Duce . . .[47]

The occupation of Fiume, which was to last over fifteen months,
as the government in Rome groped for a solution, afraid to send in
the army lest it mutinied, provided a remarkable spectacle of theatricality, licentiousness and political innovation. Mussolini observed it
with close interest from Milan and was later to incorporate a number
of its features into fascism. In addition to heavy drinking, sexual
promiscuity and drug taking (cocaine had become widely used in army
circles in the war and D'Annunzio was in all probability addicted),
there was extraordinary experimentation with dress and appearance.
The English writer Osbert Sitwell, who visited the city in 1920, noted
a prodigious array of styles on display: 'Some had beards, and had

shaved their heads completely so as to resemble the Commander himself . . . others had cultivated huge tufts of hair, half a foot long, waving out from their foreheads, and wore, balanced on the very back of the skull, a black fez. Cloaks, feathers and flowing black ties were universal . . .'[48] There were choreographed parades and marches, mock battles and public dances; and from the balcony of his residence D'Annunzio delivered histrionic speeches full of religious imagery, invective, oaths and liturgical chants, designed to create a close emotional dialogue with the audience ('the first example of such interplay since Greek times', he claimed).[49] Among D'Annunzio's most favoured exchanges (both later taken up by the fascists) were 'A noi!' ('It is ours') and 'Eia, eia, eia, alalà', a war cry, apparently of Greek origin, that D'Annunzio had made his fellow aviators use in the war instead of 'Ip, ip, urrah!'[50]

But beneath the theatricality and the hedonism ran a current of deeply subversive anger. In defying the government in Rome, many of D'Annunzio's followers believed that they rather than Nitti or the Chamber of Deputies now represented the 'true' nation and that the seizure of Fiume was therefore morally legitimate. According to Giovanni Bartoli the legionaries were fighting 'to save the honour of Italy and make more luminous and lovely the victory and VITTORIO VENETO'. He could see no justification for the attempts made by the police to arrest his friends whenever they strayed outside the city limits. He also rejected out of hand the accusations that he and the others occupying Fiume were mere 'criminals' or 'brigands'. If anyone deserved to be arrested – and shot – it was 'the craven Cagoia':

All the bile of His Indecency Cagoia was directed in vain against our enterprise. And as far as I am concerned that man, whom I have never trusted at all, should be handed over to true Italians or to a squad of black flames [arditi] and executed as an example to the traitors of the Fatherland.[51]

2

From Rhetoric to Violence, 1920–22

Towards civil war

Vincenzo Rabito inhabited a very different mental and material world from the well-educated middle-class patriots for whom Fiume and 'Great Mother' Italy were causes to fight and die for. He had served in the war; but unlike D'Annunzio or Carlo Ciseri his thoughts and feelings had not been moulded by the ideals of the Risorgimento or the aggressive rhetoric of Nationalism. He had been born in a small rural community in the province of Ragusa in the south-east of Sicily in 1899, one of seven children of an impoverished agricultural labourer. He had not attended school: his father had died of pneumonia aged forty, and like millions of other peasant children in Italy at that time, Vincenzo had been obliged to ignore the law on compulsory primary education in order to try to find work. As a result he was illiterate. Only in later life did he acquire some rudimentary writing skills – sufficient to allow him to shut himself away in a room every day over a period of seven years, from 1968 to 1975, and painstakingly tap out his autobiography with an old Olivetti typewriter on 1,027 sheets of paper, using a highly idiosyncratic oral Italian mixed with dialect, in an uninterrupted flow of words, each separated neatly from the next by a semicolon, with no sentences, paragraphs or punctuation.

Vincenzo had been called up in 1916 and been sent to the Trentino front, near Asiago. Here the brigade commander had welcomed the 'boys of '99' by telling them that they were there for one purpose, and one purpose only, 'to defend the Mother *Patria*'. 'I have no doubt that you young lads will defend *"la Patria"* as you would defend your mother if she was in danger'. Vincenzo had been involved in a brutal assault on Monte Fiore ('we walked up and up, but there were so many

dead and wounded that we had nowhere to put our feet . . . [M]ore
than half our brigade were killed by the Austrians, and we wept and
cried so much . . .'), and had lost a toe to frostbite in the ensuing
months spent high in the Alps. And all the time he had felt bitter
towards 'the whore Mother *Patria*', who was paying the 'lads' just
55 cents a day and giving almost nothing to their families, 'who
were dying of hunger, starting with my mother'. When he and his
fellow soldiers received letters, most of the writing had been crossed
out by nervous censors eager to conceal from them the anger and
low morale of their relatives back home; and their replies to their
families had only got past the censors by using phrases such as,
'we are well and are serving *la Patria* with all our heart' or, better still,
'I am longing to die for *la Patria*'. Vincenzo had ended the war on
the Piave front, but had still not learned to love his 'Mother
Patria'. Far from it: 'If I die my last words will have to be: "Spit on
this *Patria* . . ."'[1]

Vincenzo's resentment was far from unusual among rank-and-file
troops. One of the paradoxes of the First World War was that the
desire entertained by sections of 'legal' Italy to generate feelings of
loyalty to the nation in millions of peasants and workers was based
on the well-founded belief that most ordinary Italians had a weak
sense of the 'patria'. But this meant compelling the masses to fight
– which ran the risk of alienating them still further from the state.
Of the 5.5 million Italians who were mobilised in 1915–18, only about
8,000 were volunteers; and mistrust towards the common soldier was
everywhere in evidence. Discipline was harsh, even by contemporary
standards. Some 400,000 men were brought before military tribunals
during the war, and a quarter were convicted: 4,028 received death
sentences (mostly in absentia), of which 750 were carried out (the
figure for Britain was 304).[2] Military police manned machine-gun posts
behind the infantry when attacks were launched to shoot those who
faltered or tried to run away, and summary executions and decimations
were not uncommon. Very little was done to provide relief for the
troops (apart from laying on improvised brothels) and leave was
restricted to a single period of fifteen days in the year. Only after
Caporetto was it accepted that such extreme harshness was counterproductive and a more lenient approach introduced.

The lack of faith in the commitment of the troops contributed significantly to the refusal of the authorities to furnish aid to those who had been captured. This was in contrast to the practice in other countries. It was feared that if soldiers learned that conditions in prisoner-of-war camps were tolerable they would give up too easily. Accordingly everything was done to stigmatise imprisonment and hamper relief efforts, and the 600,000 Italians who ended up interned in Austria and Germany (the number of British POWs was far less, about 170,000) had to get by on rations that frequently fell below 1,000 calories a day. Around 100,000 died of hunger and hunger-related diseases – five times the figure for French prisoners, who, like the British, received regular food parcels.[3] There was an inevitable legacy of resentment. One soldier wrote sarcastically after the war of how the 'government of our *patria*' had 'completely abandoned' him and the other Italians in his camp, forbidding access to essential supplies and restricting to a minimum any communication with families (only postcards were permitted).[4]

The concern of the authorities to prevent those on the home front from knowing too much about the horrors that soldiers like Vincenzo were facing revealed deep anxieties about civilian morale. Even the humane left-wing intellectual Gaetano Salvemini urged the government to stop wounded soldiers spending time with their families in case they passed on unpleasant information to them.[5] Such unease about the public mood was well justified. The distinguished liberal politician and expert on the south, Giustino Fortunato, had initially been impressed by the stoicism and dedication shown by the peasants in his home town of Rionero in Basilicata: 'The calm, the good will, the dignity of all classes, and especially the peasantry, in this the first great unitary war Italy has fought, is astonishing, truly astonishing. Yes, Italy is made!'.[6] But from the end of 1916 he became increasingly alarmed at the number of deserters and the mounting anger of local people. By the summer of 1917 the situation was looking desperate. The women were incandescent (like 'harpies') at the fate of their husbands and sons; and their fury was directed largely at landowners like himself who were accused of conspiring with the government to prolong the conflict and deliberately massacre the poor. Deserters roamed the countryside and forests were set on fire. He warned his friend, the former prime minister, Salandra, that an insurrection or, worse, brigandage was about to erupt.[7]

In the north of the country, too, the situation looked precarious. The firms producing the goods and equipment needed for the war – some 2,000 of them by November 1918, mostly in Piedmont, Liguria and Lombardy – were subjected to strict centralised planning and control. Strikes were banned, wages and hours of work tightly regulated, and factory floors patrolled by armed guards. The pay of most industrial workers declined in real terms between 1915 and 1918, and shifts were often extremely long. A seventy-five-hour week was quite normal in 1916 at Fiat – whose workforce rose from 6,000 to 30,000 in the course of the war, as the company developed into Europe's leading producer of trucks and lorries. Food shortages were a growing problem in the cities, and in August 1917 severe rioting broke out in Turin. Barricades went up and some fifty people were killed before troops restored order. Revolutionary socialist ideas had already circulated widely among northern workers before 1915; and they continued to do so during the conflict, fanned by party activists who could point to the enormous profits being made by the employers as evidence that the war was primarily a mechanism for reinforcing the stranglehold of the capitalist bourgeoisie on the poor.

Once the conflict was over, the government hoped that the sting of popular discontent might be drawn by electoral reform, and that the grievances of the masses could at least be aired by their representatives and spokesmen inside the framework of the state. A new suffrage law was accordingly introduced in 1919, giving the vote to all who had served at the front, regardless of their age, and to every other male aged over twenty-one. This raised the electorate by more than a quarter, to 11 million. But an even more decisive change was the establishment of proportional representation and electoral colleges. Deputies would now be chosen from a list on the basis of the percentage of votes cast for their party in a province, thus severing the link between individual politicians and their local clienteles on which the liberals had traditionally relied for success at the polls. The political initiative was thereby handed to parties with the machinery to mobilise voters on a large scale – the socialists, with their enormous and fast-expanding network of trade unions, cooperatives, leagues and Chambers of Labour, and the newly formed Italian Popular Party (PPI), which was strongly Catholic in orientation and could draw on the extensive associations of the Church for support.

When the first post-war elections were held in November 1919, the socialists secured 32 per cent of the vote and 156 deputies, three times as many as in the previous legislature, and the Popular Party 20 per cent and 100 deputies. As a result, over half the new Chamber comprised politicians who were deeply sceptical of the liberal regime (the Catholics) or who were militantly hostile to it (the socialists) and saw parliament mainly as a forum for barracking and abuse ahead of the anticipated revolution. The rest of the Chamber was split between groups of social democrats, radicals and liberals, with little capacity to cooperate with one another. The upshot was near governmental paralysis and a further blow to the already deeply tarnished image of representative government in Italy. Mussolini's newly formed fascists stood for election in Milan together with Futurists and *arditi*. They won just 4,796 out of some 315,000 votes. None of their seventeen candidates, including the renowned conductor Arturo Toscanini, was returned. Mussolini thought of emigrating, while the socialists celebrated the failure of a man whom they looked upon as a traitor by staging a mock funeral through the city streets.

When Vincenzo Rabito was transferred from Gorizia to Florence in the spring of 1920 ahead of his demobilisation, he was initially excited at being sent to such a beautiful and famous place. Each evening he celebrated by visiting the brothels (which he rated much higher than those of his native Sicily: 'they were so clean, and the walls . . . were all like in a bathroom, so when you saw one girl, it looked, with all those mirrors, as if there were six').[8] But Florence soon revealed itself to be a deeply troubled city. His first assignment was to guard the street outside the Murate prison in the town centre and make sure pedestrians kept moving:

> Because all those kept in this prison were political prisoners and everyone had to pass without stopping, because the law – and us soldiers were the law – were afraid they could write some message, and a revolution could break out . . . Florence was all socialist and communist. Only the rich weren't socialists and those who hadn't been in the war. And they were all revolutionaries, because Russia had made a revolution . . . and they wanted to do the same in Italy. So month after month they were expecting the red flag to appear on the town hall.[9]

In contrast to middle-class officers like Carlo Ciseri, who felt continually under threat in Florence, Vincenzo did not feel personally at risk, despite being in uniform. He flirted with the working-class girls; and rather than reprimand the socialists, he laughed along with them (and especially with the women, who were the most vocal and passionate) when they hurled taunts at the soldiers of the Royal Guards who had been sent to provide reinforcement in the city. On one occasion he was arrested and threatened with a transfer to Libya 'to deal with the negro rebels' after being heard singing 'Bandiera Rossa' in the street at night with a crowd of youths on his way back from the theatre. But the atmosphere in Florence became increasingly menacing. Vincenzo found himself posted inside Palazzo Vecchio, 'with my rifle loaded as in war time, because the communists wanted to occupy the palace, where all the government offices were', while outside were 'thousands and thousands of Royal Guards, with machine guns placed on the balconies pointing at the demonstrators'. There was growing talk in the early summer of 1920 of 'the journalist Mussolini' and of a possible assault on the town hall by 'young fascists', eager to hoist their black flag: 'We had to open fire on them, too, if they attacked. We were therefore caught in the middle of two revolutions.'[10]

Everywhere in Italy the situation was deteriorating. Strikes, demonstrations and violent clashes between the police and socialist workers, with numerous dead and injured, were daily occurrences. The government in Rome, which in the early summer of 1920 passed from the hands of the execrated Francesco Saverio Nitti to those of the experienced (but, in the eyes of many, scarcely less odious) seventy-seven-year-old Giovanni Giolitti, seemed to have no solution to offer. 'Everyone can see that Italy is heading towards civil war, the perennial curse of its people', wrote Giustino Fortunato around this time, '. . . and everyone is calling out . . . for the providential intervention of a Man – with a capital M – who might finally be able to restore order to the country . . .'[11] In late June 1920 a revolt broke out in Ancona in a *bersaglieri* regiment that refused to be sent to Albania. Local socialists joined in from sympathy and the city quickly slid into anarchy. Neighbouring towns in the Marche and Romagna also came out in support. Vincenzo was dispatched from Florence to help restore order. He found Ancona in a state of 'war': 'We attacked the city . . . without knowing who were our enemies and who were our friends'. It took several days to impose a measure of calm and in the meantime ten of his fellow soldiers were killed and another seventy wounded. He himself got off relatively lightly: he returned to Florence with a badly bruised shoulder – and venereal disease.[12]

The sense of excitement that Vincenzo had felt when he first came to Tuscany had evaporated. Before being sent to Ancona he had enjoyed a few weeks of 'paradise', serving as a private guard in the house of one of the wealthy Florentine families that, out of fear that Red Guards might devastate their palaces, 'used to go to the barracks of St George and beg the colonel to give them four or five well armed soldiers or, better, a machine gun'. (For a sum, the colonel agreed.) Vincenzo had relished 'eating at a table, drinking well, smoking luxury cigarettes and sleeping well'. To add to his enjoyment there had been a 'beautiful and amorous maid', whom he would have considered marrying if only she had been twenty-one and not twenty-nine. But now Florence struck him as oppressive. The relative light-heartedness of the spring had given way to a much grimmer climate: 'I had become overwhelmed with sadness, as there were strikes day and night . . . and there was no chance of making friends any more.' He was compelled to remain in the city some time longer, feeling increasingly redundant as 'the big landowners turned for protection to the fascists rather than the soldiers [and] . . . we were now pointless'. In 1921 he was finally released from the army and allowed to return home to Sicily.[13]

Squadrismo

The situation in Florence in 1920 was mirrored across much of northern and central Italy, where the Socialist Party and its trade unions, grouped together in the General Confederation of Labour, was strongest. Membership soared from 250,000 at the end of the war to 2 million at the end of 1920. In southern Italy, where the economy was overwhelmingly rural, the hopes and grievances of the poor were expressed in a less overtly revolutionary form. Here, millions of returning soldiers, who had received assurances in official propaganda in 1917–18 that there would be plenty of 'land for the peasants' when the fighting was over, marched onto large estates, often in festive mood, with flags waving and bands playing, staked out individual plots and began to dig. These land occupations were mostly directed at uncultivated properties or properties that were believed to have been common land before the abolition of feudalism in the early nineteenth century and thus still belonged properly to the community. Sometimes the occupations were carried out spontaneously. Often local priests, cooperatives or ex-servicemen's associations took the lead. Only in a few areas, such as Puglia and south-eastern Sicily, was the Socialist Party a protagonist. But the prevailing sense among the middle and upper classes, as in the north and centre of Italy, was that order was collapsing.

To the dismay of the southern landowners, the government seemed as reluctant to take a firm stand against the peasantry as against the urban workers. Back in September 1919 it had issued a decree allowing the local authorities to recognise the occupation of uncultivated lands by cooperative associations for up to four years; and a year later Giolitti's government went much further, and guaranteed permanent tenure to all illegal land occupiers. Faced with what seemed tantamount to criminal weakness on the part of the state, landowners in the south began to take the law into their own hands, especially in those areas where private violence was already common. In August 1920, it was reported that the landowners of San Cipirello, south-west of Palermo, had responded to local land occupations by forming an association and, 'armed with Mauser carbines, moving in a dense column from one estate to the next, seizing those who were guarding the plots, forcing the peasants to stop working, and locking them up in farm buildings and pulling down the red flags that had been hoisted above them.'[14] More extreme measures were also used: the rates of murder in Sicily reached unprecedented levels in the post-war years, with trade unionists and peasant leaders common targets.

At the other end of the peninsula, in the border areas around Trieste and the Istrian peninsula, where the continuing occupation of Fiume by D'Annunzio and his supporters fuelled a climate of torrid nationalism and fanned tensions between local Slav and Italian communities, the summer of 1920 witnessed the first punitive raids by fascist squads. These consisted for the most part of young junior officers, still under arms or recently demobilised, who drove out into the countryside with the connivance of the local authorities and terrorised militant socialists in Slav-speaking communities. The moral imperative against fratricide that in the same months acted as a brake on Carlo Ciseri's strong inclinations to use his pistol on left-wing demonstrators in Florence could here be set aside with the thought that the Slav subversives, even if formally Italian, were ethnically outside the national fold.[15] Such early episodes of fascist violence or '*squadrismo*' would set the pattern for what was soon to be an explosion of brutal retaliatory action across much of the north and centre of the country. But for a while yet the sanctity of the idea of national unity, in whose name the war had largely been fought, held the situation nervously in check. Few wanted to be seen as casting the first stone.

The last straw for many came in the early autumn of 1920. In September, amid fears that a number of employers were about to introduce a lockout as a part of a pay dispute, around half a million workers occupied factories and shipyards, running up red or black (anarchist) flags and driving out the management. Giolitti feared a full-scale insurrection (he later pointed to the huge quantities of arms and explosives that were found abandoned in the factories as vindication for his anxieties)[16] and pressurised the industrialists into making concessions, including the principle that trade union representatives could sit on management boards. He was looking to buy time: 'Patience, patience and patience. The theory of Tolstoy', was a favoured maxim in these years.[17] He was convinced that the current turbulence in Italy was little more than a 'neurasthenic' reaction to the war, and that with tact and concessions it could be calmed and steered into constitutional channels. After all, many other countries in Europe were facing similar turmoil at this time. But few shared his optimism. Indeed many thought his leniency had become excessive and that it was time to adopt a far more robust response.

One such was the Florentine schoolboy Mario Piazzesi, now aged seventeen. Mario belonged to a middle-class landowning family, originally from Cesena in the Romagna, and like many of those who had not been old enough to serve in the war, he felt regret at having missed out on what was clearly the defining experience for his generation. He listened to the stories of veterans just a few years older than himself with a mixture of anger and frustration, eager to mitigate the sense of betrayal that so many of them felt after their return home. In 1919 he had joined the youth branch of a local civilian defence organisation, the Alleanza di Difesa Cittadina, many of whose members would soon migrate to fascism. The events of the summer of 1920 convinced him that it was time to act. In late June he confided to his diary: 'We have now become convinced in our hearts that in order to defeat the old world of the grey-beards and the new world of Asiatic madness [cast in such terms, the socialists were stripped of their Italian identity] we should occupy the piazzas and streets of the city in both spirit and body, and hold them firmly.' A few weeks later he recorded his father's intense dismay at the occupation of the factories. It was 'the end', his father said: Italy was in thrall to 'the Soviets'.[18]

In November, shortly after a general strike had been proclaimed by the socialists in protest at Western intervention in the Russian civil war, local government elections were held. The far left made sweeping gains across the north and centre of the country. In the socialist strongholds of the lower Po valley, in old provincial capitals such as Bologna and Ferrara (where a red flag now flew defiantly over the Renaissance town hall), a new mood of militancy surfaced. On 21 November some 300 armed fascists marched through the streets of central Bologna to Palazzo d'Accursio, where the socialist administration was being sworn in. The attack had been announced in advance, and women and children had been warned to stay away. The socialists had barricaded themselves inside the building. At the earliest opportunity the fascists opened fire. Red Guards threw grenades from the balconies, causing panic in the crowds that were gathered outside, and in the ensuing confusion ten socialists or socialist sympathisers were killed, seven of them by fascists. Inside the town hall an opposition councillor was shot (by a guard), providing the fascists with their first significant 'martyr'.

The change in atmosphere in the autumn of 1920 was recalled by the prominent social democrat, Ivanoe Bonomi, who at the time was Minister of War in Giolitti's government:

> After the tragedy in Bologna, the rural propertied classes were stirred to action and began to meet and organise themselves. In the towns of the Po valley young officers who had served at the front summoned their landowning friends and relatives and told them that they needed to defend themselves . . . against those who wanted to establish the dictatorship of the proletariat and repeat the Russian experiment. A spirit of battle hovered over the countryside. During patriotic ceremonies the men of order no longer remained firmly indoors, frightened of

violence, but displayed the national flag and went out into the piazza
to cheer. The slogans on walls – so much part of Italian political culture
– were now not just communist ones. Alongside the numerous 'Viva
Lenin!'s and 'Long live the dictatorship of the proletariat!' were others
celebrating the fatherland and the victory.[19]

A similar attack to that in Bologna took place shortly afterwards in
Ferrara and, in the weeks that followed, a wave of retaliatory violence
swept through the Po valley and into central Italy. Giulio Teoni, a
secondary-school student, two years younger than Mario Piazzesi,
from a prosperous family of silk merchants in the small Tuscan town
of Rassina, described how fascist violence first began in the provincial
capital of Arezzo towards the end of 1920. A former *ardito* was walking
down the main street of the town, he said, dressed in civilian clothes,
with a silver medal and tricolour ribbon pinned to his jacket. He was
confronted by two socialists, and when one of them attempted to pull
off his decoration, he took out his dagger (a distinctive *ardito* weapon)
and struck him dead. 'This episode acted like a cold shower in the city
and was the signal for the fight-back to start.' Teoni's account may
not be entirely factual: it has an air of schoolboy exaggeration. But
the romantic image of violence is telling. Teoni confessed to being
deeply excited by Mussolini and the fascists: their talk of securing
honour for the veterans and making Italy great, he admitted, appealed
'to all of us middle class boys': 'It seemed that our turn had now come
to continue the work of our elder brothers.'[20]

The sudden escalation of the fascist movement towards the end
of 1920 took many observers, Mussolini included, by surprise. There
were 1,065 new subscriptions in October–November: the following
month the figure leapt to nearly 11,000. Total membership rose from
20,165 with just 88 sections at the end of December, to 187,588 and
more than 1,000 sections five months later.[21] One important reason
for this rapid growth was a realisation that the authorities were incapable of stopping the violence. The government issued repeated
orders to the prefects to ensure the law was upheld impartially in
their provinces, but local police and army units in most places simply
turned a blind eye to what was going on. They after all tended to
sympathise with the *squadristi*: they had themselves been targets of
socialist anger and violence, and generally shared the fascists'

commitment to the war and contempt for the liberal state. Another major factor behind the surge in support for fascism was a recognition that the socialist movement was much more fragile than its brazen rhetoric had suggested. Despite all the talk of solidarity, there was often little cooperation between grass-roots leaders in one village or town and another, while at the national level major rifts were also evident – as the party's national congress in January 1921 showed, when a number of important delegates walked out to found the Italian Communist Party.

For boys like Teoni and Piazzesi, from conventional middle-class backgrounds, the attraction of fascism was not just political. Though many of them grew up listening to their parents' laments about liberalism and socialism – and agreed with them – *squadrismo* offered a chance to rebel against what often seemed the tepidity of provincial life. For two decades the leading cultural figures in Italy, from D'Annunzio to the Nationalist writers gathered around journals such as *Il Regno* and *La Voce*, had denounced the timidity, materialism and lack of idealism of Italy's conservative liberal elites. Fascism held out the prospect of 'living dangerously' (among D'Annunzio's most celebrated war-time slogans had been the Latin *'memento audere semper'* – 'remember always to be daring') and flouting bourgeois comforts and conventions in the service of a great cause – saving the nation. One of the themes running through Piazzesi's diary is the contrast between the harsh and frugal (but highly exhilarating) life with his comrades in the squad, and the genteel existence that he had been used to with his wealthy family. Interlaced with the bohemianism is a marked strain of eroticism. In May 1921 he described returning from an expeditionary raid in Arezzo. He wrote:

> The girls had prepared *vin brulé* and sweet pancakes for us. And there we all were getting high, laughing and creating mayhem. I thought of the tea in our drawing rooms, of the canapés, of the hand-kissing, and compared them to this rough wine that burns your throat, these pancakes that stink of fat, and these greasy buttocks of our female sponsors.[22]

This sense of generational revolt was encapsulated in fascism's celebration of 'youth', a category that elided easily with the long-standing aspirations for national renewal whose non-fulfilment could be equated with the liberal state's domination by a dull and cautious gerontocracy. 'Has this Italy been reduced to so lowly a condition, that she cannot bring forth from her womb anything other than an eighty-year-old man?' wrote Piazzesi after learning of Giolitti's appointment yet again as prime minister in June 1920.[23] The moral (and not just temporal) primacy of youth for the *squadristi* was reflected in the adoption of 'Giovinezza' (youth) as their principal anthem, a song that had started out in 1909 in university-student circles in Turin before being taken up by Alpini regiments in the army and subsequently, in the First World War, by the *arditi*. Its lyrics underwent various changes over the years (and were to be modified again when it became the official anthem of the fascist regime from the mid-1920s), but the sentiment remained essentially the same: an exaltation, in a strongly Nietzschean vein, of the courage, idealism and selflessness of youth (the 'springtime of beauty', as the refrain described it) and of the readiness to embrace hardship and a heroic death.

The *squadristi* were young, frequently very young. Piazzesi was eighteen when he went on his first raids. Teoni had to wait until February 1922 before enrolling in the Arezzo *fascio*, but even then he was barely sixteen. As the many carefully posed photographs of fascist squads taken in these years show, their members were often of a similar age. One study has suggested that around 25 per cent of militants in the fascist movement were under twenty-one.[24] Another has found that nearly 90 per cent of the *squadristi* in Bologna and 83.5 per cent of those in Florence were aged between sixteen and twenty-seven, and that while the great majority of the squad leaders were demobilised junior officers, more than half of their rank-and-file followers were not old enough to have fought in the war.[25] The overwhelming majority of *squadristi* came from the ranks of the middle classes: landowners, entrepreneurs, professionals, civil servants, white-collar workers, students and the self-employed. In the study of Bologna and Florence less than 5 per cent could be classified as working class. Given the age profile, it is not surprising that students made up a particularly large percentage of the squads. In Bologna and Florence more than a quarter of the *squadristi* were enrolled at university, and 17 per cent – like Teoni – in secondary school.[26]

The assaults of the fascists were carried out by 'action squads'.

These consisted typically of a dozen or so men who travelled to the scene of an attack on a socialist party building, Chamber of Labour or trade union office by train or bicycle, or in cars and trucks. The Fiat 18BL lorry, which had been mass produced in the war, was an especially favoured vehicle, and was subsequently given iconic status under the regime for the role played in *squadrismo*. Each squad had a sobriquet – Desperate, Satan, Dauntless, Lightning, 'Me ne frego' ('I don't give a damn', the slogan appropriated by the fascists from the *arditi*) or the name of a patriotic hero – and carried a banner with a skull and crossbones or some equally macabre motif. The black shirt, similarly redolent of death, was the main item of uniform (it, too, was borrowed from the *arditi*). The *squadristi* used an array of weapons: clubs (the notorious *manganello*, sometimes weighted with lead or thick leather), knuckledusters, daggers, rifles, revolvers, grenades and even machine guns. These arms were sometimes provided by local police stations or army barracks. Occasionally more bizarre weapons were used. Mantua *squadristi* became well known for hitting opponents round the head with slabs of dried cod.[27]

The exotic and sometimes ludic overtones to the activities of the fascist squads owed much to the aestheticisation of violence that the Futurists in particular had made fashionable. Their founding manifesto of 1909 had celebrated 'the love of danger, the habit of energy and rashness . . . acts of aggression, feverish sleeplessness, the double march, the perilous leap, the slap and the blow with the fist'. While in some belligerent countries the carnage of 1914–18 had begun to foster widespread revulsion among intellectuals at the inhumanity of modern warfare, in Italy the Futurists (and D'Annunzio) had continued to proclaim the grandeur of violence. Their stance was in part determined by political constraints. The fact that opposition to the war was largely synonymous with the supporters of socialism, Giolitti and parliament made it hard for them to soften their cultural line without appearing to give ground to their enemies. In a speech to *arditi* in October 1918, the Futurist leader, Marinetti, celebrated the 'spirit of renewal, the spirit of revolution, the spirit of Futurism' that had inspired the shock troops:

You became *arditi* from a love of violence and the beautiful heroic gesture. Smacks in the face for cowards, bastards and traitors in times of peace. Stabbings and hand grenades for the Teutons in war. You became *arditi* from a love of the mafia spirit and youthful arrogance . . . Beautiful triumphant mafia of the *arditi* of Italy, who love beautiful women and conquer them like trenches with an heroic gesture . . . You are the lords of the new Italy.[28]

Marinetti's sentiments echoed those proclaimed by D'Annunzio at Fiume. And it was from Fiume that much of the tone and style of fascism derived. A number of prominent *squadristi* had been in the Croatian city before joining Mussolini's movement, and they often sought to carry on the decadent and flamboyant practices that had been rife there in 1919–20. Alcohol and cocaine were freely consumed before raids (there was even a cocaine scandal involving wealthy *squadristi* in Palermo, a city that had only a very limited fascist presence before 1922). In Ferrara the 'Celibano' squad indulged in pouring libations of cherry brandy as one of its rituals (the name 'Celibano' was a drunken version of 'cherry brandy').[29] The 'beffa', or violent practical joke, which D'Annunzio had popularised through some of his most feted military gestures, both during the war and at Fiume, was used by the *squadristi* to humiliate opponents, most famously in the forced ingestion of the powerful laxative, castor oil.

An aesthetic and rhetorical celebration of violence was to be an important component of fascist culture in the years to come. The detachment from reality that such an abstracted approach could engender was to have disastrous consequences when the enemy they faced was resilient, as in 1940–43. As it was, the socialists in 1920–22 were no match for the *squadristi*. In a few towns, such as Parma and Bari, militant traditions of revolutionary syndicalism provided a platform for the formation in 1921 of armed left-wing units such as the Arditi del Popolo,[30] but in most places the socialists had no military organisation, leadership or weapons with which to resist the furious onslaught of their assailants. Confident that revolution would soon break out, they had abused their enemies with an air of invulnerability, incurring the wrath of the industrialists and landowners with their repeated strikes, often brutal control of the local labour market and inflammatory language. And all the while the socialist leadership in Rome had felt too constrained by the dictates of revolutionary faith to speak out and curb the ardour of the grass-roots activists, even though they knew well that there was no serious prospect of the Western powers allowing a Bolshevik-style regime to be formed in southern Europe.

The mismatch between the fascist squads and the socialists was well captured in a conversation that the social democrat politician Emilio Lussu had in November 1921 with a university-student friend who had served with him in the war as a junior officer. Lussu had been living in his native Sardinia, where there was very little fascism, and was keen to know from his friend – the son of a wealthy Po valley landowner – what exactly the *squadristi* were doing:

– We are restoring order.
– With fires and armed assaults?
– There was no alternative. With verbal propaganda we were getting nowhere. We needed weapons. Now we have them. We have vehicles, machine guns and rifles.
– Who gave them to you?
– Some came from the police, some from the landowners' associations.
– So that means you can now do what you like and what you want with impunity?
– No, there are also risks. Look. [He showed me a gun-shot wound on the back of his right hand that had still not fully healed.] Those brigands wounded me during a night attack.
– What brigands?
– The peasants.
– Were the peasants attacking or were they attacked?
– No, we were attacking. And we managed to beat them. Their land of cockaigne is finished. Imagine, each peasant was earning up to 40 lire a day.
– And now? . . .
– Fourteen lire. Which is still too much . . . Do you know, immediately after the war, when I walked in the street with my medals, they laughed in my face?
– And that's the reason, today, why you reduce their pay to 14 lire and cut them to pieces?
– Oh! It's easy to criticise. You needed to have been living with us. The peasants were dressing like me, and the cowman's daughter was more elegant than my sister.

– Let's not exaggerate. But still, this seems to you sufficient provocation
to justify hunger and death?

– But the world was out of joint, and we have set it right.[31]

Precise statistics for the casualties incurred are hard to find.
Government figures for 1920, when the socialists were at their most
militant, indicate that 288 people were killed in Italy in public disorders.
Of these 172 were socialists, 10 were Popolari, 51 were members of
the security forces, 51 were bystanders, and only 4 were fascists. In the
first three months of 1921, when the attacks by *squadristi* had begun
in earnest, 102 people were killed, of whom 41 were socialists and 25
fascists.[32] Figures issued by the fascists themselves for the entire period
from the foundation of the movement in 1919 until the March on
Rome in October 1922 point to 672 black-shirt deaths – though this
number is almost certainly inflated, given the importance at the time
(and subsequently) to fascism of the cult of 'martyrs'. The number
of socialists who lost their lives has been estimated at over 3,000 for
1921–22 alone.[33] No less indicative of the disproportionate character of
the conflict are the statistics for criminal charges and arrests. Official
figures show that down to the start of May 1921, 1,421 socialists had
been arrested in violent clashes with the fascists, compared to 396
fascists. In addition 878 fascists had been charged but not arrested, as
opposed to 617 socialists. Clearly the sympathies of the judiciary, as
much as those of the army and the police, were with the fascists.[34]

For the eighteen-year-old Mario Piazzesi the transition from the
fantasy of violence, as conjured up by Marinetti and D'Annunzio with
their inflammatory language, to the sober reality of bloody clashes
with the socialists was not easy – despite the disparity of forces. 'This
struggle, that in our dreams we had imagined to be a beautiful adventure of our youth, is no easy game', he wrote in his diary at the
beginning of March 1921, after witnessing the streets of Florence turned
into a battleground. 'Even those who have seen proper action in the
war have been amazed by just how much violence there is.' All over
the city could be heard the constant crack of rifle shots. Barricades
had been erected and tiles were flying, and at the end of Via Palazzuolo
he had seen a stream of blood on the pavement where two petards
had landed. In Piazza Cavour, 'there were those two bodies of reds
lying rolled over on their backs':

One act of vendetta follows another . . . people are pitted against each other as if the malign spirit of the Middle Ages had restored the old feelings of the Blacks and Whites [the two factions of the Guelfs that had torn Florence apart in the time of Dante]. It's just the same now as it was then – only the colours of the parties have changed; but the ferocity is the same and an air of hatred swirls around our heads as if it were the very breath of life.

But he consoled himself that it was worth it: 'our Italy' could not be reduced to 'an Asiatic colony'.[35]

If the socialists were the immediate enemy for Mario, they were not the main cause of the country's difficulties. The real banes of Italy were the liberal politicians and parliament in Rome, 'that truly disgusting . . . weak, lifeless, spineless and cowardly city'. The trouble with men like prime minister Giolitti, he wrote, was that they had 'turned away from the spirit of the Risorgimento and ignored the Nation'. They were running the country as if it were 'a public limited company – and badly', with no real concern for the mass of the population, whom they happily saw packed on steamships and forced to emigrate to Argentina or Brazil when things got hard. As for parliament, it was simply too corrupt, divided and weak. Fresh elections were held in May 1921 in the hope that a more stable majority might emerge. But this did not happen. The socialists lost ground, as anticipated, but not disastrously, and they remained the largest party with 123 seats, while the Popolari increased their total to 107. The rest of parliament consisted, as before, of a cluster of liberals, social democrats and others, of varying political complexions, with little cohesion. 'How', asked Mario towards the end of May, 'can peace return to Italy, lost without a pilot in a storm of blood, decadence and cowardice?'[36]

The triumph of the fascists

The exponential growth of fascism in the first months of 1921 had placed Mussolini in the position of the sorcerer's apprentice, struggling to contain a movement that risked breaking away from its radical roots and becoming a crude anti-socialist strike force in the pay of the conservative middle classes. A further danger had been presented by

Giolitti. Having failed to draw the more moderate socialists into his orbit after the occupation of the factories, he had set his sights on the fascists, hoping that with appropriate inducements they could be brought inside the constitutional fold and provide the body politic of Italian liberalism with a welcome injection of fresh blood. He had accordingly invited Mussolini to participate in his 'national' bloc in the May elections – an extraordinary act of endorsement given the extent to which the *squadristi* had been flouting the law. The risk for Mussolini was that his movement might become further divorced from its political origins, which were fiercely anti-parliamentary; but equally a foothold in the Chamber could give him a firm platform from which to control the leaders of the local squads (or *ras* as they were exotically styled, after the Ethiopian word for a warlord), who were becoming increasingly independent and powerful.

Thirty-seven fascists were returned to parliament in the elections. Among them was Mussolini, who won resoundingly in both Milan and Bologna, securing nearly 400,000 votes. All but two of the new deputies came from colleges in the north and centre of the country. The new cohort of blackshirts marked their arrival at Montecitorio with a suitably violent gesture. On 13 June they assaulted the communist deputy Francesco Misiano, who had fled Italy in 1915 in order to avoid military service and been convicted *in absentia* of desertion. Misiano tried to defend himself with a pistol but was overwhelmed by the fascists, who grabbed his weapon, brandished their own guns at him and shouted: 'Out! Out with deserters! Here we do not offend the glorious dead of the war and the revolution!' Ejected into the street, he was forced to walk down the Corso, with his head shaved and painted, and with a placard round his neck, jeered at by the crowds and spat at by *squadristi*. Inside the parliament building, the triumphant fascist deputies marched into the Chamber crying 'Viva l'Italia'. Roberto Farinacci, the *ras* of Cremona, handed Misiano's pistol to Giolitti: '. . . I consign to you the weapon of a deputy and deserter'. With characteristic nonchalance the prime minister replied: 'I cannot accept it. I do not have an arms licence.'[37] In the months that followed, Misiano was subjected to further attacks, before seeking refuge in Berlin and finally Moscow.

Mussolini was hardly in a position to reprimand his followers in the Chamber. For some months he had been calling publicly for 'a ruthless war' against the deputies of the far left: 'The reprisals of the fascists will reach them always and everywhere! Inexorably!'[38] But to maximise his negotiating position in Rome he needed to offer some reassurances to his new backers in the government bloc that the era of untrammelled violence might be nearing its end. He was thus constrained to walk a tightrope, reaffirming for his radical fascist supporters the republican tendency of the movement, its commitment to major social and economic reforms, and even his willingness to enter into a coalition with the socialists, while simultaneously stressing the need for order and discipline among the *squadristi*. In his first speech to parliament he mixed threats to the socialists ('on the plain of violence the working masses will be defeated') with offers of conciliation, albeit heavily qualified: 'For us violence is not a system, nor an aestheticism, far less a sport: it is a brutal necessity to which we have been driven. And I add: we are prepared to disarm if you, too, will disarm – your spirits, especially . . . for if we continue like this, the nation runs a serious risk of plunging into the abyss.'[39]

In the weeks that followed, Mussolini repeatedly pressed for an end to violence: he feared political isolation if the lawlessness persisted.[40] But it was hard to curb the anarchic impulses of the squads, who continued their raids almost unabated, spreading their attacks in provinces such as Brescia and Cremona to embrace Catholic workers' organisations as well as socialist ones. In July, Mussolini proposed a 'pact of pacification' between the fascists and the socialist unions – and even signed one early in August – but there was little chance of it being accepted by grass-roots members, particularly after eighteen *squadristi* were killed in a pitched battle with police and the local peasantry at a town in Liguria. There was now a crisis of authority in fascism, with many of the squad leaders in open revolt against Mussolini. Two of the most influential *ras*, Dino Grandi of Bologna and Italo Balbo of Ferrara, even went to see D'Annunzio and invite him to take over the movement. (D'Annunzio was at a loose end: Giolitti had forcibly ended the occupation of Fiume the previous December after the Treaty of Rappallo had declared the Croatian city a 'free state'.) But D'Annunzio was not interested, and with the *ras* aware that there was nobody else of sufficient stature to dominate fascism, a compromise was eventually reached: in the autumn Mussolini agreed to abandon the pact in return for the movement becoming a party – the Partito Nazionale Fascista (PNF) – with a centralised command structure and local branches that together would help offset the power of the squads.[41]

For many fascists, the change from movement to party was hard to swallow. In some cases, as with Pietro Marsich, the leading figure in Venetian fascism ('a poet and an idealist', with an outlook of 'revolutionary mysticism', according to Italo Balbo),[42] the shift towards more conventional politics was too much to bear, and they withdrew. Mario Piazzesi was certainly worried. On 4 November 1921, the third anniversary of Italy's victory in the war, he noted in his diary how he and his fellow *squadristi* were afraid that 'our fascism, this clear spring of energy, might get mired in the mephitic swamps of Montecitorio, that the youth and poetry of the movement could be contaminated by Roman alchemy, in short that our David might acquire a large paunch, a moustache and a beard'.[43] Mario presumably cast Mussolini in the role of David mainly on account of his being a slayer of the nation's enemy, rather than because of any physical parallels (apart from a shared youthfulness). But it was Mussolini's physical appearance and magnetism, as much as his rhetoric or actions, that in the next months reassured Mario and other *squadristi* that their spiritual revolution was not going to be betrayed.

When Mussolini came to review Mario's 'Disperata' squad in December 1921 it was the mysterious force emanating from the fascist leader's face that most struck the student:

> He looked at us with those large deep eyes, and then, in the silence that had been created, he moved slowly along the line. I had never seen him so close up and I felt him going by more through his liquid gaze than the physical passage of his body. He disappeared suddenly with those massive shoulders through the doorway.[44]

Others similarly claimed to be mesmerised by Mussolini's eyes. The leading Perugia fascist, Giuseppe Bastianini, had a pleasant sensation of being examined intensely as if he were an object and penetrated by a 'magnetic fluid' at his initial encounter with the fascist leader in March 1921.[45] For the journalist and psychologist Paolo Orano, later one of the fascist regime's most prominent intellectuals (and a major anti-Semite), it was the 'light devouring' eyes that struck him most at his first meeting with Mussolini in November 1922 and caused him to think: 'You, you are the one I have been awaiting for the Fatherland . . . You are the one: I recognise and obey you. Command, lead, govern.'[46] The young Bologna fascist and future editor of *Il Popolo d'Italia*, Giorgio Pini, first heard Mussolini speak in April 1921 and immediately felt that he was 'a truly new figure compared to the other politicians of the time'. When he met him in October 1923 the experience was 'truly electrifying': what remained impressed on his mind 'was the benevolent and piercing look he gave me that day'.[47]

Mussolini himself was fully aware of the importance of his personal magnetism to the success of fascism. Like many observers, he believed the horrors of the war had accentuated what the Milanese intellectual, Margherita Sarfatti (a writer for *Il Popolo d'Italia* – and also his lover) called 'the religious sense of life' and with it the predisposition of ordinary people to express their often ill-defined hopes of redemption and renewal in 'veneration for the Leader'.[48] As a revolutionary socialist in 1912–14 his passionate and often violent oratory had made him, as an early biographer said, an 'idol of the crowd';[49] and in the post-war years he honed his rhetorical skills to convey what one listener described as a sense of 'total self control' and of 'knowing perfectly how and where he wants to lead his people'.[50] The effect on audiences was frequently remarkable. The journalist Ugo Ojetti heard him speak in Rome in November 1921 and was struck by his dramatic gestures and facial expressions and the air of absolute moral certainty – 'the whole world reduced to black and white' – that so captivated his audience. And when the speech was over he watched as Mussolini was grasped round the waist by a colleague and hoisted into the air above the crowd, 'with the gesture of a priest raising the holy eucharist in a monstrance'. Next to him he saw two young blackshirts in tears.[51]

One young *squadrista* who was smitten by Mussolini from the start and felt, like Mario Piazzesi, that he offered a guarantee that fascism would not lose its initial moral force, was Giuseppe Bottai. Bottai had been born in 1895, the son of a Rome wine merchant, and after serving in the war as a junior officer, and being wounded, he had returned home with a deep sense of emotional disquiet. He had first met Mussolini in the offices of *Il Popolo d'Italia* in Milan at the end of 1918 and had been struck by an aura of ill-defined greatness and strength: Mussolini's hands in particular had seemed 'immense, gnarled and powerful' as they had picked up a hand grenade lying on his desk to show him.[52] The following year Bottai had helped set up the Rome *fascio* but, as his diary of the time indicated, he had found many of his colleagues in the movement intellectually lightweight.[53] He had tried Futurism, but that too had proved less than satisfying. After visiting the studio of the painter Giacomo Balla, he had come away feeling that Futurist art was arid and simply reflected the 'amorality of the age':

> The century is here in a nutshell: the cold application of scientific, systematic, financial logic prevails over the mental triumph of instinct, over the absence of a spiritual line, over our age's negation of religion. Never indeed was mystery so distant from the world . . . In the past the mysterious and the miraculous flourished in the most palpable things . . .[54]

Throughout 1920 he had discharged his sense of spiritual anguish onto the pages of his diary, interspersing detailed notes on his wide reading of French, Spanish and classical authors with his own romantic verse compositions and allusions to what he hoped would be a new dawn. In March he had written:

> There is a moment in the life of the individual and society when the air clears and unclouded eyes see error where until the day before they had seen sacrosanct truth . . . I feel we are fast approaching such a moment, which will be a kind of universal judgement on earth. And we will all go to it naked and pure. And whoever for excess of corruption does not have the courage to go will thereby see himself eliminated from the world.[55]

As fascism escalated in the course of 1921, Bottai's somewhat apocalyptic mindset projected a measure of religious fervour onto the struggle against socialism, and he found a new sense of vocation in Mussolini's political movement. He stood for parliament in the spring (and was elected: though he was disqualified subsequently on the grounds that he was too young) and played a leading role in the organisation of the squads in the capital. And within fascism's hierarchical framework Mussolini came to occupy in Bottai's eyes an increasingly exalted role, such that in 1924 he could be described by him reverentially as 'becoming more and more a deep mystery in my life'.[56] He was never to lose his infatuation with the fascist leader. Even in 1946 he could look back nostalgically and recall how Mussolini's eyes had imparted an 'immense and uncontainable look' and his voice had 'vibrated with echoes of the infinite'.[57]

Bottai, who was to become a pivotal figure in the fascist regime, was undoubtedly extreme in his intellectual idealisation of fascism in general and of Mussolini in particular. Many of those who got involved in *squadrismo* in 1920–22 were inspired by much less elevated motives. For some the fight against socialism was probably little more than an opportunity to display adolescent ruthlessness and bravado – as with the killers of the Cremona socialist, Attilio Boldori, who in December 1921 was brutally clubbed to death by a group of some twenty fascists. When the police asked who was responsible, the main culprit stepped forward and boldly declared: 'Me, Giorgio Passani, student, 16 years old.'[58] Some *squadristi* were to all intents and purposes psychopaths; some just petty criminals. And some perhaps both: Amerigo Dumini, a prominent figure in Florentine *squadrismo* (and later one of the assassins of the socialist leader Giacomo Matteotti) liked to introduce himself, according to Emilio Lussu, as 'Dumini, Amerigo, eight murders!' Dumini was responsible among other crimes for the killing of a socialist municipal guard and his mother in Carrara and was only stopped from stealing gold objects from their corpses with the arrival on the scene of the police.[59]

As for the huge numbers who flocked to join the fascist party in 1921–22, many were motivated by economic self-interest as much as by political or ideological considerations. Membership reached 218,000 by the end of 1921 (up from 20,000 a year before), and according to the party's own statistics a quarter of those enrolled were agricultural labourers and a further 15 per cent industrial workers (the next two largest categories were students with 13 per cent and farmers with 12 per cent).[60] This social profile was in large measure a reflection of the rapid growth in 1921 of the fascist trade union movement, which had sprung up over the wreckage of the socialist and Catholic organisations, mainly in the rural areas of the Po valley. By the late spring of 1922 it claimed nearly half a million workers. Those who entered the fascist unions did so not just from terror and coercion. Many rural labourers, smallholders and sharecroppers had themselves resented the stranglehold of the local socialist organisations and often seem to have joined the fascist unions willingly, particularly when there was the prospect of preferential treatment with the assignment of jobs. They had also become accustomed over the years in much of the north to quite brutal struggles between socialists, republicans, revolutionary syndicalists and Catholics for control of the labour force. The advent of fascism was in a sense therefore nothing very new – especially as many of the leading fascist unionists had themselves been active in revolutionary syndicalism prior to the war.[61]

But however varied in reality the impulses that led so many people to join what by 1922 had become the largest party up till then in the history of Italy, the language of crusading idealism in which Mussolini and other fascist leaders clothed their actions created a moral arsenal with which a movement rooted in violence and illegality could be legitimated and support or acquiescence justified. And this language was made all the more potent by being historically and culturally familiar. Many *ras* spoke of how their commitment to fascism emerged from a belief that they were finishing the uncompleted work of the Risorgimento. The Ferrara *ras*, Italo Balbo, who graduated from university in 1920 with a dissertation on the economic and social thought of Giuseppe Mazzini, sanctioned his *squadrismo* with talk of 'duty', 'thought and action', and 'Rome', 'which encompasses the most absolute, vast and definitive ideal'.[62] The Bologna *ras*, Dino Grandi, who described himself as a 'Mazziniano' after the war, talked of how his 'adolescent spirit' had been imbued with 'the sentiments and ideas' of the great figures of the nineteenth century, and how their thinking could be summed up in the dictum of the Piedmontese patriot Massimo d'Azeglio: 'We have made Italy, now we must make Italians'.[63]

Even more potent in many respects was the deliberate use of religious language and liturgical practices. The Risorgimento again furnished a powerful precedent. Mazzini and his democratic followers had been convinced that the cause of Italy would best attract mass support if it was presented as a passionate holy war, with 'faith', 'sacrifice', 'martyrdom' and 'mission' as cardinal concepts. More recently D'Annunzio had offered a further template, filling his speeches with sacred language and imagery and punctuating the civic life of

Fiume with carefully choreographed rituals. Mussolini built on these precedents, encouraging his supporters to view their struggle as a 'war of religion' and to construct a 'liturgy' that would induce the masses 'to believe in the holiness of the sacrifice of our dead'.[64] For, as Bottai explained in a party journal in 1923, 'religions often conquer souls and spirits through the solemnity of their ceremonials more than through the sermons of their priests; and it is through these ceremonials that the mystical afflatus frequently finds its way into hearts. So it was with fascism . . .'[65]

For Mario Piazzesi and his friends in the Florentine 'Disperata' squad, the recourse to liturgy found its most poignant expression in the cult of the dead. On 6 March 1921, after the days of bitter street fighting that had evoked for Mario the brutality of medieval factional struggles, they carried the coffins of their comrades on their shoulders into Piazza Cavour, placed them in a square, and sang 'Giovinezza' as a final salute. 'The song', Piazzesi wrote in his diary, 'rose into the great piazza, hard and full of pain, and at the end it took on a strange tonality. And our faces too became hard, suddenly aged I would say, as if our youths had fled to join the immortal youths of our fallen companions.' The theatricality of the occasion was deliberate, and Piazzesi was content to note how the local 'bourgeoisie' were 'scandalised by the profane rite'.[66] But the commemoration of the 'martyrs' of fascism – which was to be a central element in ceremonial culture throughout the regime – had a political as well as a liturgical purpose. It served, as Mussolini said, to show the continuity that existed in the eyes of fascism between 'the epic poem of the war and the drama of the revolution'.[67] The dead of 1915–18 and 1919–22 had fallen for the same glorious ideal.

The use of religious language had another crucial function beyond trying to vindicate the moral and political claims of fascist violence, a function that was to play an important role in the years ahead as the regime set out to bind the masses emotionally to the state. In stressing faith, obedience, duty, sacrifice and hierarchy, and celebrating the spiritual over the material, fascism was able to map much of its value system onto the familiar landscape of Roman Catholicism. Tullio Cianetti, a smallholder's son from Assisi, with strong Christian convictions, who was to become a prominent figure in fascist syndicalism and in due course a government minister, recalled in his memoirs how in the summer of 1922 a leading party figure, Piero Bolzon, was sent to try to persuade the diffident young fascist to become a union leader in Terni. What resonated in Cianetti's memory was the sense of an irrefutable religious logic:

'But . . .', I started objecting. 'But . . . but . . .', Bolzon interrupted me, smiling, ' . . . I will put just one question to you: do you have in you that certain faith that can make you see the beauty of a battle?' 'Yes, I certainly do, but battles are fought with weapons . . .'. 'But if you don't have faith, weapons are but idle things.' 'But without weapons, faith is not enough.' 'Love, love, my boy, is needed to guide the masses. With faith and love you will quickly make up for your inexperience. For men to believe in you, you must make them feel that you believe in them: and if you want to be loved, love them! . . . You are a man of the people and must know how much good sense there is in the poor, who may lack means but are certainly not short of intelligence and feeling . . . In your Assisi, Saint Francis' town, every street, every church, every monastery, every stone speaks to you of the great Christian ethic that has come from Heaven to teach men the true brotherhood that arises from understanding. To understand and be understood is the great secret that illuminates the ways of love and social harmony.' And so many other things Bolzon said to me. And I believed blindly in his words because I felt they came from his heart . . . I accepted with enthusiasm the destiny that was confronting me, I was ready to place my faith and my enthusiasm in the service of the great cause. Bolzon continued to talk as we walked up and down between piazza del Comune and Santa Chiara. And he expounded fascinating ideas and theories about the future of fascism, which he saw as an idea that would renew national society. I listened to him with growing admiration as if his words revealed not just ideas that were completely unknown but truths that had been lying dormant in my spirit, to which his words gave form and the breath of life. 'Many people', [Bolzon added], 'wrongly think that fascism is simply an anti-Bolshevik reaction. No, fascism will be a Revolution and Mussolini is the new man who will have a defining role in contemporary Europe. I see in Mussolini the future Leader of a great European democracy that will spread from Rome to Moscow, via Berlin.'

All Cianetti's doubts were allayed. He had a sense of vocation: 'I listened with religious attention. I felt a flame, a great flame, descend into my heart. I would leave that evening for Terni.'[68]

3

Return to Order, 1922–24

The March on Rome

The formation of the fascist party in the autumn of 1921 did little to moderate the violence of the fascist squads across northern and central Italy. The local *ras* remained very much a law unto themselves. Moreover, from a tactical point of view, as Mussolini himself realised fascism stood to benefit greatly from perpetuating the disorder and using it as a weapon with which to blackmail the government into handing over power. Neither Ivanoe Bonomi, who became prime minister after Giolitti's fragile coalition acrimoniously collapsed in the wake of the spring elections, nor his successor, Luigi Facta, an ineffectual Piedmontese lawyer who took over in February 1922, showed any sign of being able to curb the *squadristi*. The police openly fraternised with the fascists: 'The *carabinieri* travel around with [them] in their lorries, sport their party badge in their button holes, sing their hymns and eat and drink with them', reported a priest from the Veneto in July 1922.[1] And the prefects almost invariably took their side. One, Cesare Mori, a Nationalist by political inclination, who famously attempted to make a firm stand against fascist aggression in Bologna, found himself for his pains quickly abandoned by the government and transferred to a post in the far south of the country.

The cause of fascism was hugely assisted by the ineptitude of its enemies. At the end of July the elderly leader of the moderate socialists, Filippo Turati, went to the Quirinal Palace for the first time in his life to discuss the political situation with the king and offer his support for an anti-fascist coalition. But the liberals could not agree on what to do. Vittorio Emanuele Orlando talked of forming a government of national unity, but Giolitti found the idea of sharing power with the Catholic *popolari* repellent and claimed that any attempt to crack down on the fascists would 'almost inevitably' plunge the country into a full-blown civil war.[2] The trade unions then proceeded to make matters worse by calling a general strike. It was poorly supported – fewer than 1,000 of Fiat's 10,000 workers joined in – but it played straight into the hands of the fascists, who declared themselves defenders of the nation against a weak state and a still-dangerous Bolshevik threat, kept the public services running with volunteers, and launched a fresh wave of attacks. In Milan, Genoa, Ancona, Livorno, Bari and elsewhere armies of fascists, in some cases several thousand strong, rampaged through the streets in the first days of August, destroying socialist buildings, occupying town halls, forcing the resignation of left-wing councils, and leaving a trail of dead and wounded in their wake. The only serious resistance occurred in Parma, where the *squadristi*, led by the *ras* of Ferrara, Italo Balbo, were halted by troops and armed civilians led by a local socialist deputy.[3]

It was now not so much a question of if but when Mussolini's party would come to power. The organisers of the general strike had been hoping to provide an overwhelming demonstration of support in Italy for 'the defence of political and trade union freedoms' and the 'conquests of democracy'. But freedom and democracy had long been synonymous with governmental weakness, subversion and economic and social chaos, and these words did not have the emotional force to stir Italians to action. Even the most authoritative representatives of liberalism showed no desire to make a principled stand, and found political or intellectual reasons to justify their acquiescence in the face of fascism. Luigi Albertini, the distinguished editor of *Corriere della Sera*, publicly hailed Mussolini's movement as 'the extreme wing of a great national party that wanted the sacrifice of the war for the good of Italy and does not wish to see Italy die, suffocated by a stupid . . . and outdated utopia'. The eminent economist Luigi Einaudi dismissed the extremism of the *squadristi* as little more than a 'boiling over of impatience', and applauded fascism for having 'broken the spell of the red terror'.[4] The philosopher Benedetto Croce viewed the excesses of Mussolini's followers with Hegelian optimism: when, towards the end of October, it looked as if the fascists were about to seize power by force, he cheerfully sought to allay the fears of his old friend Giustino

Fortunato, saying: 'But don Giustino, have you forgotten what Marx says, that violence is the midwife of history?'[5]

For Mussolini, one of the biggest threats in the late summer of 1922 was his old rival Gabriele D'Annunzio. Luigi Facta, the prime minister, was considering using the official anniversary of Italy's victory on 4 November 1922 to launch a programme of national reconciliation. There was talk that D'Annunzio might be lured from his retreat on Lake Garda to deliver a speech calling on all Italians to bury their differences and unite behind the flag. Fortunately for Mussolini, the chances of this happening were reduced when the poet was seriously hurt falling from a window of his villa on the evening of 13 August. (He appears to have lost his balance fondling the sister of his mistress while high on cocaine.)[6] But there remained a sense of urgency, not least among many *ras* and *squadristi*, who feared that if they did not press for power at this juncture, the opportunity might be lost for good. Plans accordingly began to be made in the early autumn for a march on Rome; and in mid-October they were firmed up. They envisaged the occupation of public buildings such as post offices in the principal cities (to hamper communications from the centre and maximise the sense of confusion), the concentration of *squadristi* at muster points in central Italy, an ultimatum to the government to hand over power, and a descent on the capital and the capture of ministries.[7]

A key issue was the monarchy. Mussolini had always maintained that fascism was 'republican in tendency' but, faced with the prospect of the king ordering the army to open fire on the rebels, he quickly modified his position, declaring in a major speech in late September that the Crown had nothing to fear from his party and urging Victor Emmanuel not to oppose the 'fascist revolution'. At the same time he looked to maximise the patriotic appearance of the march by placing it in the tradition of the three attempts made by Garibaldi to capture the Eternal City in the 1860s and stressing how his party aimed to regenerate Italy spiritually, as befitted Rome's unique character and the unfulfilled hopes of the Risorgimento:

[I]f Mazzini and Garibaldi attempted three times to reach Rome, and if Garibaldi had presented his redshirts with the tragic and inexorable dilemma of 'Rome or death', this means that for the men of the

Risorgimento Rome had an essential role, of paramount importance, to play in the new history of the Italian nation. Let us therefore turn our thoughts to Rome, which is one of the few cities of the spirit in the world, with hearts pure and free of rancour . . . And it is our intention to make Rome the city of our spirit, a city that is purged and disinfected of all the elements that have corrupted it and dragged it into the mire. We aim to make Rome the beating heart, the galvanising spirit, of the imperial Italy that we dream of.[8]

The *ras* of Ferrara, Italo Balbo, was to be one of the four so-called 'quadrumvirs' heading the march on Rome (two of the others, Cesare Maria De Vecchi and Emilio De Bono, were chosen for their close links with the army). For Balbo the sense of continuity with the Risorgimento, with its romantic dreams of national regeneration, a Third Rome, and 'the people' mobilised in concord on behalf of a great cause, shaped the way he experienced the events at this time. On 24 October a huge rally was held in Naples and the final plans were made for the march on the capital. Mussolini addressed an enthusiastic audience in the San Carlo Theatre. Benedetto Croce was seen applauding 'fervently'.[9] After the speech Balbo came down from the stage and mingled with the crowds, and helped, as he recorded in his diary, to beat time to 'the two fatal syllables: "Roma"'. Outside, in Piazza del Plebiscito, thousands of people were likewise chanting 'the great word'. The following day, at a meeting of the party leaders, the administrative secretary handed out 25,000 lire to each zone commander to cover their mobilisation expenses. But for Balbo the money was not important. It was 'will' that counted – and unity of purpose. Two *ras* who had fallen out were invited by Balbo publicly to bury their differences: 'There is an atmosphere of almost religious fervour in the room . . . At my request the two men throw themselves into each other's arms. Peace is made.' Everything now seemed propitious for the attempted coup: 'The old parliamentary Italy has realised that its hour has come . . . The pact that binds us is sacred and will not be broken, whatever may happen.'[10]

The mood in the country following the Naples rally was tense. 'We are at the moment when the arrow flies from the bow, or the bowstring snaps under the pressure!' Mussolini had told his supporters.[11] On 27 October fascist squads began converging on major towns and cities, occupying telephone exchanges, telegraph offices, town halls and prefectures, in most cases without violence. Rumours and counter-rumours began to fly. 'There was a huge bedlam of reports, of denials, confirmations, and denials again', recalled the eighteen-year-old Giulio Bianchi Bandinelli, who was living in the small Tuscan town of Castellina, where almost everyone, he said, including the family he was staying with, had converted from socialism to fascism during 1921. '. . . There was enormous excitement and also a measure of anxiety.' Some of his school friends urged him to come with them to Rome; but he had no money (and it was raining): 'So I had to forgo the glory'.[12] In Arezzo, the seventeen-year-old Giulio Teoni recalled seeing posters telling fascists to assemble, and he and a cousin got hold of a couple of pistols and travelled in a cattle truck to the town of Orte some 40 miles to the north of the capital, and waited there with several thousand other blackshirts for further news.[13]

Overall, the mobilisation went less well than expected. The cold and wet, as well as deep uncertainty about how the government would respond, discouraged many from turning out, and only about 16,000 *squadristi* reached the main assembly points around Rome. Most had no weapons or food, and it was clear that the army could have dispersed them with minimal force. 'It would have taken just one regiment to massacre us', said Teoni, 'since the majority were boys or adults with no training.'[14] The prime minister met senior generals and ministers in emergency session in the early hours of 28 October, and later his full cabinet, and it was unanimously agreed that a state of siege should be introduced across the whole country, beginning at midday. A telegram to this effect was sent to all prefects at 7.50 a.m. But when Facta went to see the king at 9.00 and asked him to sign the decree, Victor Emmanuel refused. Why, is unclear: the previous evening he had apparently been determined not to bow to fascist pressure. He may have grown uncertain about the loyalty of his troops or feared that his charismatic cousin, the Duke of Aosta, had done a deal with the fascists and was planning to depose him. Or he may simply have wanted to avoid bloodshed. Whatever the reason, his decision ensured that 'the march on Rome', which had been conceived more as an exercise in political blackmail than a serious revolutionary or military operation, brought the fascists to power.[15]

Facta resigned at 11.30 a.m. Half an hour later a telegram was

dispatched to all prefects, announcing that the state of siege had been
revoked. Jubilant fascists took to the streets. The king initially asked
Antonio Salandra to form a new government, and Mussolini came
under great pressure to accept this solution, particularly from the
Nationalists. But he knew that he was now in a position to dictate
terms. 'Much of northern Italy is under total fascist control . . . Central
Italy is completely occupied by fascists', he wrote in *Il Popolo d'Italia*
on 29 October. 'The victory must not be mutilated . . . The government must be unequivocally fascist.'[16] Salandra declined the mandate,
and Victor Emmanuel turned instead to Mussolini, who arrived in the
capital on the morning of 30 October on the overnight sleeper from
Milan, where he had been staying, barricaded inside the headquarters
of his newspaper, deeply uncertain at the outset as to whether his
gamble would pay off.[17] He drove to the Quirinal Palace, dressed in a
black shirt. Victor Emmanuel asked him to form a government. He
also asked him to disband the squads, but Mussolini considered this
impossible, and it was agreed that the *squadristi* should be allowed a
victory parade through the capital before being sent home.

At the news of Mussolini's appointment as prime minister, tens of
thousands of blackshirts, together with members of the much smaller
paramilitary organisation of the Nationalist Party, the blue-shirted
Sempre Pronti (always prepared), who had often assisted the fascists
in rallies, strike-breaking and sometimes also in raids, descended on
the capital. Among them was a sixteen-year-old school student living
in Caserta, Antonio Dini. Antonio had joined the Sempre Pronti
earlier in the year, along with some ten others in his class, and on
30 October he and his friends travelled to Rome to see what was
happening. They found the streets between the station and St Peter's
thronged with *squadristi* wearing every manner of outlandish uniform,
brandishing pistols, rifles and clubs, and acting as if they were 'the
masters of Rome'. In bars, restaurants and brothels, the fascists merely
had to show their party cards to be served free.[18] In some places the
local inhabitants had the courage to vent their anger, by throwing
bricks and bottles at the 'black devils', as they called them. But this
was risky, since the *squadristi* were looking for almost any opportunity
for violence. Across the city left-wing newspaper offices and party
buildings were ransacked and burned, and prominent anti-fascists were
assaulted and their homes destroyed. The local *ras*, Giuseppe Bottai,

RETURN TO ORDER, 1922-24   61

led his blackshirts through the working-class quarter of San Lorenzo and at the first sign of opposition unleashed an orgy of violence which left a dozen 'subversives' dead.[19]

On the morning of 31 October Antonio watched with shock as fascists destroyed the Federazione Socialista in the Piazza Fontana dei Trevi, throwing books out of the first-floor window, and piling them up to make a bonfire. He hurried to save one volume, an edition of the sixteenth-century playwright, Pietro Aretino's, comedies, but a blackshirt waved a club in his direction and ordered him to put it back: 'This is subversive stuff and must be destroyed.' 'But these are classics, and can be useful for everyone.' 'But they won't be useful for the communists any more . . . That's why we're burning them.' Then the fascist relented, and said, with a sneer: 'Take the book – student – and go!' Later at lunch Antonio and his friends revealed something of the disdain that the predominantly upper-middle-class Nationalists felt for many rank-and-file fascists, loudly telling the waiter in the restaurant in the hearing of several dozen blackshirts: 'The Nationalists are not beggars but gentlemen who pay for their meals!' Fortunately the fascists were too intent on singing and eating to stop and punish them.[20]

Despite such awkward moments, 31 October 1922 remained for Antonio a memorable and exciting day, as he and his fellow Nationalists paraded with fascists through the centre of the capital for four hours amid cheering crowds and girls throwing flowers in an atmosphere that seemed 'intoxicating and heroic'. A distinguished-looking man hurried up to congratulate them: 'Bravo, boys, bravo . . . You have saved Italy! Always remember this great day, which is so important for you and the Fatherland!'[21] For others, too, there was a thrilling sensation with the events of late October that they were protagonists in a drama of momentous and historic proportions. Tullio Cianetti was 'convinced that a new era had begun for the Italian people' – a conviction reinforced by his experience of seeing Mussolini for the first time as he and his fellow fascists from Terni assembled in Piazzale Flaminio before marching down the Corso. Tullio was smitten by the fascist leader's eyes and transfixed, 'as if an imperative in my spirit obliged me to impress on my brain his image, which I wanted to know, understand and love':

When he had left my sight, I felt the sweet sensation that pleasant things leave behind after they have acted for a moment on our senses. Accustomed as I was to the venerable beards of statesmen, and to the imposing and revered old age of the great war leaders, this Leader, my Leader, our Leader, still not forty, with will-power in his jaw, made me feel certain that Italy had secured a helmsman and the youth an inspiration . . . From that moment . . . my life belonged to him, only to him.[22]

Another young man who felt intoxicated by the events of these days was Antonio Pietri, a student at Florence university and a member of the Nationalist Sempre Pronti. Antonio had grown obsessed with politics in recent months – so much so that he had begun to neglect the two activities that in the past had given him the most intense pleasure: hunting and womanising. He had become hugely proud of his blue cap and blue shirt, with its badge of a soaring eagle, and he had spent every evening with his comrades attending rallies (often with the local fascists), singing, drinking, putting up posters, and every now and then going on raids to punish socialists. He relished the feeling that the excesses of youth were being sanctioned by the new political climate, and when news came through that Mussolini had been appointed prime minister he poured out his excitement to a woman friend in a letter full of the inebriated language of his beloved D'Annunzio. He spoke of his boundless faith and enthusiasm, of how he felt ecstatic at being numbered among the pure youth of Italy, and of how he considered himself free now to abandon all self-restraint and give full vent to his idealism.[23]

But not every young Nationalist or fascist was elated by the outcome of the March on Rome. Some radical or 'pure' squadristi had a sense of deep disappointment. The entry into the city seemed more like a hurriedly staged gesture of consolation designed to get them off the scene as fast as possible, rather than a proper revolution. Mario Piazzesi felt that he and his comrades were treated 'like dogs, just like dogs', forced to make their own arrangements for food and accommodation and then lined up perfunctorily and marched down the Corso:

On the balcony of the Quirinal, the king, flanked by the two war commanders, [General] Armando Diaz and [Admiral] Thaon di Revel, saluted the revolutionaries. In front of the palace, the timid Roman bourgeoisie, their fears now allayed, waved their arms in patriotic celebration . . . We walked on and on, dazed with tiredness, until before we knew it we found ourselves back on the train. 'What! No sooner do we arrive than they send us away, do they? Without shooting anyone? What revolution is this? Or haven't we won?'[24]

Mario and his friends were not alone in their uncertainty. Many observers in those cold and damp autumn days at the end of October 1922 were far from clear as to who or what had won.

Return to order

It was not altogether surprising that there was such uncertainty over what the March on Rome and Mussolini's appointment as prime minister meant. Fascism had burst so suddenly onto the stage in the course of 1921–22; it had offered no clear programme or ideology; and its supporters had come from a great variety of political backgrounds. Its seemingly protean character was enhanced by the way it gloried in extreme and florid language, which could leave listeners uncertain as to what was really meant and what was intended principally as gesture or emotional display. Roberto Farinacci, the *ras* of Cremona, probably the most radical and violent of all the squad leaders, told the blackshirts assembled in Rome on 31 October, in a statement released to the press, that they had achieved 'the most beautiful revolution a people could ever carry out', renewing 'the glorious triumphs of the Garibaldian epic'; but he added that 'the muzzle of every rifle must today carry a flower, as an exquisite symbol that would express the will to bring peace to all spirits'.[25] Mussolini veered between similar extremes a fortnight later when he delivered his first speech to parliament as the head of government. To loud cheers from fascists and Nationalists (and also the far left), he declared that he could have turned 'this grim grey chamber into a bivouac for soldiers', but then added – to applause from many on the liberal benches – that he aimed to convert 'the revolution of the blackshirts' into a 'force for development, progress and stability in the history of the nation'.[26] Most observers felt that the advent to power of Mussolini marked

the beginning not of a revolution but of a return to order and normality
after the turmoil of the post-war years. The fact that the new cabinet
included four liberals, two *popolari*, the Nationalist Luigi Federzoni,
the eminent philosopher Giovanni Gentile, and two distinguished
military figures, General Diaz and Admiral Thaon di Revel, appeared
to offer confirmation of this. Mussolini retained the key foreign and
interior ministries for himself, and many of the positions of undersecretary were given to fascists. But overall the complexion of this
so-called National Government was reassuringly conservative. The
business community, which had been highly nervous at the prospect
of such an unpredictable figure as Mussolini being in charge, had its
anxieties allayed by the appointment of an orthodox liberal economist,
Alberto De' Stefani, as Minister of Finance. Throughout the country,
as the deputy Emilio Lussu recalled, there was a deep sense of relief:
'The time of turmoil is over! No more strikes, ransacking, or fraternal
blood . . . The law returns triumphant after its long exile. Every bell
is tolling: this is peace.'[27]

In fact the unrest and violence had not ended. Brutal episodes of
squadrismo, directed at working-class organisations and leaders,
Catholic as well as socialist, continued with little indication that the
authorities felt able to clamp down on them. In December, for example,
blackshirts, led by a *ras* who subsequently boasted in an interview
with a national newspaper of having ordered twenty-four executions,
terrorised the working-class suburbs of Turin, murdering as many as
forty people. The police stood idly by, convinced, as a report later said,
'that the government was complicit and that the fascists should accordingly be given free rein'.[28] But support for the government was not
seriously undermined by such acts of lawlessness. It was widely
accepted that the process of 'normalisation' would inevitably take
some time and that Mussolini, however good his intentions, would
not be able to bring the squads to heel overnight. Moreover, many
conservatives had persuaded themselves that fascist extremism was a
deeply regrettable but ultimately salutary expression of patriotism,
which could provide a much needed 'injection of energy' into the
governing class. The former prime minister, Antonio Salandra, for
instance, had very little sympathy for the methods of the *squadristi*,
but felt that the blackshirts had their hearts in the right place and were
working to restore the authority of the state.[29] In May 1921 he had

declared in a speech how tears of joy came to his eyes when he heard 'the *crème de la crème* of our people' singing 'Giovinezza, giovinezza', and 'proclaiming once again to the world today, that this Italy of ours is not weak or decadent . . .'.[30]

The return to 'normality' in the country was widely seen as needing to be directed against parliament as much as against the far left (or indeed the *squadristi*). After the March on Rome a number of senior fascists maintained that the cause of the 'revolution' would best be served by an immediate dissolution of the Chamber and the holding of elections. They were worried about a coalition government and the compromises that this might entail, just as some of them were anxious about the longer-term implications of Mussolini having been invested with power constitutionally by the king. ('It is not the revolutionary Mussolini who went to the king, but the king who summoned the revolutionary Mussolini', Mussolini pointed out to a somewhat nervous follower.)[31] However, the new prime minister correctly calculated that he could secure more from a legislature that was discredited and over which hung an imminent threat of dissolution, than from one newly mandated by the electorate. On 16 November 1922 he accordingly demanded of the Chamber, and was granted, 'full powers' to reform the administration and finances of the state. The mood that day among deputies after the extraordinary events of the previous weeks was cowed. There was one somewhat tentative cry of 'long live parliament' in protest at Mussolini's bullying manner, but nobody followed suit, and the words, according to an observer 'fell into a void amidst bewildered servility'.[32]

Against this backdrop of parliamentary acquiescence, Mussolini was able, in the interests (or so it could be maintained) of 'normalisation', to take a number of measures that were ostensibly in breach of the constitution. At a meeting of the cabinet on 15 December he angrily demanded authorisation 'to act by whatever methods I may hold necessary against anyone, of whatever party, faction or sect, who seeks to introduce disturbance or disorder into the nation, which has an absolute need of calm and discipline'. He then introduced a new deliberative body, the Grand Council of Fascism, which would co-ordinate the actions of the fascist party and its various organisations with those of the government. This institution was intended as a form of 'parallel' cabinet – indeed as a rival to it; and though it could be presented as an instrument for taming the party and bringing it into line with the state, its decisions were soon seen as having greater weight than those of the official cabinet. Its dubious constitutional status (and perhaps intent) was underlined at its first meeting when it declared that the date of any new elections would be decided by Mussolini: traditionally it was the king's prerogative to make such a decision on the basis of advice received from the cabinet.[33]

Another innovation that again could be presented as a means of bringing the party to heel was the setting up in January 1923 of the Fascist Militia. This was a paramilitary organisation whose declared aim was to support the police and army in preserving public order and 'defending the fascist revolution'. The fact that members of the Militia had to display 'blind' and 'total' obedience to the leadership (ultimately Mussolini) and swear an oath of loyalty to 'Italy' and not the king – who under the constitution was head of all the armed forces – made this a manifestly illegal institution, as a number of liberal commentators were quick to point out. But since the Militia could be seen as a mechanism for absorbing the *squadristi*, bringing them under the control of the state, and curtailing the power of the *ras*, conservative anxieties were allayed (though in practice many *ras* and their followers long refused to be 'absorbed' in this way). Furthermore, regular army officers were encouraged to take up positions of command in the Militia, which provided additional reassurance for the establishment.[34]

A further indication that Mussolini might be serious about curbing his more radical followers was the merger with the Nationalists in February 1923. The Nationalists were a small but highly influential party – authoritarian, monarchist and Catholic in orientation – with a strong following in the upper echelons of the army, the diplomatic service, big business and academia. They had much in common with fascists, both ideologically and organisationally, including their own paramilitary formation. But as Antonio Dini's edgy experiences during the March on Rome had shown, relations between the blueshirts and the blackshirts had not always been harmonious. Many radical fascists felt uncomfortable about the merger – even though it meant the complete liquidation of the Nationalists as a distinct party. They feared their own party would now be pulled in a sharply conservative direction. But for Mussolini the fusion had clear political advantages.

It underlined his bid for respectability; it gave him links to important sectors of high society; and it provided him with much needed cadres of able administrators. In the years to come the Nationalists would exert an influence on the regime that was out of all proportion to their modest numbers, and figures such as Luigi Federzoni and Alfredo Rocco were to be crucial in shaping the architecture of the fascist state.

In the course of 1923 Mussolini played a skilful political game. He alternated between respectability and radicalism, and kept both sides uncertain as to his true trajectory. At his first meeting with the king he had worn a black shirt: thereafter he dressed in a morning suit and top hat for royal audiences, and spats, butterfly collar and bowler hat for most other public occasions. In his speeches he touched repeatedly on traditional leitmotifs of Italian patriotism, using language that had become ingrained in the national lexicon since the time of the Risorgimento. He spoke of the need for Italy to be 'reborn', shake off its old vices, and emerge strong, feared and respected in the world and not just a land of 'museums and libraries'.[35] He referred time and again to the importance of 'order', 'discipline' and 'hard work', and of the need to mould the national character and 'make Italians' in accordance with the celebrated dictum of Massimo d'Azeglio at the time of unification ('we have made Italy, now we must make Italians'). He stressed how Italy must strive to achieve 'moral unity' and transcend the old divisions caused by factions, parties and municipalism.[36] He also made highly respectful comments about the Catholic Church, describing it as 'one of the pillars of national society';[37] and he backed up his words by reinstating crucifixes in schools and courtrooms and providing 3 million lire for the restoration of churches damaged in the war.

But interspersed with such conservative gestures and statements were far more subversive comments. For the most part these were delivered at party rallies, to *squadristi* eager for confirmation that the March on Rome was indeed the start of a revolution and that it was only a matter of time before the compromises with the old regime came to an end. Liberals could comfort themselves with the thought that the vehemence of Mussolini's language on these occasions was largely tactical – a way of appeasing rank-and-file fascists pending their 'normalisation'. But it was also the case that many of his attacks on

the Italian liberal state had been part of mainstream criticism for
several decades, and their capacity to shock was accordingly severely
blunted. This was the case with parliament, an institution that the
fascist leader persistently disparaged as corrupt and weak. As he said
in a speech to party members in October 1923, explaining why the
March on Rome had been necessary a year before:

> For twenty, perhaps thirty, years the Italian political class had been
> growing steadily more corrupt and degenerate. Parliamentarism – with
> all the stupid and demoralising associations that go with this word –
> had become the symbol of our life and the hallmark of our shame . . .
> When people could read what were referred to as parliamentary
> proceedings and see what might be described as an exchange of the
> most banal insults between the so-called representatives of the nation,
> they felt disgusted, and a sense of nausea welled up inside them.[38]

Just how much attacks of this kind could resonate, even with people
who felt little instinctive sympathy for fascism, can be seen from the
diary of Stefania Berto. Stefania had been born into an aristocratic
family in Palermo in 1882. Her husband had been killed in the war,
leaving her to bring up an infant daughter on her own. She does not
appear to have had strong political feelings: her diary is for the most
part a record of her grief, her religious convictions and her domestic
life. But she admired D'Annunzio, and had approved of his occupation
of Fiume; and she was a member of an Association for Political Culture
(largely, it seems, for social reasons), which met every now and then
to discuss the latest national events. As in much of the rest of the
south, fascism had enjoyed only very limited support in Palermo prior
to the end of 1922, but after the March on Rome there was a headlong
rush to join the party or at least pledge loyalty to it. When Stefania
attended a meeting of her association on 1 November she was horrified to discover that everybody present had decided, with what
appeared quite shameless opportunism, to come out in favour of the
new government.[39]

Initially Stefania could see little if anything to admire in Mussolini.
She considered him ambitious and unprincipled – in the past, as a
revolutionary socialist and republican, and now, as a reactionary
minister and dictator. But she wanted him to achieve one thing before

he left office: to free Italy from parliament. She wrote in January 1923, in language strongly reminiscent of the invective of the pre-war Nationalists, of her desire to see Montecitorio razed to the ground and a *café chantant* built instead on the site. In this way, she felt, the country would be liberated from the 500 or so corrupt deputies who were poisoning and polluting Italy.[40] In the months that followed, as Mussolini began to stamp his authority both on parliament and the country, Stefania's early reservations about the new prime minister began to evaporate. By the time the diary ended in the summer in 1923, she found herself defending his government staunchly to her friends. She pointed out to them how the strikes and lawlessness of the liberal period had given way to a pervasive sense of discipline, and how everyone was now able and willing to work – all thanks to the strong hand at the centre.[41]

The benefits of the 'strong hand' inevitably came at the price of freedom, and some observers undoubtedly felt deeply troubled by Mussolini's cavalier approach to parliament, the continuing brutal demolition of left-wing trade unions, the threats to the constitution, and the persistent persecution of the far left: hundreds of socialist and communist leaders were arrested in the spring of 1923. In that year the editor of the *Corriere della Sera*, Luigi Albertini, emerged as a particularly outspoken critic of fascism. But many liberals broadly agreed with Mussolini when he declared that freedom was not to be confused with licence and that the state had to take adequate steps to defend itself against subversion. ('If by liberty is meant the right to spit on the symbols of religion, the fatherland and the state, then I – head of the government and Duce of fascism – declare this liberty will never be allowed!')[42] And many also liked to believe (or hope) that Mussolini would in due course make too many mistakes – he was, after all, only thirty-nine, and the son of a blacksmith to boot – and fall discredited by the wayside, together with many of his young, inexperienced and uncouth followers.

Even the most enlightened liberals and democrats accordingly found grounds to be cheerful. The eminent economist Antonio De Viti De Marco told Gaetano Salvemini in April 1923 that the fascists had 'many merits'. They had shown that the socialists were 'a cardboard wind-screen that crumpled at the first bang' and that the country could 'easily be disciplined', provided it felt 'controlled by a guiding will':

'Today employees work harder, as they are afraid of being sacked or
beaten. The trains arrive punctually. Tax-payers readily pay their dues
because they believe they will help to sort out the budget.'[43] Salvemini
himself maintained publicly at this time that fascism was the consequence of the 'pseudo-democratic practices' of pre-war Italy that he
and other intellectuals had repeatedly criticised in journals like *La Voce*.
He said that until a return to the left meant 'the creation of a regime
that was seriously democratic' and not a reversion to the 'pseudo-
revolutionary post-war hysterics', it was 'desirable that the fascist
regime should remain in being, for better or for worse – and hopefully
for better rather than for worse. Because at present, between Mussolini
and all his possible successors, Mussolini is without any shadow of a
doubt preferable.'[44] In due course Salvemini, like De Viti De Marco,
was to become a committed opponent of Mussolini.

After the turmoil of the previous few years, the myth of 'order'
was mesmerising. It was ironic that those who had been the chief
instigators of the violence and who had done more than anyone else
to undermine the rule of law and bring the state into disrepute should
emerge as the principal beneficiaries of the widespread craving for
stability. A good example of just how seductive the idea of order was
can be seen from the diary of Bruno Palamenghi, a professional soldier
and a relative of the great statesman, Francesco Crispi. Bruno had
been born in Agrigento, Sicily, in 1863, and had served with considerable distinction in the army, rising to the rank of colonel on the Isonzo
front during the First World War. In 1917 he had been dismissed, for
no good reason he felt, and had become active after the war in a league
to support the interests of those who had suffered a similar fate to
himself, the '*Fascio* for sacked officers' (the term '*fascio*' was very much
in vogue at this time, on all sides of the political spectrum).[45] He had
joined the fascist party a few days before the March on Rome, and in
June 1923 he was appointed to the senior rank of 'Consul' in the
recently formed Militia.

After so many years of service to the liberal state, of which his
forebear Crispi had been one of the most illustrious figures, Bruno's
instincts were highly conservative, and talk of the fascist 'revolution'
did not sit very comfortably with him. But the chaos that had engulfed
the country after the war had left him with a powerful sense that it
was the March on Rome alone that had saved Italy from total collapse.

In his native Sicily the situation in 1919–22 had been one of unprecedented turmoil. The larger towns had witnessed repeated strikes,
demonstrations and clashes with the police, while huge swathes of
the rural interior, especially in the centre and west of the island, had
been reduced to near anarchy, as mafia violence, fuelled by high
unemployment, political instability and the desire of often desperate
landowners to bring the peasantry under control and halt the occupations of large estates, reached epidemic proportions. 'Armed robberies,
thefts, cattle rustling, murders, intimidation and violence of every kind
rained down, as never before, on everything and everyone', recalled
Cesare Mori, who witnessed the situation at first hand (and was later
to be entrusted by Mussolini with conducting a major operation against
the mafia).[46] In the province of Trapani alone, according to one esti-
mate, the annual murder rate was around 700 in these years.[47]

In March 1924 Bruno was invited to Rome and heard Mussolini
speak in the spectacular setting of the Teatro Costanzi. He was hugely
impressed. 'He has a penetrating expression, he captivates – he makes
himself master of all of us – he imposes – he electrifies. His voice has
vibrant power . . . and fascinates, enthrals and conquers.' And he
moved on seamlessly in his diary entry from recording this almost
alchemical sensation of control that he had experienced to reflecting
on why 'the Fascist revolution' had been so necessary for Italy:

Who can forget the state of degeneration to which the masses had
been reduced in 1920–1921–1922? There were continuous strikes – the
occupations of factories, plants, workshops and land were daily
occurrences. The railway workers had become absolute masters of the
railways . . . Everything that got dispatched was damaged – wrecked –
stolen. Property was not respected. The post and telegraph services
worked according to the whim of the employees. The *barabba* gangs
in Piedmont, the *teppa* in Lombardy, pick-pockets in Rome, *camorristi*
in Naples, *mafiosi* in Sicily, spread terror in every town, freely carrying
out persecutions – abuse – brutality of every kind – robberies – murders,
and other things – and all this because of the weakness of the
governments at that time . . . Just a few months more of that regime,
and this beautiful Italy of ours would have been finished, and would
have become worse than Russia. It pains me to have to remember, but
even the Italian army – the glorious infantry of Vittorio Veneto . . .

even they were mistreated, abused and insulted in the streets, in cafes, everywhere, by scoundrels – by scum. Without the Fascist revolution – without the March on Rome – Italy would have fallen prey to bolshevism, anarchy, bankruptcy, poverty – and we would have become the laughing-stock and joke of the other nations, worse than we were before the war.[48]

It was this almost apocalyptic vision of what Italy had been reduced to after the war that confirmed Bruno in his wholehearted support for fascism. Mussolini and the March on Rome had 'saved' the country from the abyss and restored discipline, order and respect. The fascist regime was in due course to make this reading of history in effect 'official' – the potted accounts of the events of 1919–22 that primary schoolchildren were obliged to write in their exercise books were invariably along these lines – and the idea that the liberal regime had been synonymous with chaos and could never safely be returned to, became an important factor in limiting opposition in the years ahead. Fascism might have its faults, but what was the alternative? This thought certainly seems to have been decisive in helping Bruno embrace the idea of a fascist 'revolution' and carried him over the watershed of 1924–25 into the full-blown dictatorship, where he served for a number of years as a prefectural commissioner in various Sicilian towns. The consideration that fascism itself had been responsible for much of the turmoil, that a socialist revolution had never been a serious possibility, and that much of the recovery after 1922 might have occurred anyway as the economy picked up, was not given currency.

Italy abroad

If the support of men like Bruno Palamenghi for fascism derived mainly from a belief that Mussolini had the ability to impose domestic order and resurrect the authority of the state, there was also a strong expectation that the fascist leader would be able to salvage Italy's tarnished international reputation – as Bruno's passionate reference to the danger of the country sinking even lower than before the war in the eyes of the world, suggests. Much of the impetus for fascism had come from the febrile nationalist spirit that had been generated by the 'mutilated victory' and the sense that Italy's huge sacrifices in 1915–18 had not been justly recompensed, or even recognised, by the allies. The defiant patriotism that D'Annunzio and his legionaries had directed towards Fiume had subsequently rebounded into the piazzas and been turned against the internal enemy, the socialists. Mussolini's overwhelming concern was with domestic politics in 1919–22 – and this remained the case throughout the 1920s – but he was acutely conscious of just how much success abroad could enhance his standing at home.

In his speech at the inaugural meeting of the fascist movement in Milan in March 1919, Mussolini had spoken of foreign policy in relatively restrained terms. Dynamic nations like Italy needed to be imperialist, he had said; but Italy would spread its influence in the world 'economically and spiritually' and not resort to the 'barbaric methods of penetration' used by the Germans.[49] On subsequent occasions the language of peaceful expansionism, with its echoes of Mazzini's ideal of a universal 'mission' for Italy, had been overlaid with aggressive tones more in keeping with Nationalism. At Fiume in May 1919 Mussolini had declared that the Italian people needed a 'place in the world so as to complete their mission of civilisation'. He added that Italy had 'more right to this than any other people', since it had 'created modern civilisation with the Roman empire and the Renaissance and should now for the third time speak its word of light'.[50] The first programme of the party in 1921 had stated that fascism's principal aims in foreign policy would be to secure national unity, 'even where it has not yet been achieved', and make Italy 'the bastion of Latin civilisation in the Mediterranean'.[51]

After the March on Rome, Mussolini was careful to indicate that he did not intend to embark on any new or independent path in foreign policy. He had no experience on the international stage and he needed to win the backing of diplomats and ministry officials to strengthen his position domestically and assist him in fostering his image abroad. This backing was secured: two senior ambassadors resigned, including Count Carlo Sforza in Paris, but otherwise the great majority of diplomatic staff were content to collaborate with the new government, confident that Mussolini's callowness would encourage him to defer to them. Mussolini fostered this belief by consenting to take lessons in etiquette. But there was also the hope in ministry circles that a strong government would allow Italy more effectively to press its claims, after several years in which Britain and France had been able to take advantage of the country's instability to delay finding a solution to a number of contentious issues still outstanding from the Paris peace conference. The fact that fascism was largely an unknown quantity abroad, but clearly determined to advance the nation's interests, would also be advantageous, it was believed, in winning concessions from foreign governments and furthering traditional Italian goals in such areas as north Africa, the Red Sea and the eastern Mediterranean.

Mussolini's repeated calls during his first months in power for Italy to assert itself on the international stage chimed with a widespread mood of frustration and anger in the country after the rebuffs in Paris in 1919. He talked repeatedly of the need for overseas 'expansion' in order to meet the requirements of Italy's fast-growing population.[52] He denigrated the recently constituted League of Nations as little more than a 'Franco-British duet' and an 'insurance scheme for the established nations against the proletarian nations'. (The idea of Italy as a 'proletarian nation' had been used by the Nationalists before the war to justify the pursuit of colonies.)[53] He celebrated Francesco Crispi for his commitment to Italian greatness in the world and unveiled a memorial to him in the Foreign Ministry. And on the few occasions that he travelled abroad he made it clear that he was determined to uphold Italy's right to be regarded as a great power. At a congress in Lausanne in November 1922 to discuss the peace treaty with Turkey, he demanded that the British and French delegates declare in advance that Italy would be treated on an equal footing. A few weeks later in London he attempted to have the French delegates to a conference ejected from their rooms in Claridge's hotel on the grounds that they had been allocated a more luxurious suite than the Italians.[54]

The impression created by Mussolini and his new government in Britain, as in many other countries, was mixed. A number of newspapers, notably *The Times*, were at first deeply concerned about the threats posed to parliament, liberalism and the rule of law, but others welcomed the restoration of stability and the success of the fascists in allaying the threat of socialism. Mussolini's first visit to London caused a good deal of bemusement, with the unorthodox presence of black-shirted bodyguards, renditions of 'Giovinezza' and a series of surprising and sometimes startling comments by the prime minister to journalists.[55] But in the months that followed, the uncertainty about how exactly to assess Mussolini gave way to a growing consensus that while many of his rank-and-file supporters might be deplorable, the fascist leader himself was an exceptional individual – 'unquestionably a man and a masterful man', as *The Times* conceded – with the force of personality needed to restore stability in Italy. Even liberals began to feel that the threats to freedom, though regrettable, were fully understandable given the history and culture of the country. According to the former Foreign Secretary Lord Grey, in a speech early in 1923, parliamentary government had been imposed on Italians in 1860 and had never proved very congenial to the general public.[56] A few months later King George V paid a state visit to Italy, and on his first evening conferred on Mussolini the insignia of the Order of the Bath and congratulated the country for emerging from its recent crisis 'under the wise leadership of a strong man of government'.[57]

This relatively sanguine assessment of the situation in Italy, which contributed to the acceptance of fascism and helped raise Mussolini's personal standing – at home as well as abroad – was influentially expressed by the historian G. M. Trevelyan in a public lecture at Oxford University in October 1923. According to the distinguished biographer of Garibaldi, Italy was a land that had always been dominated by cities and in which the will of the people had typically been expressed with what he called a 'row in the piazza'. With unification, a system of government that had grown up gradually in England over many centuries was introduced into a society where 'the peasant had no political traditions, and the townsman had no parliamentary training'. As a result the liberal institutions had failed to put down roots and had soon lost credibility; and when, after the war, the country was in chaos, 'the Italian tradition, three thousand years old, of the row in the piazza as the method of political action' led the socialists and the fascists to take to the streets. The fascists ('young ex-servicemen in football shirts, armed with sticks and revolvers') had been victorious, and Mussolini, 'a man of genius at the head of an armed faction', had come to power with his 'amazing *coup d'état*'.[58]

Trevelyan ended his lecture by expressing the fervent hope that the Italian prime minister ('a great man and, according to his lights, a very sincere patriot') would work to restore the operation of free government after having given Italy 'order and discipline when she most needed them'. But he underlined how profoundly different the historical traditions of England and Italy were, and urged his fellow countrymen accordingly 'not to be impatient with Italy if she is for a moment swerving from the path of liberty':

> [T]he Italians as a race have always had a leaning towards a dictator as the surest means of expressing the popular will. It is in the blood and tradition both of their city life, and of their life as a nation. Witness the names of Marius, Julius Caesar, Rienzi, Masaniello, the Capitani del Popolo of the medieval cities, and the element of dictatorship in the careers of Manin, Mazzini, Cavour, Garibaldi, and Victor Emanuel [sic], even in that most liberal of revolutions. The Italian is accustomed to turn for relief to a dictator, to put his trust in a man. The Englishman, owing to an equally great historical tradition, looks for relief to Parliament.[59]

Trevelyan's interpretation of Mussolini as a product of the deep historical traditions of Italy did much to colour British perceptions in the years to come and encourage the idea that fascism should be accepted as a natural and essentially salutary force. Senior politicians such as Austen Chamberlain, Foreign Secretary from 1924 to 1929, strongly promoted the view of Mussolini as an exceptional statesman who had almost single-handedly rescued Italy from disaster. Winston Churchill took a similar line: he announced to journalists in Rome in 1927 that if he had been an Italian he 'would have been whole-heartedly with [Mussolini] from the start to finish in [his] triumphant struggle against the bestial appetites and passions of Leninism'.[60] There was an element of political calculation in such comments. Chamberlain and Churchill certainly did feel genuine admiration for Mussolini, but they also subscribed to the Foreign Office line that the best way to curb the fascist leader's impulsiveness was through flattery.[61] But such endorsements inevitably strengthened Mussolini's hand back home, fuelled belief that he was indeed a 'man of genius', and weakened the position of his opponents.

Evidence that Mussolini was indeed impulsive ('an Etna of a man', as the editor of the liberal newspaper, the *Observer*, called him),[62] and therefore something of a liability on the international stage, came with the Corfu episode in the summer of 1923. Towards the end of August, four Italian members of an international boundary commission were murdered in mysterious circumstances in the north of Greece. Relations between Rome and Athens had for some time been strained on account of the disputed ownership of the Dodecanese islands, which Italy had seized in 1912 at the time of the Libyan war. Although the killers (who were never caught) had almost certainly come from Albania, Mussolini immediately issued an ultimatum to the Greek government demanding a formal apology, a large indemnity, and a solemn funeral for the victims in the Roman Catholic cathedral in Athens to be attended by the entire Greek cabinet. When the Greek government demurred, Mussolini ordered the occupation of the island of Corfu. A squadron of warships was dispatched, but arrived several hours behind schedule, leaving insufficient time for a peaceful surrender to be arranged. Instead the Italian commander proceeded to bombard the island's fortress, even though he was aware it was full of refugees from Armenia. Sixteen people were killed and dozens wounded.[63]

The Corfu incident – a clear challenge to the authority of the League of Nations and its central principle of collective security – attracted worldwide condemnation. The British press was especially critical, much to the indignation of Mussolini: sympathy for the Greeks, he said, defied 'every principle of international morality'.[64] For a time relations with London were very tense. Mussolini hoped to annex the island, but after a month of diplomatic activity he was forced to withdraw his troops in return for the Greek government paying compensation of 50 million lire. Postage stamps bearing the overstamp 'Corfu' were already on sale and had to be swiftly removed from circulation.[65] Despite this disappointing outcome, Mussolini did all he could to present Corfu as a major success, claiming that it had greatly raised the prestige of the nation. In a speech at the end of October to mark the first anniversary of the March on Rome, he described the episode as 'the most interesting and important experience' since 1860, in as much as Italy had 'for the first time carried out a gesture of absolute autonomy and had the courage to deny the competence of the Genevan Areopagus'.[66]

A few senior officials in the Foreign Ministry were shocked by Mussolini's intemperate behaviour over Corfu, but Italian public opinion in general appears to have been enthusiastic about the affair, seeing it as having gone some way to salvaging national honour after the 'mutilated victory'. The fact that one of the main architects of the attack on the island had been the Piedmontese aristocrat and former aide-de-camp to the king, Admiral Thaon di Revel, who had wanted a strike against Greece to help restore the country's prestige, shows how much mainstream conservative support there was for an assertive and defiant foreign policy.[67] Even the liberal *Corriere della Sera*, which was otherwise hostile to the government, backed Mussolini strongly in the crisis, criticising the British and claiming that Italy was displaying moderation and restraint towards the 'brutally offensive' Greeks.[68] Most other Italian newspapers adopted a similar editorial line. The Italian representative at the League of Nations, Antonio Salandra, pledged his full support to Mussolini and defended his country's actions vigorously, maintaining that 'no Italian government could have acted differently'.[69]

Carlo Ciseri was excited by the Corfu episode. In the summer of 1920, shortly after being demobilised and returning to his native Florence, he had recorded in his diary his sense of deep disgust at the way Italy had been treated at the peace conference and his belief that the French and the British had selfishly been bent on keeping Italy as the 'least of the great powers'. 'Our victory no longer counts for anything', he had written despondently. In the course of the next three years, frustrated in his artistic ambitions, struggling to make a living, and deeply dejected, he had found little he wanted to record in his diary. Even the March on Rome had gone by without comment. But news that Mussolini had ordered the occupation of Corfu raised his spirits and gave him fresh confidence that the trust he had shown from the start in the fascist leader had not been misplaced. 'Greece pays the price – Here is the real Italy'. And a few weeks later, on the anniversary of the March on Rome, he voiced once again his profound admiration for Mussolini and in particular his remarkable, indeed almost superhuman, capacity to overcome any obstacles in his path: 'This man is the superior being sent by God to restore peace to us, and perhaps also the honours and glories of ancient Rome.'[70]

Others felt a similar confidence in these months that Mussolini was indeed a 'superior being' whose exceptional abilities would help to restore Italy's health and standing in the world. The minister and future secretary of the fascist party, Giovanni Giuriati, wrote to Mussolini in March professing his 'most fervent faith that you are the Veltro prophesied by Dante', alluding to the famous lines in which the author of the *Divine Comedy* had described how Italy would be saved by the unnamed 'veltro' (literally 'greyhound') who would drive the forces of evil out of every town and city. (After the fall of fascism Giuriati recalled how genuine this belief had been that Mussolini was 'the man predestined . . . to chase moral and civil disorder, heresy and war, not just from Italy, but from the face of the earth'.)[71] Another minister, Alberto De' Stefani, referred in the newly founded party periodical, *Gerarchia*, to Mussolini filling 'the vacuum left by myths' and turning 'the word' into 'action'.[72] And the well-known journalist and writer, Antonio Beltramelli, published a biography of Mussolini in 1923 under the title *L'uomo nuovo* ('The new man'), in which he portrayed the fascist leader as a true son of the Romagna, a region of saints and warriors. Mussolini, he said, had 'recognised in himself the mark of God' and become 'the shepherd of crowds'. He had set out on a path 'towards an almost mystic ideal': 'the exaltation of national sentiment and the power of the State, in opposition to the democratic, pseudo-liberal, pacifist and humanitarian ideologies'.[73]

Mussolini himself was by no means altogether comfortable with such hyperbole. At the end of September 1923 he wrote to the newspaper *L'Impero*, edited by the Futurist and former *ardito* Mario Carli, saying that he had been 'literally terrified' by a recent article that had urged him to consider himself 'sacred'. He requested that his 'profaneness' henceforth be fully respected.[74] Any considerations of personal modesty aside, he was no doubt worried about offending the sensibilities of the Church at a time when he was doing all he could to secure backing from the Vatican for his domestic political battles. There was also anxiety in some sections of the party that in certain areas of the country, the south especially, support for fascism was based primarily on personal admiration for Mussolini and not enough on any ideological commitment.[75] But there were also clear political advantages in the growing exaltation of the fascist leader, especially if the impetus for the nascent 'cult of the Duce' could be seen as coming from below. It strengthened his hand hugely in his dealings not only with his liberal and conservative allies but also with the provincial *ras* and *squadristi*, whose unruliness and resistance to central control remained a major problem throughout 1923 and 1924.

Electoral reform

Admiration for Mussolini, both at home and abroad, in the course of 1923–24 rested heavily on the belief that he was an exceptional man who could return Italy to some form of normality. The persistent violations of the law by the *ras* and their followers, who strove to maintain the local power bases that they had carved out for themselves in the preceding years (sometimes in fierce competition with one another),[76] could thus continue to be overlooked as essentially transient. And the longer-term political (and moral) dangers that such acquiescence might pose in terms of steadily numbing public opinion to illegality could be wilfully ignored. After all, as Bruno Palamenghi had been driven to reflect, a 'revolution', with its many regrettable acts, had surely been inescapable given the failure of successive liberal governments to bring the post-war chaos under control. And in the minds of many, too, there was a recognition that parliamentary government had always been deeply flawed in Italy. As the notable historian Luigi Villari (son of one of liberal Italy's most renowned politicians and intellectuals) bluntly put it in a book published in England in 1924 (*The Awakening of Italy. The fascista regeneration*), one of the main aims of Mussolini from the start had been 'to combat and demolish the artificial structure which a degenerate parliamentarism had imposed on the country'.[77]

But just how far the fascist leader would go with his revolution remained unclear. Mussolini repeatedly stressed that the fascist revolution was 'spiritual' and would seek to purge the degenerate mentalities and practices of the past and create a nation of 'new' men and women: patriotic, disciplined and united. Fascism had 'something religious about it', he claimed. He wanted to 'purify, redeem and elevate' the country and 'forge the great, proud and majestic Italy of our dreams, of our poets, of our warriors, of our martyrs'.[78] Institutions were thus, in effect, of secondary importance, and Mussolini was explicit on occasions in saying that he did not intend to abolish parliament but rather to 'perfect' it by infusing it with fresh energy and morality.[79]

Few had the prescience (or intellectual honesty) of the liberal anti-fascist deputy, Giovanni Amendola. He pointed out in an article in November 1923 that the much vaunted 'spirit' of fascism was in fact wholly antithetical to pluralism and the respect for the views of others on which representative government necessarily depended. The most salient feature of the 'peculiar "war of religion"' that fascism was waging, he said, was 'its "totalitarian" spirit' (perhaps the first-ever time this term had been used), which would 'not in the future permit any dawns to be greeted other than with Roman salutes, just as it does not permit today any souls to be nurtured that do not bow down and confess the "I believe"'.[80]

Mussolini himself was a self-professed atheist, and his socialist past had been full of vitriolic and often blasphemous attacks on religion and the Church. He had talked of priests as 'black microbes', who poisoned the minds of young people and persecuted the Jews, and in 1910 he had published a scurrilous novel about a seventeenth-century cardinal and his courtesan mistress. Even after the war he had continued on occasions to launch diatribes against the Church, condemning Christianity at one point as 'detestable' and calling on the Pope to abandon Rome for ever.[81] Many early fascists had grown up with the nihilism of Nietzsche and Georges Sorel and the icono-clasm of the Futurists, and were mindful of the Pope's dismissal of the war in 1917 as a 'useless slaughter': they, too, harboured intense anti-clerical views. But Mussolini's repeated talk of the need for 'spir-itual' renewal in Italy, his calls for the reassertion of authority, discipline and order, and his passionate opposition to socialism, liberalism and the doctrines of materialism, struck a powerful chord with broad sections of the Catholic Church. The growing favour with which, after the March on Rome, the Pope and the higher clergy in particular came to look upon Mussolini – who repeatedly made clear his earnest desire for their support – was a critical factor in the consolidation of fascism.

The brutality of the *squadristi* in 1920-22 had been persistently denounced as 'barbaric' by the Church, particularly when directed at the Catholic peasant leagues, unions and cooperatives headed by the *popolari* in regions such as the Veneto, Lombardy and Emilia Romagna. Priests and members of the laity who had looked to defend the various Catholic associations (most of which were centrally controlled by the Church through the organisation known as Catholic Action) against the predatory claims of the *ras*, had often found themselves the targets of intimidation and violence. But after Mussolini's advent to power the signals coming out of the Vatican swiftly assumed a much more conciliatory tone as the Papacy sought to take advantage of the prime minister's need to reassure conservative opinion. The fusion with the pro-Catholic Nationalists early in 1923 offered some guarantee that the financial and other concessions made to the Church by Mussolini during his first months in power were not just opportunistic political moves but indications that fascism was sincere in wanting to shed its anti-clericalism and achieve a durable accommodation with the Vatican.

The fact that so many clergy had served, often with great distinction, as chaplains in the army during the First World War, had strengthened patriotic feelings among Catholics and priests and hastened the erosion of the Church's traditional hostility towards the Italian state. It was an indication of how significantly the gap between the Vatican and 'Italy' had narrowed in recent years that after his election as pope in February 1922, Pius XI had given his inaugural blessing ('as a pledge of that peace for which humanity is yearning') to the huge crowds that had gathered expectantly in the rain, aware that something momentous might occur, from the external balcony of St Peter's looking out over the city. All of the three previous new pontiffs since the seizure of Rome by Italian troops in September 1870 had made their first benediction from the *loggia* inside the basilica, symbolically turning their backs on the Italian capital in recognition of the Church's official repudiation of the liberal state.[82]

The increased benevolence of the Vatican towards the Italian state had also been encouraged by the gravitational shift in patriotism brought about by the war. The enemies of the nation, according to those who had pressed for intervention, were not only the socialists but also the old ruling elite and parliament. This made it easier for the Church to sympathise with Mussolini: if the violence of the *squadristi* was reprehensible, the anti-liberalism of fascism was in many respects welcome. The Dominican preacher, Don Guido Palagi, was among a growing number of patriotic clergy who felt able after the March on Rome to write enthusiastically (and intimately) to the 'Saviour of the Fatherland' and applaud his hostility to parliament. 'On this night', the monk said in a letter from his house high in the Apennines on 15 November 1922, 'while the icy wind was blowing on this cold steep mountain, I picked up my pen and spoke about You'. And he attached a poem of 100 verses, entitled 'The lash and the club' (*manganello*), urging Mussolini to save Rome by acting mercilessly against the Chamber:

> O lash, whistle/ without pity/ in the historic halls/ of the Capitol!/ Listen! . . ./ the sensitive Roman geese/ with their raucous croaks/ urge you on/ . . . Lash!/ Beautiful symbol of expiation,/ hurry and strike/ Montecitorio. Can you see/ those undisguised satraps? . . ./ They are . . . deputies/ . . . O provident virtue/ of the club!/ Best it is to destroy/ that brothel! . . . Even in the temple/ the Messiah lashed/ the hawkers/ and drove them out![83]

In the upper echelons of the Church, the authoritarian and anti-liberal elements within fascism resonated with those – and they included Pius XI – who had come to see the turmoil and conflict that had convulsed the world in recent decades as symptoms of the deep moral malaise that had afflicted Western society since the time of the Enlightenment, with its corrosive doctrines of rights and popular sovereignty. As Pius said in an encyclical delivered in St Peter's less than two months after the March on Rome, the absence of peace in Italy and elsewhere had been the direct consequence of the mistaken idea that political life should be rooted in the will of man rather than the will of God. True authority, and with it order, could only come with divine sanction. Any other basis for secular power was a recipe for chaos. 'Jesus Christ reigns over society when men recognise and reverence the sovereignty of Christ, when they accept the divine origin and control over all social forces, a recognition which is the basis of the right to command for those in authority and of the duty to obey for those who are subjects.' And he looked back nostalgically to the Middle Ages when authority had rested firmly on the teachings of the Church, thus creating 'that true League of Nations, Christianity'.[84]

In immediate political terms the most important impact of Pius's authoritarian outlook was on the Popular Party, many of whose grass-roots activists and supporters had experienced at first hand the brutality of the fascist squads. At its congress in April 1923, the party, led by a progressive Sicilian priest, Luigi Sturzo, emerged as deeply split over whether to continue in government. Mussolini responded by brusquely

expelling the *popolari* ministers from his cabinet. This left his parliamentary majority at risk, however – the *popolari* had more than 100
deputies in the Chamber – and he needed to pass a bill for electoral
reform that would guarantee the fascists a clear majority when the
country next went to the polls. It was widely accepted by the liberals
that proportional representation had been disastrous since its introduction in 1919, as it had heavily favoured the socialists and the *popolari*
and prevented the formation of a strong majority. A 'corrected' proportional system was now proposed that would guarantee two-thirds of
all the seats in the Chamber to the party or party grouping that got
the largest number of votes, provided it had secured more than a
quarter of the valid votes cast.

The passage of the bill hinged on the votes of the *popolari*. Pius
was known to be very unhappy about the independence of the Popular
Party from the Church. This had contributed, he suggested in his
encyclical, to 'some among the best of our laity and of the clergy'
being 'seduced by the false appearances of truth' – in other words by
radical ideas. His ambition was to restore strict hierarchical control
over the faithful, using the associations of Catholic Action as his main
tool. The opposition of many of the *popolari* to fascism seemed to
him a stumbling block to the 'pacification of society' that he was
calling for, and in July 1923, with the debate over electoral reform
growing increasingly fraught and threats and demonstrations by *squadristi* against Catholics intensifying, Pius indicated that the *popolari* no
longer enjoyed his favour. As an obedient priest, Luigi Sturzo felt he
had no choice but to resign immediately as secretary of the party. The
popolari were now in total disarray. When it came to the crucial vote
on the electoral law, most of their deputies abstained. The bill was
passed.

Any hopes the *popolari* may have had that their political emascula-
tion would bring an immediate end to their persecution and harassment
by *squadristi* were not immediately realised. This was shown by events
in the small town of Argenta, in the bleak marshlands to the south-
east of Ferrara. Here, as in so many other rural communities, the
fascists had been pressing ahead since the March on Rome with their
efforts to dominate the local peasant population. A particular area of
friction regarded youth. In 1920 the fascists had created an organisation
for students, the Avanguardia Studentesca; and in 1922 the Balilla had

been set up to recruit boys aged from eight to fourteen. (It was named after the child who according to tradition had sparked a popular revolt in Genoa against the occupying Habsburg troops by flinging a stone at an Austrian officer.) These fascist institutions were a direct challenge to the Church, which had long seen the indoctrination of the young as vital to its mission. The various youth associations of the Church were an important part of the umbrella organisation of Catholic Action.

The bespectacled young parish priest of Argenta, Giovanni Minzoni, who had served as a military chaplain in the war and been awarded a silver medal for bravery, was an active supporter of the *popolari* and a strong promoter of peasant cooperativism. His initiatives and independent-mindedness had already attracted the hostility of the local *squadristi*, who took their orders principally from the charismatic *ras* of Ferrara, Italo Balbo. On various occasions blackshirts had gathered outside the presbytery at night and threateningly sung a penitential *Miserere*. In 1923 Minzoni decided to set up a section of Catholic Scouts in the town: there was already a flourishing Circle for Catholic Male Youth and a similar organisation for young women. In July he invited the regional head of the Catholic Scouts, Monsignor Emilio Faggioli, to talk about the aims of the movement in the large hall that Minzoni had recently had refurbished (complete with film projector) for the use of his Catholic Circles. Faggioli explained how the training of mind and body provided by the Scouts would result in the formation of 'men of character'. A voice called out from the audience: 'We already have Mussolini!' Faggioli pressed on, amid loud applause, stressing that the Catholic movement was non-political and expressing the hope that the piazza of Argenta would soon be full of young Scouts singing their anthems. 'They will not enter the piazza', shouted the local fascist party secretary. 'As long as don Giovanni is here', replied Minzoni, 'they will go into the piazza'.[85]

A few weeks later, on 23 August, Minzoni was returning home late in the evening in the company of a friend. The scouting initiative had proved a success, and more than seventy local boys had enrolled. But the priest was well aware of just how provocative his behaviour had been to the fascists, and the risk that he was now running. 'With an open heart, and with a prayer on my lips for my persecutors, which I hope will not cease', he had written in his diary not long before, 'I await the storm, . . . perhaps death, for the triumph of the cause of Christ . . . [R]eligion does not allow cowardice, only martyrdom.' At the corner of a narrow street near to his house he was set upon by two assailants and bludgeoned over the head with a club. He died an hour later. The young man with him survived: his straw hat had softened the blows to his skull. Despite the general public outcry that followed the murder, the police and the courts moved very slowly, and it was not till the summer of 1925 that the trial was finally brought to a conclusion. All the accused, including Balbo, were acquitted of any wrongdoing.[86]

4

The Man of Providence

The murder of Matteotti

Elections were held on 6 April 1924. Mussolini hoped violence could be kept to a minimum – particularly in the major towns and cities, which were most exposed to foreign gaze. But there were numerous murders and assaults, countless attacks on opposition headquarters and other buildings, and frequent disruptions of rallies. Fraud and intimidation were rampant, especially in the more remote rural areas where the *squadristi* had a virtual free hand. Priests faced so much intimidation that the Vatican threatened a public denunciation. The press was largely pro-government: but opposition newspapers such as the prestigious *Corriere della Sera* were often burned at railway stations or boycotted.[1] The government slate of approved candidates (the so-called *listone*) included right-wing liberals and *popolari* as well as fascists. The opposition groups were divided and found cooperation very difficult. There were two socialist parties, a communist party, a republican party, social democrats, *popolari* and various liberals (among them Giolitti). Their failure to form a united bloc made it easier for the fascists to maintain that they were the only 'national' force capable of providing a government.[2] The turnout at the polls was high at nearly 64 per cent. The *listone* secured two-thirds of the votes (making the new electoral law in effect redundant) and 374 of the 535 deputies in parliament. Support for the government and its allies was especially strong in the south.

When parliament reopened on 30 May, the leader of the 'reformist' socialists (who had split from the mainstream party on the eve of the March on Rome), Giacomo Matteotti, a courageous and highly educated lawyer from the province of Rovigo, rose to deliver a damning indictment of the elections. He described graphically the corruption and brutality that had prevented the 'expression of popular sovereignty'. 'Perhaps in Mexico they are used to conducting elections not with ballot papers but with bravery in the face of revolvers. And I apologise to Mexico if this is not true!' In the course of his speech he was subjected to abuse and barracking from the government benches. The prominent socialist and editor of *Avanti!*, Pietro Nenni, who back in 1911 had shared a prison cell with Mussolini, described the scene:

Matteotti: We have a proposal from the Committee for Elections to confirm numerous colleges. We are opposed to this proposal . . .

(A voice: This is provocation.)

Matteotti: . . . because if the government majority has obtained 4 million votes, we know this result is the consequence of obscene violence.

(From their benches, the fascists brandish their fists at the speaker. In the centre of the Chamber the most violent try to throw themselves on Matteotti. Mussolini watches impassively from his bench, frowning, silent, making no gesture.)

Matteotti: The leader of fascism has himself explicitly declared that the government did not consider its fate as tied to the outcome of the elections. Even if it had been in a minority, it would have remained in power . . .

[Achille] Starace: That is true: we have power and we will keep it.

(The whole Chamber descends into uproar. A voice shouts: We will teach you to respect us by kicking you or shooting you in the back! Another exclaims: You are a bunch of cowards! Matteotti remains calm and allows the tumult to die down, ignoring the interruptions.)

Matteotti: To support these government proposals, there is an armed militia . . . *(Voice on the right: Long live the Militia!)* . . . which is not at the service of the state, nor at the service of the country, but at the service of a party . . . *(Shouts on the right: Enough! Enough! Throw him out of the hall!)* . . .

Matteotti: You want to hurl the country backwards, towards absolutism. We defend the free sovereignty of the Italian people, to whom we offer our salute and whose dignity we will defend by demanding that light be shed on the elections.

(The left rises to acclaim Matteotti. On the right there are cries of: Villain! Traitor! Provoker!)

Matteotti (smiling to his friends): And now you can prepare my funeral oration . . .

The 'duce' no longer hides his irritation . . . The previous day he had interrupted a speaker, saying: Twelve bullets in the back are the best remedy for enemies who are in bad faith.[3]

Matteotti was a highly regarded figure in international socialist circles, and his speech had the potential to be very damaging. Even more worrying for the government were rumours that Matteotti had assembled a large dossier on corruption in the fascist party and was about to divulge its contents. One potential scandal related to the sale of huge quantities of surplus war equipment at knock-down prices to fascist supporters, who had then sold it on. One beneficiary was the violent Tuscan *squadrista* Amerigo Dumini, who had amassed the huge sum of 1.5 million lire. He was possibly acting as a front man: Dumini had moved to Milan in the early 1920s pursued by charges of murder and arson and become a protégé of one of the most powerful figures in the fascist party, Mussolini's close adviser, Cesare Rossi. Another possible scandal related to allegations of bribes being paid by a large American oil company to senior fascists to secure exclusive distribution rights in Italy. One of those rumoured to be involved in the party's underhand financial dealings was Mussolini's younger brother and confidant Arnaldo, who had assumed the editorship of *Il Popolo d'Italia* after the March on Rome.[4] Mussolini's cynical view of human nature made him indulgent towards corruption among his colleagues (and the fascist party was to be a breeding ground of corruption during the regime); but he could not afford a public scandal at this juncture. If nothing else it would expose the hollowness of fascist claims to be redeeming Italy from the weakness and vices of liberalism.

On the afternoon of 10 June Matteotti was seized by five men as he walked along the Tiber towards parliament, bundled into a car and, after a violent struggle, stabbed to death. His assailants, led by Amerigo Dumini, had for some time formed a semi-official terror squad nick-named the *Ceka* (after the Soviet secret police), run by the treasurer of the fascist party, Giovanni Marinelli. The killers drove around Rome for several hours, apparently trying to decide what to do, before disposing of the body in a shallow grave some 15 miles outside the city. The corpse was not discovered for more than two months, but it was immediately apparent to everyone that a serious crime had been committed. By chance an alert concierge had written down the number of the vehicle, and it was quickly traced. It belonged to the editor of *Il Corriere Italiano*, a fascist newspaper under the control of Mussolini's press secretary, Cesare Rossi. The night before the murder the car had been seen parked in the courtyard of the Ministry of the Interior. Late on 10 June, Dumini came to Mussolini's office, apparently unflustered, and showed the prime minister a small piece of bloodstained uphol-stery.

The attack had been ordered by Marinelli and perhaps by Rossi, too. Both men had daily contact with Mussolini and would not have acted without his knowledge. The intention had probably been to pass the crime off as yet another 'spontaneous' gesture by undisciplined *squadristi*. Matteotti had already been severely assaulted by blackshirts near his home town in the Veneto in 1921. After his murder a false rumour was spread that a group of *squadristi* from the Rovigo area had been sighted in the capital.[5] But, against the odds, the car had been identified; and in the immediate confusion that followed the crime the fascist leadership was unable to move quickly enough to hamper the investigations and prevent the killers being arrested. Mussolini realised that his government was in serious trouble. 'If I get away with this we will all survive, otherwise we shall all sink together', he reportedly told members of his staff.[6] In an attempt to limit the damage, he ordered the initial investigations to be taken out of the hands of the magistrates and given (illegally) to the fascist Chief of Police, who interviewed Dumini accompanied by two senior members of the Militia. Dumini was in due course to spend two years in prison for the murder, but for a long time after that he was able to extract huge sums of money (in excess, it seems, of 2 million lire) from Mussolini, for all he had done, as he put it in one of his supplicatory letters, 'in the years of danger . . . for the Idea'.[7]

Mussolini strenuously denied any involvement in Matteotti's murder. The country seemed willing to give him the benefit of the doubt. In the eyes of many he still appeared the best guarantee of order and stability. There were almost no protests or strikes, even in the major cities (a sign of how swiftly the working-class movement had been broken); the king did not intervene; the Vatican urged peace ('Let him who is without sin cast the first stone', declared the *Osservatore Romano*); and in Britain *The Times* underlined Mussolini's achievements against 'Bolshevism' and said that his fall was 'too horrible to contemplate'.[8] The principal threats came from the press, the *Corriere della Sera* in particular, and from the cabinet. Several ministers indicated they would resign if the government was not broadened so as to hasten the work of 'national reconciliation'.[9] Mussolini duly brought in two well-respected Nationalists, including Luigi Federzoni as Minister of the Interior. The opposition parties decided to boycott parliament in protest at the killing in what became known as the 'Aventine secession'. But the main effect of this move was to ensure that the government would not be defeated by a vote in the Chamber. Mainstream conservative opinion remained behind Mussolini, and on 26 June the Senate backed his government by 225 votes to 21. Explaining why he had voted with the majority, the liberal philosopher Benedetto Croce said that fascism had 'done much good' and ought to be given 'time to complete its process of transformation'.[10]

But in seeking to reassure conservative opinion, Mussolini was once again at risk of alienating the radical fascists – whose loyalty was vital to his 'carrot and stick' tactics. Throughout the summer he was forced to do everything he could to allay their fears. He gave his public backing to the most violent 'intransigent' wing of the party, led by the Cremona *ras*, Roberto Farinacci. He called on his supporters to 'live dangerously'; he urged the Militia to be on its guard and not be deceived by their enemies, even when they advanced bearing 'every possible olive branch, indeed a whole forest'; and he reminded his followers that the country was calling out for strong government and not freedom.'' But the double-game was becoming increasingly difficult to sustain and risked spiralling out of control. As the *squadristi* placed mounting pressure on Mussolini to demonstrate his unreserved commitment to their fascist 'revolution', well aware that many of them would face prosecution and imprisonment if he fell, so the old elites became increasingly suspicious of his real intentions. The strain on the prime minister was visible. When the young Umbrian fascist Tullio Cianetti visited Palazzo Chigi in August with a delegation of trade unionists, he found Mussolini tired and unshaven – but still mesmerising: 'He spoke to us in a calm voice: he seemed to me a saint.'[12]

By the autumn, when parliament reopened, support for Mussolini within the ranks of the establishment was beginning to wane. On 15 November Giolitti became the first major defector from among the liberals. One factor in his decision had been a decree introduced unconstitutionally while the Chamber was in recess, severely curbing press freedom. Salandra continued to back Mussolini, but confessed to experiencing 'perplexity'.[13] The main opposition groups were still boycotting the Chamber, which ruled out defeat in a confidence vote. But Mussolini felt he urgently had to show a renewed commitment to normalisation, and he ordered a purge from the fascist party of all unsuitable elements and 'those who make violence a profession'. This did not please the *squadristi*, who showed growing impatience with their leader. Tension was heightened further when a number of senior army generals placed heavy pressure on Mussolini to curtail the independence of the Militia. On 27 December the opposition parties delivered what they hoped would be the *coup de grâce*, publishing a memorandum in the newspaper *Il Mondo* in which Cesare Rossi stated explicitly that the prime minister had been responsible for setting up the *Ceka* and ordering attacks on opponents (though he claimed not to know if Matteotti was one of them). 'We have a prime minister charged with common crimes. No nation can tolerate that such a situation should continue.'[14]

Mussolini had no further room for manoeuvre. On 29 December Salandra went into opposition, and two days later a delegation of Militia commanders told the fascist leader that unless he acted immediately to defend the revolution against the opposition, the party would seize the initiative. Already tens of thousands of armed *squadristi* were descending on towns in Tuscany and the Romagna. Rumours were rife of Mussolini's imminent dismissal and the declaration of martial law. But the king failed to make a move. Perhaps he feared civil war; or perhaps as a constitutional monarch he believed it was the responsibility of parliament to provide him with a lead. Whatever the reason, Mussolini was given a final chance to fight for his political life when the Chamber reopened on 3 January. His speech that afternoon was a direct challenge to his opponents to invoke article 47 of the constitution and impeach him:

It has been said that I set up a *Ceka*. Where? When? How? Nobody can tell us!

There has indeed been a *Ceka* in Russia . . . But the Italian *Ceka* has never existed . . .

It has been said that fascism is a horde of barbarians encamped in the nation, a movement of bandits and marauders! Attempts have been made to turn the issue into a moral question, and we know the sad history of moral questions in Italy. (*Strong signs of approval.*)

But it is not worth wasting time, gentlemen. I come to the point. Here, in front of this Assembly and in front of the entire Italian nation, I declare that I, and I alone, assume political, moral and historical responsibility for all that has happened. (*Prolonged and very loud applause. Many shouts of 'We are all with you! We are all with you!'*)

If some more or less garbled comments are enough to hang a man, then bring out the gibbet and the rope! If fascism has been simply castor oil and *manganello*, and not the magnificent passion of the very flower of Italian youth, the fault is mine! (*Applause.*) If fascism has been a criminal association, I am the head of that criminal association! (*Very loud applause. Many cries of 'We are all with you!'*) . . .

Gentlemen! You have deluded yourselves! You thought that fascism was finished because I was disciplining it . . . But if I employed one-hundredth of the energy that I have used in disciplining it in unleashing it, you would see something indeed. (*Very loud applause.*)

But there will be no need for this, because the government is strong enough to stamp out fully and for good the sedition of the Aventine. (*Very loud and prolonged applause.*)

Italy wants peace, tranquillity and calm industriousness, with love, if possible, and with force, if necessary. (*Loud applause.*)

You can be certain that in forty-eight hours following my speech, the situation on every front will be clarified. (*Very loud and prolonged applause. Comments.*)

We all know that I am driven neither by personal caprice, nor by love of power, nor by ignoble passion, but solely by strong and boundless love for the fatherland. (*Very loud, long and repeated applause. Repeated cries of 'Viva Mussolini!' . . .*)[15]

There could be little doubt as to Mussolini's intentions. It was now up to the king and the opposition to respond to the challenge. They failed to do so, and in the days that followed the liberal state was allowed to slip quietly away. The Minister of the Interior, Luigi Federzoni, instructed the prefects to enforce law and order vigorously and close down any organisations that tended to 'undermine the powers of the state' – a reference, obviously, to the far left, not to fascism.[16] The parties of the Aventine secession lingered on for a number of months, hoping there might be some reaction in the country and debating whether or not to go back to the Chamber. But they were now isolated and powerless, and it was just a matter of time before they were silenced for good. The reformist socialists were banned in November 1925. The *popolari* deputies tried to return to Montecitorio in January 1926 but were driven away by fascist guards. Finally, in the autumn of 1926, in the wake of an attempt on Mussolini's life, all opposition parties were proscribed and their reconstitution forbidden by 'the law for the defence of the State'. Italy had become a one-party state and a dictatorship.

The king's role in the collapse of liberalism was crucial. In the absence of most of the royal archives, which disappeared from Italy when the monarchy went into exile in 1946, it is difficult to know exactly what Victor Emmanuel's thoughts were. But there is enough to suggest that he, like many of his subjects, had come to regard Mussolini's authoritarianism as preferable to weak parliamentary government and what he called 'the sorzdid game of the parties'.[17] At the end of July 1924 the National Association for Veterans had voted at its congress to 'condemn absolutely' all illegality, and its president, a much decorated war hero and deputy, Ettore Viola, had gone with a delegation to see the king at his hunting estate near Pisa and present a formal request for the constitution and the rule of law to be upheld. After listening carefully to Viola's statement, the king had 'smiled grimly like a ghost' and then indicated his determination to wash his hands of responsibility, replying enigmatically: 'This morning my daughter killed two quails.' There had been stunned silence among the delegates. 'I very much like quails fried with peas', one of them had hazarded. The appeal for the defence of liberty on behalf of the millions who had fought in the war had ended in farce.[18]

The man of providence

The support of the king for Mussolini was to be a crucial element in ensuring popular backing for the fascist regime.[19] The monarchy had struggled in the decades after unification in 1860 to establish itself as a strong symbol of the nation: its Piedmontese origins, the lacklustre character of its incumbents, and the responsibility many felt it had shared for the country's poor showing in foreign policy and the (at times) brutal suppression of workers' movements, had left it with a rather tarnished image. But even in regions where revolutionary socialism and anarchism had been strong, such as the Romagna, sympathy for the royal family had often been quite pronounced at a grass-roots level. Mussolini's ostensibly republican father, Alessandro, had publicly declared his regret at the assassination of Umberto in July 1900 on the grounds that the king had been a 'gentleman' at heart.[20] It was precisely because royalist feeling was so deep-rooted in much of the country that the distinguished historian Gioacchino Volpe had written to Mussolini in June 1921 urging him to make sure that fascism did not go against the Crown. The peasants had been conditioned by the Catholic Church over many centuries, he had said, to see authority 'solely in monarchical terms' and to look to the king ('and what else was the State for them?') for justice and protection against the privileged classes.[21]

The extent to which the authority of Mussolini was closely connected to that of the king was apparent to Raffaella Valenti, a young primary school teacher, brought up in the Marche region in central Italy, who had been sent to work in the remote hilltop town of Sant'Angelo Muxaro to the north of Agrigento in Sicily in the mid-1920s. Like many schoolteachers in impoverished rural communities

Raffaella was sustained by a conviction that it was her duty to impart
not just the rudiments of literacy and numeracy but also a strong
sense of patriotism to the local children, and through them to their
parents. In her diary she wrote proudly of her 'great mission as
educator of the people'. She used songs to help her pupils learn Italian
(most would only have spoken dialect at home) and develop a sense
of love for their country; and she was particularly pleased at the way
they chanted 'We are little Italians': 'I felt at that moment that their
hearts were vibrating with love for the Fatherland'. On 10 March 1926
she received some pictures of Mussolini and immediately hung them
in each classroom next to the images of the king and queen. She got
the children to give the Roman salute, talked to them about the
achievements of the fascist leader, and made them sing 'Blackshirt'
and 'March on Rome'. She felt they were pleased: 'The Duces who
today control the destiny of the Fatherland are side by side: the King,
the symbol of national unity, and Benito Mussolini, who with a steady
hand is guiding our people to greater future power.'[22]

As with all diaries kept by civil servants, there is inevitably an element
of uncertainty about the 'spontaneity' of the sentiments expressed, but
at the very least Raffaella was keen to underline to herself, as well as
to any superiors who might read what she had written, the feelings
that she ought to have as a conscientious teacher. She certainly gave
every indication of being sincere and unreservedly enthusiastic in her
patriotism. She handed out postcards of leading fascists and members
of the royal family for her pupils to distribute or sell. The most popular
were those of the Duce, Farinacci and the Crown prince, Umberto,
for all three of whom, she said, there was 'a quite genuine idolatry' in
the town. She celebrated 21 April, the traditional date of the founding
of ancient Rome, which in 1923 had replaced May Day as the festival of
workers; and on the eve of the anniversary of Italy's entry into the
war on 24 May, she wrote of how it was the school's duty to teach the
children to love their fatherland and prepare them to sacrifice everything
for it – 'their possessions, family bonds, even their lives':

> For this reason I talked today about the last, great war. I brought it
> back to life in the imaginations and the very heartbeats of my pupils.
> Not in order to kindle animosities, but because the memory of the
> heroism of their fathers gives rise in the children to a clear sense of

their duties towards this Italy of ours, which, finally free from the Alps to the sea, requires of the children of the heroes who made it such strength of convictions, hard work and fraternal concord – which is the basis for all true greatness.[23]

What sort of impact such patriotic talk had on the children or their parents is difficult to know, but the indications from another small Sicilian town, some 30 kilometres to the west of Sant'Angelo Muxaro as the crow flies, are that it was quite limited. Milocca was a community of around 2,500 people, almost all of whom, as in so much of southern and central Italy, where industry was still very scarce, were entirely dependent on agriculture. (About 60 per cent of Italy's total labour force worked on the land in the early 1920s, according to official statistics, and a similar percentage lived in rural settlements of fewer than 10,000 inhabitants.)[24] The artisan and middle classes – civil servants, professionals and traders – accounted for a small fraction of Milocca's population: about seventy people. There was one industrial plant, a mill, which employed half a dozen men (with an extra two or three in the autumn at the time of the olive harvest). Like most Sicilian towns, Milocca was without electricity. There was also no piped water, and communication with the external world was difficult: before the completion of an asphalted road in 1929, it could only be reached along narrow mule tracks, which were hard for carts and unpassable with the autumn and winter rains.[25]

Information did not penetrate this remote peasant community easily. Much of the population was illiterate. Government figures suggested that around 40 per cent of Sicilians over the age of six were unable to read or write at this time (somewhat higher, but not by very much, than the average for Italy as a whole). But as the American sociologist Charlotte Gower found, when she lived in Milocca in 1928–29, many of those who might technically be classified as literate were in fact unable to do more than slowly trace out their names. The only printed material in circulation consisted of a few religious pamphlets and some old novels – read by a dozen or so people (mostly women) – and eight copies of a daily newspaper, seen by perhaps thirty of the town's inhabitants.[26] Radios still belonged to the future. A national transmission company (EIAR) was set up in 1927, with 40,000 subscribers (Britain had 2.5 million subscribers at this time), but coverage was only

effective in the north of the country, and not till 1933–34 was the
network extended across the whole of Italy.[27]

In these circumstances, the mental world of the people of Milocca
did not move far beyond the confines of the local community, and in
general there was little interest, as Gower discovered, in what was
happening in the outside world. The main talking point in 1928–29
concerned the arrests made in Milocca as part of the campaign against
the mafia, which the government had launched in the autumn of 1925
in a bid to show the country (and the rest of the world) that the new
regime could impose order in Sicily where the liberal state had failed.
The police had descended on the town one night in January 1928 and
seized some three dozen men. Relatives or livestock of any of the
wanted who could not be found had been taken in their place and in
the morning the main square in Milocca had been packed with 'bleating
sheep, goats, horses and mules, while the police station was full of
weeping women'. 'No one felt safe . . . Pity was mixed with fear, pity
for the unhappy animals, the bereft families, the arrested men, and
even for the police, who had come without adequate provisions and
had to beg bread from the terrified townspeople.' By the autumn
around 100 Milocchese men were in prison awaiting trial, and when
Gower arrived, a rumour spread that she was carrying out investigations and might be helpful in getting them released. The result was
somewhat paradoxical: although the entire community had descended
into 'a sort of mourning', with every arrested man being described
to her as 'entirely innocent and a true saint', the fight against the mafia
and the policy of sweeping round-ups was uniformly praised.[28]

Otherwise, events beyond the community attracted little attention.
There was some excitement in 1929 at the signing of the Lateran Treaty
and the ending of the rift between the Church and the Italian state, and
also at the forthcoming marriage of the Crown prince – though Gower
thought that interest in the latter might have been due to hopes of an
amnesty for prisoners. Nor did recent national events, including the
First World War, appear to attract much enthusiasm among the local
population. The principal teacher in Milocca, Don Pippino Angilella
(who also happened to be the postmaster and the brother of the mayor),
was keen, like the other young fascists in the town, to 'speak heatedly
of the glory of Italy, its inspiring role in the history of civilisation, and
the inevitable splendour of its future', and to stress how important the

heroic sacrifices in the war had been for the regeneration of the fatherland. But such language seems to have belonged to an emotional world
alien to that of most of the peasantry:

> The schools do what they can to . . . create patriotic feeling, but without
> noticeable success . . . The 1914–18 War seems to have been unpopular
> in Milocca and the surrounding region. No criticism was heard of the
> two men who had permanently blinded themselves with the medicine
> they put in their eyes to make themselves unfit for military service . . .
> To resort to artifice to avoid military service was simply the exercise
> of proper Sicilian astuteness. No one was pointed out as a hero of the
> War. Disabled veterans were preferred for employment in minor
> positions connected with the local government, but their war records
> were never cited in their praise.[29]

The difficulty, it seemed to Gower, was that 'Italy' was synonymous
in the minds of ordinary people with the government; and the government was 'a not too friendly entity' that imposed taxes, sent husbands
to prison, conscripted sons for the army, and on occasion deliberately
spread diseases such as cholera. (Even the recent epidemic of Spanish
flu was suspected by some as being the work of government agents.)[30]
The state was something to be endured fatalistically. Its malevolent
effects, like those of the spirits and witches that were widely believed
to have a powerful influence on health and emotional relations, could
be mitigated with the appropriate help and due precautions but never
entirely circumvented. It operated in its own sphere and according to
its rules, with little need to feel constrained by ethics or ideological
consistency. For this reason most people seemed to take it for granted
that the battle to control the local fascist party should have been fought
out between the wealthy Angilella and Cipolla families, who had long
dominated the town's rival political factions, using every possible
subterfuge and weapon. Nor did it occasion surprise that the Angilellas,
who finally prevailed in 1927, had headed a socialist movement and
organised land occupations back in 1920. Parties were tools for winning
power. Doctrines were of little account.[31]

But as in Sant'Angelo Muxaro, the figure of Mussolini appears to
have escaped the general feelings of negativity towards the state and
assumed something of an iconic status. The distinctions between

'idolatry' (the word Raffaella had used), admiration, interest, and the judicious extolling of somebody known to wield enormous power are not easy to discern. Gower found 'general enthusiasm' for the Duce in 1928 and excitement at any news reports about him, with one man going so far as to describe him as 'a saint out of paradise'; but she wondered whether such unalloyed praise might be 'due to caution in the presence of a stranger whose precise mission in the community was never understood'.[32] She was also uncertain about what to make of the passionate verse eulogies to Mussolini that were circulating in Milocca (in which the familiar form of address, 'tu', commonly used in prayers made in Italian to God or saints, was employed). Were they articles of fascist propaganda or spontaneous expressions of popular devotion? And what significance was there in the fact that two of these poems had been bought at a local fair by a young man whose father had been arrested as a member of the mafia and who earnestly wanted to be able to recite them by heart?[33]

There were probably no clear-cut answers to these questions that would allow popular attitudes to Mussolini in communities such as Milocca or Sant'Angelo Muxaro to be assessed in terms of any balance between calculation and spontaneity. Such an antithesis might indeed have appeared almost meaningless to peasants who were living in highly impoverished and precarious circumstances. In a world where natural and man-made disasters could strike at almost any time – death, disease, injury, drought, famine, earthquake, landslide, conscription, arrest, brigandage or lawlessness – any force, human or supernatural, with the capacity to stave off misfortune could be looked to with a potent mixture of hope, awe, enthusiasm and solicitude. By the later 1920s, the figure of Mussolini had assumed a powerful presence in the minds of many Italians; and the combination of eulogy and imprecation evident in one of the poems circulating in Milocca was becoming an important cultural aspect of fascism: 'Great Duce, minister of Italy . . . man of genius . . . How beautiful is that divine mind that speaks and sounds like a bell. Duce, give aid to the poor unfortunates, to the little old people who suffer hunger. The blood is water in our veins, poor afflicted Sicilians.'[34]

The development of the cult of the Duce in 1925–26 was in part a reaction to the crisis of the second half of 1924. In the wake of the murder of Matteotti, Mussolini had seemed increasingly exposed and fallible. Much of the support and confidence that he had enjoyed since the March on Rome had evaporated; and in the face of escalating pressure he had appeared incapable of decisive action. Many within his own party had sensed that the days of the government were numbered and had abandoned what Gabriele D'Annunzio had described as a 'stinking ruin'.[35] Somewhat ironically, given how reluctant they had previously been to allow the fascist leader an exceptional and unique status within the party (and so overshadow them), it was the radical provincial *ras* who had felt most keenly that Mussolini was now indispensable. They had criticised his prevarication and threatened to desert him if he made too many concessions to the opposition. But this had been the language and counsel of desperation. They had known that if Mussolini fell, they would be finished too. As Roberto Farinacci had said, it was vital to support Mussolini: his was the 'only myth' tenable in Italy.[36]

Once the crisis was resolved with Mussolini's speech of 3 January 1925, much of the impulse to rehabilitate the fascist leader in the eyes of the country and institute a cult around him came from within the party. One important political reason for this development lay in the need to put clear daylight between the Duce and the blackshirts, and enable any blame for what had recently gone wrong to be deflected towards the unruly rank-and-file elements. Mussolini could thus be transformed from a culprit into a victim – a man who had suffered at the hands both of opportunistic liberal politicians, eager to regain power after using him to slay the dragon of Bolshevism, and of his own disorderly followers. The exaltation of the Duce by the party (highlighted by the attendance of Roberto Farinacci at a ceremony in Mussolini's home town of Predappio on 16 January 1925) thus became not only an affirmation of fascism's triumph over its enemies but also a means whereby the image of Mussolini could float free of the insalubrious landscape below him. This mechanism was to have effective results in the future: in the 1930s the failings of fascism were regularly to be imputed to the Duce's incompetent, corrupt or treacherous entourage, with Mussolini himself viewed as ignorant of the sins of those around him or otherwise magnanimously forgiving of them.

The rapid development of the cult in 1925–26 inevitably owed much to the systematic elimination of the residual areas of opposition. The often brutal silencing of individual critics (such as Giovanni Amendola and Piero Gobetti, two prominent anti-fascists whose deaths in 1926 were hastened by fascist violence), the dissolution of the opposition parties, and the introduction of increased press censorship, all made it possible for the figure of Mussolini to assume, unchallenged, an exalted position. But the relative ease with which the vestiges of liberalism were crushed and the near spontaneous fashion in which the owners of many leading newspapers ceded editorial control to fascism suggest that the success of Mussolini owed as much to the weakness of any will to resist as to the severity of imposition. The prescient warning of the liberal diplomat Carlo Sforza in the *Corriere della Sera* on 21 January 1925 about the dangers of creating a climate of uncritical adulation had an air of anachronistic sobriety. Dictators were inclined to surround themselves with flatterers, he wrote; and flatterers were often 'the first to become credulous victims of the fantasies that they have invented'. It was this same atmosphere of unreality generated by the absence of press freedom and open and informed debate that had brought France to ruin in 1812–15 and 1870.[37]

Much of the momentum for the development of the cult from early 1925 came from leading party members, who helped to make public professions of the Duce's uniqueness items of fascist faith. Giuseppe Bottai wrote in *Critica Fascista* on 15 January 1925 of how he disapproved strongly of excessive adulation but had no difficulty in affirming that Mussolini was altogether an exceptional being.[38] Farinacci, who was appointed secretary of the PNF in February, was particularly assiduous in promoting the cult. He strongly supported plans to develop Mussolini's birthplace into a site of popular pilgrimage. On 30 August 1925 he and Italo Balbo came to the Romagna to inaugurate Predappio Nuova. They unveiled a bronze inscription on the house where Mussolini had been born and laid the foundation stone of the nearby church of Santa Rosa of Lima (in honour of Mussolini's mother, Rosa Maltoni). In his speech Farinacci spoke of how the fascist party was 'a religion' and of how 'its comrades in faith' would send out from Predappio a 'renewed oath of loyalty and devotion': 'And let this be the oath: "Duce, we are always at your command, in both spirit and body. Our lives are at your disposition. With you we seek only to know glory or death."'[39]

A crucial political dimension of the cult – and an important reason why Farinacci and other senior party figures were keen to promote it – was that it provided an element of cohesion for a movement that had from the outset been characterised by ideological eclecticism and uncertainty. A number of observers in the second half of 1924 had felt that the fascist government was as likely to collapse from internal conflicts within the party as from the external pressures generated by the Matteotti crisis. And Mussolini's victory in January 1925 made the problem potentially more acute: in the absence of a common enemy to instil a measure of discipline, there was a danger that the different tendencies and currents in the party – syndicalist, Nationalist, republican, Catholic, anti-clerical, conservative, intransigent – would start vying for supremacy and cause chaos. An authoritative Duce would thus help in bringing discipline to the *squadristi* – the main task that had been assigned to Farinacci as secretary. Simultaneously the cult of the Duce became a necessary common denominator in the regime, permitting fascism to remain a broad church without any fixed ideological matrix.

If the cult of the Duce served important functions within the party, its main political purpose was as a tool for the mobilisation of those for whom ideology was of little relevance. Echoing the ideas of pre-war theorists of crowd psychology, Margherita Sarfatti claimed in her best-selling biography of Mussolini, first published in 1925, that the masses had a natural propensity in times of uncertainty to adopt a heightened 'religious sense of life' and invoke a strong leader. She gave examples of ordinary people wanting to touch Mussolini or kneel before him as if he were a miracle worker. 'The stature of a man', she claimed, 'is measured both by the myth that he projects of himself and the devotion he is able to arouse.'[40] Using a similarly religious frame of interpretation, the historian Gioacchino Volpe wrote in August 1925 of how fascism had centred on Mussolini ever since it became a mass movement in 1920:

All mass movements have this characteristic: they gather around a man, and give themselves, abandon themselves, to him. Their religion is anthropomorphic: take away the man and the religion declines. To four-fifths of Fascists, Fascism is Mussolini, or rather a complex of somewhat vague aspirations that acquire meaning, substance and vital force only in as much as they are incarnated in him. His is a sublime and terrible position that cannot fail to cause him to tremble: not for his own person but for all the sincere and enthusiastic young men who see in him their guide, their infallible master, the word made flesh.[41]

The idea that fascism was religious in character, and was driven by faith, idealism and will, had been present in the movement from the outset. But it was hugely amplified in 1925–26 in ways that made the exaltation of the figure of the Duce seem a logical corollary. *Il Popolo d'Italia* regularly interpreted the relationship of Mussolini to the masses in spiritual terms, claiming that popular enthusiasm was due, as Arnaldo Mussolini suggested, to the Italian people's 'enormous messianic expectations', 'desperate longing for greatness', 'thirst for obedience' and 'desire for order, discipline and a *condottiero*'.[42] Some writers pushed the religious analogy further. A newspaper for Italian fascists abroad talked in May 1925 of how the triumph of fascism had been due not to reason but to 'mysticism' and 'emotion':

> Science claims to explain miracles, but in the eyes of the crowd, miracles exist, seduce and create neophytes. In a century, perhaps, historians will talk of how after the war a Messiah arose in Italy, who began by speaking to fifty and ended by evangelising a million; and how these enlightened ones spread through Italy and conquered the heart of the masses with faith, devotion and sacrifice.[43]

The idea of the Duce as a 'providential' figure who had saved Italy from Bolshevism and liberalism had already achieved some currency in clerical circles in 1923–24,[44] but it was the succession of attempts on Mussolini's life between the autumn of 1925 and the autumn of 1926 that allowed the concept to be widely disseminated, drawing on the twin notions of martyrdom and divine protection. Again it was senior figures in the PNF who took the lead, followed by the press, a broad array of party and local government organisations, and, increasingly in the course of 1926, by the Church. The first plot was unearthed on 4 November 1925, just a few hours before a former socialist deputy, Tito Zaniboni, was intending to shoot Mussolini as he stepped out onto the balcony of Palazzo Chigi. It led to demonstrations around the country and a flood of letters and telegrams of congratulation from politicians, both at home and abroad, celebrities (such as D'Annunzio), members of the royal family and the public. When parliament opened on 18 November, the galleries were packed, with women especially, and Mussolini was given a standing ovation. The vice president of the Chamber declared that 'without the rapid and lightning intervention of the police, you would have been nailed, like Christ on the cross, to the railings of your balcony in Palazzo Chigi'.[45]

The importance of ecclesiastical sanction in fostering the cult of the Duce was well understood by the party. In many places clergy lent their support with apparent willingness. But not always. Primo Mazzolari, the young parish priest of Cicognara, a small town of some 1,300 inhabitants on the river Po to the north-east of Parma, had long felt that the fascists were no better than the socialists in reducing the ordinary people to 'beasts'. On the evening of 5 November 1925 he listened with melancholy dismay as the bells of his and neighbouring churches rang out loudly and young fascists roamed the streets shooting in the air and invoking death on their enemies. 'They say there has been an attempt on the life of the Head of the Government in Rome . . . Why did they want the voice of the bells also to be heard in this tragic hour of criminality . . . ? To rouse a town that is resting so abruptly, to cause anxiety and fear to people who have not the faintest idea of what is going on, to terrify them with wild salvoes of gunshots . . . is certainly not the best way to show those feelings of indignation and disapproval that are appropriate at moments such as this.' The leaden sky, with its heavy rain clouds, seemed to him portentous, as if it was about 'to hurl down . . . its anger and its mercy'.[46]

In the next few days, Primo came under enormous pressure from the local fascists to hold a service of thanksgiving for the Duce's escape. He waited for authorisation from his bishop, and when it arrived, he fixed the time for 4.00 on Sunday 8 November. This did not meet the approval of the fascists. They sent a delegation to demand it be held twice, at 7.00 in the evening on Sunday and Monday. 'The service must have a politico-religious character – their exact words – because they need to see who has fascist faith and who does not (clear implication: so as to beat the recalcitrants): because they do not intend to mix with the people who normally go to church on Sunday.' Primo refused. If it was a political ceremony they wanted, he suggested they go into the piazza: 'Christ could not be made into the instrument of a political faith'. One of the leaders of the delegation, a schoolteacher, told him that if he went ahead with his *Te Deum* on the Sunday afternoon, he must sing theirs on the Monday at the time they had ordered. 'We are paying', added the Militia commander. Primo became incensed: 'The conscience of a priest cannot be sold or bought; he is not a mercenary.' 'We know who we can to turn to', the teacher said threateningly, '. . . and you will pay for your stubbornness'.[47]

On Sunday afternoon, a small boy came to deliver a letter to Primo: 'In the name of all the fascists and the population of Cicognara, I express my contempt that you did not want to celebrate a service of thanksgiving to God for the delivery from danger of our most beloved Duce. I inform you that the ceremony that you will be holding today at 4.00 will not be regarded as official.' In the town, Primo was the target of abuse and threats ('we will take him to church with kicks in his backside', said the teacher); and he saw fliers announcing that there would be a meeting of all party and trade union members the following day at 7.00. On the Monday evening a crowd of blackshirts armed with pistols and clubs escorted him into the church, and the same boy who had handed him the letter asked if he would recite the *Te Deum*. Primo resigned himself to God: 'I spoke for five minutes. The Lord knows what I said, for He alone inspired me, and I cannot even remember. All I know is that when the congregation stood up, at my request, in perfect unison, to say the Lord's Prayer, many of us were in tears.' A few minutes later the church was empty, 'and the town returned to calm and silence'.[48]

Primo had no problems the following April with holding a thanksgiving service after the second assassination attempt on Mussolini, when a mentally disturbed Irishwoman, Violet Gibson (who had initially been intending to assassinate the Pope, it seems), fired a shot at the prime minister at almost point-blank range as he was leaving the Capitol after inaugurating a congress on surgery. Mussolini moved his head suddenly at the last moment and the bullet grazed his nose. Since the previous autumn relations between the Vatican and the government had taken a further turn for the better. In a public address in December the Pope had warmly thanked the Italian authorities for all the help they had given with the arrangements for Holy Year (1925) and for 'everything that is being done in favour of religion'; and in a gesture that had struck observers as quite exceptional, if not unprecedented, he had described the joy that he had recently experienced when the prime minister had 'by the grace of God' emerged unharmed from the 'heinous crime' that had nearly cost him his life ('the memory of which still disturbs Us').[49] Against this backdrop, priests like Primo could have little doubt as to what their duty should be, and up and down the country church bells were rung and *Te Deums* sung. Public demonstrations were staged in protest and thanksgiving, and newspapers carried headlines with phrases such as 'God has saved him' and 'God has protected the Fatherland'.[50]

But it was the response to the attacks by the anarchists Gino Lucetti and Anteo Zamboni in September and October 1926 that showed how extensive the cult of the Duce had become in less than two years – since the nadir of Mussolini's fortunes in the Matteotti crisis. And it also underlined the degree to which the state and the ecclesiastical authorities were now working in partnership to encourage popular enthusiasm and make public expressions of devotion to the figure of the Duce an essential item of fascist 'faith'. In the wake of the Lucetti incident, when a bomb thrown at Mussolini's car at Porta Pia in Rome bounced off and exploded, injuring eight bystanders but leaving Mussolini unscathed, mass rallies were staged across the country addressed by prefects, party leaders and other dignitaries. In Venice the cardinal had the bells of St Mark's rung, while in Pisa the cardinal archbishop sent a telegram of congratulations and ordered the singing of a *Te Deum*. In Milan cinemas and theatres suspended their screenings and performances so as to allow audiences to attend a huge demonstration in the Piazza del Duomo.[51] Arnaldo Mussolini wrote to his brother: 'God protects you, the Italians worship you: two forces that render the criminality of the assassins futile.'[52]

Seven weeks later, the response to the attack by Zamboni in Bologna, when a bullet fired from a crowd passed through a sash Mussolini was wearing, was even more effusive. The party secretary implored the Duce in a mass rally in Piazza Colonna to recognise that his life was 'indissolubly tied to the life of the Nation': 'We would beg you, Duce, to heed the anguished heart of the people who now recognise themselves solely in the light of your life!' The Minister of Public Instruction ordered all schools to display the national flag 'as a sign of exaltation for the safety of the Duce, who has once again been visibly protected by God'. The distinguished war hero, Carlo Delcroix, urged an audience in the Politeama Nazionale in Florence to 'raise once more their devout and grateful thoughts to Divine providence, who has acted as a shield to our Leader'. And he added, using the opaque language (and logic) that was becoming characteristic of fascist rhetoric: 'As long as [the Duce] continues to represent – as he is now representing – the spirit and the needs of our people, as long as he remains loved by us, he cannot fall: if it is true that the Fatherland is immortal, he will be able to pass through the fire and will not die.' The Pope was reported as saying, 'the Honourable Mussolini is truly protected by God', and as requesting that he take greater care of his personal safety. And up and down the country it was senior clergy who led the local celebrations. In a sermon in Naples cathedral, the archbishop said that 'Providence' had for the fourth time saved the life of Mussolini, and that 'therefore there is some high destiny that must be fulfilled through his work for the greater good of our Italy and perhaps of the whole world'.[53]

The attempts on Mussolini's life in 1925–26, and the orchestrated anger that followed them, created the climate in which the framework of the liberal state could be dismantled. In the winter of 1925–26 new measures were introduced to strengthen the powers of the head of government, free ministers from parliamentary control, and allow the executive increased scope in the issuing of decree laws. A further law enabled any public official whose views did not conform to 'the general political thinking' of the government to be dismissed. Such a purge was needed, Mussolini informed the Chamber, because 'we are not a ministry, and not even a government. We are a regime. (Applause)'.[54] In the spring of 1926 a major new law, drawn up by the former Nationalist and Minister of Justice, Alfredo Rocco, sought to 'discipline' the labour movement by banning strikes, imposing arbitration by special tribunals in the event of collective disputes, and giving the fascist syndicates an effective monopoly of trade unionism. The aim was to ensure that the turmoil of the post-war period did not recur. And Rocco's law largely achieved this: despite the deteriorating economic situation of many peasants and industrial workers in the coming years, there was to be little labour unrest under fascism.

The final nails in the coffin of liberalism came in the autumn of 1926 after the attacks by Lucetti and Zamboni. With the 'provisions for the defence of the state' all opposition parties were definitively banned and it became an offence punishable with up to ten years in prison to attempt to reconstitute them, or indeed any association or body that had been banned by the public authorities. (Freemasonry and other secret societies had been declared illegal in 1925.) A Special Tribunal was created, with judges drawn from the Militia and the armed forces, to deal with political crimes, and the death penalty was made available in a number of instances, including attempts on the life of the head of government. In a move to clamp down on anti-fascism abroad, Italian citizens who in any way undermined 'the credit or prestige of the State' or caused 'damage to the national interests' when outside the country, faced up to fifteen years in gaol. A public security law gave the police the powers to send anyone suspected of engaging in subversive activity, or even of just intending to engage in subversive activity,[55] to 'internal exile' (confino) in a remote community, usually in the deep south of the country, for up to five years. A similar spirit of severe authoritarianism pervaded the new statute of the PNF, which ended any form of democracy, and stipulated that the party was to be run in a strictly hierarchical fashion under 'the supreme guidance of the Duce of Fascism'.[56]

On 4 October 1926, a few days before the statute was discussed in the Grand Council, the 'Duce of Fascism' received an important verbal endorsement from the Catholic Church at the celebrations in Assisi to mark the seventh centenary of the death of St Francis. Some months earlier Mussolini had publicly described Francis as 'the most saintly of Italians and the most Italian of saints', and the government had done all it could during 1926 to assist the ecclesiastical authorities with the commemorative events, even declaring 4 October a national holiday. The papal delegation was headed by the secretary of the Holy Office, Cardinal Merry Del Val, who travelled to Assisi in the first 'papal train' to have left Rome since 1870, receiving full military honours at stations along the route. There had been rumours that Mussolini himself might be attending, but the government was instead represented by the Minister for Education, the prominent historian Pietro Fedele. In an address, the cardinal paid tribute to the 'man who holds the reins of government in Italy', and commended him for his efforts to ensure that religion was 'respected, honoured and practised': 'Visibly protected by God, he has wisely restored the fortunes of the Nation, increasing its prestige throughout the world.'[57]

As Mussolini well knew, the public backing of the Church was vital to the success of fascism – much of the liberal state's failure to anchor

itself in the hearts and minds of ordinary people had been due to the
hostility of the Papacy over many decades. On the evening of 4 October
1926, a few hours after Merry Del Val had delivered his encomium,
Mussolini wrote to a leading constitutional lawyer, Domenico Barone,
and formally instructed him to undertake exploratory negotiations
with the Vatican, in the strictest secrecy, to see if a resolution to the
Roman question could be found. Though fascism and the Church
differed profoundly as to their ultimate goals, with fascism focused on
duty to the state and the secular glory of the nation, and the Church
looking to the service of God and salvation in the afterlife, it was clear
that both had a mutual interest in seeking an accommodation. And
not simply to avoid rivalry – though the Vatican was deeply concerned
that the totalitarian aspirations of fascism posed a major threat to the
Church's capacity to mobilise the laity, and the young especially,
through the organisations of Catholic Action – but also because each
could see in the other a natural buttress for the main coordinates of
its social vision, in which hierarchy, obedience, faith, anti-materialism,
and the subordination of the individual to the collective will, were
paramount.

Just how emotionally powerful the combination of fascism and
Catholicism could be is evident from the diary of Andreina Del Panta,
a seventeen-year-old girl living on the outskirts of Florence at Peretola.
Andreina belonged to a wealthy commercial family, and her father
had apparently been a supporter of Mussolini from an early date. She
wanted to be an artist, and the diary she kept in 1926–28 reflected her
passionate and strongly aesthetic temperament. She loved the colourful
ceremonies organised by the Church and the fascist party, and she
relished the stirring patriotic sentiments to which she was frequently
exposed in speeches, newspapers, books, and newer media such as the
cinema. In April 1927 she saw *I martiri d'Italia* ('The martyrs of Italy'),
a 'marvellous' film, she wrote, which, 'with pure artistic visions of
poetry and feeling, celebrates the heroic achievements of the Great
Men and Martyrs who gave their lives, everything, for the unity, the
greatness of our beautiful Fatherland' – from Dante and Petrarch in
the Middle Ages, to Mazzini, Pisacane and Garibaldi in the nineteenth
century, to the 'unknown soldier', D'Annunzio and Mussolini. She was
receptive to the main political message of the film: how this magnificent legacy had been criminally 'scorned in an hour of madness by

the misguided masses', and then saved 'by the pure youth of Italy
marching in 1922 under the command of the Glorious Duce . . . on
Rome, the immortal mother'.[58]

On the evening of 4 June 1927 a ceremony was held in Peretola to
commemorate St Francis. The habit the monk had been wearing when
he received the stigmata was brought in honour to the local church.
Any tensions that may earlier have existed between the fascists and
clergy, of the kind that had strained relations in communities such as
Primo Mazzolari's Cicognara, had evaporated, helped by the conciliatory signs emanating from the ecclesiastical authorities. (One signal
had been the appearance in 1926 of a book entitled *Saint Francis and
Mussolini* by a priest, Paolo Ardali, described by the publisher as 'very
close to Vatican spheres', in which the fascist leader had been compared
to the saint for his suffering and self-sacrifice, his 'lofty vision of a
superior end', and his general character, with 'all his good qualities
harmonised in an intimate, superior, calm, serene and luminous
spirit'.)[59] Andreina described how she marched slowly through huge
crowds in a cortege of blackshirts, war veterans and children, many
of them enrolled in fascist organisations such as the Balilla and Piccole
Italiane (for small boys and girls) as well as Catholic Action – restyled
as the Association for Italian Fascist Catholic Youth. When the car
carrying the relic of the saint arrived, the national anthem (the 'Royal
March') was struck up and 'a thousand arms stretched out in a solemn
act and gave the Roman salute'. The procession went on to the church,
whose tower was 'illuminated fantastically'; and the bells pealed out,
'their sound disappearing far, far away into the air, which had already
grown dark as the evening came down slowly . . . sadly!!!'[60]

Andreina's enthusiastic acceptance of fascism formed a continuum
with her Catholic faith and at times meshed with it linguistically
('obedience and respect to the Duce, now and forever', she wrote in
her diary in October 1927 after learning that commemorations of the
March on Rome and Italy's victory in the war would henceforth be
held on a Sunday to save the country two days of work).[61] And the
absence of any obvious inconsistency between the political and religious spheres was underlined by what she heard from the local clergy.
In January 1928 she went to an Epiphany (Befana) service in Peretola,
attended by teachers and numerous dignitaries, including the mayor
(now a centrally appointed official known as a *podestà*: administrative

elections had been abolished throughout Italy in 1926). The officiating cleric was the Franciscan, Padre Bernardino del Sole, from the convent of Quaracchi. He read the prayers and blessed the ceremonial flame and the national flag:

> I have blessed it with a patriotic spirit, because, although the habit I wear should keep me far from worldly affairs, I have taken part in fascism even in the most terrible moments, and I am a fascist in my soul and a member of the fascist party. Six or seven years ago this Italy of ours was so gravely ill that even the most skilled doctor would have been frightened. But now it is no longer so thanks to the tireless work of the Man whom God has chosen as the Duce of our Italy.

Andreina made a little speech to the Piccole Italiane, and felt very proud of herself. They were, she told them, 'good and kind girls, who love and respect God and the fatherland, and adore their Duce, and who promise now and forever more to be worthy of this Italy of ours, which is so great, and imitate the women of Rome who provided so many great examples of virtue'.[62]

5

Purifying the Nation's Soul

Forging new men

Luigi Federzoni was one of the key figures in the fascist regime. He had been born into a literary and patriotic family in Bologna in 1878, and like many middle-class intellectuals of his generation he had developed an acute sense of the chasm separating the dream of the new Italy, that had inspired the protagonists of the Risorgimento, from the prosaic reality of the liberal state. One of his university teachers, the distinguished poet Giosuè Carducci, whom he later described as a seminal figure in the 're-awakening of the historic sense of the nation', had summed up the disparity in a celebrated poem written in 1871 in which he had claimed that the unification of Italy had not resulted in the acquisition of 'Rome', with all its connotations of heroism, idealism and nobility, but rather in a weak and decadent regime akin to 'Byzantium'. The humiliating defeat in Ethiopia – at Adua in 1896 – had been a turning point for Federzoni. It had underlined the seeming unconcern of the country's liberal leaders for Italy's standing in the world and their craven preference instead for a peaceful 'domestic' existence.[1] Federzoni's deep sense of disillusionment and anger had impelled him towards Nationalism.

Federzoni had initially sought to make his name as a writer, and under the teasingly anagrammatic pseudonym of Giulio De Frenzi he had published a number of plays and novels (with titles such as *The Corruptor* and *The Candle Wick of the Ideal*) before reaching national attention in 1909 with an exposé of the erosion of Italian sentiment around Lake Garda. Here, in the shore-side towns, he had discovered that the locals had almost abandoned speaking Italian in a bid to ingratiate themselves with wealthy German tourists. On the walls of almost every restaurant, 'Germanically panelled in dark wood', he had found pictures of Victor Emmanuel III overshadowed by portraits of the German and Austrian emperors. Italy's most conspicuous weakness – the absence, nearly half a century after unification, of a strong sense of patriotism among the mass of the population – had stood revealed to Federzoni in a microcosm. He had urged the authorities to do something about it: impose a high tax, for example, on signs in a foreign language or at the very least stop posters being put up by the council in which Desenzano sul Lago was called Desenzano am See. He had also called on the educated middle classes to set an example by abandoning the 'servile snobbism' that made them exclaim 'Pardon!' rather than 'Scusi!' when they accidentally trod on someone's foot.[2]

From 1910 Federzoni had dedicated himself increasingly to politics. He became a founder member of the Italian Nationalist Association, played a major role in the campaign that led to Italy's invasion of Libya, and got elected to parliament in 1913. As his anxieties over the penetration of the German language into Lake Garda had suggested, he saw the health of nations primarily in terms of their capacity to assert themselves culturally as well as materially over others. Patriotism should be a dynamic force, an 'affirmation of the *people*', manifested in 'economic hegemony, colonial expansion, and the impulse to extend one's own particular civilisation to the whole world'. And if the new generation in Italy was to acquire an 'awareness of its historical mission', it would have to free itself of liberal humanitarian values ('hatred is indeed no less necessary than love for nurturing civilisation') and become 'nationalist and imperialist'.[3] In 1914–15 he had been one of the most passionate and vocal advocates of intervention, seeing in the war a wonderful opportunity for Italians finally to acquire the strong sense of nationhood that decades of weak liberal government had failed to impart.

After the war, in which he served as a volunteer officer, Federzoni had re-entered parliament and become a key figure on the far right of the Chamber. His sympathy for the fascists had seen him rewarded after the March on Rome with the Ministry of Colonies and, in June 1924, with the Ministry of the Interior. His support for Mussolini during the Matteotti crisis had been vital, and at the decisive cabinet meeting on 30 December he had vigorously countered the proposal of two liberal colleagues to resign and bring down the government.[4]

He had continued to act as Interior Minister in 1925 and 1926, suppressing opposition groups, curbing the freedom of the press, and helping to shape the authoritarian structures of the fascist state; and he had become increasingly convinced that Mussolini was personally indispensable to the regime, the only 'guarantee of its life and development', as he had told him in a letter after the assassination attempt by Violet Gibson.[5] His offer to resign on this occasion had been rejected, but after the fourth attack in October 1926 Mussolini himself had taken over the Interior Ministry and Federzoni had resumed his old role as Minister of the Colonies.

Like Mussolini and a number of other leading fascists, Federzoni had never forgotten his intellectual roots, and he had been among the 250 or so signatories of the 'Manifesto of fascist intellectuals' published in *Il Popolo d'Italia* on 21 April 1925, the anniversary of the foundation of Rome. The manifesto, which had been drawn up largely by the philosopher, Giovanni Gentile (Minister of Public Instruction from 1922 to 1924), sought to establish the main coordinates of fascist ideology and justify the assaults that were being made on 'freedom' as it was conventionally understood. Fascism was described as 'a recent and ancient movement of the Italian spirit, intimately connected to the history of the Italian nation' whose nature was intrinsically religious – 'this religious and therefore intransigent character explains the methods of struggle pursued by Fascism in the four years from 1919 to 1922'. It looked to counter the materialism of 'agnostic liberalism' and enable individuals to find their 'purpose in life' and true 'freedom' through selfless subordination to the ideal of the 'patria'. Like Mazzini's patriotic movement of Young Italy in the 1830s, it said, fascism had attracted the support of Italians through the power of its 'faith' – 'an energetic violent faith that would not tolerate anything that might oppose the life and the greatness of the *patria*'.

Among those who had signed the manifesto with Federzoni were a broad array of intellectuals. They included such prominent names as the playwright Luigi Pirandello (who had pointedly joined the fascist party in the middle of the Matteotti crisis), the Futurist leader, Filippo Tommaso Marinetti, the modernist poet, Giuseppe Ungaretti, and the journalist Luigi Barzini. Ten days later, on 1 May, a counter-manifesto had appeared in *Il Mondo*, written by Gentile's former friend and fellow philosopher, Benedetto Croce. He had finally realised that his hopes that fascism might be a force working for the reinvigoration of the liberal state had been misplaced. This 'Manifesto of anti-fascist intellectuals' had been signed by a no less distinguished collection of names (though a good many of them were in due course to come round to supporting the regime), including the economist Luigi Einaudi, the poet Eugenio Montale, the historian Gaetano Salvemini and the journalist Luigi Albertini. It had angrily taken issue with the idea that intellectuals could pledge their support to a party that was seeking to 'grace' an incoherent ideology and vicious intolerance with the name of 'religion':

> For this chaotic and elusive 'religion' . . . we do not feel inclined to abandon our old faith: the faith that for two and a half centuries has been the soul of the resurgent, modern Italy. This faith consisted of love of truth, of desire for justice, of generous human and civil feelings, of zeal for intellectual and moral education, of concern for liberty, which is the driving force and guarantee of all progress.

Appeals for the defence of freedom by liberal intellectuals had continued for some months more while newspapers such as *Il Mondo* and *Corriere della Sera* had retained a degree of autonomy. But their arguments had largely ceased to resonate in a country where dissent was being suppressed as much by disdain for 'the lovely times before Fascism', as Federzoni mockingly called them,[6] as by the repressive machinery of the state. In the early summer of 1925 *Il Giornale d'Italia* had taken violent exception to an article in a French magazine by Giuseppe Prezzolini, in which the well-known journalist had maintained that the success of Mussolini had been due to the general indifference of Italians to freedom. Such assertions, it had said, were humiliating and untrue. To allege that the population as a whole had no interest in public affairs and was content as long as the trams were running and the cafes were open, was absurd; just as it was ridiculous to say that opposition to fascism was limited to about 100,000 intellectuals 'pedantically attached' to old ideas and annoyed at no longer being able to read their favourite columnists. In reality Italians loved to argue and were passionate about liberty, and all Prezzolini's predictions about the demise of liberalism were 'built on sand'.[7] But such impassioned claims had begun to sound like whistling in the dark.

By the time he resigned as Minister of the Interior in the autumn of 1926, Federzoni was confident that the regime was moving in the direction he wanted. The liberal opposition had been silenced, and he welcomed the warmer relations that were developing between the government and the Church. He was also delighted that the radical fascists had been brought to heel and the party steered in a more conservative direction: in the spring of 1926 Farinacci had been replaced as secretary by a much more restrained and pliable figure, Augusto Turati (he addressed Mussolini deferentially as 'Presidente': Farinacci called him 'Benito').[8] And the clear subordination of the party to the state was spelled out early in 1927 when Mussolini issued a circular denouncing *squadrismo* as 'utterly anachronistic' and declaring that in 'a totalitarian and authoritarian regime such as the fascist' the prefect alone was to act as the guardian of both 'public order' and the 'moral order' in the provinces.[9] But perhaps most satisfying to Federzoni were indications that the hopes that he had entertained as a young man listening in Bologna to the lectures of the disenchanted poet and patriot Carducci, that Italy might one day fulfil the promise of the Risorgimento and become a great force in the world – Rome rather than Byzantium – could be realised through the remarkable figure of the Duce.

In the memoirs he wrote shortly after the Second World War, Federzoni displayed little overt warmth for Mussolini or fascism. His main concern at this time was to suggest that his own pivotal role in the establishment of the dictatorship had been the result largely of his determination to uphold the law and save the country from the extremism of the *squadristi*. But the diary which he kept in the first months of 1927 indicates far more enthusiasm than he later confessed to. Why exactly he decided to write a diary at this juncture is not clear. It may be that he wanted to have an accurate record of the daily difficulties that he encountered as Minister of the Colonies. In resuming his old portfolio in the autumn of 1926, he had told Mussolini that the country's possessions in north and east Africa should be considered as 'a springboard and instrument for a vaster and more varied expansion of the influence of Italy in the world', but that this would be very hard to achieve until the ministry was better resourced, had its own well-defined and autonomous sphere within foreign policy, and the 'chronic quantitative and qualitative shortcomings of the staff of the colonial administration' had been overcome.[10]

One of the most damaging features of government that he observed
in his diary was the ubiquitous atmosphere of rivalry. He noted on
3 March how the Chief of Police, Arturo Bocchini, was 'tired, exasper-
ated and distracted by the silent war that is being waged against him
by almost all the members of the Party Directorate'. Two days later
he recorded how the Minister of Finances was facing resistance from
the Ministers for Communications, Public Works, and the National
Economy. There were serious divisions within the upper reaches of
the party – for instance between 'orthodox' fascists and those with
'republican tendencies' who were conspiring to reduce the powers of
the Crown. And perhaps most worrying of all in this pervasive 'climate
of suspicions and fears . . . in which even the loyal and intelligent end
up by losing their head from time to time', were the deep rifts in the
armed forces. The Undersecretary of War was at odds with the Chief
of the General Staff, Marshal Badoglio; and while Mussolini himself
was nominally Minister for the Army, the Navy and the Air Force, in
practice the three branches continued to operate independently and
did not communicate with each other. 'All of this', Federzoni
commented presciently, 'is a recipe for a grave future crisis'.[11]

Amid this somewhat dispiriting landscape, the figure of Mussolini
stood out for Federzoni and gave him hope that the fascist regime
might succeed in restoring Italy's fortunes and international standing
where liberalism had failed. He watched Mussolini attentively, and
recorded his shifting moods with great interest. One day he found
him 'in the most appalling humour – God knows why'; on another
'sweet tempered, and keen to chat'; and on yet another 'looking tired
and repeating frequently a gesture I am familiar with, that of touching
his back and stiffening it up at the waist, as if to soothe a nagging
pain'. 'Let us hope, for the sake of Italy', he commented, 'that it is
nothing to worry about: perhaps a pulled muscle or something
nervous.' The close attention Federzoni paid to Mussolini's fluctuating
emotions and physical condition was partly due to insecurity: as the
Duce's position within the regime became ever more unassailable, so
the careers of ministers and party officials grew increasingly dependent
on the leader's personal whims and preferences. Federzoni was clearly
uncomfortable when Mussolini was cool and conversely delighted
when he smiled at him and was friendly. He got particular satisfaction when he was patted on the shoulder.[12] But like many who

came into close contact with Mussolini, Federzoni was also captivated by the Duce's sheer inscrutability and enjoyed recording and assessing the different facets of his personality.

What especially excited Federzoni was Mussolini's vision of how the regime would establish Italy as a leading force in the world. The susceptibility of Federzoni to the fascist leader's impassioned arguments was increased by Mussolini's ability to present his ideas as if they were the fruit of serious reflection and reading. (Federzoni's own intellectual proclivities were to earn him a succession of prestigious appointments in the 1930s, culminating in the Presidency of the Royal Academy of Italy, a body founded in 1926 along the lines of the Académie française to 'preserve the purity of the national character . . . and encourage its expansion and influence beyond the borders of the State'.)[13] On one occasion Federzoni was taken aback when Mussolini suddenly exclaimed with characteristic bluntness: 'They've screwed us then!' 'Who?' Federzoni asked, startled. 'The Jews. I'm reading these days Rathenau's book on Israel, and I have thought hard about the argument. I am becoming ever more convinced that this is where the confusion in our civilisation lies.' Mussolini then proceeded to 'expatiate on his anti-semitism, which I am very familiar with', said Federzoni, 'but which is one of the least well known, and most interesting aspects, of this formidable spirit'.[14]

Federzoni was particularly impressed at a meeting of the Grand Council held on the evening of 7 January 1927 when Mussolini spoke for more than an hour without interruption. It was a 'stupendous speech', he recorded in his diary, and everyone was 'profoundly moved'. Mussolini began by talking about how the 'political and spiritual conditions' of France were destined to make relations between Italy and its neighbour increasingly tense: the Republic was 'now entirely pervaded by atheistic, pacifistic, neo-Malthusian, Masonic and demo-social individualism'; and with Italy 'instead completely dominated by the fascist mentality', the two countries were 'irreconcilably antithetical'. To illustrate the degree of France's moral decline, and just how great the gap was between the two countries, he mentioned the example of a revue in a popular theatre where one of the characters was the French president's wife, and appeared on stage dressed only in a fur scarf. He continued:

> This is the situation now: in a decadent Europe, weakened by vice, perverted by exotic habits, striving deliriously to attain the dreams of

social-democratic humanitarianism, the only vital principle is fascist
Italy. Europe no longer has any faith: it does not attach any real
importance to religious values, but only to money, to the individual
and the collective instinct for survival, to the pursuit of enjoyment,
and to a peaceful life. Fascist Italy – Catholic, disciplined, war-like – will
be able to dominate Europe if it can defend its physical and moral
health. This is our programme . . . In demographic terms, Italy is better
than other peoples. But though still high, its birth rate is nonetheless
seriously declining. In twenty years' time we must be fifty, no, sixty,
million people. The reason for the lower birth rate is urbanisation, or
rather excessive industrialisation. Here is the point. We must aim for
a national economy that is above all agricultural, then maritime and
finally industrial . . . This is the policy for labour and production that
we are laying down for the immediate future of Italy.

When Mussolini finished speaking, said Federzoni, 'we leapt to our
feet and cheered'.[15]

Mussolini's vision of a Europe in the grip of immorality and decadence,
with declining population as its most conspicuous symptom, had considerable popular currency in the mid-1920s. The German philosopher
Oswald Spengler had raised the spectre of Europe's nations growing
culturally degenerate and being overtaken by the more prolific races
of Asia and Africa in his best-selling work *The Decline of the West*
(1918–23). He had portrayed the nineteenth century as a period of
rampant materialism and individualism in Europe, and suggested that
democratic systems were destined to be overturned shortly by the
forces of irrationalism and 'blood' and be replaced by authoritarian
rule: '[T]oday Parliamentarism is in full decay . . . The Caesarism that
is to succeed approaches with quiet, firm step . . . Ever in History it is
life and life only – race-quality, the triumph of the will to power . . .
that signifies.'[16] Spengler greatly admired Mussolini, and was to see him
as the only European leader who was responding to his call for a
'Caesar' to defend Western civilisation. In the spring of 1925 he sent
him a number of his political works: whether Mussolini read them at
this point is not clear. Probably not. But by 1927, when the theme of
Europe's 'crisis' was being widely discussed in the Italian press, he may
well have done.[17]

There was also a strong tradition within Italy itself of discussions about the links between decadence and population levels. In the years before the First World War these debates had been bound up with concerns over emigration – more than 8 million Italians went overseas between 1900 and 1915 – and the demands of the Nationalists for colonies in Africa as an outlet for the country's surplus workforce. Corrado Gini, to whom Mussolini turned for information when planning his demographic campaign, was one of a number of prominent Italian academics who in the early years of the century had argued for a close connection between levels of fecundity and the dynamism of peoples.[18] Nations were organisms with a life of their own and a natural tendency, when healthy, he had argued, to expand through sexual exuberance. In a book published in 1912 he had claimed that a falling birth rate was a sign that a society had reached its 'old age', and he had related this process to the prevalence of material self-interest over patriotic idealism and 'the sedentary character' of bourgeois culture.[19]

Some indication of how far these ideas had become woven into the fabric of patriotic thinking by the mid-1920s can be seen in the diary kept by Mario Carlotti, a young naval rating on board one of Italy's largest battleships, the *Conte di Cavour*. The extent to which Mario's patriotic meditations on his country and its future reflected his innermost feelings is somewhat unclear, as there are signs that the diary had to be available for inspection by his superiors: at one point an officer commented that Mario wrote with 'verve and enthusiasm'. The diary is certainly almost unremitting in its nationalistic fervour, with much talk of Italy's mission to dominate '*mare nostrum*'; and the comments on political events have a strongly formulaic feel. Thus when Mario heard of the attempt on the Duce's life in early November 1925, he talked of how the whole country was indignant, adding heavy-handedly: 'This time the people of Italy want to show to the foreigners that they are disciplined . . . and remain disciplined at their post, obedient to the orders of the Duce who wants calm and no act of reprisal'.

At one point, in August 1925, Mario reflected at length on how Italy would achieve its rightful position in the world now that order had been restored after the terrible post-war years, when the 'reds' had sought to seize control of the country. His ideas were somewhat disjointed, perhaps suggesting an attempt to digest a lecture or a talk he had heard. His central point was that while the country might lack the economic resources of the other great powers, it had an enormous relative advantage in its high birth rate, which necessitated an 'outlet' for its surplus population (Spengler had described demographic growth as 'Italy's only weapon'):

> [Italy] wants land, it wants, in short, recognition of its supremacy, sooner or later, over those who surround it, following the parabola that every population always follows, which in our case is entirely rising, while for our neighbours it is declining. And the demographic growth leads to the intellectual development of the population. In a war the side wins which has known how to produce most and has worked hardest. Arms are just a tool for victory. For us Italians, a period of intense work and intelligent diplomacy and our rights will be acknowledged!![20]

The intertwining of patriotism with population growth and an imperial mission for Italy, which constituted a major feature of Mario's diary in 1925–26, reflected an accelerating ideological trend within the regime. Prior to the establishment of the dictatorship, Mussolini's more intemperate remarks about fascist expansionism had been largely restricted to party rallies, but from the second half of 1925 the theme of empire became ever more widely discussed. In December of that year Roberto Farinacci's newspaper *Cremona Nuova* said that imperialism was 'the central idea of fascism' and that Italy's 'right' to a greater international presence arose quite logically from its sacrifices in the war.[21] In her biography of Mussolini, published in 1925, Margherita Sarfatti quoted the fascist leader as saying that imperialism was 'the eternal and immutable law of life', that arose from 'the need, the desire and the will for expansion nurtured by all individuals and people who are alive and energetic'.[22] In the summer of 1926 Mussolini himself told an American news agency that because Italy's 'racial vitality' was exceptional the country had no choice but to 'expand or to suffocate'.[23]

Against this backdrop, the public declaration of fascism's demographic campaign with Mussolini's 'Ascension Day' speech of 26 May 1927 occasioned relatively little surprise in the country. The general tenor of press comments was that the Duce's programme had the 'coherence' to be expected of a nation that had finally found its voice and its direction.[24] In a wide-ranging survey of the regime's achievements and aims, the Duce announced that he intended 'radically to transform the appearance and above all the soul' of Italy, and that a key factor in this would be to raise the population from 40 to 60 million in the space of twenty years. To those who might wonder if such a goal was wise given the scarcity of resources in the country and the absence any longer of emigration as a safety valve (the United States had recently introduced restrictive quotas), Mussolini retorted that Italy simply had no option if it wanted 'to count for something' in the world: 'I maintain . . . that the premise of the political and thus the economic and moral power of nations is their demographic force. Let us put it bluntly: what are 40 million Italians compared to 90 million Germans and 200 million Slavs . . . or the 46 million English and the 450 million living in their colonies?'

But it was not mere numbers that mattered to Mussolini. More fundamental was his belief that birth rates were an indication of the moral health of peoples: 'All nations and all empires have felt the teeth of decadence sinking into them when they have seen their levels of natality fall'. The arguments he put forward to support this claim were more emotive than rational, with sweeping assertions about how 'industrial urbanisation' and 'the infinite moral cowardice of the so-called upper classes of society' (who selfishly put wealth and material pleasure ahead of sexual reproduction) condemned a country to sterility. But the historical examples that he gave to show the supposed link between demography and the rise and fall of peoples, ranging from the decline of the Roman empire after Augustus to recent shifts in the balance of power in Europe ('we must consider that since 1870 France has increased by 2 million inhabitants, Germany by 24 and Italy by 16') made it clear that his principal concern in seeking to transform the 'soul' of Italians was not so much with domestic regeneration as with foreign policy: 'If you diminish, gentlemen, you do not create an empire. You become a colony!'[25]

The broad acceptance of Mussolini's demographic campaign and the accompanying emphasis that the regime now intended to place on 'rurality' (peasants were seen as less hedonistic than townspeople and thus more prolific: hence the warm tribute he paid in his speech to one of the poorest regions in the country, Basilicata, whose high birth rate showed that it had still not been adversely affected by 'the pernicious currents of contemporary civilisation')[26] owed much to the traditional hostility of the Catholic Church to city life. Already in 1925, when the government had set out to boost agricultural production and make the country self-sufficient in wheat by launching a national 'battle for grain', sections of the senior clergy had responded warmly to the encouragement they felt was now being given to rural life and values. The Archbishop of Perugia, for instance, had written to the clergy in his diocese urging them to give their 'full backing' to Mussolini's initiative. Apart, he said, from the laudable desire to make 'our dear fatherland' strong ('a master not a slave'), there would be undoubted 'moral and religious benefits' for the poor, 'who from contact with the green, healthy and fertile land will feel elevated to thoughts of purity and to intentions of hard work'.[27]

The Church was careful to make clear that its attitudes towards sex and procreation were shaped by religion and differed from the political concerns of fascism with national strength, but it had little difficulty in welcoming the government's emphasis on natality and the various measures taken to encourage large families. These ranged from the establishment in 1925–26 of an agency, ONMI (Opera Nazionale Maternità e Infanzia), to provide care and support for needy mothers and their children, to taxes on bachelors, subsidies for prolific couples, and curbs on abortion and the sale and distribution of contraceptives. (A new penal code in 1931 included a section on 'crimes against the integrity and the health of the race': any form of encouragement given to the use of prophylactics could result in a custodial sentence, while the practice of abortion became punishable with up to twelve years in prison.) The value of the Church's backing for the demographic campaign was well understood by Mussolini, and in 1928 he sent a telegram of personal thanks to the Cardinal Archbishop of Milan for having read out a pastoral letter on the subject of large families, in which positive comments were made about the Ascension Day speech and the government's pro-natalist policies.[28]

No less important for ensuring support for the demographic campaign, particularly among the educated classes, was the fact that it was embedded in a broader transformative programme that drew heavily on the ideas and language of the Risorgimento. In analysing the reasons for Italy's slide into what was commonly referred to as 'decadence' after the glorious era of the Middle Ages and the Renaissance, patriots of the nineteenth century had repeatedly focused on what they had seen as the 'vices' of ordinary Italians – vices that had been exacerbated, if not caused, they felt, by long years of corrupt and oppressive foreign rule. Excessive individualism, materialism, scepticism, factionalism, indiscipline, indolence and an absence of martial spirit were among the main defects of the national character that were commonly seen as responsible for Italy's political, economic and cultural decline. Supporters of the national movement had regarded the generation of civic morality as a necessary premise for political revival, with independence emerging as the product and expression of the new spirit. The fact that unification had been achieved primarily through diplomacy and foreign arms had left the moral agenda of reforming the character of the Italian people unfulfilled.

This moral reading of the country's problems had flowed over into post-unification Italy and done much to erode the credibility of liberalism. The shortcomings of the kingdom were widely attributed to the inability of the representative institutions to remedy the old defects. Parliamentary government had seemed simply to reflect, even amplify, the traditional vices, especially as the suffrage broadened and new swathes of still 'unmade' Italians entered the political arena. Corruption and military defeat were just two of the most conspicuous facets of the new degenerate 'Byzantium'. The various Nationalist and other intellectuals who had gathered around journals such as *La Voce* in the years before the First World War had criticised Giolittian Italy in terms of the failure of the country's leaders to create the consciousness that patriots such as Mazzini had called for. Mussolini, though a revolutionary socialist at the time, had himself endorsed this perspective, telling the editor of *La Voce* in 1909 of how vital it was 'to form the spiritual unity of the Italians': 'A difficult task, given our history and our temperament, but not impossible. To create the "Italian" soul is a superb mission.'[29]

Fascism had from the outset looked to gain legitimacy for its revolutionary aims by connecting with the regenerative language that had long been at the heart of debates about the nation. In the months after the March on Rome Mussolini had punctuated his speeches with references to the old Italy being 'dead', to a 'new immensely vigorous' Italy being made, and to how the country was now experiencing the 'fourth rebirth of our immortal race'.[30] In an interview with an

American newspaper in May 1924 he had claimed that the central problem with Italy ever since the Middle Ages had been the gap between the richness of its cultural life and its 'civil education'. He had said that Massimo d'Azeglio had summed up the issue in his famous aphorism shortly after unification about the need to 'make Italians' now that the country itself had been brought into being. He had added: 'Fascism is the greatest experiment in our history in making Italians. What do I mean by the phrase "making Italians"? I mean that we must create something that destroys the imbalance between Italian civilisation and Italian political life, this evil that has tormented our history for all these generations.'[31]

The idea that fascism would regenerate the nation by creating 'new men' and 'new women', whose discipline, energy and fecundity would enable Italy to dominate a continent that was weakened by materialism and humanitarianism and sliding into decadence, was aired with growing insistence by Mussolini after the establishment of the dictatorship. In the summer of 1925 he announced that fascism must become a complete 'way of life', in which the prevalent values would be bravery and love of risk, 'abhorrence of all that is sedentary', 'revulsion towards craven comfort' ('panciafichismo'), discipline at work, respect for authority and 'pride in feeling Italian every moment of the day'.[32] The damage caused by the failure of the liberal state since 1860 to harness the masses and bind them into a strong and purposeful collective unit, would be brought to an end. The nation would acquire the character of an efficient army: 'Every one of you must think of himself as a soldier', he told a party rally on the third anniversary of the March on Rome, 'even when you are not in military uniform; even at work, in the office, in the factory, on the construction site, in the fields; a soldier bound to every other element of the army, a molecule that feels and pulsates with the entire organism'.[33]

At one level, Mussolini and others of his generation who had grown up with the crowd theories of Le Bon and Nietzschean ideas of elite leadership probably believed that the character of the masses could be moulded with relative ease. Perhaps carried away with his radiant vision of fascist ascendancy in Europe, he expressed the rather surprising view to the Grand Council on 7 January 1927 (at least as Federzoni recalled in his diary) that Italy was already 'completely dominated by the fascist mentality'. Such optimism drew on a tradition common among Italian intellectuals of considering the problems posed by the rural and urban poor in largely paternalistic and educative terms. ('Ordinary people ['il popolo'] are like big children', Mussolini informed the readers of the *Daily Express* in 1925, 'that need to guided, helped and, if necessary, punished'.)[34] But another strand of thought that had become closely linked to discussions of Italy's national revival since the early nineteenth century suggested that the task of creating 'new' men and women might in fact not be so easy. In his more sober moments Mussolini acknowledged this. As he told a gathering of party leaders in October 1930:

> We need time, a great deal of time, to complete our work. And I am not speaking here of the material but of the moral work. We have to scrape off and crush the sediments that have been deposited in the character and mentality of Italians by those terrible centuries of political, military and moral decadence between 1600 and the rise of Napoleon. It is a prodigious undertaking. The Risorgimento was merely the beginning, as it was the enterprise of just tiny minorities. The world war was profoundly educative. It is now a question of continuing on a daily basis the task of remaking the Italian character. For example, we owe it to the culture of those three centuries that the legend grew up that Italians cannot fight. It required the sacrifice and heroism of Italians during the Napoleonic wars to demonstrate the opposite. The Italians of the early Renaissance, of the eleventh, twelfth and thirteenth centuries to be precise, had temperaments of steel, and brought all their courage, their hatred and their passion to bear in war. But the eclipse we suffered in those centuries of decadence weighs still upon our destiny, as yesterday, as today, the prestige of nations is determined almost exclusively by their military glories, their armed might . . . This enterprise is my cross and my mission . . .[35]

Purification in action: the campaign against the Sicilian mafia

Despite having earned the bitter enmity of the *squadristi* in Bologna in 1922 and been sacked from his position as prefect of Bari after the March on Rome, Cesare Mori was determined to resurrect his career.

His distinguished record of public service since the 1890s and his close links with conservative politicians, particularly Nationalists, stood him in good stead. 'You will surely find a way of refuting the myth that you hate fascists', one high-placed friend reassured him: 'Whoever applies the law impartially . . . restores the authority of the state. And the fascists, if they are in good faith, ought to be the first to acknowledge this.'[36] In March 1923 another of his contacts reported a conversation with Luigi Federzoni in which the Nationalist leader had expressed 'sympathy and respect' for the former prefect and concluded emphatically: 'He will rise again!'[37] Mori endeavoured to hasten his rehabilitation by making it quite clear that he bore no grudges towards the blackshirts and that his dream was to return to Sicily, where he had spent many years before the First World War as a police officer combating banditry and organised crime, and 'fight once again fascistically, as I have always fought'.[38]

Mori had literary ambitions, and to help pass the time pending a new appointment he wrote poems in the decadent style of D'Annunzio and also a book about the Sicilian mafia with the deceptively romantic title of *Between the Orange Blossoms and Beyond the Mist*. Like most other contemporary commentators, he regarded the mafia not as a formal criminal organisation – certainly not a unitary one – but more as a cultural phenomenon in which individuals or groups, located for the most part in communities in western and central Sicily, were able to commit crimes with impunity, thanks to the traditional weakness of the state and the refusal of local people to cooperate with the public security forces. The solution, he claimed, was for the police and the courts to demonstrate that they were stronger than the criminals by making sure that they had powerful enough tools to arrest and convict anyone suspected of being a *mafioso*, leaving innocent Sicilians to rally gratefully to the side of the authorities, inspired by the 'loftiest ideal of the Fatherland and Justice'. He was hopeful this could now be achieved. He had detected a new spirit of blowing 'through the flowering orange trees, the purpling vines and the waving fields of grain' – a spirit generated by the experience of the war and characterised by 'intensity of work, fervour of thought, and light of faith'.[39]

In June 1924 Mori's hopes of rehabilitation were realised when he was appointed prefect of the western Sicilian province of Trapani. His efforts to introduce some stability here after the lawlessness of the post-war years earned him many enemies, not least because he concentrated his energies heavily on purging the local fascist party, whose ranks had been infiltrated, he believed, by the mafia. Protests reached Rome. The former Minister of Public Instruction, Giovanni Gentile, whose family came from the province, complained to Luigi Federzoni in the spring of 1925 that the government 'should never have given a position of responsibility to someone with Mori's past'.[40] But Federzoni was keen to back Mori: it was well known that operations against organised crime in the island inevitably resulted in political casualties, given the degree to which *mafiosi* always looked to entwine themselves with those in power. If Mori's actions led to unruly elements being eliminated from the party, so much the better. Mussolini was of a similar persuasion. In the autumn of 1925, with pressure mounting on the party secretary to stamp out the remaining vestiges of criminality and *squadrismo* among rank-and-file fascists, Mori was promoted to the prefecture of Palermo.

The campaign he waged against the mafia in the course of the next couple of years led to thousands of arrests, with the police descending on small towns at night and seizing the wanted men – or in their absence their relatives or property. The police lacked concrete evidence in many cases to link individuals to specific crimes and relied instead on the claim that the term '*mafioso*' indicated membership of a 'criminal association'; and since 'criminal association' was a permanent offence, somebody could be summarily arrested and then held indefinitely in prison on the grounds that he had been caught in flagrante delicto.[41] As was widely pointed out at the time, this opened the door to serious injustices, not only because, as Mori himself said, 'the mafia' was not strictly an organisation, at least in the rural centres of the Sicilian interior, but also because in popular parlance the epithet '*mafioso*' could denote somebody who was proud or assertive, but not necessarily criminal. Even more problematic was the fact that the term was freely used as a weapon with which to tar opponents in the bitter factional struggles that raged between rival families in almost every Sicilian town. The police were constantly in receipt of defamatory anonymous letters denouncing individuals as *mafiosi*.

In these circumstances, decisions about whom to arrest almost inevitably became political. In Corleone, for example, the police maintained that the 'criminal association' had its headquarters in the local

Agricultural Circle, 'otherwise known as the *Casino* [club] of the Mafia'. When they arrived in the town in the early hours of the morning of 20 December 1926, the 159 people they were looking for were all believed to be closely involved with this Circle. The leading members of the Agricultural Circle were prominent in the faction that controlled the municipal council – a faction which supported a controversial deputy called Giovanni Lo Monte and which had long been contending power with a rival faction in Corleone headed, until his murder in 1915, by a charismatic socialist called Bernardino Verro. Lo Monte's followers had backed the government in the 1924 elections, and the police at the time had given them a clean bill of health saying that the socialists were in fact the real 'mafia'. But the victory of Lo Monte's followers caused problems for the town's fascists, who subsequently found themselves unable to take independent initiatives and attract recruits.[42]

The police case against the arrested men depended largely on hearsay. This was evident from statements made to the investigating magistrate and at the trial. A member of the Militia confirmed the police claim that the Agricultural Circle was known as the '*Casino* of the Mafia' and denounced those who frequented it. Another fascist referred to the 'so-called group of the mafia', with 'a circle in the piazza in front of the urinals', whose building was 'commonly' called the '*casino* of the mafia'. However, a number of witnesses were clearly very unhappy with the way their testimony was being used. 'The names I gave in my declaration belonged to people who went along to the Circle, and not to mafia people', objected one. 'When I named those men to the police', another said, 'I referred only to public opinion, according to which the opponents of the socialists were *mafiosi*.' One man denied that there was any 'party of the mafia', and pointed out how easily epithets got thrown around in Corleone to smear enemies: 'I cannot admit that I belonged to the party of the honest and that my opponents were dishonest. That is not true. The opposition list, like ours, was made up of respectable people. In every party, there are honest and dishonest. Giving the label "mafia" to the opposition is as outrageous as my being called a "social communist"'. The significance accorded to the term '*mafioso*' also caused some problems. 'Most people did not regard him as *mafioso* if by that you mean a criminal', said a priest, 'because in Corleone the word gets applied to someone who simply adopts a brazen manner.' The local bandmaster sought to defend one of his pupils saying: 'I used to . . . clip him round the ear when he made a mistake in some piece of music and he never tried to hit me back. If he had been a *mafioso* he would have reacted differently'.[43]

The political dimensions of the campaign against the mafia forced Mori to watch his step very carefully. But he was assisted by the general direction in which the tide was flowing in fascism, with Mussolini eager after 1925 to bring the provincial *ras* under the control of the prefects and purge the party of disreputable elements. Against this backdrop Mori decided to launch an attack on the most prominent Sicilian fascist, a young oculist of somewhat radical views called Alfredo Cucco, who had dominated the party in Palermo since before the March on Rome. Cucco had grown increasingly critical of Mori in the course of 1926, and was a barrier to the reconstruction of fascism on the more conservative footing envisaged by the prefect and many of the island's influential aristocratic landowning families. In December Mori asked the *carabinieri* commanders, in the strictest secrecy, to provide him with information about 'infiltration by mafia and criminals' of local fascist party sections or unions. Armed with this information, and a series of trumped-up personal charges, he succeeded in getting Cucco and his leading supporters expelled from the party early in 1927.[44]

In the months that followed, fascism in the province of Palermo was entirely rebuilt, with the landowning aristocracy – which up until then had largely stood aloof from the regime – taking over many of the key positions. Mori's own position was cemented in May, when in the course of his Ascension Day speech Mussolini devoted a large section to the campaign against the mafia, proudly listing the size of the various 'criminal associations' that had been rounded up by the police, and inviting 'the press of all the world' to publish the figures and acknowledge that 'fascist surgery' had been 'truly courageous and truly swift'. 'From time to time', he declared, 'I hear sceptics suggesting that we are going too far in Sicily, that an entire region is being humiliated . . . I reject such suggestions with scorn.' He congratulated Mori warmly on his achievement and offered him his 'cordial greetings' (several Palermo deputies leapt to their feet at this point and applauded), and he quoted figures to show the fall in crime rates in the island, saying that these were the best tribute that could be paid to the prefect. He ended by announcing that the campaign would only come to an end when there were 'no more *mafiosi*' and every memory of the mafia had been 'blotted from the minds of Sicilians'.[45]

Such defiant ambitions accorded well with the hyperbolic tone of the Ascension Day speech, with its proclaimed goal of transforming the entire 'soul' of Italy. But the reality on the ground in Sicily suggested that Mori's draconian measures were not having quite the salutary effects intended. The arrest of one 'criminal association' with links to a particular political faction frequently left the way open for a rival political faction to move in and secure control of the municipal admin- istration. But as the barrage of letters sent to Mussolini in the course of 1927 suggested, the purged social environment did not give the impression of being morally much superior to what had preceded it. One problem was that all the documentation relating to the *fasci* in the province of Palermo in 1921 to 1926 had apparently been stolen. This meant that the political credentials of those charged with recon- structing the party were often hard to verify – with sometimes rather surprising results. Thus in Corleone, the man who was entrusted with the task of rebuilding the local *fascio* after the members of the Agricultural Circle had been arrested was a certain Colonel Vinci. But according to Alfredo Cucco, Vinci had 'for years been a *popolare*, an anti-fascist and head of the subversives, to the point of having been cautioned about this by the political and military authorities'.[46]

For many observers in the island the problem of the mafia remained as serious as ever, whatever the claims of Mussolini about the success of 'fascist surgery'. In August 1927 Mariano Fazio wrote to the Duce to express his horror at what was happening in his small town of Ventimiglia to the south-east of Palermo. He reported that in the previous November Mori had proposed the dissolution of the communal administration, headed by a certain Calì, 'who acted as the mayor, and friend to the local mafia'. Then in April, 'to everyone's amazement', Calì had been nominated as the town's *podestà*, while the Communal Secretary, one Brancato, who had earlier been denounced as affiliated to the mafia (and whose brother was wanted by the police), had been released from prison and was now 'controlling the political and administrative situation on behalf of criminals'. Fazio blamed this state of affairs on Mori's close personal friendship with a leading veterinary surgeon, who was a relative of the Communal Secretary of Ventimiglia, and who had used his connections with the prefect and other influential figures in Palermo not only to get Brancato freed from gaol but also to have the local *fascio* dissolved and its reconstruction entrusted to Calì and his friends – who had formerly been expelled from the party for opposing Mussolini during the Matteotti crisis.[47]

This unedifying picture in relation to the mafia was replicated in numerous further protests sent to Mussolini and other senior party figures in the course of 1927. It underlined just how difficult it was going to be for fascism to break with the corrupt political behaviour that had so damaged the image of the liberal state, especially in the south of the country, and create 'new' Italians. The town of Bagheria, for instance, to the east of Palermo, had been a political stronghold of a famous oculist and senator called Giuseppe Cirincione. Cirincione was a friend and colleague of Alfredo Cucco, and when Cucco fell, Cirincione was pulled down in his wake. 'A cyclone of slanders', he wrote to the Sicilian general and former Minister of War, Antonino Di Giorgio, in January 1927, in a desperate appeal for help, 'threatens to hurl into the mud forty blameless years of hard work.' He had been suspended from his university post, and the reason, he had heard, lay in his supposed 'links with . . . the mafia!' Mori was to conduct an inquiry into his family background ('on behalf of [Giovanni] Gentile and the Minister [of Public Instruction, Pietro] Fedele, who both have grudges against me'), and the starting point was to be a report by an aggrieved magistrate 'whom I had removed from Bagheria last year because he was a protector of the mafia, as was shown by an inquiry I had instigated'.[48]

One reason why Cirincione was being investigated was that the police had apparently found in the homes of some of those who had recently been arrested letters he had sent while a deputy in reply to requests for favours: 'These are electoral letters, and in Bagheria they are an unmitigated nuisance, as the deputy has traditionally been considered a person you solicit for anything. Like my predecessor . . . I answered everybody, regardless of rank or character, and in my own hand.' How could such documents be regarded as criminal? And anyway, had not his entire career shown that he had always been a resolute opponent of the mafia?

Everything I have done shows my hostility towards that rabble . . . In my local administration (Bagheria), I chose the councillors personally, and not a single *mafioso*, or relative of a *mafioso*, has got in . . . In order to make life harder for *mafiosi*, I had the rural guards replaced by sworn policemen. But I had to struggle manfully to get my way, and the prefect of the time sent me his warmest congratulations, and I still have them. From then on the countryside here has been free of crime. It is only because [the magistrate] and the *mafiosi* hate me, that I have had to suffer the humiliation of seeing them credited rather than me.[49]

But the pendulum of factionalism had swung against Cirincione. With his fall the task of rebuilding the fascist party in Bagheria was entrusted to one of his opponents, Onofrio Corselli. Once again eyebrows were raised and letters of complaint reached the authorities. As the police had to confess, Corselli had been involved in a coalition that had fought the 1924 elections backed by 'all the militant mafia'. But they did not think Corselli was at fault for having failed to sever his links with the mafia bloc. Quite why, they did not say.[50] As the disgraced and disenchanted Alfredo Cucco indicated in a long report sent to Rome in 1928, the situation in Bagheria was no different from that in other towns in western Sicily, where 'mafia and former anti-fascists' were now firmly ensconced in power.[51] But for the time being Cucco's opinion counted for nothing. However, in 1931 he was finally acquitted of all charges against him and his rehabilitation began. He continued his career as an oculist, taught demography at Palermo university and published books on the dangers of birth control and racial degeneration. In the spring of 1943 he was made a national vice-secretary of the party.

The growing confusion in the island caused increasing consterna-tion in Rome. Mori was summoned to the capital to explain. 'What the devil is going on in Sicily?' Augusto Turati, the party secretary, asked him, alluding to the torrent of complaints and protests that he was receiving. 'I no longer understand anything'.[52] Mussolini was rather more supportive. He had to be: he had not only given his unequivocal backing to Mori in the Ascension Day speech, but he also recognised that the fight against the mafia had become a litmus test at home and abroad of the capacity of fascism to achieve what liberalism had been unable to effect and of its determination to create a new and morally regenerate Italy. The foreign press was taking a huge interest in the campaign, and tributes to Mori and his work appeared in newspapers from Norway to Argentina. *The Times* of London spoke of the success of the fascist government in finally breaking the mafia and ending the climate of fear in the island, and of how 'the simple and superstitious peasantry' of Sicily referred to the prefect with awe and gratitude as 'Santo Mori' and had placed him 'among those saints who work miracles'. A former American ambassador to Italy, Richard Washburn Child, wrote a series of widely translated sensationalist articles on 'the uprooting and throttling of the world's deadliest secret society, which for centuries terrorised four million people with the "dark, the knife, silence!"'[53]

But despite this huge acclaim, Mori sensed the vulnerability of his position. He had not only antagonised many within the party – who saw his brutal elimination of Cucco as confirmation that he was still an anti-fascist – but he was also attracting growing criticism from influential conservatives such as the well-regarded General Antonino Di Giorgio. In the spring of 1928 Di Giorgio told Mussolini of his fear that Mori had lost all sense of proportion, and that the sheer scale of the arrests – the official figure stood at 11,000 – and the crude methods being used were causing widespread anger. Victims of criminals had been lumped together indiscriminately in the mass round-ups with the criminals themselves, 'for no other reason than that they had had contact with them'. The courts, faced with the almost impossible task of trying hundreds of people simultaneously, and under huge political pressure not to call into question the work of the police, were inevitably committing gross injustices – which risked discrediting the entire legal process. And to make matters worse, said Di Giorgio, the hopes that the regime had of overcoming the traditional alienation of the peasantry from the state were being undermined by class prejudices: wealthier people were routinely spared as 'victims' of the mafia, while the vulnerable poor were being sent to prison for 'crimes' such as delivering a blackmail letter, under threat of death if they failed to do so.[54]

Mori quickly sought to counter the opposition of Di Giorgio (whom he disliked: 'old clientelistic and Masonic mentality – meddler – intriguer against the Militia – antifascist – [said] that I had threatened the jury at Termini – has always accused me of hegemonic ambitions'). He dug up evidence of Di Giorgio's supposed links with the mafia and sent a report to Mussolini. He said that one of Di Giorgio's political supporters was head of the Mistretta 'criminal association' and that the name of Di Giorgio's brother had appeared in a document found in the house of an arrested man. Mussolini, who was growing increasingly weary of Mori's campaign and the trouble it was causing, and coming to realise that 'fascist surgery' was hardly the answer to such a complex problem as the mafia, summoned Di Giorgio to Rome and put the allegations to him. Di Giorgio was incensed that his criticisms of Mori's work could be attributed to base self-interest and alleged criminal connections. He refused to accept Mussolini's offer of a military command outside Sicily and he returned to Palermo, where he confronted Mori in a violent altercation and apparently slapped him in the face.[55]

To bolster his position in Sicily, and deflect criticism in Rome, Mori strove to present himself as a model fascist prefect, dutifully carrying out the regime's goal of forging new Italians. He agreed with Mussolini that the liberal state had abandoned the masses and left them without any clear sense of what it was to be a citizen. To illustrate the scale of the problem he told the First Regional Congress of Fascist Teachers in 1926 of his encounter with a poor shepherd boy 'alone in the murky solitude of a *latifondo* of ill repute'. 'His father? Wanted, and in America. His mother? Sick, and alone in the village with two babies. The village? Far away. How far? He did not know; he never went there. God, prayer, school? Nothing. The King, Italy, the nation? Nothing. Rights, duties, the law, good and bad? Nothing.' It was the duty of the island's educators, he told the teachers, to rectify such moral neglect and ensure that 'the great soul of Sicily, which in the past had become lost as in a moonless night', should burst forth again 'proud and naked like once the Spartan virgins on the sand' – and this new soul would be 'composed of love and inspired by one faith: God, King and Fatherland'. Mori sent a copy of his speech to Federzoni and to every school in the island.[56]

To spread the message of fascism, and comply with the emphasis on 'ruralisation', Mori assiduously toured the agricultural centres of the Sicilian interior, cultivating direct contact with the masses, and relishing the sobriquet accorded him by the press of the 'peasant prefect'. Some of the places that he went to had never before seen a prefect (a fact that he stressed), and in an effort to ensure that the image projected of the state was both engaging and benign, everything was done to ensure that his visits – which usually took place on Sundays – had a strongly festive atmosphere. 'In all quarters, in the streets and in houses, there were flowers and laurel wreaths', said a newspaper account of Mori's trip to Roccamena. 'Balconies were draped with carpets, hangings, embroideries and silk; at every street corner and in the piazza there were flags and arches decorated with greenery.' The band from nearby Corleone provided music; the banner of the agricultural union was baptised, first with holy water by the parish priest and then with champagne; and Mori ('greeted as ever by a frenzy of exultant cheers and cries') smiled as he began his long speech, 'almost chatting with the peasants'.[57] Press reports of other visits gave a similar picture of enthusiasm, with crowds shouting 'Viva Mori', 'Long live our saviour' and 'Down with the mafia', and 'hurricanes' of applause.[58]

Whether the impact on the local population was as positive as the tightly controlled press liked to suggest is difficult to know for sure. In all probability not – at least in 1926. Cucco, who toured the province alongside Mori prior to his downfall, gave a very different picture of the atmosphere of the official visits that year in his unpublished memoirs – though his account was inevitably partisan. Mori's height, imposing martial bearing and unfamiliar northern accent left audiences cold, he said; and the fact that the prefect surrounded himself with police was a further source of alienation. Cucco's own speeches, in which he emphasised the importance of using the party's youth organisations to re-educate the young and so meet the Duce's goal of 'removing the evil tares from souls, characters and habits', were greeted with 'great warmth and applause'. 'But as soon as Cesare Mori stepped forward, a sepulchral silence descended on the piazza and the crowd.' And the military language he used, with talk of the 'merciless campaign' he was waging against the mafia only coming to an end when the 'wicked beast' had been slain for good ('its head crushed beneath the iron-shod hooves of your sturdy mules') was received, so Cucco claimed, with 'dismay' and 'fear'.[59]

During his last two years as prefect in 1927–29, Mori complied vigorously with the regime's ideological programme. He extolled the Duce: 'the Man who never speaks in vain'; 'the Man guided by God'; 'the Man on account of whom the whole world envies us . . . for whom we will march together into the joyous dawn that already gilds the horizon'.[60] He proclaimed that Sicilian fascism would be 'essentially rural' and celebrated the peasantry: 'In the figure of the Sicilian peasant . . . silent, industrious, and riveted to his place of work on the sun-baked *latifondo*, I see not only the worker of today . . . but also the bold pioneer who affirms the primacy of Italy beyond its shores.'[61] And he repeatedly sought to underline how the values and moral impetus of fascist Italy stemmed from the sacrifices of the First World War, encouraging the erection of monuments to the fallen, and urging his audiences, in some of his most florid prose, to feel themselves bound in one community with the glorious dead. As he said at the unveiling of the memorial in Balestrate, in the piazza in front of the Mother Church:

> Here, citizens, is the Fatherland and with it God. Here is the Fatherland in which our whole being is immersed and obliterated. Here is duty, here is honour, here is sacrifice. Here is the symbol of the supreme holocaust . . . Here speak the souls as they rise up high along the purest paths of feeling, beyond all human suffering, in the glow of boundless faith, towards the sacred fire of the Ideal which is called Italy. Only by being worthy of them in actions can these dead be honoured . . . And because this is so, I stand here before this monument content . . . Because, citizens, from this and the other monuments, which thanks to filial heroism and fraternal love adorn this ardent land . . . Sicily has finally leapt forth, the true Sicily, the Sicily of the Vespers – martial, Savoy, fascist Sicily.[62]

This 'true Sicily' was a land purged of vice whose energies would be directed to the greatness of the nation ('today with the plough, tomorrow, if God wills it, with bayonets.').[63] And crucial to Italy's future, as Mori dutifully emphasised, was demographic growth. Among the initiatives that he took in furtherance of the government's pro-natalist campaign was the distribution, on Christmas Eve 1928, of 26,300 lire to the heads of 101 large local families. (The money was drawn from a national fund of over 2 million lire that Mussolini had assigned for prizes to prolific couples.) The gesture was essentially symbolic, given the relatively small sums and numbers involved, but Mori took the opportunity, as so often in his speeches, to interweave the sacred with the profane and suggest that compliance with the demands of the state was also a religious duty. He told his audience that strength lay in numbers, that children had always been and would continue to be Italy's greatest asset, and that everybody should 'have faith' and 'persevere in their work of procreation', mindful of the 'warning of Christ, who has ruled and comforted us for twenty centuries, not to lose heart', and 'in obedience to the will of the Duce, in whom are co-joined the greatest future and the greatest fortunes of the nation.'[64]

Given such language, it is little surprise that Mori was able to count on strong backing from the Church hierarchy for his activities in Sicily – certainly from 1927. The archbishops of Palermo and Monreale gave him their unequivocal support, and senior clerics as well as parish priests often appeared alongside him when he toured provincial towns. In June 1927 the leading Catholic journal, *La Civiltà Cattolica*, carried a long article praising Mori's work in Sicily. It claimed that the mafia had flourished in the past thanks to the 'misrule of the old Masonic liberalism', but was now finally being destroyed through 'a new and legitimate, but more resolute, exercise of authority'. It commended Mori's close collaboration with schools and his acts of charity – including making donations to the families of arrested men. It also underlined how for the 'work of moral restoration' to be lasting, the full cooperation of 'all honest citizens and especially priests' was needed, so that in contrast to 'the indifference or agnosticism' of the liberal state, 'the exercise of authority can resume its full force illuminated . . . by the light of reason and faith, but more still warmed by Christian benevolence and love'.[65]

The convergence of Catholic and fascist morality was well illustrated in the vigorous support that Mori gave to the work of the National Anti-blasphemy League. As he said in October 1928 in a long speech to the Palermo branch of the League, much of which was devoted to the importance of improving the moral heath of the nation through a higher birth rate, swearing, like immodest female attire (of which he was a stern public critic), corroded 'religious and family sentiment'. Conversely, the suppression of blasphemy would lead to 'the elevation of religious feeling and the formation of a religious conscience'. This in turn would have beneficial consequences for the population, since – and he quoted the study of a young German demographer, Richard Korherr (future head of the statistical bureau of the Nazi SS), which had recently been translated into Italian, 'with that marvellous preface by Benito Mussolini' – 'the extinction of true religious feeling is the cause of the decline of births, and the worm that gradually kills our civilisation'. In furtherance of the crackdown on swearing, Mori had warning posters placed around the city, while designated 'vigilance inspectors', carrying official identity cards, were authorised to patrol the streets and public places.[66]

For Mori (as for Mussolini) the backing of the Church was not only important for the work of moral reconstruction. It was also crucial for mobilising mass political support. This was evident in the prefect's last major undertaking in Palermo. In March 1929 he had to oversee the vote that took place in the province, a few weeks after the signing of the Lateran Treaty and the formal conciliation of the Vatican and the Italian state, as part of a plebiscite held across the country for a single list of 400 centrally chosen parliamentary candidates. As he told a meeting of local mayors and party leaders, the primary purpose of the plebiscite was to demonstrate to the outside world that Italy was fully united behind Mussolini. To this end an overwhelming 'yes' was imperative. 'I want the plebiscite to be totalitarian both in reality and on paper'. He told them to remember how fascism had imposed its will in the past, by 'having recourse where necessary to that piece of wood called the *manganello*'; and if any attempts were made at sabotage, the authorities should intervene 'fascistically'. Those in charge of the polling stations had to be 'mentally agile and of secure faith', and should ensure that 'duplicate' voting slips were ready in advance. There was to be a carnival atmosphere, with music and flags, and since the clergy were now the 'friend, ally, and collaborator' of the regime, they had to play a full role: 'The parish priests will do what we have a right to demand from them'. And for a bit of added 'spice', he said, he would scrutinise all the voting lists after the election: 'Whoever has failed in his duty will have to settle his accounts with me.'[67]

Mori described the plebiscite in characteristic military language as a 'review in the open': 'Either here with us, or there against us'. On the eve of polling the local press was instructed to carry prominently in large letters a terse warning: 'Voting YES is a sacrosanct duty. To abstain is cowardice and treachery. To vote NO is desertion. MORI'.[68] The results were perhaps not surprising. The turnout in the province of Palermo was 92 per cent, slightly higher than for the country as a whole, and there were only 320 'no' votes and more than 190,000 'yes' votes. Of the 'no' votes, 297 were in the city of Palermo alone. In the overwhelming majority of Sicilian towns there was not a single vote against. Nationally there were 136,000 'no' votes and more than 8.5 million 'yes' votes. The American anthropologist Charlotte Gower observed the plebiscite in the town of Milocca and watched as the local men were collected in groups and marched to the polling stations escorted by the band. She overheard one person saying: 'We will vote as they tell us, but God knows what is in our hearts.' She was unable to discover exactly what he meant.[69]

Mori's efforts to defuse the growing disquiet in Rome by 'polarising everything on fascism and the Duce', as he put it in some private notes, turned out to be unsuccessful.[70] On 23 June 1929 a brief telegram arrived from Mussolini informing him that he was being retired 'for reasons of seniority'. He was only 57 and was bitterly disappointed. He moved to Rome, where he did his best to keep the issue of the mafia alive, delivering a forthright speech to the Senate in March 1930 calling for urgent economic intervention in Sicily to ensure that the problem of crime in the island was resolved definitively. His remarks were not appreciated: as far as the government was concerned, the mafia had been eliminated and was not to be alluded to again.[71] Mori faced similar hostility in 1932 when it came to the publication of his memoirs, *Con la mafia ai ferri corti* ('At close quarters with the mafia'). He had proposed alternative titles such as 'Lictorial dawn over the orange blossom', no doubt hoping to draw the sting of party criticism, but his publisher, Mondadori, was clearly more concerned with marketability. The dust jacket initially showed an armed bandit peering menacingly from beneath a heavy cloak, but this had to be withdrawn hurriedly after protests that it was morally offensive to Sicily. It was replaced with an image of Mori in a black shirt standing shoulder to shoulder with a Greek Orthodox priest. A number of deputies asked whether 'unauthorised' autobiographies by state officials should be banned. Mussolini refused to intervene, and publication proceeded – with vitriolic reviews from the more radical fascist press.

Mori was hurt by the reception given to his book, which he regarded as 'a hymn to Sicily, fascism, the regime and the Duce'.[72] But the government clearly wanted to project a new image of the island, and indeed of southern Italy as a whole – one from which all reference to organised crime had been removed. In July 1931 Mussolini ordered the prefect of Milan immediately to sequestrate a journal which had published an article entitled 'L'arcisantissma camorra': 'camorra', he said, was a term of 'disparagement and defamation of Italians' and to allow it to circulate was 'an imbecility that damaged the moral prestige of the Nation'.[73] Mori hoped to resurrect his literary career by writing short stories and poems, but his attempts to get them published came to nothing. He had to be content with spending the remaining years of his life as president of a land reclamation consortium, overseeing irrigation works, building roads and canals, and draining marshes, in Istria – a position that he had no doubt been offered with the intent of getting him as far away as possible from Sicily. He died in 1942.

During the 1930s Mori had to face additional disappointment as he received numerous reports from friends and former colleagues in Sicily indicating that the scourges of crime and the mafia were as bad as ever. The catastrophic economic conditions of the island, endemic corruption, and the ban on reporting anything that might contradict the official line that fascism had solved the problems that liberalism had failed to deal with, all contributed to a bleak picture. In December 1931 a lawyer wrote to him about the chaos around Termini Imerese:

As for public security, strong orders are issued but people go ahead regardless and murder and rob at will. Where is it all going to end? Even [the *podestà* of Termini] . . . has been held up and robbed. I realise that hunger, after two bad harvests, has not improved things; but it is above all the lack of general faith in the authorities that is to blame. In almost every town, the mafia bosses have had their sentences reduced and are back from *confino*, leaving the small fry behind. In Caccamo, a dangerous place, the Azzarello brothers, supreme mafia bosses of Sicily . . . were proposed by the local authorities for *confino*, but were then let off . . . Scandals such as this make honest people sick, and do nothing but encourage criminals.[74]

A few months later another friend reported on how dangerous life had become around Cefalù with 'hold ups, highway robberies and violent thefts': 'God preserve us, for we are going through a wretched time; and what is particularly bad is that the newspapers have been ordered to keep quiet.'[75] But despite the best efforts of the local fascist authorities to impose press censorship, something of the truth occasionally seeped out. In June 1933 Mussolini told the prefect of Palermo to take strong action, as he had heard that 'criminal associations' were again flourishing.[76]

No less dispiriting was the persistence of the unscrupulous factionalism that had for so long plagued the life of Sicilian towns. The suppression of elections and the imposition of rigid centralisation in the fascist party had failed to have the beneficial effects imagined. Indeed there are signs that the situation was growing worse in the 1930s as the deteriorating economic climate intensified the competition between clienteles for jobs and resources. A Sicilian deputy raised the problem in parliament in April 1932, saying that across the island partisan disputes had grown 'terrifyingly bitter': 'Slander can be an instrument of vendetta for the old displaced camarillas. Intolerant of the new order, they flood the province and the capital with denunciations and anonymous letters, sowing disquiet, mistrust, and suspicion of crime'.[77] The province of Palermo appears to have been particularly insalubrious, as Mori's departure opened the door for his many enemies to move onto the offensive. 'People have become obsessed here and see *mafiosi* everywhere', a magistrate from Misilmeri told Mori in 1930:

> . . . Men of unblemished character, who in the past risked having their heads shot off for standing up to the mafia, are now in grave trouble with the *carabinieri* simply because some trouble-maker decided to have them branded as *mafiosi* . . . Much of the work that Your Excellency achieved in the province of Palermo has been undone through ignorance or ineptitude.[78]

The limits of the Duce's grandiose talk of transforming the 'soul' of Italy, which had caused Luigi Federzoni and other members of the Grand Council to leap to their feet and cheer in January 1927, were all too evident. Traditional patterns of behaviour proved resistant to change, and hopes that the fascist party might become a training ground for a new elite imbued with a 'fascist mentality' and freed of old debilitating habits were not being realised. Reports from every-where in Italy in the 1930s spoke of pervasive corruption, municipalism, clientelism, profiteering and infighting in the PNF. The situation was considered to be especially bad in the south of the country – the delegates who attended the National Council of the PNF which was held in Sicily in 1933, with the specific purpose of injecting some moral momentum into fascism in the area, came away horrified with what they saw[79] – but the picture elsewhere was often little better. This was perhaps not surprising given that fascism's claims to renew the nation had originated in the exercise of untrammelled personal power by local *ras* and the exaltation of youthful lawlessness, unaccountability, partisanship and violence.

If the shortcomings of the party were one major impediment to the creation of 'new' Italians, the impoverishment of the masses was another. Mori's celebration of the peasantry, in keeping with the regime's policy of 'ruralisation', had gone hand in hand, as elsewhere in the country, with a strengthening of the political and economic power of the major landowners. The introduction of the 'battle for grain' in 1925 inflated the price of wheat through raised tariffs and enabled the often inefficiently farmed large estates or *latifondi* that covered much of the island (and southern Italy) to return higher profits. At the same time, the post-war increase in smallholdings, which had been encouraged by the land occupation movement, slowed dramat-ically after 1924, and new farmers were often forced to sell up after a revaluation of the lira in 1926–27 left them struggling to meet their mortgage repayments. The new balance of power in the countryside was evident in official pay indexes which showed a drop of 28 per cent in agricultural wages between 1928 and 1935.[80] The reality in many places may have been far worse, as employers were often able to disregard with impunity settlements agreed by the state-controlled unions. The same was equally true in the case of industry.

With emigration overseas no longer an option, desperate peasants had little choice but to move to the cities in a bid to find work. This made a mockery of the regime's desire to halt what it saw as the morally corrosive effects of urbanisation. The situation in Palermo was not untypical of the picture nationwide. In 1931 a quarter of those living in the regional capital were immigrants, and despite the best endeavours of the authorities to stem the flow, the influx from the countryside continued unabated during the next five years, pushing the population up by nearly 30,000. Housing was in short supply, and in 1931 more than half of the city's residents were living in one- or two-room dwellings, about twice the figure for a decade earlier.[81] A report of 1938 spoke of how 'huge working class quarters' had been pulled down and the population resettled in 'cramped and miserable homes without sun or light', where tuberculosis was rife and poverty 'absolute'.[82] Cities elsewhere in the peninsula faced similar pressures. The industrial centres of the north-west struggled to cope with the immigration from regions such as the Veneto, Emilia Romagna and Tuscany – and, for the first time, the south.[83]

Overcrowding and destitution in the cities were compounded by severe corruption. In Palermo, embezzlement, fraud and racketeering were widespread. The situation was made worse by the reluctance of the authorities to intervene strongly for fear of exposing the truth too publicly. The British consul in the city observed with growing dismay the prolonged scandal surrounding the disappearance of 40 million lire from the municipal budget in the mid-1930s and concluded in a report to the ambassador: 'As far as Sicily is concerned, [fascism] has done nothing to purify the administration . . . I am told by old residents, graft is as prevalent as it was under all previous regimes . . . Even when dishonesty is brought home to a Government employee he is not punished in a manner to deter others from following his example.'[84] Criminal gangs controlled the city's food markets, taking cuts of over 20 per cent on traders' takings; state contracts were awarded to cartels submitting tenders that were clearly fraudulent; and the public services were reduced to chaos. An official report in 1939 found that the main hospital could no longer get syringes as suppliers knew they would never be paid.[85]

Such a moral and material environment was hardly conducive to the success of the regime's campaign to increase the population of Italy by 20 million in the space of two decades. Mussolini tried to set a good example by adding two more children to his family, in 1927 and 1929, bringing the total to five, and he assiduously scanned local authority reports and the demographic statistics that newspapers were obliged to carry for any signs of progress. Prefects were praised or reprimanded accordingly: 'From the municipal bulletin . . . I note that between the last census and today the population of Como has declined by 27 stop if all the provinces of Italy were to follow this brilliant example the Italian race would have its days numbered stop tell the *Podestà* to do something for large families stop Como needs it'.[86] But the general trend in the birth rate across the country from the late 1920s was one of steady decline, falling from nearly twenty-eight per thousand of the population in 1926 to a little over twenty-two ten years later. In parts of the north and centre it even dropped below replacement levels. The situation was not helped by the conspicuous failure of many senior fascists to practise what they preached. Ahead of a meeting of the Grand Council in 1937 to introduce a new raft of demographic initiatives, Mussolini decided to compile a list of the number of children that each of the council's twenty-nine members had fathered. He found that the average was only 1.9.[87]

Mussolini had to concede that his hopes of bringing about a moral transformation of Italy were misplaced. As his disappointment and frustration mounted, he grew increasingly vituperative and misanthropic, railing in private against the seemingly incorrigible defects of his fellow countrymen. By the later 1930s he frequently attributed the failure of his regime to mould Italians into a more vigorous and disciplined people to a genetic legacy – to the fact that a large element of the population was descended from slave stock. In between violent lovemaking, glorying in his own energy, and boasting of himself as a 'giant', a 'gladiator', a 'savage', a 'wild animal', an 'eagle', and a 'force of nature', he told his young mistress Claretta Petacci how in reality many Italians greatly resented his attempts to make them more virile and martial, and would much prefer to have an easy life. They could not wait to see him go, he claimed, so that they could return to being the 'craven beggars' that they were before:

> For thirty years I have been studying why some of the Italians are so cowardly. They are descended from slaves. Think how many slaves must have copulated with women. And basically only fifty generations have gone by – not so many, then. And now this slave blood is surfacing again . . . If they had a mark on their heads I would destroy them all, exterminate them. They are the dross, the shame of the nation. They are the eternal whingers, those that cannot bear to change the way they behave.[88]

In the company of others, Mussolini's language was often less coarse and bombastic than with his lover, but the scorn was equally vehement. 'Have you ever seen a lamb turn into a wolf?' he asked his son-in-law, Galeazzo Ciano, in January 1940. 'The Italian race is a race of sheep. Eighteen years are not enough to transform it. You need 180, or perhaps 180 centuries'.[89] A few weeks later he announced that the only way to deal with Italians was to keep them 'lined up and in uniform from morning to evening' and administer 'stick, stick, stick'. And in June 1940, after the Italian forces had made a first humiliating showing in the Second World War, with the invasion of France, he complained to Ciano of how his grandiose dreams of 'making Italians' had been cruelly dashed: 'It is the raw material that I lack. Even Michelangelo needed marble in order to make his statues. If he had only had clay, he would simply have been a potter. A people that for sixteen centuries has been the anvil cannot, in a few years, become the hammer.'[90] Mussolini may have found comfort in the thought that he was part of a long tradition of illustrious reformers, ranging from Savonarola to Mazzini, who had been eager to change the character of Italians. But the consequences in human terms of his ambitions were in reality little short of disastrous.

6

Spaces for Dissent

Defending liberalism

In the course of 1925, the diaries of Benedetto Croce, Italy's most internationally acclaimed scholar, grew increasingly gloomy. His belief that the violence of fascism was an unfortunate but somehow necessary expression of the turbulent spirit generated by the First World War and would in due course pass, leaving Italy's liberal institutions strengthened and enabling the country to resume the long and steady march towards freedom that had begun with the Risorgimento, had proved unfounded. For a time after the establishment of the dictatorship in January he felt an uncharacteristic urge to become active in politics. He joined what remained of the Liberal Party, and pressed Giovanni Giolitti and its other elderly leaders to close ranks, take the fight to the country and set out a clear programme in defence of the principle of freedom. The dogmatism of fascism had to be countered with similar assertions of faith, he felt. 'Like all those who fight for an ideal we need to repeat the words of Luther before the Diet of Worms: Here I stand. I can do no other. God help me. Amen!'¹ But in his heart he knew that the battle was lost: with the government rapidly tightening the noose around the opposition, many of his former friends were defecting or withdrawing demoralised from the fray.

In October 1925 Croce travelled to Turin and met with the liberal senator Alfredo Frassati, the long-time editor and majority shareholder of the prestigious and still anti-fascist newspaper, *La Stampa*. Publication of the daily had been suspended on government orders since the end of the previous month, and Croce learned of how Giovanni Agnelli, the owner of Fiat, was pressing, with encouragement from Mussolini, to buy Frassati out and change *La Stampa*'s editorial stance (as duly happened). 'The visit to Turin yesterday and the talk with Frassati', Croce recorded in his diary, 'kept me awake until the morning in sad meditation. Painful sense of suffocation at the suppression of press freedom; rebellion of my spirit at this injustice, simultaneously violent and hypocritical.' In the course of his nocturnal reflections he came to the conclusion that his only hope of not succumbing to enervating depression was to disengage himself as best he could from the plight of Italy and focus instead on being true to his inner self, as was indeed his main duty as a philosopher. Given the nauseating spectacle of 'so many compromises and so many betrayals' that he saw all around him, he feared he might be banned from publishing in Italy and thus have little chance of engaging with his fellow coun-trymen and educating them to a better future. But he was comforted by the thought that there were still other Italians who shared his views: 'Let us go forward then with courage and faith.'[2]

However, his despondency deepened in the coming months. He belonged to the Senate, whose members were appointed for life by the king and might therefore have been expected to display a greater spirit of independence than their counterparts in the lower house. But in December the Senate hurriedly debated and passed the law that brought an end to press freedom in Italy. Croce was so disgusted by the cowardice of his fellow senators that he was inclined to abandon the sittings and return to his home in Naples. But he remained, 'in order not to leave alone the few friends that are speaking against [the law]'.[3] The new legislation required all journalists to belong to a professional body controlled by the state, and Croce now knew that editors would be disinclined to publish anything he wrote or even mention him other than in disparaging terms. His one consolation was that he still had his own journal, La Critica. He hoped (and his hope turned out to be correct) that the government would feel it counterproductive, given his international standing, and unnecessary, given La Critica's limited circulation, to ban it. La Critica continued in existence until after the fall of Mussolini and even evaded the stipulation that publications should carry the date of the 'fascist era' ('year one' being 1922–23) in accordance with a new calendar introduced in 1927.[4]

The space for voicing dissent was growing smaller and the pressure from the state was mounting. In the course of 1926 thousands of liberals, socialists and communists fled abroad to escape persecution or arrest. Many went to Paris, where those with sufficient resources and contacts set up parties, newspapers or organisations to keep alive the struggle against fascism. In the wake of the attempt on Mussolini's life in September 1926 by the anarchist Gino Lucetti, who had returned from France to carry out his bomb attack, a campaign of growing vitriol and abuse was directed at the exiles, and one Rome newspaper decided to write to known opposition figures in Italy calling on them to condemn the anti-fascists abroad in no uncertain terms. Croce was furious at such a menacing demand. He urged his friends to follow his example and not to answer. Some did, others, fearful of the consequences, did not. The newspaper duly published the letters of those who had responded and alongside listed the names of those who had failed to do so. Under their names it printed the threatening words of the ghost of Caesar to Brutus on the eve of his defeat in battle and subsequent death: 'Thou shalt see me at Philippi.'[5]

A few weeks later the last of the four assassination attempts on Mussolini provided the trigger for a wave of attacks by *squadristi* across Italy. Croce was not spared. In the early hours of the morning of 1 November more than a dozen blackshirts broke into the house where the sixty-year-old philosopher, his wife and four daughters were sleeping, terrorised the servants with guns, and smashed doors and windows and almost anything else they could find (though Croce's books were left untouched), before fleeing into the night. The police were immediately summoned by neighbours, but they did not turn up for five hours. Croce was determined to carry on with what he now regarded as the best contribution he could make to the opposition to fascism – writing a history of liberal Italy. But it was difficult. 'In the morning I resumed historical readings, and took notes from books I had previously read and marked up; but there was such a crowd of friends coming to ask for news about what had happened last night that I could hardly continue the work, from which I had resolved not to be distracted.'[6] The prefect of Naples dropped by to offer his commiserations and promise a full investigation and severe punishments for those responsible. In the event none of the culprits, most of whom were already well known to the police, ever faced any charges.[7]

The purpose of assaults such as that endured by Croce was as much to frighten colleagues and friends as to intimidate the victims themselves. Those with sufficient profile and moral resolve not to feel easily browbeaten managed to keep up their links with the liberal philosopher. They included the senator and distinguished expert on the problems of southern Italy, Giustino Fortunato, and Croce's lifelong publisher, Giovanni Laterza. But many of Croce's former contacts began to melt away, as the authorities had hoped. The fact that two policemen were now permanently stationed outside his house provided a further deterrent. According to the government, they were there for Croce's own safety, but their main purpose in reality was to monitor those who visited him and follow him whenever he went out. The informal social gatherings that in the past had taken place on Sundays, when scholars and writers had freely dropped by to converse and exchange ideas, rapidly petered out. And those who had once been proud to speak to him or to shake his hand, avoided him in public when there was a risk of being seen – although they were usually willing, as he recalled, to exchange 'friendly and warm greetings in deserted streets and in solitary corridors'.[8]

A further measure of surveillance came from the Political Police Division ('Polpol'). This was instituted by the government in the autumn of 1926 as part of the raft of new measures designed to stamp out all remaining opposition to fascism. Directed by Mussolini's recently appointed Chief of Police, Arturo Bocchini, an efficient and cynical former prefect, whose rapid rise through the civil service had begun early in the century under Giolitti, Polpol was soon operating a network of thousands of spies and informers both in Italy and abroad. It had a huge budget at its disposal – 50 million lire in 1927–28 – nearly half the total assigned to the running of the country's entire police force.[9] Polpol worked in conjunction with the local police authorities, and in order to overcome the practical difficulties that this sometimes entailed, another vast tentacular organisation, OVRA (it was unclear exactly what the initials stood for), was set up from the late 1920s, also run by Bocchini, which was able to act with greater autonomy (and thus secrecy) across the entire country. One of the main tasks of the secret police, as Croce well knew, was to intercept and copy the incoming and outgoing correspondence of those under surveillance – a further major bar to his freedom of expression.

In these circumstances, Croce's principal contributions to keeping the cause of anti-fascism alive – aside from his academic writings – lay in acts of solidarity and support. He travelled the country seeing old friends and any new contacts who were willing to meet him. (He kept records of these trips, but carefully avoided writing down names in case the diaries should fall into the wrong hands.) He also provided financial aid to anti-fascists in exile and helped them to get books published. When he was abroad, his presence had the added advantage of drawing the attention of the international press. In September 1928 he went to Paris with his daughter and Giovanni Laterza, and in addition to discussions with French scholars and research in the Bibliothèque nationale, he met up with such prominent exiles as the ex-prime minister, Francesco Saverio Nitti; the former head of the *popolari*, Don Luigi Sturzo; and the socialist leader, Filippo Turati (earlier political differences had now been laid to rest beneath the common cause of anti-fascism). He also went to Père Lachaise cemetery to visit the grave of the brilliant liberal intellectual, Piero Gobetti, who had died in Paris two years before at the age of just twenty-four, after being assaulted repeatedly by *squadristi*.[10]

His visits to Rome often proved dispiriting. He derived some satisfaction from seeing Giolitti, who despite his extreme age continued to speak out in the Chamber against fascist legislation. But in July 1928 Giolitti died. Croce attended the funeral along with a few friends, but he was sickened by the failure of the king and the Crown prince to come and pay their respects to a man who had been prime minister five times over a period of almost thirty years and who had dominated Italian politics for most of Victor Emmanuel's reign. Croce experienced a similar sense of dismay at what appeared to be moral cowardice, indifference or opportunism on other occasions. In November 1928 he voted against a new law that made it mandatory for the Grand Council to be consulted on all questions of a 'constitutional character', including the workings of parliament, the powers of the Crown, and the succession to the throne. This was a huge assault on the prerogatives of the monarchy and on the Statuto that the king had sworn to be faithful to on his accession.[11] But Victor Emmanuel offered no visible show of protest, and in the Senate, as Croce noted ruefully in his diary, 'only nineteen of us voted no'. The subservience of his fellow senators ('once staunch democrats, republicans, Freemasons and socialists, now turned fascist . . . fearful . . . and suspicious of any free discussion') pained him deeply.[12]

Croce could take some heart from the reception accorded to his *History of Italy from 1871 to 1915*. He intended the book as a tribute to what, with hindsight at least, seemed the considerable achievements of the liberal era, and he hoped that the work might inspire some people, the young in particular, to question the disparagement that was being systematically heaped by fascism on the decades of parliamentary government.[13] He was worried that the authorities might attempt to seize the manuscript if they knew exactly what he was writing, and he accordingly broke with his conventional practice of releasing draft chapters first in *La Critica*. When the book was finished in December 1927, he sent a copy discreetly to London, and began to make soundings about a possible English-language edition. He also travelled to Bari to hand over the manuscript in person to Giovanni Laterza. He was accompanied by Laterza's small daughter in an effort to conceal the true purpose of the journey from the police.[14]

The book was published in January 1928, and the first edition of 5,000 sold out in the space of a few days. Other editions followed, and during the course of the next fifteen years around 40,000 copies were printed, making it considerably more successful than a rival (and far more critical) account of liberal Italy by the eminent pro-fascist historian, Gioacchino Volpe, which first appeared in 1927 under the title *Italia in cammino* ('Italy on the march') . Mussolini came under strong pressure from party colleagues to ban Croce's book, but he knew that such a move would be counterproductive and that it would be far better publicity for his regime to show the outside world that fascism had a tolerant face and had nothing to fear from allowing even such a distinguished opponent as Croce to speak out freely. Instead, instructions were issued to the press to ignore the work; and when this proved unrealistic, given the widespread interest that it was generating, to make sure that it was systematically ridiculed and condemned. Arturo Bocchini kept a watchful eye on the situation, and the agents of Polpol and OVRA were careful to take note of those seen buying copies or reading it in libraries.[15]

What induced people to buy Croce's history, and exactly what they made of it once they had read it, is hard to assess in general terms. Old friends such as Giustino Fortunato certainly welcomed the work enthusiastically for its 'exaltation of the fifty years of our Italian national life that are so much scorned in the present hour',[16] but others legitimately wondered why, if the achievements of Italy in the decades before the First World War had been quite as positive as Croce suggested, the entire edifice of liberalism had collapsed so easily in the space of a few years. Some might also have been inclined to speculate on the author's precise motives in publishing the book. It was all very well for Croce and other anti-fascists such as Gaetano Salvemini (who wrote an approving review in exile in London) to look back and celebrate the work of men such as Depretis, Turati and Giolitti and the progress that the country had made under the parliamentary regime, but had they not themselves spent years loudly criticising the liberal state for its corruption, lack of idealism and failure to live up to the promise of the Risorgimento? Was there now perhaps a sense of guilt?

A more fundamental difficulty lay in the vision of history that Croce himself had so long forcefully championed. If, as his account of liberal Italy implied, the roots of fascism were to be found in the proliferation from the end of the nineteenth century of 'unhealthy' currents of irrational thought, it was difficult to avoid the conclusion that the neo-idealism that he, Giovanni Gentile and others had made into such a powerful strand in Italian culture, with its celebration of 'spirit' as the supreme driving force in life, had itself undermined rationalism. Furthermore, if 'spirit' had caused Italy to make progress through liberalism, what was to say that the forward 'march' (to use Volpe's term) was not now legitimately continuing with fascism? This was a concern of the young anti-fascist intellectual Giovanni Ansaldo. In February 1928, shortly after returning from three months in *confino* (internment), Ansaldo wrote to Giustino Fortunato, to say that he had finished Croce's book with a glow of satisfaction: 'Everything that happened from 1870 to 1915 was inevitable . . . and everybody deserves top marks'. But he had then been confronted with an uncomfortable thought: 'Why should Italy, and all Italians, . . . winners and losers, also not deserve top marks from 1915?' Croce's historicism, in other words, offered him no answer to the question, 'why fight, why resist?'[17] Ansaldo soon decided not to resist any longer and instead to collaborate with fascism.[18]

Croce carried on studying and writing in Naples for the remainder of the regime, harassed but not openly persecuted, his movements watched, and his incoming and outgoing post – including letters from his wife and daughters – opened, copied and carefully archived. In due course Bocchini's police accumulated over 1,300 files on his various correspondents, with additional folders for material forwarded to Mussolini for his personal perusal. Croce's books were mostly erudite studies of philosophy, literature and history, destined for a limited academic audience, and they rarely dealt in any explicit sense with fascism. But they were nevertheless scrutinised by the censors and their publication and distribution often hampered. Croce continued to make public gestures of opposition. In 1933 it became compulsory for members of national academies and learned societies to take an oath of loyalty to the regime: Croce refused to comply. But two years later he disappointed a number of his remaining admirers by agreeing to donate his senator's gold medal to the government at the time of the Ethiopian war to help boost the country's gold reserves. He did so, he told the president of the Senate, Luigi Federzoni, 'in the name of the fatherland' and not because he approved of the government's policies. The distinction was perhaps rather too uncomfortably subtle for many.

That Croce was permitted to write and publish with a relative degree of freedom under fascism was due not just to his international stature and the regime's fear of incurring foreign opprobrium if it tried too obviously to stifle a voice of such distinction. The fact was, as Mussolini knew, that Croce's ideas had little resonance in Italy and posed no serious threat. As many young intellectuals later recalled, reflecting after the Second World War on why they had not opposed fascism, liberalism belonged in their eyes to a world that was synonymous with weakness, failure and chaos. Any return to the political system that Croce and his elderly friends remembered nostalgically would simply be to turn the clock backwards.[19] As the liberal anti-fascist law professor, Piero Calamandrei, noted in his diary in April 1939, the students he taught at Florence university all believed that the success of Mussolini after 1922 showed that his ideas were right and those of his opponents wrong, and that fascism was the best regime 'because it is successful' and thus 'corresponds historically to the needs of the present'. They accordingly accepted it almost without question. The sense of living in a 'total moral vacuum' was one reason, Calamandrei said, why he was driven to keep a diary (whose contents, if known, could have earned him *confino*, he acknowledged): he wanted to bear witness for posterity to the 'atmosphere in which today we are suffocating'.

> If we are indeed the melancholy survivors of a dying civilisation, this notebook could in a few centuries fall into the hands of some historian and seem a document not without some interest. The daily memories of an ordinary man at the time of Julian the Apostate, wedded to the old paganism and recording the last sighs of a civilisation on the point of extinction, would today be of great value.[20]

Secret police

If the agents of Polpol and OVRA kept close tabs on Croce, their main targets were the much more active and organised opponents of the regime on the far left. Their success in infiltrating the ranks of subversive groups at home and above all abroad during the late 1920s and early 1930s helped ensure that the widespread socio-economic discontent generated by the downturn in the world economy did not get converted into revolutionary unrest. Mussolini was immensely proud of his secret police. 'Do you have any idea what OVRA is?' he boasted to his lover in 1937. 'It is something I created. It is the strongest organisation in the world.'[21] As so often with the Duce (and never more so than when he was with Claretta Petacci, the object of his sexual infatuation nearly thirty years his junior), there was an element of unbridled exaggeration in these remarks. But it is certainly true that OVRA was very effective in limiting dissent within the regime, and equally true that Mussolini was the principal driving force behind it. He took an extremely close interest in its activities and findings, and conferred with Bocchini almost daily (until Bocchini's sudden death in 1940 following a characteristically Lucullan dinner and an encounter with a twenty-five-year-old aristocratic mistress).[22]

The success of OVRA and Polpol was not due so much to their scale – the staff in Rome responsible for overseeing Bocchini's networks of informers numbered no more than 375 in 1940.[23] More important was the psychological impact on a society in which scarce resources and the often arbitrary and unpredictable workings of the machinery of the state (and the party) made rivalry, mistrust and fear staple ingredients of everyday life for millions of people. The very fact that 'OVRA' did not have an officially recognised meaning as an acronym – Mussolini apparently coined the name as a contraction of the word for an octopus, 'piovra' – was intended to heighten the air of mystery surrounding the organisation.[24] Numerous diaries and memoirs attest to the baleful impact of this pervasive climate of uncertainty under fascism, in which incautious remarks or actions could be reported and lead to sanctions. And it was the mere possibility of being in trouble with the authorities, rather than actual intervention by the police, that gave rise to the anxiety and with it self-restraint. This reduced the need for repression – which statistics for institutions such as the Special Tribunal of the State might suggest was not particularly severe, certainly when compared to other totalitarian regimes. It tried a total of just 5,620 people between 1926 and 1943.[25]

If the agents of the secret police worked primarily in public spaces, fascism also had ways of patrolling the domestic realm. The phone network was extensively tapped by a Special Confidential Service, which by 1938 employed 462 stenographers to record the calls not just of possible subversives but also of leading party figures (whose private lives Mussolini monitored closely – in part for reasons of blackmail).[26] Conversations in the home could also be reported by envious neighbours or even by disaffected members of the same family. As diaries often reveal, parents were concerned to make sure their children did not make unwise remarks. They warned them accordingly, and in some instances resorted to their own forms of policing. Perla Cacciaguerra, a girl with ardent fascist parents (and a pro-Nazi grandmother) living in a small town in Tuscany during the Second World War, had become firmly anti-fascist – in part, it seems, out of teenage rebelliousness. She discovered that the maids in the house had been instructed to spy on her, and when in June 1944 she expressed pleasure at the news of the fall of Rome, her father was quickly informed: 'This evening Papà was furious with me and gave me a huge amount of grief. Grandmother was the usual witch'.[27]

The spies of OVRA and Polpol were recruited from many different walks of life – journalism, law, business, the priesthood, trade unions, the aristocracy, universities, the civil service, the arts. Women were well represented, and accounted for about 15 per cent of the agents who reported directly to Bocchini and a significant proportion of the extensive subsidiary networks run by the spies themselves.[28] The motives for becoming an informer inevitably varied. They might range from political zeal, to a thirst for travel or adventure abroad, to simple financial need. But in many cases people became spies in order to escape an embarrassing personal situation. For instance, many of the civil servants recruited were former policemen or officials of the Ministry of the Interior whose careers had been terminated by involvement in corruption – typically accepting bribes in return for allowing illegal gambling joints or brothels to continue in operation.[29] The well-educated and highly plausible lawyer, Carlo Del Re, who was responsible for the betrayal and arrest in 1930 of the Milan members of the recently founded democratic socialist movement, Giustizia e Libertà (Justice and Liberty), agreed to become an OVRA agent after facing bankruptcy and probable imprisonment for debt.[30]

The most useful agents for OVRA and Polpol were subversives who could be induced to reach a 'compromise' with the regime in return for immunity from prosecution or in some cases simply for money. The destitution to which so many Italian communists and socialists were rapidly reduced after 1925 often made the task of turning them relatively easy, and the success of the fascist state in breaking up the clandestine organisations of the left from the late 1920s was largely due to their infiltration by turncoats. In many cases the process of softening up was encouraged through severe harassment, and even the most ideologically committed were vulnerable. By the time the veteran revolutionary socialist Costantino Lazzari was brutally assaulted by three fascists led by Achille Starace inside the Chamber of Deputies on 9 November 1926 – on the eve of his seventieth birthday – he was financially desperate. He had even been driven to pawn his parliamentary medals in a bid to support his wife and daughter. His poverty and physical injuries were compounded by a sense of bitterness towards his colleagues: he believed many of them had capitulated too quickly to fascism. Bocchini was well aware of his plight (his 'terror of tomorrow without bread', as he put it), and in July 1927 he met Lazzari and persuaded him to cooperate. Lazzari furnished one report for Polpol, but then repented. Bocchini promptly took revenge, ordering his agents to spread the word in anti-fascist circles abroad that the old socialist leader had 'become the confidant of the Italian police in return for money'. A few months later Lazzari died a broken man.[31]

The experience or prospect of internment or prison were powerful tools at Bocchini's disposal. The student, Aldo Romano, who in the mid-1930s was to be one of the most active spies monitoring the intellectuals frequenting Croce's house, reached his 'compromise' with Polpol after having his sentence of *confino* commuted to the lesser punishment of *ammonizione* (a type of house arrest) and being allowed to return to Florence to complete his university degree. The former secretary of the Communist Party in the south of Italy, Ugo Girone, was arrested in March 1929 and agreed to a 'compromise' with the police while in the Regina Coeli gaol in Rome. He was released in May and sent to France, from where he delivered numerous reports on the Trotskyite left and the activities of his former mentor, Amadeo Bordiga. The immediate material benefits of collaborating with Polpol are evident from a receipt issued at the time when Girone was being 'newly fitted out' following his decision to compromise and preserved in the police archives. It refers to 'two automobile journeys to the judicial prisons with 3/4 of an hour wait, plus another 1/4 of an hour wait in Corso V. Emanuele to buy shirts, collars and other items for Dr Girone. Total cost 33.50 lire. Rome 8.4.1929'.[32]

The infiltration of exiled subversive circles by Polpol agents added to the enormous sense of insecurity and mistrust that had already become such a marked feature of the far left as a consequence of the bitter ideological cleavages within socialism and communism from the later 1920s. The rancour, resentment and isolation that these divisions could cause again played into the hands of the fascist police, providing them with potential new recruits and assisting greatly with the work of repression. The case of a former associate of Mussolini, Maria Rygier, provides a good example of the psychological contortions that hardship and political extremism could produce. Maria was the daughter of a Polish sculptor and had been active in revolutionary socialism in Milan before the First World War. In the early autumn of 1914 she had suddenly converted from being a committed neutralist to supporting the cause of intervention, and had subsequently become a contributor to Mussolini's *Il Popolo d'Italia*. Her political path after the war is somewhat unclear. She had backed the annexation of Fiume and set up an Anti-Bolshevik Union in Rome, but according to a memoir she published later in exile, her activities after 1922 ought to have led to 'many years in prison'. Instead she was left untouched by the fascist government until early in 1926, when the police suddenly raided her home in Palazzo Borghese and uncovered evidence of her involvement in Freemasonry.[33]

Her violent reaction (according to the authorities) to the police raid resulted in her being sent to a hospital psychiatric ward. It seems that she was only spared incarceration in a lunatic asylum through the intervention of a rich Tuscan landowner, Gian Francesco Guerrazzi, a personal friend of Mussolini and of many prominent fascists, whom Rygier had become friendly with when they had worked together on behalf of interventionism. Rygier was released and moved to Paris, where she became active in Masonic circles; and it was through her new contacts that she obtained documents which claimed to show that back in 1903–04 the young Mussolini had been an informer working for the French police and spying on socialists. She published the allegations in a pamphlet in 1928, but her hopes that these potentially damning revelations (which almost certainly had no substance in fact) would earn her acceptance by Italian anti-fascists proved illusory. She found herself denounced to the French League for the Rights of Man as a fascist spy on the basis that she was apparently able to travel backwards and forwards to Italy without any difficulty. At the same time the principal coordinating body of anti-fascism in Paris warned its members to steer clear of her on the grounds that she had been a passionate Nationalist in the war and then 'violently anti-Russian and anti-Bolshevik': 'We do not know what she is now doing and what her political contacts are.'[34]

Her rejection by the Italian anti-fascists left her embittered. In the spring of 1933 she decided to approach in strict confidence her 'protector', Gian Francesco Guerrazzi, and offer her services to the regime. In his diary Guerrazzi registered his bemusement and his delight at renewed contact with 'this strange woman': '[Her] trust in me – to the point of confiding her most intimate and jealous affairs to me – I have never forgotten; nor her courage . . . and intelligent work for the national cause during the war'. He recorded how Rygier had written to him to profess her 'immutable faith' and desire to return to Italy, and how she had described 'the persecutions she had suffered' at the hands of the anti-fascists and reassured him that she was now a 'correct person' and that he had nothing to fear from having dealings with her. She had offered to help the government penetrate French

Masonic circles with fascist agents. Guerrazzi went to see the president of the Chamber of Deputies, Giovanni Giuriati, who told him that he had been 'imprudent' to have contact with such a 'savage enemy of Fascism and Mussolini'. But Bocchini was far less condemnatory – and extremely interested:

> Bocchini was clearly up to date with Maria Rygier's situation. And without any prompting from me, he said:
>
> If M.R. wants to return to Italy, I will give my personal guarantee that she will not experience any problems . . .
>
> I replied:
>
> But she has written atrocious things against Mussolini . . .
>
> But [Mussolini] is very generous and has forgiven plenty of others . . .
>
> . . .
>
> Bocchini tells me that the link with M.R. would be very useful, and that to start with, and to keep the contact going, I should ask her about the current attitude of French Masonry towards Italy.
>
> I give him my promise.
>
> We agree that I will send whatever I have to him marked: personal.
>
> He says goodbye to me with great courtesy.[35]

It is not clear how much, if any, material Rygier supplied to Bocchini: the death of Guerrazzi in September 1933 probably ended her willing-ness to collaborate. She remained in exile until the end of the war, when she returned to Italy and resumed her political activities – now as a monarchist and a member of the Liberal Party. In 1946 she published a memoir about her time in France in which she denounced the 'nause-ating' manner in which the dictatorship had succeeded in penetrating the ranks of the anti-fascists with its spies and agents provocateurs.

Fear, evasion and silence

In a society that had made political faith and conformity the corner-
stones of public morality, there was inevitable anxiety about being
judged, found wanting and reported, and it was often children, who
inevitably had to face many of their own insecurities, that were most
alert to adult fears. One such was Giuliana Rossi, an intelligent small
girl from Genoa, who for a few years from 1928 kept a diary of her
most vivid impressions. She was very conscious of politics, because
her uncle admired Mussolini greatly while her father did not, and she
had to listen to the two of them arguing. She herself knew about the
Duce: she saw him constantly in the newsreels of the state film
company LUCE that from 1927 had to be shown in cinemas prior to
the main programme. 'Whenever I think of him, I always seem to see
him making gestures from a terrace, and then with his arms crossed
waiting for the applause from the huge crowd beneath him. In my
view the Duce would really have liked to be an actor.' Giuliana was
a member of the party youth organisation, the Piccole Italiane, but
her father clearly made it a point of honour to resist complying with
the regime's dictates. When on 28 October 1929, the anniversary of the
March on Rome, he suddenly put on a black shirt to go to the office
to avoid being singled out, she was shocked: 'I never thought that
papà, who hates politics and discusses with uncle in such a strong and
confident voice, could ever be afraid.'[36]

Manoeuvring in a society where people knew they were being
watched, and trying to express some measure of dissent and maintain
personal dignity in the face of pressures from the party and the state –
and the often no less strong moral injunction to avoid compromising
one's family – was very difficult. For the father of the teenage girl
Angela Martina, living in the Alpine foothills of the Valle Seriana to
the north-east of Bergamo, the struggle to keep some semblance of
faith with his old socialist principles was made all the more difficult
by the catastrophic economic situation of the early 1930s. This was so
for many who had taken part in the political battles of the immediate
post-war years. In the province of Bergamo, where the workforce
consisted primarily of small peasant farmers, rural labourers and textile
workers, unemployment jumped from 8,000 in 1928 to over 35,000 at

the end of 1932 and more than 43,000 in December 1934, while the salaries of those fortunate enough to retain a job saw a decline in real terms in the order of 20 per cent in the same period. Not surprisingly, as in many other rural regions of Italy, the exodus from the country-side proved impossible to contain.[37]

To help keep the family afloat, Angela had to accept a poorly paid job in a cotton factory. But her father doggedly refused to take out member-ship of the fascist party and remained unemployed. In August 1935 the fifteen-year-old recorded in her diary (which shows some signs of subse-quent rewriting as a memoir) making a trip with her father deep into the woods near their house, lying down in the sun and asking him to sing 'their' song – the old socialist anthem 'Su fratelli e su compagni' ('Up brothers and up comrades') – 'the song he taught me at home, taking me to the space under the stairs of a small attic above the kitchen'. He did so, and since they were 'in a safe place' – back at home they had to be careful, as Angela's godmother, who lived next door, was strongly pro-fascist – he went on to teach her verses of the anarchist lament, 'Addio Lugano bella' ('Farewell lovely Lugano'). Angela asked her father why he was not able to get a job. After all, he had six children to support. 'Perhaps I would find one – or, rather, I would certainly find one', he replied, 'if I took out the party card'. 'Then why don't you get one?' Angela asked. 'After all, I am enrolled in the *Giovani Italiane* [the youth organisation for teenage girls that followed on from the Piccole Italiane]':

You, like all boys and girls, are enrolled 'ex officio', as we say. You start having the party card even before you go to school. But the men of my generation, we don't want to accept a regime that has been imposed by force. We want liberty and democracy.

What do you mean?

I mean liberty is something good that you win day by day, thinking with your own head and not with somebody else's . . . The anti-fascists want respect for people, which is something fundamental . . . Some fascist laws are good and have rescued us from miserable situations. But I still think that if there is no democracy, if workers cannot choose their own representatives in Parliament, if there aren't unions that protect the workers . . . the regime is wrong.[38]

Angela found his rigid commitment to such principles rather difficult to accept, not least morally: after all, was she not in effect being
forced to go out to work to support his inflexibility, thereby sacrificing
her own education and future? (She loved reading and studying, and
was eventually to become a teacher.) Furthermore, fascism seemed
perfectly pleasant from her perspective, even if there was a degree of
coercion involved. Given the very limited freedoms traditionally
accorded to women, Angela, like many girls, welcomed the social
opportunities that the party activities provided: 'I, too, have to do the
"fascist Saturday" [paramilitary instruction was compulsory on
Saturday afternoons for members of the fascist youth organisations
from June 1935] and go to the gym in uniform . . . But I like putting
on the black skirt and the white blouse. And I meet boys and girls of
my own age in the gym, and we can laugh and play together.' All this
was just so much 'candyfloss', her father retorted: 'Let's stop. These
are topics that are a bit too grown up for you. But one day you will
understand how much it has cost me to stay faithful to my principles
and my ideals.'[39]

Angela was clearly still very fond of her father, but the price he
was made to pay for remaining true to himself at a time when the
only realistic prospect of work was through party membership ('PNF'
was often jokingly said to stand for 'Per Necessità Familiare' – 'for
the sake of the family') illustrated how strong the coercive reach
of the regime was. It also showed how difficult it was for anti-fascist
ideas to be passed to a younger generation. (Angela was to remain
resistant to his views.) It was perhaps pressure from his family, and
the prospect not only of destitution but also of seeing himself
condemned or even rejected by those he loved, that in the end
persuaded Angela's father to compromise. When war broke out with
Ethiopia in October 1935, he agreed to serve in the army, despite his
ideological opposition. He was called up, but in the event was never
sent to Africa – so depriving him, it seems, of the opportunity to wipe
his political slate clean. He managed to find a job in 1937 in a metal
factory, but only for a short time. By the start of the Second World
War, with his health in serious decline, he was reduced to travelling
around the countryside on his bicycle searching for food.[40]

The capacity of the regime to punish anti-fascists by harming
members of their family might lead to mediation through 'unofficial'

channels in a bid to limit the damage. The fact that the party was riddled with traditional clientelism (and corruption) could facilitate the process. The father of the Turin schoolboy, Arturo Gunetti, was eager not to compromise his left-wing principles: his cousins had been prominent local communists, and one had been sent to prison for his beliefs by the Special Tribunal in 1928. He accordingly refused to allow his son to enrol in the fascist youth organisation, the Balilla. Arturo was the only boy in his class not to be a member, and his teacher, an ardent fascist who ran the school's youth groups, retaliated by failing Arturo in his end-of-year exam for promotion to the fourth year, even though he had achieved consistently good marks. In desperation Arturo's mother decided to go behind her husband's back. Through a neighbour, she contacted the headmistress, who was known to be unsympathetic towards the fascists. The headmistress suggested that Arturo should try to win round the teacher by helping him out during the summer holidays with gardening – for which the teacher had a passion. Arturo did so, and after six weeks the mother was able to persuade her husband to back down and permit the boy to join the Balilla. The teacher, duly mollified, altered Arturo's marks and let him move up into the next year.[41]

Though the wife's stratagem could in a sense be seen as a small victory 'against' fascism, in as much as the teacher had rescinded the punishment, the fact was that Arturo was now a member of the Balilla. This left the father feeling extremely uncomfortable. He tried to preserve a semblance of resistance by making sure that his son took off his uniform the moment he got back home. But on one occasion a member of his cousins' militantly left-wing family happened to be in the house when Arturo returned from school in his fascist clothes after his regular Thursday morning parade, forcing the father into desperate self-defence: 'Look, don't get angry. Otherwise he wouldn't have been able to go to school . . . Drop it, please, my nerves are already bad. Because if I hadn't . . . if I hadn't enrolled him, I couldn't have sent him to school any more. And I'm not in a position to pay for him to be taught privately . . . And there's no way I could have kept him ignorant.' In an attempt to salvage a small measure of dignity and reaffirm his political credentials he shouted at Arturo: 'Go and get changed at once!'[42]

Urban working-class families such as Arturo's in general felt more vulnerable than their middle-class counterparts, and with justification: nearly three-quarters of those tried by the Special Tribunal were industrial workers, compared with about 15 per cent from the middle classes and 10 per cent from the peasantry.[43] The chances of being left untouched by the fascist authorities increased with influential connections and wealth. Giulio Bianchi Bandinelli, for instance, belonged to a well-known Tuscan noble family. His father worked for the Banca d'Italia in Florence before retiring early to indulge his passion for bee-keeping and use an inheritance to buy the fashionable bathing resort of Scoglio della Regina in Livorno. Like most of those in his circle, Giulio was from the start strongly sympathetic to fascism, and he recalled in his memoirs the general feeling among his friends that they were finally 'in good hands' after Mussolini came to power. He joined the party in the mid-1920s and was made an officer in the Militia. For want of anything better to do, he then ran his father's bathing station for a time before his wife, a niece of the rector of Florence university, persuaded him to take a degree and become a secondary school teacher (Giulio also had academics in his own family: his cousin Ranuccio was a brilliant young archaeologist with burgeoning sympathies for communism).[44]

Giulio was not a very conscientious fascist, but in the upper-class circles in which he moved, nobody, he recalled, felt at all concerned that they might be denounced as an anti-fascist. They told jokes quite openly about Mussolini, though not with any sense of hostility: almost everyone he knew readily accepted the regime, reassured by the behaviour of the king ('as long as he was happy, we could be happy, too') and by a feeling that there simply was no alternative. As a teacher he was supposed to set an example and conform to party directives, but he rarely did so. He found fascist rallies, with their huge raucous crowds, 'boring', and he never bothered to go to hear the Duce's speeches when they were broadcast live in the piazzas. He was meant to wear a uniform on Saturdays. But he did not do so; and he was not rebuked: 'I never owned a uniform. I just had the black shirt, and I only put this on occasionally, because usually I "forgot". The head teachers in their turn "forgot" to notice. One head teacher was a passionate fascist, a puny man, who used to turn up on Saturdays in a ridiculous uniform with boots bigger than himself. Not even he made a comment about the uniform.'[45]

Almost the only unsettling memory that Giulio had of the fascist period was the curious silence of his father. 'During fascism', he recalled, 'he never expressed any judgement either for or against the regime . . . He read *La Nazione* every day and happily listened on the radio to the news and propaganda broadcasts of the regime, but without ever making a comment. I sometimes revealed my enthusiasm, for example for the trans-Atlantic flight of [Italo] Balbo. He would let me talk, but without ever adding a word.'[46] In all likelihood, as a patrician who had grown up in the cultivated circles of liberal Tuscany, Giulio's father had little sympathy for the crude populism of fascism, but given his penchant for a quiet life he opted for studied silence as the best strategy for preserving his dignity without compromising himself or his family. He also avoided a potential breach with his son, who was left free to accommodate himself to what Giulio called a 'rose-water dictatorship' untroubled by obvious paternal censure. Giulio sensed the advantages of the arrangement and acquiesced: 'As I had no reason whatsoever to want to know what he did not wish to tell me, I always respected his reserve.'[47]

Silence featured tellingly in another wealthy Tuscan family, that of Anna Caredio. She recalled growing up in the small town of Bagni di Lucca in the 1930s and observing how the various members of the household positioned themselves in relation to the regime. Anna's father, Edgardo, insisted on loudly telling the latest joke he had heard about Mussolini or reading out in a comic stentorian voice the head-lines in newspaper articles – to which those present responded by quietly shaking their heads and smiling. But on Sunday afternoons the situation became more awkward when a lawyer friend and earnest fascist used to drop by, and Edgardo invariably felt spurred into making cynical and irreverent remarks about 'the new man'. The lawyer would listen impassively and then gruffly say: 'Edgardo, remember that if Mussolini had not come along we would have had communism!' This, said Anna, always halted her father dead in his tracks, for like many people she knew who had reservations about fascism, he was forced to admit that, compared with the Bolsheviks, Mussolini was 'the lesser of two evils'. But one member of the family, her grandfather, was implacably hostile to Mussolini: '[H]e was always silent, but when he heard these arguments he left, slamming the door.'[48]

Sometimes, silence was not just a form of passive dissent but also, at some level, an awkward admission of impotence. This was the case, it seems, with Ettore Castiglioni, one of the most outstanding Italian mountaineers of his generation. Ettore was born into a wealthy Milanese family, and from 1925, when he was sixteen, he kept a highly introspective diary in which he recorded his innermost thoughts and feelings about the music, literature and art that he loved so passionately, but with almost no mention at all, in fifteen years of detailed entries, of Mussolini or the fascist regime. However, Ettore was far from indifferent to politics. On 10 June 1940, the day on which the Duce announced Italy's entry into the Second World War, he suddenly poured out his horror at what he called the 'most ignominious action' in the country's history and 'the criminal madness' of Mussolini. He noted bitterly that the events unfolding were just 'the logical conclusion to which the dictatorship was leading us': 'The Italian people, who for 18 years have endured slavery without knowing how to rebel, have merited no other fate than to live out to the bitter end their shameful tragedy and to endure the most horrific experience of blood and destruction in order to be worthy of redemption.'[49]

A few weeks later, sitting high in the mountains, Ettore felt an overwhelming sense of disgust not just towards his fellow countrymen but also, to a degree, towards himself, realising that his passion for climbing had been driven partly by a desire for evasion and flight:

> Despite feeling profoundly Italian, and despite my efforts to try to distinguish what is essential in our people from the transitory elements of a criminal regime, all my pride has now been shattered by the shame of being Italian, by the shame of my own powerlessness to rebel and redeem. In these circumstances all I could do was flee among the mountains, where I can still forget, and where I can still rediscover my life and the sense of living it without ignominy.[50]

On one occasion during the war, in a gesture of defiance, as his nephew Saverio Tutino recalled, Ettore filled his lungs and cried out as loudly as he could amid the solitude of the Alps: 'Down with the Duce!' The words echoed around the mountains, 'but fortunately', said Saverio, 'nobody could hear us.'[51] After the fall of Mussolini in the summer of 1943, and the subsequent occupation of northern and central Italy by the Nazis, Ettore was able to demonstrate his contempt for the regime by working with a group of fellow soldiers to help anti-fascists escape into Switzerland. But he died of exposure and exhaustion on 12 March 1944 while attempting, with perhaps a certain degree of symbolic appropriateness, to cross the border secretly into Italy over the Passo del Forno alone at night.

For millions of middle-class Italians, who did not enjoy the wealth, the status or family connections of those such as Giulio Bianchi Bandinelli, Anna Caredio or Ettore Castiglioni, 'dissent', in whatever form, was usually something to be carefully avoided on pragmatic grounds. This was noted by the Florentine schoolboy, Pietro Ambrosini, in the detailed diary he kept from 1936, when he was eleven, until the end of 1943. Like many other sensitive children growing up under fascism, Pietro, who was an only child, often found himself puzzled by the ethical and emotional challenges that the regime engendered. Realising that his parents found it awkward to talk about them, he used his diary to air thoughts that he could not discuss openly. His anxieties came to a head in the spring of 1942 when he was assailed by a 'sea of doubts' regarding both the war and fascism. He had an acute feeling that numerous other people had the same ideas as he did, but dared not voice them:

> not so much out of fear, I think, but rather from a form of shame, as if it was obscene to say them. Or perhaps it is so as not to admit that they had been wrong, and have to confess that they were naive in having believed all the bombast that they fed to us. Because to begin with, and there is no point in denying it, we all of us believed it, some more and some less, and so now we prefer to be silent and keep on going, hoping that it will finish soon and not too badly. At this point I think I have written nonsense [Pietro had started his entry confessing that he was perhaps unwise to put his thoughts in writing], so I will stop and go back to bed, but it is for some time that I have been wanting to vent my feelings, and I have done so tonight.[52]

Pietro's father worked in a machine shop, and the sense of economic and social insecurity that coloured his outlook on life fostered political conformity. He encouraged his son to be a diligent member of the Balilla, and Pietro responded by becoming the favourite pupil of the gymnastics teacher who ran the school youth group, and earning promotion to the rank of 'caposquadra' (squad leader). (He was the best in his class at stripping down the 'model 91' rifle.) His mother proudly sewed his new badge on and told him how important it was always to 'aim to stand out in life'.[53] But in December 1937 Pietro suddenly found his moral universe challenged. The gymnastics teacher had announced that he was volunteering to fight in Spain, but a friend of Pietro, who had absorbed 'strange ideas' from his anti-fascist grand-father, claimed that the teacher would in that case be fighting against fellow Italians: 'I replied that this was all bullshit made up by his grandfather, because it seems to me impossible that Italians would be fighting alongside the communists, and if it was true the papers would have said so.' Pietro claimed that the grandfather was 'a liar', and the two boys came close to blows. But they stopped in time, 'because it is dangerous to be heard discussing certain things in the middle of the street'. Pietro's father advised him in the future to steer clear of his friend.[54]

But other children in Pietro's class also heard reports about Italians enrolled in the International Brigades. When the gymnastics teacher returned wounded from Spain a few months later, having lost an eye, he gave a talk to the school about the conflict ('almost as if he had come back from a football match rather than a war'). A girl suddenly asked him if he had been fighting against Italians. The teacher became angry and demanded to know who had told her about the Brigades. The child, who was clearly quite confident (she was the daughter of a lawyer), replied that 'it was now common knowledge' and that even some newspapers – though she did not know which ones – had referred to the fact. The atmosphere in the assembly was growing tense, but the teacher managed to recover the moral high ground by joking that if there had been any Italians among the communists he had not been able to recognise them as they were all running away. The children burst out laughing and the head teacher quickly stepped in to start a rendition of 'Giovinezza' and bring the proceedings to an end. Pietro commented in his diary that the girl should have remained silent as her indiscretion had almost ruined the holiday the pupils had been given that day to mark the occasion.[55]

Another issue that in 1938 caused the thirteen-year-old Pietro to begin doubting fascism's monopoly of truth and justice was anti-Semitism. He had become quite friendly with two Jewish girls in

his class, and when in the spring they announced they were emigrating to the United States because they no longer felt safe, he was
horrified: Mussolini would never persecute the Jews, he declared. He
was accordingly deeply troubled later in the year by the government's
introduction of racial laws ('I don't understand too much about this
business of the Jews . . . but taken one by one they seem good people').
When his French teacher was forced to leave the school because of
the new legislation, Pietro and most of his classmates applauded the
teacher loudly when he made a farewell speech ('I don't know if what
we did was good or bad'). Only one member of the staff, a priest,
tried to explain to the children what was going on, and he amazed
them by saying that in his view 'everybody should be able freely to
practise the religion they are born into'. When Pietro's father heard
this, he was alarmed. The priest had been very ill advised to make
such a remark, he claimed, 'because some things are better thought
and not spoken, especially at school'. And perhaps sensing Pietro's
growing restiveness, he told him forcefully not to talk about these
matters, adding that 'if they have made certain laws, it means that
they needed to be made and that's the end of it.' 'My mother too has
told me not to get mixed up in things that are above my head.'[56]

The level of risk involved in making injudicious political comments
was often hard to calculate. Apart from anything else, the authorities
responded very arbitrarily, as numerous memoirs and police reports
attest. Moreover, denunciations could intersect with disputes of a
non-political character in ways that were frequently difficult to antic-
ipate – as the writer Ignazio Silone observed in his well-known satirical portrait of rural life in fascist Italy, *Fontamara*, written in 1930. In
Fontamara, a fictitious but in many ways representative small community in Silone's native region of Abruzzi, the local people are in dispute
with the fascist *podestà*, who has diverted the town's main water
supply in order to provide irrigation for his newly acquired estates.
In a bid to break the opposition of what he calls the *'cafoni'* (boors),
the *podestà* sends in *squadristi*, who terrorise the community and then
interrogate the peasants. Their ingenuous answers to the question,
'who do you support?' are used to damn them. One man says 'poor
people' and is branded as 'a socialist'; another says 'everyone' and is
marked down as a 'liberal'; while another shouts 'down with taxes'
and is described as an 'anarchist'.[57]

Silone's peasants view fascism with resignation and impotence: 'Faced with every new government, a poor *cafone* can only say: "Let's keep our fingers crossed". Just like in summer when huge clouds appear on the horizon, and it is not up to the *cafone* to decide if they will bring rain or hail, but the Eternal Father.' They regard those in power as corrupt and rapacious – 'every government is always composed of robbers' – and feel an overwhelming need to do whatever it takes to survive in the face of pervasive injustice and uncertainty. This feeling was probably shared, in real life, by millions of Italian peasants.[58] Silone wrote *Fontamara* while in exile in Switzerland suffering from a deep personal crisis (which led him to therapy with Carl Jung) and an urge, as he said in a letter in 1930, 'to repair the damage I have caused, to seek redemption, and to help the workers, the peasants (to whom I am bound with every fibre in my body) and my country'.[59] He had for some years been a leading figure in the clandestine Italian Communist Party but also a spy in the service of OVRA. His desire to extricate himself from the clutches of the fascist regime, and to make amends, was apparently connected to the arrest, torture and imprisonment of his younger brother for subversion.

In rural communities in northern and central Italy, the risks of being reported to the police might be heightened by the legacy of the disputes and divisions of the post-war years. The village of Gazzo Bigarello, for instance, near Mantua, had been the scene of bitter struggles between the fascists and the socialists in 1921–22, as Guido Morselli, who came from a local peasant family, recalled in his memoirs. Guido, who was a young child at the time, remembered an occasion when his father and elder brother were going to work in a cart pulled by two oxen. They were stopped by *squadristi*, who tore off his brother's 'new red cap', beat the dog, and humiliated his father by forcing him to make a fascist salute to their banner. The feelings of rancour in Gazzo Bigarello simmered on long after the March on Rome. One day in the spring of 1928 Guido's uncle went with three other men into a bar where they were to meet a friend from Florence. Behind them, as they were eating, was a young fascist listening to their conversation and pretending to play cards. When the friend from Florence came in he saw a large picture of the Duce hanging on the wall. He unguardedly joked: 'Look, if we didn't have him, we would be better off in Italy.' The next morning the fascist reported what he had heard to the police. The five men were immediately arrested for insulting the head of the government. Three of them later died in gaol, including Guido's uncle.[60]

In contrast, perhaps, to more urban environments where socialism had stronger roots, there seems to have been little pressure on the villagers of Gazzo Bigarello to show loyalty to their left-wing past by avoiding collaboration with fascism. Guido himself became a member of the party youth organisations and proudly went on leadership courses in the Trentino and Rome. Similarly the community as a whole happily took advantage of a new hall and bar run by the fascist leisure organisation, the Opera Nazionale Dopolavoro, which staged dances for adults and children, with free servings of rice, pork and parmesan. But the betrayal of the five men to the police led the local peasantry to close ranks in a gesture of social solidarity, and the father of the fascist was universally ostracised. Nobody would play cards or bowls with him any more, or even speak to him. One morning the old man got up, walked to the nearby railway line and threw himself under a passing train. In May 1945 Guido's cousin, the son of the uncle who had died in prison, succeeded in tracking down the fascist himself on the shores of Lake Garda, and would have murdered him but for the intervention of the *carabinieri*.[61]

The severity of the punishment meted out to the five men in Gazzo Bigarello suggests that there may have been evidence that they were linked to organised subversion, for in the context of the agricultural and industrial depression that hit Italy in the late 1920s and early 1930s, the overwhelming concern of the authorities was to ensure that criticism, anger and dissent did not coalesce into coherent anti-fascism. There were certainly strong signs of popular disaffection during these years, as unemployment soared and industrialists and landowners frequently broke the pay settlements negotiated with the trade unions, pushing down wages and depressing working conditions. The law of April 1926 that gave the fascist syndicates a monopoly of the representation of labour had made strikes illegal, but official figures nonetheless indicated 74 strikes across the country in 1929, with more than 3,000 individuals being prosecuted, over half of them women. The most troubled sector was that of textile manufacturing in Lombardy.[62] The general situation remained fraught in 1930 and 1931, with reports everywhere showing widespread working-class hostility towards the government – though the anger was often mitigated by recognition that economic conditions in many other countries were far worse. Only from 1932, with the introduction of huge welfare and public works programmes in accordance with Mussolini's newly declared policy of going 'towards the people', did the regime's concerns about mass discontent begin to abate. The success of OVRA and Polpol in breaking far-left cells also helped to allay anxieties.[63]

The illegality of strikes was clear-cut, but how the police and the courts should deal with seemingly anti-fascist remarks or gestures was rather more problematic. The public security law of November 1926 banned statements that were 'seditious or damaging to the prestige of the authorities or in any way dangerous to order' as well as the 'displaying of flags or emblems that are symbols of social subversion, of revolt or of offensiveness towards the state'. But weighing up whether to prosecute somebody for making an irreverent comment or joke about the regime, or daubing a piece of vulgar graffiti about Mussolini in a toilet, or sporting an item of red clothing, or failing to turn up to work on May Day, was not an easy matter – particularly as people often learned to provide imaginative excuses or explanations for their actions. When a Turin factory worker, Decimo Baglione, was reported by a member of the Militia for uttering the word 'bastardo' during the transmission of Mussolini's speech on 10 June 1940 announcing Italy's entry into the war, he managed deftly to deflect the charge of defamation: 'Interrogated in the police station, Baglione admitted that he had pronounced the word "bastardo", but claimed that he was directing it at himself, because, having a criminal record, . . . he would not have been able to enrol as a volunteer . . .'[64]

Humour was a particularly awkward terrain, for, as under all dictatorships, jokes proliferated during fascism. However, the infrequency with which the police appear to have taken action in relation to 'barzellette' (jokes) – even when, as was often the case, these poked fun at the government's bombastic claims, or highlighted corruption and inefficiency, or satirised the behaviour of Mussolini and other leading figures (such as the party secretary, Achille Starace, who was a particular butt in the 1930s) – suggests that the authorities believed that laughter at the expense of the regime was rarely threatening or damaging. Indeed in most cases it was probably rightly seen as indicating a form of benign accommodation with a reality that there was no possibility of changing.[65] Even so, humour did occasionally have a provocative edge that might be regarded as subversive, as in the case of the man nicknamed 'iron whistle', who every Monday morning rode his bicycle into the market in Soresina, near Cremona, a former left-wing stronghold, whistling tunes from the opera *Andrea Chénier* (which was set in the French Revolution), with a dog called 'Giolitti' in the basket attached to his handlebars. The fascists felt taunted by his spirited behaviour and repeatedly threatened him and told him to change the dog's name ('you tell him to change it'), not least because the local people found the weekly spectacle of the man shouting, 'quiet, Giolitti!', or, 'be a good boy, Giolitti!', highly amusing. His obstinacy led in the end to his arrest.[66]

If somebody was considered to be of good political and moral character, the chances were that the police would be lenient, particularly if the offence seemed to have essentially non-political motives. This was apparently what happened with an employee at one of the Fiat factories in Turin, Giovanni Cerutti. He was reported in August 1935 by a fellow worker and member of the Militia, Bernardo Perrero, for having allegedly said that Mussolini was 'frightened of England', that 'the English are a hundred times better as soldiers and as a nation', that 'even the Italian army is against the war in Abyssinia', and that 'Italy is the worst country in the world and we Italians the most useless'. When interrogated, Cerutti claimed that in the three years he had worked at Fiat he had often discussed football with Perrero, and that Perrero had recently been taunting him about how badly his team, Torino, had been playing. In a 'stupid attempt to get his own back . . . he began to talk about the conflict between Italy and Ethiopia, knowing it would work, because his colleague belonged to the Militia and felt very strongly about such matters.' After inquiries, the police were reassured that Cerutti was of 'good moral conduct and a hard worker'. He was presumably let off.[67]

In some circumstances, even being of seemingly good character might not be enough to save someone from losing their job. Mario Azzalin was typical of many thousands of landless labourers from the Veneto who was forced in the 1920s and 1930s to migrate in a desperate attempt to find work. After spells abroad in factories in Belgium and France, he had taken a job for four months assisting with the land reclamation programme in the Pontine Marshes near Rome, leaving behind his family in Belluno in northern Italy. The following year, with opportunities severely limited back in his native region, he had returned to the Pontine Marshes and secured a position in a workshop run by the National Association for Veterans in the newly built town of Littoria. But the strain of trying to support himself, his wife and seven children on 100 lire a week took its toll. On 17 July 1936 he was reported by three colleagues for 'insulting the Head of the Government by spitting on the radiator of a tractor on which was written "Viva il Duce"' and for 'speaking badly of the regime and saying that it would be better if the negus came and governed Italy'. Azzalin admitted in his defence that he had often complained about his financial difficulties, but he denied having blamed Mussolini or anyone else: he had come to accept, he said, that 'after travelling around so much I had to be content with whatever pay they chose to give me'. The only political remark he remembered making was: 'And then we go and civilise the Abyssinians.' Since Littoria was something of a showcase for the regime, the authorities may have been less inclined to tolerate any form of truculence or dissent. Azzalin was sacked with a formal caution, and sent back to Belluno, where his future employment prospects were inevitably grim.[68]

What induced Azzalin's fellow workers to denounce him is unclear. Quite possibly – and the same may have applied to Bernardo Perrero when it came to reporting his supposed friend Giovanni Cerutti – the dynamics of fear produced by a totalitarian environment led those who had witnessed imprudent remarks or behaviour to be worried that if they did not report them to the authorities they might themselves risk an accusation of complicity. Such anxieties, especially among the economically insecure, could prevail over feelings of social solidarity, or basic humanity, even in a small peasant community, as a forty-four-year-old builder's labourer, Lorenzo Boccaccio, found to his cost in the spring of 1933. Boccaccio lived in Maranzana, a Piedmontese wine-growing centre with barely a thousand inhabitants in the hills south-east of Asti. He may not have been the most respected inhabitant. According to a police report, he was 'not fond of work and [was] much given to drinking', and although married with four children, he tended to spend whatever money he had 'on parties and loose women', leaving his family poor. But he had served in Libya and in the First World War, and had not been an active socialist (though he was suspected of having 'socialist sentiments'); and while never a party member, he had not stopped his children joining the fascist youth organisations.[69]

On 27 March 1933, Boccaccio had joined five other villagers for an evening of carousing in a hamlet outside Maranzana. After consuming around 20 litres of wine (though the estimates later varied), the six men had staggered back into the village in the early hours of the morning singing, according to their own account, 'popular and country songs'. After stopping at the house of one of the group and taking on board another couple of litres, Boccaccio, a teenage boy called Antonio Gabeto, and an impoverished small sharecropper, Giovanni Benazzo, had emerged into the cool night air and proceeded down the Via del Littorio, singing as they went, presumably quite boisterously. At some point Boccaccio had found himself alone. He had sat down on a bench outside the town hall and fallen asleep. He had woken with a start after rolling heavily to the ground, and had made his way home just as the town clock was striking four, no doubt more or less oblivious to what had taken place.

Unfortunately for Boccaccio, a number of villagers were willing, whatever their exact motives, to testify against him when they were interviewed by the police. One said that Boccaccio and his friends had been heard singing 'an old socialist song' of rice workers, while another claimed that they had actually been declaiming the 'Red Flag' and had done so for at least five minutes. Often when individuals were accused of subversive gestures of this kind, they could secure leniency or even pardon through the fact of having been drunk and therefore temporarily irresponsible. But not in this case. Perhaps Boccaccio's reputation for being somewhat idle and a poor family man offended the traditional Piedmontese work ethic and Catholic morality too much. Whatever the reason, he became one of the 13,000 or so troublemakers of various kinds – whether political dissidents, petty criminals, homosexuals or, as in his own case, somewhat dissolute elements – sentenced to a period of *confino* (internment) in a remote community in the south of the country. Benazzo was also sent to *confino* – though his straitened circumstances led to the punishment being commuted to *ammonizione* (house arrest) after several months. The young Gabeto got away simply with *ammonizione*.[70]

Boccaccio spent his term of *confino* in Grassano, a town in the region of Basilicata. He stayed there a year before being amnestied: a factor in his early release may have been an appeal that his eighteen-year-old son sent to the Duce, begging that his 'unhappy father who is suffering in some far-off place and so makes his family suffer, too' be allowed to return home. Another man who in 1935 was sentenced to *confino* in Grassano, before being moved on to a more remote village, was the anti-fascist intellectual from Turin, Carlo Levi. During the time he spent in this isolated area of Italy, Levi became conscious of how for the mass of the peasant population the idea of political consent or dissent was effectively meaningless given the inveterate hostility of the poor towards all forms of government. 'For the people of Basilicata, Rome means nothing: it is the capital of the *Signori* [gentlemen], the centre of a foreign and malicious state.'[71] For Boccaccio, too, and for his friends, whose brief escape from the precarious poverty of their everyday lives into a world of drunken revelry and song had cost them dear, fascism must similarly have seemed as if it was something largely alien and hostile – an embodiment of capricious power that offered little more than liberalism before it.

7

Imparting Faith

Schools

The small Tuscan town of Bagni di Lucca, where Anna Caredio lived with her father Edgardo, who loved telling jokes about Mussolini, had a long history of welcoming distinguished visitors: Montaigne, Montesquieu, Metternich, Byron, Shelley, Lamartine, Heine and Dumas were among the many distinguished foreigners who had been attracted to its wooded hills and celebrated hot springs and baths. But as the primary school teacher, Albina Chiodo, found when she arrived in the community during the Matteotti crisis in the autumn of 1924, most of the permanent residents of Bagni were rural labourers whose aspirations and general level of culture were dispiritingly low. The first thing that struck her was just how filthy the small children were that she was responsible for in the second and fourth years, and she made it her task immediately to take them out to a fountain and scrub them clean. She was horrified at their ignorance – many did not even know in which year they had been born – and shocked by their indiscipline and absenteeism. Their poor health also alarmed her, and she noted frequent serious illnesses and sudden deaths in the diary that she kept over the next four years as a record of her struggle to have some impact on those she taught.[1]

Given the tremendous political insecurities that had attended the creation of the Kingdom of Italy and the awareness of the enormous gulf separating the patriotic elites from the great mass of the population, education had been considered from the outset to be a vital tool in the process of 'making Italians'. The emphasis, certainly at the level of primary schooling, had traditionally been not so much on imparting knowledge – it was after all questionable how much benefit most

peasants would derive in adult life from being literate and numerate –
as on moulding the moral character of children so that they grew up
to be hard-working, obedient, truthful and patriotic – and accepting
of their station in life. As Michele Coppino, the author of a major
reform act of 1877 that had made education free and compulsory to
the age of nine, had declared, the principal purpose of primary schools
should be to ensure that the masses were 'content to remain in the
condition that nature had assigned to them, and not encourage them
to abandon it'. And he had added that the main task confronting
teachers should be to 'create a population that is instructed as far as
it can be, but which is first and foremost honest and industrious, useful
to the family, and devoted to the fatherland and the king'.[2]

But as Albina was to find in Bagni di Lucca, the capacity of primary
education to influence the young was restricted by various factors.
Although the law of 1877 had allowed mayors to fine the parents of
any children who failed to attend, the reality was that most peasants
felt they needed their offspring to help look after livestock or work in
the fields, especially in the spring and summer months; and sanctions
were generally regarded as futile. A survey of a Romagna province in
1886–87 had discovered that in only three out of forty communes had
attempts been made to impose fines for truancy; and in just five had
proper lists been drawn up of those who were absent.[3] Another
problem was that the costs of primary schooling had been placed on
local councils, and there was often neither the money nor the will to
pay for adequate equipment or space. In 1928 Charlotte Gower found
that in the Sicilian village of Milocca the authorities could not enforce
attendance because the rooms were simply not big enough to hold
all the children. She also noted that in the second year girls were only
permitted to come to class if they had underwear, 'which their grand-
mothers dispense with entirely, and which few of their mothers own'.
As a result, she said, it was only the wealthier and more ambitious
families who bothered to send their children to school regularly.[4]

The sense that schools were failing in their mission to 'make Italians'
had become acute in the years preceding the First World War, as
persistent social and political unrest had led a growing chorus of
commentators to point an accusatory finger at the education system.
The problem was considered not only to be one of inadequate
resources – though various official reports had underlined the

alarmingly primitive conditions in which many teachers were forced to work, especially in rural communities. There had also been concern that the system was too accessible, allowing children to proceed relatively easily from primary to secondary school and then on to university, generating expectations and ambitions that could not be matched by the country's limited job market. Many had seen the spread of revolutionary socialism as directly linked to the growing army of unemployed or frustrated secondary school and university graduates who turned their intellectual armoury in anger against the state. As the Undersecretary in the Ministry of Public Instruction wrote in 1924, looking back over the liberal period: 'I had the painful impression of seeing children who were playing with fire. And more than once I found myself saying that the most dangerous illiteracy was not that of the poor who cannot read and write but the illiteracy of the educated classes.'[5]

Another major complaint about schools in the Giolittian period, closely related to the anxieties voiced by intellectuals about the lack of inspirational ideals in public life, had been that they were too dominated by positivism – concerned more with disseminating dry information and handing out certificates and diplomas than seeing education as an essentially spiritual process of moulding children morally and emotionally. The fact that many teachers had been socialist supporters in the pre-war years had given an added edge to this criticism. The philosopher Giovanni Gentile had been among those who had called most loudly for an injection of his and his friend Croce's neo-idealist principles into the classroom. After the war – which had intensified the debates about the scholastic system (one of the most influential educationalists of the period, Ernesto Codignola, had blamed the defeat at Caporetto on Italy's inadequate schools)[6] – he had taken a leading role in championing reforms. Early in 1920 he had joined a number of other well-known figures including Piero Gobetti and Giuseppe Prezzolini in launching a passionate appeal for a 'Fascio of national education' to raise teaching standards, lay the foundations of 'the granitic national unity and greatness of the fatherland' and create 'the solid national consciousness' that the country lacked.[7]

In 1923, as Minister of Public Instruction, Gentile had introduced a series of reforms to tackle the main criticisms that had been levelled at the education system for a generation. These were described by

Mussolini (rather misleadingly given their very conservative character) as 'the most fascist' of laws. Gentile set out to promote quality over quantity ('few schools, but good ones'), and the ultimate goal, as Mussolini said, was to ensure that the universities produced a ruling class 'properly prepared for the great and difficult duties' of regenerating the Italian nation.[8] For the vast majority of the population, schooling would now end at fourteen, with the last three years being spent in a new tier of 'complementary schools' that offered no access to higher education and whose curriculum was built around basic vocational skills. One of the consequences (and aims) of these changes was to debar working- and lower-middle-class children from climbing the academic ladder and, instead, to leave the secondary schools to a social and intellectual elite steeped in those subjects such as classical studies (especially Latin), literature, history and philosophy that were believed to transmit the spiritual essence of Italy. (Science was seen as intrinsically cosmopolitan and materialistic.) Religion, too, was accorded a prominent place, above all in primary schools. Gentile was himself a non-believer, but he saw Catholicism as a 'peculiarly Italian institution' and 'store-house of national tradition' that could serve to reinforce respect for hierarchy and authority.[9]

From 1925, as Albina found in Bagni di Lucca, teaching was subjected to a process of increasing 'fascistisation'. Mussolini declared in December of that year that schools 'at all levels and in all their instruction should educate Italian youth to understand fascism, to renew itself in fascism and to live in the historical climate created by the fascist revolution'.[10] From the evidence of her diary (which she kept largely to provide solace in the midst of so much frustrating ignorance and immorality), Albina appears to have had no difficulty in adjusting to the new political climate. Like many primary school teachers she had always regarded her pedagogic 'mission' as being framed by Catholic morality and patriotism. Fascism, she might reasonably feel, was seeking to do little more than strengthen these two key ideological poles.[11] She recorded her excitement at attending a convention of the National Association of Fascist Teachers in Lucca in the spring of 1927 and listening to the uplifting words of the Superintendent for Schools ('he made me forget my considerable tiredness and dissatisfaction'). A few months later she learned to her dismay from a newspaper that she had recently missed a meeting of 'fascist primary school teachers'. She enjoyed going to such meetings, she wrote, 'because they make me feel that my spirit is restored, for a number of reasons'.[12]

One thing that particularly appealed to her about fascism was the way it struck an emotional chord with the young. 'How these children feel fascism!' she wrote in April 1926 as she prepared to take her pupils off to church for a service of thanksgiving 'for the escape of our Duce' from the most recent attempt on his life. Mussolini's epic struggles against the socialists – her own home town of Sarzana in Liguria had been the scene of a particularly bloody battle between blackshirts and socialists in June 1921 – the heroic March on Rome, and now the Duce's providential deliverance from assassins' bullets, furnished a powerful narrative with which to illustrate the importance of the 'patriotic sentiment' that she regarded it as her principal duty to impart. She was delighted to find in the summer of 1926 that the pupils in the fifth year had spontaneously wanted a picture of Mussolini in their class-room and had got together and paid for it themselves (she marked its arrival by having them all stand in front of it and deliver a Roman salute 'in unison'). She was also extremely pleased when the children tried to wear something approaching a party uniform – a marked contrast to their usual clothes: 'I am beginning to see little black smocks and shirts. How smart they look!'[13]

But getting across the main messages of fascism to the young was still an uphill struggle for Albina. She worked hard to enthuse her pupils. She gave what she hoped were spirited talks about Mussolini and the achievements of fascism, discussing the First World War and the heroic sacrifices of the Italian soldiers, praising the king and other members of the royal family, and celebrating major anniversaries such as 28 October and 24 May. But she had just three hours of lessons each day. This was simply not enough, she felt, to counter the perni-cious influence of the children's families, where drink, dancing, indis-cipline and general dissoluteness seemed rife: 'Only somebody living in the midst of people of this kind, born merely to have pleasure, can understand and feel pity.' After more than three years in the commu-nity she was experiencing a deepening sense of despondency. Her fourth-year pupils struck her as typical: 'Instead of striving to find out as much as possible about our beautiful peninsula, they compete to see who can know the least.' And it was not just their attitude to learning that depressed her; it was also their persistent immorality. In the summer of 1928, in one of the last entries in her diary, she wrote: 'To educate! That is my mission, but one I cannot fulfil. I have pupils who make me blush for the way that they behave outside school.'[14]

Albina's sense of frustration was not helped by the many reminders she received from educational experts at conferences and in a steady stream of books, manuals and articles in professional journals of how, in contrast to the 'agnosticism and indifference to supreme national goals' of the liberal era, fascism aimed to forge the Italian people into a 'strong spiritual unit'.[15] It was her duty to help realise this, she was informed, by engaging with the children, using every emotional tool she could muster. For, as one of the regime's leading educationalists explained, 'we know that a primitive mind will only allow itself to be stirred by the vivid, the picturesque, and the simple representation of drama'. To illustrate the point, he suggested how a teacher might set about presenting a particular episode from the post-war period when three people, one of them a schoolboy, had been murdered by communists in the Piedmontese town of Casale Monferrato. The young victim, Scarfoglio, should be brought to life:

> Create not a ghost but a living creature, and then you will see how the children will follow him, will tremble with fear, will push their way through the crowd in order not to lose him, will shield him, and when they see him fall, they will cry, they will curse the heinous, bestial attack, and will yearn to follow his example and dream of sacrificing themselves, not for this or for that ideal, but like Scarfoglio, like the boy from Casale, who was one of them.[16]

Making use of examples, presenting living models for children to imitate and emulate, had long been considered an essential tool of primary school teaching, given the particular importance attached to moral over intellectual training. The increasing emphasis placed by fascism from the mid-1920s on the need radically to transform the Italian character led to the figure of Mussolini being employed more and more as a template in school textbooks and lessons. The 'cult of the Duce' was thus regarded as serving a specifically pedagogic function within a refashioned education system – one whose primary goal, as the Minister of Justice, Alfredo Rocco, said in 1927, was to break with the deleterious 'agnostic' approach of liberalism, with 'its absence of moral content and identity', and 'shape the new Italian, worthy of the new history of Italy and able to understand it and fulfil it'.[17] Mussolini, according to another member of the government in 1926, was to be considered 'the prototype of the new Italian'. His character and values would be transmitted to the people by 'furnishing us with the living model of the ethical and political individual whom we must resemble'.[18]

The transmission into schools of Mussolini as an exemplar, and of fascist doctrines in general, was assisted by a general willingness on the part of both publishing houses and authors to produce texts that conformed to the directives of the regime. Self-censorship was widely applied, and probably did more to ensure that educational books were adapted to the prevailing climate than government-imposed constraints. Already in 1924 the writer Franco Ciarlantini pointed out to his publisher Arnoldo Mondadori that the front cover they were proposing for his new fifth-year primer, *Love and light*, showing two small children kissing, would have to be changed, given the pressure the Church was successfully bringing to bear on school texts in the wake of the Gentile reform: 'Kisses, even of little children, are asking for trouble: the clericals would boycott us'.[19] Three years later, when the political climate had grown still more restrictive, the publisher Enrico Bemporad diligently reminded one of his authors of her responsibilities. She should ensure the 'greatest possible harmony between the book and the physiognomy of Italian schools . . . between the book and the content and practice of the Catholic religion . . . between the book and the national ideals . . . between the book and the style of life championed by Fascism . . . between the book and the legislation of Fascism . . . between the book and the general directives for the physical health of the new generations.'[20]

The fact that new texts for schools proliferated from the later 1920s indicates that there was no shortage of writers willing to demonstrate their commitment to the regime's goals. Saverio Grana, for instance, suggested how the Duce might be represented in the classroom in his 1927 book (subsequently reprinted and expanded), *Mussolini spiegato ai bimbi* ('Mussolini explained to children'). Italy after the war, he said, had become 'worse than an African tribe or at least a fine lunatic asylum', with strikers everywhere stealing and committing arson and even burning whole families alive. The reason why Italians had behaved

like this was simple: they had lacked a strong leader. 'Ordinary people
are children, like you, and are sometimes even more gullible than you.
And above all, like you, they need to be set on the right path and led
by men of faith and conscience.' Another factor behind the chaos had
been the godlessness of socialism – which was why Mussolini had
restored religion to the country. That the Duce was acting with God's
blessing was shown by the way he had been shielded 'miraculously'
from four assassination attempts, 'four signs that the divine will wanted
our Fatherland saved from revolution and ruin'. 'And even if Mussolini
was not for us Italians like a celestial saviour, his life . . . should be
made known to you children, and to all children, as an example and
a model.'[21]

The suffusion of the primary school syllabus with references to the
Duce and fascism accelerated from 1929 when a standardised state
textbook was introduced with material chosen and approved by a
ministerial commission. But the 'fascistisation' of the teaching environment was already well advanced before this date. Coercion certainly
played its part. A law of January 1927 relating to civil servants exposed
any teacher who did not display sufficient enthusiasm for the regime
to possible dismissal. But there was also a large degree of unprompted
fervour, especially among the younger generation for whom the
defence of Catholicism by Mussolini was often seen as the major
reason for supporting fascism.[22] This was especially the case with
women, who made up the great majority of primary school staff. As
one female teacher in the Abruzzi, born in 1901, recalled:

> I wanted to become a teacher as I felt attracted by the mission of being
> an educator . . . I enrolled in Catholic Action and taught catechism to
> the girls . . . When communism started to incite the working classes
> into hating their employers and to spread materialistic and atheist ideas,
> I was against it and welcomed fascism as a liberator, so much so that
> in 1926 I founded the women's *fascio* in Montorio al Vomano, and was
> its secretary until 1929.[23]

It was the enthusiastic support of the staff for fascism that Maria
Teresa Rossetti, an intelligent middle-class girl from Padua, found
particularly stimulating. She began keeping a diary in 1926 when she
entered her intermediate school at the age of eleven. Her teacher

spoke with passion about Mussolini and how he had marched on Rome 'to save Italy from civil war', and she told the girls of their duty to help build 'the future Italy, great and powerful, worthy daughter of ancient Rome'. In December 1926 a shrine was created in the school to the memory of the unknown soldier, with a rifle, sword and helmet, and a bronze effigy with a laurel crown. Maria was moved: 'I like that wall so much; it is the holiest in the building.' When a few months later the headmaster gave a lecture to her class about the foundation of the fascist movement, describing how in March 1919 Mussolini and a group of just 'thirty men' had taken an oath to make Italy 'great and strong', she recalled his stirring words: 'With Benito Mussolini the Italy of the centuries of Rome has been restored, the Italy of our fathers, powerful and beautiful! For the greatness of Benito Mussolini: Eia, Eia, Alalà!'[24]

Maria's receptiveness to the rhetoric of her teachers was no doubt facilitated by the environment in which she was growing up. Her parents were well educated (her father was an engineer) and patriotic and moved in respectable urban professional circles. A similar cultural milieu, in which talk of Mussolini and fascism could be comfortably grafted onto a rich bedrock of references to ancient Rome and the Risorgimento, enabled another middle-class girl, Zelmira Marazio, to respond with equal enthusiasm to her school environment. Zelmira was born in 1921 in the Borgo Po district of Turin and brought up in a household of women teachers. None of the adults, she recalled in her memoirs, was seriously interested in politics, but there was considerable sympathy for Mussolini, if tinged by primness. Her mother used to relate how when she first heard his name it had reminded her of the famous Calabrian bandit, Musolino; and she added: 'In fact he has got brigand's eyes.' On other occasions she would say: 'That saying of his, *me ne frego* [I don't give a damn], is vulgar. But he's a good man. He's increased the pay of schoolmistresses, from love of his mother, who was a teacher herself.'[25]

Zelmira loved books: stories about ancient Rome and Edmondo De Amicis's patriotic classic, *Cuore*, were among her favourites. She learned about Garibaldi and the Thousand from the collection of children's poems, *Il Cestello* by Angiolo Novaro – though she was worried when she first read the lines 'Alone at the top of the bridge / His forehead bathed in an ocean of light / Italy's fate in his hand /

The *duce* stood guard'. 'For me there existed only one *duce*, him, Mussolini.' But her mother helpfully explained that Garibaldi also deserved that noble title for what he had achieved in 1860. At her primary school there was a shrine to the First World War with a red lamp constantly burning in front of a bronze plaque of General Diaz's victory bulletin and an inscription with the names of former pupils who had been killed. Zelmira would stop as she passed, stand to attention and make a Roman salute. She was a member of the youth group, the Piccole Italiane, and recalled the excitement she and her friends felt as they put on their uniforms of black pleated skirts and white blouses and set off to party rallies singing songs, their arms stretched wide to make their capes billow in the wind.[26]

Zelmira's memories of her childhood in Turin were of a time of emotional fulfilment. She loved the Duce (as her parents were separated he provided something of a surrogate father), and claimed to have experienced in fascism a comforting sense of what it was to be truly Italian, with present and past merging and holding out a promise almost of an earthly paradise:

> Fascism filled our lives, and gave us all that we could wish for and even more . . . Our freedom was to be able to grow physically and spiritually, to prepare ourselves for a radiant future, to believe and to obey so as to make the fatherland greater. Ours was the best of all possible worlds . . . For myself and my friends being fascist was the same as being Italian. There were no alternatives, nor could there be any. The reality in which I was immersed was a coherent whole . . . Centuries of suffering, humiliation and struggle had emerged into the luminous spring of the Risorgimento, and then, after the abject interlude of Umberto's *Italietta*, into the still more splendid spring of fascism. 'Hail, oh people of heroes / hail immortal fatherland. / Your children are reborn . . .' And at the top of everything there was him, the Duce.[27]

Zelmira's obsession with Mussolini was stimulated primarily by the uncritical cultural environment in which she found herself in Turin. Her mother, though deeply patriotic, had the typical 'restraint', she said, of the city's educated bourgeoisie and disliked the coarse and populist aspects of fascism. But this did not diminish Zelmira's enthusiasm. She avidly read the daily reports about the Duce in *La*

Stampa and *Gazzetta del Popolo*, watched him in LUCE newsreels in
the cinema, and often debated with her elder sister after supper whether
or not he was a greater genius than Napoleon. At a certain point when
she was in her early teens she found the parameters of her feelings
for Mussolini challenged uncomfortably. She and her classmates had
recently seen documentaries of the Duce stripped to the waist
threshing wheat. One of her friends, Fiorenza, suddenly asked her as
they were walking through the Parco Valentino if she found Mussolini
sexually attractive. Zelmira became confused:

> I had never seen him in this way, and I could not picture him as
> somebody to embrace and kiss: for me he was a god. 'I don't know, I
> couldn't . . . Yes, I like him, but as a lover . . . I can't imagine it.' 'I like
> him, also as a man. He is so handsome, strong and powerful. I would
> like to have a man like that.' Her words sounded as confident and
> irrefutable as mine were tentative. There was also the question of his
> age. 'How old is he?' I asked nervously. 'I'm not sure. Anyway, does it
> matter? He's got so much health and charm. I could die for him.' I
> was more confused than ever and walked on in silence as Fiorenza
> talked to me about him and smiled. Suddenly her face looked serious.
> 'Supposing he got ill? And died?' The Duce, die? It was not possible.
> 'What would happen to us without him? What would become of Italy?'
> The thought dismayed us. It was as if the sun were to go out. Did we
> not sing at that time: 'God has sent you to Italy / as he has sent the
> light'? Fiorenza pulled herself together first. 'What are we talking
> about? He is fine. He is strong and handsome. He will live till he's a
> hundred.' But that conversation left me rather uneasy. I realised that
> you could admire this man in a different way to the way I did. For me
> he was 'the man of Providence', the culmination of Italy's history, the
> person in whom that history found its consummation and meaning.
> He was the sun of my life.[28]

As Zelmira recognised, much of the allure of the Duce to her as
a child had come from the degree to which he closely fitted the traditional templates offered by Italian history and Catholicism. And given
the regime's claims that fascism belonged essentially to the same
(Italian) cultural matrix as Roman Catholicism, and given, too, that
the Gentile reforms had accorded a new prominence to religious

instruction in schools (with priests often delivering it), teachers could feel they were fully entitled to borrow familiar religious images to help provide fascism with the 'spiritual' charge that it was seeking. In Zelmira's local nursery in Turin small children were taught a poem about the young Mussolini and his mother Rosa which contained strong echoes of conventional representations of Christ, Mary, and the Holy Family:

> Rosa was her name / Benito was her child / The house was humble / With no trace of garden. / All day could be heard / The sound of the hammer, / Like the harness bell / Rung by the lamb. / On his mother's knee / Benito sat doing his homework / Tracing the words in the book / With his finger. / Rosa was her name, / A name that means thorns / But he was her flower, / Benito, her son. / And kissing his forehead / She said to him: – you are mine! / But she knew he belonged to Italy / And to God.[29]

The interweaving of fascism with traditional Catholic precepts can be discerned in numerous primary and intermediate school exercise books. In the town of Boscotrecase to the south-east of Naples, for example, a thirteen-year-old working-class boy, Alberto Allocato, produced a fairly typical set of essays in the course of his final year of education in 1928–29. On 28 October he wrote about the March on Rome. He said that Mussolini was 'a gentleman and a patriot' who had saved the country from the civil war 'caused by the socialists led by Lenina [corrected by the teacher to 'Lenin'] who were going to hand Italy back to foreign rulers'. He concluded: 'We should consider that Mussolini was the son of a blacksmith who was a poor man but rich in heart and mind . . . Glory and praise to those that respect Italy. For Benito Mussolini. Eia! Eia! Eia! Alalà.' The Duce's humble origins featured again in a piece about the Balilla in December, where Mussolini was described as coming from a poor family, loving birds, and having a 'gentle and good heart'. On one occasion the young Mussolini saw an old man hoeing, took the tool from him and worked the soil in his place for six hours. But this son of a blacksmith, who had even been arrested as a vagabond, had ended up as the head of the blackshirts: 'Nobody has been able to control and command Italy. But he has been able to do so. He is ready to fight for the Fatherland,

and to shed his blood in war, together with the fascist regime, together with us Balillas, who with outstretched arms cry: Excelsior! To us!'[30]

In subsequent compositions Alberto wrote about such topics as Santa Lucia, carnival, emigrants, reading, Palm Sunday, resurrection and Garibaldi. He did an essay on the Blessed Carmela d'Auria – a peasant girl from the nearby town of Boscoreale whose intense faith and charitable works had led her to die in the odour of sanctity in 1908 – and made a list of dialect proverbs with their corresponding Italian translations: the celebration of local culture was widely seen by educational experts as an important stepping stone towards a love of 'the greater Fatherland', Italy.[31] He copied out the patriotic ballad, La spigolatrice di Sapri ('The gleaner of Sapri'), as well as improving quotations about the importance of hard work and thrift by Samuel Smiles, Benjamin Franklin, Cesare Cantù and other writers. In an essay on the aviator and polar explorer Umberto Nobile ('the true fascist, the true Italian') he returned to the theme of humble origins, saying that the person who brought most honour to his country was not one born

in riches and graceful castles, but one born in a hovel. Jesus, who was born in a stable and then found himself in the stars, gave us the example. Mussolini, too, was the son of a primary school teacher and a blacksmith; and then from blacksmith he rose to be head of government. And Nobile as well, the son of a trader, came to be called 'Explorer of the North' . . . And for Umberto Nobile: Eia! eia! eia! Alalà. Excelsior![32]

Tensions with the Church

The interlacing of fascism and Catholicism and the active support given to the government by many clergy, at all levels, was undoubtedly of huge benefit to Mussolini in anchoring the regime among the masses. But the totalitarian ambitions of fascism were threatening to the Church, above all the belief that the individual should find meaning and fulfilment primarily through the state. The value system to which the 'new Italian' was expected to subscribe was certainly not unwelcome to the Vatican: obedience, discipline, faith, sobriety, social solidarity, respect for authority and a disdain of bourgeois materialism and individualism ('a mindset totally antithetical to the fascist mentality', as Mussolini repeatedly stressed)[33] could all be comfortably accommodated to the Church's teachings. Much more troubling was the idea that Italians were being moulded with a primary aim of creating a strong nation that could spread the influence of Italy in the world, if need be, through war. As a secret report by an informer on the mood inside the Vatican noted early in 1926, there was growing concern among those around the Pope about the 'spiritual climate' of fascism and a fear that in the future 'the fire of statalist idolatry . . . and nationalist paganism . . . might prove worse than the frying pan of demo-liberalism and Freemasonry'.[34]

Of particular concern to the Church were the fascist party's youth organisations. These were brought together in 1926 in a single association, the Opera Nazionale Balilla (ONB), headed by the athletic and good-looking former *ras* of Carrara, Renato Ricci (who had an unusual amount of socialist blood on his hands). Although Catholic education, to be delivered by specially designated chaplains, was incorporated into the activities of the ONB, so as to ensure 'the fusion of religious fervour with patriotic ardour', the new centrally coordinated national body posed a clear challenge to the youth associations of Catholic Action, which the Vatican had long regarded as instrumental in safeguarding the hearts and minds of children for Catholicism. The ONB consisted of four sections: the Balilla, for boys aged eight to thirteen, the Piccole Italiane, for girls of the same age, the Avanguardisti and the Giovani Italiane, for boys and girls, respectively, aged between fourteen and eighteen. To these were later added the Figli della Lupa ('Children of the She-Wolf') for children aged between six and eight. Membership was not made compulsory until the late 1930s, but parents who did not want their children to join the ONB had to provide schools with a written explanation.[35]

The principal function of the ONB was to prepare the young for their future roles in society: boys to be soldiers and girls to be the mothers of warriors. After all, as Mussolini proclaimed with characteristically aphoristic terseness in 1934, 'War is to man as maternity is to woman.'[36] Boys dressed in uniforms, paraded, sang marching songs and engaged in competitive sports. Girls practised first aid, danced around poles, went to concerts and attended courses on such topics as flower arranging, embroidery, knitting and typing. Part of the training for future maternity consisted of a military-style drill, in which

girls were passed in review carrying dolls 'in the correct manner of a
mother holding a baby'.[37] Guns were central to ONB culture, and in
1930 Ricci called publicly for every Balilla gym to be furnished with
them, on the grounds that practising with real weapons was indispensable to the formation of true men. One much-favoured ceremony,
repeated in piazzas up and down the country, consisted of a member
of the Giovani Italiane handing over a rifle to an Avanguardista, then
to a Balilla and finally to a Figlio della Lupa, as if it were the torch
of life.[38]

The regime aimed to use the ONB to supplement the limited impact
of schools and impart directly the true spirit of the fascist revolution
('libro e moschetto, fascista perfetto' – 'book and musket, perfect
fascist'). To this end it ordered the disbanding in 1927–28 of all rival
youth groups, including the Catholic Boy Scouts. The negotiations for
the settlement of the Roman Question, which had been proceeding
in fits and starts secretly for several years, were placed in jeopardy.[39]
The Pope publicly lamented that the huge benefits fascism had brought
to the Church ('how much good has been done, how much evil has
been brought to an end') were now being undermined by the hostility
towards Catholic Action, but the Duce replied peremptorily that the
'system of totalitarian . . . preparation and education of the Italian
man' was 'the fundamental task of the state' and could not be compromised.[40] Mussolini's brother, Arnaldo, widely considered a devout
Catholic, urged the Pope to bear in mind that fascism and Catholicism
shared the same ideological matrix: fascism was inspired by 'the religious and spiritual essence of *romanità*' just as it was '*romanità*' that
had invested the Church with much of its greatness: 'Not to feel this
connection between Catholicism and our nation is to deprive the
religious idea of one of its greatest historical forces'.[41]

But for both sides the prize of an end to the Roman Question was
too great to miss. Mussolini soon compromised and allowed the youth
groups of Catholic Action 'with chiefly religious ends' to continue:
only the Boy Scouts remained banned on the grounds that they had
a 'semi-military character'.[42] The negotiations resumed, and on
11 February 1929, in a magnificent ceremony at the Lateran Palace,
the Vatican's Secretary of State and Mussolini signed the Lateran Pacts.
This brought an end to nearly seventy years of formal dispute between
Church and state. 'Italy has been restored to God and God to Italy',

announced the *Osservatore Romano*. In return for recognising the territorial settlement of 1870 as final, the Vatican City was made a fully
independent state with 44 hectares of land. The Pope received an
indemnity of 750 million lire plus a further 1,000 million in bonds as
compensation for the loss of Church property since 1860. An accompanying concordat declared Catholicism to be the official religion of
the state and gave the Church a number of important privileges, such
as the exemption of trainee priests from military service. Most significant as far as Pius XI was concerned, the concordat guaranteed the
position of Catholic Action and its organisations, 'in so far as they
carry out their activities independently of all political parties . . . for
the diffusion and realisation of Catholic principles'.

In practice, the concordat did not bring an end to the rivalry between
the ecclesiastical authorities and fascism for the control of children.
Tensions were to explode into another full-blown breach in the summer
of 1931, when Mussolini ordered the closure of Catholic youth circles
and the Pope publicly condemned the regime for its 'pagan state
worship' and its opposition to 'the natural rights of families and the
supernatural rights of the Church'. But a compromise settlement was
again soon achieved. Just how fierce the competition frequently was
can be seen in the letter sent by the president of the ONB in the
province of Vicenza to the heads of local party organisations in July
1929, in which he said that fascism must 'at all costs' control the young
and resist the insidious threats from Catholic Action:

> We must therefore aim at totalitarianism. Every young person must
> be marshalled in our ranks; nobody must escape our control . . . And
> we can, and must, achieve more: the schools will soon be reopening,
> and we must accordingly, without fail, set to work to recruit new
> members. It does not matter if the Balilla sections are not fully or
> perfectly equipped. What matters is that no child should be outside
> our ranks and subjected to somebody else's propaganda.

He was particularly concerned to raise the number of teenage
Avanguardisti:

> If children aged 14 to 18 are not in our ranks, they will slip from our
> grasp forever, because they are not even subject to the broad control

of schools. Every sacrifice must be made in order to increase the *Avanguardisti*, to dress them and to educate them militarily . . . The future security of Fascism, in other words of the Fatherland, is at stake.[43]

Reports rained into the Vatican of instances where the fascist authorities were doing everything they could to steer young people away from Catholic groups. The atmosphere in many places was rendered intimidating. Sometimes it was also unseemly. In the village of Rocchetta Nervina on the French border, in March 1932, the funeral of a twelve-year-old boy who had belonged both to the local Balilla and the Catholic 'Company of Saint Luigi' was marred by an ugly altercation between the blackshirts and the 'Luigini' over who should carry the coffin. The parents had wanted the Luigini to do it; the blackshirts had protested; the parish priest had said nothing, and the parents had got their way – leaving the priest exposed to the wrath of the fascists.[44] Instructions were frequently issued to the effect that membership of fascist youth organisations was to be regarded as incompatible with belonging also to a Catholic association, on the grounds, as the president of the ONB in the province of Messina said in a circular, that even 'religious education' could only be safely ministered 'under our control'.[45] In Senigallia in February 1930, a group of intermediate schoolchildren who had been attending Mass in the cathedral were summoned to the fascist party headquarters after the service and told they should no longer belong to the association of Italian Catholic Youth. Attempts were then forcibly made to confiscate their membership cards.[46]

Sometimes the rivalry between fascism and the Church strayed into the realms of blasphemy, as senior party representatives incited the young to direct their religious fervour towards secular figures. In Tuscany the Catholic hierarchy were very uncomfortable about the activities of the well-connected avant-garde writer Fernando Agnoletti, who, according to the Bishop of Prato and Pistoia in December 1931, had become something of an 'official orator' in the province of Florence. Agnoletti, the bishop said, had recently given a speech to children in the Teatro Banchini in Prato on the occasion of the Giornata del Balilla (Balilla day). He had told them: 'Remember that in Italy Saint Luigi is no longer the patron saint of children, as he once was.

Today your saint is Balilla. And you must pray to him in the same way that you pray to the saints for strength . . . because Balilla hurled a stone and you must hurl a grenade.'[47] Much more alarming was an episode that occurred a few months later in the town of Acireale in eastern Sicily when a prominent party official from Catania told an audience of young people that Catholic Action was incompatible with fascism, that for fascists 'the only god is Mussolini', and even that they should smash crosses. The bishop went to protest to the local party secretary and received a suitably Catholic reply: such remarks were indeed regrettable and should not recur: 'errare humanum est, perseverare diabolicum!'[48]

Another recurrent complaint of the clergy was that the fascist youth organisations often seemed determined to make it hard for children to attend church services – for instance, by scheduling drills and parades for the whole of Sunday morning. One result of such obstructionism, according to a senior figure in the Vatican, Monsignor Giovanni Pizzocolo, in January 1930, was that thousands of young people were being prised away from Catholicism, much to the alarm also of the parents, who saw their offspring 'no longer taking the sacraments, failing to observe feast days and heading towards a decidedly pagan life'. By way of consolation, Pizzocolo reported to the Pope that two of Mussolini's own sons, Bruno and Vittorio, had recently purchased a crib in a shop in Rome and had put some coins in a collecting box for missionaries, and that he had personally taken the opportunity to send Mussolini a letter, with a relic and two images of the Blessed Giuseppe Cottolengo, signed and dedicated to the boys. He was delighted to have received a grateful note back from the Duce, saying: 'Now that the image and relic of the Blessed Cottolengo have entered into the Mussolini household, may the Divine Providence, of whom the Blessed is the supreme Saint, work to smooth the path of many things for the good of Religion and the Fatherland'.[49] Neither Pizzocolo nor the Pope could have had any illusions about Mussolini's own personal faith, but it was public gestures that weighed most with the Church (and indeed with fascism).

The fascist youth organisations had the further disadvantage, as far as the Church was concerned, of exposing children to vice. Much concern was expressed about outings to the cinema and theatre and the way in which girls and boys were able to meet and mix quite easily at party events. The enormously popular ONB camping holidays, especially the annual showpiece of the Campo Dux – a week-long training exercise for Avanguardisti held from 1929 in a wooded district outside Rome – were regarded as particularly perilous, in as much as teenage boys were left unsupervised some of the time and so exposed to the temptations of the city. Priests were reported to patrol red-light districts in an attempt to curb underage sex,[50] but they faced the problem that promiscuity was not only often condoned by ONB leaders, eager to promote a manly and martial spirit among the adolescents, but even actively encouraged. When in 1931 the Avanguardisti of the Umbrian town of Città di Castello went to a rally in Perugia, they were taken to a brothel by those in charge as part of the day out. A young Catholic boy who refused to go was apparently teased mercilessly by others in the group.[51]

For all the regime's declarations that Roman Catholicism was to be respected and promoted as an integral element of Italian identity, it was clear to some at least that the use of organised religion to buttress the activities and secular goals of fascism risked seriously compromising the Church. If chaplains were present at ONB camps and led the young in Christian prayers – in between the sports and gymnastics events, lectures and twice-daily salutes to the king and the Duce – it was very hard to avoid the perception that Catholicism's claims to being a faith founded on love and peace sat very uncomfortably with the value system being championed by fascism. As one trenchant report to the Vatican stated in 1931:

> The government wishes to create young people who are war-like and with no inhibitions and scruples, nurtured on hatred, ready to commit violence and vendetta, proud to serve fascism even by beating and killing. Love, gentleness and forgiveness are regarded as vices of weak souls who are incapable of understanding the spirit of fascism, which is not only a party, but a doctrine, an ethic and a new religion.[52]

But for millions of Italians the incongruity was probably not self-evident. What, after all, did real faith mean – the faith that could drive people to risk martyrdom and death in the name of truth – if not, as Mussolini later said in a slogan, a capacity to believe, obey, and, if necessary, fight?

Beyond reason

The values of fascism and those of Catholicism did not seem at odds to Carlo Ciseri. They formed an emotional continuum – and he was a highly passionate young man living in a society that continually stressed the superiority of faith and enthusiasm over rationality and scepticism. His disgust with parliament and the socialists immediately after the war had been tempered by his excitement at the rise of Mussolini; and his support for the Duce and fascism remained undimmed throughout the 1920s as he at last found a stable job managing a hotel in Florence. Carlo kept up his diary, albeit intermittently now that he was a married man with a growing family to take care of, and in it he recorded his great admiration for Mussolini and his pride in fascist Italy. He found it moving that the Duce had risen from such humble origins: in 1928 he cut out a favourite photograph of the king alongside Mussolini – 'the man of the people who has elevated himself to the level of the man of royal blood and guides a Nation, reaching out to the people'. In the summer of 1929 he wrote an entry about the epic flight of Italo Balbo with a squadron of thirty-five planes across the Balkans to Odessa, underlining how important it was that Italy's international prestige ('the prestige that we have always lacked') had risen greatly thanks to fascism: 'That prestige that one day will restore to Rome its ancient splendours together with the reins of all European, and perhaps world, politics.'[53]

For Carlo, the essence of fascism was faith, and in October 1934 he had what seemed to him a wonderful opportunity to show his fervour, when a lavish ceremony was held in Florence on the twelfth anniversary of the March on Rome to mark the reburial of thirty-seven 'fascist martyrs' in the crypt of the church of Santa Croce. Like Catholicism, fascism attached huge importance to the cult of the dead. The fallen in the First World War together with the blackshirts who had lost their lives fighting against the socialists from 1919 to 1922 were the objects of intense official commemoration – in speeches and monuments and in the names of public buildings, party sections and streets. The 'fallen of the Militia' were also widely glorified. An anthology published by the party in 1935 with photographs and biographies of 370 fascists killed defending the revolution between 1923 and 1931 contained a characteristic mixture of religious and military imagery, with a frontispiece of a flaming crucifix flanked by fasces and erect bayonets, and an invocation to the fascist dead:

GOD, you who light every fire and strengthen every heart, renew each day my passion for Italy.

Make me ever more worthy of our dead, so that they – the strongest – may reply to the living: HERE!

You nourish my book with Your wisdom and my musket with Your will . . .

When the future soldier marches beside me in the ranks, may I hear his faithful heart beating . . .

Lord! Make Your cross the insignia that goes before the banner of my legion.

And save Italy, in the DUCE, always and at the hour of our beautiful death.

Amen.[54]

The church of Santa Croce in Florence had particular resonance. It contained the graves of some of the most illustrious Italians, including Machiavelli, Michelangelo and Galileo, and had been the subject of a celebrated patriotic poem of the Risorgimento, Ugo Foscolo's *Dei sepolcri* ('On tombs') (1806), in which the idea of the nation as a spiritual community of the living and the dead had been powerfully expounded. Reburying the 'fascist martyrs' in this hallowed site was thus a powerful symbolic statement of the regime's desire to bring together the past and the present into a seamless whole. A group of Catholics protested to the Bishop of Florence about the involvement of the clergy in the ceremony: 'Those it is now wished to glorify as martyrs were violent, bloodthirsty men who died trying to kill and certainly did not belong to the multitudes of Christian citizens'.[55] But the bishop felt unable to heed such a minority view and, after a solemn service in the cathedral presided over by senior clerics, each of the thirty-seven coffins was carried through the streets of the city preceded by a banner bearing the martyr's name and the word 'Presente!' (Here!). The press underlined how the event testified to fascism's success in unifying the nation through religious enthusiasm:

> ... [T]he entire Italian soul is preparing itself for this rite, reaching out towards it as to a supreme and intimate source of religious energy without which life would be a colourless succession of meaningless days . . . The civil liturgy of fascism testifies to the discipline of the masses and their great faith in the Duce.[56]

All the leading members of the fascist party had arrived in Florence for the ceremony, which was broadcast live on the radio around the country. For Carlo the idea of seeing the Duce in the flesh was a thrilling prospect. On the morning of 27 October he put on his *bersagliere* uniform – that Mussolini had also been a *bersagliere* during the war gave him a feeling of particular affinity – and set off for the city centre: 'I was thinking as I went through the streets that today I would be able to hear the living voice of Mussolini, which I had always listened to on the radio, and then only a few times. A great day, then, an exceptional day ... a day of joy for me because today I was going to hear and see Mussolini.' What exactly went wrong during the next few hours, causing him to return home in anguish, is not certain. In all likelihood the problem lay in the fact that the proceedings were rigorously controlled by the party, with the composition of the cortège planned and monitored in such a way as to highlight the role of *squadrismo* and the PNF in the formation of the regime.[57] Carlo had never been a squad member; nor had he ever joined the PNF. And somehow his commitment to fascism had been impugned in the course of the day, leaving him distraught. That evening he wrote in his diary: 'It is true that I am not a member, but that does not count – it should not count. What really matters is Faith: Believing – and I believe. I firmly believe.'[58]

Carlo was to retain his faith, above all in Mussolini, until the end of the regime, determined – like others who kept diaries or wrote memoirs about their experiences under fascism – to protect the confidence that he had placed in the regime from the unsettling idea that it might have been naive, misjudged or even wholly reprehensible. For many intelligent and well-educated young men and women, the value system of fascism, with its stress on belief, selflessness and anti-materialism, had a compelling quality that made it extremely difficult, even when common sense and humanitarianism indicated that support might be inappropriate, to find a moral key that would permit an exit. This was the experience of a young student at the university of Pavia, Alberto Caracciolo, later to be a distinguished philosopher of religion, who felt impelled at the end of the Second World War to reflect on why he, like almost all his contemporaries in the prestigious Ghislieri College, had not opposed fascism in the later 1930s. He admitted that not all the students had been fervent supporters of the regime: while some had indeed experienced fascism as 'a true religion, a view of life', others had evinced a cooler and less committed attitude. But the fact remained, he said, that almost nobody, so far as he could tell, had been in any serious sense an anti-fascist.[59]

Alberto had been born in 1918 in a small town in the Veneto. His father, a doctor, had been broadly indifferent to politics, and Alberto had grown up without any particular sense of ideological or emotional attachment to the regime. Even at his secondary school, the dominant values had appeared to him to be more those of traditional patriotism than of fascism. But after he had left home and enrolled at university, he had found himself in an environment in which it had been hard not to get drawn into politics, particularly towards the end of the 1930s when the tone of public life had grown increasingly strident. As a well-educated Catholic he had felt an instinctive dislike for the crudeness of party rallies, the blind adoration of the Duce, and the way in which fascism presented itself 'as a total conception, as a religion', with the state as 'its god' and war as the 'supreme act of the cult', with glorification of the desire to kill and be killed. But despite these strong feelings of antipathy, he had been unable to identify within himself sufficient moral grounds for rejecting a doctrine that was 'present everywhere and was acclaimed by all'. Indeed he had blamed himself for his failure to share the general enthusiasm: 'I made every effort to feel that love, but in vain. And I regarded this failure as a shortcoming of my moral being.' And this sense of guilt was underpinned by intellectual doubt:

Was it possible that millions and millions of people were deluded and that I alone – or that small group of opponents that I knew – was right? Was it not more likely that we were wrong? Moreover, while dogmatism may, on the one hand, . . . inspire resistance and hatred as a result of the marmoreal certainty with which it presents itself and condemns its adversaries, it cannot, on the other hand, fail to induce a certain sense of doubt, especially among hesitant and timid spirits.[60]

But it was not just the force of collective pressure that had impelled him towards conformity. There had also been elements within the actual value system of the regime that had attracted him and left his moral defences blunted. One was the fact that fascism had presented itself as a heroic, self-sacrificing and 'difficult' ideology, and branded its enemies as effete, egotistical and cowardly. Such an image had resonated with Alberto: after all, what young man would have wanted to risk being seen as weak, selfish and materialistic by his peers? More important still for Alberto had been the centrality of faith to fascism, for what had most alarmed him about liberal doctrines was the threat that they posed 'once accepted, to the religious sphere'. But liberalism had anyway lost its credibility in his eyes as a result of the uniform picture that had been painted of Italy before 1922 as a country in which atheism, hedonism and 'moral abandon' had reigned supreme. And it was out of the chaos of the post-war years that fascism had emerged as a reaction – a necessary reaction, Alberto and many of his friends had been inclined to argue, whose less pleasant aspects, including violence and the suppression of freedom, had to be endured as an inevitable stage in the nation's historical evolution.[61]

As for millions of other Italians, Alberto's relationship with fascism was extremely personal: the chemistry of impulses that impelled so many people to support the regime or to acquiesce in it necessarily varied from individual to individual according to circumstances. But a powerful common denominator in generating adhesion, above all for intellectuals such as Alberto, lay in the capacity of the regime to offer a species of Faustian pact in which the excitement of participating in a new and revolutionary political order that would propel Italy to greatness was made to seem highly attractive, not least given the traditional tedium and impoverishment of so much of provincial life. And as long as faith was manifested (above all a belief in the Duce), there was considerable space for individuals to inject their personal ideas and hopes into what was deliberately conceived as being a broad church. As the journalist Giuseppe Melis Bassu recalled of his time as a student in Sardinia in the later 1930s (and his recollections are similar to many of his age group and middle-class background):

> You should bear in mind that fascism was also, and above all, a receptacle into which . . . everyone put what they wanted of their hopes, their personal view of life, and their own public philosophy, even if it was only. crude. The horizons and boundaries of heresy were very wide, precisely because fascism was weak from an ideological point of view. So, everything could get bundled into this automatic – and I would say natural and almost physiological – adhesion: religious faith – there was broad support from the priests – the desire for order and respect for the law, the possibilities of economic improvement . . .[62]

The degree to which enthusiasm and faith acted as poles towards which those living under fascism not only felt drawn, but also (as with Alberto) believed they ought to be drawn, is well illustrated in the diary of the young middle-class girl from Padua, Maria Teresa Rossetti. Like her engineer father, Maria was of a scientific cast of mind (she went on to study physics at university) and, running through her diary – and perhaps one of her reasons for keeping it – was a desire to monitor her emotional responses, not least because she sensed that the rational streak within her was threatening to weaken and even call into question her 'orthodox' feelings. In February 1932, for example, the seventeen-year-old went with the rest of her class from school to see a film about the First World War, *Battaglia dal Astico al Piave* ('Battle from the Astico to the Piave'). It was a little long, she thought, but she liked its patriotic character: it ended with images of the king and Mussolini, and a vision of Italy as a woman with a turreted crown on her head wrapped in the tricolour and giving a Roman salute. But Maria was unsettled by the way that the students in the audience got wildly excited and repeatedly booed any reference to France. She came away with an awkward sensation that the film had been screened for 'a purpose'.[63]

Such lurking doubts about the morality of the regime's intentions caused her to feel guilty at times and left her wondering in her diary if she would ever be capable of experiencing truly passionate 'love for the fatherland'. The atmosphere at home did not help much, as her parents showed little interest in politics. Her worries were allayed in December 1932, when Croat nationalists in the Yugoslavian town of Trogir on the coast of Dalmatia destroyed a number of stone lions, symbols of former Venetian domination, in a gesture of defiance against the local Italian community and old claims by the government in Rome to sovereignty over the area. Thousands took to the streets in protest, in Padua as elsewhere. Maria joined in, and she was delighted to discover how ardent she felt as she stood in the piazza with her fellow students shouting and chanting. It was a revelation to her, a moment of joyous release. She had a strong sensation of being 'united in a single faith with all the Italians and prepared to give my life for the great fatherland'. Now, she wrote, she understood what patriotism really meant: it meant the 'annihilation' of the individual 'in order to be born again in the universal life of the fatherland'. To her huge relief, she had found that she too was capable of abandoning herself to such transcendent feelings.[64]

In the course of the next few years, Maria's enthusiasm for fascism was unalloyed, and she was able to record in her diary her feelings of excitement and pride at being part of a great national community that was united in both spirit and purpose around the figure of the Duce. In March 1933 she visited Rome and was impressed by the grandeur of the city centre. A vast new building programme was underway to showcase the monuments of the ancient imperial capital. Thousands of medieval houses and churches had recently been demolished in the area of the Roman forums to make way for a giant thoroughfare, chiefly for military parades – the Via dell'Impero – connecting the Colosseum to the monument to King Victor Emmanuel II and Italy, the Vittoriano. She saw Palazzo Venezia, which since 1929 had become the headquarters of the government, and looked up towards the balcony and the prime minister's office, the 'volcanic workshop from which comes all the energy that makes Italy great and beautiful'.[65] And she visited the Exhibition of the Fascist Revolution, which had opened the previous October to mark the tenth anniversary of the March on Rome. It was housed in the Palazzo delle Esposizioni, a Beaux Arts building in Via Nazionale, whose nineteenth-century facade had been transformed by the addition of four towering black fasces, modernist in design and nearly 80 feet high, placed boldly against a backdrop of red – as if to highlight the nation's metamorphosis from old liberal effeminacy to new fascist virility.

The exhibition had been designed by some of the most talented architects and artists of the period, including Mario Sironi and Giuseppe Terragni. It set out to chronicle the years in Italy from 1914 to 1922 using thousands of original documents and photographs displayed in rooms of often great aesthetic originality. On the surface, the political narrative was paramount, with Mussolini and the other fascist leaders as the protagonists, but the underlying message was that fascism was a supremely spiritual movement whose purpose was to reconnect the people to the nation and enable Italy to fulfil its true destiny in the world. The most striking section came at the end. One room had a reconstruction of Mussolini's newspaper office in Milan, with the phone receiver lying on the desk, as if he had just been called away hurriedly, and with cases of documents framed to resemble death notices detailing the assassination attempts on his life. Another, the last, the Shrine of the Martyrs, was a darkened hemispherical space dominated by a huge cross bearing the inscription 'For the immortal fatherland' and surrounded by the word 'Presente!' written up around the walls a thousand times on small oblong plates. As the organisers had intended, it was these final rooms with their evocation of death and immortality that made the greatest impression. Maria wrote:

It is very suggestive and moving . . . There are a huge number of relics of the fascist martyrs, the Duce's handkerchief soaked in blood from his wound. With your soul thus prepared for religious feelings, you enter the shrine of the martyrs: a dark circular room with illuminated glass rectangles bearing the word 'presente' on the top three-quarters of the walls. Below, in a purplish blue half light, are lots of banners. You move silently around a platform with a tall cross rising out of it, while in the far, far distance you hear choirs singing patriotic hymns. You come out slightly dazed, partly also because there are no windows and the heat gets to your head.[66]

The eighteen-year-old Maria freely admitted in her diary at this time to being totally captivated by fascism and above all by Mussolini: he had saved Italy from ruin and restored the country's ancient glory, and

was now 'labouring tirelessly so its people may continually be first in
the world'. Her sense of pride in the nation's achievements was almost
boundless. 'I felt so moved, I could have cried', she wrote in April 1933
after crossing the new road bridge that linked Venice to the mainland
– 'the biggest bridge in the world, built in just two years'. And the
following year, on the anniversary of Italy's entry into the First World
War, she experienced the same comforting feeling of belonging to a
great collective whole that she had enjoyed eighteen months earlier
at the time of the protest demonstrations over Trogir. Listening to
the radio as young people all across the country did gymnastics in
unison to orders transmitted from the Foro Mussolini in Rome, she
was overcome by 'a powerful sensation': 'The whole of Italy appeared
to me to be stretching out in its blue sea under its golden sun, with
thousands of strong smiling children on it, as the clear and incisive
words of the Duce greeted them and gave them words of encouragement and comfort.'[67] It was a vision fully in keeping with the regime's
most radiant propaganda posters.

Maria's enthusiasm remained undimmed in the next couple of years.
It reached its zenith in the spring of 1936 with Italy's conquest of
Ethiopia in the face of sanctions by the League of Nations and 'the
cold egoism and the hostility of the whole world'.[68] But during 1937
and 1938 Maria began to experience growing doubts as Italy drifted
closer to Nazi Germany and the regime embarked on policies that
made the young university student wonder if her faith in the regime
had been entirely justified. She feared that the various laws that were
being brought in to 'reform customs' and get rid of such 'bourgeois'
practices as handshaking and the use of the polite form of address,
'Lei', might make the country look ridiculous; and she was deeply
troubled by the introduction from the late summer of 1938 of racial
legislation, which struck her as contrary to all principles of humanity
and justice. The fact that a number of her physics professors were
forced out of their jobs added to her alarm:

> The most beautiful sentiments (love of the fatherland, of the family,
> of work, of humanity) have vanished beneath false ideas. Freedom – of
> thought and the press – is a meaningless word. Books and works of
> art must have one theme only: fascism and the Duce. The newspapers
> sing one chorus: adulation . . . Mussolini himself, whom I once admired

as the most complete genius, seems to me to have lost his sense of equilibrium. Pity has been banished and cruelty, in the form of the campaign against the Jews, has been elevated into patriotism.[69]

The clouds had seemingly parted and the light of reason shone through. Certainly in the next few years, as the racial laws intensified and the country became embroiled in a war for which it was unprepared, alongside a German ally that Maria, like many other Italians, feared and loathed, her hostility to the regime accelerated. But she found it difficult to shake off years of enthusiasm and blind trust and accept that independent thought was morally superior to faith. Back in 1932 she had been enormously comforted to discover that she was capable of allaying the nagging doubts of rationality through immersion in transcendent and selfless joy. Likewise, just two weeks after confiding to her diary her horror at Mussolini's behaviour and the direction that the regime had taken, she happily recorded her elation at the prospect of the Duce coming to Padua on 24 September 1938. Her excitement was so great, indeed, at his impending visit to the city – which took place in the middle of the Czechoslovakian crisis and the threat of European war over Hitler's demands for annexation of the German-speaking Sudetenland – that she found it almost impossible to sleep the night before.[70]

On 24 September Maria joined the crowd of several hundred thousand packed into the Prato della Valle, the largest square in Italy, to listen to Mussolini announce to the world that any attempts by Britain and France 'to settle accounts with the totalitarian states' would find Italy standing shoulder to shoulder with Germany. His speech was interrupted by repeated cheering, rising at the end, when he proclaimed the readiness of the 'entire Italian people' to go to war if necessary, to a near frenzy. Maria was swept along in the excitement:

I did not miss a word of the speech or an expression on his face and came away with a marvellous impression. He is an exceptional man who emanates an immense force, capable of shackling endless multitudes. His face is unique and inimitable, full of strength and sweetness, hard and human. You should have seen how he smiled at the cheering and with what perfect style he made the Roman salute! To behold that face is to feel ready for anything, for any sacrifice, for any struggle . . . I shouted and shouted so much that I lost my voice and was hoarse the whole day, but I felt such enthusiasm as I will never forget.[71]

By the time Italy entered the Second World War a little over eighteen months later, Maria's willingness to be transported by enthusiasm had come to an end. She now looked on fascism with an unwaveringly critical eye: the attack on France was 'an act of cowardice' for which Italy would have to be held to account 'before history', while Mussolini had lost all semblance of genius and become a man whose 'ambition, levity and incapacity to reason' had propelled Italy towards ruin. By the spring of 1941 he was 'a traitor, an anti-patriot and an anti-Italian'.[72] The disenchantment that Maria felt was certainly shared by numerous others, especially, it seems, among the urban middle classes. But the dialogue between faith and reason was by no means simple in the face of adversity, and for many the challenge of war and the threat of defeat often worked to accentuate blind trust – whether from mounting desperation, moral coherence or a sense of honour. Almost invariably in such instances the military disasters that befell Italy were blamed not on Mussolini, but on those around him, who had criminally 'betrayed' their leader. The Duce was thus a victim rather than a culprit. How else could the faith that millions had for so long expressed in him not appear absurdly misguided?

One of those who retained his convictions after 1940 and refused to accept that his belief had been misplaced was Francesco Pinelli. Francesco was a few years younger than Maria, but like Maria his conversion to fascism – as he described it in his memoirs – was the product more of his school and social environment than of parental or family influences. He began to feel drawn to fascism after being sent away to a Catholic boarding school in Pistoia at the beginning of the 1930s when he was twelve. He regarded the austerity and discipline of the college as oppressive and the repeated obligation to get onto his knees and pray as little short of a torment. His moment of liberation came on a Sunday morning towards the end of March 1932 when he attended a fascist rally in Piazza Mazzini and found himself surrounded by a great sea of banners and flags and crowds of men, women and children in uniforms, exultantly singing patriotic songs and hymns. It was a striking contrast to everything that he had been used to. He was thrilled. In the weeks and months that followed he took part in other rallies, and soon felt himself becoming completely captivated by the fascist youth movement.[73]

Individual teachers played an important role in Francesco's political formation. He recalled how a few weeks after the Pistoia rally, on the anniversary of Italy's entry into the war, a young woman teacher whom he particularly liked had talked to his class in a graphic manner about the way in which the troops returning from the front had been derided, rebuked and reviled – words that he had not fully understood at the time, but whose general meaning he had gathered from the context – by socialists and anarchists. The soldiers had even had their medals ripped off them, she had said, and it was only through the greatness of Benito Mussolini – a man who had risen from the humblest of backgrounds – that their dignity and honour had eventually been saved. Francesco had been horrified by what he heard. His father had been in the war and had won four bronze medals and a cross, which he kept proudly in a case back home. The thought that he might have been one of those who had been insulted was horrifying to Francesco. He felt his affection for Mussolini and fascism growing stronger than ever.[74]

After two years at the Catholic boarding school, Francesco moved in 1933 to another school in Pistoia, run by a passionate fascist and officer in the Militia, who greeted everyone with a Roman salute – including any friends or relatives who were visiting the boys. Here Francesco participated in all the activities of the party youth organisations and finally, after a good deal of begging, managed to persuade his father to buy him an Avanguardista uniform. With his commitment to fascism becoming ever more robust, he went on to a college in Prato, where he took a course on fascist and military culture. He found it compelling. He recalled the texts that he had to study – all of them widely prescribed for use in intermediate schools: *Primi elementi di cultura fascista* ('First elements of fascist culture') by Asvero Gravelli, *Cultura fascista* ('Fascist culture') by Giuseppe Steiner, *Corso di cultura militare* ('Course of military culture') by Giuseppe Liguori, *Elementi di cultura militare* ('Elements of military culture') by Alberto Baldini, and a collection of Mussolini's speeches. The teacher, a certain Professor Massa, was inspirational. Francesco was now completely in thrall to the regime.[75]

Just as it was for Maria, the most intoxicating moment for Francesco
came when he saw Mussolini at close quarters. It was in May 1938, on
the occasion of Hitler's visit to Florence. The eighteen-year-old
Francesco was standing with thousands of others in Piazza della
Stazione waving a small tricolour flag that his mother had made and
shouting 'Duce! Duce!' interspersed every now and then with 'Führer'.
Suddenly Mussolini was no more than a few feet away from him, next
to Hitler, his arm outstretched in a Roman salute to acknowledge the
applause of the delirious crowd. He turned in Francesco's direction;
and Francesco had the strong impression, as many did when they
found themselves in proximity to Mussolini, that he was looking
directly into his eyes. The Duce's gaze seemed overpowering, and
Francesco was left with an extraordinary sense of emotional turmoil.
His irrational devotion to the fascist leader remained with him, he
said, for a long time and helped to sustain him when serving in the
army in the dispiriting campaigns in the Balkans and elsewhere
between 1940 and 1943. His spiritual journey away from fascism only
began in earnest after the end of the war. But he confessed that it was
a very slow and painful process.[76]

The difficulty Francesco faced in breaking with fascism was inevitably determined by the degree to which he had pledged himself
emotionally, morally and intellectually to the regime. Depending on
their background, circumstances and character, others certainly found
it easier to put the past behind them; some, harder still. In many parts
of the country, especially the remote rural areas where the party often
enjoyed only a rudimentary presence, fascism resonated faintly most
of the time, and then chiefly through the figure of Mussolini – and
though the image of 'the Duce' was undoubtedly strong enough to
impinge on the minds of millions of peasants, in the end he could
perhaps disappear from their mental landscape without too much
sense of loss. But for millions, especially among the educated middle
classes who had found themselves immersed in a world where party
organisations, schools, newspapers, radios, cinemas and rallies made
it almost impossible to avoid exposure to the powerful emotional
cocktail that constituted fascist 'faith', the imprint of a regime that
lasted for nearly a generation was not so simply removed. And in
emphasising that fascism was a form of 'faith', the regime was able
to draw itself into realms of belief and feeling that frequently went

beyond the trappings of mere public display and penetrated intimate mental recesses.

The diary of the schoolteacher Primo Boccaleri suggests the extent to which fascism could work itself into the moral being of an individual, entwine itself with conventional faith and generate a framework of conviction with the capacity to sustain an individual through adversity. As with many diaries written by civil servants as records of professional activities, there are inevitably questions about how far the language used and sentiments expressed reflect what the writer believed somebody in his position ought to be saying and feeling – even if the document was intended for at most a private audience (of family, say), and not for public scrutiny – rather than mirroring real thoughts and emotions. After all, the expectations placed on teachers, especially primary school teachers, were high: the pedagogic literature of the regime regularly spoke of education in religious terms, with 'mission' as a key concept. Boccaleri himself was praised in one of the most widely circulated journals for teachers, *I Diritti della scuola*, in September 1942 for his 'serene and enthusiastic apostolate, as mobile as an apostle and as constant in his faith as a saint'.[77] But the articulation of such values, if indeed somewhat speciously, is indicative at the very least of a measure of genuine aspiration.

Primo was born in 1909 into a peasant family in the province of Alessandria. His father died when he was young, and a local priest took him under his wing and helped to secure him an education in a seminary. After working for a time in a cotton factory, Primo married in 1936 and trained as a teacher, qualifying in 1939 and taking jobs in various schools around Novara. Following the invasion of Yugoslavia by Italian and German forces in the spring of 1941, he was offered a post in the village of Torrette, a community of some 150 houses and 1,200 inhabitants on the coast of Croatia. Despite opposition from his family, he decided that it was his duty to accept. On 3 December he set off: 'I say goodbye to my wife and relatives. I am serene. In my conscience I feel I am setting out on a great mission for my Fatherland and an imperious fascist commandment to carry out my duty in full and at whatever the cost.' He travelled to Zara, where he met up with a number of other colleagues destined for schools in the newly occupied territory: 'We are animated by the same faith. The same ideal is burning in our veins. Perhaps the same fate awaits us. Without doubt the same victory.'[78]

Like Albina Chiodo in Bagni di Lucca, Primo was shocked at the lack of discipline and the dirtiness of the children in his charge. Their parents seemed little better: they were profligate and inclined to excessive talking; and they lived promiscuously in squalid and overcrowded accommodation. After his first day at the school Primo returned to the small house that he was renting in the village, conscious of the enormity of the task that lay ahead of him. He knelt down and sought inspiration, thinking of his wife, his daughter and Italy:

> Kneeling beside my bed, I pray . . . My mission has begun. I ask God for health so as to give me strength for my work. I pray to God to increase my love for the fatherland and my faith in the Duce. I ask God long to preserve my Duce for the sake of an ever greater fatherland. I ask God to grant me too the victory of life and civilisation in this land.

The following day he felt invigorated by a surge of love and joy – the same sensation of joy that he had experienced when he received his first communion – and he was delighted to discover that when he held up two large pictures of Mussolini and the king the children clapped:

> Duce, Majesty, I am here in your names. I will bring to this land all my heart, my fascist and Italian faith. Duce, I will teach here not only our sweet tongue but also our ideals: at whatever cost.[79]

Primo believed he had two main aims for what he called 'the apostolate of my Italian-ness'. One was to impart the rudiments of civilisation: cleanliness, punctuality and discipline (he made the children salute, and sit and stand in silence for long periods, their hands behind their backs). The other was to engender love for the fatherland and the Duce in a region that the government in Rome believed had always rightfully belonged to Italy. He described the tricolour flag to the children, and after just a week he even tried to teach them 'Giovinezza', despite their ignorance still of Italian. (The prefect of Zara had mildly rebuked him for not having taught it already.) In the evenings he wrote up his diary, his thoughts turning often to Mussolini for guidance in dealing with a population 'that does not even have a sense of civilisation':

Duce, how dear you are to our heart as Italians, to our love as fascists, we your believers, your fighters! You who have restored our cities and our villages; you who have caused the humble but respectable dwellings of our wise and industrious peasants and workers to be kissed by the sun and by health.[80]

In the next few weeks Primo managed to teach the children some patriotic songs and began making them aware of the new civilisation to which they belonged. He was assisted by the village priest, who ensured that Mass was now celebrated in Latin rather than Croat. On 23 March Primo gave his pupils a dictation: 'Today the tricolour flag, white, red and green, is flying in every window in Italy. On 23 March 1919 the Duce founded Fascism and began the war against the communists. The Duce wants peace in the whole world. He wants God in every school and work in every home, and with work, peace and justice.' At the bottom of the page the children had to draw and colour in a fascist banner.[81] On 21 April Primo commemorated the foundation of the city of Rome and delivered a lecture to all the pupils on the greatness of their capital city. On 9 May, the anniversary of the declaration of empire, he recorded in his diary his sense of pride and pleasure at the progress that the local people were making:

The truth is that this fine population is on an accelerated march towards our faith and our life. This is the sweetest and most beautiful joy imaginable, because it is the result entirely of my own hard work each day as a teacher, as an educator, as a fascist.[82]

But Primo's optimism was somewhat misplaced, as the resistance movement against the Italian occupation was becoming quite vigorous in the area, with troops regularly being ambushed and killed by partisan fighters, aided and protected by local people. On 14 June 1942 the Governor of Dalmatia, Giuseppe Bastianini, summoned Primo and other teachers to a meeting and spoke to them angrily about how 'this scum of a population' was repaying 'the love of the Mother Patria'. The fervour with which Bastianini spoke left Primo morally disarmed: exhortations to fascist faith offered little room for contradiction or doubt:

His words are passionate. There is a need to act with inflexible justice. In the next few days the blackshirts under his command will burn down everything, to the last haystack, where an ambush could take place or there might be the slightest sign of revolt. These will be days of fighting, days of *squadrismo*. As a loving father he remembers those who have fallen. He recalls the cowardly kidnapping of the female teacher in Stretto [a few miles down the coast from Torrette], and he swears revenge – and exalts us in the oath we have taken. You cannot be good fascists if in such circumstances you do not feel the need to be ferocious fighters. Return the bite of a dog with the bite of a wolf. Dalmatia, with such orders, will very soon receive its baptism of blood which will purge it of all Yugoslavian original sin, and it will be clothed in the tricolour cloak of justice and peace of our Italy.[83]

Primo was stirred by Bastianini's words, and pledged in his diary to do all he could to help:

Excellency, I have returned home with your orders coursing through the blood in my veins, and I will not move from here until your face is illuminated by the peace that you will have established in this land with justice. I will collaborate with the apostolate or with the revolver, as the occasion requires, in the name of the Duce.[84]

In the next few days he warned the people of Torrette not to listen to those who harboured rebellious feelings; and he told the children to urge their parents to love Italy and have the courage to report anyone who did not. On 17 June a list of those who had sided with the partisans was issued. It included nine families in Torrette. Primo thought this must be a mistake. But when that same day he heard gunfire as Bastianini's men went into action his thoughts moved from any sense of pity towards a reaffirmation of his fascist convictions:

The blackshirts are in action. O why cannot I join them and taste the joy of combat in the service of my Fatherland. I have begged His Excellency the Governor for this great favour. Would that God had granted that he would listen to me. I see the members of the Militia passing who have avenged my colleague kidnapped in Stretto. They have killed some 40 rebels and destroyed their houses . . . The horrors committed show how fully the soul of this people has been brutalised through enslavement by Moscow and perverted by 20 years of former Yugoslavian government.[85]

Not surprisingly the atmosphere in Torrette was now ugly and Primo was forced to close the school. He found himself walking the streets alone, and he feared for his life. His 'mission' to Dalmatia was over. He returned home to his wife and daughter, and continued to serve as a dedicated teacher until his death in Novara in 1965. In September 2009, following a request by the Italian Association of Catholic Schoolteachers, the town council of Novara agreed to honour his memory by naming a park after him on the north side of the city. Just how, in the years after the Second World War, Primo had come to view his passionate engagement with fascism and to what extent he had been able to consider that his faith in the Duce and the regime had been in any sense misguided, is not known. Probably, like millions of others, he had found some way of drawing a line under it, at least in public. The citation read:

Schoolteacher. Born in Piovera (Alessandria) 24/7/1909 – Died in Novara 17/10/1965. Man of learning, of sensitive feelings, educator, capable of transforming general human values into individual educational journeys. Citizen of outstanding human and social vocation.[86]

8

The Politics of Intimacy

Adoring the Duce

Whether the Bologna housewife who wrote 848 letters to Mussolini between 1937 and 1943 had ever enjoyed sexual relations with him is not certain. Quite possibly she had. Though the rambling, neurotically charged and rather obsessive character of much of the correspondence might be taken as consistent with a delusional state of mind, there are strong indications that she had had at least one rendezvous with Mussolini – in Cattolica on the Adriatic coast near to the resort of Riccione where he regularly spent the summer holidays with his family. She clearly seemed to believe that she had given herself to him and that he had reciprocated:

> My great lord and beautiful Duce. I have done nothing but trouble you, but you have always been generous in supporting me, because you have experienced the love that I have felt for you and still feel, and I will always love you. And you too have loved me, and your love has felt so sweet and beautiful that my heart will never forget it. I feel your love strongly, and this gives me the strength to remain yours and wait.

And it was not just a matter of sentiment. In another letter she described the intense physical desires she had experienced on a visit to the Duce's birthplace in Predappio, when she had 'grabbed the dear little bed' and suddenly imagined being alone with him in the house: 'So many kisses and caresses I would give my dear Benito. I would embrace him so he could not escape!'[1]

How many of these letters ever found their way onto the Duce's desk is not known. Like other correspondence posted to Mussolini in

Rome, they were opened by the staff of the Segreteria Particolare del Duce, the office that had principal responsibility for his relations with the general public. The Segreteria Particolare was never officially an organ either of the government or of the fascist party, but it grew rapidly in size and significance in the late 1920s as the cult of Mussolini developed into a central pillar of the regime. By the early 1930s it was employing around fifty civil servants, divided between Palazzo Venezia and Palazzo Viminale, with others drafted in from various ministries as occasion required. It was the task of these officials to sift through the 1,500 or so letters that arrived for Mussolini every day and decide which ones should be forwarded for his personal scrutiny – up to 200 – and which of the remainder merited a positive answer (in which case the Duce would be given credit in the response – otherwise his name was omitted in the reply and an impersonal formula used instead). By the time of Mussolini's fall, the Segreteria had accumulated a massive archive, with more than 565,000 files and millions of cards recording individual items of correspondence. Over 480,000 of the files were sent for destruction in the summer of 1943.[2]

The Bologna housewife was probably just one of the innumerable women whose desire for contact with the Duce had resulted in a fleeting sexual encounter. Mussolini informed Claretta Petacci, his principal mistress in the later 1930s, that most of the women he had made love to he had seen only once and had never met again: 'They were always people who came to me to ask for some favour or other.'[3] In Rome he regularly received female visitors in Palazzo Venezia at 11 a.m., but that did not rule out opportunities at other times. 'I'm tired of all these women', he told Claretta in December 1937, though evidently with the aim more of bragging than complaining. 'I've had so many of them. When I was first in Rome there was a constant stream of women in the hotel. I had four a day. Some of them just went with me once out of curiosity to see how I did it.'[4] Claretta herself was far from being the sole object of the Duce's affections. She had to compete jealously with (among others) two mistresses of much longer standing: Alice Pallottelli De Fonseca, by whom Mussolini had fathered two children – 'they are mine . . . the voice of blood is infallible' – and Romilda Ruspi – whose son he was reluctant to recognise – 'there is nothing of me in him'.[5]

Mussolini was proud of his sexual vigour, and despite the official

image of himself as the dutiful husband of Donna Rachele (Rachele
Guidi, a strong-minded peasant woman from Predappio, whom he
had married in 1915 after having cohabited with her for six years) and
loving father of Edda, Vittorio, Bruno, Romano and Anna Maria, he
was content for an unofficial portrait to circulate of a man of priapic
inclinations. After all, as Carlo Delcroix said in his 1928 biography of
the Duce, *Un uomo e un popolo* ('A man and a people'), those in a position of command had a compelling physical need to love – though he
added that it was important that they did not get distracted emotionally, which is why they were drawn by 'providence' to women who
were 'able to give themselves without demanding in return'.[6] Mussolini
certainly reassured Claretta from time to time that he did harbour
romantic feelings towards her, and even that he loved her, but he was
careful to underline that this was very much contrary to his nature.
Ever since he had been to a brothel as a young soldier, he said, he
had regarded all the women he had been with as 'like those in the
whorehouse. For my carnal satisfaction'.[7] And his appetite was huge:
at one point he claimed he had been seeing fourteen different women,
with three or four coming to him each evening:

> At 8 there was Rismondo, at 9 Sarfatti [Margherita Sarfatti, the well-
> known art patron and critic, and Mussolini's biographer], at 10 Magda
> [Magda Brard, a talented French pianist], and then a fearsome Brazilian
> woman who would have been the death of me if a storm and hurricane
> had not brought down a piece of wall. This gives you an idea of my
> sexuality. I didn't love any of them. I had them because I liked them,
> I enjoyed it.[8]

Though Mussolini endeavoured to keep his lovemaking as perfunctory as possible, there is little doubt that his relations with women
consumed a huge amount of his time. In 1938, as Italy drifted irrevocably into an alliance with Germany and Europe slid towards war, he
typically phoned Claretta a dozen or more times a day to check on
what she was doing, explain how he was trying his best to extricate
himself from his other relationships, allay her insecurities, and arrange
trysts with her. And he often confessed that he could not stop fanta-
sising about her from the moment he woke up. Even when delivering
speeches his mind might be shifting narcissistically between the

delirium of the crowd and the infatuation of his young lover. (He liked nothing better than to sublimate the adrenalin rush on such occasions into passionate sex.)[9] On 23 October 1937, for example, he proudly showed her a recent portrait photograph of himself, pointing out how he could fully understand why women were so attracted to him ('what a strong, powerful chin . . . look at that nose . . . the mouth'), and then invited her to stand hidden just behind the window as he went out onto the balcony of Palazzo Venezia. When the crowd erupted Claretta was swept up by the surge of emotion:

> The shouting becomes frenetic, the roar grows like an explosion, rising with a crash to a frenzy . . . Hats in the air, handkerchiefs, radiant laughing faces . . . They seem mad. It is a delirium, something indescribable, an inexplicable feeling of joy, of love. It is a torment of the soul overflowing into the cry of jubilation.[10]

In most instances, it would seem, the Duce's lovers – past and present – could expect to reap some form of material benefit from their relationship with him, as long as they posed no discernible threat to his reputation. But if there was a suggestion of danger (and the persistence with which the Bologna housewife contacted him led the staff in the Segreteria Particolare to ask questions about her sanity),[11] the response from Mussolini could be much less sympathetic. This was the case with a woman with whom he had had an affair before the First World War, Ida Dalser, and who had borne him a son, Benito Albino, in November 1915. Dalser maintained she was Mussolini's wife; and more alarming from Mussolini's point of view, she may well have had documentary proof of the fact. There are good grounds, indeed, for believing that Mussolini had married Dalser, who came from the Trentino and was thus technically an Austrian subject, in a church service in 1914, and then in December of the following year, while recovering in hospital from an illness contracted at the front, had agreed to marry his long-standing partner, Rachele Guidi, in a civil service, and legitimate their daughter Edda, born in 1910. In the eyes of the Italian state a religious wedding on its own was not legally valid at that time (it was for the Austrian authorities), which would have allowed Mussolini some space for manoeuvre, especially in the chaotic circumstances of the war.[12]

To complicate matters further, Dalser had been the owner of a successful beauty salon in Milan, and in the autumn of 1914, around the time of her probable marriage, she had sold it in order to help Mussolini set up *Il Popolo d'Italia* following his split from the socialist party. She had also been involved in the financial transactions surrounding the creation of the newspaper, and was aware of the huge sums of French capital that had been invested in it. She could thus corroborate the awkward charge that the nationalist Mussolini had in effect 'sold' himself to a foreign power.[13] Dalser was accordingly a great liability to Mussolini as his career developed after the war. Her bitterness towards the man who had betrayed her and economically ruined her meant that she (and her family) had no qualms about lobbying politicians and journalists in a bid to secure reparation. Her story also had the potential to be seized on by Mussolini's enemies, at home and abroad, and used to discredit him. Mussolini did his best to silence her after 1922 – and had as many compromising documents as possible seized (including all the relevant ecclesiastical records, it seems) – but Dalser still posed a big threat.

On 19 June 1926, as Dalser was on her way to a meeting with the Minister of Public Instruction, who was visiting Trento, she was seized, beaten and placed in a straitjacket. She was taken to a police station, where a doctor, who was also a member of the Militia, signed papers ordering her immediate confinement in a mental hospital on the grounds that 'in her present state of over-excitement the insane could cause harm to others'. Dalser's brother-in-law was told to hand over the ten-year-old Benito Albino (whom Mussolini had formally recognised as his son). When he refused, the boy was arrested and assigned to the guardianship of a local party official, before being sent away to various boarding schools. He never saw his mother again. In 1932 his surname was officially changed from 'Mussolini' to 'Bernardi'. He died ten years later in a lunatic asylum near Milan.[14] Ida remained incarcerated in psychiatric institutions for the remainder of her life, first in Trento and later in Venice. She wrote numerous letters of appeal to Mussolini but they never got beyond the walls of the hospitals: the doctors recorded 'graphomania' as a symptom of her insanity. The Duce did not appear to have problems with his conscience: in December 1938, a year after Ida's death, he told Claretta that Dalser had simply been one of the unfortunate 'mistakes' in his life and that she had 'gone mad'. He denied that the boy was his: 'Too many have been attributed to me.'[15]

The issue of bigamy aside, one of the most awkward aspects of the Dalser affair was that it risked undermining a key dimension of the myth of the Duce as it developed during the later 1920s: that of the all-seeing, humane and protective father figure. As the writer Corrado Alvaro observed in 1934, much of the extraordinary appeal of Mussolini to the masses lay in a widespread view that he was in some sense omniscient and could intervene to rectify their wrongs in accordance with an 'old ideal of justice'. And even when he was not aware of a specific grievance, it was commonly felt that he would act to remedy it just as soon as it came to his attention.[16] Mussolini assiduously played up to such beliefs. The editor of *Il Popolo d'Italia* recalled how the Duce telephoned him on one occasion after reading in a newspaper of a mother who was living with triplets, seven other children and a sick husband in a single room, telling him to send someone to the poor woman 'immediately' ('because we must not lose time with the usual bureaucratic headaches') with a gift of 3,000 lire in his name. In reporting the charitable gesture in *Il Popolo d'Italia* the next day, the editor was told to emphasise how Mussolini had spotted the story tucked away in a corner of 'one of the many newspapers that he reads and notwithstanding the huge burden of work that he was saddled with'.[17]

Stories of Mussolini's benevolence abounded and gave rise to what became one of the most pervasive phrases (and sentiments) of the regime: '*se lo sapesse il Duce*' (if only the Duce knew). Anecdotes to substantiate the generosity of the Duce were spread both in print and orally, and their moral charge was often increased by being placed in a context which showed that Mussolini was never too busy with the affairs of state to stop and deal with the plight of an individual. In his 1928 book *Mussolini da vicino* ('Mussolini close up') the well-known writer Paolo Orano described coming across the Duce surrounded by papers, and being asked for his opinion about an author who had just written to request assistance. Orano confirmed that the man in question had indeed had a hard life and was weighed down with debts, and Mussolini promptly declared that he needed to be 'saved' and wrote out a cheque for 10,000 lire – despite the fact that the author was not known to be a fascist sympathiser.[18] Nor was it just financial support that the Duce was willing to find time to provide. Valentina Leonardi was struck by an episode recounted to her by her father, who was a deputy, when Mussolini had been passed a telegram from a Sicilian coastguard as he sat on the ministerial benches during a debate in the Chamber. The telegram had read: 'I beg Your Excellency to make Signor . . ., a coastguard like me, marry my daughter Rosina, whom he has seduced.' Mussolini had smiled and instructed the relevant minister to make sure that the request was granted.[19]

Genuine acts of charitable intervention by the Duce were supplemented by rumours and myths to create a climate of often quite extraordinary expectancy – one which, according to Orano, could probably only be fully explained in religious terms. Whenever something was not right, he noted – a road was poorly maintained, a car was travelling too fast, a school was dirty, streetlights were not working, or somebody was spreading malicious gossip – it had become almost second nature for people of all classes to exclaim: 'If only Mussolini knew! – If only I could tell Mussolini!'[20] That such expressions were not just rhetorical, at least as far as the poor were concerned, is suggested by the way in which stories circulated among the peasantry of the Duce travelling incognito in the countryside to see for himself what was going on and to put things right. The idea of a powerful figure moving secretly in the midst of the common people to remedy their injustices is common to the folklore of many rural societies, but the traditional character of the conceit is just as likely to have been seen as providing confirmation of the likely authenticity of the narrative as indicating its possible speciousness.

Among labourers in the Pontine marshes, for example, numerous tales circulated in the 1930s of chance meetings with Mussolini. Typical was one that an immigrant worker from the Veneto had heard about an old woman foraging for fuel in the countryside near Sabaudia in winter. She had suddenly come across Mussolini out hunting, dressed in large boots and carrying a shotgun over his shoulder. The Duce had asked her what she was doing. She had told him that she was being forced to search for scraps of plants in order to make a fire, as she had no money to buy any wood and was so cold that she could not sleep. He had said: 'Have no fear. Mussolini will send you plenty of wood.'[21] It is not clear in this instance if the supposed encounter had been considered unintentional or if the Duce was thought to have gone hunting deliberately so as to come across ordinary people. However, in most of the Pontine marsh stories the suggestion is that Mussolini was travelling around on his own with the specific aim of meeting the poor, usually on a motorbike and in disguise. Rosina Menin, who had moved to the marshes with her family in 1934 when she was eleven, recalled many years later:

> He was passing our house and came in, and for a time we really couldn't work out who it was, because he was dressed, it seemed, so as not to be recognised. He asked my father two or three questions . . . I was small and wasn't very interested in what he was saying . . . and then he suddenly disappeared . . . He left when he saw that he must have been recognised. He had his motorbike. And he also went on his motorbike to Malconsiglio . . . when there were workers there. And he stopped to ask the workers how things were going and if their companies were paying them well and if they were happy. Then they recognised him and knew who it was: 'It's Benito Mussolini!!!' And he sped off on his motorbike. That's what the workers said . . .[22]

In cases where the story clearly had a more factual basis, it was not uncommon for the narrator to indicate that something quite remarkable or extraordinary had occurred. Tullio Lucetto, for instance, who worked in the Pontine marshes as a young man, recalled seeing Mussolini several times in the early 1930s, and despite the fact that he had been beaten and sent to prison by local fascists for failing to turn up for a parade on a Saturday, he felt no animosity towards the Duce himself. Once Mussolini had come to Latina to thresh wheat, and Tullio remembered how he had stopped after an hour's work, dressed and washed, and gone to the union official to be paid 'just like an ordinary peasant'. On another occasion Mussolini had given an address, and when he had stepped out to speak, 'he looked to me a Christ on earth':

> Even in April it could rain here on feast days, and the weather was bad. Then he arrived . . . and the clouds went and there was sun. It seemed like something from God. And when he had finished making all his speech, down came the water again. How often did we think: was this Duce some kind of Saint Anthony or what![23]

The idea that the Duce was endowed with remarkable powers and yet was at the same time down to earth and unexceptional – 'like an ordinary peasant' – was at the heart of much of his popular appeal. It encouraged the belief that he was highly accessible and that intimate contact with him was both natural and (for him, too) welcome. At times the combination of proximity and awe could lead to what might look, paradoxically, like irreverence, as the young Zelmira Marazio found on one occasion when travelling on a train through the Pontine marshes in the mid-1930s – and her discomfort appears to have been shared by her fellow passengers. While she and others in the carriage were gazing out of the windows at the expanses of well-farmed and drained fields with their straight new roads and gleaming white urban settlements, a middle-aged man suddenly turned and exclaimed:

> Do you see, do you see all this cultivated and fertile land? Until yesterday this was a land of poverty and malaria. Who has brought about this transformation? An ordinary little man ['*ometto*'], yes, an ordinary little man has managed to do all this. An ordinary little man with a big heart and an even bigger head. He has created a new Italy.

A 'murmur of approval' rippled through the compartment – and Zelmira joined in, though she smiled at the thought that the word '*ometto*' was quite inappropriate to use about the Duce.[24]

The 'ordinariness' of Mussolini in the eyes of the general public was reinforced by the huge emphasis that was placed on his role as a family man. Though in reality he was never very close to his wife or children (his brother Arnaldo was probably his only true confidant), the carefully controlled publicity surrounding his domestic life created an image of relative normality onto which millions of Italians could map themselves. Episodes such as the premature death of Arnaldo in 1931, the affliction of his daughter Anna Maria with polio in 1936, the death of his second son Bruno in 1941, and the weddings of three of his children in the 1930s, provided occasions for mass outpourings of emotion, with hundreds of thousands sending letters, telegrams, poems and gifts of every kind to express their commiserations or congratulations. Members of Mussolini's family were themselves frequent targets of requests for help, with children writing to whichever son or daughter seemed appropriate, asking for intercession with their father, while women in particular approached Donna Rachele ('Noble Lady', 'Most Gentle Noble Lady', 'Most Excellent Signora', 'Noble Signora', 'Distinguished Signora', 'First Lady of Italy') requesting her direct assistance or else intervention with her husband.

The desire to feel organically linked to Mussolini and his family found additional expression in the names given to children – there was a surge in boys being christened Bruno, for instance, in 1941 – or in requests to the Duce to stand as godfather to a newborn child. The incidence of people writing to Mussolini to inform him that their most recent offspring would be called 'Benito', or 'Italia', or 'Romano', or some other suitably fascist or patriotic name appears to have gone up during the war, perhaps as a consequence of a genuine hope that it might bring luck in difficult times as much as from any calculation of possible material reward ('At dawn this auspicious day is born our fourteenth daughter to whom we will give the fateful name Italia. Stop . . . We raise devoted thought to beloved Duce wishing for greater fortunes for beloved fatherland', a peasant couple telegraphed Mussolini on the anniversary of the March on Rome in 1941).[25] Many opted for 'Vincere' ('Win') which presumably had to be discarded or changed into something less embarrassing such as 'Vincenzo' after 1943. The letters and telegrams asking Mussolini to be the godfather at a baptism also seem to have increased in the war, though there is no indication that these requests were ever granted.[26]

From a political point of view, the most significant dimension of the engagement of the masses with Mussolini's family lay in the development of Predappio into a focal point for the cult of the Duce. As in the case of many Christian shrines – Loreto, for instance, or Assisi – the site derived much of its emotional charge from a conspicuous combination of the humble with the exceptional. A tour included a visit to the simple house where the Duce had been born in 1883, with its peasant furniture (Mussolini specified that the mattresses should be stuffed with maize leaves), the nearby church of Santa Rosa of Lima – built in 1925–28 in honour of his mother, Rosa Maltoni, the local schoolteacher – and the cemetery of San Cassiano, where visitors could hear Mass and pay their respects at the tombs of his parents. San Cassiano was extensively rebuilt between 1929 and 1932 around the Mussolini family chapel and crypt, to act as the culminating point of 'pilgrimages' to the town.[27] The body of Mussolini's father, Alessandro, the village blacksmith, was moved to the cemetery in 1932 from its original resting place in Forlì: after his wife's death in 1905, Alessandro had gone to run an inn, 'The *bersagliere*', on the outskirts of Forlì, together with his mistress, Anna Guidi. She already had five daughters, and one of them, Rachele, in due course became Mussolini's wife.

The number of visitors to Predappio increased rapidly from the later 1920s, with mass trips being arranged by the party, schools, military associations, sports clubs, and all kinds of professional bodies. The parish priest of San Cassiano, Don Pietro Zoli, kept a register of signatures in the cemetery and proudly passed on to Mussolini information about how many people had attended each day, with indications as to their provenance and social background ('every class of person . . . from all parts of Italy and abroad').[28] Newspapers also carried regular reports, especially when prominent individuals were involved: the king and other members of the royal family came to pay their respects in 1938. By the time the town had reached the height of its development in the later 1930s, with the construction of a broad central avenue (Via Benito Mussolini), a large piazza where visitors could assemble before going up the simple wooded footpath to Mussolini's birthplace, a party headquarters in a severe modernist style, and a massive new church dedicated to Saint Anthony of Padua, some 5,000 a day were signing Don Pietro's register. However, with special trips organised by local party associations, the numbers could be much greater – as in June 1937, when Pesaro decided to demonstrate its devotion to the Duce by sending 15,000 of its townspeople to Predappio.[29]

The regime encouraged visitors to Predappio to act as if they were 'pilgrims' and to display the appropriate sense of respect and devotion. Many perhaps saw the trip chiefly as an opportunity to enjoy themselves on a day out with friends, and acquire postcards or other souvenirs (the theft of maize leaves from the mattresses was a constant problem).[30] But the indications from letters and other sources are that the conscious replication in Predappio of the traditional features of a Catholic pilgrimage often encouraged feelings of a genuinely religious nature (perhaps at times overlaid with sexual impulses). A report on a typical trip made in 1937 by 820 members of the party's national association of peasant women (*massaie rurali*) certainly suggests some spontaneous reverence:

The previous evening, the *massaie rurali* decorated coaches and lorries with wild flowers from their fields and they also brought enormous bunches of them to lay on the tombs [of the Duce's parents]. The endless queue of *massaie*, in their characteristic costumes and their arms filled with flowers, was a splendid, lovely sight . . . Then the *massaie* heard a mass for Mussolini's parents, celebrated in the Predappio church . . . Then, with religious emotion they visited the Duce's house, poor, rustic like their own, where a mother has worked, loved, suffered, living a life like theirs, simple and loving, a life of sacrifice and happiness, teaching Her Great Son goodness, discipline and self-sacrifice.

One *massaia* was reported to have 'religiously kissed' everything she could touch in the house.[31]

As this report suggests, the impulse towards intimacy sprang as much, if not more, from the idea that Mussolini inhabited a different sphere as from a feeling that he was at the end of the day just an '*ometto*', an ordinary little man – the offspring of a humble schoolteacher and a village blacksmith. Among the thousands of letters that each week reached the Segreteria Particolare del Duce from men, women and children across the country were a fair proportion that looked to engage with Mussolini using both the language and the forms of prayer. Given the emphasis placed by the regime on the 'cult of the Duce' and more generally on the category of faith, the deployment of religious templates may in some cases have been part of a calculated desire to ingratiate. Often, though, the letters were of such an intense and sustained character, above all when triggered by an important event – Mussolini's escape from an assassination attempt in June 1932, the declaration of empire in May 1936, the Munich agreement of September 1938 – that it is hard to avoid the impression that they were, as the writers themselves frequently admitted, the product of a spontaneous emotional 'out-pouring'.

A good example of how intimacy could be stimulated by religious reverence is a letter written by a young woman in Genoa after listening to a speech of Mussolini on the radio on 30 March 1938 describing the readiness of Italy's armed forces for war and his own role as commander in any future conflict (he was made First Marshal of the Empire that same day). As so often with female admirers, the language is suffused with an overtly erotic dimension:

Forgive me if I, just a humble woman, dare to write to you and use [the familiar form of] 'tu'. But when I turn to God I do not use [the formal] 'Voi' or 'Lei' and You [Tu] for me are a God, a supernatural being sent to us by a superior power to guide our beautiful Italy to the destiny assigned to it when Romulus and Remus founded Rome, which will become, if you continue to guide us, mistress of the world . . . You, my Duce, are the greatest soldier, and what is more important the most loved . . . Forgive me again, but my heart was so filled with enthusiasm by your divine words transmitted through the radio that I had to unburden myself and tell you of all the admiration and all the love that we women feel as well and how your words inspire the most vivid and genuine enthusiasm. My Duce, for a long time you have been talking of coming to Genoa. Genoa awaits you with all its heart, and I have such a desire to see you even if only at a distance and confirm that you are not a myth, but a man, and hear for once your passionate words not through the radio but from your lips. I am waiting for you soon, my Duce . . .[32]

There seems little reason to doubt that this young woman felt her forwardness was justified by a genuine belief that Mussolini had an exalted, almost divine, status. It seems quite likely, too, that her desire for close contact with the Duce was fuelled by the growing uncertainty of the situation in Europe in the late 1930s and the threat of war. The many tens of thousands of letters, cards and telegrams sent to Mussolini in the wake of the Munich agreement, mostly by women (men, certainly young men, inevitably felt more constrained in celebrating such an event), hailing him, typically, as 'the man destined by Providence for the salvation of the peace of Europe', indicate just how much hope resided in him at this time and how readily in these circumstances he became invested with a religious aura.[33] And the fact that similar language and sentiments can be found in private diaries, such as that of the seventeen-year-old Tuscan schoolgirl Athe Gracci, where there was clearly no intention to flatter or secure personal gain, suggests that the religious dimension of the image of the Duce was largely spontaneous (and buttressed in her case, too, by palpably strong romantic feelings).

Athe was a highly intelligent and articulate young woman from the small town of Pontedera, with a yearning to escape the seclusion and boredom of her provincial life (and her oppressive father). The diary she kept from 1938 was largely an account of a stormy love affair, in which her passion for her boyfriend was counterpointed with her often no less intense feelings for God, Italy and Mussolini. In April 1939, after breaking up (temporarily) with Enzo, she wrote in her diary of the sense of 'liberation' that she was now experiencing:

> Now that I have no love . . . I am passionate about political events. It is like a liberation . . . For I have a heart that needs to love, and I now feel great satisfaction in the love of my Fatherland, as I love the Duce above everything else. Because the Duce makes me tremble with excitement, because I only need to hear his words to be transported in heart and soul into a world of joy and greatness.[34]

In the months that followed, Athe's love for the Duce became inter-woven with her anxieties about the situation in Europe. On 30 August 1939, with the Second World War about to break out, she found herself confiding her hopes and fears to her diary in a prayer-like form:

> O Duce, Duce of our life, commander of an entire people, everyone places their love in you, everyone hopes in you, and if you do not succeed in securing peace, your people will still be faithful to you; and we will admire every aspect of you just the same: your smile, your words, your actions. Thank you, O Lord, for having given to Italy the pride and joy of a unique man, the pride and joy of having a man admired and envied by all the world.[35]

By now Athe was back together with Enzo, and when Italy entered the war on 10 June 1940, she was able to encapsulate her feelings of hope and trepidation at what might lie ahead in a simple and laconic formula: 'I love the Duce, I love Enzo, above everything else.'

However strong the psychological and cultural impulses impelling people 'spontaneously' towards the Duce, the regime itself also set out deliber-ately to promote close contact with the leader. The liberal state was criticised for having failed to bridge the gap between the masses and the institutions – between 'real' and 'legal' Italy. Fascism intended to rectify this. The steady stream of letters that ordinary Italians sent each day to Mussolini was a material equivalent to the ecstatic cheering of crowds and an indication of the regime's spiritual dynamism. (Silence, by contrast, signalled failure: 'In recent times the requests for my photograph have dropped sharply', Mussolini lamented in the summer of 1943.)[36] As Arnaldo Mussolini explained in *Il Popolo d'Italia* in May 1926 in a piece entitled 'The Man and the Crowd', the manner in which Italians felt drawn enthusiastically towards the Duce showed how fascism had successfully overcome the disorientation of the previous regime and tapped into popular cravings for 'spiritual unity' and 'order'.[37] Another article in the same newspaper the following year stressed how important it was for a people historically prone to anarchy and individualism to be directed with 'unanimous discipline' towards an 'infallible' leader.[38]

Similarly, contacting the Duce was encouraged as a mark of faith, a sign of an individual's willingness to open his or her soul to the leader. Many commentators linked such a manifestation of intimacy to the feelings of religiosity that fascism believed was essential to political life. According to the journalist Giorgio Pini, writing in 1927, a people needed to have a focal point towards which to direct its 'civil religiosity'; and this was particularly the case in Italy, which had always lacked a great figure to 'act as a national symbol, a divinity, a unifying myth and a source of inspiration'. Mussolini, with his 'complete human personality', he suggested, fulfilled this role in a way that neither Cavour, nor Mazzini, nor Garibaldi had been able to do.[39] In this context, an unburdening of the heart to the Duce, especially in times of difficulty, could be regarded as a laudable political gesture. By the 1930s such highly personalised forms of communication had come to be regarded as quite normal. 'When do you write a letter to Mussolini?' asked *Corriere della Sera* in an article in 1936:

> Not always, but on practically every occasion, at a difficult time in your life . . . When you are looking around and don't know who to turn to any more, you remember that He is there. Who, but Him, can help you? . . . The Duce knows that when you write to him it is out of genuine sorrow or real need. He is the confidant of everyone and, as far as he can, he will help anyone . . . And where is the Duce? . . . He is anywhere. He is even – have you not felt it? – in that gloomy little room downstairs where you, poor thing, were writing of your sufferings. Have you not felt that he was listening to you?[40]

Another factor contributing to the huge volume of correspondence with Mussolini was, somewhat paradoxically, the ideological weakness of fascism. Commentators from a very early stage had pointed out that support for the government, especially in the south, derived far less from belief in the party or what the party stood for than from admiration for the Duce. And this situation persisted, aggravated by the inability of the regime to establish doctrinal coherence. 'While I would have liked it to be monolithic', recalled the journalist Ugo Indrio of the 1930s, 'I realised that within fascism there were various fascisms, various currents . . . and that the only unifying element was the myth of the leader and his presumed infallibility.'[41] The lack of clarity as to what exactly fascism represented made the figure of Mussolini, as much by default as by design, the emotional lynchpin of the regime. For fascists of a strongly intellectual persuasion this was deeply galling. 'Mussolini', wrote Giuseppe Bottai in his diary in May 1943, in near despair at the lack of initiative being displayed by all those around him as the country slumped towards defeat, 'has stripped us of those very qualities with which we could and should have served him. What use is faith when you have no idea what you are having faith in? Faith to a man, in politics, can only be faith in the ideas that he incarnates. Take away the ideas, and all you have left is corporeal, physical faith.'[42]

Linked to the ideological hollowness of fascism was also a deep dissatisfaction, which intensified in the course of the 1930s, with both the state and the party bureaucracy. Despite the regime's claims to be forging new men and women and ridding the country of the vices that had bedevilled liberal Italy, corruption and clientelism proliferated on what appears to have been an unprecedented scale. The PNF, which expanded rapidly during the 1930s under the secretaryship of the dull-witted and zealous Achille Starace, reaching a membership of more than 2.5 million by the end of the 1930s, became almost synonymous with malpractice, with unscrupulous local party officials using their positions to feather their own nests and favour relatives and friends. Nor was the party leadership in any way immune. Indeed it is hard to find a single senior figure who was not at some point the subject of allegations of serious misconduct. In a few cases, such as that of the Milan *ras*, Mario Giampaoli, who was accused of financial and sexual corruption, blackmail, extortion, drug-taking and gambling, or the Bologna boss, Leandro Arpinati, who faced similar charges, action was taken: both were sent to *confino*. But in many instances very little or even nothing was done.[43]

The pervasive feelings of frustration and anger at the inefficiency and corruption of the regime had the curious effect of helping to elevate the Duce into a position of apparently blameless isolation high above the fray. The fact that Mussolini himself was regarded as self-sacrificing and wholly honest (and he was certainly not financially rapacious) assisted the process. From his exalted position, it was hoped, Mussolini would be able to intervene to sort things out once he was informed of what was going on. Hence the ubiquity of the phrase 'if only the Duce knew'. Reports from OVRA in the 1930s suggest that this rather paradoxical tendency for discontent with the party or the local administration to strengthen faith (or at least hope) in the Duce was most pronounced among the poorer classes. Agents frequently noted, not without surprise, how Mussolini was widely seen by ordinary people, especially in more remote rural areas, as ignorant of what was going on and as 'betrayed' rather than as personally responsible for what was taking place. As one informant wrote in August 1932:

> In a rapid tour around southern Italy we have been able to observe how public opinion is almost everywhere – and strangely – becoming ever more sympathetic to the Duce and ever less so to Fascism, which is viewed through the prism of local squabbles and the conduct of party leaders. This conduct is not always – indeed is hardly ever – exemplary . . . The masses seem every day to become more and more attached to the Duce, who is never blamed in any way at all for the faults that are attributed to the local party officials.[44]

If dissatisfaction with the local situation engendered the desire, or perhaps the need, to keep the figure of the Duce in an uncontaminated moral bubble, the rancorous disputes and rivalries that characterised the life of the fascist party also encouraged professions of faith in Mussolini. The infighting and the ease with which anyone in office might fall from grace created an atmosphere of pervasive insecurity, and expressions of devotion to the Duce might afford a measure of protection against the vagaries of political life. Mussolini exploited this situation by maintaining extensive files on the misdemeanours of senior party figures and using the information as a tool for keeping them loyal. This worked particularly well in the case of potentially awkward individuals like the radical ex-secretary of the PNF, Roberto Farinacci, one of the most notoriously corrupt figures in the regime, who dominated the life of his home town of Cremona as if it was a personal fiefdom, abusing and manipulating the law almost at will. Mussolini amassed enormous dossiers on his financial, sexual and other offences, but ensured that he remained broadly acquiescent by turning a blind eye to most of them.[45]

The mechanisms whereby the corruption, competitiveness and insecurity of much of provincial life might work to foster the cult of the Duce is well illustrated by the case of a young Sardinian writer, Edgardo Sulis. Edgardo was born in 1903 into a middle-class family in the small town of Villanovatulo in the province of Cagliari. His father, Antonio, had backed fascism from an early date and during the 1920s his fortunes had risen, enabling him to acquire a number of substantial properties around the town. But by the end of the decade rumours and anonymous letters had begun to circulate that the family was living beyond its means and that Antonio's administrative practices in the local branch of the Istituto di Credito Agrario per la Sardegna, of which he was secretary and cashier, might not be entirely above board. Among the principal enemies of the family was the *podestà* of Villanovatulo. When a government inspector was brought in to examine the books of the Istituto, he found a deficit of 42,000 lire and indications of forgery. On 16 May 1932 Antonio committed suicide. In a final letter he stressed that he died believing still in fascism and recalling as evidence of his faith how he had supported Mussolini in the difficult times that had followed the Matteotti crisis.[46]

Edgardo now set out to restore his family's honour and fortunes. His first tactic was to rally as many 'friends and partisans' to his cause as he could and undertake a systematic campaign of denigration of his father's enemies, including the *podestà*. But this proved ineffective, as official inquiries turned up nothing of any significance against the *podestà*. Edgardo then decided on a more extreme course of action. In August 1932 he and his brother Italo incited their followers to break into the offices of the town hall and denounce the *podestà* and his administration, 'exploiting the discontent which more or less openly always courses through the population of a place like this', as a police report explained, 'both because of its native riotousness and the profound hostility elicited by any demand for payment by the communal authorities'. Edgardo – whom the prefectural authorities described as a young man consumed with 'vanity and megalomania' – and Italo were arrested for this serious breach of the peace, found guilty and sentenced to *confino* in a mountain town in Molise.[47]

Edgardo's future looked bleak, but he possessed a secret weapon: a hymn to the Duce that he was planning to publish under the title *Imitation of Mussolini* – an allusion to the famous fifteenth-century devotional work by Thomas à Kempis, *The Imitation of Christ*. Fascism, according to Edgardo, was 'the new political religion', whose truths had been revealed by Mussolini, 'the incarnation of the glories and the sufferings of the Italian people': 'O Comrade, you who come from the era of materialism, you must believe in the Fatherland without seeing it, as you believe in the existence of God. Who guarantees for you the existence of God? His Church. Who guarantees for you the existence of the Fatherland? Fascism'. The Duce had 'sacrificed the dragon of the regions, the ogre of municipalism, the solitary beast of separatism to the Nation', and he had given his people a sense of mission. And he himself was a paragon of virtue: 'You should imitate Mussolini alone. You should have no other model but Mussolini.' And 'imitation' entailed experiencing a 'love which invades every thought and action, sometimes so unconsciously that you are sublimated . . . into perfection'.[48]

Edgardo wrote to Mussolini and asked him to provide a preface to the volume. He said that his dream was to repay the family's debts through his literary efforts and restore the honour of his father. 'It is a holy work', he claimed. Whether moved by Edgardo's personal plight or impressed by the book itself, the Duce signalled his favour through the Segreteria Particolare and the *Imitation of Mussolini* was able to proceed towards publication. This allowed Edgardo to start appealing against his *confino* sentence. He was now the author of a forthcoming work of unimpeachable fascist orthodoxy – and towards the end of 1933, shortly before the book came out, Edgardo and his brother were allowed to leave Molise. Even better, once the *Imitation of Mussolini* appeared in print, Edgardo found himself welcomed into influential intellectual circles and in the summer of 1934 he had an official audience with Mussolini himself along with other writers and journalists.

He began to receive a monthly stipend from the Duce's secret funds, and in the course of the next few years he was able to secure substantial supplementary grants in return for agreeing to write whatever might please Mussolini: 'Do with me what You like, order me as You will, since Your command and only Your command has the force of goodness'. His professions of faith in the Duce had paid off.[49]

Quite what the balance was in Edgardo's mind between calculation and sincerity in his paeans to the Duce cannot be known with any certainty. But in the case of many of the leading figures of the regime the manifestations of devotion were clearly genuine. Giuseppe Bottai, for instance, felt deeply hurt by the Duce's growing coolness and detachment in the later 1930s, and he recorded his pain in his diary. The final straw came on 17 January 1941 when he received a perfunctory phone call from Mussolini, telling him, without a glimmer of human warmth, it seemed, that he was being sent to fight on the Greek front. He was left devastated:

I put down the receiver, mechanically. I gaze ahead of me into the void. My fourth war arrives in this way, dehumanised, from my Leader. A terrifying solitude. Something that for more than twenty years had been beating in my heart suddenly stops: a love, a faith, a devotion. Now I am alone, without my Leader.[50]

Three days later he added as a further reflection:

A Leader is everything in the life of a man: his beginning and his end, his aim and his purpose, his point of departure and his finishing line. If he goes, there is a searing loneliness inside. I would like to rediscover my Leader, restore him to the centre of my world, rearrange this world of mine around him. I am afraid, truly afraid, that I will not be able to do this again.[51]

But despite the sense of being rejected, he refused to acknowledge any diminution in his own loyalty. Before going into action, he wrote to his wife from the front line in March 1941:

I did not receive from my Leader as I left the salute from man to man, which my soul as a faithful follower alone longed for. But I am faithful to him, through and beyond this pain that I bear inside me like a cross, and I dedicate my death to him . . .'.[52]

Bottai's intimate relationship with Mussolini had a strong physical as well as spiritual dimension. He was fascinated by the Duce's every gesture and expression, and he liked to observe his body closely and analyse its changing contours.[53] In December 1935 he recorded in his diary how Mussolini had grown more refined and noble in appearance over the years as he had increased in moral stature. He noted specifically how his hands, which had seemed 'immense, gnarled and powerful' at their first meeting in Milan in 1918, when Mussolini had picked up and shown him a hand grenade on his desk, had now become 'small, delicate and almost feminine, like those of a midwife'.[54] Another prominent figure in the regime whose love of the fascist leader had a pronounced physical element was the Duce's son-in-law, Galeazzo Ciano. He sought almost slavishly to imitate Mussolini's poses, facial expressions, staccato delivery and exaggerated cadences, and, as his diary indicates, he relished being in close proximity to him on a near daily basis. In the final entry, after he was dismissed as Foreign Minister in February 1943, he wrote: 'Our parting was cordial. This makes me very pleased, because I love Mussolini, I love him very much, and what I will miss most will be the contact with him'.[55]

Tullio Cianetti, who was a member of the Grand Council from 1934, confessed in the memoirs he wrote in prison in 1943–44 that his relationship with the Duce had been based on a form of infatuation that had prevented him from seeing reality. Whenever doubts had entered his mind, his 'faith' had demanded that he put them aside. Even the chain of military disasters after 1940 had not done much to alter his feelings: he had become used to what he called 'Mussolinian miracle-working', and for over twenty years had been brought up in 'the political school that makes individuals act and think in terms of the man who knows, foresees and achieves everything, leading them to exaggerate the divinatory gifts of the dictator'.[56] In April 1943, less than three months before the Allies landed in Sicily, Cianetti was appointed Minister of Corporations. He could hardly contain his joy at working alongside a 'man I have loved so much' and 'a great figure of history'.[57] He wrote excitedly to Mussolini:

I 'sense you' Duce, because all the best part of my spiritual life has been illuminated by Your faith, which is our faith, the faith of every Italian . . . I feel proud, Duce! I do not know, Duce, if I have what it takes to be a Minister; but I know how immense my faith is in You. From my painful childhood, to my youth and my combative adulthood, I have learned that the heart, and thus faith, can reach where the brain cannot go. And, I swear, it is to faith that I will principally look to guide me so that I can always be worthy of your esteem.[58]

The economics of intimacy

The majority of the many millions of Italians who wrote to Mussolini did so because they faced economic hardship. Requests for subventions, jobs, pensions, the award of contracts, or assistance with securing loans or sorting out bureaucratic problems, had long been part of the clientelistic politics on which liberal Italy had been built. Deputies had depended for electoral success largely on promising to reward their voters with financial concessions extracted from the government. The abolition of elections under fascism had certainly not ended clientelism at a local level, as the career of Roberto Farinacci and many other provincial *ras* amply demonstrated, but the emergence of the cult of the Duce as the central pillar of the regime had greatly encouraged people to turn directly to the head of government for aid. This trend accelerated in the early 1930s as the regime increased its programmes of welfare support in response to the ravages of the Great Depression. Though clientelistic practices were in some respects officially frowned on as inherently servile and thus unbecoming of the 'new' Italian, in reality little was done to discourage supplications to Mussolini. What better sign of faith was there than having the humility and the trust to turn in one's hour of supreme need to the Duce?

From the outset fascism had regarded itself as a movement of the spirit, determined to counter the corrosive materialism of both liberalism and socialism, and when it came to power it had no specific new policies for dealing with the widespread unemployment and poverty in the country. Nor did it hold out to the masses any new dreams of economic betterment to replace those that it had left brutally shattered in the destruction of the socialist movement. Many of the government's early initiatives were intended primarily to allay the anxieties of the establishment and win over the conservative business community. Reduced public expenditure, the lowering of tariffs, and the abolition of various taxes contributed to the boom in manufacturing that occurred (as elsewhere in Europe) in 1923–25. In agriculture, the 'battle for grain' was of benefit principally to large arable farmers. So, too, was the programme of 'integral land reclamation', which was introduced from the later 1920s with the aim of raising production levels through extensive investment in irrigation works, road building and reafforestation. Private landowners were supposed to contribute to the cost of the schemes, but in the absence of serious penalties for non-compliance, many failed to do so.[59]

The increased state control over labour that took place in the second half of the 1920s, with the monopoly of workers' representation by fascist unions and the banning of strikes, was widely talked about as a staging post towards what was known as 'corporativism'. Many leading fascists had been influenced by the pre-war ideas of the revolutionary syndicalists. They had talked of constructing a more modern and equitable political system by having every economic category in the country – employers as well as employees – represented on an equal footing within corporations so that the nation's resources could be harnessed rationally to the needs of the collectivity: a so-called 'third way' between capitalism and socialism. But in practice fascism was never in a position to control the industrialists to the same degree as the workers, and though some government measures – such as the revaluation of the lira in 1926–27 – were taken in opposition to the wishes of parts of the business community, the fascist economy in general tended to favour the middle classes more than the peasants and urban labourers.

The deflationary policies of the later 1920s that followed the revaluation of the lira, together with the still-limited industrial base of the country, meant that the Great Depression had a less severe impact on Italy than on many other European states. However, there was still considerable hardship. Wages were cut by around 25 per cent between 1928 and 1934; and although the cost of living also dropped sharply during the same period, the fact that the average working week was reduced by about 10 per cent meant that many industrial labourers were probably on balance worse off than before. Some fascist leaders welcomed the economic asperity for the improvements that it might bring to the Italian character. Bottai suggested that it would 'have valuable psychological and moral consequences by enforcing a more rigorous way of living'.[60] The most damaging effects of the depression were felt in the countryside, where the shift towards wheat production that the 'battle for grain' had encouraged was accelerated by the collapse of the export market for goods such as citrus fruit, olives, nuts and wine. Small peasant farmers now faced serious difficulties. Unemployment rose sharply and consumption declined, especially in the southern regions, where the traditional safety valve of overseas emigration and remittances had been shut off as a result of the United States and other countries introducing strict quotas after the war.

The government responded to the country's economic hardships with an enormous increase in state expenditure. In the 1930s the outlay on welfare schemes, including maternity benefits and family allowances, went up from 1.5 billion to 6.7 billion lire – more than 20 per cent of the country's total receipts from taxation – thereby creating the prototype of a modern welfare state.[61] The pace of land reclamation projects and other public works programmes accelerated, and the regime was able to claim that it had spent more in this field in just ten years than liberalism had done in sixty.[62] Two important new agencies were established – the Istituto Mobiliare Italiano (IMI, 1931) and the Istituto per la Ricostruzione Industriale (IRI, 1933) – to rescue ailing banks and businesses. IRI in particular proved immensely important for the development of the Italian economy, intervening to save enterprises ranging from steelworks, shipyards and shipping lines to electrical and machine-tool industries and the telephone system. The aim initially was to provide capital and managerial advice that would enable companies to be restored to financial health and then sold back to the private sector, but in practice many of the firms remained fully or partially under the control of the state. On the eve of the Second World War it was estimated that the Italian state owned a larger proportion of the industrial sector than any other European country outside the Soviet Union.[63]

The regime liked to present IRI as an aspect of the 'corporativist state'. This was inaugurated in 1934 with the creation of twenty-two vertically structured corporations of employers and workers, each (supposedly) articulating the needs of a different sector of the economy.

But in practice IRI remained largely independent of these new institutions. Indeed the corporations turned out to be much less important than government propaganda initially claimed. In theory they were supposed to regulate wages, levels of production and conditions of work in accordance with the general needs of the community, but in practice their powers remained limited, with most of the key economic decisions continuing to be made by the party-controlled workers' unions, the autonomous employers' organisation, Confindustria, and Mussolini. But this did not stop an enormous amount being written in Italy and abroad about the corporativist state. In 1935 the anti-fascist historian Gaetano Salvemini, who had emigrated to the United States to teach at Harvard, noted how 'Italy ha[d] become the Mecca of political scientists, economists and sociologists' eager to examine a system that appeared to offer a revolutionary solution to the evils of both capitalist individualism and communist collectivism.'[64]

As many reports from prefects, party officials and OVRA agents revealed, the government initiatives in the early 1930s to mitigate the effects of the Great Depression greatly enhanced the standing of the Duce in the country. 'The overwhelming majority of the population, not least because of the blind faith that it has in the head of the government, [is] convinced that the regime is doing everything possible to weather the world storm . . . It is now a general conviction that all that could be done to alleviate the hardship faced by the working classes has been swiftly implemented by the government.'[65] The widespread feeling (assiduously fostered by propagandists) that fascism was showing itself better able to provide effective answers to the great political and economic problems posed by the twentieth century than other political systems, did much to undermine any residual sympathies in Italy for the liberal or socialist opposition.[66] By the time the regime celebrated its tenth anniversary in 1932 – a year that culminated in the inauguration of the Via dell'Impero in the centre of Rome and the opening of the Exhibition of the Fascist Revolution – there was a remarkable feeling throughout the country of a nation united around an adored and internationally envied leader.

Some sense of the intensity of feelings binding Italians to the Duce at this time can be gauged from the many tens of thousands of telegrams and letters that poured into the Segreteria Particolare del Duce in response to the thwarted attempt on Mussolini's life by an anarchist in June 1932. The common theme running through the often fervid expressions of gratitude at his deliverance, sent in by men and women from all walks of life – from deputies, party officials, archbishops, priests, civil servants and professionals, to the humblest workers and peasants (many of them scarcely literate) – was that of an act of attempted 'parricide' in a community conceived of as an extended family that was both divinely ordained and divinely protected. And since 'Providence' was manifestly working to safeguard Mussolini and Italy (and the two were commonly seen as identical – 'you are Italy and God has consecrated Italy to the glory, the victory and the life of the world'), the enemies of the country were necessarily considered 'traitors' who merited no mercy. And since, too, Mussolini was the 'father' of the nation, his 'sons' had a duty to avenge him. Some of the most intimate and passionate letters were those that offered their personal services, or those of their children, to help track down and kill 'the repugnant serpents' that were threatening the life and future of Italy.[67]

Many of those who appealed to the Duce for financial or other help did so from a belief that he occupied a position of absolute power and also from a sense that he would view supplicants with the kindness of a father and the charity of a man blessed by God. In the innumerable letters that reached the Segreteria Particolare in the 1930s from peasants in the province of Rovigo – a province that in the immediate post-war years had been almost entirely dominated by the socialist movement led by the local deputy Giacomo Matteotti – Mussolini's omnipotence and benevolence resonate like leitmotifs:

'I turn to You who does all and can do everything . . .'

'For us Italians you are our God on earth, and so we turn to you faithful and certain of being heard . . .'

'All our hope is in You whom we love as a father . . .'

'Duce, I venerate you as the Saints should be venerated . . .'

'Excellency, I place myself in your humanitarian hands . . .'

'I have a mother, but you occupy the first place in my heart . . .'

'My Duce, kneeling at your feet, I beg you for a crust of bread for all my life . . .'

'You who help everyone, help, O Duce, a poor old woman who has nothing . . .'

'I hope you can help me!! But if You cannot, who can? . . .'

'Father of us all, dearest husband . . .'

'Father of Italy . . .'

'Father of the poor . . .'

'Supreme benefactor of the working people . . .'[68]

The chances of requests for help being heeded depended on a number of factors. After being received in Rome, a letter would normally be forwarded by the Segreteria Particolare to the local prefect, who would check up on the supplicant's political and moral credentials, make sure that genuine hardship was involved, and ascertain if any assistance had already been given. If he advised that the case had merit, then an appropriate sum might be awarded ('The Duce has deigned to concede to you . . .'). Requests for personal subventions would normally result in grants of no more than a few hundred lire, but in exceptional circumstances, or where a request was being made on behalf of an organisation such as a school, far larger sums might be involved. Visits made by the Duce to a particular town or province could lead to a concentration of awards to individuals or bodies in that area. Likewise, notable events in Mussolini's family life – such as the marriage of his son Vittorio in 1937 or of Bruno the following year – might result in sudden surges in financial generosity.[69]

The desire of the regime to link as many initiatives as possible directly to the person of the Duce meant that the financial reach of the Segreteria Particolare was enormous, with awards being made in Mussolini's name for the building of roads, houses, schools, churches and cemeteries as well as assistance to millions of needy individuals, newly-weds, parents of prolific families and war widows. The precise sums in question are hard to ascertain, but each year tens of millions of lire were available for the Duce's own personal distribution from the secret funds of ministries, the police, the Bank of Italy and various other sources. To mark the foundation of the empire, more than 56 million lire was spent on 'donations and offerings' between May 1936 and January 1937 alone according to the Segreteria.[70] Nor was it just money that was involved. Mussolini's generosity could extend to domestic appliances (such as sewing machines), clothes and food. In the province of Rovigo 3,770 quintals of flour, 435 of bread, 66 of pasta, 60 of rice, 850,000 'popular rations', and 60,000 items of clothing were distributed in the winter of 1933–34 in the Duce's name. 'Even the humblest of workers and the poorest of labourers knows the Leader is concerned about them', one local newspaper observed.[71]

The impact of Mussolini's personal beneficence on individuals or communities was often considerable, not least because a sense of impoverishment might be bound up closely with ideas of inveterate neglect by the state. The files of the Segreteria Particolare are full of letters from grateful recipients eager to capitalise on the feeling of having been singled out with a further communication that would reinforce the sense of personal connection with the Duce. Typical was a collective statement written by the inhabitants of the remote community of Collecroce, near Nocera Umbra, in the hills to the east of Assisi, thanking Mussolini in December 1938 for his help in providing them with an aqueduct for their village. As so often it was the Duce's extraordinary omniscience as much as his generosity that was deemed to be remarkable:

> You who know how much we have suffered for lack of water can understand our uncontainable joy and infinite gratitude. We used to feel truly forgotten by everyone. And the legend about the origins of our village, handed down to us by our forebears, had seemed ever more true: . . . One day God passed through these mountains carrying on his shoulders the sack in which was contained the seed of every town in the world. Our seed fell through a hole made by a thorn, down here, and God did not notice, neither then nor later. But You, DUCE, with your all-seeing gaze, that penetrates into the labyrinths of the

past, you understand all the causes of present day ills . . . You, DUCE, though beset by the most pressing work, have seen and have thought even of us. We feel so proud of this gaze, more than if the eyes of all the world had been fixed on us.[72]

Icon

Mussolini's 'gaze' – the mesmerising eyes that transfixed so many direct viewers, or, as here, a more metaphorical focus directed towards a community – was a crucial component of the intimate relationship of the masses with the leader. One of its most conspicuous manifestations was the presence in millions of homes up and down the country of portraits of the fascist leader. Many of the men, women and children who wrote to Mussolini asked in their letters for a photograph, preferably signed; and down to the early years of the war, a high percentage of their requests was granted, it seems. Sometimes a specific picture was sought. One young woman, who said she had for years prayed for the Duce daily and never forgotten to put flowers in front of the photographs of him that she 'guarded with jealous care', asked for an image taken some years before that she had been unable to track down:

> You were dressed elegantly in civilian clothes . . . Your smiling eyes highlighted your pale and adorable face! Beneath your jacket around your neck there was a brightly coloured scarf that fell at an angle across your shirt front. You were standing with your left leg in front of you with the knee slightly bent. Your right hand was resting on a beautiful stick . . . How attractive your masculine figure was! You were talking to a group of friends. Do you remember it, Excellency?[73]

There could be various reasons for wanting a photograph. Some women may have regarded Mussolini as a 'star', whose image could be set alongside other pin-ups of the interwar years. In certain instances, acquiring and displaying a photograph of the Duce might have served as a mark of commitment to the regime to help deflect malicious insinuations of anti-fascism. But in a society where images were widely regarded as having tutelary powers, it seems probable that in many cases the presence of the Duce's portrait in a home had a more 'anthropological' function. Letters often referred to the reassurance that Mussolini's picture provided, especially in times of difficulty: 'In our family', wrote one woman from Parma in the spring of 1941, 'the devotion to You and to our cause is . . . complete and absolute . . . Your eyes, to which ours are turned a hundred times a day, tell us that we have good reason to believe blindly in the victory and the glory of Italy.'[74] A young peasant girl working in the rice fields of Emilia spoke of her pleasure at seeing images of Mussolini in the newspapers and of how she liked cutting them out and keeping them. But her motives were not those of a simple 'fan', it seems: 'I say to myself: "The Duce has been our saviour." I learn the hymns where there are words that refer to you and I often sing them. You are the father of every Italian.'[75]

The distribution of Mussolini's photograph encouraged a reciprocal traffic in images from members of the public. Large families requesting a subvention or simply wishing to register their pride at having produced so many offspring for the fatherland would send the Duce a studio portrait showing parents and children lined up, unsmiling, often in fascist uniforms, looking neat and disciplined. Another, and sometimes more intimate, dimension to this dense exchange of pictures was that involving 'santini' – giving Mussolini a favoured image of a saint, frequently with an accompanying explanation of why it would bring him special help or protection. Typical of many thousands of such cases, most of them involving women, was that of a teenage girl who felt encouraged by God to write to the Duce in July 1941 after learning that he had a particular veneration for Saint Teresa of the Baby Jesus (Thérèse of Lisieux), who had saved him from the first attack on his 'holy existence':

> I wanted to send You this image, with the relic of the Little Saint of the Roses. I particularly treasure it, as it was sent to me by the sister of the saint, Mother Agnes of Jesus, but I am happy to part with it for You, Duce, who are so deserving. Keep this holy image on you always, Duce. It will protect you and save you from every danger and will enlighten your great intelligence. Saint Teresa of the Baby Jesus will in this way quickly procure, from the Lord, the victory of your arms, which every heart feels absolutely confident of achieving.[76]

The contradiction inherent in this letter – the claim to feel 'absolutely confident' of victory, yet urging the Duce to seek the intervention of Saint Teresa – indicates just how much the impulse towards intimacy with the Duce was built upon the search for reassurance. The frequency with which people wrote about 'miraculous' happenings – a newborn baby raising its arm in a Roman salute, the sun suddenly coming out when the Duce's voice was broadcast on the radio, a newspaper photograph of Bruno Mussolini sucked into the sky on a windless day a few days after Bruno's death in a flying accident in 1941[77] – or the eagerness with which they reported what seemed to be auspicious dreams, are further signs of a longing to allay anxieties and doubts and see their trust in the regime confirmed. The extent to which many dreams brought together fascist and Catholic imagery suggests how the two frameworks of faith could operate in people's minds in symbiosis rather than in opposition. Ersilia Reale, for instance, described to Mussolini in November 1942 how the previous evening she had fallen asleep while praying and had dreamed that the Duce, at the head of an army and a sea of banners, was genuflecting before Pope Leo XIII – himself leading a great host of followers. Mussolini had tried to speak, but the Pope had stopped him and said: 'I will pray for you!' He had then made a sign to show that Italy would be victorious. This was a clear indication, said Ersilia, that the Duce would win: 'Whoever is divinely inspired cannot fail'.[78]

More vivid was the dream of Rosina Leto from the small town of Crucoli in Calabria, who told Mussolini, in April 1941, of how she had seen herself on the terrace of her house at night, under a clear starry sky with a brilliant moon flooding the entire landscape with light:

> The heavens seemed closer and closer to me, and I raised my eyes and saw carved in the sky your figure walking onwards and onwards, and I immediately gave a salute. But you walked straight ahead and took no notice of anyone. Further back, tied together in a bundle, were our tricolour flag, the fascist symbol, a fascist banner and the German flag, and hanging from them was a huge swathe of gold and silver medals, all shining. Further back still was a great battalion of soldiers singing happily, and behind them was the figure of an angel guiding everyone with open arms and carrying in his right hand a gilded sash on which was written in large and clear letters the word: VICTORIOUS.

The dream had been so bright that Rosina had woken up. In describing it in detail to Mussolini she presumably hoped that it would somehow acquire increased authority and significance, though in her conclusions she sounded rather less confident than Ersilia: 'I hope my dream comes true, and that we will soon experience the victory and greatness of our dear Fatherland.'[79]

Since Mussolini afforded for millions of Italians an intimate point of reassurance and hope, it is perhaps not surprising that the moments of most intense engagement with him were often those of actual or impending loss or grief. At such times the Duce could provide a justification for suffering. Many soldiers in the Second World War wrote last letters voicing contentment at laying down their lives for Mussolini ('I was born for the war of Mussolini, and for him I wish to die';[80] 'Duce, when you receive this letter I will already be dead, fallen on the field of honour with your name preserved in the depths of my soul').[81] Of course, there may have been an element of pragmatic calculation with at least some of these expressions of loyalty: a hope that the widow or parents would gain a better pension. And the same might apply to the many wounded soldiers who wrote to the Duce to express their continued faith in him and the fascist cause. But the fervour and apparent spontaneity of so many of the letters suggest that the main aim was to establish meaning for the sacrifice that had been incurred. Franco Oldrini, a former Fiume Legionary, was perhaps unusual only in the level of his effusiveness. In April 1941, in the course of the campaign in Greece, he was hit by a mortar, as a result of which he had to have a leg amputated. Shortly after the operation he wrote to Mussolini to say that his spirit was 'still strong', his morale 'very high', and his love of the Duce 'more than great':

> With the pure and great faith You have instilled in us, Duce . . . with the love of a son for his father, of a fascist for his Duce, of a blackshirt for his Leader, I took up my rifle . . . Duce! Attached to my bed is Your Effigy of when you were wounded and were on crutches, and I kiss Your Crutches – which I will soon have to use; I kiss them with passion, because making myself equal to You in physical suffering, I will come to resemble You more in the ideal. For the blood given in Your name to the Fatherland; for the willing gift of my limb, Duce, I thank You![82]

Some of the most poignant letters written to Mussolini were those from relatives who had lost a son, a husband or a brother fighting in the Ethiopian campaign or in the Second World War. Again it is impossible altogether to discount a financial incentive with such correspondence. But once more the passionate language and the recurrence of words that resonated with religious significance – 'blood', 'sacrifice', 'holocaust', 'martyrdom', 'faith', 'holy cause' – suggest that the cult of the Duce operated in its most internalised and intimate form as a point of ethical reference whose validity derived largely from the fact that it dovetailed with deep-rooted Catholic templates. To take one example from many hundreds of similar letters preserved in the Segreteria Particolare del Duce relating to the invasion of Ethiopia, that of a semi-literate peasant woman from a village near Cosenza whose brother had been killed in January 1936, 'with the name of Your Excellency and of our Italy on his lips':

But my eyes are not weeping. Although I am just a poor peasant woman for whom his arms were very precious, as they were strong and helped me to cultivate the small field that I rent, I nevertheless feel boundless pride that one of my blood has offered himself up of his own will to his Duce and the Fatherland, heroically sacrificing himself. And may the selfish and arrogant world know that the poor and noble women of Italy are, and always will be, ready to offer up their lives too, at one sign from Your Excellency.[83]

9

A Place in the Sun

Defying the world

Exactly why the six-year-old Albertina Roveda decided to start keeping a diary is not certain. Perhaps it was a suggestion from her new schoolteacher to help improve her writing – which to begin with was shaky and uncertain. Or perhaps it was from a sense that the world around her was confusing, and as a late child of rather elderly parents, with two grown-up brothers, it was not easy to find someone with the time to explain to her exactly what was going on. Her family were keen fascists; her teacher 'loved' Mussolini; and she herself was enrolled in the Piccole Italiane. But despite all the enthusiasm that she encountered for the Duce, it was clear that many people, including her brothers, were extremely unhappy in 1934 about the economic situation in the small town of Colle Umberto in the province of Treviso where she lived. In recent years unemployment had forced many to emigrate, and the situation showed little sign of improving. On 1 January 1935 one of her brothers, Carlo, exclaimed over his scrambled eggs at breakfast: 'Leave and live, or stay and die'. Albertina was left puzzled: 'I did not understand'. Two days later she found that Carlo was leaving home to serve in the army in Africa.[1]

Fascism had long talked about Africa as a possible panacea for the nation's economic ills. 'Our peninsula is too small, too rocky, too mountainous to be able to feed its 40 million inhabitants', Mussolini had declared to parliament in 1924.[2] The colonies of Eritrea and Somalia, which Italy had clung onto after withdrawing from Ethiopia in the wake of defeat at the battle of Adua in 1896, were regarded as possible areas of development, and in the mid-1920s a series of brutal military operations were undertaken in Somalia in an attempt to eradicate local resistance. But it was Libya that was the main focus of the regime's early imperial ambitions, with suggestions that hundreds of thousands of Italian peasants might happily be settled amid the fertile oases and palm groves if only the territory could be properly subjugated. Here, too, military activities were intensified from the mid-1920s. As Giuseppe Bottai explained shortly after Mussolini had paid a high-profile visit to Tripoli in 1926, fascism needed to assert itself in the Mediterranean and repair the damage done by liberalism:

> The imperial future of the Italian nation hinges in large part on the Libyan coast and on the political efficiency of its hinterland. It should not be forgotten that *mare nostrum* is not ours. The Mediterranean is everything to us, and yet we count for nothing in it. We are penned in this sea thanks to the criminal inertia of past governments and the power of other countries.[3]

The idea that Italy should have as a main foreign policy goal the strengthening of its position in the Mediterranean was certainly nothing new: it had been advocated by liberal politicians from at least the 1880s. But the damage that had been done to the country's *amour propre* at the Paris peace conference, and the refusal in particular of the British and French to grant Italy a share of the former German colonies, led fascism to amplify the rhetoric of *mare nostrum* as part of its campaign against the alleged greed and selfishness of the old imperial powers. Albertina's schoolteacher had no hesitation in referring proudly to the Mediterranean as *mare nostrum*. Albertina was puzzled: 'I really don't understand why it is ours. The ancient Romans could say this because they had a great Empire.'[4] But the notion of dominating the Mediterranean gathered momentum in the late 1920s, fuelled by the regime's celebration of ancient Rome and its culture – epitomised in the placing of a series of giant marble and bronze maps illustrating the phases of growth of the Roman Empire along the western side of the new Via dell'Impero in the heart of the capital – and by the suggestion that the hardship created by the Great Depression could be alleviated through 'a place in the sun'.

In Libya military activity was intensified at the beginning of the 1930s under the governorship of Marshal Pietro Badoglio and his deputy, Rodolfo Graziani, a ruthless general soon to be feted by the regime as a quintessential fascist 'new man'. Badoglio and Graziani aimed to stamp out the resistance of the Senussi tribesmen in the eastern half of the colony by severing the links between the largely nomadic local population and the small mobile army of mujahideen fighters, led by an elderly and charismatic warlord, Omar el Mukhtar. To this end around 100,000 people, for the most part women, children and old men, were marched across the desert and interned in a series of barbed-wire compounds erected around Benghazi. Without proper sanitation over 40,000 died from disease and malnutrition. To isolate the mujahideen still further and prevent supplies reaching them from British-controlled Egypt, Graziani ordered the construction of a 275-kilometre barbed-wire barrier, 4 metres deep, running south from the port of Bardia. The final stages of the operations against the rebel forces and their families were carried out with clinical efficiency. Bombers supported the ground troops and dropped high explosives and mustard gas (illegal under the Geneva Protocol of 1925, which Italy had signed) on enemy positions. No prisoners were taken. In September 1931 el Mukhtar was captured and after a summary trial hanged in front of 20,000 of his loyal Bedouin followers. He was immediately hailed as a martyr throughout the Arab world.

With Libya largely subdued, the regime's attention turned increasingly to Ethiopia, a long-standing object of Italian imperial ambitions, whose conquest might serve to remove the shame of Adua, consolidate Italy's holdings in east Africa, and place strategic pressure on the British in Sudan and Egypt. In the autumn of 1932, buoyed by the success of the celebrations for the tenth anniversary of the March on Rome, Mussolini asked the Minister of Colonies to draw up plans for a possible attack. These sparked off a prolonged debate among the leading military authorities – the Chiefs of Staff of the army, the navy and the air force, and the Chief of the General Staff, Marshal Badoglio – about how the operations should best be conducted. The debate exposed how little coordination there was at the top of the armed forces. Though nominally the most senior general, the Chief of the General Staff had no powers of effective command over the three services. The only person who could impose a degree of centralised control was Mussolini, who from the autumn of 1933 held the War, Marine and Air Force portfolios (not to mention those of the Foreign Ministry, Interior Ministry and Ministry of Corporations).[5]

The decision to invade Ethiopia was taken against the backdrop of the new international situation created by the accession to power of Hitler in 1933. Mussolini calculated that with Britain and France distracted by developments in Germany, there would be little opposition to Italian aggression in Africa, provided it were swift. There was also the question of Austria: any action in Ethiopia needed to be completed before Hitler (who at this point was far from being considered an obvious ally by Mussolini) moved to annex Austria and posed a threat to Italy – which had largely German-speaking provinces in the Alto-Adige – on its northern border. At the end of 1934 a secret memorandum was issued to the country's senior political figures to prepare for the 'total conquest of Ethiopia'. Nine months later, on the evening of 2 October 1935, Italians gathered in piazzas up and down the country to hear the declaration of war transmitted over loudspeakers from the balcony of Palazzo Venezia. 'Fascist and proletarian Italy', the Duce declared, was moving in unison to secure its rightful living space and avenge the injustices of which it had long been a victim:

> Blackshirts of the revolution! Men and women of all Italy! . . . Listen. A solemn hour is about to strike in the history of the fatherland. Twenty million Italians are at this moment occupying the piazzas in every corner of Italy . . . Twenty million people: one single heart, one single will, one decision . . . It is not just an army that is moving towards its objectives, but an entire people of 44 million souls; a people against whom attempts have been made to commit the blackest injustice: that of depriving us of a little place in the sun . . . We have been patient for thirteen years, during which the noose of selfishness that has stifled our natural energy has been pulled ever tighter! With Ethiopia we have been patient for forty years. Enough![6]

Albertina, who had often helped her father in the blazing heat of summer in the fields of Colle Umberto, was again left rather perplexed: 'The teacher has said that the Duce wants to give the Italians a place in the sun. It seems to me that we have got plenty of sun in my town.'[7] For all its naivety, it was a telling comment: how far was the Ethiopian venture in fact being propelled by rhetoric and passion rather than logic? But her scepticism was not widely shared, and as news came through of early victories, support for the war escalated rapidly. When in the second week of October the League of Nations condemned Italy for violating the Covenant, and fifty-two of its member states voted to apply economic sanctions, a mood of extraordinary defiance swept through the country. Such distinguished liberal critics of the regime as Luigi Albertini and Vittorio Emanuele Orlando were swept along in the surge of patriotic excitement and pledged their support to the government, while the eminent socialist Arturo Labriola apologised for his former opposition to fascism and returned to Italy from exile in France. Even Benedetto Croce offered his qualified backing. Among those who volunteered to fight in Africa was the sixty-one-year-old physicist and Nobel laureate, Guglielmo Marconi.

The letters of support for the invasion that poured into the Segreteria Particolare del Duce in late September and early October 1935 condemned the unspeakable egoism and hypocrisy of Britain and the other Western imperial powers, and looked forward excitedly to avenging the military humiliations of the past and bringing civilisation to a barbarous people – not least Catholic civilisation. (The Church provided overwhelming backing for the war, with seven cardinals, twenty-nine archbishops and seventy-five bishops offering public endorsements in the press.)[8] A man from Naples echoed the views of countless others in asking Mussolini how a country like England, 'so rich in territories and money', could possibly 'grab from our plate a piece of meat that will serve to feed millions of hungry people', while at the same time defending an immoral, slave-trafficking country like Ethiopia?[9] A woman from Milan told the Duce that everyone she spoke to was firmly behind him as there was a general feeling that the current situation in Italy could not continue ('there is only hunger') and a widespread conviction that Britain was being criminally selfish in not letting Italy have what it deserved: 'You cannot imagine how much bitterness there is among our people towards England and its hostility to us.'[10]

In the view of many, the opposition shown by Britain in particular to the invasion of Ethiopia was the product of fear – fear that Italy with its new spiritual energy and unified sense of mission was resurrecting the glorious military traditions of ancient Rome and would soon be able to threaten the imperial dominance of the increasingly materialistic, corrupt and effete older powers. Typical was a letter from a man in Pavia who told the Duce that fascist Italy could not fail to be victorious against the 'cautious, decrepit democracies, bloated with wealth': 'The Italy of the Caesars and the Augustuses was the master of the known world. This is why England is ungrateful to you and to Italy. It is afraid of its own decadence, which is already apparent.'[11] Very often linked to this idea were suggestions that the British were profoundly jealous of Italy and its extraordinary leader ('they envy us and wish that you were not so just, so upright and so human . . .') and were determined to block the country's 'right of legitimate expansion', its 'historic mission', and the advance of 'Christian Civilisation' out of a preoccupation that Italy would secure 'all the primary resources that it needs' in Ethiopia, become rich and economically independent, and develop into a major commercial force in the world.[12]

Some correspondents urged Mussolini to show the true spirit of fascism in Ethiopia by laying aside humanitarianism and treating the barbarians with the ruthlessness that they deserved. After all, Italy was now threatened by countries with enormous military resources at their disposal and the best way of warning them off was by displaying 'diabolical savagery' in east Africa and 'saturating the plains of Somalia and the forests of the Tigre in a week with gas bombs'.[13] A group of Bologna university students, who were hoping to volunteer to fight in Ethiopia, called on the Duce to avenge the humiliation of 1896 by conducting a 'war to the limits' against the 'inhuman, vile . . . bestial Abyssinian people'. Any means were justified:

WE WANT AN OFFENSIVE AERIAL WAR. CHEMICAL WEAPONS SHOULD BE USED ON A LARGE SCALE AS MODERN WAR DEMANDS . . . Duce, we are not impetuous or blood-thirsty. We are Italians and we want to keep our sacrifice to a minimum, especially when it is a question of fighting animals like the Abyssinians. What force do treaties have? They only apply to weak states . . . How can anyone check if Italy does or does not use gas? . . . Chemical weapons are expensive, it is true, but the Italian people are ready to make the financial sacrifices required to save their sons who will be needed as the productive forces of tomorrow's Empire.[14]

Amid the general chorus of enthusiasm for the war, a few voices of dissent could be heard, especially in those areas of the Po valley where socialism had in the past fostered a culture of anti-militarism and anti-imperialism. In the small town of Vezzano sul Crostolo near Reggio Emilia, a watermelon seller was reported to the police for telling his customers in September 1935 that the Ethiopians were in the right, 'because we are the ones who are breaking into their homes'. He added that Mussolini's real purpose in fighting was to justify the economic hardship inflicted on ordinary people, 'since they will now say we must tighten our belts'. In some instances it was the wisdom of falling out with powerful states that was called into question, as in the case of a Forlì railway worker who was arrested after declaring over a cup of coffee in a bar that Italy was wrong to antagonise Britain, as it was a hugely wealthy nation that had 'conquered Napoleon Bonaparte, Wilhelm II and others'. A shopkeeper in Cremona with a track record of making rather negative remarks about the government was sentenced to three years in *confino* for saying in a restaurant that Britain had been correct to impose sanctions and that the present war would prove no more successful than those that had been waged by liberalism, when Italy had only 'managed to seize a few stones and some sand'.[15]

But such notes of scepticism were as almost nothing amid the near universal acclaim for a war that it was widely believed would provide opportunities for mass settlement and at last make Italy wealthy: rumours abounded in 1935–36 of the great fertility of Ethiopia, of wonderful gold and diamond mines, and of vast unexplored oilfields.[16] There was also a powerful sense that Italy was asserting itself in the world, avenging past insults to the nation's dignity, and wiping away the image of weakness that liberalism had saddled it with. Carlo Ciseri, who had been drawn to fascism in 1919–20 from a feeling of disgust at the disparagement of the Italian army's contribution to the First World War, both at home and abroad, saw Ethiopia as a chance to demonstrate to the world that the nation would no longer put up with being treated as a second-rate power. On 3 October 1935 he cut out from a newspaper a photograph of fourteen gold medals awarded to men who had fought at Adua in 1896 and pasted it in his diary. Beside it he wrote:

> It is right that we look for a place in the sun given that our dear French and English allies, after promising us heaven and earth to get us into the war, pushed us aside when it came to dividing up the booty, leaving

us, as always, to play the part of Cinderella . . . <u>Enough!</u> Italy is no longer the land of mandolins and songs. Today Italy is a nation, a people, conscious of its worth, that knows what it wants and how to get it. The Italy of 15 years ago is finished, dead. <u>Enough!</u>[17]

Carlo did not volunteer to go to Africa – although four years later, with his hotel business in Florence in crisis at the outbreak of the Second World War, he did – but many of those who enlisted in the army in 1935 set off for Africa with a similar sense that the attack on a sovereign member of the League of Nations was justified in the light of the many trials and humiliations that Italy had suffered in the past. Espedito Russo, a twenty-five-year-old from a modest middle-class family in the small town of Altavilla Irpina in the province of Avellino, was typical of countless others in his largely unreflective absorption of the regime's rhetoric of a righteous and inexorable march into a glorious future as expiation for earlier sufferings. When he was called up on 6 August 1935 he noted in his diary that he felt happy 'to avenge the fallen of 1896': 'The past was very painful. The slopes we faced were difficult and covered in brambles. Today our holier, more radiant ascension begins . . . The Fatherland is calling us to assert the rights of Italy'. And when the war began on 3 October he recorded his trepidation and pride at taking part in an event of such momentous significance for Italy:

The historic hour has struck. We are entrusted with a task that has excited five continents and has summoned us together, sons of the Italian fatherland, with pure pride, with arms and with courage.

We will be proud to follow our Duce, step by step. With this battle Italy will gain the most beautiful victory. Oh! May God ensure that in the soul of us legionaries the memory is ever alive of those who died as heroes, shedding their blood in sacrifice for the Fatherland. The war that has brought us into the land of Africa was foretold by many; now it is up to us, sons of great Italy – beautiful, strong, prolific and fascist – to win the victory. It is up to us to avenge the error of Versailles . . .

We want Italy to be great: every Italian has said this. And you Benito Mussolini, you who control the destiny of the Fatherland, protect and guide our loved ones in Italy . . .

Today Italy is quivering with excitement; our dear ones tremble and pray. But we are calm, with a smile on our lips, saying to ourselves: 'now is the time'.

Today the youth of Italy has leapt forward as one man, ready to bear arms and carry into the barbarian land the symbol of Rome, symbol of greatness, civilisation and strength.[18]

Espedito had a frustrating war. He remained stationed in Eritrea as a quartermaster, and his repeated requests to be allowed to serve at the front in Ethiopia went unheeded. Early in 1936 he succumbed to a tropical illness, and after repeated spells in hospital, was forced to return to Italy. But throughout his time in Africa he continued to write his diary, which he dedicated to his wife, Elisa; and no doubt in part from a wish to impress upon her the strength of his fascist faith, he filled the pages with stirring observations about the justice of Italy's cause. He spoke of the clash between 'the ancient civilisation of Rome' and the 'barbarian hordes of Abyssinia' and of how 'the hand of the man who controls the fate of one of the most powerful nations in the world will smite inexorably the heads of those who have sought to block our righteous path and . . . rob us of our place in the sun'. And he condemned all who were eager to see 'our civilisation shattered, and hurl us down into the mud, into the black and putrid mud in which that most civilised country, England, is wallowing, as it tries to thwart us as the supreme defender and henchman of filthy, slave driving, and cowardly beggars . . . Proletarian and fascist Italy, the Italy of Vittorio Veneto and the Revolution: arise!'[19]

Conquest

Once the invasion had been launched, Mussolini could not afford anything other than a crushing victory. Fascism had for years celebrated the values of war and denounced the weak humanitarianism of the liberal regime that had left the dreams of the Risorgimento shattered with the defeats at Custoza and Lissa (1866), Adua and Caporetto. On the face of it, success in Ethiopia should not have been difficult to achieve. The army of the emperor Haile Selassie numbered no more than 300,000 men, and was feudal in both its spirit and its organisation, with loyalty owed to individual warlords (*ras*). Though most of the troops had access to modern rifles, there were no military planes, very few machine guns, and virtually no artillery. Against these ramshackle forces, Mussolini mobilised the largest army ever seen for a colonial war. Initial plans had suggested that three divisions would be sufficient, but Mussolini wanted to be safe and decided to send ten divisions (and eventually twenty-five). In all, around 650,000 men were dispatched to east Africa, together with two million tons of supplies. They were supported by 450 aircraft, including more than 200 bombers.[20]

Despite this massive superiority, the lack of passable roads in Ethiopia made it hard to keep such large forces adequately equipped. After the initial successes (including the capture of Adua on 6 October, which brought jubilant crowds into the streets across Italy), the campaign stalled badly. But the lack of military progress was largely concealed by the regime's brilliant success in mobilising public opinion against the League of Nations and the sanctions, which came into effect on 18 November 1935. Though these economic measures in fact had limited impact, given that they were only partially applied by some states and oil was excluded, there were widespread fears in the autumn of financial collapse. A huge press campaign was launched to encourage Italians to contribute to the nation's metal reserves and boycott foreign goods. Women were a particular target. In Cremona posters appeared around the city urging housewives to take a solemn vow: 'I promise in the name of my dignity as a fascist and an Italian not to buy, for myself or my family, either today or ever again, foreign products.'[21] Theatres and cinemas reduced their opening times to save electricity; restaurants introduced restricted menus; and motor vehicles were converted where possible to gas or alcohol.

The culmination of the regime's campaign of patriotic mass mobilisation came on 18 December, when across the country couples were invited to donate their gold wedding rings publicly to the state and receive in return a steel substitute as a sign of their sacrifice. The 'Giornata della Fede' ('Day of the wedding ring', though 'fede' also means 'faith') was from a political point of view hugely effective in that it asked individuals to donate their most private and intimate possession to the regime, leaving the millions who took part enmeshed more deeply than ever in the web of moral collusion that fascism was so adept at spinning. In Rome the ceremony was presided over by Archbishop Angelo Bartolomasi, the chief prelate of the armed forces, who stood on the steps of the Altar of the Fatherland, alongside many of the leading figures of the state, surrounded by smoking braziers, choirs and bands, with huge crowds in Piazza Venezia below, as the queen – who rarely appeared in public – inaugurated the day's proceedings with an emotional speech, broadcast live by radio across the country:

> In ascending the memorial of the Vittoriale [not, as more properly, 'Vittoriano': the regime was keen to press the association with 'victory' rather than 'Victor Emmanuel'], united with the proud mothers and wives of our dear Italy, to lay on the altar of the Unknown Hero my wedding ring, symbol of our first joys and of extreme renunciations, in a purest offering of devotion to the Fatherland . . . we call, along with our glorious dead of the Great War, before God, for 'Victory'. For you, young sons of Italy – you who are defending its sacred rights and opening new avenues for the luminous march of the Fatherland – we hope to see in Africa, redeemed by you, the triumph of the civilisation of Rome.[22]

The enormous success of the day's events – in Piazza Venezia the demand to follow the queen's example was such that within a few hours every one of the 45,000 replacement metal rings had been distributed – owed as much to the powerful support of the Church as to the propaganda machinery of the state. After all, for many Italians a wedding ring had a strongly sacramental character, and the sanction of the Church undoubtedly helped to ease moral pangs. The Pope himself refrained from making a public statement, but across the country senior clergy gave their backing to the Giornata della Fede, frequently suggesting, as the Archbishop of Oristano said, that the donation of gold to the fatherland would raise the Abyssinian people from the 'most abject religious and moral level' in which they currently languished and bring them closer to 'the true faith, that of our Catholic religion, which is the fountainhead of civilisation and progress'.[23] Cardinals offered gold chains from their pectoral crosses to support the 'crusade', and a number of bishops swapped their gold episcopal rings for steel ones. Nuns freely surrendered to the state the rings that symbolised their marriage to Christ.[24]

The combination of institutional and collective pressure with spontaneous enthusiasm resulted in around 70 per cent of married adults in Rome and perhaps 50 per cent in other major cities (rather less in the countryside, it seems) surrendering their rings.[25] Many of those who chose not to donate them commissioned substitutes from jewellers or else contributed gold in other forms. Benedetto Croce and Luigi Albertini gave their senator's medals; the playwright Luigi Pirandello sent Mussolini four medals, including that for the Nobel Prize for Literature which he had been awarded the year before. There were very few reports of protest or resistance – though since a principal aim of the Giornata della Fede was to demonstrate to the outside world that the country was united behind the government, it was hardly in the interest of the authorities to draw attention to gestures of opposition. One case of dissent that did attract publicity was that of Prince Filippo Andrea Doria Pamphili, a prominent Roman aristocrat married to an English wife. His refusal to offer any gold or to display the tricolour flag as prescribed on 18 December resulted in an attempt by fascists to break down his door. The name of the street next to his palace was pointedly changed from 'vicolo Doria' to 'via della Fede'.[26]

The enthusiasm for the campaign in Ethiopia was reinforced by a barrage of emotions and images transmitted through songs, postcards, advertisements and films in which themes of beauty, sensuality and exoticism competed with lurid press accounts of 'barbaric' practices such as slavery, infibulation and child sacrifice.[27] The notion of the 'black Venus', whose cultural genealogy stretched back, via the contemporary American entertainer Josephine Baker, to traditional stereotypes of Somali beauties and the erotic fantasies of Marinetti's Futurist novel *Mafarka* (1909), was used in posters to sell products as diverse as coffee, insurance and chocolate. Pornographic photographs of African women were said to be circulating in their millions in Italy by the spring of 1936, despite government efforts to ban them.[28] The most famous popular song of the time, 'Faccetta nera' ('Little black face'), had as its central conceit the liberation of a 'beautiful little Abyssinian girl' from her benighted environment and her relocation to Rome where she could be 'kissed' by an Italian sun, see the Duce and learn the laws of a civilised society – whose only form of slavery was the 'slavery of love'. The extraordinary success of this piece lay as much, it would seem, in its successful bracketing of erotic possession, Italy's civilising mission and loyalty to fascism, as in the jaunty carefree tune with its suggestion that the subjugation of Ethiopia would be simple.

With enthusiasm for the war so strong and public opinion avid for success, Mussolini needed victories. He had replaced the elderly and in his view too cautious fascist commander, General Emilio De Bono, with Marshal Badoglio in late November, but in the next few weeks the military situation showed few signs of improving, with Italian troops at times being driven back before superior enemy numbers. Mussolini became increasingly alarmed. At the end of December he sent Badoglio a telegram authorising him to 'use any kind of gas . . . even on a massive scale'. Badoglio had in fact already begun employing mustard gas (or 'insecticide' as he euphemistically liked to call it)[29] – he knew of its devastating effects from his time in Libya – and during the next three months around 1,000 heavy bombs filled with the chemical were dropped on enemy positions or, more lethally, sprayed as a vapour from aircraft, killing combatants and non-combatants alike and poisoning rivers and lakes.[30] Shells filled with arsine (a compound of arsenic) were also fired. The balance of advantage tipped decisively towards the Italian forces, and when in February Mussolini suggested it might be beneficial to use bacteriological weapons, Badoglio said this was unnecessary as the enemy was sufficiently weakened.[31] The little paper tricolour flags that Albertina Roveda's patriotic school-teacher made the children stick on the map of Ethiopia hanging on the classroom wall in Colle Umberto, to show the advance of the Italian army, moved towards Addis Ababa.

Mussolini was not especially concerned about the reaction of world opinion to the use of illegal weapons, and he made little attempt to conceal the transport of hundreds of tons of chemicals through the Suez Canal during the months of the campaign.[32] Since the League of Nations had been so successfully portrayed as a selfish instrument for preserving the interests of the wealthy powers against the just claims of 'proletarian' Italy, why should fascism feel overly worried about breaking international law? And anyway, to moralise now about gas seemed deeply hypocritical as well as self-serving: the British

Empire had hardly been built with kid gloves. Mussolini and his senior diplomatic officials accordingly had few qualms about lying and dismissing the allegations of atrocities as calumnies designed to discredit the regime. When a leading figure in the Foreign Ministry, Baron Pompeo Aloisi, asked what line he should take on gas in Geneva, Mussolini told him to say that the substance being used in Ethiopia was quite harmless and simply knocked troops out of action for a few hours, and that it was only being employed spasmodically as a reprisal for the barbarous crimes being perpetrated by the Abyssinians.[33] When photographs reached London of mustard gas victims, the Italian Embassy batted them away as cases of leprosy. It was also suggested that the British themselves might in fact be cynically supplying chemical weapons to the Ethiopian army.[34]

Inside Italy, there was blanket censorship about chemical weapons, and the regime firmly rebutted allegations about their use as defamatory. Even if the enemy was subhuman in its barbarism and the plutocracies odious in their moralising, it would not have done much for the image of either fascism or the armed forces to suggest that victory had been facilitated by 'unheroic' means. (Only in 1996 did the Ministry of Defence finally admit publicly that mustard gas and arsine had been used in Ethiopia.) With public opinion so enthusiastic about the war and hostile to the League of Nations, Mussolini knew that the idea of an international conspiracy to blacken the image of fascism would be widely credited and that any reports of atrocities filtering through from overseas would be generally discounted. In the little Tuscan town of Bagni di Lucca, Anna Caredio recalled how the atmosphere in late 1935 and early 1936 was one of excitement, with 'Faccetta nera' and other popular songs such as 'Africanina' ('Little African girl') and 'Ti saluto e vado in Abissinia' ('Farewell, I am off to Abyssinia') being sung everywhere, and people talking eagerly of the prosperity Ethiopia would bring. But one day her father Edgardo came to the house looking deeply shocked and reported that somebody had heard from a foreign radio station that the Italians were winning because they were gassing the Ethiopians: 'That's why this war appears to be more like a stroll than a war.' Anna's mother immediately dismissed the claim as 'propaganda'; her grandfather was rather less certain. Edgardo remained troubled: he was very proud of the 'honourable' way that Italy had fought in 1915–18. Anna, who was only eight at the time, did not know what 'gas' was – though she immediately sensed that it was something she could not possibly mention to her teacher.[35]

In Africa itself, the troops were aware that gas and atrocities were not subjects to be reported, either in correspondence (which was censored) or openly in conversation. Giuseppe Bottai wrote lyrically in his letters to his wife back home about the 'historical necessity' of the campaign and the joy he felt at being involved in a war that was a 'work of art . . . in its fervent poetry'.[36] The account that he published in 1940 of his experiences in Ethiopia conveyed a similar sense of aesthetic exhilaration at Italy's civilising mission. But in his private diary he recorded less attractive aspects of the campaign that could not be made public. In February 1936 he noted that soldiers were being told not to touch bomb fragments in case they were contaminated with mustard gas, while a few weeks later he expressed his revulsion at the way ordinary middle-class officers were 'confusing cruelty with heroism' and perpetrating 'episodes of bestiality', including the 'cold and calculated slaughter' of native non-combatants. Galeazzo Ciano told him of how the party secretary, Achille Starace, had used a group of prisoners for target practice, aiming at their hearts. When he had got to the fourth victim, he had stopped and exclaimed, 'In this way, they don't suffer enough!' Thereafter he had shot them first in the testicles and then in the chest. 'Eye witnesses have reported these details. Naturally, since they must not talk about them, they all speak *sotto voce*.'[37]

The extent to which soldiers in Africa felt shocked or uncomfortable at what they experienced depended on a variety of factors. In Bottai's case, his disquiet was not with the campaign in general, which he regarded as entirely legitimate, but with the crude behaviour of petty-bourgeois non-intellectuals (like Starace), whom he instinctively despised. And in general, as the numerous diaries that were kept during the campaign in 1935–36 reveal, the prevalent feelings among the troops were of great pride in the achievements of fascism and of confidence that the methods employed were appropriate given the barbarism of the enemy and the benefits that would accrue to Ethiopia in due course from the introduction of superior Italian civilisation. Only occasionally, it seems, did participants in the war latch onto a moral framework that enabled them to view what was going on with a critical eye. Most were safely corralled inside a value system where patriotism, devotion to the Duce and obedience to the fascist regime intertwined with an exaltation of military virtues and a disparagement of liberal humanitarianism to blunt expressions of doubt or dissent. And the enthusiasm of the Catholic Church for the invasion of Ethiopia provided powerful endorsement for the idea of a 'civilising mission', in whose name almost any form of conduct or action might in the end be justified.

One of the very few diarists who (in private) voiced general opposition to the war was Vasco Poggesi. Vasco had been born in 1912 into a humble family of moderately left-wing views (though his parents were not in any serious sense anti-fascist) in the small Tuscan town of Reggello. He had been forced for financial reasons to finish school at twelve, but he had a strong academic and creative streak: he enjoyed acting with his father and loved reading. While he was in the army he passed much of his spare time devouring works by Victor Hugo, Tolstoy and Dostoevsky: their sense of humanitarianism and social justice appealed to him. In the spring of 1935 he was sent out to Somalia, and left full of enthusiasm. 'Young people', he wrote, 'do not calculate or reflect very much: they have the spirit of adventure in their blood and want at this time to be heroes in the eyes of their fine comrades and of all the Nation.' But as he sailed south through the Suez Canal he realised, not without a twinge of guilt, that he did not feel quite as patriotic as perhaps he should. 'We are all Italian', he affirmed; but the truth was that he only really felt at ease with people from his 'beautiful land of Tuscany': '[S]ometimes you feel a bit lost in the Babel of dialects and you long desperately to find a friendly face, and a clear and distinct voice that you can only hear in Tuscany.'[38]

After arriving in Kismaayo in southern Somalia, Vasco was uncomfortable. All the talk was of imminent war. He did not want to go to Mass at Easter, as he felt, in another rush of heterodox individualism, that Christianity should not be supporting the idea of killing – particularly when the motive was not self-defence or the protection of vital interests but simply the suppression of people with a different language and culture. He was employed on fortifications and other building projects, but quickly found himself loathing military life: it was enervating and corrupting (everybody was involved in theft) and produced the 'almost complete annihilation of the spiritual self'. He regarded his superiors as incompetent, stupid and craven: they were concerned only with safeguarding their careers, 'which could be ruined permanently by a bold gesture or a sincere word'. And he became increasingly alarmed by the ever more insistent talk of hostilities in the summer of 1935. He wanted desperately to go home, not because he was a coward, but because he could not stomach the idea of 'going and slaughtering poor devils whose only crime was that they were still not civilised'. His one satisfaction was the post from Italy and particularly the sports news: 'Who has won the football league? Who is the winner of the Grand Prix of Tripoli? How has the Giro d'Italia ended?'[39]

Vasco felt out of step with his comrades and increasingly isolated. He was certainly proud to be Italian and even prouder to be Tuscan: he got extremely irritated by the arrogance of soldiers from Rome who boasted about the Via dell'Impero, the Vittoriano and the Lido of Ostia when in his view Tuscany was the real cradle of the nation's culture. But he also admired the British, the French and other peoples of the world, and could see no good reason to hate them. And why was Italy, whose strength had always lain in its glorious cultural and artistic traditions and the 'power of its spirit', now trying to dominate the world by force of arms? He thought the sudden demand for 'a place in the sun' illogical and unjust and found the demographic campaign and the arguments about the need for expansion totally bewildering: 'If there are lots of us, why should we try to increase our numbers? They tell us: so as to be in a position to secure other lands and dominions. But why must we put ourselves in a position to secure other lands? Because there are many of us, too many. It's a vicious circle.'[40]

When war was finally declared at the beginning of October 1935, Vasco found the enthusiasm of his fellow soldiers grating. The arguments they used to justify the invasion, not least the idea that Italy would bring civilisation to a benighted land, struck him as deeply hollow:

Is our aim really to shine light where there is darkness, or is it rather to conquer a rich and fertile region? . . . No, I do not consider our action against Abyssinia justified. First and foremost because I hate war and violence. Secondly, because an attempt is being made on this occasion as well to conceal behind a mask of humanity and civilisation what in reality is an act of aggression against an enemy that has only its courage and its fury to oppose us with. Therefore I criticise the behaviour of my Nation. Am I a discordant note in what is – or is said to be – a concert of harmony and complete approval? Yes. I am not a sheep. My mind is not so blinkered as not to see good and evil. And what we are doing is evil.[41]

How, he wondered, could the Church give its blessing to such a war? And how could people be so blinded by the rhetoric of 'glory', 'youthful bravado', and 'heroism'? And what was this 'fatherland' for which everyone was being asked to make such sacrifices? Was it really the mothers, the fathers, the brothers and the sisters who were anxiously waiting back home (many of them in vain) for the return of their loved ones? Or was it rather (and here Vasco offered a premonition of his future career as a communist trade union official) something 'infinitely more restricted and despicable', a clutch of 'big capitalists, big industrialists and big diplomats who provoke wars in order to fill their coffers or out of wretched personal prejudices.'[42]

Vasco, who was fortunate to return to Italy in the spring of 1936 without having seen action, was, as he would have been the first to concede, something of a maverick. Others who went out to Africa in 1935–36 certainly had some of their initial ardour tempered by the unsavoury reality of what they experienced – the inclemency of the terrain and the climate, the ubiquity of disease, the squalor and poverty in which most Ethiopians lived, the boredom of so much of military life, and the stark contrast between the fantasy image that was often harboured of 'black Venuses' and the unhealthiness of so many of the prostitutes who traded in sex ('nick-nick'). The scale of the slaughter and the rough justice that was frequently meted out to the locals by the Italian authorities as a deterrent also appeared at times to be deeply shocking. And numerous diaries and letters referred with anger to the corruption and incompetence of the officers ('a shameful camorra – if the Duce knew about it, he would shoot at least half of the scum who command us').[43] But unlike Vasco, the great majority of those who served in Africa remained convinced that Italy was fully entitled to its 'place in the sun' and that the suffering and brutality were relatively small prices to be paid for the benefits that would soon

accrue to Ethiopia as well as Italy from the civilising mission brought
by fascism.

The willingness of so many soldiers to accept the rhetoric of the
regime is partly explained by the fact that the war was very one-sided,
with many of the enemy casualties being brought about from the
relative safety of the air. Italian losses amounted to only about 4,500
dead, as against anything between 70,000 and 275,000 on the Ethiopian
side. Most of those who reported their feelings in diaries or in letters
displayed consistently high levels of morale and enthusiasm throughout
the campaign. When Giuseppe Bottai arrived in Africa in October, he
wrote excitedly to his wife about meeting Galeazzo Ciano at an airfield
in Asmara amid 'embraces, cheering, and incredible celebrations' and
immediately setting off with him on an air raid in which they dropped
eighteen bombs on an enemy village – which he had found thrilling:
'You cannot imagine how I feel "at home" here.' Three months later,
his exhilaration was undimmed, and he talked of his heart being
'swollen with joyous and youthful emotion' and claimed that there
could be 'no lovelier destiny' for a man of his mature years than to
march behind 'unfurled banners'. In February, he witnessed several
days of fighting: compared to the static monotony of 1915–18, he said,
they had been 'beautiful' – 'mobile, agile, sensitive, protean', a 'blazing
adventure' whose flames had 'not yet fully died down'.[44]

The celebratory and aestheticising vision of war that the regime
had taken over from Futurism and the sense of excitement at fascism's
civilising mission in Ethiopia were by no means confined to intellectuals like Bottai. A young telegraph operator from Montepulciano,
Mario Saletti, was characteristic of many with quite limited education
but some academic aspirations who felt drawn in the privacy of a
diary to the florid language that the regime had made fashionable.
His fervour was accentuated by the overlapping of his fascist and his
Christian faith. After arriving in Ethiopia towards the end of 1935, he
wrote of his 'pride' at being among the first 'to bring the breath of
civilisation to this uncivilised land' and of his certainty that Italy would
be victorious given the justice of the cause: 'Forward, comrades, our
march, guided by a genius, who is supported by a divine ray, is irresistible. We will win!'[45] He frequently invoked God, and talked of his
work in Ethiopia as his 'calvary'. His prose exuded great fervour as it
hovered at times between prayer and profane rhetoric:

Africa! Africa! . . . I feel that you are more dear to me than life! . . . Is
it perhaps the feeling that one day you will be the land of a blessed
people that makes you dear to me? Is it perhaps the sense of the good
that we are all doing for those who will come later that binds us so
tightly to you? Duce, here, more than anywhere else, we understand
you. O blind Halcyon [presumably he meant 'Albion'], be warned that
your spears are destined to be hurled in vain as they shatter against
the barrier formed by myriad heroes, who, inspired every one of them
by the example of a great man, run the gauntlet of danger with the
verve of the ardent youth who is about to throw himself into the arms
of his beloved![46]

Like Bottai, Mario showed no visible sign of losing enthusiasm or
confidence as the months passed. After attending Mass on Easter
Sunday in April 1936 he reflected on why he felt so satisfied at being
in the army in Ethiopia, despite the fact that he was such a long way
from home:

Although I am far away from my family and deprived of some of my
freedom (even on the best days), how is it that I feel calm, indeed
almost happy? It is the sense of having done my duty, the awareness
of serving the cause of the fatherland and fascism in the manner best
suited to my abilities. Thank you, O Lord, for making me worthy to
understand what is beautiful.[47]

Numerous diarists and letter writers spoke, like Mario, of the pride
they felt in serving the fatherland and fascism, bringing the blessings
of civilisation to a region of barbarism, and defying Britain and the
other members of the League of Nations. But most of those who
went out to Ethiopia in 1935–36 probably viewed their time abroad in
predominantly more mundane terms: as a relief from unemployment
and hunger back home, and also, in many cases, as a welcome opportunity for novelty and excitement. The images of Africa that circulated
in the interwar years through films, postcards, advertisements, journalism, popular fiction, travel writing and various other sources
fostered impressions of a romantic land in which exotic experiences
(not least sexual) would be freely available. As a twenty-six-year-old
medical officer from Lecce, Manlio La Sorsa, freely admitted at the

start of the detailed diary that he kept in Africa in 1936, his main
motive for wanting to go out to Ethiopia was 'the thought of being
able to have a rather adventurous life' in a country that was 'so alluring
and mysterious':

> It is my intention to record in this diary the impressions that I will
> have during my journey in Africa . . . I have always hugely enjoyed the
> natural spectacle of dense forests inhabited by lots of ferocious animals,
> of vast deserts, of rivers filled with crocodiles, of villages devastated
> by locusts, of caravans wiped out before some dry and abandoned
> oasis, etc . . . No film has ever excited me as much as [the 1930 American
> documentary] *Africa speaks*, and others like it.[48]

But as a conscientious fascist, Manlio did not want to emphasise
pleasure too much. He quickly added that his trip was also ('indeed
above all') 'a duty' and 'a mission', and that he would do everything
possible to win the admiration of his superiors and the love of his
fellow soldiers.[49]

Manlio had a university degree in chemistry and pharmacy and his
mind was in many respects cool and analytical. But from the outset
he was determined to display to himself (and to anyone who might
happen to read his journal) appropriate flights of patriotic ardour. He
set sail for Africa on 12 February 1936, saluting the fatherland with
typically fascist hyperbole – 'farewell, great Italy: never have you
appeared as sublime in your titanic force as now'. After arriving at
Massaua on the Red Sea ten days later he recorded with excitement the
reports he heard of the heroic achievements of the Italian troops, who
had been 'renewing the deeds of our indomitable *arditi* and the glorious
ancient legions of Rome'. When news came through at the end of
February of the 'resounding victory of Tembien' (when the armies
of two Ethiopian *ras* were destroyed, primarily as a result of being
bombed from the air with mustard gas) he was intensely proud but
also slightly disappointed: 'As I write these notes, my heart exults with
true and burning patriotism, I tremble with joy and contentment at
the great victory, and I feel regret at not being among the first combatants and the first glorious dead!'[50]

How much Manlio knew at this stage about the use of gas is not
clear, but he would have been under few illusions a week later when

he visited two Italian airfields at Mai Edaga, south of Massaua. Any moral scruples that he might have experienced were wholly concealed beneath a sense of awe at the power of fascist modernity and a feeling of irritation rather than pity that the Ethiopians were choosing to fight and die rather than surrender, 'as a result of not having understood that [Italy] desired only to bring the torch of civilisation to lands where no ray of civilisation had ever shone'.[51] He was especially impressed by the airport for bombers:

> This one is of vast and extensive proportions, built according to the most modern technical criteria, and richly endowed with enormous and powerful hangars and huts for the personnel, intelligently adapted to the land and the climate . . . The airport is truly imposing and colossal, capable of holding more than 160 aeroplanes, most of which I saw lined up outside the hangars and already fitted out with massive, heavy calibre bombs containing mustard gas, and all set to take off and drop their lethal cargo on the enemy hordes . . . To see these horrifying and yet marvellous mechanical frames is moving.[52]

There were no discernible chinks in Manlio's moral armour. He was able to witness thousands of Ethiopian corpses strewn across a battlefield almost with dispassion: they were a regrettable but necessary price for making 'our dear fatherland greater, stronger and more respected' and bringing civilisation to 'this dark and shadowy land'.[53] And just how much the antithesis between fascist modernity and African barbarism could dull his capacity for ethical discrimination was underlined by the way in which he talked about the contingents of Libyan Arab soldiers deployed on the Italian side, who had terrified the Ethiopians with their cruelty:

> People will say that they used barbaric, ferocious and inhuman methods, but it was the only way for us to deal effectively with a barbaric and inhuman population. And we Europeans, who are easily moved and readily forgive, would never have been capable of committing the vandalic acts that were indispensable for keeping this treacherous and ignorant people in check and snuffing out any desire on their part to resume hostilities.[54]

Manlio remained stationed in Ethiopia for some months after the Italian forces had entered Addis Ababa early in May 1936 and Mussolini had formally declared victory (though in reality large parts of the country still remained unsubdued). He was able to travel around the northern parts of the colony and witness the burgeoning fruits of civilisation. In August he admired the fine road winding through the mountains from Axum to Asmara, with its viaducts and bridges – 'a true masterpiece that only the genius and the manpower of Italians would be able to accomplish'. He observed how trade and commerce seemed to be taking off, with new shops springing up and local people successfully imitating ('just like the monkeys do') the business practices of the Italians. And he was struck by how quickly the Catholic Church had made its physical presence felt, with small churches, votive chapels and sanctuaries, built by the troops, dotting the landscape. Indeed, the momentum of progress was already such, he felt, that he was certain Addis Ababa would in a few years' time become like one of the great capital cities of Europe, while the country as a whole, under 'the wings of eternal Rome, with its work, its songs, and its riches', would be completely 'transformed and renewed'.[55]

Manlio's confidence in the righteousness of the invasion was strengthened by a sense of excitement that the errors and humiliations of the liberal era had at last been expunged. Italy was now firmly set on a course to prosperity and greatness thanks to the genius of Mussolini. Millions of fellow Italians shared in this feeling of a past expiated and of a future more in keeping with the hopes generated by the Risorgimento and inflamed by Nationalism and fascism – and it underpinned much of the general euphoria surrounding Ethiopia. 'The Italian people, under the dynamic leadership of the Duce', wrote Manlio, reflecting in August 1936 on the success of the campaign, 'have accepted this expedition with enthusiasm and with Roman spirit, trusting in their own Chief, conscious of their own needs and of their own destiny'. Everything had been brilliantly planned so as not to repeat 'the mistakes made by governments in the unfortunate colonial wars of the past'. The military operations themselves had been prepared in every minute detail, and the 'most modern methods of warfare' employed to dazzling effect, particularly the use of 'aeronautic material'. And in this way, the torch of Italian civilisation, that had been 'passed down the centuries from generation to generation, growing ever brighter, ever more dazzling, until it reached its present radiance', could now illuminate a people that had hitherto been consigned to 'the most desolate barbarism'.[56]

Such confidence helped Manlio to see Ethiopia in a glowing romantic light. Between descriptions of persistent local resistance, arrests and hangings, he had little difficulty in engaging in flights of poetic fantasy in which the countryside around him appeared a Garden of Eden in its lushness and beauty, and the land as a whole an arena for emotional luxuriance:

> How beautiful are these starry nights of Africa! What sweetness, what love, what goodness is in the heart beneath this sky illuminated by the white disc of the moon, which fills the soul of whoever dreams of his fatherland, his mother, his wife awaiting him with a sense of beatitude and profound, calm felicity.[57]

Perhaps not surprisingly in this frame of mind Manlio's thoughts turned readily to sexual adventure. He was after all a conscientious fascist; and had the regime not always encouraged and celebrated manifestations of virility, energy and youthful exuberance as central elements of its ideology? 'How much should I like to live my life totally, intensely, thoughtlessly, almost with desperation. Drink every last drop from the chalice of happiness, and so be able to say: 'I am growing old, it is true, but I have lived my youth to the full and have no regrets.'[58]

Sex had hovered around the conquest of Ethiopia from the outset, and its potential availability had undoubtedly been one of the attractions for many men going out to serve in Africa. The respectable face of sensuality in 'Faccetta nera' was complemented by cruder songs, such as a version of the popular 'Valtzer d'amore' ('Waltz of love') that Manlio recorded in May 1936:

> Down here in Africa/ we will keep our vices up/ doing *nick nick*/ in the shade of the palms./ Down here the *tukul* [hut] will be our retreat/ and we will be able to put on the best display/ making love to black girls and mulattos/ and turn out a string of babies *caffè-latte*.[59]

Countless opportunities presented themselves, and Manlio, like other soldiers, was repeatedly solicited. But he faced something of a dilemma. As a young fascist male he ought to have few qualms about flaunting his sexual potency whenever the occasion arose; but as a representative of a superior civilising race should he not be spurning all physical contact with local women?

As was often the case with those who kept diaries in Ethiopia, 'dirt' and 'smell' were two categories that served to mediate a cluster of often competing emotions. In early July, Manlio found himself taken into a house by a girl during a storm. She took off his glove, caressed his hand, and sang, and then lay down on a bed. As the rain beat down outside he was torn between the impulse to secure sexual gratification and revulsion at the woman's lack of cleanliness – no doubt genuine but also symbolically convenient in terms of creating an appropriately 'fascist' response to the rival demands of virility and racial hierarchy:

> I had to make an effort to suppress the disgust that I felt. Anyway she deserved compassion and gratitude. She was after all no dirtier than others . . . She clutched me ever more tightly . . . But her embrace repelled me . . . A nauseating and unbearable smell made it hard for me to breathe and it was absolutely impossible for me to overcome the repugnance and disgust at such a neglect of cleanliness. Luckily the rain stopped. I got up with my senses unsatisfied and frustrated. I tried to make her understand that I could not stay any longer. She was unable to hide her disappointment and a certain humiliation at not having been able to make her general superiority as a woman – and that of her race – prevail . . . But I am not all that bad or impolite . . . I feigned a certain tenderness and sympathy, said goodbye to her and promised to return when the moon was out.[60]

Manlio's hopes of a romantic sexual adventure in Africa were realised a few months later when he spotted a beautiful woman of uncommonly proud bearing while walking through the streets of the northern Ethiopian town of Dessie. She answered his gaze and invited him to her house. She turned out to be wealthy and upper class, and this time there were none of the physical or psychological impediments that had marred his experience with the common prostitute. He must have felt, as his vivid description of the encounter in his diary suggests, that his dignity as a fascist male could not be impugned – given the woman's aristocratic superiority and a *mise en scène* worthy of a novel by Gabriele D'Annunzio (there is even a suggestion that drugs were involved, as he appears to have lost consciousness at one point): 'I pointed towards her bed: she said yes. The servants withdrew. Sprawled on the simple Abyssinian bed . . . in the weak light of the setting sun that was coming in through a small opening, I held in my arms the most beautiful Ethiopian woman that up till then I had known.'[61]

The euphoria of victory

In Italy, the progress of the Italian forces in Africa was eagerly followed throughout the country during the winter and spring of 1935–36. In Turin, Zelmira Marazio, who was fourteen at the time, remembered how in her classroom there was a large map of Ethiopia – just as in Albertina Roveda's school in Colle Umberto in the Veneto – on which little banners were pasted to mark the places that had been conquered: Adua, Axum, Makalle, Amba Aradam, Amba Alagi. She and her friends were given names of soldiers who wanted to be adopted by 'war godmothers', and they wrote letters to them 'brimming with high-flown phrases'; they received back tiny photographs of young men with beards standing beside their tents, with rolling hills in the background. In church, priests called for prayers to be said to help the army in bringing Roman civilisation and Christian faith to Ethiopia and breaking the chains of slaves, while in the convent of the Monte dei Cappuccini a plaque was dedicated by the friars to the most famous Italian missionary to Ethiopia in the nineteenth century, Cardinal Guglielmo Massaia. Zelmira herself was swept up fully in the excitement of the campaign; she kept her own map at home to chart the advance of the troops and dreamed of going out to Africa 'to teach the little black children and turn them into faithful subjects of fascist Italy'.[62]

In Genoa, a ten-year-old schoolgirl, Sandra Cironi, wrote enthusiastically in her diary of how slaves were being freed from their shackles, of the gratitude of the Ethiopian people, and of how sanctions were a 'crime' against a country that 'had saved' the Western powers twenty years before and was now bringing 'civilisation where barbarism reigns'.[63] In Milan, a Jewish gem merchant, Roberto Cohen, stated

confidently in his diary that Italy's 'most beautiful' victory would mark
the onset of Britain's decline. The English, he claimed, fully deserved
their fate: 'The ignominy and ingratitude of people! What was the
point of 700,000 dead to help save the British Empire! . . . We will
never forget this, you English barbarians . . . We must advance: England
will realise we are no longer a bunch of guitar players!'[64] By contrast,
in Rome, Monsignor Domenico Tardini was deeply dismayed at how
everybody in Italy appeared 'to have gone mad': 'The people are
exultant at the thought of war and, educated in violence, believe they
can conquer the whole world.' And the clergy were doing nothing to
encourage restraint or reflection: they were themselves almost
uniformly 'shrill' and 'bellicose', with the bishops being particularly
outspoken: 'They are the most . . . inflamed and unbalanced of all.
They offer pure gold, pure silver, rings, chains, crosses, clocks, pounds
sterling. And they talk of civilisation, of religion, and of Italy's civilising
mission in Africa.'[65]

In Padua, the twenty-year-old university student of physics, Maria
Teresa Rossetti, was tempted to 'dance and sing' to show her joy when
she heard that the Italian forces had entered Addis Ababa on 5 May
1936. Her excitement spilled over almost uncontrollably into her diary.
Despite the hostility of the entire world, she wrote proudly, Italy had
managed to carry out 'the greatest colonial enterprise recorded in
history':

Just seven months, but now the name of Italy flies gloriously from
everyone's lips and demands the enthusiasm and the admiration of the
world. Seven months: and those who still thought they were dealing
with a wretched *Italietta*, torn apart by parties, without strength or
passion, with an *Italietta* that they imagined they could reduce to
hunger, must now bow their heads in reverence before one of the
greatest nations in Europe . . . O shades of Crispi, of Oriani, and of
a thousand others, you who struggled all your lives for a colonial Italy,
worthy of its traditions, behold her now, all victorious, imposing the
'Roman peace' on the world and carrying the greatest and most radiant
of civilisations into the land of Africa, thus renewing the splendours of
the ancient Latin empire! Behold her and rejoice in your tombs, for
she is heading towards a future of glory and victory.[66]

Maria's enthusiasm on 5 May was shared by some 30 million Italians,
who, to the sound of wailing sirens, emerged into the piazzas to hear
the news of victory. In Rome 400,000 people packed Piazza Venezia
and the surrounding streets to listen to Mussolini declare that the
war was over and that Ethiopia was now '*de iure* and *de facto* Italian'.
Such was the acclaim that he was compelled to come out onto the
balcony ten times to acknowledge the cheering. Meanwhile a choir
of 10,000 children sang a newly composed 'imperial hymn' on the
steps of the Vittoriano. Four days later, under arc lights, an even more
ecstatic crowd applauded as the Duce hailed the 'reappearance of the
empire after fifteen centuries on the fatal hills of Rome' and announced
that the king had assumed the title of Emperor 'for himself and his
successors'. He asked the crowd if they would be 'worthy' of the
empire that he had given them. And when the cry came back resoundingly 'yes', he declared that their response was 'a sacred oath' that
bound them before God, 'in life and in death.'[67]

Among those in the crowd that evening was the distinguished journalist and art critic, Ugo Ojetti, who witnessed the scenes of jubilation
from a flat on the corner of the Corso overlooking Piazza Venezia. His
description of the occasion was cast in strongly religious terms –
just as his first account of seeing Mussolini had been, back in 1921,
when the spectacle of the fascist leader held up before his adoring
followers had reminded him of a priest raising aloft the holy eucharist.
Even the sudden appearance of the Duce on the balcony is seemingly
miraculous. In Ojetti's case, as in so many others, the borderline
between authentic experience and expression, and self-conscious arti-
fice, is hard to discern:

> The longer we wait the more we feel charged with a sense of electricity,
> radiating through us and sharpening our minds, so that not only the
> present but also the future and the past seem clear and distinct: the
> past of Rome. I feel a hand on my shoulder: 'Exactly two thousand
> two hundred years since the first Punic war: 264 BC, 1936'. It is the
> Rector of the university, De Francisci. .. . . 'Du-ce, du-ce, du-ce'. The
> chanting begins each time on the far edge of that sea, as if those
> furthest away were trying to get close to Palazzo Venezia with their
> voices, unable to do so in person. Suddenly the rhythm intensifies . . .
> Three blasts of a trumpet. Down below they haven't heard, and are

still shouting, crying, calling out. And then there he is, erect and motionless, his face square, his hands on the marble of the balcony. When did he step out? When did he become visible? It seems that he had always been there, and that those broad shoulders had forever been in the middle of the huge window, made of marble like the sills and mullions . . . Every word he utters is like a deliberate step forward, firm and accentuated: 'Finally Italy has its empire.' Then there is a warning: 'Your cry is a sacred oath that binds you before God . . .' With one statement after another he had filled us with such burning passion and raised our spirits to such heights that this short and infinite word seemed in this way to the people like a natural invocation beyond life. A cry comes back in response as if to say, yes, God is already in everyone's heart. At that moment the piazza, under the great canopy of the sky, resembles a temple.[68]

Pietro De Francisci, a distinguished professor of Roman law who had recently been Minister of Justice, was not the only prominent academic to be swept up in the enthusiasm in Piazza Venezia that spring evening. Sitting together on the steps of the Vittoriano, looking out over the sea of faces gazing up excitedly towards the balcony of Palazzo Venezia, were a dozen or so of the country's most talented historians. They included Gioacchino Volpe, Carlo Morandi, Federico Chabod, Alberto Maria Ghisalberti, Ernesto Sestan and Walter Maturi. As Mussolini proclaimed the reappearance of the Roman empire, they found themselves drawn into the surge of collective joy: 'A noise like thunder rose up from the huge crowd', recalled Volpe. 'The emotion seized us too. And all of us, on those steps, turned and embraced each other.'[69] Like Ojetti and De Francisci they no doubt had a sense of the past and the present merging into a spiritual whole and creating the kind of morally unified national community that Mazzini and so many other intellectuals had dreamed of since the early nineteenth century.

A more sober perspective on the triumph of fascist civilisation in Africa was offered the following month in Geneva. On 30 June the Ethiopian emperor, Haile Selassie, delivered an appeal to the League of Nations. As he rose to speak, he was heckled and booed by Italian journalists, who had been issued with whistles for the occasion by the recently appointed Foreign Minister, Galeazzo Ciano, Mussolini's

son-in-law.[70] Haile Selassie reminded the delegates of the promises of
help they had made eight months earlier when sanctions were introduced and of the assurances given that aggression would not be
allowed to triumph. He then proceeded to denounce the systematic
deployment of poison gas against his people, 'in violation of the most
solemn promises made by the nations of the earth that [they] should
not be used against innocent human beings'. He said that at the end
of 1935 the Italian forces, fearing defeat, had dropped tear-gas bombs
and barrels of mustard gas on his troops. When these tactics had
proved largely ineffective, they had resorted from late January to more
deadly methods, which it was his duty, he declared, 'to denounce to
the world':

> Special sprayers were installed on board aircraft so that they could
> vaporise, over vast areas of territory, a fine death-dealing rain. Groups
> of nine, fifteen, eighteen aircraft followed one another so that the fog
> issuing from them formed a continuous rain . . . The very refinement
> of barbarism consisted in carrying ravage and terror into the most
> densely populated parts of the territory, the points farthest removed
> from the scenes of hostilities . . . These fearful tactics succeeded. Men
> and animals succumbed. The deadly rain that fell from the aircraft
> made all those whom it touched fly shrieking with pain. All those who
> drank the poisoned water or ate the infected food also succumbed in
> dreadful suffering. In tens of thousands, the victims of the Italian
> mustard gas fell . . .

> I . . . come myself to bear witness against the crime perpetrated against
> my people and give Europe a warning of the doom that awaits it, if
> it should bow before the accomplished fact . . .

> I ask the fifty-two nations not to forget today the policy upon which
> they embarked eight months ago, and on faith of which I directed the
> resistance of my people against the aggressor whom they had
> denounced to the world. Despite the inferiority of my weapons, the
> complete lack of aircraft, artillery, munitions, hospital services, my
> confidence in the League was absolute. I thought it to be impossible
> that fifty-two nations, including the most powerful in the world, should
> be successfully opposed by a single aggressor . . .

On behalf of the Ethiopian people, a member of the League of Nations,
I request the Assembly to take all measures proper to ensure respect
for the Covenant . . .

I ask the fifty-two nations, who have given the Ethiopian people a
promise to help them in their resistance to the aggressor, what are they
willing to do for Ethiopia? . . .

Representatives of the World I have come to Geneva to discharge in
your midst the most painful of the duties of the head of a State. What
reply shall I have to take back to my people?[71]

In the spirit of appeasement, the delegates turned a deaf ear to his
entreaties. Four days later they voted to lift the sanctions against Italy.
The credibility of the League of Nations was irreparably compromised.
Haile Selassie went into exile in Britain, where he remained until 1941.

With the conquest of Ethiopia, Mussolini reached the pinnacle of his
popularity in Italy. The king, who had wept with joy on hearing of
the taking of Addis Ababa and then stayed up all night poring proudly
over a map of Africa, awarded him the country's highest military
honour for having won 'the greatest colonial war in history'.[72] From
his villa on the shores of Lake Garda the elderly D'Annunzio wrote
to congratulate Mussolini on his achievement, saluting the Duce 'in
immortality'. He described the victory as an 'incomparable and courageous gesture' that had left his soul stirred 'by a kind of spiritual
revelation'.[73] In the Senate, the Nobel laureate physicist Guglielmo
Marconi hailed Italy's triumph in Africa as the heroic culmination of
the 'ideals of the Risorgimento' and applauded the 'titanic work' of the
country's leader: 'Against the most insane and immoral coalition that
history has ever seen, Italy has pitted its indomitable courage, its
unshakable unity, binding itself around the Duce, certain of Him and
for Him.'[74] Other tributes poured in from all quarters, and propagandists hurried to proclaim Mussolini as an instrument of God: 'divine',
'infallible', 'ineluctable', a 'genius', a 'Caesar', the 'founder of a religion'
('the name of this religion is Italy').[75]

    Mussolini himself responded to the adulation by growing ever more
detached and aloof. It was as if he now believed in his myth and no

longer saw himself as a common mortal. Colleagues complained that he was becoming increasingly deaf to the opinions of others and wanted to rely exclusively on his own intuitions when making decisions. His faith in the primacy of the irrational, already such an important dimension of the fascist *Weltanschauung*, progressively strengthened: 'I have never made a mistake when I followed my instinct; I have always gone wrong when I listened to reason'.[76] In official photographs he assumed stiff, unsmiling and sculptural poses, often wearing a helmet – an icon rather than a man. And the extent to which this abstracted, dehumanised image corresponded to an inner conviction about his own exceptionality, a feeling that he now towered above the sea of mediocrity around him, is evident from the diaries of his mistress Claretta Petacci and his son-in-law Ciano. They record the brutal scorn he felt for his fellow Italians and his hubristic self-exaltation. In the course of a typically violent session of lovemaking with Petacci in 1937, he announced his desire for a monument to himself standing erect, gazing far into the distance, brandishing a sword at least 2 metres long, with a helmet on his head to symbolise the empire. It should be 'colossal': 'I want children to say: "This was Mussolini"'.[77]

The affair with Petacci started in the late spring of 1936 – coinciding almost exactly, it would seem, with the proclamation of the empire. The infatuated twenty-four-year-old was the daughter of an eminent doctor (the Pope's personal physician) and had first met Mussolini in 1932 after spotting him driving his Alfa Romeo fast on the road to Ostia and ordering her chauffeur to accelerate and pursue him. A string of impassioned letters and intermittent encounters ('You who dominate the world smiled at me' . . . 'You telephoned me, and when I hear your voice it is as if . . . the rays of the sun were a magic lute on which vibrated the most beautiful song of life')[78] culminated in a torrid sexual relationship that was to last until the couple died next to each other nine years later in a burst of machine-gun fire on the shores of Lake Como. From the outset Petacci pandered to Mussolini's feelings of omnipotence and virility, and her influence did nothing to attenuate the insidious distortions of reality that fascist rhetoric was prone to foster. On 12 May 1936, when she was still rather shyly using the polite form of 'you', he was her 'sweet savage', she his 'little Servilia' – after the name of Caesar's mistress.[79] Three weeks later she was employing the intimate form, '*tu*', and the full force of her passion, which was to keep the Duce in thrall for the rest of his life, had been unleashed:

> My great love. I adore you. You were beautiful this evening. Your masculine face, aggressive like a lion, violent and majestic, seemed to be radiating sparks of force. Your figure is like a single concentrated pulse of potent life, of marvellous youth, and such is the invincible vibrant feeling, such the sensation of formidable will, that you make me shudder. It is like a hail, a blast of superiority, of greatness, of youth, that strikes, smashes and stuns, leaving in its wake ecstasy and admiration. I am overwhelmed. I see you as a giant of beauty and power . . . At thirteen, when I was ignorant still of everything, I had already offered my whole life to you. Now I breathe your breath, I live sublime dreamlike moments near to you . . .[80]

With hubris and euphoria enveloping not only Mussolini but the entire country in 1935–36, sober assessments of reality were hard to find. 'A grand illusion, the history of a dream', was how the Neapolitan journalist, Ludovico Greco, who had been a university student in the later 1930s, summed up the events of the time.[81] In truth, the conquest of Ethiopia had been ruinously expensive, in both economic and political terms. It had cost in all probability well over 40 billion lire, or the equivalent of almost the entire national income for a year; and this just when the outlay on welfare was rising steeply, reaching nearly 7 billion lire in 1940, more than quadruple what it had been a decade earlier.[82] Intervention in the Spanish Civil War in 1936–39 compounded the country's financial plight. One result of such spending was that Italy was in no position to invest in developing its armed forces either numerically or qualitatively at a moment when other countries were embarking on huge rearmament programmes in preparation for the impending European war. Further problems were generated by the League of Nations sanctions, which left exports searching for new markets and accelerated the push towards self-sufficiency ('autarky'), as imports had to be replaced by ersatz goods – wool, for example, by 'lanital', made from milk. With its currency reserves running out and its budget deficits out of control, the country was lurching towards ruin.

From a political point of view, the international condemnation of the invasion of Ethiopia propelled Italy away from Britain and France and closer to Nazi Germany. The door was not yet closed: the Western powers' fear of Hitler left Mussolini with considerable room for manoeuvre. Indeed, it was mainly anxiety that Italy might be driven into the arms of Germany that had caused the League of Nations to grow acquiescent over Ethiopia. But Mussolini's instinct was that the future of the West lay with the aggressive newer nations of Italy and Germany with their faith-driven ideologies, and that the era of the old democratic powers with their timid bourgeois values was coming to an end. By the autumn of 1936 when he signed a treaty of friendship with Germany and announced that Berlin and Rome formed an 'axis' in Europe, his confidence in this intuition was strong. A year later, following a state visit to Germany when he was idolised by the Nazi elite and a crowd of nearly a million heard him deliver a speech in a thunderstorm at an outdoor rally in Berlin, he had a euphoric sense that he and Hitler together could bestride the world. As he boasted to Claretta after his return:

They are loyal, and they have felt the power of the [fascist] regime. They understand that if one falls, both fall: we are too closely united. And they have realised that Italy is serious. They are a fine people. They know how to do things on a big scale. Imagine, they are still talking about me. They are fanatical about me. The [German] officers admired my serene, calm force, my easy sense of command. The students – there are twelve million of them – were amazed at my speech . . . The ordinary people are completely conquered. They have felt my force . . . The crowd for the speech was so big you could not see where it ended. They have never given such a reception before, not to kings, not to emperors, not to anyone. Yes, I have conquered them. They have felt the power . . . The red banners behind us, the rays of light, the torches . . . We passed like two gods on the clouds.[83]

Defence of the Race

Sexual fears

When in the summer of 1936 the journalist Ciro Poggiali set sail from Naples for Ethiopia as a special correspondent for his newspaper, the *Corriere della Sera*, he knew there would be many things he could not report. He was relatively sanguine about this. He had worked for the *Corriere* since 1923 and like most journalists he had accepted pragmatically the transition from liberalism to fascism and the restrictions on freedom that this entailed. Looking back some years later, he felt no inclination to pass any general judgement on the regime, but he did think there were some aspects of the government's attitude to the press that had been 'rather curious', and even 'a touch paradoxical'. Why, for example, had so much been done to hide the fact that there was widespread resistance still in Ethiopia after May 1936? It had after all taken many other countries decades to subdue their colonies. And why had the difficulties in making such a disadvantaged country prosperous been played down, when it was again well known that other colonial powers had struggled to develop their territories? 'But that is how it was', wrote Poggiali. 'They did not want to sow pessimism or create alarm in the minds of the Italian masses, who were thought to be as prone to despondency as they were to enthusiasm.'[1]

Certainly everything possible was done after the declaration of victory to encourage optimism by talking up the wonderful opportunities that were now available. In May 1936 an article in the leading party journal *Gerarchia* talked of the 'inexhaustible resources', hitherto only minimally exploited by the indigenous population, that would soon become unlocked in Ethiopia through 'rational, systematic and progressive colonisation': 'We can state without a shadow of doubt that the agricultural horizons open to our farmers have become so broad that it is hard to discern their real limits.' The prominent fascist Asvero Gravelli described the huge riches that Africa would bring, stressing in particular the great potential that lay in the production of bananas, 'the gold of the plant kingdom'. And in the pages of *Il Popolo d'Italia* the well-known travel writer and journalist Mario Appelius portrayed Ethiopia as a veritable El Dorado, claiming that 'vast possibilities' lay in its subsoil. The presence of gold was 'definite': it was confirmed by hieroglyphics in the Valley of the Kings, which had even specified the precise location, in the west of the country, between the Balassa and Abar rivers. There was also platinum, as well as nitrate, enormous quantities of sulphur, and extensive deposits of iron.[2]

As a seasoned journalist, Ciro Poggiali strongly suspected that the official image of Ethiopia would turn out to be largely a mirage, and he decided to keep a diary in which to record impressions and episodes that would not be suitable for publication. Already on his journey down to Africa he had come across a seamier side of life in the new colony. On board the steamship were a number of women destined for employment in a brothel in Asmara. One of them told Ciro that she was not going to leave Ethiopia until she had made at least 400,000 lire – which she reckoned would take her a little over a year, at fifty men and 1,000 lire every day: 'That will even mean I can stop work and pay for my son to study up to university'. The prostitutes gave rise to some tensions, as they risked being forcibly repatriated if they accepted clients on the ship. Two men came to blows over one of them: Ciro suspected that blood would have been shed if they had been Neapolitans or Sicilians. The woman in question apologised philosophically: 'It would be so easy to calm your hot blood with a good professional caress . . . Morality forbids it. And it is not we who have made morality.' The need for discretion was underlined by the presence among the passengers of missionaries and nuns.[3]

The departure of white prostitutes for Ethiopia reflected a growing preoccupation of the government. Mussolini had launched the demographic campaign in 1927 in part because of his publicly declared fears about the threat posed to the West by the coloured races. The dangers of miscegenation in the African colonies horrified him. In 1934 he had angrily ordered the sequestration of the novel *Sambadù amore negro* ('Sambadù negro love') for 'offending the dignity of the race': the front cover had shown a white woman embracing a black man (though the story was in fact quite 'orthodox', in that it ended with the Italian woman recognising her lover's barbarism and Sambadù returning to his tribe in Africa).[4] Once the Ethiopian campaign had begun, the sexual overtones of many popular songs were a source of consternation, and the government tried from the spring of 1936 to have 'Faccetta nera' banned. When this proved impossible it sought to make the wording more 'dignified' – 'when we are together with you' became 'when we are near you'.[5] And no sooner had victory been declared than steps were taken to introduce strict racial segregation and urge wives to join their husbands out in Africa as quickly as possible. In the meantime, the Minister of Colonies told the new viceroy of Ethiopia, Rodolfo Graziani, to set up brothels – if need be, mobile brothels – staffed solely with white women, 'with an absolute ban on access to the natives'.[6]

The problem the government was up against in Ethiopia became apparent to Ciro when he landed in Asmara. The port was brimming with Italian troops, and there was only one brothel with white prostitutes – a large building with wooden cells, and two entrances: one for ordinary soldiers, who bought a ticket for 15 lire (which they could use on any day, but not after 8.00 in the evening), the other for officers and respectable civilians, who paid 25 lire and had to wear a tie and (for some reason) no safari jacket. The women serviced both sets of clients, and were known to be making on average 1,000 lire a day. They were clearly struggling to meet the high demand. Consequently, as Ciro found, there was still plenty of trade for the local prostitutes, who operated in a well-appointed cluster of buildings in a designated quarter of the town ('the civilisation of prostitution here is evidently higher than with us'). To stop customers going through the wrong doors, the adjacent houses had the words 'family home' written in Italian on the outside. Ciro came across one young prostitute crying loudly. The *carabiniere* who had just been with her said she was upset because he had given her 10 lire when she had wanted 20. Ciro suspected that the problem was in fact that 'this young representative of Italian order' had reneged on a promise.[7]

As Ciro could see, attempts by the government to introduce strict racial segregation, and stop sexual contact between Italians and the local population, were likely to prove hard to implement. From the outset the colonial authorities certainly did what they could. They kept blacks and whites apart as far as possible in public places – including on buses – and drew up plans for urban development that would enable the Italian community to live separately from Ethiopians.[8] And in the spring of 1937 a law was passed that made marriage between blacks and whites and the keeping of an African mistress ('madamismo') crimes punishable with up to five years in prison. But in practice such measures were not very effective; and the situation was not helped by the fact that a number of senior Italian officials in Ethiopia persisted in having relationships with local women. An additional problem lay in the shortage of contraceptives – Ciro heard of a pharmacy in Asmara that sold out of its newly arrived consignment of 1,000 in just one day[9] – and the risks of infection and pregnancy were accordingly high. Exactly how many mixed-race children were born in the colonies under Italian occupation is not known. Estimates suggest a figure of perhaps 10,000 from 1936 to 1940.[10]

Lurking behind the government's efforts to keep the Italians and Ethiopians apart were various anxieties. Mussolini himself was prey to a particularly squalid cocktail of fears and prejudices. In a well-known published interview with the German writer Emil Ludwig in 1932 he talked judiciously of how race was a 'sentiment' rather than a reality, and of how the 'strength and beauty' of a nation was often the product of a rich admixture of races over the centuries.[11] But in private he harboured less attractive views. He told a senior diplomat in May 1936 that it was vital to prevent Italians having sexual relations with Africans, as 'a race of half-castes' would become 'our worst enemies'. He did not explain just what he meant.[12] In the company of Claretta he was especially unguarded. He informed her in 1938 that he had been a racist since 1921, and he stressed the importance of making Italians racially conscious so that they did not breed half-castes and 'ruin what is beautiful in us'. He regarded the situation in France – which had a Jewish prime minister and a black vice president of the National Assembly ('not olive skinned, but black as ink') – as a warning of the dangers of not having clear racial awareness. He suggested that France would soon be swamped by coloured people as a result of the great susceptibility of Frenchwomen to the sexual potency of negro men.[13]

Alongside such racial stereotypes about blacks were equally racist views about the Italians themselves. Mussolini often railed against the shortcomings of his fellow countrymen and claimed their vices were due to the fact that many were descended from slaves. He told Claretta in 1938 that it was the Italians of servile stock who cohabited with black women in Ethiopia. And he made it clear that he regretted having to allow such 'scum' to go to Africa simply in order to give them jobs: 'This is the civilisation we are taking down there.'[14] Ciro was an educated middle-class Tuscan, and he harboured similar ideas to Mussolini – though in his opinion the moral fault line was more a regional one. After several months in Ethiopia he became despondent about numerous aspects of Italy's administration of the colony. He attributed the problems largely to the fact that too many southern Italians were being sent to Africa:

They are too backward to have authority and impose what is called European civilisation. Some of them are perfectly happy in the filth of the mud huts [tukuls], because in their Apulian or Calabrian village they have never known anything better. To hear people talk about the prestige of the race is laughable. If you take away the colour of the face, what difference is there between some of our ragamuffin fellow countrymen, miserable physical specimens, who have been sent here God knows why, and the Ethiopian peasants who by contrast have very beautiful physiques and appearances?[15]

One of the concerns of Ciro about the poor quality of administration in Ethiopia was that it would alienate further an already disenchanted local population. In September 1936 he spent a day in the court in Addis Ababa observing proceedings. He was horrified: 'I do not have a high regard in general for the workings of justice, but this is too gross a miscarriage'. Since none of the Italian magistrates spoke Amharic, or made any effort to learn it – the officials who came out to Ethiopia were all elderly and were looking to retire soon, as service in the colonies counted double in pension terms – everything had to be done with interpreters. The results were farcical. Ciro watched as the public prosecutor (a southerner) spoke rapidly in abstruse legal language, and the black translator ('whose Italian is enough to ask for a cup of water') passed on a version of what was being said, trying to sound as confident as possible (if he hesitated he knew he would lose his job): 'The accused says that he was living in his *tukul* with his wife and children and sister-in-law. Where are you going? The onions are. How much for hundred? I go to Florence.' Nobody seemed phased by the gibberish. The consequences of such 'justice', said Ciro, were that innocent people were often sentenced to 'atrocious punishments' without having the faintest idea of what they were charged with or why.[16]

Ciro was aware that the gap between rulers and ruled in Ethiopia was perilously wide. The fact that Mussolini had insisted, against all advice, on governing the colony directly, without the mediation of the local *ras*, did not help matters. Rebel attacks on Italian forces continued on an intense scale throughout the summer and autumn of 1936, and the viceroy, Graziani, responded by ordering the wholesale destruction with mustard gas of villages that displayed support for the enemy.[17] Although by the end of the year many of the key warlords had been captured and summarily shot, heavy resistance still continued. Ciro and other correspondents were banned from reporting any adverse news; and on 3 February 1937, the same day as information came through about a serious Italian defeat in which more than two hundred troops had been killed, including seven officers, a dispatch arrived from Rome requiring every journalist to sign a declaration saying they would not transmit anything at all that might suggest fighting was continuing, as the official line in Italy was that 'the war is over.'

A little over a fortnight later, two young Eritreans threw nine grenades into a crowd of Italian officials during a ceremony in Addis Ababa to mark the birth of a son and heir to the Prince of Piedmont. Seven people were killed and around fifty wounded (including Graziani). Ciro was an eyewitness to the attack and was himself struck by shrapnel fragments. While his wounds were being dressed in the local hospital he could hear the sound of rifle fire as the reprisals started. He hurried into the streets to see what was happening. It was an ugly sight:

> In the absence of a military or police organisation, the task of the vendetta has been undertaken by all the [Italian] civilians in Addis Ababa, and carried out with lightning speed using the methods of the most authentic fascist *squadrismo*. They go around armed with

manganelli and iron bars bludgeoning any natives they come across in the streets. There are mass arrests. Crowds of negroes are driven with tremendous lashes of heavy whips – like herds of animals. Soon the streets around the tukuls are strewn with bodies. I see a driver who, after knocking an old negro to the ground with a blow of a club, thrusts a bayonet right through his head. It goes without saying that this slaughter is directed against innocent people who know nothing about what has happened. Without this swift reaction by the citizen body – ferocious, but well timed – the hundred thousand native inhabitants of Addis Ababa (the whites number fewer than three thousand) could have risen up and slaughtered us: this is the explanation given subsequently . . . I try to get permission . . . to telegraph my newspaper. In vain. The orders from Rome are categorical: Italy must not know about it.[18]

Between 3,000 and 6,000 Ethiopians were randomly killed in reprisals in the space of just forty-eight hours. In the weeks that followed thousands more were executed, deported or sent to concentration camps. Graziani proposed razing the old city in Addis Ababa to the ground. Mussolini thought this excessive, but he did agree that any Ethiopian leaders 'even remotely suspected' of opposition should be shot.[19] Graziani accordingly instructed Italian commanders throughout the colony to proceed to ruthless wholesale purges: 'Be aware . . . that I have undertaken the totalitarian elimination here of Abyssinian chiefs and notables and that you must apply in full the same measures in your territories.'[20] When evidence came to light of possible links between rebels and the most important Coptic Christian centre in Ethiopia, the ancient monastery of Debrà Libanòs, Graziani ordered its 'complete liquidation'. According to official figures more than 400 monks were shot, though the total number of victims, including sympathetic local laity, teachers and students, may well have been closer to 2,000.[21] Graziani also had itinerant singers, fortune-tellers and witches executed on the grounds that they served as possible conduits of information about the resistance.

Graziani had long enjoyed a reputation for ruthlessness. He justified his ferocity intellectually by quoting the likes of Caesar and Machiavelli ('my lords and masters') and politically by asserting that the building of a new world necessarily involved the destruction of the old.[22] But

the exceptional brutality of his measures after the attack in February –
which had almost cost him his life – began to seem excessive even to
the fascist leadership in Rome, particularly as the rebel resistance in
Ethiopia showed every sign of intensifying, not diminishing, during
the second half of 1937. Graziani was inclined to blame the deteriorating situation on the failure of colleagues to shed their residual
'sentimentalism' and understand what needed to be done with the
enemy: 'Eliminate them, eliminate them, eliminate them, as I have
been preaching against everyone else's illusions from the first day of
assuming my office.'[23] There were suggestions that the physical injuries
he had sustained had taken too heavy a toll. Graziani tried to counter
such claims by sending the president of the Senate, Luigi Federzoni,
a series of photographs showing himself stripped to his underwear,
his body covered in scars, in various unusual gymnastic poses.
Federzoni decided not to circulate the pictures to his fellow senators
in case they started asking questions about Graziani's mental health.[24]

Graziani was replaced as viceroy at the end of 1937 (he was rewarded
for his services in Africa by being made a marquis), and his successor,
the Duke of Aosta, adopted a less ruthless strategy, with more trials
and fewer summary executions of opposition leaders. But the resistance
in Ethiopia remained as strong as ever: in the spring of 1940 a leading
commander in the colony reported that the moment Italy entered the
Second World War on the side of Germany, it would require no more
than a handful of British or French troops to conquer Abyssinia, given
that the 'great mass' of the population would rise up and support them
in driving out the Italian forces.[25] In 1939 the Minister of Colonies could
still describe to parliament the wonderful material benefits that 'the
formidable world historical reality' of the Italian empire would be
bringing 'proletarian Italy' through mass settlement and access to
'precious metals, meat, milk, wool, skin, cotton, oil seeds and cereal'.[26]
Had Mussolini ever taken the time (and risk) to visit Ethiopia, he might
have understood better how unlikely such hopes were and just how
easily the colonies and all their attendant fantasies could be blown away.

When Ciro left Ethiopia in September 1937 he could already see
that the prospects for the colony were not good: 'I depart . . . with a
far from rosy picture of the situation: the unrest is spreading and
strengthening'.[27] The costs of the enterprise in financial and human
terms were clearly proving to be far greater than he or anyone else

DEFENCE OF THE RACE

had anticipated, and though he showed no signs of becoming an opponent of the regime in any serious sense of the word, he did wonder, when he landed in Messina on 3 October and saw the acute poverty of the local population, if the country's scarce resources might not have been better directed elsewhere:

The sight on the quay is both picturesque and pitiful. Every time a steamship arrives from Africa the people of Messina come out and play music on cylinder pianos, hand-organs, guitars and mandolins for the returning passengers. There are hawkers, priests, friars and nuns – who knows if genuine or not – with things for sale, travelling jugglers, even a little cart with a small stove for frying fish on the spot, sellers of flasks of wine, fruit and hardboard suitcases. But above all there is a crowd of people in rags begging. They are asking for bread, clothes, money, cigarettes, anything. To fetch a packet of cigarettes, children will throw themselves into the sea. These are the signs of the profound poverty of the city and of Sicily in general. The captain of the ship is furious: he had requested in vain to dock in the commercial harbour so as to avoid this wretched spectacle. I remember that perfidious article that *The Times* published on its front page when Italy decided to invade Ethiopia. 'Italy', it said, more or less, 'is about to spend several billion lire. Even assuming it does manage to conquer the territory of Abyssinia, this will not mean that it has secured completely the riches of Abyssinia – which are only latent riches and also 5,000 kilometres from the peninsula. How much better if those billions could instead have been devoted to the totalitarian regeneration of Sicily, which is a potential earthly paradise waiting to become a real paradise and richly productive, if only every strip of its coastal, interior or mountain land could be given the water that it lacks. With the billions . . . Italy would have on its doorstep that agricultural and non-agricultural wealth that it is going in search of so far away with its risky enterprise.' However much inspired by traditional English egoism, perhaps the article was not entirely wrong.[28]

Making imperialists

The conquest of Ethiopia, the growing involvement of Italian forces in the Spanish Civil War on the side of the Nationalists from the end of 1936, the ever closer alliance with Nazi Germany, and the accelerating drift towards a general conflict in Europe, heightened the regime's preoccupations with forging a new, more martial, Italian character. For Mussolini in particular, a disdain for the mass of Italians was coupled with a growing conviction that the country would only realise its full potential if the fascist experiment in reshaping minds and bodies was racked up to a fresh level of intensity. 'We must learn to think imperially', he told a meeting of party officials in August 1936. 'It is not easy . . . Yet it is absolutely vital to create an imperialist mentality and psychology.' The following year he declared (echoing the famous dictum of d'Azeglio): 'Now the empire is made . . . we must make imperialists.'[29] His obsession with reshaping his fellow countrymen was fuelled by a hubristic sense of personal greatness – encouraged by adoring crowds, obsequious colleagues and an infatuated mistress – and by an attendant fear of ageing: 'I still have so much to do, so many things in mind. I am a force of nature. When I am unleashed nobody can stop me – like a hurricane, a storm, an earthquake. Ah, old age is revolting', he exclaimed characteristically to Claretta in March 1938.[30]

The focus on reshaping the mindset and behaviour of Italians had the political virtue of deflecting blame for what went wrong in these years away from both Mussolini and fascism. If the subjugation of Ethiopia had proved far more difficult than anticipated and the resistance movement remained strong, it was not because the invasion was poorly thought out and the methods of direct rule insensitive and inappropriate. The problem was that Italians had failed to behave in a manner that would command respect. Fascism accordingly needed to accentuate its programme of moral and spiritual regeneration. As Mussolini explained in a secret speech to the party's National Council in October 1938, one of the main causes of a recent rebellion in the Amhara region of Ethiopia was a 'lack of racial dignity' on the part of the occupying forces. Initially, he claimed, the Amhara people had accepted Italian rule:

> But when they saw the Italians going around more dishevelled than they were, living in the *tukuls*, and taking their women, they said: 'This is not a race that is bringing civilisation'. And since the Amhara are the most aristocratic race in Ethiopia, they rebelled . . . This is why

the racial laws of the Empire must be rigorously observed . . . If we are to keep the Empire it is necessary for the indigenous people to have a very clear and overwhelming impression of our superiority.[31]

Mussolini's concern with inculcating an 'imperialist' mentality and a sense of 'racial dignity' proved especially attractive to intellectuals and students, many of whom had become concerned in recent years that the momentum of the fascist 'revolution' had slowed. From the beginning of the 1930s, when the economic impact of the Great Depression had heightened fears of popular discontent, the regime had been particularly determined to reach out to the educated classes and prevent them being seduced by rival ideologies such as communism. On the whole its efforts had been successful. Inspired by such influential journals as Bottai's *Critica Fascista*, which from its launch in 1923 had explicitly aimed to engage the young in debate and form a new ruling class, countless periodicals had sprung up to air issues of fascist culture and ideology. Many of them were linked to the party's student organisation, the Gruppi Universitari Fascisti (GUF). In 1934 an annual national competition for students known as the Littoriali had been initiated to encourage discussion among the most able young minds of key political and other topics. At the same time the state had solicited the support of artists and writers by adopting an ecumenical approach to matters of style and by extending greatly the sphere of public patronage through commissions, exhibitions, prizes, pensions and subsidies.

The Littoriali proved particularly effective in engaging young intellectuals. Those who took part almost invariably found them to be stimulating and entertaining. Students were entered into preliminary provincial rounds by their GUF sections, and submitted written dissertations – judged by a panel of experts – or else made oral presentations at conferences devoted to themes such as 'elements of fascist culture', 'colonial studies', 'military studies', 'literary and artistic criticism' and 'racial studies'. The winners from each university then proceeded to the national finals, which were held amid great publicity, every year in a different city, over the course of a week in the spring. Fidia Gambetti, who after the war was to become a prominent figure in the Communist Party, remembered how extraordinarily heated the Littoriali debates could be, with Bottai sometimes stationing himself among students in the back row and making deliberately provocative interventions – much to the annoyance of the more conservative professors.[32] The brilliant young writer Giaime Pintor was thrilled to discover the founder of Futurism, Filippo Tommaso Marinetti, arguing loudly in his session in the Trieste finals in 1939. He called the Littoriali a 'most beautiful institution'.[33]

Paolo Emilio Taviani, a minister in several Christian Democrat governments between the 1950s and the 1970s, described the Littoriali in retrospect as being 'no different from, and nothing more than, games played today by young people, television quiz shows, or many literary prizes'.[34] The Littoriali could certainly be sportive and enjoyable. But they had a far more serious political purpose than Taviani liked to suggest, as they aimed to engage the most talented Italians of their generation very publicly in the intellectual and cultural life of the regime and curtail the moral space in which dissent of any serious kind could germinate. The prizewinners – who in addition to a prestigious gold badge bearing a stylised 'M' (for Mussolini) monogram often received coveted positions in the party or other jobs – included many of the leading figures in twentieth-century Italian arts, literature and politics. Among them were the writers Giorgio Bassani, Vittorio Sereni and Franco Fortini; the publishers Edilio Rusconi and Alberto Mondadori; the film-maker Michelangelo Antonioni; the painter Renato Guttuso; the economist Franco Modigliani; and the politicians Aldo Moro and Pietro Ingrao.[35]

The Littoriali, and more generally the GUF and their journals, also helped to inject fresh ideological impetus into fascism at a time when the party seemed to have lost much of its initial moral and intellectual energy and be succumbing, under its obtusely unimaginative secretary, Achille Starace, to conformism, opportunism and corruption. Early in the regime such prominent figures as Roberto Farinacci had hoped that the PNF would act as a dynamo to drive forward the fascist revolution, create a new elite, and reshape the Italian character. But these aspirations had declined in the later 1920s. And with Starace in charge from 1931, the party grew into an increasingly bloated and arid bureaucratic machine whose principal purpose, aside from catering to the unsavoury ambitions and clientelistic needs of local placemen, was to regulate and control. Detailed party directives of often mind-numbing banality were issued in relation to almost every aspect of fascist life.

Uniforms and minutely choreographed parades, ceremonies and rituals
appeared to have become the essence of the regime.

With liberal democracies in crisis almost everywhere and Europe
growing polarised between the extremes of left and right, many in
Italy felt that the regime should acquire a sharper ideological edge
that would help define it clearly in relation to the other totalitarian
powers. The mood among young intellectuals was one of growing
radicalism in the later 1930s – and the Littoriali and the journals of
GUF offered a forum for the elaboration of new ideas around issues
such as race, imperialism, decadence and moral regeneration. Many
older intellectuals also believed that fascism had lost its way in recent
years and needed to recover the revolutionary elan that had characterised it at the start. One such was Paolino Ferrari, a property surveyor
and senior Militia officer from Emilia Romagna, with a degree from
the university of Perugia. Paolino had served in the army at the end
of the First World War and had been a supporter of fascism almost
from the outset, taking part in the March on Rome. He had later
served as secretary of the *fascio* in the town of Salsomaggiore, near
Parma, but in the course of the 1930s he had become increasingly
disillusioned with the direction the regime was taking. Such was his
disquiet that towards the end of 1938 he decided to start keeping a
diary in order, as he wrote, to record 'the betrayal of the fascist
revolution and its leader' by 'antifascist criminals' – those who had
manifested systematic hostility to 'ideal Fascism'.[36]

The problem with the regime, Paolino reflected in the summer
of 1939, was that it had lost the spiritualism of the 'time of heroic
squadrismo'. The rot had begun to set in as far back as 1923 when
opportunists had been allowed to enter the party and corrupt it.
Mussolini had been 'like the founder of a universal religion'; but as
with all founders of religions he had seen his work 'polluted by the
dishonesty of place-seekers, profiteers, dealers and windbags'. And
now those who had struggled and suffered so much to establish the
fascist faith were not even admired, he felt. Worse, they had become
widely disparaged and regarded as a threat:

All faiths, all religions, have imposed respect for their apostles and their
founders. How could this grotesque inversion of spiritual values have
come about whereby the fact of having been among the first

proponents, the first heroes, the first martyrs of fascism, is now considered, in the fascist regime itself, as no different from having been among the enemies of fascism?[37]

Paolino was particularly angry at the damage that he felt Starace had done to fascism. He did not doubt Starace's loyalty to Mussolini nor his capacity for hard work. The problem was his lack of a 'superior spirituality and an understanding of the psychology of the Italian people'. The consequences, he wrote in November 1939, shortly after Starace had been dismissed as party secretary and replaced by a young air force commander, Ettore Muti, were that all the country's traditional vices had been allowed to flourish unchecked:

> Starace . . . has reduced Italian Fascism to the lowest moral level that it has ever reached in its tumultuous twenty year history. Attention has been paid to external trappings and forms: countless new uniforms of all kinds, displays of eagles on every cap . . . a clamping down on hand-shaking . . . But not only have the worst defects of the Italian people not been countered, but, whether deliberately or not, they have been supported and nurtured. Thus undisciplined individualism, unbridled opportunism, disregard for the spirit of the law and bureaucratic blindness have received plenty of encouragement through the politics of personal preferences, personal favours, recommendations and the camorra of the dishonest.[38]

Paolino's anger at the failure of fascism to bring about moral renewal in Italy chimed with the mood of intensified concern within the party – led by Mussolini himself – at the need for an austere morality that would enable the country to meet the challenges of empire and war. ('Italy can never be Prussianised enough', the Duce told his son-in-law in June 1938. 'I will not leave the Italians in peace until I have two metres of earth over me.')[39] In keeping with public pronouncements by Mussolini and other senior party figures, and with debates in the Littoriali, GUF journals and the press more broadly, Paolino summed up the problem as the persistence still in Italy of materialistic 'bourgeois' values, whose supreme exponents were Judaism, Freemasonry and the rich democracies. He felt the need to fight the 'Masonic, Jewish and xenophile rot of anti-fascism' and the 'mercantile spirit' of the bourgeoisie was all the more pressing given that the domestic battle lines mapped onto the ideological cleavage in Europe following the Ethiopian campaign and sanctions – a cleavage that would only be ended 'with the rubble of the empires of the demo-plutocratic nations'. Indeed, in December 1938 Paolino thought that Europe was heading irrevocably towards war:

> [A] conflict has opened between the heroic spirit of the ordinary Italian people and the associated forces of Judaism, Freemasonry and plutocracy, which will end with the destruction of the older and more degenerate forces – in other words those opposed to Italy.[40]

Paolino had no serious doubts about the Duce: the two elements in Italy 'worthy of the universal destiny connected with the race' were 'the Leader' and the 'common people' (not the bourgeoisie). But in denouncing the failure of the regime after so many years to tackle the issues of vice and corruption, Paolino could not help speculating on why Mussolini had not done more. How come, for instance, he had been so tolerant of his son-in-law, whose decadent millionaire lifestyle struck many people as symptomatic of all that was wrong with fascism? 'Whenever in the cinemas Movie Star Count Galeazzo Ciano appears on the screen with his extravagant fur coats with fox collars or his generals' uniforms, there are grim, deeply thoughtful silences, that say far more than anything spoken aloud.' Paolino's answer to the conundrum of Mussolini's curious passivity was to suggest that he had become so heavily preoccupied with the big inter-national questions that he regarded 'the miserable little men who fool around with decorations, uniforms and camorra intrigues in the same way as Christopher Columbus would have regarded the rats and cock-roaches living in the bilges of the vessels on his famous expedition' – to be tolerated as long as they did not pose a danger to the enterprise. It was thus probable, he thought ('indeed there are those who are absolutely certain of it'), that 'as soon the Duce reached port, he would, like the good captain that he is, see to a total cleansing of the ship, with special disinfection of the most dubious parts'.[41]

Paolino was certainly correct in supposing that issues of foreign policy had absorbed more and more of Mussolini's attention in recent years. But the 'good captain's' navigational skills were much less sound

than he liked to assume. Buoyed by elation after the Ethiopian
campaign and emboldened by the example of Nazi Germany, Mussolini
began from 1936 to commit Italy to a course that it would find increasingly hard to sustain – certainly in material terms. With the outbreak
of the Spanish Civil War he agreed to send 50,000 troops to support
the rebel Nationalist forces of General Franco. The Italian soldiers
took heart from the idea that they were fighting – as their letters often
indicated – for the defence of 'Christian', 'Latin' or 'Catholic' civilisation against godless Bolshevism, as well as for the greater glory of
fascism and the fatherland.[42] But despite Mussolini's assumption that
the war would be short, it was soon evident that a modern conflict
in Europe was likely to prove dispiritingly prolonged. In March 1937
three Italian divisions were routed at Guadalajara, and in order to
salvage the honour of his fascist 'new men', Mussolini was sucked
ever deeper into the war, sending huge quantities of aircraft, artillery,
machine guns and armoured vehicles to Spain at a cost of at least 8.5
billion lire by the spring of 1939. Much of this materiel never returned
to Italy.

The intervention in the Spanish Civil War hastened Italy's seemingly
inexorable drift into the arms of the Third Reich. When Mussolini
visited Germany in September 1937 the Nazis went out of their way
to impress him. They laid on huge military parades and staged the
most spectacular army manoeuvres the country had ever seen (though
Marshal Badoglio reassured the Duce that the Italian forces were
superior).[43] In a speech delivered to an outdoor rally in Berlin, Mussolini
spoke (in German) of how the similarities between fascism and Nazism
demonstrated the historical parallels between two nations that had
achieved unity in a similar way and at nearly the same time, and he
stressed just how much their world views had in common: hostility
to communism and materialism, a belief in will as the principal motor
of history, an exaltation of work and youth, a commitment to the
virtues of discipline, courage and patriotism, and a scorn of easy living
and comfort. He said that the Rome–Berlin Axis existed to promote
peace in the face of the 'dark forces' that were operating to foment
war, and he ended by insisting that the two peoples, who together
constituted 'an imposing and ever-increasing mass of 115 million spirits',
should be united 'in one unshakeable will'.[44]

Mussolini came back from Berlin confident that the Axis powers would prevail in any future conflict. His Foreign Minister, Ciano, wondered if it might not be advisable to begin immediately what he called, with the insouciance of a young man who spent most of his afternoons playing golf and womanising, 'the supreme game'.[45] In the next few months Mussolini withdrew Italy from the League of Nations, signed an anti-Soviet pact with Germany and Japan, and acquiesced (albeit uncomfortably) in Germany's annexation of Austria. On 30 March 1938 he addressed the Senate on the state of the armed forces. Far from being weakened by involvement in Africa and Spain, as some foreigners had suggested, he said, Italy had been strengthened morally and materially by its recent experiences. It could now swiftly mobilise 8 or even 9 million men, up to 5 million of whom would be for the front line: 'You must agree, honourable comrades, that this is an imposing mass.' The young had been superbly trained in the youth organisations. The army was magnificently equipped. And perhaps most important of all there could henceforth be unity of command at the top in a way that would eliminate dangerous rivalry between politicians and generals: 'War in Italy will be guided, as it was in Africa, at the orders of the king, by one man: the man who is speaking to you.'[46]

The clause 'at the orders of the king' could hardly conceal the fact that this was a severe slight to Victor Emmanuel, who under the constitution had sole command of all the armed forces. But there was little concern in the atmosphere of heightened ideological fervour that had seized the regime since the Ethiopian campaign for political correctness. After Mussolini's speech (which Badoglio and Admiral Thaon di Revel proposed should be printed and disseminated across the country) a special session was convened in the Chamber of Deputies to create the title of First Marshal of the Empire and confer it upon the Duce. To soften the subversiveness of the move it was suggested that the king should also be given the title. The decision was taken in ten minutes. The deputies, led by the president of the Chamber, Costanzo Ciano, marched to the Senate to have it ratified. Galeazzo Ciano tried to stop his father taking this blatantly unconstitutional step. 'But we are in a revolution!' Costanzo shouted at him. The Senate accepted the new measure – also in ten minutes – amid much cheering. Starace closed the session, shouting: 'For the fascist Senate, eia, eia, alalà!' A large crowd of deputies and senators proceeded, arms linked, to Palazzo Venezia to inform the Duce of their decision. A couple of Piedmontese politicians suggested they should also go to the king: by the time the cortège reached the Quirinal Palace, it had dwindled to three people.[47]

Five weeks later, on 3 May, Hitler arrived on an official visit to Italy. Mussolini was determined to project an image of imposing military strength, great prosperity and discipline. Every section of the itinerary was carefully scrutinised in advance. Shabby buildings were painted, demolished, or concealed behind artificial facades, streets repaved, trees planted and appropriate works of art installed (a copy of Donatello's Renaissance statue of Saint George, a suitable prototype of the fascist 'new man', was erected along the route of the motorcade in Florence).[48] For six days the Nazi leadership was feted. Huge cheering crowds, and countless swastika banners adorning balconies and lining streets, conveyed a sense of great popular enthusiasm for the friendship between the two countries. There were spectacular parades, military reviews and naval demonstrations, as well as visits to exhibitions and museums. Hitler was hoping to secure a military convention with Italy. However, Mussolini was not yet ready to commit to a formal alliance, as it made little sense to break irrevocably with France and Britain until he had seen just how far these countries were prepared to go to maintain his friendship.

Mussolini was delighted with the impression made on the Germans during the visit, seemingly unconcerned that in striving so hard to project an image of military strength he might be encouraging Hitler's belligerent plans. He described to Claretta with almost childish glee the amazement he believed the Germans had felt at the navy and army displays, and their admiration in particular for the newly introduced *passo romano*. This marching step was one of several measures that he had recently sanctioned as part of a campaign to reform Italian customs, crack down on bourgeois softness, and engender an 'imperial mentality'. To most observers it looked like an imitation of the German goose-step, but Mussolini claimed that it was in fact Piedmontese in origin and that it was important to adopt it to dispel the myth that Italians were physically inferior (the king could not do it – he had abnormally short legs – and was mortified). The new march was intended as a manifestation of 'will' and 'moral force'.[49] The Germans were left 'astonished', Mussolini told Claretta:

They could never imagine anything like it. There they were, their eyes shining, transfixed. They didn't know what to say. Those [naval] manoeuvres were perfect. And then this morning they watched the *passo romano*. They were surprised and full of admiration. They said to me: 'It took us years to teach our soldiers this march. You've got it perfectly in a few months. It's wonderful.' I can't tell you how impressed they were when the heavy and very long guns came by; and the tanks. They were terrified by the power of our army. They hadn't imagined . . .[50]

Some senior military observers, including Marshal Graziani, knew that much of Italy's military equipment was in fact out of date and more or less obsolete: the tanks in particular were very light (and in some cases had wooden dummy guns).[51] But Mussolini preferred to see the world in more reassuring terms. At a time when many Italians were growing deeply uncomfortable about the friendship with Germany and alarmed at the intentions of the Nazis,[52] he liked to convince himself that he was in control and that Hitler did not in fact pose a serious threat. Indeed, he told Claretta, the German leader was really not much more than a boy at heart:

We laughed a lot today, because, you know, when he is not acting officially, [Hitler] is very nice [*molto simpatico*], and laughs and jokes . . . With me he is always a bit intimidated, I have to say, as if respectful. But I manage to make him laugh. We talked about what position the Delphic oracle in Paris will take at the end of [our] talks, and we laughed a lot . . . You know, these Germans are extremely nice and Hitler is a big child when he is with me . . . Hitler was emotional when he left, he was crying. He said to me: 'These have been the most beautiful days of my life. I will never forget them. Six dream-like days.'[53]

A rather different impression of the relationship between Hitler and Mussolini was gained by the young archaeologist and art historian, Ranuccio Bianchi Bandinelli. He acted as interpreter during the visit. Hitler, he felt, certainly behaved rather obsequiously towards Mussolini; and Mussolini responded by speaking to Hitler in an offhand manner (in German, with a strong Romagna accent). But there was no sign of any affection, certainly on the Duce's part, as Hitler's intellectual and artistic pretensions clearly irritated the Italian leader (and even Bandinelli: 'At last, at last, I understand Böcklin and Feuerbach', he heard Hitler mutter as they stood in Piazzale Michelangelo looking out over Florence), and left him at risk of losing face. Coming out of the Baths of Diocletian in Rome Mussolini decided to chance an observation on the contrast between the ancient world, where architecture was anonymous, and the present, where architects clamoured for recognition. 'But', said Hitler, 'we do know the names of architects of antiquity. We know the name of the architect of the Propylaea on the Acropolis in Athens, and of the Parthenon – Phidias'. Mussolini turned for help to Bandinelli, who suggested that the German Chancellor was talking about Greece, whereas 'you were referring to the Roman world where the individual obliterated himself before the majesty of the Empire'. Mussolini was delighted at this platitude. 'What about Vitruvius?' said Hitler. Mussolini was left floundering again, and it was down to Bandinelli to salvage Italy's honour by pointing out that Vitruvius was now known only through a treatise, not a building.[54]

Edginess and mistrust – on both sides – were in fact to characterise the relationship between the two Axis leaders for the next seven years. If Mussolini tried to convey in his brusqueness towards Hitler (and in his boasting to Claretta) an air of superiority, in reality he felt increasingly in awe of a man who had already displayed a breathtaking capacity for ruthlessness in both domestic and international politics, and of a country that seemed to have acquired the kind of discipline and resolve that he had dreamed of for his fascist 'new men'. '[The German] people is formidable, dangerous', he said to Claretta in February 1938. 'If that mass sets itself in motion it is terrifying, compact – like a single man'.[55] And running through his mind by way of contrast to the ideological fanaticism and resolve that he had seen in Nazi Germany – with racial arrogance (and its complement, hatred) somewhere near its core – were reports of his own people's dissolute behaviour in Africa or the scenes of servility that he had encountered when he visited Sicily in May 1937: 'They flung themselves at my knees, and hurled themselves under the cars, to hand in their petitions . . . Truly ugly sights.'[56]

Mussolini's response was to accelerate the 'reform of customs' in the course of 1938 and 1939. As he told his son-in-law in March 1938

after ordering the bombardment by Italian planes of the civilian population in Barcelona in support of General Franco's offensive in
Catalonia (thousands were killed and injured in three days of heavy
air strikes), he would much rather Italians 'excited horror at their
aggression' than 'pleasure as mandolin players': 'This . . . will raise
our standing with the Germans, who love total and ruthless war.'[57] All
possible measures accordingly needed to be adopted to encourage
Italians to be 'less nice' and teach them to be more 'odious, tough
and implacable: in other words, masters'.[58] From the beginning of 1938
the polite form of address, 'Lei', was condemned as a foreign import
with connotations of 'servility' and a fierce campaign was waged to
replace it with the more fraternal and manly 'voi'. Handshaking was
declared 'soft', unhygienic, and Anglo-Saxon, and banned in public
and at work: the more martial 'Roman salute' – with the right arm
extended at an angle of 170 degrees, hand open and fingers together,
as one of Starace's directives specified – was to be used instead. Civil
servants were obliged to wear uniforms for work, and coffee drinking
was discouraged as bourgeois and decadent. And to underline the
importance of physical fitness party leaders were required to take part
in gymnastic displays and jog in public.

The most extreme and brutal of the 'anti-bourgeois' measures was
the introduction of racial legislation. The drive for strict segregation
in Africa that had led to the decree of April 1937, making it illegal for
Italians to have sexual relations with blacks, had from the outset been
linked as much to a concern to bolster the consciousness of the 'new
man' as to fears of biological contamination. For young intellectuals
in particular, the desire to inject renewed ideological intensity into
fascism and strengthen its claims to future dominance against the
decadent liberal democracies, gave the concept of 'race' enormous
allure. As Luigi Preti recalled of the second half of the 1930s, when
he was a brilliant young law student in Ferrara (and a winner of the
Littoriali), the nationalistic fervour of the time went hand in hand
with an acceptance of the 'imperialistic myth' and a belief that fascist
Italy with its superior spiritual mindset (into which the category of
'race' slotted naturally) would sweep all before it:

The university students embraced the nationalistic and imperialistic
myth with passion and conviction, and saw in the Duce the *princeps*

juventutis, the beacon of the new generations summoned by history to a great and enviable destiny . . . National pride was like a wine, blurring the outlines of reality in [their] minds. They saw Italy at the summit of power and glory confronting the democratic nations, who were effete and incapable of keeping up with Mussolini. And if one of the more enthusiastic students uttered the word 'war' – almost to invoke it – he imagined . . . a kind of triumphal march . . . before which the enemies of fascism, lacking any idealistic drive, would quickly surrender to avoid certain defeat.[59]

The extent to which young intellectuals were keen to regard the category of race as something ideological and educational can be seen from an article written by the twenty-six-year-old Indro Montanelli in December 1935 for *Civiltà Fascista*, the journal of the National Institute of Fascist Culture. Montanelli, later one of Italy's most successful journalists, was enthusiastic about the Ethiopian campaign, enrolling as a volunteer in the autumn of 1935 and commanding a unit of native troops. He was disparaging about the martial qualities of the Abyssinians, but like many well-educated middle-class Italians, he was also troubled by the behaviour of his fellow countrymen: they needed to acquire a greater sense of 'racial dignity':

> There are two racisms: one European – and we will let the blond-heads to the north have a monopoly of this; and one African – and this is a catechism which, if we do not know it already, we must quickly learn and adopt. We will never be dominators without a strong sense of our predestined superiority. There is no fraternising with negroes . . . No indulgences, no love affairs . . . The white must command.[60]

Montanelli was wounded in December 1935, but stayed on in Ethiopia as a press officer. He enjoyed his time in Africa, describing it as 'like a beautiful long holiday given to us by the Great Father as a reward for thirteen years of school'.[61] He did not practise what he preached. however: he purchased himself a twelve-year-old Ethiopian wife from her father for the equivalent of 500 lire. He left her behind on returning to Italy.[62]

The campaign against the Jews

The introduction of racial laws, the fostering of anti-Semitism and the encouragement given to biological debates were undoubtedly influenced by the growing friendship with Nazi Germany. But no direct pressure was ever applied by Berlin. In the weeks that followed Hitler's official visit in May 1938, the issue of race was aired with mounting stridency in the press, with the relationship of the Jews to Italian society emerging as a central point of focus. In July the government published a manifesto, drawn up by ten prominent Italian academics, laying down 'the bases of fascist racism'. It declared that race was a 'purely biological' concept and that the overwhelming majority of Italians were of 'Aryan origin' and 'Aryan civilisation'. It claimed that the regime had always acted with racial motives in mind and called on Italians to 'proclaim themselves, frankly, racists' in a way that would elevate them 'to an ideal of superior consciousness of themselves and of greater responsibility'. And it stated bluntly that Jews did not belong to the Italian race: 'The Jews represent the only population that has never been assimilated in Italy because it is composed of non-European racial elements that are absolutely different from the elements that have given rise to the Italians.'[63]

From the autumn of 1938 legislation was introduced stripping Jews of their rights. Mussolini was well aware that such measures would come as a shock to many Italians. The country's 48,000 Jews had long been fully assimilated into national life, and Mussolini himself had denied in the past that they constituted a problem of any sort. Moreover, Jews had been disproportionately well represented in the party from the outset. Aldo Finzi, Undersecretary of the Interior at the time of the murder of Matteotti, was Jewish. So, too, was Margherita Sarfatti, Mussolini's mistress for much of the 1920s and a pivotal cultural figure of the regime. Guido Jung, Minister of Finance from 1932 to 1935, was also Jewish. But in the context of the regime's growing obsession with hardening the Italian character, the very unexpectedness and ruthlessness of the anti-Semitic laws served to give them a perverse logic. As Mussolini explained to a meeting of the National Council of the PNF in October 1938, the legislation would provide a further 'heavy punch in the stomach' to the bourgeoisie and help create a more pitiless and aggressive cultural environment in Italy: had the belligerence of the ancient Romans not derived in large part from their being 'racists to a quite extraordinary degree'?[64]

The fact that Catholicism had for centuries nurtured a deep vein of hostility towards the Jews undoubtedly eased the reception of the anti-Semitic laws in Italy. Pope Pius XI certainly protested at the more extreme aspects of the new racism, issuing the encyclical *Mit brennender Sorge* in 1937 and telling Belgian pilgrims in September 1938 that anti-Semitism was 'unacceptable'. But, as Farinacci and other leading fascists repeatedly liked to underline, the Church itself had a long history of enclosing the Jews in ghettos and actively persecuting them, and was thus in no position to take a serious or effective moral stand against the fascist measures.[65] Indeed, a number of prominent Catholic clergy and intellectuals emerged as among the most outspoken supporters of the racial legislation, and the Pope was obliged to refrain from condemning the laws – which debarred Jews from marrying 'Aryans', teaching in schools and universities, owning more than 50 hectares of land, being members of the fascist party, and serving in the armed forces – as much from a fear of splitting the Church as from a concern with possible government retaliation. The Vatican confined itself to trying to secure more favourable treatment for Jews who had married Catholics or had converted to Christianity.[66]

Most leading fascists gave their backing to the anti-Jewish laws (as did the king, who signed them – though he did confess to Mussolini that he felt sorry for the Jews),[67] whether from political expediency, moral conviction, or a belief that such measures might strengthen the fabric of the nation and bolster the revolutionary profile of the regime. The educationalist Nazareno Padellaro wrote in the newly established periodical *La Difesa della Razza* (The Defence of the Race) that 'consciousness of race' was 'more perfect and more mature' than 'national consciousness', and underlined the importance of teaching children that they were superior to blacks and racially distinct from Jews. In the same journal the writer Julius Evola stressed how racism would give 'a more concrete foundation to national unity', while the journalist Giorgio Almirante described the anti-Semitic campaign as 'the biggest and most courageous act of self-recognition that Italy has ever attempted'.[68] The Minister for National Education, Giuseppe Bottai, used his periodical *Critica Fascista* to proclaim the 'eminently spiritual' character of fascist anti-Semitism, which summed up 3,000 years of Italian 'history, thought and art'.[69] At a more popular level, a huge number of magazines and newspapers spread the racist message through the medium of satirical articles and cartoons that lampooned the somatic features of blacks and Jews and caricatured their supposed defining traits: infantility in the case of Africans, mercenariness and moral depravity in the case of Jews.[70]

Some of the most influential support for the campaign against the Jews came from university circles. The arrest of a number of prominent Jewish intellectuals as members of the clandestine opposition movement, Giustizia e Libertà, in 1934–35 had already given rise to speculation in the journals of GUF about connections between anti-fascism and Judaism. This line of thought was hugely encouraged by the outbreak of the Spanish Civil War, which helped to resuscitate old theories about Bolshevism as an intrinsically Jewish ideology as well as myths of an international Jewish conspiracy.[71] In a much discussed book published in 1937, the prominent academic and rector of the University for Foreigners in Perugia, Paolo Orano, argued vigorously for a fundamental incompatibility between Jewish identity, which he saw as inherently Zionist, and Italy's need to defend its 'national patrimony in every field and manifestation, at the centre of which stands the immense work of the Church, which is entirely Roman and entirely Italian'.[72] And once the anti-Semitic laws were passed, the GUF journals and the Littoriali competitions acted as powerful vehicles for the dissemination of racial ideas. Many university professors openly endorsed the campaign against the Jews; many acquiesced; very few protested at the new measures or at the dismissal of their colleagues.[73]

The reports of OVRA agents indicated widespread public incomprehension at the anti-Semitic legislation and a general feeling that the government was simply imitating Germany or perhaps acting under duress in some way from Hitler. Many people liked to think that Starace rather than Mussolini was the driving force behind the laws, given the Duce's 'profoundly good and Italian character'. Some thought that Mussolini must have had evidence that Italy was indeed the victim of an international Jewish plot. One common rumour that circulated as a justification for the new measures was that the Duce had been endeavouring, out of his usual sense of beneficence, to secure large supplies of grain from France in order to ensure that ordinary people were fed in the event of war. He had approached a major financial company, the Assicurazioni Generali of Venice, headed by Edgardo Morpurgo, a Jew, to underwrite the deal. When Morpurgo had insisted, as the price for his agreement, on being in charge of the new 'Italian Grain Monopoly' company, Mussolini had, it was said, flown into a rage, seeing the demand as an indication of 'the international Jewish will to insinuate itself even more deeply into the internal affairs of our country'. His response had been to crack down on the Jews.[74]

Along with the incomprehension, according to the reports, there was considerable public sympathy. Accounts of Jewish army officers committing suicide in despair at their patriotic credentials being so brutally called into question occasioned particular pity. Some OVRA agents sensed that sympathy for the Jews was more pronounced among the working classes, and that professional people in cities such as Milan were inclined to think that the measures might well be justified given the growing Jewish control over many aspects of national life, particularly the economy. A number of reports referred to anger – especially in regions such as Piedmont where Jews had long featured prominently in public life – and sometimes to gestures of defiance: but any such manifestations of resistance tended to be quite minimal. In most instances the expressions of hostility or indignation were linked to a specific or local episode, rather than being directed in a general way at the new legislation or at the government – for example, when the bust of the much revered former Jewish prime minister, Luigi Luzzatti, was suddenly removed from the hall of the Banca Popolare in Milan.[75]

As the months passed, the incomprehension and much of the sympathy evaporated, and public opinion became increasingly obsessed not with the campaign itself but with the way the laws were applied. This had a paradoxical result of generating in many places anti-Semitic feelings where perhaps none had previously existed. The legislation of the autumn of 1938 stipulated a number of grounds for exemption or 'discrimination' – for example, in the case of families of men killed in the First World War, Libya, Ethiopia or Spain, or for volunteers in these conflicts, or for those who had joined the fascist party before the March on Rome or during the Matteotti crisis. This inevitably led to often desperate efforts by Jews to show that they fell into one of the categories. There was much recourse to string-pulling and bribery, and those

Jews who managed to secure immunity from the full impact of the laws were frequently vilified as accessories to an aspect of the regime that was widely hated, especially by those who lacked the contacts or the means themselves to benefit from clientelism and corruption. Farinacci was rumoured (with justification) to be particularly unscrupulous about taking money from wealthy Jews: half a million lire for securing their 'discrimination', a million for 'Aryanisation'.[76]

By the summer of 1940 the reports of OVRA agents suggest that popular attitudes towards the Jews were fast converging with the crude stereotypes being disseminated in party propaganda. This was especially so in the cities, where the hardships arising from autarky and war made public opinion prone to conspiracy theories and susceptible to anger at what looked like preferential treatment. The capacity of some wealthier and better connected Jewish families to circumvent the laws could be taken as evidence of inherent Semitic immorality and cunning (and materialism). At the same time the fact that the Jews were being persecuted gave rise to the logical assumption that, whatever their previous feelings, they were now inevitably hostile to fascism and Italy and thus a threat to security – particularly, some suggested, given their historic propensity for intrigue.[77] According to one informer in April 1940, there was a common belief in Rome that the Jews should be placed in concentration camps in Africa or Sardinia, because 'with their hatred, and their wicked, intelligent and extremely powerful campaign [against Italy], they constitute the gravest moral danger to our nation'.[78]

The idea that the Jews were an enemy within intensified after Italy entered the war. Agents frequently referred to popular anger at the government's failure to clamp down harder on the Jews and stop them from spreading defeatist propaganda or from spying. The army's disastrous showing from the autumn of 1940 fuelled speculation about Jewish plots. A report from Milan in November 1941 said that party members were incensed at the way Jews were being permitted to undermine the war effort – and even insinuate themselves into important positions – and it claimed that many people wanted the Jews to be made to wear distinctive badges, 'so that they could be shunned by everyone like lepers'.[79] In the same month an OVRA agent in Venice noted that the anti-Semitic German film *Süss l'ebreo* ('Jew Süss') was being warmly applauded at every screening in the San Marco cinema.[80]

Malicious gossip about the privileges wealthy Jews were allegedly able
to secure was widespread, even when the individual in question had
such impeccable 'patriotic' credentials as Oscar Sinigaglia, a hero of
the First World War, a leading figure in the occupation of Fiume and
one of the most important industrialists of the interwar years. As an
informer, himself clearly racked with resentment, wrote in a report
from the fashionable Alpine resort of Merano in September 1941:

> In the restaurant of the Albergo Parco in Merano, Engineer Oscar
> Sinigaglia from Rome and his wife, née Mayer, both Jews, are taking
> their meals at the table next to mine. Although they are both in excellent
> health, they have received medical authorisation to have a special diet:
> meat every day, white pasta and white bread. Even the hotel staff are
> surprised by this and make unfavourable comments about it. The same
> staff, in common with the staff in other hotels, are surprised that in
> general those belonging to the Jewish race always manage to obtain
> privileges, in contrast with the sacrifices that other social classes rightly
> have to put up with.[81]

The lack of resistance to the anti-Semitic laws, despite the widespread
disquiet and anger that many Italians expressed when they were first
introduced, dismayed anti-fascist observers. In Trento, Ernesta Bittanti
Battisti, the widow of the well-known socialist politician and patriot,
Cesare Battisti, recorded in her diary in the autumn of 1938 her horror
both at the compliance with the new legislation and at what such
general passivity revealed about the regime's insidious success after
so many years in eroding the moral defences of ordinary people:

> The law is a reagent that brings out the worst instincts in Aryans. It
> exposes stupidity and ignorance, and revives superstitious hatreds . . .
>
> The reaction of Aryan Italians:
>
> *One*: in public, no protest.
>
> *Two*: in private, rumours of petitions presented by one or two senior
> figures . . .

Three: supine obedience to the orders to remove the names of even distinguished Jews from cultural, intellectual and business associations . . . One professor who had come out of a meeting of an elite cultural institute, which had that day struck off the names of eminent Jews, said to me: 'In fact we had all been opposed.' When I asked him why, then, they had acted as they did, he replied: 'We are all sheep' (this is what they are reduced to after sixteen years of an absolutist regime).[82]

What for Ernesta was craven conformism, might be seen by intellectuals (and others) as compliance in testing circumstances with the primary fascist virtues of 'obedience' and 'belief'. The twenty-three-year-old university student, Maria Teresa Rossetti, was in private horrified at the new laws – which resulted in a number of her physics teachers being expelled. But just a few days after condemning the legislation angrily in her diary, she found enormous satisfaction at being able to show her unbounded 'enthusiasm' for the Duce publicly when he visited Padua.[83] Giuseppe Bottai likewise regarded the anti-Semitic campaign as something of a test of his fascist 'faith'. Colleagues had imagined that he might be opposed to the laws.[84] In fact, as Minister of National Education, he proved a zealous enforcer, stipulating such measures as strict racial segregation during university exams and the exclusion of Jews from schools and public libraries. His backing for the laws, he noted in his diary, stemmed from a conviction that the principle of authority was vital to fascism: 'The orders of the Leader must be accepted or not accepted'. Non-acceptance was only conceivable on 'irresistible moral grounds'.[85]

A further constraint on resistance to the anti-Semitic legislation lay in fascism's disdain for bourgeois humanitarianism. As the anti-fascist law professor, Piero Calamandrei, observed ruefully on a number of occasions in his diary in 1939, many of those who had grown up under the regime had learned to be scornful of the values that he, as a middle-aged left-wing liberal (who considered Britain and France to be his real 'fatherlands'),[86] held dear. They regarded feelings such as sympathy and pity as little more than relics of a morally redundant civilisation and inappropriate to the forward march of history and the struggle for the victory of great ideals to which fascism was committed. Looking at the young intellectuals around him, Calamandrei was deeply pessimistic about the future: 'How will we be able to persuade them that sentiment is not sentimentalism, that goodness is not weakness, that humanity is not "humanitarianism"?'[87] It particularly pained him that his own son, Franco, a university student, showed no regret at the persecution of the Jews: he simply gave 'a half smile without a glimmer of indignation' – though he hoped that this was because Franco thought that any display of his inner feelings would be a sign of 'sentimentalism and weakness'.[88]

The fact, too, that the regime emphasised that fascist racism was essentially 'spiritual' in character (and thus superior to its coarser Nazi counterpart) – despite the claims in the manifesto of July 1938 and journals such as La Difesa della Razza about the purely biological foundations of race and the need to preserve Italy's 'ancient purity of blood' – also helped to disarm potential critics, not least in the Church. The sense that the campaign against the Jews was a logical corollary to an affirmation of the nation's cultural identity, with Catholicism at its core, enabled intellectuals to overlook the perverseness of saying that Jews could never be spiritually assimilated, however 'Italian' they might appear (including being converted to Catholicism), and give their backing to the new legislation. Leading Catholic periodicals such as La Civiltà Cattolica and Vita e Pensiero lent support to the anti-Semitic campaign, while in a much publicised speech at the university of Bologna in January 1939 the rector of the Catholic University in Milan, the distinguished psychologist and Franciscan father, Agostino Gemelli, recalled how the Italian people, thanks to Mussolini and the conciliation of 1929, had at last become 'one of descent, of religion, of tongue, of customs, of hopes, of ideals', with 'tragic' (but inevitable) consequences for those 'who cannot be part of this magnificent fatherland, both on account of their blood and their religion'. This was the reason why, he said:

> we have once again seen carried out, as on so many occasions in past centuries, that terrible sentence that the Deicide people has brought upon itself and for which it goes wandering through the world, unable to find the peace of a fatherland, while the consequences of that horrendous crime pursue it everywhere and all times.[89]

The regime focused much of its attention on universities for the propagation of the racial campaign. Party circulars stipulated the establishment of chairs of racism across the country; new courses were introduced from the autumn of 1938 in topics such as racial demography, racial anthropology, racial statistics and racial anthropometry; and the journals of GUF called stridently for an aggressive application of the anti-Semitic measures – and their intensification: 'We will put up with them no more! Out of our cafes, out of our restaurants, out of our theatres and our cinemas: one decree: civil death!'[90] In these circumstances it was hard for young intellectuals not to be caught up in the increasingly strident atmosphere. Often it was teachers and professors who applied pressure, whether from ideological conviction or, as Calamandrei imagined more cynically, simply from a desire to further their careers.[91] Francesco Pinelli, who was nineteen at the time and a passionate supporter of the regime, recalled how he and his student friends had all bought and read *La Difesa della Razza* on the instructions of their literature teacher. Those who could not afford it, had borrowed copies from friends. Francesco remembered how there was a Jewish student in the class who suddenly found himself the target of insults. One day he did not turn up. He was never seen again.[92]

For most Jews the introduction of the new legislation came as a bolt from the blue. Elements of cultural anti-Semitism had certainly been in evidence for some time – though this was the case in nearly all European countries. The growing friendship with Nazi Germany had also been grounds for increasing anxiety. But Mussolini had on various occasions given public reassurances about the position of the Jews in Italy; and the enthusiasm for fascism displayed by much of the Jewish community from the outset ostensibly made it very hard – or so it seemed to the Milanese dealer in precious stones, Roberto Cohen – for anyone to claim that the Jews posed a political threat to the regime. As his diary makes clear, Roberto was sincerely patriotic and enormously proud of what Italy had achieved with Mussolini ('O Italians of Mussolini, we are still strong! Remember us, you ancient Romans!). When in September 1938 he learned of the racial laws, he was incredulous and struggled to identify a rational explanation. As a wealthy and cultivated man, he imagined that envy had to be involved:

Racism in Italy! Mussolini has suddenly decided to copy Germany! Purity! Purity of race? Right, out with the Jews! But first get hold of their property! Italian Jews – you who are perhaps more patriotic than anyone else! You who did not know you were semites! You too will have to suffer like the others! Faults? Too intelligent! Too much money! A crisis of jealousy and not of anti-semitism![93]

Roberto was one of around 6,000 Italian Jews who managed to emigrate – he went to the United States in 1939 and remained there for the duration of the war. Those who stayed behind and did not have the wealth and the political influence of the likes of Oscar Sinigaglia, faced growing financial hardship, insecurity and persecution (culminating in a government order in May 1942 conscripting Jews for heavy manual labour). Samuele Varsano, for instance, was a university-educated chemist, originally from Salonika, who in the mid-1930s was employed by the Montecatini company in a secret factory at Sarzana producing mustard gas for the Ethiopian war. On 6 November 1938 he was sacked from his job. Thereafter nobody else dared to employ him: the huge press campaign against manifestations of bourgeois 'pity' scared off those who might otherwise have been inclined to help. Like Roberto, he found the suddenness of the anti-Semitic campaign difficult to comprehend:

> Until a short time before, the Italians did not even know what anti-semitism was, and in a great number of cases they did not know what Jews were. We had always lived with them and among them . . . It was therefore natural that most people felt these persecutions were profoundly unjust and showed their sympathy for the victims when they could. But the regime wanted Italians to be hard and therefore condemned any form of sympathy as reprehensible pity (*pietismo*). Fear then did the rest.[94]

The regime pursued the campaign against 'pity' vigorously. A restaurant owner in Rome who was reported to have given additional helpings of meat to Jewish customers had his business closed down; the directors of a firm in Milan who bought a gold watch for a Jewish colleague when he lost his job were expelled from the party.[95] Mussolini was particularly determined to prevent any displays of sympathy: as far as he was concerned the main purpose of the anti-Semitic campaign was to encourage a hard racist mentality, and the last thing he wanted was to engender a humanitarian backlash. He boasted repeatedly to his mistress Claretta in the autumn of 1938 of his own determination to show utter ruthlessness: 'These revolting Jews, they need to be destroyed, all of them. I will slaughter them, like the Turks did . . . I imprisoned 70,000 Arabs: I will be able to imprison 50,000 Jews . . . They are scum, enemies and cowards. . . . I regret not having been brutal enough. They will see what Mussolini's steel fist is capable of doing. I will destroy them.' He simultaneously scorned the weakness of his compatriots: 'These pitying and craven Italians . . . Now they are crying for the Jews: "But why, what have they done, poor things, how sad". Yet does none of them ask what they would have done with us if there had been 44 million Jews and 50,000 Christians?'[96]

Samuele Varsano managed to survive the growing strictures of the regime, living in Rome with his family. He narrowly escaped the round-up of more than 1,000 of the city's Jews by the Nazi and fascist authorities in October 1943: the victims on that occasion were subsequently deported along with around 6,000 other Italian Jews to camps such as Auschwitz. Countless others proved far less lucky than Samuele, even when they enjoyed the friendship and protection of powerful political figures. This was the case with the prominent Turin banker, Ettore Ovazza, a committed supporter of the regime, who had joined the fascist movement shortly after the First World War and had been among the more than 230 or so Jews who had taken part in the March on Rome. In 1935 Ettore had founded a newspaper, *La Nostra Bandiera*, to champion the cause of Jewish patriotic commitment to the regime and oppose Zionism, and that same year he had been made a Knight of the Colonial Order of the Star of Italy for the support that he had given to the development of Libya. Early in 1936 he had been invited to participate in a guard of honour outside the tomb of the royal family in Turin.[97]

Ettore's response to the anti-Semitic laws was to regard them stoically as a 'necessary sacrifice' – and not to lose faith in fascism. With the help of influential friends – among them, paradoxically, Paolo Orano, whose 1937 book on the Italian Jews had done much to pave the way for the new legislation – he secured 'discriminated' status. He steadfastly remained in Italy even as the situation worsened in 1939–40 and Jews were forced to take increasingly desperate steps.

There were many stories of affidavits being secured from friends to say that children were the result of extramarital affairs with Catholics (such offspring could be classed as 'Aryan'); and Ettore knew of people who exhumed relatives from the Jewish cemetery in Turin and had them reburied as Christians in a similar bid to claim Aryan status. Ettore continued to believe that Mussolini had been driven to anti-Semitism simply to appease the Nazis, and that once the war was over the situation for the Jews would return to normal. In October 1943, a few weeks after Italy had surrendered to the Allies and German forces had occupied northern and central Italy, Ettore was taking refuge in a hotel in the Alpine resort of Gressoney. He appeared to underestimate the danger he faced: he had a signed and dedicated photograph of the Duce which he thought might protect him. His faith was again misplaced. He was turned over to the Germans, taken to Intra on the shores of Lake Maggiore, and shot in the cellar of a primary school by the SS along with his wife and fifteen-year-old daughter.[98]

Curt Gutkind was another Jew whose faith in Mussolini was tragically misplaced. Curt was a German academic, with a passion for Italian history and culture. As a young man in the 1920s he had taught in the university of Florence. His enthusiasm for fascism was such that in 1927 he had published a book, *Mussolini e il suo fascismo*, with essays by a number of prominent intellectuals including Balbino Giuliano and Gino Arias, and a preface written by Mussolini himself. A German edition had followed. According to Curt, Mussolini was the reincarnation of a Renaissance *condottiero*, a leader of genius who had swept away the discredited liberal parliamentary system (which represented 'neither the state, nor the nation, nor the people') and mystically united the masses in a common will. This new sense of collective purpose would lead in due course to the realisation of 'the great dream of the third Rome'.[99] Curt had returned to Germany in 1928 and had lectured in Heidelberg and Mannheim. But in the spring of 1933, following Hitler's advent to power, he had been forced to resign his academic post on account of his being a Jew. After two years in Paris he had managed to secure a job in Oxford, before being appointed a reader at Bedford College in the University of London in 1936.

Curt could have applied for British citizenship. But with the outbreak of the Ethiopian war and the imposition of sanctions, he had been determined, as he told Mussolini in a letter in September 1938, to demonstrate publicly his 'faith in this New Italy that I now regard as my true fatherland'.[100] He had accordingly braved the opprobrium of his English colleagues, enrolled in the London *fascio*, and in April 1936 acquired Italian citizenship. But a little over two years later, with his book, *Cosimo de' Medici. Pater patriae, 1389–1464*, about to be published by Oxford University Press, he had learned that he would be stripped of his citizenship under the new anti-Semitic laws and debarred from returning to Italy, where his Roman Catholic wife had a house in the Veneto, which they visited every year. Curt turned to the Duce in desperation, pointing out his long-standing devotion to fascism. He also went to see Balbino Giuliano, who since contributing to his volume in 1927 had risen to a position of considerable influence in the regime, serving as Minister of National Education from 1929 to 1932. Balbino agreed to write a letter of support. But it turned out to be little more than lukewarm in tone. In November 1938 Curt lost his Italian citizenship. He was now stateless.[101]

On 11 June 1940, the day after Italy entered the Second World War, Curt was arrested as an 'enemy alien' and sent to an internment camp at Bury in Lancashire. The previous January he had applied for British citizenship on the basis of five years' residence in the country. But the application had not been processed. He was detained in Bury for three weeks. He was able to send one short letter to his wife, Laura; but she was not allowed to visit him. The principal of Bedford College wrote to the Home Secretary asking for Curt's case to be reviewed: she confessed that she knew little about Dr Gutkind's private life and political affiliations, but could confirm that he was 'a distinguished scholar'. But by the time her letter arrived on 6 July it was too late. On 1 July Curt had been boarded on the *Arandora Star* at Liverpool, bound for a camp in Canada along with 1,200 other Italian and German internees. At 7.00 the following morning the ship was struck off the north-west coast of Ireland by a German torpedo. It sank half an hour later with the loss of more than 800 lives. Curt's body was never recovered. Laura had not been informed that her husband was being sent abroad, and she learned of his presumed death through friends. She wrote to Anthony Eden, to the

Home Office, and even to the Queen Mother, hoping for some form of compensation. She got nothing. In March 1942 she received her husband's effects, that had been left behind in Lancashire: a few papers and a volume of the works of Dante.[102] Whether Curt's decision to forgo the writings of Italy's most celebrated 'national' writer marked a bitter repudiation of the country that had so cruelly rejected him, is not known.

II

War

In thrall to Germany

With tension in Europe growing in the course of 1938 and a general war looking increasingly likely, as Hitler turned his attention from Austria to the Sudetenland in Czechoslovakia, Mussolini became ever more obsessed with Claretta Petacci. Colleagues may have found him aloof, impervious to discussion and deaf to the opinions of others – and they themselves, torn by mutual rivalries, were afraid to present unwelcome truths to him for fear of incurring his displeasure – but Claretta had no difficulty in commanding the attention of the Duce for many hours each day. Her jealousy made her insistent: she was battling to prise him away from two long-standing lovers, Romilda Ruspi and Alice Pallottelli. But Mussolini himself appeared no less determined to allay Claretta's insecurities and encourage the adoration of his 'dear little Walewska' (as he liked to call her, after Napoleon's mistress). Claretta carefully recorded his outbursts of passion in her diary: his repeated declarations of love, his confessions to being a 'slave' of her 'flesh', his reveries about her 'delicious little body' and his insistence that she should 'adore' his body as much as he did hers. And every time they had sex, she made a note of it: a perfunctory '*si*' (yes) underlined, usually with a brief indication as to his level of ardour.[1]

On a typical day in 1938, Mussolini would spend an hour or two in the afternoon with Claretta in the private apartment, built by a Renaissance cardinal, that he had set aside for her on the first floor of Palazzo Venezia. In between lovemaking, sleeping, listening to music on the radio, eating fruit and having Claretta dress him (something he enjoyed), he would reminisce about his wild childhood and

youth, launch tirades against whichever nation or race he felt particularly indignant towards at the time, lament his countless unsatisfactory
relationships in the past, complain of his weariness at having to deal
still with so many women (including his wife), reassure her that she
was the only person he had ever truly loved, and promise to do his
best to be more faithful. Either side of the daily trysts, Mussolini
would telephone Claretta typically a dozen or more times, from early
in the morning to late at night, checking up on her movements, telling
her of any ailments he might have (his stomach ulcer was a regular
source of pain and distraction), saying how much he was thinking
about her and reassuring her of his love. Some days they spent entirely
together, on the slopes of the ski resort of Terminillo in the winter
and spring, or amid the dunes and pines of the Lido di Ostia in the
summer and autumn.

Mussolini certainly had a capacity for hard work, but with his mind
clearly elsewhere much of the time, his ability to maintain a detailed
grip on the five ministries for which he was responsible, as well as keep
abreast of all the complexities of international affairs, was bound to
suffer. He liked to believe that instinct spared him the need to grapple
with pedestrian facts or even reasoned discussion. He told his son-in-
law in December 1937 that he regarded his own instinct as 'infallible'
and that he wanted to have as his epitaph the line: 'Here lies one of
the most intelligent animals that ever appeared on the face of the
earth'.[2] (He also informed him, no less disturbingly, that he shared the
view of a French philosopher that 'genius lies in the genitals'.)[3] And
certainly many of Mussolini's monologues, as recorded by Claretta in
her diary, are almost self-consciously feral in their lack of intellectual
finesse, whether he was discussing the Jews ('these pigs . . . a people
destined to be completely slaughtered. You know what we are for them,
don't you? Dogs, that's what they call us . . . *goym*, which means dogs
. . . Puoh! . . . I detest them'); or the English ('a disgusting people . . .
They think only with their arses . . . They hate anyone exceptional as
a matter of principle . . . Their only great man was an Italian, Disraeli');
or the Spanish ('they are lazy, lethargic . . . Eight centuries of Muslim
domination – that's why . . . they eat and sleep so much').[4]

The absence of serious discussion was most glaring in relation to
the armed forces. Mussolini had assumed control of the Army, Navy
and Air Force Ministries in 1933, but he had not instigated any serious

planning to deal with the eventuality of a general war. His reference in 1936 to the country having '8 million bayonets' was much bandied around in the press; but such rhetoric belied the fact that there was a serious shortage of rifles, machine guns and artillery, and the firepower of Italian divisions was thus considerably less than that of many other armies. Tanks were also a major problem. The General Staff had failed to appreciate the importance of armoured vehicles (partly because they were still thinking of a static war in the Alps: 'men, mules, rifles and cannons' were the keys to an effective fighting unit, according to Badoglio),[5] and this error, along with the country's growing insolvency, meant that the only type of tank available in 1939 was a very small 3-ton machine. Similar deficiencies dogged the air force and the navy. The relative weakness of the industrial base meant that it took nearly five times as long to construct an aeroplane in Italy as in Germany, and the main fighters produced by Fiat were far slower and more lightly armed than the new generation of Spitfires and Messerschmitt 109s. The fleet was impressive in size, but its guns were poor; and largely because of the admiralty's refusal to cooperate with the other services it had no aircraft carriers or air cover of its own, which made it hard for Italian ships to leave port.[6]

A number of factors contributed to this catastrophic lack of realistic preparation. One was the regime's obsession with the primacy of 'will' and 'faith', which helped to perpetuate the anachronistic idea that it was the superior 'spirit' of an army that would enable it to win victory. Federzoni recalled how Mussolini once said at a meeting of the Grand Council that if a conflict broke out he would not stay in Rome but would 'mount his horse' and ride to his command post – a sign, he thought (at least with hindsight) of the Duce's romantic vision of war.[7] Even more fatal was the existence of a political climate that worked against openness and honesty. To reveal unpalatable truths in a regime that was continually seeking to stoke up the fires of enthusiasm might be taken as an indication of an overly sceptical and un-fascist mindset. And given the ceaseless jockeying for position among the leading figures in the regime, it was often much safer to hide unwelcome facts and so avoid giving unnecessary ammunition to jealous rivals (or indeed Mussolini). The Duce's remoteness compounded the problem: it came as a rude shock to Mussolini to discover in August 1938 that the Minister of Finance knew about the serious shortages of artillery, whereas he, as Minister of War, did not.[8]

The full extent of the disparity between the facade and the substance began to dawn on Mussolini only a few months before the outbreak of the Second World War. On 29 April 1939 he told the Council of Ministers that the army was being run in an 'unacceptable' way. The figures that he had been given for equipment and manpower had 'never been exact': 'We have been deceived about the heavy guns. The artillery we have is insufficient and old. The same applies to the Air Force: there is always some gap between the published figures and the real ones'.[9] The Foreign Minister, Ciano, who was present at the meeting, noted ruefully in his diary that the Duce's remarks coincided with the disturbing rumours that he had heard. It was a 'tragic' situation, he suggested – though he did not care to reflect on his own responsibility for having encouraged such a bellicose foreign policy in recent years while failing to ascertain, or indicate to Mussolini, the country's true state of military preparedness:

> Headings have been inflated. The number of divisions has been multiplied, but in reality these divisions are so small that they are not much bigger than regiments. The stores are empty. The artillery is old. Anti-aircraft and anti-tanks weapons are completely lacking. There has been a lot of bluffing in the military sector, and the Duce himself has been deceived: but it is a tragic bluff.[10]

That the Duce had allowed himself to be deceived for so long said much about his state of mind in 1938 – a hubristic sense that the material truth was not entirely relevant given that fascist Italy and Nazi Germany were spiritually dominant and held the future of the West in their hands. He regarded the old democracies as effete, decadent and craven, and in no position to offer any serious resistance to the vigorous new nations of Europe. France with its declining birth rate, loose morals and lack of racial dignity was especially degenerate. He told Claretta in July 1938 that the French were a 'hotchpotch of races and scum, a haven for cowards', with a cringing respect only for those who were stronger than themselves – which is why they were completely terrified of the Germans, 'who had bludgeoned them': 'These French pigs will be frightened of us when we beat them. Then they will understand what the Italians are like . . . Puah, they are contemptible.'[11] And a few months later he dismissed them as 'thirty million spineless and gutless people', who had been corrupted by 'alcohol and syphilis'.[12]

The British fared little better in his estimation. They were 'terrorised' by the idea of war – as was only to be expected of a people that 'has made a religion of eating and playing games', loved animals and could not bear to get their clothes wet in the rain ('people who carry an umbrella can never . . . understand the moral significance of war, because they cannot love that supreme, inexorable violence which is the chief motor force of world history').[13] As with the French, demographic statistics provided clear evidence of decline: there were 4 million more women than men in Britain, and 12 million people over the age of fifty, and this preponderance of 'the static masses' over 'the dynamic masses of youth' led to an inevitable desire for 'peace, compromise and an easy life'.[14] Among the upper classes especially, pederasty was rife, while the growing numbers of women who were opting for Caesarean section to avoid the pain of childbirth was a further sign of moral degeneration.[15] It was hardly surprising in these circumstances that the British empire was everywhere crumbling:

> When you get to this point, an imperial power no longer scares anyone, and in fact the Arabs are no longer frightened, the Indians make fun of it, South Africa is looking to break away, as is Australia, while Canada will be sucked up like an egg at the first opportunity . . . England is now in the stranglehold of destiny.[16]

His view that the democracies were incorrigibly weak inclined him to believe that they would not risk war – and that if they did fight, their resistance would be short-lived (he talked of using poison gas to ensure rapid victory).[17] He accordingly had no qualms in 1938 about encouraging Hitler to pursue his aggressive designs on Czechoslovakia; and when in September the British prime minister, Neville Chamberlain, urged him to use his influence to restrain Hitler, indicating that London might accept a partial annexation of Czechoslovakia, Mussolini took the opportunity to gain international credit by brokering a much-acclaimed deal at Munich. He relished the fact, as he said afterwards, that Chamberlain had 'licked his boots', and announced to loud

applause in Rome that for the first time since 1861 Italy had played a
'preponderant and decisive role' in Europe.[18] His instinct was now
stronger than ever that Britain and France had no stomach for a conflict.
When, in January 1939, Chamberlain paid him a visit in a last attempt
to prise Italy away from Nazi Germany, he was visibly scornful of the
British prime minister's bourgeois demeanour (and umbrella).[19] Two
months later Hitler completed the annexation of Czechoslovakia and
Mussolini responded by launching an invasion of Albania, a country
that had for some time been a de-facto Italian protectorate.

His success in Munich gave Mussolini a sense of extraordinary
elation – less for the outpouring of gratitude in Italy (the tens of
thousands of letters and telegrams that were sent to Rome hailing his
genius in preserving peace in Europe did not sit very comfortably with
the 'imperial mentality' that he was trying to forge – even if most of
them did come from women),[20] and more for what it indicated to him
about the march of history. He told Claretta excitedly on his return
that the old democracies had demonstrated their inability to control
events. In future the 'dictatorships' alone would dominate the international order: 'There has to be only one at the helm, to command.
Today Germany is the greatest power in the world'. And he was not
concerned, it seems, about the Nazi leadership dragging Italy into a
war for which it was unprepared. Indeed, he had come away from
Munich feeling once again that Hitler was in thrall to him. The Führer
had been 'very nice': 'Deep down Hitler is a real softy ['sentimen-
talone']. He had tears in his eyes when he saw me. He really loves
me, very much.' He had repeatedly waxed lyrical about Italy: '"Ah,
Italy, Italy, how beautiful it is . . . You don't know what an effect your
art has on me. I should have been an artist."' And he had gone
out of his way to show his desire to be accommodating. He had talked
of the difficulty of halting an army once it was unleashed: '"But if
the Duce wants it, it will be done" . . . Hitler really adores me.'[21]

Non-belligerence

With instinct and emotion rather than discussion and reason driving
so much of Italian foreign policy, there was no realistic prospect of a
return to cordial relations with the Western democracies. In the spring

of 1939 Hitler began to speak of Poland as his next target after
Czechoslovakia. Mussolini talked of pushing on from the occupation
of Albania deeper into the Balkans: to Greece, Turkey or Romania.
And despite the growing indications of public anxiety at the enormous
risks that the country was facing, Mussolini believed the moment had
come to conclude a formal alliance with Germany. He announced it
in May, without any consultation of colleagues; and the terms of the
Pact of Steel (the Duce's initial preference had been for 'Pact of
Blood') were drawn up almost entirely in Berlin, with little being
done by Rome to place restraints on its partner. Italy committed itself
to supporting Germany in any defensive or aggressive war in which
it became involved; and although there had been much talk of the
need for Italy to buy time for rearmament, no temporal clauses were
inserted into the treaty. The Germans repeatedly told Ciano that they
were not planning an imminent attack on Poland. And Ciano was
apparently reassured. But no sooner was the pact signed than Hitler
issued secret orders to his generals to make preparations for the invasion of Poland.[22]

Mussolini probably sensed that events were moving faster than he
had anticipated. In the weeks that followed the signing of the pact
he repeatedly ignored requests from Hitler for a meeting – while
continuing to indicate to Berlin that Italy would support Germany
fully in the event of a war. He may have hoped that he could continue
to exploit German aggression, as he had in the previous four years,
to secure further territorial gains. When in August it became clear
that an attack on Poland was impending, Ciano (who was fast realising
his own naivety with regard to Hitler) was sent to Germany to explain
that Italy was not ready to fight in what would almost certainly become
a generalised European conflict and to request a delay of two or three
years. But despite what he had unctuously said to Mussolini in Munich,
Hitler had no intention of stopping at this juncture. He was confident,
he said, that France, Britain and Russia would not enter the war;
and he told Ciano (to his great relief) that he was not expecting any
direct Italian help with the invasion of Poland. He also invited Italy
to consider taking Yugoslavia or Greece as its part of the deal. Mussolini
was initially hesitant, but when, towards the end of August, it was
announced that Hitler had signed a pact with the Soviet Union (to
Mussolini's astonishment: Italy had not been consulted or informed

in advance), he became more confident and issued fresh orders to the army to prepare for a limited war in the Balkans.[23]

When Britain declared in the wake of the Nazi–Soviet pact that it would guarantee Poland's independence, it became clear that the conflict would in fact not remain localised. Hitler pressed Mussolini to say whether or not he would support Germany. Fear of repeating the behaviour of the neutralists in 1914–15 inclined Mussolini to say yes. But faced with overwhelming evidence that the army was desperately short of basic equipment and in no position to sustain a prolonged campaign, he told Hitler on 26 August that he would intervene 'immediately', but only if Germany supplied, among other things, 6 million tons of coal, 7 million tons of petrol and 2 million tons of steel – impossible quantities, as he knew. Hitler scathingly remarked that Italy was acting towards Germany just as it had done at the outbreak of the First World War. In order to deflect accusations of cowardice and disloyalty, the Italian public was informed on 1 September in an official press release that the Council of Ministers had decided to refrain from military action ('non-belligerence' was the authorised formula) in keeping with the Duce's long-standing desire to achieve 'peace based on justice' in Europe.[24] In reality, as Mussolini confessed ruefully to Ciano, the army had only ten divisions ready to fight.[25]

Like millions of other Italians, the twenty-three-year-old university student, Maria Teresa Rossetti, was hugely relieved at the agreement reached at Munich on 30 September 1938. She had seen Mussolini a few days before he had travelled to Germany when he had come to Padua to deliver a speech, and she had been captivated by his magnetism and had found herself cheering him wildly. Though she may not have joined the crowds that lined the route of the Duce's train as it travelled back from Germany over the Brenner Pass to Rome, with people, as one eyewitness noted, on their knees in gratitude before the man whom they now looked upon as the 'Angel of Peace' rather than the warrior 'founder of the Empire',[26] she was certainly reassured by the thought that Italy had as its leader 'a great and tireless genius' who was doing all he could to raise the standing of his country in the world.[27] But Maria had recently begun to be plagued by doubts and anxieties. Doubts about the racial laws (which seemed morally execrable), doubts about the campaign to reform customs (which she feared made Italy look ridiculous), and anxieties about the Nazis, who seemed to be dragging Italy remorselessly into their orbit. Indeed, as she noted in her diary, people were saying that the anti-Semitic legislation had been 'imposed' by Hitler and that Italy was 'now a colony of Germany'.[28]

In the months that followed, Maria's sense of trepidation increased. She was fearful of the growing friendship with Germany and did not trust Hitler, who, she imagined, might soon turn his predatory instincts on Italy and take Trieste and Trento. The patriotic hopes and dreams that had given her so much inspiration in the course of the previous decade were fast turning sour. At the end of March 1939, a fortnight after Hitler had completed the invasion of Czechoslovakia and made a mockery of the Munich settlement, she wrote disconsolately in her diary of how Italy, which had been raised up so high in the years following the First World War, was now being 'hurled into an abyss of internal slavery and German protection'. It seemed to be acting 'solely out of ambition, with no thought for the fatherland and its people':

> Yesterday when I was sitting in the Institute of Physics, I saw an Italian flag waving high in the blue sky. And that flag did not allow me to study, and did not leave my mind in peace. My beautiful dear flag, this is how I would always like to see you: flying high in the sky, triumphant, noble, proud of a free people, strong and great![29]

Maria had been hugely enthusiastic for the regime up until 1938, and the 'freedom' for which she was nostalgic was above all Italy's capacity to remain independent and not to 'bow its head obsequiously to every whim' of Germany and align itself with the party of 'injustice and violence'.[30]

As reports from the secret police indicated, the anxieties and doubts that Maria had about the direction in which the regime was heading from the end of 1938 were widely shared across the country. The campaign to stamp out use of the polite form of address 'Lei' was seen by many as unnecessary, irksome and absurd, not least because it was generally felt there were 'far more serious problems weighing on the nation'.[31] Even in shops that had signs up telling people to use 'voi', most customers carried on using 'Lei' – though according to an agent in Genoa this was usually from absent-mindedness rather than wilful obstinacy. The middle classes were particularly resistant to using 'voi', it appears, since they regarded 'Lei' as an important indicator of education and status which they were not willing to forgo – certainly not to please Starace, whose own uncouthness was often considered to be driving the campaign. An OVRA spy in Milan noted particular irritation among telephone subscribers, who found their calls being cut off by the operators if they were overheard using 'Lei'.[32]

The campaign against the Jews was an additional source of complaint and grievance, according to the agents ('how could the Duce, a good father and family man, have allowed certain measures against people whose only fault was to have been born to Jewish parents?').[33] So, too, was the persistent corruption in the party, and the feeling – and this had the clear potential to damage the image of the Duce himself – that members of Mussolini's own family were profiting illicitly from the regime. Ciano ('the Cardinal-nephew', as he was sometimes disparagingly called) was particularly disliked for his extravagant lifestyle. His fortune was said to amount to billions, and he was rumoured to be shipping much of it out of the country.[34] The general impression of the informers was that Mussolini was still viewed as a model of probity and a source of hope and reassurance in a time of international crisis, but there was a growing feeling that he was too cut off, and surrounded by people who lacked the courage to tell him what was really happening. He needed to get rid of the likes of Starace and Ciano: 'Oh if only Mussolini would return to the old simplicity, put a stop to the uniforms, and go around among the ordinary people a bit and hear of all the sufferings they are having to endure . . . he would quickly see how much he would rise in the estimation of the public.'[35]

But it was the friendship with the Nazis and the prospect of Italy being dragged into a war against its will that caused most anxiety during 1939. 'If the Duce does not get off the German wagon quickly, he will be forced to make Italian troops march for the triumph of Pan-Germanism in Europe!'[36] In the cities of northern Italy in particular, where economic and cultural ties with France had traditionally been strong, the alliance with Germany was widely resented. Anti-German feeling was especially pronounced in Milan and Turin – and among all classes, it seems.[37] In Rome and the south there was rather less concern at the prospect of a war with France, but here too there was deep mistrust of Hitler's intentions and a widespread belief that the 'friendship' being displayed by the Germans towards Italy was just a façade. As an agent in Naples reported, it was felt that the arrogance, rapaciousness and ruthlessness of the Germans would in due course lead them to 'extend their claws into us Italians and make us become part of the Reich. It is the dream of the Hohenstaufens that is being played out . . .'[38]

The signs of mounting popular disquiet among many sections of the population in the months leading up to the outbreak of the Second World War led the regime to be especially assiduous in its work of control and repression. The Pact of Steel could after all lose a good deal of its credibility if there was much manifest opposition to the course being pursued by Mussolini. One agent in Rome, who was concerned that the Duce might be becoming impervious to criticism, felt emboldened to point out to his superiors that the ecstatic reception given to Mussolini when he appeared in public in Piazza Venezia should not be taken at face value, 'if one considers that the majority of people present on such occasions are regularly summoned, at least twenty-four hours in advance, by their respective local party groups, to be made ready, and in some ways ordered, to participate enthusiastically'.[39] Another informer in Bologna, who was worried that the economic suffering of the poorer classes might trigger subversion, suggested that the heavy-handedness of the police was in danger of being counterproductive. He mentioned the case of some fifty local peasants who had apparently been sent to *confino* for expressing surprise that Mussolini's sons had acquired property worth many millions of lire, and wondering where their money had come from.[40]

Particular care was taken when Mussolini made high-profile visits to towns or cities. But as his trip to Turin on 14 May 1939 showed, it was not always possible to guarantee that all vestiges of dissent were kept hidden. The widespread hostility in the Piedmontese capital to the alliance with Germany together with traditional loyalty to the king – who was rumoured to be at odds with the Duce over foreign policy – meant that there was considerable anxiety in party circles about the reception that Mussolini would be given. Security was accordingly stepped up – so much so that many thought that the city's patriotism was being insulted. The streets were cleared in advance of beggars, the unemployed, prostitutes, and anyone else who might cause a problem, and over 20,000 police and members of the Militia were brought in from the provinces to lead the applause of the crowds. Large numbers of elderly peasant women who had never been to Turin before were also mobilised from the surrounding countryside and promised that Mussolini would be hugely generous to them. They turned out to be especially effusive, and in some cases obligingly went down on their knees as he passed by.[41]

Much of the visit was a success, not just because of the heavy security precautions, but also, as one informer said, because 'in truth, a clear distinction is still drawn here between the figure of the Duce and the party'.[42] The problems arose when Mussolini went to inaugurate the new Fiat plant at Mirafiori on the outskirts of the city. The authorities knew in advance that there was likely to be trouble among the 50,000 workers, who were unhappy with pay and living standards as well as with broader issues of foreign and domestic policy. In the days before the Duce's visit the walls of the factory toilets had become so covered with abusive graffiti that it had been difficult to get them cleaned in time. To avoid mass absenteeism, the employees were obliged to arrive early in the morning and have their cards stamped. But the fears that Mussolini would be given a cool reception turned out to be well founded. Despite frantic gesticulations by Starace, who was standing on the podium behind Mussolini urging the crowd to show more enthusiasm, there was little applause, and the Duce's attempts to engage the audience through his customary technique of questions and answers proved unproductive. Finally, his patience snapped. After asking the workers if they recalled a major speech he had made about industry in 1934 and getting only a ripple of 'yes-es', he shouted: 'If you don't remember it, read it again!', and turned and walked off the platform.[43]

In the days that followed the debacle at the Fiat factory, Mussolini toured other parts of Piedmont and the Val d'Aosta. There are indications that in the smaller provincial towns and in the countryside enthusiasm for the Duce was stronger and more spontaneous than it had been in Turin.[44] He certainly returned to Rome on 21 May feeling buoyant and confident that the magnetism that he had come to regard as so intrinsic to his personal and political identity was as powerful as ever. He could not wait to tell Claretta about the trip, and phoned her as soon as he got back. Claretta, as ever, kept a detailed record of their meeting in Palazzo Venezia:

> I enter at 16.00. He is at the desk. He is very well. He sees me come in, smiles and puts both his hands over his eyes, pointing his index fingers at me and smiling . . . 'It's been so many days! I have thought about you constantly. Come here, give me a kiss . . . It's been a wonderful, truly beautiful trip. I've done thousands of kilometres. No, nothing: I've been very faithful to you. More than faithful, even in my thoughts. When I go on these political tours you can rest assured. Fanatical scenes, delirious, mad: they were weeping, kneeling, shrieking, arms stretched out . . . There was a woman who said to me: "Duce, speak some more!" "I've just been speaking", I said. She said: "Duce, you don't know how beautiful your voice is!" . . . And then I remember another who suddenly fainted as I passed. She went: "Ah Duce . . ." and puf! Down she went, doubled in two over the barrier! . . . A woman of about thirty . . .'[45]

In all likelihood, those who wept, knelt and held out their arms to the Duce in the late spring of 1939 did so in part because they hoped desperately that war in Europe might yet be averted, and husbands, brothers and sons be spared another conflict. Despite the accentuation of radicalism in the party that Mussolini himself had done so much to encourage with the anti-bourgeois measures since 1936, the dominant version of the myth of the Duce at this time was not that of the ruthless revolutionary warrior but of the bringer of peace and social justice.[46] The more extreme elements in the party, students in particular, were certainly becoming increasingly vocal in their enthusiasm for war; and a number of informers noted that among the poorest sections of the population there was some support for the idea of a conflict on the grounds that things could not get any worse economically and might improve for the 'proletarian nation' if the plutocracies were defeated. But most official reports into the state of public opinion in the summer of 1939 spoke of 'unlimited' and 'absolute' confidence in the Duce, and a belief that Mussolini would again, as at Munich, save the peace of the world, or at the very least act to curb Nazi Germany.[47] 'Everybody has faith in Mussolini', Bottai wrote in his diary in August after noting, rather to his dismay, how few even of his friends had an appetite for war. 'They expect a "miracle" from him. The Italians of the "big star", as ever.'[48]

As tension in Europe increased in July and August 1939, Mussolini kept a low public profile. He spent a lot of time with Claretta at the Lido of Ostia and at Riccione, complaining about the stupidity of the British and the French in taking a stand over Poland, and making out that his refusal now to do anything was sagacious. ('"It was pointless making so much fuss . . . In this way they will simply end up provoking and irritating the Germans . . . These English will make asses of themselves, you know! . . . Everyone is amazed at my silence. What do they say? Of course I am keeping silent!" He gives a Mephistophelean smile.').[49] The reticence of the Duce at this critical juncture gave rise to a host of rumours. Most of them were tailored to keep intact the myth of the heroic leader that so many millions of Italians had invested in for nearly two decades. There was speculation that he had been stricken by a kind of arteriosclerosis after having been forced to make a sudden landing of a plane in a storm. There was talk of his having being wounded – notably in the jaw – as a result of being set upon by an assailant (whom he had then slain). And there were suggestions that he was selflessly planning a *coup d'état*, to install Marshal Badoglio as military dictator and allow the country to extricate itself from the alliance with Nazi Germany, thus sparing Italians the horrors of war.[50]

In reality he simply could not decide what to do. When Ciano came back from seeing Hitler in the second week of August, 'disgusted' at the realisation that the Germans were bent on war ('they have deceived us and lied to us'), Mussolini was torn between staying neutral or honouring the Pact of Steel, joining the conflict alongside the Nazis and taking the opportunity to secure 'his share of booty in Croatia and Dalmatia'.[51] Two weeks later he was still paralysed by indecision – horrified at the thought of following in the footsteps of the man against whom fascism had defined itself from the very outset, Giovanni Giolitti.[52] He found himself revealing his bewilderment to Claretta. After being forced on the evening of 27 August to make a brief appearance on the balcony of Palazzo Venezia to acknowledge the crowds that had gathered for the ceremony of the changing of the guard, he hurried to find her:

'Did you see, my dear? They needed to see me and I smiled and gave them encouragement . . . and I made a gesture as if to indicate that things are going better. These people don't want war and they are beseeching me silently and calmly. From all over the world they are writing to me and asking me to mediate . . . What can I say. I can intervene . . . but let's wait and see. I don't know what to do.'[53]

After several more days of indecision, the announcement that Italy would adopt a position of 'non-belligerence' in the face of the war in Europe was greeted with widespread relief across the country. When Mussolini broke his long silence with a broadcast speech to party leaders on 23 September, the comments of people in the street, as reported by OVRA informers, indicated a general lightening of the public mood and a feeling of reassurance that the stance taken by Italy in the crisis had been approved by the Duce: 'Finally he has come back to life! Now we feel better!' one person was heard to say in Bolzano. 'In these times of crisis in particular, we need to know that he is ever watchful, and above all that he is in good health, and that he is blessed by God, because they had been describing him as nothing short of paralysed! At heart we are a bit like the little child that has to feel his father's hand guiding him while he is walking!'[54] At the other end of the peninsula in Brindisi, a worker voiced a similar sense of gratitude that Mussolini was not paralysed and that the decision to be 'non-belligerent' could therefore be seen as enjoying, in effect, providential sanction: 'To lose the Duce is like saying that a ship has lost its rudder. After all, he is protected by the Divine hand.'[55]

According to the informers, many people believed that the Duce had always wanted peace and blamed the outbreak of war in Europe on the arrogance and inflexibility of the British and the French. But mixed in with general support for the stance taken by Mussolini were notes of disquiet, especially in the north of the country where the alliance with Germany was most resented. The idea that the Duce had become surrounded by inept and dishonest people – which was often used to explain why Italy was so unprepared for war – was more widespread than ever. The phrase, 'if only the Duce knew' ('which everyone goes around repeating when faced with an umpteenth example of alleged incompetence or dishonesty by a politician') was reported to be bandied about insistently.[56] And rumours of the king, the Crown prince, Badoglio or even Italo Balbo intervening to extricate Italy from the clutches of the Nazis persisted well into the winter of

1939.[57] At the same time there was also a significant current of opinion that Italy ought to have honoured its alliance with Germany irrespective of its state of military unreadiness, either on the grounds that neutrality was humiliating after all the martial posturing of the previous few years, or that Germany was looking irresistible and Italy ought not to shun the opportunity to share in the spoils of victory.[58]

As the fourteen-year-old Florentine schoolboy, Pietro Ambrosini, discovered, some of the most vocal support for Italy's entry into the war on the side of Germany came from university students. They saw the destruction of the old plutocratic powers and the creation of a new international order as the culmination of their dreams of a fascist revolution. He noted in his diary in the autumn of 1939 how the headmaster of his *liceo* was under increasing pressure from the local GUF organisations to make his pupils participate in demonstrations in favour of Italy's entry into the war, and on 24 November Pietro was taken along to protests staged outside the British and the French consulates. Whistles (distributed by students) were blown and songs were sung declaring that England would be reduced again to 'a little island of fishermen' ('England, England, your fate is already sealed') and calling for Nice, Corsica and Savoy to be handed to Italy. One person tried to tear down the Union Jack but fell and was seriously injured. Pietro felt awkward: his father was afraid of Italy joining the conflict and would have beaten him if he had known he had taken part. And he himself was not able to feel much enthusiasm: 'All things considered, I have to say these demonstrations seem to me stupid affairs. It also strikes me that the people who gathered to watch us were not really convinced.'[59]

Pietro had been having doubts about the regime for some time and wondering if it could be quite as admirable as the radical university students liked to make out and as he was encouraged to believe at school. A friend, whose grandfather was an anti-fascist, had for a while been planting seeds of uncertainty in his mind (much to his father's alarm); and the forced resignation of his Jewish French teacher in December 1938 had upset him greatly. When in January 1940 Pietro bumped into the teacher again he was shocked to find him looking dishevelled and run-down. His concerns about the morality of fascism intensified:

He spoke to me with his heart on his sleeve, exactly as if I was a grown up . . . I realised that he had a desperate desire to unburden himself to me because, as he said at one point, his few friends had all turned their backs on him. At the time I happily listened to him, but on reflection, I think I would have preferred not to have met him, first of all because the pain it has caused me has been so great that I cannot get it out of my mind, and secondly because it has filled my head with a load of doubts that had already been beginning to take shape for a while.[60]

As Pietro noticed, the situation in Florence had grown increasingly tense in the preceding months (and the same was true of larger towns and cities across the peninsula) as the international crisis had become intertwined with the anti-bourgeois campaign and the drive to forge a racialist and imperialist mentality. The previous April his friend's anti-fascist grandfather had been brutally set upon by a member of the Militia after refusing to take his hat off and salute at a parade to celebrate the annexation of Albania;[61] and by the early autumn of 1939 *squadrismo* was making a reappearance on the streets following calls by the Duce for intensified efforts to enforce the radical directives of the party and eliminate dissent. The law professor at Florence university, Piero Calamandrei, noted in his diary at the end of September how the atmosphere in the city was similar to that of January 1925, with dozens of people being assaulted by fascist squads armed with *manganelli*. He had heard that in Rome a senior member of the party executive had spoken with satisfaction of 45 litres of castor oil being administered in five days. 'This shows', the official had said proudly, 'how our civilisation compares to that of the Germans: those the Germans would have shot, we expurgate.'[62]

For Calamandrei, one of the most distressing aspects of the crisis of the second half of 1939 was the uncritical attitude displayed by so many intellectuals. A few days before the outbreak of war in Europe he found himself talking to the distinguished writer Giuseppe Prezzolini. Prezzolini assured him that the 'cowardly English and French' would be too frightened to fight; and if they did fight, they would simply 'disappear from the face of the globe'. Prezzolini justified his confidence by explaining that Germany, Italy and Russia were the new proletarian peoples fighting against capitalism – as if, noted

Calamandrei, capitalism did not exist in Italy and Germany: 'To think that this is the Prezzolini who with [the journal] *Voce* taught how preconceived ideas should be set aside and problems examined in depth!'[63] No less dispiriting – and equally indicative, he believed, of how successful fascism had been in depriving even highly intelligent people of rationality and sound moral judgement – was a meeting of his university law faculty in June 1939 at which the brewing crisis in Europe was discussed. Everyone who spoke said that Italy was in favour of peace; and they all went on to say that if war did break out, the fault would lie with France, which was ill disposed towards Italy:

> It is deeply disturbing and distressing that an assembly of representatives of 'higher culture', and lawyers to boot – in other words people who are supposed to be good at conducting arguments – should turn reality on its head in this way and not understand that somebody who wants peace must necessarily hate implacably those few criminals who for decades have been preparing war. These people deserve this master they have got.[64]

If he despaired of many of his colleagues, he found the moral and intellectual vacuity of most of the university students he encountered terrifying. One of the most brilliant, the young Jewish writer Franco Fortini, confessed to him in the course of a long conversation in September 1939 that fascism had deprived his generation of any capacity to think: 'If [fascism] were to fall tomorrow, and it was up to us young people to rebuild Italy, we would not know what we wanted'.[65] Calamandrei sensed that part of the problem lay in the unremitting emphasis that the regime had placed on faith and obedience, which had restricted the parameters of discussion and left people insulated within a kind of emotional bubble and 'incapable of appreciating the force that certain moral principles, which they do not feel, have for others'.[66] But connected to this was another even more alarming issue: the disjuncture that the regime had cultivated between language and reality and the encouragement this had given to the long-standing rhetorical traditions in Italian culture. Words had become as much vehicles for the generation of sentiment as tools for intellectual argument or windows onto truth: 'Alas . . . we are, without being aware of it, bookish people who see the world through fantasies . . . For decades we have been confusing our desires with reality, our poetry with history.'[67]

The abyss that fascism had opened up between words and reality, and the appalling consequences this had when Italy was confronted with the fact of war, was something that the young philosopher Alberto Caracciolo reflected on amid the wreckage of Mussolini's regime in 1944. Alberto recalled how during the 1930s he, like millions of other young Italians, had heard about war, had talked about war, and had invoked war, in an almost matter-of-fact and natural way, 'as something necessary and redemptive'. As a member of the GUF at Pavia university in the late 1930s he and his fellow students had been enthusiastic at the prospect of a conflict: something that 'from a human and Italian point of view' may have been 'a stupidity and a crime', but which from a fascist perspective 'was nothing other than the most fitting and coherent culmination and epilogue of the entire work of the movement'. But when war had actually arrived, and young men had begun to die, houses to get bombed and destitution and hunger to spread, the reality had come as a brutal shock, for hardly anyone 'had understood before that this, and this alone, was what he himself had been calling for with all the force that his throat could muster in the piazzas and in the streets'.[68]

Alberto found this extraordinary disjuncture difficult to understand. It led, rather humiliatingly, to many of his contemporaries doing all they could to avoid military service as they suddenly realised that the ideals in which they were supposed to believe (and in which they had perhaps thought they genuinely did believe) were in fact 'purely words repeated so as to be heard, names without objects'. The best explanation that he could come up with had been offered to him by a friend who had suggested that the capacity to appreciate fully that an articulated concept might have repercussions in the real world was blunted in a political system where the individual was deprived of any effective will or responsibility: 'In a dictatorial regime you get used to the notion that whatever and however much is said, everything has to happen or not happen according to the will of the Leader. As a result the importance of words is lost.' According to the historian Tacitus, one of the causes of the decadence of the Roman empire was that 'we lost even the names of things'; in the case of the fascist regime, Alberto proposed, this should be amended to 'we lost even the things of names'.[69]

For Alberto, as for so many of his generation, the journey into disillusionment was very complex as well as painful. How quickly the rhetoric of enthusiasm began to crumble in the face of the harsh realities of war, varied greatly from individual to individual. In cases where fascist ideology had been very strongly internalised – as with Giorgio Forni, a young law student from Pescara – sufficient emotional defences might be constructed to ensure a high degree of resilience. Giorgio had been born in 1919, the son of an industrialist. In the later 1930s he was drawn to the School of Fascist Mystical Theology (Scuola di Mistica Fascista), an institute founded in Milan in 1930 to promote an intensely spiritual version of fascism centred on the cult of the Duce ('the fountain, the one and only fountain, of the mystical theology is in fact Mussolini, exclusively and solely Mussolini').[70] The school had many admirers in Catholic circles and enjoyed close links with the Catholic University in Milan.[71] It aimed to fashion a new political elite, and among its teachers were some of the most prominent intellectuals of the regime, including Berto Ricci, Julius Evola and Asvero Gravelli.

As the diary he kept from 1938 until 1940 shows, Giorgio was a fervent supporter of the international mission of fascism. He endorsed the view of Mussolini that Italy should replace the plutocracies as the dominant imperial power in the world. As he wrote in May 1938:

> Imperialise, imperialise, imperialise. Cross frontiers, export goods, intelligence, labour. The 'stay at home' *Italietta* is finished. We must be present everywhere. Hold high this flag of ours . . . We dream of being great in order to give much: we want to refashion the 'think imperially' of Anglo-Saxon small-mindedness into a reality of magnanimous Roman greatness.[72]

The ruthlessness of the Nazis certainly filled him with some consternation in the months that followed, but he was excited by the thought that the coming war in Europe would be 'our war', the war of a generation that would finally realise the dreams of greatness that had begun 'on the battlefields of the Risorgimento' a hundred years earlier. The German occupation of Czechoslovakia was undoubtedly brutal and provocative, but fascist Italy, he wrote on 18 March 1939, should welcome it and all that ensued: 'For we recognise the inevitability of history. For we recognise the rights of the strong. For we despise the impotent schemings of the weak.'[73]

Giorgio was frustrated at Italy's 'non-belligerence'. He longed to see his country join the war. But he knew it was his duty stoically to bow to the will of the Duce. On 16 May 1940 he wrote:

> We obey. But there is so much sacrifice in obedience. Of all the tests that he has set us, this one of staying quiet and not fighting yet is the hardest. But when we are released, we will be like springs that have been compressed to their limit, and our thrust will carry us to the sky.[74]

A little over a fortnight later, with Italy's entry into the conflict on the side of Nazi Germany imminent, Giorgio wrote of the excitement that he felt at being confronted with 'destiny'. He described how he and his generation longed, through war, to be able to convert 'the marvellous and incredible work of the Revolution' into an entirely new culture and society, transforming what had been a 'moral impulse' into 'a style, a system, a way of life'. And what gave him particular gratification was the thought that this radical metamorphosis would be sanctioned by Christianity: 'If this comes about, it will be a reward for our torment. We believe in it. It is an ideal of revolution that for the first time believes in Christ and the saints.'[75]

Giorgio was killed on 1 January 1941 fighting on the Greek front, his enthusiasm for the war blunted by the disastrous performance of the Italian forces ('too little skill, too little organisation') and a realisation that the regime's hopes of forging a revolutionary mindset had not been fulfilled. Those around him, he noted, still displayed 'too little will to act'.[76] For Mussolini as well, the gulf between his ideal of the ruthless fascist 'new' man – bellicose, disciplined and fearless – and the reality of the great mass of Italians, who, as the reports of the party and the police continued to indicate during the first months of 1940, remained eager for peace and highly anxious about being drawn into the conflict alongside Germany, was profoundly disconcerting. The contrast was made all the more galling by the breathtaking efficiency of the Nazi war machine, and the ease with which Hitler was able first to subjugate Poland and then in the spring of 1940 to sweep into Norway, Denmark, Belgium, Holland and France.

In his frustration and embarrassment at Italy's non-belligerence,

Mussolini railed with growing acerbity at his fellow countrymen. The Italians were a 'race of sheep', he told Ciano in January 1940. It was humiliating to stand by while other nations were making history: he would drag his people into the conflict, if need be with 'kicks in their backsides'.[77] He was certain that Germany would be victorious and that Italy's continued neutrality would leave the country relegated to 'division B of the European powers'.[78] On 18 March he met Hitler, and made it clear to the Nazi leader that he would enter the war as soon as he was sure that the hostilities could be concluded swiftly. He now appeared more convinced than ever that the Germans would win. He told the Council of Ministers that Italy must fight at all costs: 'A nation that avoids the supreme test of its history is a nation of pigs.'[79] But the abusive and bellicose talk was not backed up by serious military consultations. It was only in early April that he informed his army and navy staff (in very general terms) that Italy would fight – though rather confusingly his 'war plan' envisaged staying on the defensive on almost every front.[80]

The contrast between German aggression and Italian passivity became increasingly marked. When Hitler launched his spring offensive against Denmark and Norway on 9 April, Mussolini remained indecisive and continued to vent his spleen on his fellow countrymen. On the afternoon of 11 April Claretta found him slumped dejectedly against an armchair on the floor of the apartment in Palazzo Venezia, almost in the dark:

'Yes, I am bad tempered because I feel ill and I could break everything, smash everything!! Yes: even you!

'I hate these riff-raff ['marmaglia'] Italians! While [the armies in northern Europe] are tearing each other to pieces, here they're living in fear and serenity! This much praised serenity of the Italians is beginning to make me sick . . . For eight months I've been able to measure the temperature of these people. I've taken their pulse, and I have to say they nauseate me. They are cowards and weaklings. They are frightened: these bourgeois pigs who tremble for their stomachs and their beds! . . . And now when the French or the others come and attack them with their cannons, they will still be thinking that it's better to be having a quiet time in the cafe! Ah, you know, it's absolutely useless: you can't undo three centuries of slavery in eighteen years of a regime! It's disappointing and soul destroying to see that I've failed to change these people into a people with steel and courage! . . . With all the problems the French and the English have been causing us, I'd have not a moment's hesitation in grabbing them by the throat. But these Italians, no, these people, no: they want their creature comforts, their coffee, their women, their theatres . . . Yes, my dear, I'm worried, worried and disgusted! I didn't think after years of exercise and kicking them in the shins that I would still be having to deal with these weak and craven people! But they shouldn't think they will get out of this unscathed, unless they want to be disqualified from at least the next fifty years of history . . .'[81]

Pressing the button

Less than a month later, the Germans attacked France. The news came as a complete surprise to Mussolini: Hitler knew that it was too risky to confide any details of his military plans to Rome as in all likelihood they would be leaked (Ciano and his circle were regarded as particularly untrustworthy).[82] As the forces of the *Wehrmacht* pushed forward, it looked increasingly probable that the conflict would very soon be over, and reports on the state of public opinion in Italy indicated a notable shift in the general mood: earlier fears of being dragged ill prepared into a dangerous conflict against Britain and France were replaced by a widespread feeling that Italy should join in before it was too late and make sure that the Germans did not take all the credit and gains and become too dominant in Europe.[83] There was much relief, and in some quarters a sense of elation. Mussolini, it seemed, had made the right choice after all in backing the Nazis, and the claims that the egoistic democracies were decadent and moribund and that the future lay with the young fascist nations appeared to have been vindicated. And among the poorer classes in particular, informers noted excitement at the thought that a new era of greater social and economic justice might be opening up for Italy.[84]

Towards the end of May, with the defeat of France appearing imminent, Mussolini finally decided to enter the war. He spent much of the 27th in a state of nervous excitement, playing tennis, arguing with Claretta (she suspected him of sleeping with one of her rivals, Romilda Ruspi, at lunchtime) and holding meetings. By the evening he had more or less made up his mind. He hurriedly placated Claretta, said it had been a 'heavy day' and told her he had a lot to do: '"Everyone is waiting for me to press the button!"'[85] The next day he informed the Chief of the General Staff, Badoglio, of his decision to fight. On the morning of the 29th he held a short meeting with the heads of the army, navy and air force, at which he announced that Italy would join the conflict any day from 5 June. He confirmed that on land the armed forces should expect to remain on the defensive, as there was 'nothing spectacular' they could do, while the navy would attack enemy shipping wherever possible. He also declared (though without having in fact received any formal authorisation from the king) that he would be in supreme command and that he would transmit his orders to Badoglio, who would then pass them on to the respective Chiefs of Staff on the ground. Nobody raised any objections.[86]

On the evening of 10 June Mussolini stepped out onto the balcony of Palazzo Venezia to announce the declaration of war against France and Britain. The moment had finally arrived, he declared, to 'break the chains' that were shackling Italy in the Mediterranean and embrace the struggle of the 'young and fecund peoples' against those who were trying to monopolise the world's wealth but who were 'impotent and nearing their sunset'.[87] Among those listening in the huge crowds in the piazza was a nineteen-year-old student at Rome university, Elvira Menichini, who had been ordered by her faculty to attend. After the Duce's brief speech, she recalled:

> a roar rose towards the sky. I too was seized with elation and clapped my hands vigorously. At that moment I was an Italian girl . . . with feelings of anger towards 'perfidious Albion' that had inflicted those humiliating sanctions on us. My mother and my grandmother loved England, where, when they were younger, they had gone shopping for elegant outfits – ones that even had strips of ivory or whalebone in the corsets – umbrellas and fans. But me, no, definitely not. The war offered us an opportunity, not to be missed, to shake off that crippling yoke. I clapped my hands – it is true – but afterwards, as the piazza slowly emptied and I headed with my friends towards the station to go back home, I felt my initial enthusiasm cooling. Dark forebodings

shot into my mind. I had an unfamiliar sensation of fear and dismay –
and unfortunately, and to my great grief, this was also painted on the
faces of my father and my mother, who were still young. I then realised
that I had brothers in their twenties, and that the word 'war' concealed
for everyone a future of suffering whose vastness and end were
unknown.[88]

The Duce's speech was broadcast live across the country. Among
the many millions who listened to it on the radio was Don Luigi
Serravalle, a priest based in the small town of Robecco, a few miles
to the east of Voghera in Lombardy. Ever since the Germans had
launched the invasion of France, Don Luigi had sensed that a declaration of war was imminent. As he bicycled around the local villages,
busily conducting religious services, organising processions and helping
to promote the newly inaugurated shrine of the Madonna of
Caravaggio at Fumo, he had noticed signs of growing grass-roots
party activity, with schoolchildren marching in the streets, singing
revolutionary songs and demonstrating against England.[89] At 10.30 in
the morning of 10 June the *podestà* and the secretary of the *fascio*
called on him to say that the Duce would be addressing the nation
later that day and that the church bells were to be rung and drums
played at 5.30 to summon the townspeople. Don Luigi needed to check
that he had the permission of the bishop, and set off on his bike to
Voghera, around 10 kilometres away. But it took him some time to
establish for sure that he had ecclesiastical authorisation. He was only
able to start back from Voghera at 4.45:

Luckily I had the wind behind me and I raced at top speed. In Casteggio
I found the Via Emilia decorated with flags and six young drummers
were already playing their little drums. There seemed to be something mysterious in the atmosphere: a mixture of enthusiasm and
anxiety . . . At about 5.15 I was in the courtyard of the presbytery,
where I found the *podestà* who had come to see about the ringing of
the bells and to invite me to go to the town hall with the other
authorities to listen to the speech. I was sweating heavily and had to
go and change all my clothes. I was soaked, as if I had fallen in water.
At 6.00, the Duce, having appeared on the balcony of Palazzo Venezia
to thunderous applause, delivered a strong speech in which he

announced that the declaration of war had already been consigned to
the ambassadors of France and England. His speech was interrupted
several times by applause; and the applause at the end went on and
on. The people of Robecco, who had assembled in the courtyard of
the town hall when the bells rang, also listened. At the news of the
declaration of war – which people were expecting, anyway – many
eyes were filled with tears.[90]

The generally muted response in Robecco was probably typical of
many small rural communities where the party organisations operated
on a limited scale and most families had painful memories of relatives
killed or wounded in the First World War. Often too, in regions such
as Lombardy, there was some residual left-wing anti-militarist culture.
This was the case in the town of Gazzaniga, to the north-east of
Cremona, where the nineteen-year-old Angela Martina heard
Mussolini's speech on 10 June in the piazza with her father, a former
socialist. The majority of people, she noted in her diary, already knew
in advance what the Duce would say:

> We listened in silence to the vigorous words, the bombastic phrases,
> and the frenetic applause in Piazza Venezia. Then people began to
> make comments. The fascists and some young people appeared
> enthusiastic. The men were worried. The women, especially the oldest
> ones, who had already lived through the painful experience of a war,
> returned to their homes grief-stricken. 'It will be a lightning war', said
> the optimists. 'In three months' time it will all be over.' 'Who knows
> what will happen?' thought the pessimists and the prudent, my father
> among them. 'War is always war: you know when it begins, but not
> how it will go and when it will end. And anyway, how prepared are
> we Italians for this conflict?[91]

In the larger towns and cities, the greater presence of party organisations may have helped to leaven enthusiasm for the declaration of
war, but this could be offset, as the fifteen-year-old schoolgirl in
Naples, Pasqualina Caruso, noted in her diary, by fear of enemy
air-raids. Pasqualina went to listen to the speech 'of our great Leader'
in Piazza Carlo III with her aunt. She was excited by the Duce's talk
of 'breaking chains' and seizing control of 'our sea' and by his

references to 'the great ally Germany, and its great leader the Fuehrer, Rodolfo [sic] Hitler'. But she was worried about what 'the English dogs' might do to Naples:

> I go home, where my sisters and I . . . talk about this war, which is so new for me as I have not seen one before (except the African one). It is evening, and everything is dark, as it has been now for several days. But this evening the streets are even darker, and what's more our hearts are churning with fear of an aerial attack. England promised Italy before it took to the field, that if it declared war it would destroy its most beautiful cities, especially Rome and Naples.[92]

In Florence, too, as another fifteen-year-old recorded in his diary, the feeling of excitement was offset by an immediate fear of air raids and an almost surreal sense of the gap between the destructive potential of a bombardment and the protection available. But unlike Pasqualina, Pietro Ambrosini found it very hard to see how anyone could be enthusiastic at all about the declaration of war. He speculated on why he appeared to see things differently from others. Perhaps it was because he had grown up with a father who was 'a peaceful man in love with the quiet life' and a mother who had always told him about just how horrific the events of 1915–18 had been. Pietro listened to the Duce's speech in a bar, where the radio had been turned up to full volume. Everyone present knew what the announcement was going to be, he said, but when Mussolini spoke, they nevertheless 'all applauded like madmen'. He found this very curious: it was certainly true that France was now beaten and that England would probably soon ask for an armistice. But it would surely not be a 'lightning war' as in Poland.[93]

The next morning Pietro's headmaster delivered a patriotic address to the school and a message was read out from a government ministry about what action to take in the event of an air raid. Rolls of gummed paper were then handed out to stick on windows. Nobody knew quite what to do, and every pane of glass ended up looking different (and a mess from the outside):

> We came out at 11 and I went for a short walk with [my friend] Lucia. The city has all of a sudden undergone a visible change. People are

going around in a hurry, goodness knows why, and little Italian and
German flags are on display in all the shop windows. In some places
people have already put up signs with the word VINCERE! [win] and
there are long queues outside the stationery shops as people look for
rolls of gummed paper, almost as if they are afraid that someone will
come and bomb us this very day.[94]

A fortnight later the appearance of the city had been transformed
more radically still. There were pictures everywhere of Mussolini
wearing a military helmet and posters of an English soldier with his
hand cupped behind his ear and underneath the warning: 'Quiet, the
enemy is listening to you!' But the main change was the great proliferation of banners with the word 'VINCERE'.[95]

Mussolini was certain when he declared war that the fighting was
almost over. All he needed were 'a few thousand dead' to ensure Italy
a seat at the peace table. Accordingly (and to Hitler's bemusement)
the army of 300,000 men, massed in the north-west of the peninsula,
was ordered to remain on the defensive for ten days after hostilities
had formally begun. Only when Paris had fallen and the French
requested an armistice was the decision made to attack. Ciano noted
in his diary on 19 June that the Duce's 'elusive dream' had always been
'glory on the field of battle'.[96] But without serious planning, the chances
of success were limited. The artillery was positioned too far to the
rear, and the air force had not received any training in bombing enemy
positions in the Alps. As a result the infantry were thrown against
well-defended forts with very little chance of prevailing. All along the
line the Italian advances ground to a near halt, and by the time the
armistice came into effect on 25 June almost no French territory had
been taken. In the meantime Italy had sustained nearly 4,000 casualties
(compared to just 104 on the French side). Inadequate clothing and
footwear (rubber-soled boots made of the milk-derived cloth lanital)
had resulted in more than 2,000 instances of frostbite.[97]

As reports on public opinion showed, the indications of just how
badly prepared Italy was for a major conflict reinforced the general
feeling of hope – and relief – that the fighting would be short-lived.[98]
But for those committed fascists who had seen war as the pinnacle of
their revolutionary longings, the poor performance of the country's

armed forces could result in a paradoxical desire for the hostilities to continue in order (somehow) to purge society of its defects. Paolino Ferrari, for instance, had for many years been dismayed by the failure of the regime to live up to its early promises of moral regeneration. He welcomed the outbreak of war, describing it in his diary on 10 June as 'the holy war that the best Italians have for decades been waiting and yearning for to free the Fatherland from the hegemony of the French and English in the Mediterranean and bring about the definitive completion of national unity'. But the incompetence displayed in the first days – such as the fact that British planes had been allowed to bomb Turin factories for two hours without resistance after apparently being mistaken for Italian aircraft – as well as the absence among broad sections of the population of any military ardour, led him to reflect that the only chance of saving both the country and fascism from decadence was through the war itself: Italy had 'to renew itself or perish'.[99]

Mussolini, too, moved in the same mental orbit. He viewed the world in terms of the ebb and flow of spiritual energy, of moral decline and regeneration; and like some latter-day Savonarola, he surveyed the events unfolding in June 1940 with the eye of an austere preacher for whom success and failure were to be regarded as the fruits of virtues or vices. As he told Claretta on 21 June, the collapse of France was an indication of the country's decadence, a decadence from which he was still striving desperately to save his own people:

'[The French] really are a people that should perish: arrogant, conceited, full of egoism and vanity. They had already been decadent in 1914–15: if it hadn't been for our help, they would have lost the war then as well! This disaster goes to show what happens to a people without discipline, and lacking any moral sense: it has slid down the slope of laziness, alcohol and perversion. It's a slope our people, who are still corrupted by impure elements, are in danger of sliding down. I will make the dangers of alcohol crystal clear to these Italians. My campaign against the vices of liquor and gambling will be ferocious! A people without dignity cannot live – and they are abandoning themselves too much to various cocktails and all the other imported filth! There's too much, too much to do. Unfortunately the raw material is resistant.'[100]

But for the moment, at least, it did not look as if his failure to refashion his people in the way he had hoped would matter too much given that the war appeared effectively to be over (though he persistently compared his fellow countrymen unfavourably at this time to the much more disciplined, obedient and dutiful 'Prussians').[101] The main issue to hand was to reap the rewards of an easy victory. In July Ciano was dispatched to Berlin to press Italy's claims to large swathes of territory, including Nice, Corsica and Malta, and huge parts of northern and central Africa. But Hitler by now had the full measure of his ally's worth and suggested instead that they wait until Britain had been defeated before making any decisions. Meanwhile the fascist press discussed Italy's imminent dominance of the Mediterranean, and there was talk of creating an Italian sphere of influence that stretched from north-west Africa and Spain across Europe to the Balkans, Turkey and even the Middle East. It was generally agreed that Palestine should be acquired by Italy, because of the Church's moral claims to the Holy Land and the fact that one of Victor Emmanuel's ancestral titles was 'King of Jerusalem'.[102]

The prospects for Italy were looking relatively good in the late summer of 1940. Many of the anxieties voiced by the public in the previous months about the alliance with Germany and the risks that the country might face in taking on France and Britain diminished. Even those with anti-fascist leanings could sometimes find their moral reservations blunted by the thought that perhaps the Duce had after all judged the march of history well, and that maybe his talk of peace with social justice provided justification for Italy's aggression. An indication of how complex the issues could appear to someone who had managed to preserve a capacity for independent thought can be gauged from the diary of Maria Carazzolo, an eighteen-year-old student from the small town of Montagnana in the Veneto. Maria came from a distinguished left-wing family – her father had been a socialist deputy – but she found it difficult in July 1940 to weigh up the respective merits and demerits of the fascist and the democratic causes, not least when she had to place into the equation issues such as patriotism and the fact that student friends would be serving in the Italian army:

Who ought to win? On the one side the rich, on the other side the poor. Certainly the poor. On the one side the free peoples, on the other

side the tyrants. Certainly the free peoples. And so? The ideal of liberty
is much stronger, yes. But perhaps if we were to win that would bring
in its wake the fundamental justice of wealth, and then the tyrannies
would disappear smoothly of their own accord: that would be the ideal.
But how to avoid the thought that our victory would sanction the
iniquity of the German invasions and lead to the torments of the Poles,
the Norwegians and the Belgians continuing indefinitely? If instead
England won, these small states would triumph, and there would be
the joy of seeing them rise again. Quite so. But the victory of England
would mean the indefinite continuation of its wealth and of our poverty,
and would result in our defeat and hunger, desperation, the loss of the
little we have, and probably communism. The latter are one-sided
considerations, it is true, but I cannot stop myself being Italian. And
so? Our victory? The victory in other words of Hitler and Mussolini?
The assassins of liberty? Ah! Never, never! No, let England win. But
what if this were to mean the death, say, of a certain Erminio: is this
not also a horrifying consideration? I have not got the courage, nor
perhaps the right, to say: it does not matter.[103]

Italy's unprovoked invasion of Greece in October 1940 was to provide
Maria with a way out of her moral maze: 'Nothing now distinguishes
us from Germany. The Italians who kill the Greeks are no different
from the Germans who kill the Poles and the Belgians. And like the
Germans we will have to pay.'[104] But in the meantime she, like millions
of Italians, could find no obvious grounds for abandoning the faith that
they had invested for many years in the regime – or at least in its leader.
Reports from the party and the police suggested that the combination
of relief at having apparently backed the winning side in the war,
gratitude that so little Italian blood had been shed, anger towards the
British for prolonging the conflict and trying to safeguard their selfish
material dominance of the world, and hope in the face of uncertainty
of a better future, led to a widespread renewal of confidence in
Mussolini and a persistent desire to see him located within the realm
of the sacred.[105] Letters of devotion continued to pour into the Segreteria
Particolare – such as one from Paola Dotti on 28 June 1940:

My creed and my prayer. I believe in You, Duce, just and strong, the
liberator of oppressed humanity. I believe in Your teaching full of

sacrosanct truth. I believe in You, Duce, the Man sent by God to preach once again the Doctrine of Christ and correct what has been falsified by egoism . . . I believe that Your daily toil irradiates the light of God, and that everything You undertake is part of the great mission assigned to You by the Almighty. May God in heaven lessen the great burden on the Duce and ensure that everyone in the world understands as soon as possible the meaning of the Roman era.[106]

12

The Road to Disaster

The Greek debacle

During the late summer of 1940, Mussolini toyed with various plans for launching a war in the Balkans. On 15 October he announced to a meeting of ministers and army generals (for some reason the representatives of the navy and the air force had not been invited) that Greece would be invaded in a fortnight's time. Hitler had warned his ally on a number of occasions in the preceding weeks about the dangers of taking on fresh enemies. As far as he was concerned Italy would already have its work cut out dealing with the British in Egypt. But Mussolini thought that Hitler might be trying to deter him out of jealousy at the prospect of Italy stealing some of Germany's limelight. He also believed that a campaign against Greece would be swift and easy: he told his son-in-law a few days before the invasion started that if they could not beat the Greeks quickly, he would 'resign as an Italian'.[1] And since the fighting would be over soon, little thought was given to the problems that might arise from heavy autumn rains, the mountainous terrain and the shortage of roads. Nor was the fact that Albania lacked ports large enough to keep a major army adequately supplied seen as an issue.

Ciano was as convinced as his father-in-law that the campaign against Greece would be simple. He told a senior Italian diplomat in the summer of 1940 that a single strike on Athens by just 200 bombers would be sufficient to bring the Greek government to its knees.[2] He also hugely underestimated the strength of the enemy forces and their will to fight. This was partly because he had excessive confidence in the secret campaign that had been undertaken by the government to suborn Greek politicians and generals with millions of lire. Similar attempts at bribery had been made in Ethiopia in 1935–36 and Albania in 1939.[3] The former ambassador to London, Giuseppe Bastianini, recalled going to see Ciano on 24 October 1940 to express his alarm at the forthcoming invasion. Ciano had told him not to worry: 'everything ha[d] been seen to' and the campaign would in effect be a 'military stroll'. When Bastianini had suggested that the Greeks would respond to an unprovoked attack by fighting like lions, Ciano had smiled knowingly and indicated that Bastianini was seeking to learn too much. He had then winked and rubbed his thumb and index finger together.[4]

The invasion began on 28 October, the anniversary of the March on Rome. For Piero Calamandrei the lack of public outrage at this latest act of aggression by Mussolini was a further sign of the moral corruption wrought by the regime: 'We are so deep in the mud that this genuine act of violent highway robbery by brigands (with apologies to brigands) does not arouse indignation; indeed, it almost seems like a routine administrative matter.'[5] In the ensuing weeks he chronicled (not without some sense of personal guilt) further signs of the degradation of 'the eternally gossiping, idle, cowardly and impotent people that we middle class Italians are'.[6] There was the case of a woman who had been overheard on a tram by an elderly man telling a friend that the bread now on sale gave her stomach pains. After she had got off, the man had escorted her to a pharmacist and forced her to drink half a glass of castor oil (or else face 'something worse'). According to Calamandrei the man was probably not a police informer but a fascist doing what he thought was his civic duty. Another episode was reported to him by a university colleague, Professor Bracci. Bracci's son had taken an exam for entry into secondary school. In answer to the question 'Say who, after your parents, is the person you love most', the boy had written about his sister. A few days later Bracci had heard from the examiners that every one of the other thirty-nine candidates had written about the Duce.[7]

Calamandrei's horror at the moral turpitude of fascism was especially marked when it came to the corruption of the fascist elite. He learned, for instance – and he was keen to stress in his diary that there were numerous eyewitnesses to testify to the truth of what he was relating – that during the Greek campaign Ciano and his entourage were based in Bari, where they commandeered a large hotel in the centre of the town and a villa in the countryside nearby – at a cost to the municipality of 80,000 lire. Each week government officials arranged for some twenty girls to be transported to the hotel for wild night-time orgies. The windows were flung open, so the neighbouring houses had a clear view of what was going on. Between 300 and 400 soda siphons were supplied every evening for the principal party game, which consisted of the officers and the girls dividing into two teams and squirting jets of water at each other's genitals and hacking at clothes with pairs of scissors: the girls aiming at ties, the men, led by Ciano, lunging at bra straps and knickers. All this, said Calamandrei, with acute consciousness of the profound indignation that such antics had occasioned in the local population, when ordinary Italian soldiers were dying across the Adriatic in the mountains of Greece.[8]

The Greek campaign went disastrously from the outset, with the Italian troops quickly bogged down in the rain and mud and then driven back into Albania by a fierce enemy thrust from the north-east. Mussolini had informed Hitler of his plans only at the very last moment, knowing that the German leader would have tried to stop him and hoping to be able to pull off a quick and sensational victory that would restore Italy to some parity with its ally. The humiliation in the Balkans was soon compounded by other setbacks. On the night of 11 November half of Italy's entire battle fleet was put out of action by a British aerial torpedo attack on the harbour of Taranto. Very little had been done in the months before the outbreak of war to ensure that this crucial base was adequately defended; and although Mussolini was justly proud of the size and quality of the Italian navy, neither he nor his chiefs of staff had grasped just how vital air protection would be in a modern conflict. As a result Italy still had not a single aircraft carrier in 1940. In Libya, a few weeks later, Rodolfo Graziani's huge but ill-equipped army of 220,000 men was routed by 30,000 British troops supported by several hundred tanks. More than 130,000 prisoners were captured, and film footage of interminable columns of demoralised and poorly clothed soldiers found its way into cinemas around the world.

The reports on the state of public opinion in the autumn of 1940 indicated that blame for the severe reverses was attributed primarily to the 'traitors' around Mussolini – the widely reviled Ciano in particular – and not to the Duce.[9] This was little consolation to Mussolini himself, who, as Claretta revealed in her diary and letters, was reduced at this time to a state of near psychological prostration at seeing so many of his hopes suddenly dashed. Claretta had undergone a major operation for an ectopic pregnancy on 27 August, and as a result of her long convalescence she was unable in the last months of 1940 to see Mussolini as often as previously and sustain the physical and emotional ardour which had done much to fuel his megalomania since 1936. In a desperate effort to keep up her lover's spirits (and stop him from losing interest in her – which he showed every sign of doing) she wrote imploring notes to him from her sickbed. She reminded him of how she was his lucky 'little mascot'. She reassured him that he would inevitably be victorious in the end, given his greatness, genius and indomitable will. His one error had been to place too much faith in those around him:

> You cannot fail to win. You are the Man of the titanic struggle and victory. You are too great to have doubts or fears. You still have the light of genius to illuminate Your path. You still have the power to crush and destroy treachery. You still have the courage, the love of battle, the thirst for victory.
>
> Only one mistake: the generous judgement that You have made of the dwarves that surround You. In your great and infinite humanity you have not wanted to file them under the heading of 'incompetent'.
>
> But this cannot stop the thunderous march of Your legions: even if it seems that there must be a momentary pause, ants cannot hinder the progress of the giant, and Your natural force is such as not to allow impediments or brook delays.
>
> You will be victorious, Ben, my great Ben, because that is how it must be thanks to Your people, and thanks to Your ceaseless work of construction over the years. You will be victorious, because Caesar knows the march of glory even if his followers are not good.
>
> My small and humble voice of friendliness, though weakened by illness and disappointment, is Yours and belongs to You in every moment of Your life. It will always murmur in your heart the word of faith and absolute and devoted love, which – even if downcast by your pointless and inconceivable acts of treachery – retains the pure and spotless light of the dawn of life.[10]

For Antonio Brunello, as for countless other young men who served on the Greek front, the gulf between the confident rhetoric of Mussolini before the war and the harsh realities of poor planning, equipment shortages, and defeat, proved to be deeply unsettling. But Antonio, who had been born in 1915 into a modest family in the small town of Thiene near Vicenza, had grown up under the regime; and nothing either in his experience or his education – which had not progressed beyond primary school – had equipped him to conceive of anything different from fascism. As the diary that he kept from the time when he first joined the army in 1936 shows, he did not harbour particularly strong political views. Nor was he in any obvious sense a committed fascist. But without a clear alternative to the regime, it was hard for the feelings of disappointment and anger that he felt during the war to crystallise into overt opposition. When in July 1943 he and other soldiers in his unit learned of the fall of the Duce, the predominant sensation that he had was one of disorientation: 'Everybody in our group was under thirty, and nobody was able to imagine what Italy could possibly be like without fascism.'[11]

Antonio was sent out to Albania to join the fighting against the Greeks at the end of 1940. He had already tasted action on the French border in June, and had been deeply alarmed at the failure of the Italian forces to get past the enemy's Alpine defences – despite their overwhelming numerical superiority – and at the air of disorganisation pervading the army. But he had remained optimistic: the war would soon be over. Amid the snow and mud of Albania, however, the upbeat tone of his diary gave way to a more sober mood as he realised that many of the claims that fascism had made were unfounded. On 20 January 1941 he wrote:

All those speeches about greatness and a longing for expansion. All that desire to make the Italians and the world believe that we are strong and invincible. All those things that put together signify pride. Yet in my view this pride has without knowing it chosen to come and dig its grave right here, in the middle of these wild and savage mountains of Albania. Over there, on the other side, are people who are gritting their teeth, like us – men who are showing a fighting spirit that is no less strong than ours. But they have an ideal. They are defending their land, their Fatherland and their families; and this is a sacred cause that we, here, cannot have![12]

In the weeks that followed, as news of the scale of the defeat of the Italian forces in Africa filtered through on the radio, Antonio continued to reflect on the enormous gulf that separated the rhetoric of the regime from the dismal reality. There was no sense of anger in his diary: the tone was more akin to one of Christian resignation. The tragedy that was unfolding seemed to provide confirmation of the vanity of human wishes and the dangers of hubris:

> Little by little Italian East Africa [Africa Orientale Italiana] is becoming English East Africa [Africa Orientale Inglese]. The initials don't even have to be changed! Quietly our Empire is going up in smoke. Our 'place in the sun' is being occupied by others and we are returning to the shade. And in this way all that arrogant posturing that marked the pre-war years is evaporating, all that mania for greatness, that mad desire to demonstrate to the world that Italy is a strong and powerful country. We are now being put to the test and events are showing what in fact we are capable of, even when the word 'VICTORY' was proclaimed by 'a supreme will'. Let us hope that somebody is gradually realising that you do not make war with empty words.[13]

Whether in Antonio's mind that 'somebody' was Mussolini (and the reference to 'a supreme will' in some way ironic) is not entirely clear. As the diaries and letters of ordinary soldiers indicate at this time, the encounter with defeat and suffering in the winter of 1940–41 led not so much to indignation at having been misled by the Duce as to an affirmation of more traditional articles of faith – God, the saints, family, home community.[14] The war, after all, was still far from over. Things might yet turn out well and Mussolini (and the years of trust placed in him) be vindicated. But in the meantime, as a young peasant from the province of Cuneo, Giuseppe Gazzerino, was at pains to underline to his sister in March 1941, it was to conventional Catholic talismans that many appeared to look for solace in the face of death:

> Rita, I am making the companions of the squad who are serving under me recite the Holy Rosary every day in the tent. I wish you could see

how passionately they all pray and how pleased they are for me to be leading them in the Holy Rosary. So, with our prayers and the prayers of all the Italian people, we hope that God and the Holy Virgin will help us soldiers and soon give us victory and peace to the world, and we can soon come back to our homes.[15]

For another young peasant – Osvaldo Cosci, a smallholder from Viareggio – the main elements of his emotional landscape to which he clung for hope were similarly religious and familial. The diary he kept from 1940 to 1943 was largely a factual account of daily events in the army and contained no comments on either Mussolini or fascism – not, it seems, because Osvaldo was apolitical (after the war he became active in the Christian Democrat Party) but rather because his overriding concern was simply with survival and returning home to his loved ones. On the night of 8 March 1941 he sat in the shadow of Mount Tomori in southern Albania knowing that he was about to be sent into battle against the Greek lines. He was aware that the words in his diary might be his last recorded thoughts. He was unable to sleep:

> I recite all the prayers I know, but a bit confused, with happy and sad thoughts mixed in. My *Mamma* far away, my *Papà*, my dear little sister, my little brother, all my relatives far away, my home, the church, the town where I was born; close at hand, the battle, the explosions, the cries, the wounded. Sitting with a blanket on my shoulders, I look up at the sky which is partly covered in stars, with groups of white clouds shaped like sheep, and a beautiful moon, and I pray to the Lord to let me return to my *Mamma*. I cannot sleep, and in the light of the moon I am writing this diary, which, with God's help I will continue tomorrow . . . Behind to our left, covered in snow, the massive shape of Mount Tomori is a spectacular sight in the light of the moon. I don't know if I am writing properly because I cannot see very well.[16]

The offensive began on 9 March and met with determined resist-ance from the Greeks. Two weeks earlier Mussolini had declared in a broadcast speech that the country's military fortunes would improve greatly in the spring. Spring, he had said, was 'our season', the season of fascism; and the war had in fact been going on not just for eight months but ever since 1922, 'from the day when we hoisted the banner of our Revolution against the Masonic-democratic-capitalistic world'.[17] In order to guide the military operations and raise the morale of the troops, Mussolini had arrived in Albania in person at the beginning of the month. But his presence made no difference. As Osvaldo recorded graphically in his diary, several days of horrific fighting at close quarters, in mud, snow and freezing conditions, with inadequate weapons and lice-ridden clothing, ended with the Italian advance grinding to a halt. Keeping a diary gave Osvaldo a measure of reassurance: with friends and fellow soldiers dying or being maimed all around him, the idea that he was the author of a narrative that had yet to reach a conclusion provided some hope that he was destined to live to complete the story.

If in the face of death humble soldiers like Osvaldo found solace in thoughts of the family and God rather than the myths of fascism, there were still millions who derived inspiration from the ideology of the regime and above all from the image of the Duce. The reports on public opinion drawn up by party and police officials in the first months of 1941 indicated extensive anger at the setbacks in Africa and Greece, particularly among the urban middle classes. But much of the hostility was directed, as before, not towards Mussolini himself but towards the supposedly incompetent or even treacherous figures around him. Ciano remained a favourite whipping-boy.[18] The brilliantly successful German-led offensive in Libya in April 1941, which ended with the British being driven back into Egypt, and the no less decisive German intervention in Greece in that same month – when the entire peninsula was overrun by Nazi forces in the space of just three weeks (much to the embarrassment of Mussolini) – resurrected concerns about Italy being a hugely subordinate partner in the Axis. Nonetheless, there was a widespread feeling that Mussolini had made the right choice in entering the war on the side of Hitler and that Italy would emerge on the winning side. 'What would have become of us if the Duce had not concluded the alliance with Germany?', and 'look at how correct the judgement of the Duce has been, alone against everyone else', were typical of the comments overheard by secret agents in the late spring and early summer of 1941.[19]

Letters and poems continued to pour into the Segreteria Particolare in Rome each day, extolling Mussolini and his God-like abilities and voicing complete confidence in Italy's victory. In some cases the principal motive of the writers may have been to secure a material benefit. For many, it seems, a more pressing desire was to feel close to a man in whom so much trust had been invested for twenty years. Often the writers chose to remain anonymous or simply (and perhaps coyly) put their initials at the end. Hardship and fear readily amplified the desire for intimate contact. 'Dear Duce', a Neapolitan woman wrote in February 1941 – and she was typical of countless others who wanted to be in touch with Mussolini at this time:

> I hope this reaches you. My desire to communicate to you my unshakeable faith in the final victory is so great! I understand your moments of painful anxiety in this supreme struggle. But I feel that you will overcome everything and everyone, because your law is divine law. In you I see an Apostle of God. The prize for all you are doing for our dear Fatherland you will receive from Him, for everybody together would never be able to give you a sufficient reward. I continue to pray for you and for our dear Fatherland.[20]

For many, the experience of hearing Mussolini's voice provided the spur to putting pen to paper. One anonymous writer, who had tried to get into the Teatro Adriano in Rome on 23 February to listen to the speech in which Mussolini predicted that good fortune would come in the spring, but had been forced instead to stand outside with the crowds, sent the 'adored Duce' an effusive four-page letter the following day, describing his words as 'waves of pure oxygen' that had removed all the doubts and uncertainties of the previous weeks. He expressed his gratitude for the 'sublime efforts' Mussolini was making to secure social justice for everyone.[21] Another writer, probably a woman (though only initials are given, and the text seemed deliberately to conceal the gender of the author) wrote to Mussolini immediately after the speech in a way that highlighted how much the sense of intimate contact with the leader engendered feelings of security and purpose – and implicitly a renunciation of responsibility:

> Our dear Duce. At last we have found you again! Once more your powerful voice has rung out, making us weep with emotion; and it seemed to us that it was the voice of Italy itself rising to issue a

challenge to the whole world that was listening . . . We know that the common people are like a big child: and our people, so sensitive and impressionable, are more so than many others; and since the challenge assigned to us by destiny is indeed supremely hard . . . little by little the enemy propaganda managed to penetrate the soul of many Italians . . . Now you have returned . . . Duce, we suffer the most terrifying ordeals with you and for you, but do not abandon us in this most solemn hour. Come back and be entirely ours: clutch us in your strong fist. You have said it: 'The spring is near'.[22]

Many soldiers also wrote effusive letters to Mussolini. In fact the cult of the Duce appears to have been more resilient among the armed forces than on the home front, where morale became increasingly eroded by food shortages and bombing from the late autumn of 1941, especially in the big cities. Rank-and-file troops may have been put under pressure by their superiors to pen expressions of loyalty to the Duce in order to demonstrate the political faith of a unit. Since the correspondence was monitored, the more cynical among the writers might have hoped to gain benefits of some kind by being seen to comply. But the sheer number of postcards and letters that poured into the Segreteria Particolare from the front line in 1941, and the fervent language that they contained, suggest that contact with Mussolini served a genuine psychological function in bolstering morale. This was especially evident when soldiers took the trouble to spell out, as they very often did, why they believed that the cause for which they were fighting was just, and why they expected Italy ultimately to prevail.

Almost invariably in these letters it was not the Greeks who were the enemy: it was the British. And the aim of the war was to end the existing international order and secure greater social justice and a fairer distribution of the world's wealth. If Britain had enjoyed military success in Africa, this was because it had more material resources at its disposal than Italy: in due course, the superior moral claims and stronger will of fascism would prevail:

To Benito Mussolini. Great Genius not just of Italy but of the entire Universe!! Greetings! We all understand the historical and social reasons for the present conflict: a war of democracy against greedy, monopolistic, exploiting plutocracy . . . We look forward to Fascist Italy . . . winning a certain and glorious victory under the guidance of the Duce! – a victory that will guarantee everyone work and wealth tomorrow...[23]

Duce! We will win without a shadow of a doubt, because Rome is eternal. It is the immortal soul of all the peoples passing through the world, in whom it has planted the Divine Spirit and is now spreading Fascist Civilisation: – the new lay word of Christianity . . .[24]

Our cause is a Holy Cause – built on work and peace (true peace, not armed peace), which is the mission of Fascism . . . Even if we had to wear sackcloth and eat crusts of bread, we would never complain, provided the British yoke is broken once and for all and Imperial Rome rises again . .[25]

For some soldiers, the Duce was the person to whom they wanted their final words to be directed. Once again the balance between idealism and self-interest is often very hard to discern in the writing of such letters. In the case of a note found in the pocket of Federico Toloti, who was killed in Albania on 7 April 1941, the hope might well have been that a profession of faith would help to secure his widow some financial support – though that does not necessarily mean that the political sentiments expressed were for that reason any less sincere:

Let my warrior's spirit go to you, Duce. I die: I die content to have served with faith and honour for the greatness of the fatherland. Long live the Duce, long live the King.

What saddens me is to leave my wife, both for the love I have always had for her and she for me.

Salute for me gloriously my wife Eustachio Grata. Her husband Toloti Federico, via Pescara, 5, Valtesse (Bergamo). Salute to the Duce.[26]

Sometimes the intention was manifestly more moral: to endow death with meaning, value and dignity. Enrico Remondini, a former *squadrista* from Trieste who was killed fighting in Slovenia in 1942, was keen to demonstrate – presumably to himself as much as to the outside world – that his life had been devoted to an ideal and that his sacrifice was worthwhile:

> Duce, when you receive this letter I will already be dead, fallen on the field of honour with your name guarded in the depths of my soul.
>
> I have served the cause with faith and fervour.
>
> Neither the pettiness of men, nor the desperation of poverty, nor the injustice of fate, nor the sin of conceitedness have ever caused the flame of my fascist faith to waver . . .
>
> Duce, I die poor, like the saints in the years of the armed revolt, but I am happy to have lived far removed from the false allure and self-interest of a mercenary faith.
>
> Who dies for the fatherland is uncontaminated by spiritual old age.
>
> Duce, you have made Italy greater, now make Italians greater. For victorious Italy *eia eia alalà*.[27]

Giuseppe Caronia, who after the war was to become a distinguished architect, was full of optimism when he went to serve in Albania in September 1940. He was twenty-five years old and came from a well-known academic family in Palermo. Like many middle-class Italian intellectuals who had grown up under the regime, he regarded fascism as a given: there could be grounds here and there for criticism of the party, of individuals, or of certain aspects of policies, but the regime was fundamentally beyond reproach. Moreover, as events in Europe in the previous few years had shown, the tide of history was flowing decisively in favour of the Axis powers, with the democracies too weak to match the moral vigour of fascism. There were question marks over the future map of Europe or exactly when the war would finish, but, as he found himself musing in his diary (with a hint of disquiet), Italy's eventual success was something that he took for granted: 'How will it end? When? Or better, I know it will end with our victory – this is so obvious that I don't mention it (but is this blind certainty not levity perhaps?): but how will the new peace be established and what will the new Europe be like?'[28]

A few days before Italy declared war on Greece, Giuseppe reflected on the reasons for which he was fighting. As a self-conscious intellectual who in his spare time wrote articles about architecture, sketched out plots and screenplays for films, and devoured works by authors as diverse as Steinbeck, Machiavelli, Maugham, Mantegazza, Pirandello, Napoleon, Kayserling and Caesar, it seemed logical to him to pose ethical questions. But the emphasis placed by the regime on faith and unthinking obedience, certainly in the political sphere, left him feeling uncomfortable and trying to find good grounds for reining in his speculative instincts:

> Aim of the war? What does it matter now? We are in the dance, so let's dance . . . Can the adventure not be an end in itself? Why am I thinking too much? And if I do think, am I not bound to reach the conclusion that all this is great and beautiful? Italy is waging war in order to expand, to dominate at sea its Mediterranean empire. 'Grave and historic hours swirl in the skies of the Fatherland'. I am living these hours with dignity. Why think? Why should I have to think about the why, the how and the wherefore? . . . [E]nthusiasm, faith in the imperial idea, understanding of the fatal necessity of the war, of this war: this is what we must think and believe.[29]

Giuseppe was doing his best to be a good fascist. Even if he struggled somewhat with the overall aim of the conflict (though he did persuade himself at one point that Albania and Greece naturally belonged to Italy on the grounds that the frescoes in local churches were similar to those in Sicily), he was happy to think that the campaign would assist greatly with his personal development ('I have always considered that my not having participated in a war was a huge gap in my formation, in my life').[30] What gave him particular satisfaction was the idea that military service would purge his spirit of residual bourgeois values, temper his will, and broaden his spiritual outlook beyond the narrow confines of his life back in Palermo:

> I have learned to appreciate hundreds of things on the material plane: the joy at not having lice, of sleeping when I like, of eating when it suits me . . . But on the spiritual plane I have further strengthened a number of attitudes and beliefs; I have defined my anti-bourgeois personality more clearly. Hatred of four walls, of what is restricted, of closed horizons. I appreciate tents, the open air, the mountains and valleys, even when the weather is bad. I hate to imagine via Giovanni Pacini, with its street, its doorway and its staircase, and the office in

via Houel, as my parameters . . . Discipline, learning to keep silent, obey, suppress, do things I do not like. Getting used to action. Action, because something must be done even if it seems futile, superfluous, boring. Learning how to give orders. Making sure orders are carried out. Initiative, responsibility, practical sense.[31]

Witnessing at first hand in the course of the next few months the disastrous conduct of the Greek campaign – the lack of planning, the poor leadership, the chronic shortages of equipment – severely challenged Giuseppe's confidence in the regime. But he found it very difficult to admit that the setbacks in Africa and the Balkans demonstrated that fascism was somehow fundamentally flawed. In the first place, faith was central to his value system. This blunted his willingness and capacity to criticise: after all, was it not in adversity that 'faith' was supposed to be most tested? ('There is only one evil in the world: cowardice. There is only one path to salvation: courage . . . I am convinced there is only one way to view the world: with faith').[32] Moreover, if the regime had made mistakes, the proper response was not to lose heart but to press on and secure victory, and then for the young men of his generation who had fought in the war to step in, purify fascism, and make it stronger than ever:

I too recognise many errors, many faults, in our regime; but the only thing now is to win, not to despair; hoping, yes, in a new revolution. But what would it lead to? By being victorious, we, yes we, would be able to make ourselves heard both inside and out, and put many things right.[33]

Giuseppe was endeavouring in adversity to think and act as a fascist intellectual. If the spirit of fascism had failed to penetrate fully the soul of the nation, the answer, as the Duce himself had argued, was to intensify the work of regeneration. The Minister of National Education, Bottai, was similarly minded. As commander of a battalion of Alpini in Albania in the first months of 1941, he, like Giuseppe, was profoundly shocked by the incompetence that he encountered. He told his wife confidentially early in February that the army had remained impervious to the regime's 'renewing energy' and had failed to understand that the fascist revolution was a 'revolution of methods and mentality'.[34] A few weeks later he was even more despondent. He talked of the 'common people' having been made 'the scapegoat' for a wholly inept and irresponsible military and political ruling class whose 'faith' had been 'opportunistic' rather than sincere.[35] His spirits lifted somewhat with the German offensive in April, but he still acknowledged that fascism had failed to achieve its mission, and that it would be up to the younger generation, his son Bruno included, to take the struggle forward:

> I will resume my work, and reignite within me my residual faith . . .
> I aim to make Brunetto into a 'man'. The word 'vendetta' is often used
> in the jargon of our so-called ruling class. I will teach Bruno to avenge
> my disappointment and bitterness with nobler and more virtuous
> actions than those that I was entrusted to accomplish.[36]

Like Bottai, Giuseppe did his best amid the chaos of the Greek campaign to cling onto his 'residual faith'. But it was not easy. In February 1941 he was sent on leave to the Albanian capital of Tirana. In between reading, playing football and going to the cinema he spent a lot of time in cafes discussing with colleagues the problems facing the regime. Some of those he spoke to were very pessimistic. The well-known journalist Indro Montanelli claimed that the disastrous performance of the army was the result of twenty years of 'enslavement and moral impoverishment of the Italian people'; and he added that back home it was generally believed that Italy was completely under the thumb of Germany. Giuseppe was indignant. Italy had not gone to war for Germany, but with Germany, he told Montanelli. It was only natural that Germany should now be doing the lion's share of the fighting, given its superior military resources. As for the idea that the Italians had been vitiated by fascism, that was manifestly untrue. The French had fought badly – and they came from a liberal regime. The problem was a much broader one: 'It is humanity that does not want to fight, not Italians.'[37]

But Giuseppe was struggling. After all, was it not precisely against bourgeois humanitarianism that fascism was supposed to have pitted itself? And if Giuseppe's own sympathies were strongly with 'humanity' and its instinctive aversion to war (his admiration for the writings of Stefan Zweig and John Dos Passos pointed firmly in this direction), where did this leave him with regard to his fascist faith? Some of those

he talked to in Tirana claimed that Mussolini had been deceived by
his incompetent colleagues and that the Italian people had been
reduced, as a result, to a spineless 'flock of sheep'. Others maintained
that the only people who should have a major stake in Italy after the
conflict were those who had fought, and fought well. Such views
angered Giuseppe increasingly in the spring of 1941. They seemed to
be based on an unthinking endorsement of militaristic values. What
was needed after the war was not just a regeneration of fascism, but
a 'revolution' to change mentalities and avoid the kind of calamity
that had befallen Italy with the Greek campaign:

> When we return, we will need to sort out lots of things. Heavens, we
> will have to carry out our revolution. There is too much idiocy about.
> There are people saying that 'those of us who have fought the war
> should get this and that'. 'No', I shout, 'this is all wrong. It is precisely
> against this mentality that we have to fight. You do not become
> important just because you wage war. These are false values that need
> to be destroyed: this superficial exaltation of war, this mania for
> believing we are born warriors, this idea that risk is necessary. For
> God's sake, this has been the mistake: to want to take risks. You do
> not put at risk the destiny of a people – the fruit of centuries of
> struggles, the sacrifice of millions [sic] of lives, the Risorgimento, the
> Great War, fascism itself, for no good reason . . .'[38]

But, as Giuseppe was beginning to realise, it was not just the
perversity of certain core fascist values that was alarming. The Greek
fiasco had also laid bare a terrifying degree of levity – an absence of
serious planning without which no modern war could hope to succeed:

> What a disaster Greece is! If we didn't have this absurd operation in the
> Balkans, we could have sent the 35 divisions that are now deployed here
> to Libya, where they would have achieved very important and decisive
> results. But even if we accept that the action in Greece was necessary,
> why not begin in October by sending at least fifteen divisions and not
> just six? Good God, such incompetence does not bear thinking about.[39]

He himself had tried to defend the poor performance of the army to
Montanelli by claiming – as many others did – that Italy simply lacked

the material resources of the other major powers. But he now realised that this was not a sufficient explanation. The problems ran much deeper – to the heart of the fascist state, and perhaps of Italian society itself:

I have seen too many stupid, too many absurd, things – illogicality, disorganisation, distrust, frivolity; lack of urgency, lack of cohesion and lack of any unity of purpose . . . So many ineffectual people, so much energy wasted. And it's said that all our failures have been due to economic constraints. But, Jesus Christ, they hand out ammunition to us in dribbles. Before firing a shot . . . we have to ask for twenty permissions and fifty authorisations. We concentrate twenty-four batteries in one single sector: why don't we just have four that can fire instead of twenty-four that don't fire? In order, [we are told], to have the right concentration when the moment comes. But, Jesus Christ, we are only up against four batteries in total . . . We are dealing with the idiocy of the commanders, the incompetence of the Militia, the brute ignorance of the rank and file soldiers. People who are unable to carry out orders, infantrymen who have never fired a rifle . . . We need to do things seriously . . . That's what the Germans do . . . They study beforehand, thoroughly, in every detail, what is going to be done, and see how it will be carried out on the ground – on that particular piece of ground, in those conditions . . . They work out the force that you need to deploy . . . We make approximate calculations on a bit of paper, by improvisation or hearsay . . . I know now what to make of the Royal Italian Army and the Germans. I have my ideas on the Germans, on how the nations stand in relation to one another, on what needs to be done in Italy, on what Italy should aspire to – on the corruption, the incompetence, the superficiality, the ignorance and the irresponsibility.[40]

In the space of a few months Giuseppe had passed from confidence, and excitement at the prospect of being able to expand his spiritual horizons as a young anti-bourgeois fascist, to a position of anger and uncertainty. Like many of his background and generation – middle-class university graduates who had experienced the intellectual gymnastics of the GUF and the Littoriali – he had never seriously contemplated becoming an opponent of the regime. It was a question

instead of harnessing the pulses of dissatisfaction and idealism that
he and others felt into forces that might act to reshape the regime
from within. As Giuseppe's immediate contemporary, Ugoberto
Alfassio Grimaldi, later a distinguished journalist and historian (and
prominent socialist), said when reflecting just after the war on why
he and his friends had remained loyal to the regime up to its collapse
in July 1943, nobody that he knew had ever thought of working against
fascism. There was a sense that the real history of Italy had begun on
28 October 1922, and that to return to the 'chaos and utopia' of the
liberal era, or to contemplate any political system other than fascism
(in some form), was out of the question:

> Outside [fascism] was the ancient era, or the jungle. We, who sometimes
> teasingly, but with an underlying note of seriousness, liked to call
> ourselves 'the anti-fascists of fascism', never thought for a moment
> before 25 July [1943] of combating the ills of fascism by linking up with
> the forces outside it . . . I was still profoundly convinced that fascism
> had formulated correctly the problem of how to move beyond the old
> democratic world, uncoupling the political life of the country from a
> system that was now exhausted . . . It was within fascism and not
> against it that we had to erect the barricades – not to overturn it, but
> to free it and reshape it.[41]

And the most resilient aspect of fascism, according to Ugoberto, was
the idea that Mussolini was a man of incomparable genius: 'Of the
various dogmas that we had to shatter in order to escape from fascism,
the hardest to break was undoubtedly that of the infallibility of the
Duce.'[42]

Like Ugoberto, Giuseppe found it hard to extricate himself morally
and intellectually from the embrace of fascism. It was extremely painful
to recognise after years of immersion in orchestrated enthusiasm and
propaganda that the beliefs that the regime had striven to encourage
had been misplaced. The anger that he felt at the incompetent conduct
of the Greek campaign and the general ineptitude of the army was
more the anger of a zealous reformer than of an outright heretic.
Amid the maelstrom of feelings that assailed him in the early months
of 1941 it was difficult to stop the redemptive myths that the regime
had done so much to foster from rising to the surface and softening

his doubts. On 14 April 1941, a week before he stopped writing his diary, he found himself in a small cemetery near Tirana. He was overcome with a profound sense of how beautiful it would be to sacrifice his life for the cause of Italy and be buried in such a spot: 'To die for the fatherland, for an ideal. And here, here would be a peaceful resting place for my remains. What more could one wish for?'[43]

Looking to the Soviet Union

If the Greek debacle caused widespread dismay, so too did the signs that the war would be prolonged. On the home front, food shortages added to the discontent, especially in the cities. In Milan the poet Magda Ceccarelli De Grada recorded in her diary on 28 April 1941 that the meat ration had fallen to just 150 grams a week: 'People are starting to be very hungry all the time, as there is not enough to eat (chickens and fish have reached astronomical prices)'. A few days later, when she came out of the butcher's shop, dispirited, with an unboned joint of three-quarters of a kilo – which was meant to feed a household of four for a week – she noted that her legs were shaking so much she could hardly walk. Similarly the shop assistants in the dairy, who might have been expected to fare better, complained about finding it difficult to stand. Her one consolation, as a woman with anti-fascist and left-wing sympathies, was that hardship might soon trigger unrest. 'If the food situation deteriorates at this rate', she wrote on 26 May, after the meat ration had dropped to 80 grams, 'there is hope of a swift solution'. Stories of the rich stockpiling food had fuelled popular anger, and she was surprised protests had not broken out already: 'Why do the people, the real people, those who are hungry, not react?'[44]

Magda was forty-eight in 1941 and married to a commercially unsuccessful but well-regarded painter, Raffaele De Grada. She had been born into a relatively modest Tuscan family with socialist sympathies, and though neither she nor her husband had been active anti-fascists, the intellectual circles in which she moved had inclined her increasingly towards opposition in the later 1930s. Her network of friends and contacts included writers and artists such as Eugenio Montale, Carlo Carrà, Arturo Martini, and Giorgio De Chirico. But it was the activities of her son, Raffaellino (whom she adored) that probably did most to crystallise her hostility to the regime. Raffaellino was one of the founders early in 1938 of *Corrente*, a journal that brought together a number of highly talented and progressive intellectuals whose dissatisfaction with the regime shaded increasingly towards outright dissidence with the approach of war. In the autumn of 1938 Raffaellino was arrested on suspicion of subversion and spent a month in the San Vittore prison in Milan. His father was furious at the risk posed to the family, and withdrew into his art: 'I get the impression that for some time he has become detached from us', wrote Magda, 'because we are too dissimilar and rebellious, and feel too strongly about things that are of little interest to him. Basically we are ruining his life.'[45]

Magda's growing isolation from her husband, her intensifying hostility to fascism and her mounting sympathy for communism were among the factors that led her to keep a diary in which to confide her thoughts and feelings once the war broke out. She knew it was risky, and she took care to refer to her friends with their initials only and to make sure the notebooks were well hidden (though she still had to destroy ten pages hurriedly in March 1943 after Raffaellino was arrested and eight policemen came to search her flat). Her continual hope was that the anger caused by the military disasters and the increasing food shortages would generate mass protests and a political crisis. But nobody was prepared to take the initiative. 'Everyone is talking, everyone is cursing, everyone is furious', she wrote on 12 December 1940. 'But nothing comes of it. There is no organisation. There are no leaders. We lack the three hundred or the thousand who are willing to risk their lives in the piazza.'[46]

In the weeks and months that followed her frustration grew: 'If this Italian people does not acquire a full sense of consciousness and does not rebel, we are again lost, and forever'. She was forced to recognise that the regime had been remarkably successful in reducing the masses 'to the most numb and craven silence'.[47] The friends of Raffaellino from the *Corrente* circle who gathered in her flat were inclined to blame the working classes for their 'cowardice' and their 'connivance with fascism'. And Magda was certainly prepared to accept that the passivity of the ordinary people in the face of 'the hunger, the suffering, the danger and the wretched lack of preparation for this war' was 'unsatisfactory'. But then what were these middle-class intellectuals themselves doing, 'apart from chatting in the bar and warming [themselves] up in front of the makeshift heater, sipping the last few drops of tea?'[48] Given such pervasive torpor, salvation, it seemed, would have to come from outside. When on 22 June 1941 Germany launched its attack on the Soviet Union, Magda was ecstatic:

> O my diary, the great day has arrived! I am laughing and crying with joy. At last everything is clear. The weight under which we were oppressed has been lifted, and we are free to believe and hope. Germany has declared war on Russia . . .
>
> There will be new persecution. Many of us will disappear, many will be imprisoned, but victory will come. The red army has mobilised against the tyrants: the whole world is on its feet. The real war is now beginning.
>
> The great socialist Fatherland has moved . . . Our hour has struck . . . Everything is pure and new, our breath is light, our eyes are shining: we have rediscovered our faith intact.[49]

Like Magda, the anti-fascist professor of law Piero Calamandrei observed how dissatisfaction with the conduct of the war led to widespread resentment, but not to concerted opposition. There were certainly plenty of gestures of protest. He heard in January 1941 that Mussolini had been forced to abandon a visit to wounded soldiers in a hospital in Rome after being received with shouts of 'assassin'. (A subsequent visit proved more successful, but on this occasion the injured had been replaced in the beds with policemen). Hostile remarks were being daubed on walls ('you have taken our iron, our copper and our rings; now you are taking our sons'). And people were refusing to buy the 50 cent stamp with Hitler and Mussolini – and making jokes about it ('they have even forced us to lick his backside'; 'you don't know with these stamps whether to spit on the front or behind'). But the entry of the Soviet Union into the war did not fill Calamandrei with the same excitement as Magda. On the contrary, the growing sympathy for communism that he noticed among a number of prominent intellectuals served merely to confirm him in his jaundiced view about the essential fickleness of the Italian bourgeoisie, who stood by passively and waited for help from whatever quarter it might come, whether from Germany, from England or, as now, from Russia.[50]

Mussolini decided that it was imperative for Italy to join Germany in the offensive against the Soviet Union. By the autumn of 1942 he had committed some 230,000 troops. Only about half of these ever returned. In the battle on the Don and the ensuing retreat in the winter and spring of 1942–43 around 25,000 Italian soldiers were killed and 70,000 taken prisoner, of whom 60,000 died subsequently in captivity. Many more were wounded or suffered frostbite. Those who participated in the campaign in general found it easier than in the Balkans to understand why they were fighting. Fascism had after all come into being to counter the supposed threat of a socialist revolution in 1919–22. There was also a religious dimension. The Catholic Church saw no justification for the war in Europe from 1939 and condemned what it saw as the brutal paganism of the Nazis. But for decades it had denounced the godless materialism of the far left, and for a few months at least in the summer of 1941 many Italian clergy felt able openly to support the invasion of the Soviet Union. The Italian soldiers who travelled east to the Ukraine could thus frequently reassure themselves of the holiness of their cause.

The diaries and letters of the ordinary men who took part in the Russian campaign mingled comments about the cold and hardship with nostalgia for their families and for the sights, sounds and rhythms of their life back home. The absence of church bells was a common source of regret. But most, it seems, were able to find solace in the idea that they came from a superior civilisation, and that the propaganda of the far left about the benefits of communism was, as fascism had repeatedly assured them, entirely false. Giuseppe Venturino, a young primary school teacher from the prosperous little town of Montà d'Alba to the south-east of Turin, was typical of numerous others who described the appalling desolation of the villages that he passed through in eastern Europe, with their 'shacks of straw and mud, dirty, full of lice, fleas and flies', with evident relish. ('The least of Italy's towns is a city compared to these . . . No Soviet paradise!'). And the 'barbarism' that he observed was not simply material. He also noted indications of what seemed to be the spiritual inferiority of the local people, who 'all day long' chewed sunflower seeds and watched the Italian troops passing by 'with indifference'.[51]

In many cases, the principal moral filter through which the campaign was viewed was religious rather than political. There was often a

sense – as there had been in Ethiopia – that it was fascism's capacity
to advance the cause of Roman Catholicism that provided the main
justification for the use of force. Ivo Manica, who came from the small
Alpine village of Castellano in the province of Trento and served in
the 9th 'Pasubio' Infantry Division, recounted what he called his 'anti-
Bolshevik crusade' in a series of twenty-seven letters sent back to his
family from the eastern front between August 1941 and December
1942. Like Giuseppe Venturino, Ivo was never to return to Italy. But
he managed to sustain a high sense of morale throughout the campaign
and remained ostensibly confident – right up to the time of the Russian
counter-offensive on the Don, which left him, like many thousands of
others, missing, presumed dead – that the 'triumphal advance' of the
fascist forces would end in glorious success. Every soldier, he told his
brother early in 1942, was able to endure the appalling conditions in
Russia because they had been given the order, 'victory': 'And we will
certainly win, because everybody feels they will win, and are convinced,
indeed certain, of victory.'[52]

Faith, as both Catholicism and fascism had underlined to Ivo, was
a supreme virtue; and it was faith that he was determined to exude to
his family, and faith that inspired him and that he hoped to transmit
to the Russian people. There were signs everywhere, he said, that the
'red paradise' was in reality a 'hell': the peasants were poor, barefooted
and in rags, and their offspring, who went around almost naked, were
taught in schools that God did not exist and that men were descended
from monkeys. Christians had been persecuted, and Jews (and 'thus
capitalists and usurers') had assumed positions of leadership and exer-
cised total control over the population in many communities. But the
'Jewish-Bolshevik clique' had fled before the fascist advance, and the
Italian forces were being welcomed as liberators. Their arrival had
created a huge surge in religious feelings, with locals attending Mass
and bringing their children to be baptised. 'They do not know God
or the baby Jesus . . . If you show them a holy image, they look at it
in amazement. If you have any, send them to me', Ivo told his niece.[53]

For those with particularly strong fascist convictions, the Russian
campaign could be accommodated quite comfortably to more radical
aspects of the regime's ideology – certainly for as long as the forward
advance lasted. Ottaviano Plet was a twenty-eight-year-old shop assis-
tant in a food cooperative from a small town in the province of Udine

in Friuli. He was a member of the 63rd Legion of the Militia, and set off for the Soviet Union in July 1941 full of confidence after being addressed by the Duce at a huge rally in the football stadium in Mantua. The rhetoric of fascism came readily to his pen: 'A day of sunshine for our spirits . . . The whole legion is drawn up in tight formation as if forged from a block of steel . . . to acclaim and render homage to the standard bearer of the great justice. There he is! He saw us all, and spoke to us. He is without doubt the man on whom victory will shine, as he is worthy of it.'[54]

By the end of August Ottaviano had reached southern Ukraine. He began excitedly to note signs of the failure of communism: 'So rich, but so poor, this Ukraine . . . What has Bolshevism done in twenty years? What has it done? Nothing!!' He wrote primarily for his wife, Claretta, and his prose at times became quite sexual in tone – as when he got to the town of Balta and talked about how the local '*mujiks*' (peasants), who were so attached to their land, could never in the long run have been duped into believing in 'the famous paradise of workers'. The doctrines of Marx would have seemed to these 'timid *tovariches*' like the seductive charms of a beautiful woman: 'But when you have married her, the castle built on lovely illusions collapses. You see her for what she truly is in all her deformed, repugnant nakedness'.[55]

Exactly how long Ottaviano was able to keep his strong fascist convictions alive is unclear. He stopped writing his diary after the first engagements with Russian troops, in January 1942, as the winter cold was growing almost unbearable, and he left no record of the remainder of the eastern offensive or of the long retreat towards Italy in the first months of 1943 – which he had the good fortune to survive. No doubt the collective ethos of the Militia helped to curb any precipitate weakening of his morale, in private as well as in public. Certainly Ottaviano still felt sufficiently buoyant at the end of October 1941 to register his pride at the thought that on the anniversary of the March on Rome he was following, as one of 'Mussolini's soldiers from Friuli', in the footsteps of the first generation of *squadristi* – of whom he evidently liked to regard himself as a 'son':

Dogged perpetuators of the era of the *manganello*, twenty years on, we have come to strike your 'Paradise'! No longer, like then, when mother *squadrismo* had to enter the piazzas to clean our towns and our

cities of that pestilential plague of Bolshevism. Instead we are now
here to root it out of its den . . . Victory! YES!!![56]

As a Militia member, Ottaviano may have been particularly drawn
to the bellicose images and myths of the regime, but others who were
less ideologically committed also seem to have found the rhetoric of
fascism easily applicable and apparently heartening in the face of
adversity. A young artilleryman from the small town of Isera near
Trento, Valerio Conzatti, who showed no signs of having especially
strong political feelings, began writing a diary the day before he went
into action against Russian forces on the Dnieper river in September
1941. He was clearly anxious, and hoped to be able to acquit himself
well and not compromise the prestige of an army that had fought
heroically on the Piave in 1918 and had now sent troops nearly 3,000
kilometres from the 'Mother *Patria*'. He described the action itself in
the aestheticised language that fascism had taken over from Futurism
and made popular. The smoke from the explosions rose into the air,
'blossoming from the ground like a fairy-tale bloom'. The tracer bullets
resembled 'a fantastic train of sparks' as they shot through the sky
with alternating reddish and silvery lights. The fighter planes wove in
the sky overhead like 'wild colts'. The thunder of the cannons was
'the voice of the Fatherland calling', while the troops were 'fused
spiritually with steel', their eyes 'shining with joy and satisfaction'.[57]
      As the advance through Ukraine slowed in the following weeks,
and the work of hauling the artillery through thick mud and soon
snow became ever more gruelling, Valerio used his diary to reflect on
the justifications for the campaign. Fascism's highly polarised world
view, and inbuilt sense of superiority in the face of opponents who
were demonised or disparaged, made it relatively easy to construe the
invasion as an act of liberation. ('We are passing through the Russian
countryside as liberators . . . and can see perfectly the situation . . .
of outright abjection to which the Russian people has been reduced
and forced to live in.') The peasants had been crushed by twenty years
of 'red tyranny', he wrote: they had lost all freedom and happiness,
and had nothing to sustain them now except 'political propaganda
conducted in every manner and by every means'. But the increasingly
determined resistance shown by the Red Army in the winter of 1941–42
troubled him. If the Russian people had been so brutally repressed,

why were they fighting doggedly, and indeed heroically? Perhaps, he surmised, there was something 'infantile' in their character. Or perhaps their bravery was a sign of the 'new face and soul' of emancipated Russia that the fascist forces had succeeded in awakening.[58]

Valerio died of typhoid fever in south-eastern Ukraine in November 1942. Whether his views on the Russians, or on the validity of the conflict, or on fascism, changed much in the last months of his life is unknown. His diary stopped at the end of 1941. In all likelihood the need to invest his sacrifice with moral purpose – in circumstances where the only realistic alternatives to continuing to believe in the cause he was fighting for were desertion or despair – ensured that he, like millions of others serving in the Italian army, kept faith broadly with the regime. Letters and diaries from the eastern front continued regularly in the course of 1942 to denounce the barbarism and atheism of the Soviet Union and see the fascist cause as fully justified.[59] 'You should be proud to have a husband who is fighting against those who do not know the Catholic religion', a rural labourer from Basilicata informed his wife in February 1942. 'It is not against Russia that we have to fight here, but against bolshevism, which believes it can dominate the world.'[60] Another common soldier told his family in August 1942 that he saw Italy's 'mission in these lands that have denied the Lord' as 'a holy crusade'.[61]

Even when direct contact with ordinary Russians led to a revision of stereotypes, there was rarely any sign of willingness to call into question the campaign. The intensely patriotic officer, Giuseppe Armellino, who came from a modest family of smallholders in Piedmont, set off for the eastern front in the summer of 1942. He was inspired, as he wrote in his diary, by 'love of the fatherland, and faith in God and in the Most Holy Madonna of Pompeii'. He also had a passionate desire to prevent 'the red Tsar' ('he who is destined to replace Satan') from imposing his 'barbarous laws' on Rome. However, when he reached the Ukraine he was pleasantly surprised to find that communism appeared to have had a less deleterious effect than he had supposed, and that the family bonds among the local peasants had not been entirely destroyed by free love. But neither this revelation nor the experience of defeat did anything to alter his basic convictions. When he arrived back in Italy in May 1943 he wrote of his joy at being part of a society where religious sentiment was rightly prized: 'There can never be anything great and immortal among the Bolshevik people, who deny every spiritual good.'[62]

In the case of prisoners of war, diaries and letters also indicate a determination very often to preserve morale by remaining loyal to fascist Italy, in both public and private. Officers frequently made it a point of honour to ensure that they and their fellow soldiers daily saluted the king and the Duce in front of their British captors. Among them was Riccardo Martini, a young *caposquadra* in the Militia. He was a peasant farmer of modest education from the small Umbrian town of Citerna, and was one of hundreds of thousands of Italians who ended up interned in camps in Africa and India. The detailed diary that he kept from the time of his capture in January 1941 until his arrival back in Italy in March 1946 ran to over 800 pages. It was testament to a strong desire to remain true at all costs to the political creed that he had embraced passionately for many years: 'For me fascism was not a party; it was a religion, like the one my mother taught me as a child'.[63] Time and again he recorded the defiant rebuttals he made of claims by the English guards that he and other Italians were 'deluded' and did not believe in the cause for which they were fighting:

> I am a soldier of the fascist Italy of Mussolini . . . Everything I have done has been from personal conviction, and not because, as you claim, I have been ordered to do it. I have embraced this faith with all the enthusiasm a young fascist can have.[64]

Riccardo was transferred from Egypt to a camp in South Africa at the end of 1941, and he and his fellow prisoners were given more freedom to make the Roman salute and openly express their loyalty to the Duce and the king. Riccardo's faith remained undimmed. On Christmas Day 1942 he prayed to God to 'bless our most adored leader Benito Mussolini, who restored peace between Italy and the Holy See', and to 'return Rome, once the teacher of civilisation, to the position that you yourself have willed.'[65] Seven months later, news of the fall of Mussolini came as a 'thunderbolt'. He did not understand what could possibly have happened: 'We have been away from the mother *Patria* for too long and know nothing'. As he told his younger sister soon afterwards in an imaginary letter, he felt totally disorientated:

My mind is still in turmoil after the events of these last few days . . .
Since my earliest years I have lived in the organisation of the ONB,
and from 1933 I have always been with young people, first as their
instructor and later as their commander. I feel this collapse now more
strongly than anyone else. Who can possibly believe that the sun has
set? Who can ever convince me that everything has passed? For me it
is like saying tomorrow that I have never been a prisoner. Benito
Mussolini, the Duce of fascism, cannot have disappeared from Italy;
he can never have left his people when it was more vital than ever for
him to stay close to them. Here, in the concentration camps, nobody
believes he has gone, apart from that wretched clique of warrant-officers
and a few medical officers . . . No, Giuseppina, I cannot believe this.
The Duce can never betray. The Duce loves his people too much.
Everyone, my dear little sister, can betray, but not our beloved Duce.
I believe in the Duce in the same way as I believe in God; and I believe
that God has sent the Duce for the good and civilisation of the world.[66]

According to Riccardo, the reports in September 1943 that Mussolini
had been rescued by German troops produced wild celebrations in
the camp. And when, later in the year, the prisoners were moved to
a camp in Pietermaritzburg, he described the soldiers waving black
flags, displaying pictures of Mussolini in the windows of the trains,
shouting 'Duce, Duce, Duce', and singing 'Giovinezza' and other fascist
songs.[67] But the strain of resilient faith that ran through Riccardo's
diary for over five years had a sad and mundane finale when he returned
to Italy in the spring of 1946, a year after the death of the 'great and
immortal Duce of Fascism'. He got home to find his mother dead
and his fiancée, Delfina – for whom he had primarily kept his diary
(in order to show her what he had been through) – was now engaged
to someone else. The diary ended with Riccardo professing his
passionate love for Delfina and begging her to come back to him, but
then watching distraught as her new boyfriend arrived on a motorbike
to take her off to vote in the administrative elections. It was a scene
that underlined dramatically how much had changed politically since
he was last in Italy.[68]

Disintegration of the home front

On the home front, the situation in the cities became increasingly bleak in 1942. Aerial bombardments disrupted production and sapped morale. By the end of the year some 25,000 dwellings had been destroyed in Turin and around 500,000 people had moved out of Milan. Shortages of food and fuel for heating caused severe hardship, and essential items such as shoes, soap and medicines all but disappeared from shops. Petrol supplies dwindled; private cars were requisitioned; and the streets of many towns grew eerily silent and empty. With rationing, adults were restricted to little more than 1,000 calories a day, but corruption and administrative inefficiency meant that it was very difficult to secure even the most basic items. Those with money turned to the black market, which flourished: in Rome by the spring of 1943 eggs were exchanging hands for fifteen times the official price. In so far as ordinary people had the energy to be angry, it was mostly against profiteers and the rich, especially in the party, that they vented their spleen. '"Today", said a typical report from Milan early in 1942, "Fascism is synonymous with *camorra*, racket, exploitation of the weak, injustice, immorality." Such phrases are on the lips of everybody, and are repeated like a constant refrain.'[69]

Destitution was especially severe in the southern cities. Naples, Taranto, Palermo, Messina, Catania and other ports became the targets of intensified bombing raids from the late autumn of 1942 as British and American advances in north Africa opened the way for an attack on what Churchill called 'the soft underbelly of the axis'. Magda Ceccarelli De Grada found the hunger, poverty and corruption in Milan horrific. But when she went to Sicily in September 1942 as a birthday treat to visit her son who was stationed on the island, the proverbial exotic delights of the Arabic palaces and churches, the palms, the mountains and the sea were vitiated by levels of suffering and squalor on an altogether different scale:

> Palermo has things of indescribable beauty . . . but they are all in streets of irredeemable filth; and the ragged people that stream by put the loveliness in the shade for me, because the grimness, the disease and the poverty evident in their rags is totally overwhelming . . . How can

people be allowed to live in such degradation? I would like everything
to be swept away and rebuilt . . . Is it surprising if the adults are stunted,
with short legs and rachitic heads and have poison in their characters?
You only need to look at the children. Ragged, with shirts in shreds,
bloated stomachs, emaciated shoulders and wrinkled skin. I saw three
of them begging: a terrifying sight. There were tears behind my glasses
and my heart ached. They were three skeletons, three little old men,
but their immense black eyes were filled with so much evil. No need
to show us the Russian children in the 'Luce' films![70]

Magda spent only a few days on the island. She noted German
troops everywhere, 'well fed and neat in perfect khaki uniforms,
standing on their own with an air of disdain . . . while our scruffy
soldiers roam the streets like so many stray dogs'. She was appalled
by what she saw, but at least had the satisfaction of feeling she had
experienced the war 'at close quarters'. This was real tragic suffering,
unlike in Milan.[71] Another woman who witnessed the situation in Sicily
in the summer of 1942 with horror was Mussolini's eldest daughter,
Edda, the wife of Ciano. She went to work as a Red Cross nurse in a
hospital in Monreale, a few miles outside Palermo. Shortly after she
arrived in May she wrote a candid letter to her father alerting him to
the disastrous state of the island and the potential political dangers
he faced:

The city near to the port is all but flattened and even parts of the main
streets are half destroyed. Terror is written on everyone's face . . . The
problem of food is becoming increasingly serious. After the last air raid
on 9 May the population was left without bread for six days, in part
because the stores were hit, but mainly because not one of the 300
ovens was working. Nobody thought of using their authority to get
them reopened. There has been no water for about a month, the
telephones are not working, and there is only sporadic lighting . . .
The civilians here feel abandoned and say so. At the moment they are
not rebelling, but the local party leader tells me that if no provision is
made for bread and pasta, something will happen . . . Medicines are
needed, clothing, and transport to get this wretched cannon fodder out
of the city . . . When asked for lorries, the military commanders
promise two on one day, and on another, none. For God's sake, they

should give fifty at a time and get the evacuation under way . . . As for the soldiers, I have been told by the Federal Secretary that they are making a more unseemly show of fear than the civilians, fleeing like rabbits into the countryside. But this is nothing. When the air raid is over, they stand idly by instead of rushing forward to help, in contrast to the Germans who set to work. The population used not to be able to stand the Germans: now they not only put up with them but admire them for their sense of organisation and their altruism. To sum up: send provisions. In particular bread and pasta (that is all they are asking for), medicines and clothing. I am in a civil hospital, where the people are lying naked in their beds and the surviving family members come and ask for the piece of bread their relative has saved from his board . . . I have been in Albania and Russia, but I have never seen suffering and pain on this scale. I personally have the impression of having ended up by chance somewhere a thousand miles from the Fatherland and civilisation. For the time being people are still saying the DUCE does not know what is going on. Now you do.[72]

Party and police reports supported Edda's view that the desire to keep Mussolini insulated from responsibility for the unfolding catastrophe was relatively strong still in 1942. Indeed in smaller rural communities the cult of the Duce appears to have remained largely intact right down to his fall in July 1943.[73] Letters continued to pour into the Segreteria Particolare each day pledging total loyalty and devotion to Mussolini and expressing confidence in ultimate victory. The influx of correspondence was especially heavy on 29 July (his birthday) and following a broadcast speech on 2 December – the first for more than a year – in which he exhorted Italians to show sterner resolve and greater hatred for the enemy.[74] But in the major cities there were growing signs in the second half of the year that the old idea of the Duce as the hapless victim of traitors and evil or incompetent counsellors was crumbling. Reports suggested that he was now being blamed personally for the military disasters and for the pervasive inefficiency and corruption in Italy. The number of people cautioned or arrested for insulting the Duce increased significantly from the end of 1942.[75]

Popular anger found some measure of political orchestration. Clandestine newspapers, often linked to embryonic communist, socialist or Christian democrat anti-fascist groups, began to circulate; and strikes broke out, culminating in more than 100,000 workers downing tools in Turin in March 1943. But in general the manifestations of dissent were still limited. The evidence from police reports, letters and diaries suggests that the dominant mood was one of growing detachment, with references to 'Italy', 'the Fatherland', 'the nation' and 'fascism' quietly disappearing from daily discourse and being replaced by allusions to private feelings as the main manifestations of identity in public – personal hardship, suffering and pain in particular, but also resentment towards individuals or groups who seemed to be faring better. Commentators noticed a growing tendency to escapism: cinemas became more crowded than ever.[76] And even the figure of Mussolini was subjected to the processes of disengagement. The journalist Paolo Monelli noted how in Rome in the winter of 1942–43 the Duce was not so much 'unpopular' as 'forgotten'. Despite all the propagandistic clamouring of the press and the radio, the talk was of Hitler, Churchill, Stalin and Roosevelt, but 'not of him'.[77]

The curious atmosphere of withdrawal, mingled with shame and anger at shattered illusions, was well captured by the young writer and film-maker, Federico Fellini, in a short story broadcast on the radio station for the armed forces in September 1942. 'The Little Man [ometto] in the Mirror' is a fable about an undistinguished middle-aged accountant, who suddenly finds himself confronted one day by his reflection while standing alone in his bedroom. The reflection invites him to enter the glass. He does so, and emerges into a mysterious cloudy world, where voices and images from his past accost him and demand to know about his promises. A small boy asks why he has not grown up to be a king, as he had once said he would, with a crown, a uniform, a white horse and armies of obedient soldiers. A young man enquires after his girlfriend, Mirella, to whom he had declared undying love and sworn to marry: why had he not kept faith with her? Others crowd around, seeking to discover what has happened to his intentions to become a poet, to be a writer and to own a beautiful house and garden. Each turns away from him angrily, shouting: 'Wicked man! Coward! You have betrayed me. Be gone!' The 'little man' calls to them to come back: he will keep his promises. But to no avail. He returns to his bedroom in tears and smashes the mirror.[78]

In Florence, the seventeen-year-old schoolboy Pietro Ambrosini observed the onset of the eerie atmosphere of silence and denial with his customary astuteness. In the spring of 1942 he confessed in his diary ('even if it could seem to be blasphemous') that Mussolini had probably been wrong to commit Italy to a conflict that was now beginning to look as if it would be lost. And he was convinced that many others felt as he did, but dared not say so openly – less from fear and more from a sense of intense embarrassment at having been taken in for so long by the regime's triumphalist rhetoric. Symptomatic of the quiet withdrawal of trust, he felt, was the fact that everybody he knew was now listening to the bulletins of the British station, Radio Londra. In mid-November, with the German and Italian forces falling back across north Africa after the Battle of El Alamein, he won an essay competition on the theme: 'How I have experienced the conflict overseas'. He did not think it very likely that he would be able to take up his prize – a trip to Libya once the war was over. Even in his school the map of Africa festooned with little German and Italian flags had been taken down.[79]

Pietro sensed that behind much of the silence was shame at having been complicit in a regime whose vain and ruinous pretensions now stood painfully revealed. Some of his teachers remained defiant in the face of what was happening and insisted on making the Roman salute and declaring 'Viva il Duce!' at the start of lessons. Even in the early summer of 1943, with the British and Americans poised to invade the south of the country, the headmaster gave an address to the whole school on the 'inevitable victory' of Germany and Italy. ('He is a fanatical fascist, and I think he is truly convinced of what he is saying'.) But most of the people that Pietro knew seemed to be caught in a kind of psychological limbo – unable any longer to subscribe to the old tenets and axioms and yet unwilling to admit that what they had supported for so many years had been wrong, and perhaps evil – however much they now sensed this to be true ('woe betide anyone who says such things, even if everyone is thinking it'). Italy was starting to split in two, Pietro observed presciently at the end of 1942. But the division was not so much between fascists and anti-fascists as between 'those who believe still in Mussolini and those who are starting to believe in him a little less'. Such a dichotomy did not bode well: 'All in all I think this is not a good thing.'[80]

13

The Final Act

The fall of the Duce

On the night of 9–10 July 1943 American, British and Canadian forces landed in Sicily. They met with relatively little resistance. The morale of the civilian population had been shattered by bombing raids, hunger and the steady disintegration of the administrative machinery of the party and the state. Across the island the invading forces were greeted with relief and often with unbridled enthusiasm. For many of those who were still convinced fascists, the spectacle of people waving and cheering and crying 'Down with Mussolini!' and 'Down with Italy!', and of women walking arm in arm in the streets with American soldiers, was deeply galling. It also presented a direct challenge to the core of their identity. The forty-three-year-old Tuscan Aldo Bacci, one of more than 200,000 Italian soldiers stationed in Sicily, was taken prisoner near Palermo on 22 July. His immediate reaction to the 'cowardice' of the 'drunken crowds' who were treacherously destroying the 'glorious edifice built in 22 years of struggle' was to start a diary and defiantly set down in writing his determination to remain true to his political faith until his dying day. 'Fatherland, Duce, Family, I live to avenge you and to punish'.[1]

Aldo was to remain in captivity for nearly three years and his disgust at the behaviour of his fellow countrymen was an important factor in sustaining his commitment to fascism. One of the principal aims of the regime had been to purge Italians of their vices and forge 'new men': if Italians were now displaying many of their old weaknesses, did this not provide clear evidence that fascism had been correct in its goals and necessary? The failure of the revolution to date had no doubt been due in large measure to the paradox of having to rely too much on unregenerate individuals for the renovation of society. But after the war fascism would be able to look to a less corrupt and more resolute leadership and to a fortified ideal:

> In a short time the whole world will see a natural rebirth of this ideal, its foundations made firm with blood and magnified and purified by men tempered in their faith and feelings by the hardships, anguish and dangers arising from the deliberate attempt of Masonic and Jewish capitalism and moribund democracy to save itself. If Fascism must emerge materially defeated from this massive struggle, it must nonetheless emerge morally victorious.[2]

Two days after Aldo was captured, as news was filtering through to Rome of the fall of Palermo, a special meeting of the Grand Council was held in Palazzo Venezia – the first to take place in four years. Discussions carried on deep into the warm summer night, with Mussolini surveying in a somewhat disjointed manner the conduct of the war and who was most to blame for what had gone wrong. He bluntly asked the twenty-seven leading party members gathered around the table what they now wanted: 'War or peace? Unconditional surrender or a fight to the end?'[3] His words, as Giuseppe Bottai noticed, were shot through with languorous scorn, his tongue sliding characteristically over the letter 's' as he often did when he wished to convey contempt ('*Fassismo!*, he hissed at the most passionate moments of his diatribe. In the way he pronounced the word, he already seemed to be dismembering his creature.')[4] There followed a number of ill-focused interventions: most of those present, Mussolini included, appeared to have no precise idea what the meeting was for. At the end a motion tabled by the president of the Chamber, Dino Grandi, was passed by nineteen votes to seven calling upon the king to resume the full military powers that were accorded to him under the constitution. Among those who supported the measure were Bottai, Federzoni and Ciano.

Late in the afternoon of 25 July, after a routine day's work, Mussolini went to see the king, unaware in his own mind that anything momentous had happened. In theory the Grand Council was simply a consultative body and any decisions it took did not have constitutional force. But Victor Emmanuel had come under growing pressure in the preceding weeks from a number of senior politicians, Grandi included, to intervene and try to extricate Italy from the conflict. After a great deal of reluctance, probably occasioned more by terror at what the Germans might do by way of retaliation than fear of taking a stand against Mussolini after more than twenty years of passivity, the king had agreed to act.[5] The Duce began the audience in his customary fashion by summarising the current political and military situation. Victor Emmanuel then broke in to say that the morale of the army had collapsed, that the war appeared irremediably lost, that Mussolini had become the most hated man in Italy, and that Marshal Badoglio would be taking over as prime minister. Mussolini was left dazed. As he emerged from the meeting he was arrested by a group of *carabinieri* and driven away in an ambulance.

The early evening of 25 July 1943 was warm and sunny in Rome. Rumours circulated on the streets. There was talk that the Grand Council meeting had not gone well for the Duce, that he had set off in irritation for his summer residence of the Rocca delle Caminate near Predappio, and that the king had convened a session of the Privy Council. But rumours, like jokes, were a common medium of social intercourse in an environment where acute anxiety, insecurity and impotence jostled constantly with a longing for some semblance of hope. In reality few believed that anything truly serious or extraordinary had taken place or was about to occur. As the evening wore on, however, the atmosphere became febrile. In the Caffe Aragno, on the Via del Corso, the customary throng of artists and literary figures gathered after 9.00 p.m. to discuss the day's events. A journalist spotted the poet Vincenzo Cardarelli sitting silently in a corner and asked him for his thoughts on the current situation. He addressed him with the banned polite form, 'Lei'. A Militia officer overheard the remark: '*Lei* is no longer to be used!' he shouted. 'I'll speak as I like', came the retort. 'What's wrong with you all this evening, you seem mad!' exclaimed the officer. A fight broke out. Tables, trays and bottles began to fly. Then suddenly, with the officer on the floor under a heap of chairs, the Sicilian writer Corrado Sofia burst into the cafe crying: 'They've arrested Mussolini, they've arrested Mussolini'.[6]

To the journalist Paolo Monelli, who was present, it felt like the dramatic finale of the opera *Cavalleria rusticana*. People started

shouting and embracing one another, and burst onto the street. At
10.45 they gathered round the radio for an expected announcement.
Normal transmissions had been interrupted and for a time there was
a disconcerting silence. Then came a brief and sober statement that
His Majesty the king and emperor had accepted the resignation of
Cavaliere Benito Mussolini as prime minister and head of government
and had nominated in his place Marshal Pietro Badoglio. Almost at
once the silence of the night sky in Rome was broken by sounds of
cheering and singing. A group from the Aragno set off down the Via
del Tritone crying 'death to Mussolini, down with fascism' and calling
on people to get out of bed. Soon excited crowds were everywhere.
Party badges and insignia were torn off and thrown to the ground
and pictures of Mussolini were hurled from windows. In front of the
Quirinal Palace there were scenes of jubilation.[7] Immediately after the
communiqué of the Duce's resignation Badoglio himself had made a
declaration on the radio that as 'jealous custodian of its ancient traditions' Italy would honour its word and continue fighting alongside its
German ally. But amid the carnival atmosphere his words went largely
unheeded.

The twenty-five-year-old Milena Milani, who had already made quite
a name for herself in literary circles, participating in the Littoriali for
poetry while a student at Rome university and writing for the GUF
journal *Roma Fascista*, had spent the afternoon of 25 July in the grounds
of the Villa Borghese. It was a Sunday, and she had felt carefree and
happy. She had ridden her bike under the trees and rung the bell loudly,
enjoying the sensation of her hair floating free and her skirt billowing
around her, and then sleeping out in the open air on the grass until
after the sun had gone down ('I had no idea what I would be doing
the next day . . . Like everyone else, I always lived for the moment').
As she rode back into the centre of the city down Via Veneto, she
noted how thick and brilliant the stars were that night. She got to
Piazza Barberini towards midnight and found herself face to face with
enormous crowds:

I had to get down from the saddle. Everyone was shouting: 'Fascism
is finished'. The pavements were awash with waste paper. People
seemed to have gone mad. There were party badges underfoot as you
walked: everyone was tearing them off their jackets and throwing them

on the ground. Some people were burning portraits of Mussolini, others were hacking off fascist symbols. Where were the fascists? I pushed my bicycle through the streets. Via del Tritone was seething with vast screaming crowds. Everyone in the city had abandoned their houses. Windows were lit. Men and women were embracing one another: they thought that the war was over as well. Nobody had given any attention to the words of Badoglio on the radio: 'Italy will honour its word'. Did anyone go to bed that night? An era was ending. Two decades were disintegrating in front of my eyes . . .[8]

Similar explosions of collective joy occurred in many towns across the country on the night of 25–26 July, but the most significant demonstrations took place in the northern towns, and especially Milan. Here, in the birthplace of the fascist movement, exultant crowds roamed for hours through the city centre to cries of 'Viva Badoglio and 'Viva il Re', breaking into the houses of leading fascists, ransacking party headquarters and newspaper offices – including those of *Il Popolo d'Italia* – and hurling official documents, newspapers, posters, banners and anything else they could seize that was combustible onto enormous bonfires, heedless of the blackout. People risked their lives clambering high up ladders or out onto precipitous balconies to reach and deface symbols of the regime. Busts and statues of the Duce were smashed or dragged clanging through the streets. Everywhere there were tricolour flags and ribbons. There were also a few red flags, though a more common symbol of left-wing sympathies were the pictures of Matteotti that were taken out of concealment and put on display.

Running through the euphoria were strains of intense anger. But according to one eyewitness, the main focus of popular hostility seemed to be the corruption of the party rather than any broader, more overtly political, issues. Dino Villani was a cultured middle-aged man, with rather ambivalent feelings towards the regime. He worked in the advertising section of the food company Motta. On the morning of 26 July he took a train from Varese to Milan, uncertain as to what exactly the news of the previous evening had meant (had the Duce really been removed from all positions of power?). However, he was confident that Badoglio would now sue for peace. He heard reports of crowds breaking into the houses of wealthy party officials and looting bottles of wine and liqueurs, pots of jam and other luxury goods. He noted the silence and despondent faces of the 'fascist fascists' and listened as some passengers felt emboldened to express their satisfaction with what had happened, declaring in loud voices how it was time that the 'government of thieves' was ended. This description of fascism, said Villani, was the one that was most commonly heard. In his view it was justified, given that so many scandals had been systematically covered up and that even within the party itself the ranks of the have-nots had far outnumbered 'the cohorts of the satiated'.[9]

But it was the escapist and carnival character of so many of the demonstrations that struck many contemporaries. People went through the streets chanting vulgar rhymes, singing abusive songs, parading mannequins, sometimes daubed with excrement, and performing parodies of the Duce. Wild rumours flew, in which the theme of mental instability was common. There was talk that Hitler had committed suicide (the glum expressions on the faces of German soldiers was said to be evidence of this) and that Mussolini had gone mad and been found ranting to the walls of his room – which is why he had been taken away in a Red Cross ambulance on 25 July.[10] Even when it came to acts of revenge, the prevalent tone, as Piero Calamandrei noted in Florence, was often light hearted: a ritualistic slap in the face in front of a ring of bystanders. The most serious episode that he heard of was a fascist official being forced to swallow his party badge as onlookers taunted, 'Go on, be brave, you can do it!' Calamandrei was initially thrilled by the fall of Mussolini, feeling united once again with his fellow countrymen in the surge of collective joy. But as the days passed he had a growing sense that an absence of either realism or conviction risked leading the country towards disaster.[11]

Indeed, it was often convinced and long-standing opponents of the regime, such as Calamandrei, who found the scenes of jubilation after 25 July most disconcerting. What did the joy say about the levels of civil and political morality in the country after two decades of dictatorship? The twenty-year-old anti-fascist from Siena, Bruna Talluri, who had links with the Giustizia e Libertà circles in Turin, wrote in her diary of experiencing 'shivers of nausea' at the sight of so many people who until recently had been 'screaming their fascist faith in the piazza' suddenly pledging themselves to democracy: 'At dawn on 26 July, after twenty years of fascist regime, you could not find one man who had the courage to justify his former faith. In their hearts everyone had been an antifascist, even those who had most profited from it.'[12] The communist supporter Magda Ceccarelli De Grada wrote similarly in her diary on 26 July of 'shuddering' at the manner in which the newspapers had overnight cynically abandoned fascism and at the spectacle of people who had a short time before been applauding the Duce hurriedly removing his picture from their walls: 'If I had been a fascist they would have had to take those pictures away from me by force. Not a word about this man. He disappears ignominiously . . .'[13]

But for many of those who hurled their portraits of the Duce out of the window, tore off their fascist badges, and cheered in the streets it was almost certainly the hope that the war was about to end – a longing for relief from suffering as much as any considered rejection of the past – that underpinned the outpourings of emotion at the end of July 1943. Zelinda Marcucci, a young seamstress in the town of San Casciano near Florence, who for months had been waiting anxiously for news of her beloved fiancé, Bruno, in north Africa, described in her diary feeling 'mad with joy' at Mussolini's fall. And when four days later a rumour emerged that peace had been declared, she and her fellow townspeople were ecstatic:

I raced down the stairs and reached the piazza. People were running from every street. Everyone was embracing. I did not know if what was in front of me was real or a dream. It was real. People were shouting, crying out, 'Viva il Re' and 'Viva Badoglio' . . . Suddenly the announcement came on the radio that the news was false. But nobody wanted to believe it: [they were convinced] it was 'Peace'. They were rejoicing with happiness. Then at 12.15 the soldiers assembled and levelled their guns at the townspeople, who were in a feverish state. Everything collapsed. The news was false. For some moments I felt insane. The bells were pealing. People were screaming, weeping, shouting. Even the men were emotional. In all my life I had never experienced anything like it. And now I don't know what to think, and only ask the Lord to give me the strength to overcome whatever I have to in order that I too can share happiness.[14]

As it became clear in the days that followed that the replacement of Mussolini with Badoglio would not necessarily bring an end to the fighting, Zelinda, like millions of other Italians, became increasingly anxious about the future. The issue was not simply whether the country could realistically expect to break with its Nazi allies and extricate itself from a conflict that it had been instrumental in causing. Apart from anything else, how could the Germans acquiesce in Italy suing for peace at such a vital juncture of the war? It was also a question of what to believe in and whom to trust after twenty years of being encouraged to invest such uncritical faith in fascism and the Duce. The king and Badoglio would struggle to command great authority: they had both been heavily implicated in the regime. What then, as Aldo Carugati, a young artillery corporal from Lombardy, wondered on hearing in a prisoner of war camp in the north of England of the fall of Mussolini, could fill the void?:

How will all those people feel who had turned a man into a supreme, infallible, leader, almost a God? How will those people feel who had placed all their trust in him and believed in his words more than in God himself? Their disillusionment will know no bounds. And here my mind turns to the eternal problem, to the thought of how fleeting and fallible are the hopes placed in a man, however great he may be, and how the course of events belies the words of such people.[15]

Aldo vowed in his diary never to commit himself in the future to any worldly creed or ideology. The great surge in the popularity of Pius XII in the summer of 1943 suggested that many were similarly inclined to look to the Church for leadership. A photograph of the Pope in a white tunic flecked with blood, standing in front of crowds, his arms flung wide as if in crucifixion, as he visited the San Lorenzo district of Rome after an allied bombing raid on 19 July had left more than 1,000 dead and 6,000 injured, soon became iconic. Yet, as Aldo had suspected, there were also huge numbers for whom it would be a psychological struggle to accept the Duce's fall from grace after so many years of exaltation. Even the eighteen-year-old schoolboy, Pietro Ambrosini, who had continually been encouraged by his parents to take a very detached and pragmatic approach to politics, confessed to finding it impossible to think badly of Mussolini. He felt 'dumbfounded'

and 'bewildered' by the news on 25 July: 'It is as if I had suddenly
found out that my father is a rotten egg or some such thing'. And
however much he tried, he could not shake off 'all those things that
they have taught us from primary school onwards about Mussolini
and fascism . . . Perhaps I am stupid, but there it is.'[16]

The fact that one of the central dynamics of the regime had been
the interplay between frustration at the shortcomings of the state and
hope that any wrongs would in due course be righted by the Duce,
made it easier to insulate Mussolini from outright vilification. As Dino
Villani noted in Milan, popular anger might be directed primarily at
corruption in the party. Moreover, radical fascists had long claimed
that the regime was being undermined by disloyal or lukewarm
elements. The events of 25 July could confirm this view. For Carlo
Ciseri, the hotel manager from Florence, who twenty-three years
earlier had experienced an epiphany hearing Mussolini speak in Milan,
the tragedy for fascism had always been the weak, incompetent and
perfidious elements surrounding the Duce – and they had now betrayed
him. Carlo was a prisoner in a camp in western Kenya when he learned
of the Duce's dismissal. The news made him physically sick: 'I was
overcome with a kind of vertigo that left me stunned and confused
and prevented me from speaking'. And in the days that followed he
found himself becoming angry with those who now sought to
disparage Mussolini and welcome the advent of liberty (or 'anarchy'
as it always was in Italy, he said):

> These people . . . refuse to acknowledge and refuse to remember the
> moral, material and political resurrection that was greeted with
> unanimous enthusiasm by the entire people and which stirred and
> captivated not only the spirits of all Italy but of Europe and the whole
> world . . . Until they bring me concrete and tangible evidence, I will not
> be able to believe the infamy that is being hurled in the face of a man who
> passionately wanted our greatness. Have there been any errors? . . . Until
> now he can be accused of only one, namely of having too much goodness,
> which in a man of government can be called weakness. Certainly this is
> strange in someone of his kind . . . Indeed if he had imitated, if only
> partly, the ferocious Stalin (just to take an example), purging all the scum,
> we would perhaps not have come to this.[17]

According to Carlo, Mussolini had been the victim of 'villainous treachery'. Other fascists agreed, and their vehement anger poisoned the air in the remaining months of the war.

Unconditional surrender

Exactly what Badoglio and his new ministers – whose photographs were published in the newspapers showing only their heads so as not to draw attention to the fact that they would all have been sporting fascist party badges in their jacket lapels until a few days before[18] – intended to do after 25 July was unclear, even, it seems, to themselves. They were terrified of how the Germans would react to Mussolini's arrest. Even when they began putting out feelers to the Allies in mid-August for an armistice, everything was done to persuade the Nazis that Italy was still committed to carrying on fighting and making sure that the talks were blanketed in secrecy. For a long time there was not even any radio contact between General Castellano – who was sent (slowly, by train) to Portugal to negotiate with the British and Americans – and the government in Rome. But the Germans were understandably mistrustful, and as the days passed they dispatched reinforcements to the peninsula. The Americans and British were also wary of Italian intentions, and stepped up their aerial bombardments. In this climate of intense fear and mutual suspicion, the lines of communication became imperfect and misunderstandings grew; deliberately so, it would seem, given how reluctant the Italian leadership was to assume responsibility for what was now occurring. The consequences were catastrophic.

The Allies wanted to conserve the bulk of their forces for the anticipated landings in France and were not in a position to commit to a full-scale invasion of the peninsula. They needed the cooperation of Italian troops to secure and hold Rome pending the arrival of Allied units from a bridgehead south of the capital. Accordingly when on 3 September General Castellano signed the terms of Italy's unconditional surrender at Cassibile in eastern Sicily, it was agreed that all airfields and ports would be secured and Rome defended with the 60,000 or so soldiers that were stationed in and around the capital – three times as many as the Germans had in the area. It was also made clear that the Allies would decide when exactly in the following days the armistice was announced publicly, as any declaration would need to coincide with their plans for the landing on the mainland. But Badoglio was still haunted, it seems, by fear that the Germans would get wind of what was happening. He failed to tell even his closest advisers that an armistice had been signed. He also claimed not to know its contents.[19]

The armistice was announced on Allied radio in the early evening of 8 September. No preparations had been made by the government in Rome: Badoglio maintained that he had not been expecting the declaration so soon. '*Siamo fottuti*' ('We are screwed'), the prime minister declared at an urgent meeting of the king and his ministers in the Quirinal Palace.[20] A number of those present suggested that they should renounce the armistice and continue fighting with the Germans. This, it was pointed out, would hardly do much for the country's credibility. At 7.45 Badoglio went on air to confirm the surrender and order the immediate cessation of all hostilities against the British and Americans. But he also added cryptically that Italian forces should 'react to attacks that may happen to come from any other source'. This could presumably only mean the Germans. But no clear orders had been issued to the army, and nothing was now done to secure the ports and airfields and defend Rome as the armistice required. The only action taken by the commander of troops in the capital, before fleeing, was to instruct an armoured corps to withdraw to Tivoli so as to avoid 'grave and futile losses'.[21]

At dawn on 9 September the king, Badoglio and more than 200 generals and senior officers abandoned Rome to its fate. They left in convoys of cars for Pescara on the Adriatic coast, where they were to embark for the safety of Allied protection in the south of the peninsula. Across the capital there was an uneasy mixture of euphoria that the war was finally over and deep uncertainty. As the journalist Paolo Monelli recalled, most people imagined that the Nazis would now simply withdraw to the north. The intermittent machine-gun and mortar fire that was heard in the distance was assumed to be the sound of German units retreating. But in the absence of any radio broadcasts, there was no confirmation. Rumours circulated that Mussolini had died after an emergency medical operation and that Allied forces had landed at Civitavecchia and were nearing the city.

Lorries packed with cheerful Italian soldiers raced through the streets. Bystanders applauded, believing they were off to fight any straggling German contingents. Girls stood in front of houses waiting to greet American and British soldiers.[22]

Only slowly during the course of 10 September did the full horror of the situation begin to dawn. Government offices stood ominously empty and phones went unanswered. The journalists at the news agency, Stefani, had no official information to report. Smoke rose from behind Piazza Colonna and scraps of paper floated in the air over the centre of the city as the archives of the Foreign Ministry were burned in the courtyard of Palazzo Chigi. Reverberations of gunfire and explosions continued unabated: far from receding, they appeared to be getting closer.[23] Newspapers confidently declared that the fighting would soon be over, and one front page carried a large picture of Garibaldi and a title stating that the Germans had surrendered.[24] But by the evening there were insistent reports that the Nazi forces were closing in on the city, and that the only resistance was coming from individuals, groups of students and pockets of soldiers. By the morning of 11 September it was clear that the Italian army had dissolved and that the Germans were in control of all key points of the capital.

Elsewhere in Italy – and beyond, in the occupied territories of Greece, the Balkans and southern France – confusion and panic spread rapidly. A fourteen-year-old girl, Vittoria Cozzi, recorded the escalating chaos around the town of Treviso in the Veneto as local people realised that the army was disintegrating and that they would be at the mercy of the Germans. Vittoria came from a wealthy middle-class Venetian family, and had the robust patriotism and firm Catholic morality characteristic of someone of her background. Her age and emotional intelligence made her particularly alert to indications of fear. She had decided to keep a diary after being sent to stay with her grandmother in a village in the summer of 1943. She addressed the entries to her boyfriend, Filippo. When the armistice was declared, she raced into the street and watched as her neighbours – or at least most of them – cried with joy and sang far into the evening: 'The pure and simple of heart were happy – The others not.' She herself felt elation, albeit tinged with considerable shame and sadness: 'An ugly peace – Unconditional surrender – But what does it matter, Filippo – Beautiful or ugly, it is peace – peace'.[25]

Her joy was short-lived. On 10 September came the first signs of the army's collapse:

> The Italian army is defeated – the Fatherland destroyed. Soldiers are arriving in groups of four or five, ragged, barefooted, bundles on their backs – their faces disfigured – the horror, the terror, of the situation. To begin with it was men from a barracks in Treviso who were deserting because of the treachery of an officer who was a paid up fascist. They were cheerful and arrogant. Then a soldier appeared – the typical cannon fodder . . . his face sunken and expressionless, with that ill fitting grey-green uniform, too long and too wide, and the cap too big. He was trudging beside a bicycle, bent under the weight of enormous packs, looking like a frightened rabbit. At that point I realised it was all over. When it was just the hotheads deserting, it was something that could be contained. But if Ordinary Joe is deserting too, that's the end . . .[26]

Two days afterwards, as she walked to Mass through the thick early-morning mist, she watched as streams of young men passed with frightened expressions on their faces, 'like children terrified by something horrible they do not understand'. They were intent on getting back home, but more often than not ended up in the hands of the Germans. Later in Treviso she saw crowds of women with children in their arms and men 'who seemed to have lost their virility' standing in the streets outside their houses, waiting with incredulity in their eyes ('what have they done to us – what are they doing to us?'). She caught sight of a German soldier on a truck staring at her. She blushed with a mixture of indignation and shame: 'It was a terrifying look – I went as red as fire – Never in all my life would I have wanted to be blushing for what the Italians are doing in front of a German.' Everyone was waiting anxiously for news. For many there were painful memories of the autumn of 1917 when Austrian and German troops had swept into the Veneto after the defeat at Caporetto:

> So many people in the city . . . Soldiers and prostitutes – When the nation falls apart, out come the dregs with their very short skirts, cleavages revealed and faces covered in paint – It is terrifying how history repeats itself . . . Everyone was waiting from one minute to

the next for the German invasion. The sky was grey and it was muggy. It seemed as if a finger hovered frighteningly in the air. People had the urge to escape – to escape towards a purer sky – to be able to breathe – to live.[27]

In some parts of Italy and the occupied territories abroad people heeded the call of Badoglio for resistance to the Germans, out of whatever combination of pride, anger or loyalty to the king. In places the fighting was determined and fierce – as on the island of Cephalonia, where the majority of the Italian garrison of some 12,000 troops ended up being massacred by German units, or in Naples, where the Nazi occupying forces were driven out after four days of street fighting ahead of the arrival of Allied troops in the city on 1 October. But in the absence of orders from the top, most rank-and-file Italian soldiers concluded they had little choice but to jettison their rifles and uniforms and seek refuge. Many were rounded up by the Germans, who took about a million prisoners. The civilian population was also in general too demoralised to offer much active resistance, not least because they were forced to contend with German troops who felt little but contempt for their erstwhile allies and behaved accordingly. On 13 September Vittoria learned that a picture of the Duce had been set up on a bridge near Treviso and that the Germans were shooting at the legs of anyone who did not salute.[28]

On 12 September, Mussolini was freed by the Germans in a commando raid on the hotel on the Gran Sasso mountain in central Italy where he was being held prisoner. After discussions with Hitler, he was installed at the head of a Nazi-dominated puppet government, the Italian Social Republic – or the Republic of Salò as it was commonly known, from the small town on the shores of Lake Garda where some of the key ministries were located. The peninsula was now split in two, with the Germans dug in from the autumn of 1943 in a series of heavily fortified defensive positions running across the Apennines to the north of Naples. To the south of this line, in the territories liberated by the Allies, Victor Emmanuel and Badoglio had established the Kingdom of the South. But like the Republic of Salò this state enjoyed very little autonomy, and most of the southern provinces were ruled directly by the Allied Military Government. The king desperately tried to enhance his standing by entering the conflict as a fully fledged 'ally'.

But the British were firmly opposed. Victor Emmanuel declared war on Germany on 13 October (with what little remained of his army: some twenty poorly equipped divisions), but he was allowed to do so only with the ill-defined status of 'co-belligerent'.

For millions of Italians the catastrophic events of the late summer and early autumn of 1943 were agonising. Apart from the suffering, the fear, the anger and the shame, there was a realisation for many that the very idea of 'Italy', which generations had been taught to love and revere, had been called into question. The fact that the regime had striven for more than twenty years to appropriate the country's past and claim that two millennia of national life had reached a glorious summation in fascism made it all the more difficult to discern the moral and political contours of the future. 'What Italy should we now live for, think, make poetry, teach and write?' asked the former Minister of Public Instruction, Giovanni Gentile, at the end of 1943 after having pledged his support to the Republic of Salò (not to have done so would have been 'supreme cowardice and the demolition of all my life', he claimed).[29] '. . . Today's incalculable disaster is not the foreign invasion and the devastation of our cities . . . It lies in our spirit . . . in the dissolution of what had been our common faith'.[30] And his one-time friend and fellow philosopher, Benedetto Croce, who had attempted to find solace in the idea that fascism was essentially just a historical aberration, was haunted by a similar feeling. He lay awake at night racked by the thought that 'everything that . . . Italians had constructed, politically, economically and morally over a century', had been 'destroyed irremediably'.[31]

For the twenty-one-year-old student from a socialist family, Maria Carazzolo, in the town of Montagnana to the south-west of Padua, excitement at the armistice and reports of British and American landings in southern Italy quickly gave way to dismay that, contrary to her expectations, Badoglio had done nothing to fortify the Brenner and defend the Veneto. As it became clear that the north and centre of the country were being overrun by the Germans and the far south by the Allies, she confided to her diary her sense of disorientation and shame: 'What is it that is still Italian? . . . Where, where are we to look for Italy – the true, pure and independent Italy?'[32] For another student, Angelo Peroni, who had also been brought up in an anti-fascist environment, the humiliation felt even more intense. Angelo had witnessed the scenes of iconoclastic joy in Milan following the fall of Mussolini and had hoped that Italy would now be able to redeem itself after twenty years of collective guilt: 'We have all been cowards. We have allowed ourselves to be called fascists in the face of the world'. It was a question of the educated elites setting an example and turning the credulous masses ('these puppets of mud'), who had been duped by Mussolini, into real 'men'. But his illusions were left shattered after the armistice. 'Yesterday evening, when the announcement first came, I did perhaps smile, it is true', he wrote in his diary on 9 September. 'But I was quickly forced to weep, thinking what the name "Italian" means: traitor, coward, buffoon.' His despondency increased in the days that followed as reports indicated the extent of the 'servility' and the absence of 'moral consciousness': 'It is utterly ignominious to be called Italians!'[33]

In October 1943 Angelo learned that he was due shortly to be called up to serve in the army by the Republic of Salò. He vowed never to put on the 'uniform of assassins'. He was looking forward to a future in which he would be able to write and make speeches and re-educate the Italian masses ('apostolate and mission are becoming sources for ambition'); and inspired by his passion for Tolstoy and Mazzini he set about drawing up a programme for an 'Anti-political Association of Universal Brotherhood' to promote the struggle everywhere against political parties.[34] His family thought it best for him to train as an officer and find some means later, if he still wanted to, of escaping. But Angelo was adamant about not doing military service: 'None of my friends will obey the call up', he observed. He managed to lie low and evade the draft until the spring of 1944, when he got across the border into Switzerland. He later became involved with partisan units operating in northern Piedmont, and survived the war to become a teacher, a writer and an active member of the Communist Party.

The distinguished mountaineer Ettore Castiglioni was another anti-fascist who was determined to find some form of personal redemption after the shame of the armistice. Ettore was a junior officer and ski instructor serving with the Alpini near the Swiss border when news came through of Italy's surrender. Six weeks earlier he had been ecstatic at the fall of Mussolini: amid the general euphoria he had felt reconnected with his fellow countrymen for the first time in two decades. He had smashed pictures of the Duce in Alpine hotels and refuges, and had proudly written out in his diary, 'entirely in capital letters, this marvellous word LIBERTY'.[35] During the course of 9 September he and the unit under his command had waited with growing consternation for orders as to what to do. When none had arrived, and reports emerged that the Germans had occupied the nearby town of Ivrea, he and his fellow soldiers had reluctantly decided to take off their uniforms and seek safety. It was, he confessed, one of the saddest days of his life.[36] In the weeks that followed he used his knowledge of the Alpine passes to help Jews and political refugees escape into Switzerland. But it was hard, he confessed on 26 September, to escape a bitter sense of anger and shame:

> The sudden dissolution of the army, swept away like a castle of playing cards by the wind; the German occupation passively endured, with almost no attempt at resistance despite the numerical weakness of their forces; the fact that we allowed ourselves to be disarmed like a flock of sheep . . . – these are humiliations that touch every Italian so deeply that it will be hard to know how long it will take for our honour as men to be restored and for us to be able to hold our heads up and look the world in the face without blushing with shame and humiliation.[37]

The determination of Ettore to find solace for the ignominy of defeat by doing what he could to support a nascent resistance movement in northern Italy against the Germans and the Republic of Salò was common to those who had long harboured feelings of deep hostility towards fascism. And even for some who had supported the regime strongly – like the twenty-four-year-old Piedmontese officer Nuto Revelli, who had grown up believing fervently in all aspects of fascist ideology – the trauma of defeat could precipitate a sudden conversion. Nuto had served in the campaign in Russia in 1941–43. His horror and anger at the suffering had slowly turned him against fascism in general and the Nazis in particular. When the armistice was announced he made what he later described as an 'immediate and instinctive choice'. As the Germans rolled into his home town of Cuneo, he ran to his house, grabbed his three automatic weapons, threw them in a rucksack, and set off into the mountains to link up with others who were prepared to fight as partisans, convinced that the only 'fatherland' worth believing in was 'that of the poor devils who had paid for the sins of "others" with their lives'.[38]

But for many millions of others who had embraced fascism with varying degrees of enthusiasm, the decision to be made after September 1943 often appeared far more fraught. Giovanni Pirelli, the son of the wealthy industrialist Alberto Pirelli, had been passionate about the war from the outset, viewing it as an idealistic struggle between the decadent materialism of the plutocracies and the superior spirituality of fascism. A spell in Berlin in 1942 had left him uneasy about the Nazis: their morals struck him as 'absolutely pagan'. But he had still believed in fascism, hoping only that it would one day be purged of its corrupt elements and become 'purer' and more egalitarian.[39] He was in southern France at the time of the armistice: the surrender, he wrote in his diary, was an act of 'treachery'. He was captured and given a choice between imprisonment and fighting with the Germans. He found it hard to decide. A third option, to be a labourer, seemed more palatable, if still undignified: 'I am prostituting myself, I know, but how can I do anything different and not follow all my comrades?' He then changed his mind, and chose to be a prisoner. But he managed to escape from the barracks that he was being held in, and crossed over the Alps into Italy, where he was able to work in his father's factory in Milan. He joined the partisans in the early spring of 1945.[40]

Only around 10 per cent of the million or so Italian soldiers arrested in September 1943 agreed to fight with the Germans. They included a majority of Militia members. Most of the remainder ended up, like Giovanni's comrades, being interned in camps in Germany and Austria and working in frequently inhuman conditions in mines, arms factories and other industries. The motives of those who consented to support the Nazis were inevitably mixed, but as the historian Roberto Vivarelli recalled it was often the question of honour that was paramount. Roberto, who was thirteen at the time of the armistice, had grown up in a strongly fascist environment. His father had taken part in the March on Rome, and as a staunch monarchist and Catholic he had always regarded Mussolini's regime as the embodiment of the Italian nation: 'For him fascism was the fatherland and the fatherland was a religious principle'. He had volunteered to fight in 1935 and again in 1940; and in 1942, shortly before being killed by partisans in the Balkans, he had written to Roberto's mother to confirm his commitment to fascism: 'You who have been my life know that I die happy. The cause for which I am dying and for which I have modestly fought since my youth, is well worth my sacrifice.'[41]

Roberto regarded the armistice as an act of consummate treachery on the part of the king. He and his friends in the local fascist party section in Siena had already been outraged by the disloyalty shown by Victor Emmanuel a few weeks earlier in dismissing Mussolini, and had immediately taken to flaunting fascist badges they had not normally worn. 'We had been taught to "believe, obey, fight", and we continued to believe with absolute faith; we were fully ready to obey; and to fight was our highest aspiration.' The news on 8 September compounded their defiance and anger. 'The Germans were the allies of fascist Italy and that meant Italy *tout court*, because no other Italy existed. And seduced by the myth of the Rome–Berlin axis we had learned to love our allies.' To abandon the Nazis at such a juncture appeared the acme of disgrace – not on account of what the Nazis stood for (Roberto said he had no idea about the atrocities against the Jews) but simply because they were allies. Roberto remembered being moved by a broadcast on the radio from Germany by Alessandro Pavolini – soon a key figure in the Republic of Salò – who spoke of how the shield of the House of Savoy on the white band of the Italian tricolour had now been removed and replaced by a single word: 'Honour!' The following summer, still only fourteen, Roberto set off to Lombardy to enrol in the newly constituted fascist paramilitary organisation, the Black Brigades.[42]

As Roberto admitted, he had been encouraged both by his father and by fascism to see the world in uncompromising black-and-white terms. But for the eighteen-year-old Florentine schoolboy, Pietro Ambrosini, the dogmatism of the regime had always been undercut by his parents' scepticism. In October 1943 he was aware that he would shortly be called up for military service by the Republic of Salò. He was uncertain what to do. He had no desire to risk his life 'without knowing what for', and though he had believed in fascism ('like all other young people'), he thought that things had now changed and that the fascists had become 'a band of thugs'. In the end, with his parents' support, he decided to go to Switzerland. His father was able to procure him a false passport through a rich business contact, and on 12 November he set off. But his conscience still troubled him. Was he a coward? What would he have done if he had not got the passport? Perhaps he might have gone with his socialist school friend to help the partisans in the mountains. Even now, he reflected, he could join them. But surely it would be much safer with acquaintances in a villa in Lugano? At this point he ended his diary:

> Well, dear diary, I leave you with all these doubts of mine. When all is said and done, there is only one thing that I regret: that as a schoolboy I stupidly went in a demonstration through the streets of the city calling for our country to enter this dirty war.[43]

With Italy humiliated in defeat, overrun by occupying forces, and split in two, the instinct of many, like Pietro, was to turn, and where possible, walk away. And if they could not walk away (and inevitably most were unable to) the desire for comfort and understanding amid the horror led millions – and women in particular, it seems – to fall back on the certainties of their Christian faith. For Maricilla Piovanelli, a young mother and writer in Varese, the disaster befalling the country was best explained as a punishment for the sins of the people. She entrusted her future fate to the 'guardian angel of Italy, the Pope, in whom, alone, all our hopes reside'.[44] For Domenica Corti, an elderly housewife in Ancona, the fact that news of the armistice arrived on the feast of the Blessed Virgin Mary's birthday was no coincidence. She recorded in her diary her belief that what was occurring should be endured patiently as something 'inevitable', given that 'we are very poor in arms, in bread, in everything, and are rich only in the blood of our poor sons'.[45] And for Mariannina Pastore, a nineteen-year-old student in Milan, the devastation she witnessed all around her was proof of just how wrong the regime had been to elevate politics into a religion. She felt that the nation, in truth, had nothing to do with God, despite everything that she had been told in school. Nor was it reasonable for fascism to regard its so-called 'martyrs' as 'saints'. It was the individual who was sacred, and, beyond the individual, the family – as the Catholic Church taught. The 'fatherland' and the 'superhuman heroes' she had been brought up to worship were simply false gods, 'deities that are falling'.[46]

For many others, too, it was tempting to hold the very concept of the 'nation', which Italians had been encouraged so insistently to venerate from the time of the Risorgimento, as the root cause of the disasters. And rather than struggle to decide whether the 'fatherland' now properly resided in Mussolini, fascism and the Republic of Salò, or in Victor Emmanuel, Badoglio and the Kingdom of the South, it seemed better to jettison national politics entirely as an arena of identity. But renunciation could be fully as dangerous as commitment, as the young university student from Puglia, Angelo Galiano, realised in the spring of 1944 as he agonised over whether to heed the call-up for military service by the Republic of Salò. He had been in the army in Rome at the time of the armistice and had gone into hiding in a friend's house. On 15 March he attempted to work out what to do, reflecting in his diary on the morality of his options. His starting point was the gaunt realisation of what might happen if he did not enlist: he would be a deserter and liable to find himself in front of a firing squad.[47]

He did not feel much sympathy for the king and Badoglio, but he could not bring himself to blame them for what had happened. It was surely the fascist regime that had been principally at fault, blinding people to reality with its inflammatory and illusory propaganda. The young in particular had been seduced by the intoxicating rhetoric and lured down the ruinous path to war.[48] This was why in the months since the armistice he had felt unable to support the Republic of Salò. Indeed his reflections since 8 September had made it almost impossible for him to fight on any side – not, he believed, because he was a coward, but simply because no cause seemed to him to be justified. To fight now would be to support a civil war against fellow Italians. Moreover, the second element of what he considered to be a sacred trinomial of God, fatherland and family had disappeared, leaving only God and the family to demand his love and loyalty. Love of the fatherland, he thought, had hitherto served to bind people together in nations; but this same patriotism had also driven countries to compete with one another for supremacy, with the disastrous consequences that all could see. In the future mankind should dispense with nations and be united by love of humanity alone.[49]

As a result of his deliberations, Angelo decided to remain in hiding in Rome and not join the army of the Republic of Salò. There was always a risk that he could end up being executed; but against that was the fact that the authorities would probably not be looking for him, as the record of his birth was kept in the registry office in his home town in Puglia, which was in the Kingdom of the South. There was also a very good chance that the British and Americans would soon be in Rome. In March, as he was writing his diary, Allied forces were launching furious assaults on the German lines around Monte Cassino, just 80 miles away, hoping to link up with the bridgehead they had established in January at Anzio, to the south of the capital. Their casualties were huge – around 100,000 in four months of fighting – but towards the end of May they finally managed to break through. On 4 June they entered Rome, two days ahead of the Normandy landings. Angelo was able to come out of hiding and head back to Puglia. After the war he became an active member of the Socialist Party.

Civil war

In the territories occupied by the Allied forces in the south of the country, food shortages, black marketeering, inflation, disease, home-lessness, broken infrastructures, corruption, petty crime and banditry all took a heavy toll on society. In Sicily mafia activity flourished again on a huge scale. It was an unedifying spectacle that invited sober reflec-tions on the attempts of Mussolini to forge a new Italy and new Italians. There appeared to be little remorse or shame at the disaster that had befallen the country. As the Calabrian writer Corrado Alvaro noted with a mixture of horror and amazement, public opinion seemed to think that 'national dignity' and 'national honour' consisted simply of trying to curb the swarms of shoeshiners and prostitutes that thronged the streets.[50] It was almost as if people were relieved to be liberated not just from fascism but from 'Italy' ('I hope that the Anglo-Americans will never go away . . . They have a vision of life that is different from the miserable one that we have known up to now', wrote a Neapolitan in a letter in January 1944.)[51] To those conscious of history there was a bitter sense of déjà vu. 'Oh, we never change . . . the eternal Italian psychology of looking to foreigners for salvation', Piero Calamandrei wrote ruefully in his diary.[52]

The moral as well as material chaos of southern society felt to many observers like a return to a pre-modern world, with people living from hand to mouth, heedless of a common good, and trusting only to themselves and their families in the desperate struggle to survive. To the writer and once enthusiastic fascist, Curzio Malaparte, it was as if people had suddenly been stricken by an extraordinary medieval plague that somehow kept the flesh intact but gnawed away at the soul, leaving everyone 'defiled, vitiated and debased'.[53] Norman Lewis, a young intelligence officer serving with the British forces in Italy in 1943–44, thought Naples was a city that had been 'pushed . . . back into the Middle Ages'. Almost the only discernible source of social solidarity came from the remarkable outpourings of popular religiosity. 'Churches', he noted in his diary in March 1944, 'are suddenly full of images that talk, bleed, sweat, nod their heads and exude health-giving liquors to be mopped up by handkerchiefs, or even collected in bottles.' And he recorded how crowds were flocking to the Campi Flegrei outside the city at the weekend to watch a twelve-year-old girl to whom the Virgin Mary was said to have appeared on several occasions and offered messages of comfort.[54]

In the centre and north of the country, the hardship, suffering and sense of moral decay were scarcely any less than in the south. Corrado Di Pompeo, a civil servant working in the Ministry of Corporations in Rome, kept a diary of the German occupation of the city from September 1943 to June 1944. He described the daily shortage of rations, the lack of gas and electricity, the destruction caused by bombing raids, the children roaming the streets in search of food (and scrawling the word 'bread' on walls in desperation), the disappearance of the once numerous cats from the piazzas ('Where have they gone? Without doubt, all into the pot!'), and the graffiti that every morning reappeared in the streets, having been whitewashed over the previous day, hailing the Soviet Union and denouncing the Germans and fascism. He had nothing good to say about the Republic of Salò – except that it was acting as a partial brake on 'the German barbarians' – or about the king, or indeed about the British and the Americans. But he longed for the Allies to get to Rome so that he could be reunited with his wife – for whom he was writing his diary. She was living in the Kingdom of the South and could not contact him. He dreamed of her at night cooking pasta for himself and his children, and he realised that like most other people all his political idealism had evaporated and been replaced by a simple yearning for domestic happiness. It left him feeling frustrated:

If only there was a goal, an ideal . . . nothing, we feel nothing any more . . . the sense of patriotism has gone, like the love for a woman who has betrayed us. We have been reduced to robots, beasts without reason who eat to live and live to eat, and nothing else. The only thing that moves us is affection for the family.[55]

Mussolini likewise looked to fill the void of disillusionment with domestic affection – though in his case, the affection was for his mistress. On 28 October 1943, after a separation of a little over three months (part of it spent in prison along with other members of her family) Claretta received a phone call summoning her to Villa Feltrinelli at Gargnano, on Lake Garda, where Mussolini had installed his residence. As she was driven to meet the Duce by a German SS general, she recited the rosary and prayed to Santa Rita, the patron saint of impossible causes, to help calm her nerves. The reunion was characteristically intense:

I feel I am fainting . . . He takes my hand and supports me. We look at each other, trembling violently . . . We enter the room in silence, our eyes locked together . . . Then we sit down on the sofa . . . Slowly my voice comes back, and we talk for a long time. He is bitter, grief stricken, nauseated – he speaks of this poor crucified Italy, of those Italians who have destroyed everything in a few hours, of his martyrdom – the humiliations suffered. The torment of seeing the work of twenty years destroyed . . . We begin to get cold. We go to bed and talk the whole night without stopping . . . He tells me that he has thought about me constantly, every hour, every moment, every minute, that he loves me deeply, that I am the last and the true love of his life . . . that I am his soul, and that our future, like the future of the country, depends on the war.[56]

Mussolini did his best, with what energy he was able to muster in his despondency and bitterness, to assert his authority in the Republic of Salò. He made passionate appeals for the defence of the 'fatherland' against the advancing British and American forces – and also against the king, Badoglio and the other 'traitors' of 25 July. In January 1944 he had five of those who had voted against him at the Grand Council meeting executed in Verona. Among them was his son-in-law, Ciano.

At the same time he endeavoured to bolster support among the masses
by reviving the anti-bourgeois spirit of the early fascist movement,
introducing such radical measures as the 'socialisation' of large firms
and the election of workers onto boards of management. But despite
such policies, and despite all the government's efforts to link the
Republic to 'la patria', and invoke the names of Mazzini, Garibaldi
and other heroes of the Risorgimento, active support for what was in
reality a German-dominated puppet state was limited to a small
minority. This angry, zealous and increasingly beleaguered minority
received backing from a ramshackle network of brutal security forces,
run largely by the Nazis.

Many of those who found themselves serving in the Republic's
small conscript army headed by Marshal Graziani were impervious
now to the allure of fascism. Among them was Danilo Durando, a
university student from Milan. He was called up in February 1944 and
was sent to Germany for training. He hated the Germans ('you who
consider yourselves the chosen race . . . you who teach us, during our
instruction, to mistreat and despise prisoners and kill them if they are
a nuisance . . . can you possibly be the best?'). And when Mussolini
came to review his regiment in July 1944, he could detect nothing
inspiring in the once charismatic leader standing a few feet away from
him: 'He is ugly: his face is spotted with the purple blotches of someone
with liver disorder. He is deflated, thin.' And two months later, posted
high in the Alps on the border with France to defend Italy against the
advancing Allies, he strove desperately to convince himself (and
perhaps those who might later read his diary) that he was serving 'the
fatherland' and not the 'little republican fascist state' run by 'criminals'
and 'hyenas':

> Patria? Yes, at certain moments I feel that this great mother exists, even
> if the Italians are now for the most part a vile, amorphous, despicable
> mass . . . I, a poor *alpino*, amid these peaks and mountains, feel that
> la Patria still dwells here, on account of the blood shed by others.
> Something indestructible, immortal, built on the sacrifice of thousands
> of martyrs, on blood and pain . . . I am not fascist, nor are my
> companions. We are Italians. Our sacrifices are not recognised. In fact
> they are laughed at. Everything is lost. I know that tomorrow, if
> I return, I will be taunted . . . I don't mind: indeed that is precisely why I

am carrying on. I am here only for my fatherland. That's enough . . .
I can show that someone is still able to suffer right to the end and so
stop people saying tomorrow that all Italians, all of them, are spineless.[57]

Danilo's sense that he belonged to a fatherland composed of those
who had laid down their lives in the past for the patriotic ideal was
shared by others who were now willing to fight and kill the supporters
of the Republic of Salò. The members of the resistance movement
that developed from the autumn of 1943 among soldiers fleeing the
German and Italian authorities were often inclined to believe that they
too were heirs of the heroes of the Risorgimento. They regularly
invoked the names of Garibaldi and Mazzini, and appealed to the
'honour of Italy', 'the ideal of the fatherland' and the 'independence
of the nation'.[58] Many found it very difficult in the immediate after-
math of the shock of Mussolini's fall and the announcement of the
armistice to adopt any clear political stance. But in due course their
objectives often crystallised as representatives of the communists,
the socialists, the Christian Democrats and the other anti-fascist
parties that were fast emerging in the major cities of the north and
centre in 1943–44 began to infiltrate the partisan formations and
draw them into their orbit.

As the resistance movement spread, Italians fought against Italians
in what became a bitter civil war. The celebration of violence and the
rejection of humanitarian values that had been central to fascism
ensured that the forces of the Republic of Salò had little compunction
about acting brutally towards their enemies. At the same time a desire
to assuage some of the humiliation of defeat by showing that they
could behave as ruthlessly as their Nazi allies also encouraged atrocities. Torture, rape, public executions, the displaying of corpses
(frequently with crude inscriptions pinned to the bodies to indicate
their crimes), and the annihilation of whole communities that had
provided assistance to partisans were all features of the struggle.
Estimates as to the scale of the resistance have varied greatly. There
was never a 'mass' popular rising, as communist mythology later tried
to suggest, but the numbers involved were certainly far from negligible.
The government of Salò maintained that more than 80,000 'rebels'
were at large by the early summer of 1944. By the spring of 1945, when
the Allies broke through the German defensive lines in the northern

Apennines and entered the Po valley, this figure had probably doubled. According to official calculations, over 44,000 partisans lost their lives between September 1943 and April 1945 and a further 10,000 civilians died in reprisal raids. Exactly how many fascists were killed in the same period is unknown.[59]

The diaries written by civilian observers in northern Italy during the last months of the war reveal communities oscillating between numbed resignation, bewilderment, fear and hatred. And the hatred flowed in different directions, with little consistency or sense, very often, of political preference or orientation. A common loathing of the Germans was accompanied by widespread feelings of anger towards the security forces of the Republic of Salò. But as Giovanni Collina Graziani, an elderly doctor in Faenza, underlined in the 'chronicle' that he kept (to make up for the absence of local newspapers) as a detailed record of what happened in the small town in the Romagna between the armistice and the summer of 1945, this anger was less a reflection of any generalised or deep-rooted opposition to 'fascism' as dismay at the failure of the government better to protect the population against German reprisals. The leitmotifs of his diary were inertia, hunger, poverty and terror ('more for the deportations than the aerial bombardments'), with hostility towards Mussolini and the fascist authorities significantly attenuated by a belief that they were as much victims of the Nazis as everybody else.[60]

In many rural areas the peasantry found themselves caught mercilessly between the hammer of the government and the anvil of the partisans – with the former meting out savage punishment to those who aided the 'rebels' and the latter, in their desperation for food, shelter or information, often exacting and insistent in their demands. Don Antonio Borghi, a priest in Castel del Rio, a village in the mountains to the south of Bologna, recorded the constant pressures on himself and his parishioners during 1944 – pressures made worse by the fact that from the later summer the community was directly on the front line. Don Antonio suggested that abhorrence of the Germans was not accompanied by very much sympathy for the partisans. In May he was forced to read out to his congregation, and post up in the church, an edict from the mayor stating that those who provided the 'bandits' with any form of assistance would be shot and that any community offering them shelter would be burned and razed to the ground. 'Everyone can imagine the dismay of the population at finding itself caught between two lines of fire: the partisans and the Germans. Threats from both sides and punishments inflicted by one or the other according to whoever happened to be imposing his will.'

Don Antonio's depiction of the partisans was deeply unsympathetic. He portrayed their frequent raids on the village for food in the following months – which inevitably put the lives of the local people at risk – as being scarcely less brutal than the actions of the German troops. How accurately his feelings mirrored those of the peasantry is not certain. They might have done; though traditional feelings of charity towards fellow 'Christians' in need probably helped to reduce any anger or resentment at being placed in serious jeopardy. The hostility of Don Antonio was undoubtedly due in part to the left-wing sympathies and anti-clericalism of many members of the resistance. In October he heard from a fellow priest of how partisans had taken shelter in the nearby church of Montefune, lit fires and covered the walls with smoke. They had opened the tabernacle and used it for storing tins of food. And to cap it all, they and their female companions had, 'without any consideration, profaned the house of the Lord'.[61]

To the north-west of Castel del Rio, at Casteggio in Lombardy, another priest, Don Luigi Serravalle, was equally troubled by the behaviour of the partisans. He had been left profoundly disorientated by the armistice ('O Lord, have mercy on us. Save our Fatherland . . . It's almost the case that we do not know who are our allies and who are our enemies'), and neither the advance of the allies nor the spread of the resistance movement inspired him with much confidence. In September 1944 a group of men came down from the hills and machine-gunned a German lorry, leaving dead in the crossfire a boy who had gone to pick up cartridge shells. Don Luigi recorded the incident in his diary as the sorry work of 'the rebels, or, as they like to be called, partisans or patriots'. On 26 April the following year partisans occupied the town and ordered him to ring the bells to announce the end of the war. He was dismayed at the behaviour of the victorious troops, fearing that they would unleash an orgy of vendetta rather than bring a 'Christian peace, the peace of the Lord, the true peace':

I so disliked hearing that Partisan who came to order the bells to be rung say to a woman who was weeping during the celebrations as she thought of her two sons who were prisoners in Germany – one of whom had not written since October: 'Cheer up, Signora. If something bad has happened to your sons, they will be avenged. I myself', he continued, 'have this morning avenged my brother by killing two Fascists in Casteggio.'[62]

In larger towns, where residual socialist traditions survived among sections of the working classes, attitudes towards the resistance were likely to be more positive than in rural communities. In the north-eastern city of Belluno, for instance, many of the young men living in the artisan quarter of Borgo Prà proudly gave assistance to the local partisan formations. The Borgo had been the target of raids by *squadristi* before the March on Rome. It was still regarded with suspicion over twenty years later by the fascist authorities, who nick-named it 'little Russia'. However, as the schoolboy Peppino Zangrando recounted in the diary that he kept in the last months of the war, not everybody in the neighbourhood was left-wing. There were a few fascists, 'who emerge only during the day and never on their own'. They included a particularly hated individual who went around in a camouflage uniform with a Beretta automatic rifle and hand grenades telling the women that the Germans would soon win because they had a deadly 'secret weapon' to deploy. 'When he turns up the women stop talking about the shortage of sugar, flour, or soap, and go back home so as not to be compromised.'[63]

But in other parts of the city there was general indifference to the partisans. Peppino lived in the newly constructed Cadore quarter, populated in large part by public sector workers, many of them immigrants from the south ('refugees from Africa'). The only 'real collaborationists' here were among people employed outside the province. Those who worked in the city, he said, neither supported the resistance nor opposed it and simply looked to get by as best they could, using the black market if need be and waiting for things to return to normal: 'In general people say they are fed up with politics and the war.' He noted that there was a lot of jealousy towards the wives of soldiers serving in the Republican army who got an allowance and additional free rations of food. There was much anger, too, towards the peasantry:

The boys despise the peasants because they say they are getting rich through the black market at the expense of us in the city. I have also heard that some of the peasants dislike the partisans because they take their cows without paying, giving in exchange a piece of paper promising to pay them after the war. Understandably some of them prefer to give their cows to the Germans, because they pay straight away . . . I have the impression that the peasants are tough nuts with everyone.[64]

Relations between the boys in the Borgo Prà and the Cadore quarter could be tense: 'They call us fascists and themselves partisans, and then stones get thrown'. Peppino himself had cousins in the resistance, and he got on well with the Borgo boys and played football with them. But in general the animosity created by the traded insults and the intermittent scuffles was lessened by the shared experience of grief and suffering. Death, as Peppino observed in February 1945, had become so commonplace that it was now woven almost incidentally into the mundane fabric of everyday life and casual conversation:

People attend funerals and go into mourning, it's true. But the next day they resume their grim lives as before, waiting to hear of other deaths or to escape their own. The boys say that someone has been 'eliminated', somebody else 'liquidated', and somebody else 'cleaned out'. Some use the term 'pruned', which is clearly of peasant origin because it refers to the trimming of the vines; others with more education talk of a person having 'given his phosphates to nature'.[65]

Peppino turned fourteen in February 1945, but he and his family were in little mood to celebrate. They learned that month that a number of their cousins had been captured by the Germans along with other partisans. For some time, with the war entering its final stages, the resistance movement in the hills and mountains around Belluno had been growing in strength. Attacks on fascist forces were intensifying; and these attacks were being met with brutal reprisals. On 10 March ten partisans were taken from prison and hanged from trees in a wood above the city in retaliation for the killing of three German soldiers a few days earlier. Peppino's cousins were not among them. A week later Peppino heard that four corpses were hanging from lamp posts in the city's main square. He hurried to the scene. On the way he was told that the Nazis had forced a young partisan – a girl scarcely older than himself – to act as executioner and place the nooses around the necks of the condemned. The spectacle in Piazza Campitello was gruesome. His cousins had again been spared; but two of the men he knew:

> I don't recognise the nearest ones, but in front of me, over to the right, towards the gardens, is Bepi, and a little further back, on the left, is Ciro. A cold wind blows through the piazza and ruffles the trousers of the four men, their faces bent on their shoulders and their tongues swollen. A few Germans are horsing around on bicycles under the gallows, and the girls that they are carrying on their crossbars, their faces thickly make up, laugh and tug on Bepi's trousers as they pass.[66]

Piazzale Loreto

Early in April 1945, after a lull in fighting during the winter months, the Americans and British launched a fresh offensive against the German lines across the Apennines. They quickly broke through into the Po valley. They reached Bologna on 21 April and the other major towns of the north in the next few days. In some places, notably Milan, local partisan formations succeeded in liberating the city ahead of the Allies. As the Germans retreated, the roads leading up to the borders with Switzerland and Austria became clogged with fleeing troops. Resistance fighters manned roadblocks everywhere, searching for prominent fascists. On the morning of 27 April a column of cars, trucks and armoured vehicles was halted by communist partisans of the 52nd Garibaldi Brigade just south of the small town of Dongo on the western shore of Lake Como. After several hours of parleying, they agreed to let the Germans proceed but insisted that any Italians should be handed over. In the corner of one lorry, hiding under a blanket and wearing a German helmet and greatcoat, they discovered Mussolini.

Mussolini was taken to the town hall of Dongo. Here he was joined by Claretta: she and her brother had been found travelling in the same column disguised as the Spanish consul and his wife. The Duce spent the night with his mistress under guard in a farmhouse in Bonzanigo, while in Milan resistance leaders debated what to do with him. Some favoured turning him over to the Allies; the majority wanted him to be dealt with immediately by a popular tribunal. The following day, according to the most plausible version of events, Walter Audisio, a prominent partisan and communist, arrived in Bonzanigo with an armed unit. He escorted Mussolini and Claretta to a waiting car (Claretta stumbling on the wet cobbles in her black high-heeled suede shoes). The couple were driven a short distance to the gates of the Villa Belmonte in the hamlet of Giulino di Mezzegra and made to get out. Whether Audisio read the death sentence ('By order of the general command of the Army of volunteers of liberty, I am charged with rendering justice to the Italian people') is unclear. Possibly not. Claretta threw her arms around Mussolini. Audisio told her to let go. He pulled the trigger of his sub-machine gun. It jammed, and he had to borrow another: a French weapon taken from one of the fascists arrested the previous day, with a small tricolour ribbon tied to the end of the barrel. He unleashed a short burst of fire and Mussolini died almost instantly. It was 4.10 in the afternoon. Claretta failed to get out of the way and was also killed, unintentionally, it seems.

Audisio then drove to Dongo to supervise the execution of another fifteen leading fascists who had been captured by the partisans. Among those shot in the late afternoon of 28 April in the central piazza over-looking Lake Como were Alessandro Pavolini, secretary of the recon-stituted fascist party from September 1943; and Nicola Bombacci, a founder member of the Italian Communist Party who had gravitated to fascism in the later 1930s and become a close supporter and friend of Mussolini in the Republic of Salò. Before the final order to fire was given, the condemned men raised their arms in fascist salutes and shouted 'Viva l'Italia!' Audisio apparently retorted angrily: 'What Italy?' To which the reply came back: 'Our Italy, not yours, you traitors'. Bombacci was said to have cried out: 'Viva Mussolini! Long live socialism!' Pavolini's final words were 'Viva l'Italia. Long live fascism.'[67] The bodies of the executed men were then bundled into the back of a lorry, which set off for Milan. It stopped on the way to collect the corpses of Mussolini and Claretta and arrived in Piazzale Loreto, on the north-eastern side of the city, in the early hours of 29 April.

A young journalist of Swiss origin, Antal Mazzotti, was among the thousands who thronged that morning into Piazzale Loreto to witness

the final macabre act of fascism. In the preceding months he had been
looking for signs that the catastrophe that had befallen Italy might
induce a sea change in the behaviour of ordinary people and lead to
a rejection of the conformism, emotionality and flight from responsibility that had characterised Mussolini's regime. At times he had
been hopeful. He had learned, for instance, in the spring of 1944
from the owner of his favourite second-hand bookshop in Milan that
the surge in demand for escapist literature – romantic novels and
thrillers – was being matched by a strong interest in history, politics,
philosophy, sociology and religion (the *Life of Jesus Christ* by Giuseppe
Ricciotti was doing particularly well). He was intrigued, he wrote in
his diary, by 'this thirst for culture and truth, this need to find bearings
and secure guidance in the midst of the vacuum, the mental chaos,
and confusion of ideas that the dictatorship has bequeathed to us'.[68]

But the scenes in Milan at the end of April left him with an uncomfortable sense of déjà vu. The streets in the centre were thronged with
people sporting tricolour and red cockades and giving clenched-fist
salutes. 'Of fascists, there is not a trace.' And when the partisans staged
a victory parade in front of the Duomo, he was struck by the sight
of three girls in red berets and shorts, with cigarettes in their mouths,
carrying sub-machine guns, who looked very similar to the women
auxiliaries of the Republic of Salò (though the latter had worn skirts).
Anti-fascism, at least in its communist variety, and fascism seemed to
him two sides of the same coin. Both were manifestations, he wrote,
of that 'malignant force' that generates 'fresh words of command and
fresh symbols' but without changing the essential components of the
political equation: 'Tyranny at the top, credulity and conformism at
the bottom: new masses, and new minorities thirsting for power and
able once again to delude.' New wine in old bottles – or vice versa:
'The transposition of one political mythology into another.'[69]

Antal was able to get close enough in Piazzale Loreto on the morning
of 29 April to see how the corpses had been arranged. Mussolini was
propped on top of Claretta. His head was on her chest, and he had a
banner of the fascist party stuck in his right hand. She seemed to be
asleep. His face was sallow, sunken and rigid, the mouth half open and
the jaw fixed in a grotesque grimace at once 'bestial' and 'truculent'.
All around, the heaving crowds were shouting insults and clamouring
to discover the identities of the other bodies. Some people were

spitting on the corpses; others kicking them. Antal experienced very mixed emotions: a 'vindictive anger close to satisfaction' at seeing so much public scorn for the man responsible for what had befallen Italy, and a sense of revulsion at the disrespect being shown to the dead. For a short time he was able to stomach the scene, reflecting that the 'abyss of evil' perhaps requires another evil, with 'everyone swept up in the same tragedy, victims and executioners by turns'. But after a while he had to leave, and went home to record his impressions in his diary.

A couple of hours later he was drawn back to Piazzale Loreto, conscious that this was an episode of profound human significance as well as a defining moment in the history of Italy:

While I was away the 18 corpses had been dragged a few metres further forward. Four of them, including Mussolini and Petacci, hung by their feet, head down, like butchered animals from a girder above an adjacent petrol station. I was told that this had been done so that those furthest away could see Mussolini and the woman. What had once been their shirts now dangled down, leaving the chests of the four white and exposed. The crowd was huge, monstrous and eager, seething and pressing in the immense piazza with a kind of constant, low, indistinct roar. Some people were standing upright on top of the girder as if to act as guards or simply to get sight of such a vast crowd. One had a machine gun, and every now and then he brandished it, laughing. After fifteen minutes I felt fed up once again with everything and was unable to stay and deal with the spectacle of the dead on the one hand and the ugly surge of the living on the other. I left, pushing my way out angrily with my elbows, desperate to get rid of the knot in my throat. I was railing – and God knows what I was saying – against everyone, including that foul beast of a crowd that in the past would have rushed to any piazza in Italy to scream deliriously for Mussolini.[70]

Epilogue

The Turin university student Zelmira Marazio could not bear to see the graphic photograph of Mussolini on the front page of the *Gazzetta del Popolo* on 30 April. Her elder sister brandished the picture in her face as she lay on a sofa: 'Look at how Mussolini has finished. Hung up by his feet in Milan . . . That's him, your God.'[1] Zelmira had been one of the 5,000 or so women auxiliaries who had volunteered for service in the Republic of Salò, and the end of fascism, and more particularly the death of the Duce, led to a period of deep psychological crisis in her life as she sought to come to terms with years of seemingly misplaced trust. She also found herself in immediate danger. The vicious cycle of reprisals that had characterised the later stages of the war in northern Italy did not come to a halt in April 1945, and it is estimated that at least 20,000 fascists were hunted down and killed over the next two years. Among them were dozens of women auxiliaries.[2] In response, clandestine formations such as the Mussolini Action Squads, the Fasci of Revolutionary Action and the Italian Anti-Bolshevik Front continued to carry out terrorist acts in the name of fascism well into the 1950s.

For Zelmira, as for millions of Italians who had invested varying degrees of personal commitment in Mussolini's regime, the path away from fascism and into the new democratic Republic that formally came into being with a referendum on 2 June 1946, was far from simple. In her case the process of adjustment was made all the more difficult by the fact that she had intertwined her political convictions closely with her religious faith. There was no simple way for her to discard the former without damaging the latter. For weeks after the end of the war she and the family with whom she had taken refuge went daily to church to recite alone together the rosary and the fascist

'Prayer of the Legionary'. They could not bring themselves to alter the final lines: 'And save Italy, Italy and the Duce, for ever, and in the hour of our beautiful death'. They did not want to accept that Mussolini had died: 'For us he remained beautiful, great, luminous, as we had loved him'. But they had nagging doubts. How could God have abandoned the 'poor hard-working' Italians and given victory to the mercenary Allies? How could God have let the Duce, 'the man of Providence', meet such a humiliating end?

For some time she and her friends in vain sought answers to these questions. In the end it was a priest who gave Zelmira the comfort she craved, telling her in the course of confession that it was not the best people who triumphed but the strongest, and that she was suffering in the same manner as Christ: 'He, before everyone else, was misunderstood, insulted and betrayed.'³ Consoled by this thought, Zelmira eventually achieved a measure of internal peace. She left her native Turin and went off to rebuild her life as a teacher in the very different environment of Sicily. She did not experience regret or guilt about her past: she had loved the *patria* just as much as the partisans, she believed. She remained a teacher for over thirty years and never spoke about her youth. Only towards the end of her life did she decide to write a memoir, in order, as she said, 'to show what fascism had meant' to her generation.⁴

Carlo Ciseri was a generation older than Zelmira. He had never been caught up quite as wholeheartedly in fascism, but he too found adjustment to life in post-war Italy hard. For him, Mussolini's regime had encapsulated everything that he cared for deeply: patriotism, the unity of the nation, the greatness of Rome, the legacy of the Risorgimento, the pursuit of empire, the nobility of Catholicism, the primacy of faith over materialism. He returned home early in 1946, after almost five years in prison camps in Africa, to find a country humiliated by defeat and, as after the First World War, prey to ideological divisions: though this time it was the Communists and Socialists who were pitted against the newly formed Christian Democrat party, backed by the Church, rather than against the liberals. He felt a huge sense of loss:

Oh, Italy . . . today I cannot see you as you once were, as painters depicted you and poets sang you. I search, I try to evoke it again in my mind, but in vain: I cannot summon up the Italy of Carducci and D'Annunzio with its myrtles, its laurels and its golden orange groves . . . [t]he Italy that I saw, I felt, I loved.[5]

There is nothing in his diary, which he kept until his death in 1984, to suggest that Carlo had second thoughts about fascism. The regime became, as for Zelmira, in effect a closed book: one about which he preferred to remain silent, but which probably contained in his memory more good pages than bad. After returning from the front in the First World War he had vowed angrily never to concern himself with politics again. Mussolini had succeeded in overcoming his disenchantment; and for more than twenty years he had filled his journal with press cuttings and tributes to a man whom he regarded to the very end as both great and good. After the Second World War Carlo once again turned his back on the public sphere. Politics disappear from his diary and there are no reflections or comments on either the past or the present. He seems to have become absorbed almost exclusively in his family and his hotel business – in which he was successful: from 1956 he was a manager of the Plaza Hotel Lucchesi, on the north bank of the Arno, which over the years welcomed a string of celebrities.

For millions of other Italians, too, the inclination quietly to forget was overwhelming. The Church strongly sanctioned this impulse, discouraging any systematic reckoning with the past. Ever since the fall of Mussolini it had been calling loudly for forgiveness, pointing out that the Christian principle of brotherly love counselled against anger and revenge. It had also been looking to deflect attention from its involvement with the regime by proclaiming the fundamental incompatibility of Christianity with totalitarianism. This meant saying, in effect, that anyone who was a Catholic *ipso facto* could not be (or, indeed, have been) a fascist and that the best remedy for what Italy had been through was to embrace God and abstain from any witch-hunts.[6] This may in part explain the growth in devotion in these years. The leading socialist, Paolo Treves, who had spent the war working for the BBC in London, noted with alarm on returning to Italy in 1945 how public opinion strongly favoured drawing a veil over fascism. In an article entitled 'The Conspiracy of Silence', he reported a widespread conviction not only that fascism had ended but that it had never really existed, as everyone had been playing 'a double game' and had not believed in it: 'In other words, book closed.'[7]

Other lines of thought contributed to the view that what had occurred between 1922 and 1945 did not warrant close scrutiny. The prominent journalist Indro Montanelli was one of a number of influential writers after 1945 who used traditional stereotypes of the national character to suggest that fascism had not been taken seriously by most of the population: Italians were by instinct too anarchic, too individualistic, too disobedient, too sceptical, too opportunistic and, at root, too humane ever to have embraced fascist ideology (in contrast to the Germans). Mussolini himself was subjected to a similar process of political neutralisation. He was portrayed in newspapers, magazines, memoirs and biographies in the post-war years as little more than an *homme moyen sensuel* – a not untypical family man, prone to histrionics and womanising: a mildly comic, even slightly pathetic figure, not a zealot like Hitler. In short, as a future leader of the Christian Democrat party, Aldo Moro, maintained in an article written towards the end of the war, fascism had failed entirely in its aims to influence Italians: 'It has not disturbed the traditional and fixed currents of ideas and ways of life; it has not extinguished the guiding ideal of the dignity of man and man's spiritual and political freedom'.[8]

It was scarcely suprising in these circumstances that there was little general appetite for a systematic purge. Those in the various anti-fascist parties and groups whose experience of the regime, the war and the resistance had led them to believe that a thorough cleansing of society was necessary to cure the country of its ills, felt deeply frustrated. In the spring of 1945 Bruna Talluri, an idealistic young woman from Siena who since 1943 had been in close touch with Giustizia e Libertà and other left-wing organisations, confided to her diary her conviction that Italians must at all costs take responsibility for what had occurred under fascism: 'In this moment of chameleons and heroes of the last five minutes, we should not forget anything'. The local National Liberation Committee asked her to look into the political background of a former prefect. She did so, and reported that he had been a convinced fascist and should not continue in office. She was then told that she was 'mistaken'. If the ex-prefect had indeed worn a black shirt, he had done so only because he had been required to do so by his office. He had always, in fact, 'been a great friend of the . . . partisans. Amen!' 'We are rushing too quickly towards national reconciliation under the banner of "let us love one another", and I foresee nothing good. You cannot change a situation like that created by fascism without altering the ruling class which has supported and tolerated this state of affairs.'[9]

The reluctance after 1945 to conduct any general purge was reinforced by the onset of the Cold War and the unwillingness of the Christian Democrats, the Catholic-backed centrist party which dominated government down to the early 1990s, to see the public sector cleared out and replenished with communists and socialists. The British and Americans for broadly similar reasons failed to insist on the country conducting a critical examination of its recent past. Rather more surprisingly, the far left was also inclined to favour forgiveness over punishment. This was partly because the official Marxist interpretation of fascism was that of a brutal capitalist dictatorship in which the mass of the population had been victims (and therefore not just blameless but probably uncontaminated too). But it was also a result of a deliberate decision by the communists to open their ranks to former fascists, intellectuals especially, and allow them to atone for their past errors by serving a new ideological cause. In order to avoid accusations of 'turncoat', converts often rebuilt their pasts. The 'dissidence' that had impelled many university students, for instance, to become critical of the regime and call for increased radicalism from the mid-1930s could be presented with hindsight as 'anti-fascism'.[10]

Without a significant purge, the post-war state showed remarkable continuity from the fascist period. A survey in 1960 found that 62 of the country's 64 prefects had been civil servants under Mussolini. The same was true of all the 135 police chiefs and their 139 deputies.[11] And many senior figures in the army and the judiciary had likewise established their careers during fascism: the man appointed in 1957 as president of the Constitutional Court, Gaetano Azzariti, had served between 1938 and 1943 as president of the Tribunal of Race – the court which adjudicated on issues relating to the fascist racial laws. Of course, not all these officials had shared the virulently illiberal views of fascism: some in fact claimed in self-defence that they had been covert anti-fascists who had taken on major positions of responsibility precisely so as to shield people against the more vicious aspects of the regime. But inevitably large parts of the bureaucracy of the Republic were staffed with men and women who had been brought up to believe that democratic principles were far from healthy.

Post-war Italy accordingly gave out conflicting messages about fascism. On the one hand the main political parties involved in the reconstruction of the country after 1945 publicly proclaimed their commitment to the so-called 'values of the Resistance'. These shaped the deliberations of the Assembly that met in 1946–47 to set out the ethical foundations and institutional framework of the Republic. According to the new constitution of 1948, the Republic was to be the antithesis of fascism: democratic, liberal and decentralised. It would have an elected president, an executive answerable to parliament, proportional representation, a strong Chamber of Deputies, a Constitutional Court, regional government, an independent judiciary, and mechanisms for allowing the general public to propose or repeal legislation. It would also guarantee a broad raft of civil and political rights. The resurrection of the fascist party was banned 'in any form whatsoever'; and a subsequent law stipulated heavy sanctions for groups or associations that denigrated the 'values of the Resistance', and for those individuals who publicly celebrated 'the exponents, principles, achievements or methods of fascism'.

On the other hand these clear rejections of the country's recent past were undercut in practice on numerous fronts. In December 1946 the Movimento Sociale Italiano (MSI), a party whose ideology derived directly from the Republic of Salò, was founded by unrepentant former fascists. Despite extolling the virtues of Mussolini and his regime, it was allowed to continue in being. In the following decades it regularly secured around 5 per cent of the vote and thirty deputies in parliament. Similar apparent inconsistencies with the constitution abounded elsewhere. These were encouraged by the much greater importance attached by successive Christian Democrat governments to curbing the communists than to suppressing or condemning the far right. Indeed, large swathes of the constitution itself were for many years regarded simply as aspirational or 'programmatic' and not implemented. Thus apart from in Sicily,

Sardinia and the Alpine fringes, there was no regional government until the 1970s: the prospect of the communists holding power in areas such as Emilia Romagna, Tuscany and Umbria, where support for the far left was concentrated, was unacceptable. At the same time a delay in the creation of the Constitutional Court until the later 1950s meant that many of the illiberal laws and legal codes that had been introduced by the fascists in the meantime remained on the statute book, despite being in clear breach of the democratic precepts of the Republic.

A particularly perverse aspect of the confusion surrounding the status of the 'values of the Resistance' in the new Republic related to the prosecution of war crimes. An amnesty for political and military prisoners issued in June 1946 in the burgeoning spirit of conciliation excluded those who had been responsible for 'especially heinous tortures'. But the judiciary often decided that the atrocities perpetrated by fascists against members of the resistance in 1943–45 had been neither 'tortures' nor 'especially' brutal. Thus the captain of a unit who had allowed a female partisan prisoner to be tied up, blindfolded and repeatedly raped by his soldiers was considered not to have committed 'torture' but 'only the maximum offence to the honour and modesty' of the woman.[12] By contrast former partisans frequently found themselves branded by the police and judges as common criminals rather than resistance fighters. They were accordingly excluded from the amnesty. In 1954 the Supreme Military Court went so far as to rule that the Republic of Salò had been a legitimate government, 'albeit through error'. Those who had fought for it had therefore not committed a crime, whereas partisans had been irregular troops and so could not claim the protection of military law.[13]

The consequences of the failure to prosecute war crimes in any consistent or thorough manner were far-reaching. Many of the most senior figures in the fascist state who had not been captured and executed in 1945 escaped serious punishment There was also no set of trials, comparable to those of Nuremberg, in which the regime's responsibility for the outbreak of the Second World War, the atrocities committed in Libya, Ethiopia, the Balkans and elsewhere, and such domestic policies as the racial laws and the persecution of the Jews could be publicly aired and condemned. As a consequence the Republic failed to define itself – and be defined by the outside world – clearly and openly in relation to fascism. The moral uncertainty surrounding official attitudes towards Mussolini's regime was evident when high-profile public examinations were made in other countries of some of its darker aspects. When two documentary programmes were screened by the BBC in 1989 about the invasion of Ethiopia and the failure of the Allies and the Italian authorities after 1945 to allow the extradition of 1,200 former fascists wanted for war crimes in Yugoslavia, Greece and Africa, the Italian ambassador in London issued an angry protest at what was considered an unwarranted attempt to diminish Italy's standing in Europe. The Italian state television company Rai purchased the documentaries, but they were not allowed to be broadcast.

The most consistent and committed upholders of the 'values of the Resistance' were the parties of the far left. For a short period the communists and the socialists were included in the country's ruling coalition, but in the spring of 1947 they were ejected by the Christian Democrat prime minister, Alcide De Gasperi, in a move that permanently broke the unity of the post-war anti-fascist front. In the following decades the communists remained a powerful presence in Italian politics, regularly polling between a quarter and a third of all votes in elections. But they were never able to enter government and overturn the monopoly of power held by the centrist coalitions whose underlying *raison d'être* was specifically to keep them out of office. The communists strove hard to define themselves, especially from the 1960s, as a distinctively Italian party, independent to a degree from Moscow and committed to a democratic road to socialism, to be reached with the establishment of intellectual and cultural 'hegemony' over society. But they never succeeded in dispelling either the deep suspicions of a majority of Italians or the ideological opposition of the Church.

One consequence of this political situation was that the cause of anti-fascism in the Republic was identified most strongly with a party whom millions never felt able to trust. The communists assiduously celebrated the partisan struggles of 1943–45 and did what they could to ensure that 'the values of the Resistance' remained the ethical foundation of the state. They used their large network of institutes, foundations and societies, their many newspapers and journals, and their commanding presence among the country's leading writers, film-makers and academics to generate within Italian society a powerful current of political opinion whose moral and emotional charge derived heavily from its commitment to the fight against fascism. This fight, which had begun heroically with the resistance, still needed to continue, it was felt, in the decades that followed against the forces of reaction that were believed to lurk beneath the thin democratic facade of the Republic. But the capacity of this stream of anti-fascist thought to become pervasive in the way that the communists hoped was limited by the very fact that it was identified so closely with a specific party – a party against whom the centre and the right could consistently over the years mobilise their followers to vote at all costs in elections.

The dominance of the left in Italian intellectual life down to the 1980s ensured that a majority of the studies of fascism were ideologically inflected. Broadly speaking, the success of Mussolini was viewed by historians in terms of the weakness of the Italian bourgeoisie from the time of unification as a national ruling class. Faced with the revolutionary challenge of the socialists and communists after the First World War, landowners, industrialists and other conservative groups turned, it was argued, to the blackshirts as a paramilitary force to smash the left, and then cooperated in establishing an authoritarian regime to hold the masses in check and ensure their continued social and economic supremacy. Largely absent from such an approach to fascism – somewhat paradoxically given its left-wing matrix – was any serious wish to investigate whether Mussolini's regime had been successful in engaging with ordinary men and women. Politically this was understandable. To suggest that fascism was in any sense 'popular' not only weakened the case for maintaining that it had been a dictatorship from which the country had been 'liberated' by the resistance, but also ran counter to a basic tenet of Marxist-inspired thinking, namely that power was essentially the product of material force.

The end of the Cold War removed the pillars on which the post-war political system had rested. With communism defeated, the need for the Christian Democrats as a bulwark against the left disappeared. Between 1991 and 1994, against a backdrop of mounting anger at the state of the country's public finances, the parties that had monopolised Italian public life for more than forty years were swept away amid a huge corruption scandal known as 'Tangentopoli' ('Bribes-ville'). And with the communists discredited by the fall of the Soviet Union, anti-fascism and the 'values of the Resistance' were open to attack from conservatives as little more than aspects of an unscrupulous and evil ideology. From the mid-1990s the resistance and all it stood for were subjected to fierce public assaults. At the same time powerful efforts were made to rehabilitate those who had supported the Republic of Salò (and by extension fascism in general) as high-minded patriots serving a regime whose negative image could be attributed to a degree to self-serving communist propaganda. Leading the 'revisionist' cause were the supporters of the man who dominated Italian politics for nearly two decades from 1994, Silvio Berlusconi. His allies included the heirs of the neo-fascist MSI, the National Alliance, a party that secured over 15 per cent of the vote in the 1996 elections.

For reasons that might in part have been linked to the left's underestimation of just how much emotional power words and images can have when culturally charged and largely uncontested, Berlusconi's extraordinary dominance of the media went unchecked. Much of his popularity derived from a capacity to exploit his control of television in particular to help foster a personality cult. He engaged in a direct and highly personal way with his supporters, and managed to project a powerful combination of ordinariness – an average man who loved nothing better than to tell jokes, watch football, sing and flirt – with exceptionalism: someone whose remarkable gifts had taken him from a relatively modest background in Milan to a position as one of the world's richest, most powerful and most talked-about men. He traded skilfully on hopes that the governmental instability that had been such a hallmark of Italian politics since the Second World War was finally at an end, and that under his firm leadership the growing crisis in the public finances would be averted and people would continue to enjoy very high levels of prosperity. His political language was studded with religious terms and symbolism.[14]

To what extent Berlusconi consciously drew on Mussolini for polit-ical inspiration is uncertain. Nor is it possible to gauge how far the prime minister's appeal to the Italian public was linked to the intersec-tion of his image with the complex tissue of memories and ideas bequeathed by fascism. But it is undoubtedly quite remarkable that the leader of a political movement whose exaltation of faith, enthusiasm and obedience, intolerance of dissent, and celebration of violence and war, resulted in the greatest moral and material catastrophe in the country's history, could still in the twenty-first century be regarded as a person to be invoked publicly as a source of inspiration and solace. At a press conference in December 2011, a month after he was forced to step down from government in an attempt to stem the disintegration of the country's public finances after ten years of poor growth and excessive borrowing, Berlusconi announced that he was reading Mussolini's final letters to Claretta:

> I have to say that I see myself in many aspects of those letters . . . [Mussolini] was right when he said that it was useless to govern Italy and also impossible . . . The man who rules Italy has no real power. At most he can ask for a favour, but cannot give orders. The Duce wondered: 'What sort of democracy is this?'

When it was suggested to him that fascism was not exactly a democracy, Berlusconi replied light heartedly: 'Well, it was a democracy in a minor way'. The ability to blur the contours of reality with linguistic imprecision and emotion would have been understood by Mussolini. In answer to a question about how many 'aspiring Clarettas' he had known, Berlusconi quipped: 'Hundreds'. Laughter and applause broke out from the substantial audience of assembled journalists.[15]

The degree to which fascism has managed in recent decades to shed many of the remaining vestiges of opprobrium surrounding it can be seen in the fate of Mussolini's body. After the spectacle of desecration in Piazzale Loreto, the Duce's remains were interred in an unmarked plot in the cemetery of Musocco in Milan. But their whereabouts were an open secret. On the night of 22–23 April 1946, two members of the self-styled Democratic Fascist Party, led by Domenico Leccisi, climbed over the perimeter wall and stole the corpse. It was recovered a few months later (minus a leg) from the Charterhouse of Pavia, where it had been consigned by Franciscan monks. It was subsequently reburied in secrecy in the Capuchin convent of Cerro Maggiore in northern Lombardy. Requests from the Duce's family to have the remains back for interment in the family vault of San Cassiano, near Predappio, went unheeded.

In May 1957 Adone Zoli was appointed prime minister. He was a leading figure in the Christian Democrat party, who in 1946 had strongly backed the proposal of the secretary of the Communist Party for an amnesty of all political crimes committed since 8 September 1943. But Zoli lacked a clear majority in parliament for his new government, and had to rely on the support of the far right. Among the deputies of the neo-fascist party, the MSI, was now the man who in 1946 had stolen the Duce's body, Domenico Leccisi. Zoli had been born in Cesena, but his family originally came from Predappio, and he knew Mussolini's widow, Rachele, well. One of his first acts as prime minister was to allow the remains of the fascist dictator to be released from hiding and returned to the place of his birth. On 30 August 1957 two Capuchin friars dragged a wooden soap box holding the Duce's body from the back seat of an American Packard car outside the gates of the San Cassiano cemetery and handed it over to Rachele. On the evening of 1 September, with a throng of faithful supporters looking on, their right arms raised in salute, the chest was laid in the crypt of the Mussolini family mausoleum.[16]

In the years that followed, the crypt became a site of pilgrimage for countless fascist sympathisers. Many signed their names and wrote tributes in the register placed in front of the tomb: a large stone sarcophagus, with above it a marble head of the Duce in a niche flanked by fascist symbols. The numbers leaving their signatures appear to have remained relatively constant over the decades: between several dozen and a few hundred a day, rising on certain occasions to a thousand or more, and sometimes, on key anniversaries, to several thousand.[17] Numerous others have come and gone anonymously. Since 1983 the lifting of the ban on the sale of fascist memorabilia has encouraged the influx of visitors to Predappio, whether casual tourists or convinced neo-fascists. Under the guise of assisting the 'historiographical knowledge' of the regime, three large souvenir shops now stand on the town's main street, the Viale Giacomo Matteotti, selling all manner of black shirts, banners, uniforms, photographs, paintings, pamphlets and books (most of them celebratory), statues, calendars, *manganelli* (clubs) – with inscriptions such as *'molti nemici, molto onore'* ('many enemies, much honour') – trinkets, DVDs and badges.

The three principal anniversaries of fascism – Mussolini's death and birthday (28 April and 29 July respectively) and the March on Rome (28 October) – have developed in recent years into occasions for major rallies by the far right. On the Sunday nearest to each date supporters of fascism, usually several thousand in strength, assemble in Predappio and march from the town centre to the cemetery of San Cassiano. They include women and men, young and old. Many wear black shirts and sport fascist insignia. There are speeches, songs, chants of *eia eia alalà*, and salutes. The procession is preceded by a huge wooden cross and led by a Lefebvrian priest, Padre Giulio Tam (suspended from administering sacraments by the Church) who recites the rosary. An important organisational hub for the commemorations is the Villa Carpena, a few miles outside Predappio. This was the farmhouse and summer retreat of Mussolini and his family, where Rachele lived until her death in 1979. It was subsequently used by her youngest son Romano Mussolini (a notable jazz musician and artist). It was acquired in 2001 by a businessman and fascist sympathiser, who turned it into a museum and study centre to promote understanding of the achievements of Mussolini and his regime.

Almost all of the many tens of thousands of visitors to San Cassiano who have left messages in the registers placed in front of Mussolini's tomb have done so in a spirit of admiration. The sentiments expressed, like those in the letters written by their forebears to the Segreteria particolare del Duce, often have a very intimate quality. Religious phrases are common. Among the principal grounds given for esteem are Mussolini's devotion to his country, his personal probity, his success in restoring Italy to greatness in the world, his hostility to communism, his achievement in giving Italians unity and a clear sense of identity, his defence of the Church, and his commitment to order, discipline and obedience. In many cases he is invoked as somebody who would have been able to save the country from its present chaos and decline. Often there is deep regret at the way he was 'betrayed' by his own people. The following is a representative selection from some of the recent registers:[18]

Dear Benito, I am Andrea. I and my friend Carlo have managed to bring 53 people here at one go. I promise that from now on this will always be the case. (15 April 2005)

Homage to a man who has been such a part of the history of my family and the construction of my being as a man. (3 May 2005)

I am only waiting for the moment when a comrade [*camerata*] with sound ideas will arise from the ashes and seize the reins of Italy, which has fallen prey to political hacks and corrupt people, and make it triumph. You will remain forever in the history and hearts of those who have fought, and continue to fight, to keep Your memory living and eternal. (26 June 2005)

From Turin to Predappio with a lump in my throat. So many kilometres to pay homage to the greatest of us all. Proud to be fascist and sad not to have lived the two decades of the regime in person. Honour to the Duce of Italy. (22 August 2005)

So many positive and negative things have been said about this man. One thing for sure is that this family of his did not get rich through the party. This should be an example and warning to today's politicians. (9 September 2005)

As I promised you a few years ago, today I have brought you my son as well, who is now 20 months old. Naturally he, too, is a *balilla*. Every time I pay homage to you is a unique sensation for me. In today's world a charismatic figure and an outstanding fighter would enable us Italians to be respected and feared throughout the world. Please return. (15 January 2006)

There are ideas that are eternal. And your idea of a true people cannot and must not die. He alone is Italian who believes in a nation based on identity, culture and uniform Christian thought; on loyalty and true respect for others; and not on daily lies. You said that we can be great. It is true!!! (4 March 2006)

After these painful elections in which the reds have returned to power, we come to pay our respects to the man who covered Italy with glory. To the Duce, with honour! (13 April 2006)

Ciao. What should I write? I am just a fourteen-year-old girl from Brescia, who lives in a hamlet of 150 people, Cecina. I know only that you did great things for Italy. You are still living for us, in all our hearts. (23 April 2006)

The struggle of blood against gold, of work against capitalism, of spirit against matter. Yesterday, today, tomorrow, proud to be fascists and ITALIANS! (11 June 2006)

Great Duce, Italy needs you. We in the south have been too abandoned; only you had the desire and the will to have an Italy that is all equal. We are with you always, even from down here! (23 July 2007)

You alone believed in a strong and free Italy and you loved your people unto death. You are the Father of every ITALIAN worthy to be called by this name. In my heart for ever. (8 August 2007)

If you could see how low our poor Italy has sunk, return, reincarnated in one of us! Now and forever. (1 September 2007)

On 28 April 1945, Italy died . . . Without you there is no Italy. After more than 50 years, we ordinary people come still to find you, perhaps praying that on that day in 1945 you did not die. Italy mourns for you; the people 'invoke' your name, because you and only you were able to make Italy into a great state. You loved this country, as only few can love. You will be forever in our hearts. With affection. (7 September 2007)

In this sad and insignificant present, where the pursuit of success is not the offspring of certainties and convictions, YOUR figure is exalted more and more, and your absence hard to bear. But we will forge straight ahead. WE BELIEVE. We cannot OBEY YOU, but we will certainly fight. Goodbye for now, DUCE OF ITALY. (9 October 2007)

We have won! Those false merchants of utopias have disappeared from the soil of Italy. Now in Bergamo we will fight to send away the extra-communitarian charlatans. Honour to the Duce. Independent Padania [the name given by the Northern League to the north of Italy]. Black Padania. (2 May 2008)

Only under your wise guidance did Italy become a 'nation', a nation that was feared, respected, fruitful and envied. But people who forget their own history, their own greatness, have no future, as they have no memory of their past!! Honour to you, immortal. (22 May 2008)

It is always greatly moving to be here . . . In this silence of death you understand fully the meaning of the word PATRIA . . . One day we will perhaps be as you wanted us to be! Rest in peace. In the end, you have been proved right: lies cannot long be hidden in the march of history . . .! THE 'VELLA' FAMILY. (16 August 2009)

On 8 July 2009, my grandson, Mauro, was born, a new Son of Italy. I will speak to him about You and of the great Love that you had for this Fatherland of ours, so humiliated and despised. You will be his example of Will, of Love and of Strength and may the God of Italy bless him! (17 August 2009)

Although I am someone with opposite political ideas to yours, I offer my salute to a person who was 'allegedly' honest, convinced of his Italian identity and proud to be Italian, in contrast to the sentiments that dominate the brazen politicians of our own day. (12 September 2009)

Dear Duce, since you were the true heir of Julius Caesar, we had to refound the Roman empire. Now, with Italy devastated by the mafia and by the communists, what would you say? Let us hope that things change soon. (29 January 2010)

Dear Duce, we have returned here after a year, to find you. In this period of enormous confusion, we truly need your charisma and your force of personality to carry Italy forwards. You and the memory of fascism will never die. You are always in our hearts. Honour and faith to the Duce. (19 February 2010)

There's only one thing I criticise you for: the war, and all its tragedies. In everything else you were a great man, even in the cruel and barbarous expiation of your sins. (3 April 2010)

I have just arrived from Tuscany to see once again my Duce, the one true and great Italian who was the first to give the people a sense of nation. With all my honour I will carry with me the ideals that the fascist movement has given Italy . . . Because now is the night . . . But soon a new day will dawn! Men die, but not ideals. *Viva il Duce*. (5 June 2010)

You have always been the greatest statesman of Italy. You loved your people and made them prosper. You gave them work and ideals. We will never forget you . . . Soon your successor will come and remove all traces of corruption . . . Benito Mussolini, the Great! (1 January 2011)

The shame of Piazzale Loreto is only partly cancelled by the dignity of this chapel, which calls for respect for the one ruler of united Italy who gave the nation an image and a respectability that it had not had before and not had since. (19 July 2011)

Italy, that you loved so much, is losing its dignity in the eyes of the world. Your prophecies are coming true: 'History will prove me right!' Rest in peace. (30 September 2011)

If you were here, we would not be in this mess. People are hungry, and the young are desperate, have no work and cannot plan for the future . . . I know that from up there you can see everything . . . ENLIGHTEN US! I continue to fight. You were a GREAT MAN, NUMBER ONE. With so much esteem. (14 September 2011)

History is written by the victors. That is why there are only a few of us today who understand what you were able to bequeath to Italy in a few glorious years, perhaps the only years since the Roman empire in which the Italians felt truly proud. (2 March 2012)

Ciao Benito, I have returned . . . I am here to cry out against these thieves who are killing our Italy . . . If, and by what means, we can get out of this CHAOS, I don't know . . . I can only say that once again it was your idea that was best, and I so much hope that we can return if not exactly to how it was before at least to something approaching it . . . We need a great LEADER, honest and effective. TO US, DUCE! (30 April 2012)

Notes

Preface

1   T. Mazzatosta and C. Volpi, *L'italietta fascista (lettere al potere 1936-1943)*, Cappelli, Bologna 1980, pp. 19–20

2   The great majority of these are in Pieve Santo Stefano. I have read all those that can be consulted for the period from 1919–43. There are a huge number of diaries for the years 1943–5. Of these I have looked at a selection – using the catalogue to gauge their potential interest and significance.

3   A. Maddison, *Statistics on world population, GDP and per capita GDP, 1–2008 AD* (1990 International Geary-Kharnis dollars), in http://www.ggdc.net/MADDISON/oriindex.htm

4   Cf. I. Kershaw, 'Consensus, coercion and popular opinion in the Third Reich: some reflections', in P. Corner (ed.), *Popular Opinion in Totalitarian Regimes. Fascism, Nazism, Communism*, Oxford University Press, Oxford 2009, p. 38

5   For a good introduction to the genre of diaries, and the difficulties of using this form of 'life writing' as an historical source, see I. Paperno, 'What can be done with diaries?', in *Russian Review*, vol. 63, 4 (October 2004), pp. 561–73. For more literary and psychological perspectives, see the entry on diaries and journals in M. Jolly (ed.), *Encyclopedia of Life Writing [electronic source]: autobiographical and biographical forms*, Fitzroy Dearborn-Routledge, London 2001, http://www.credoreference.com/entry/routlifewrite/diaries_and_journals_general_survey. Also, W.J. Wiener and G.C. Rosenwald, 'A moment's monument: the psychology of keeping a diary', in R. Josselson and A. Lieblich (eds), *The Narrative Study of Lives*. Vol. 1, Sage, Newbury Park, 1993, pp. 30–58

6   For example: S. Duranti, *Lo spirito gregario. I gruppi universitari fascisti tra politica e propaganda (1930–1940)*, Donzelli, Rome 2008; L. La Rovere, *Storia dei Guf. Organizzazione, politica e miti della gioventù universitaria*

fascista (1919–1943), Bollati Boringhieri, Turin 2003; id., *L'eredità del fascismo. Gli intellettuali, i giovani e la transizione al postfascismo 1943–1948*, Bollati Boringhieri, Turin 2008

7   Cf. J. Hellbeck, *Revolution on my Mind. Writing a diary under Stalin*, Harvard University Press, Cambridge, Mass. 2006

8   Kershaw, 'Consensus, coercion and popular opinion in the Third Reich', pp. 42–4

9   P. Corner, 'Everyday fascism in the 1930s. Centre and periphery in the decline of Mussolini's dictatorship', in *Contemporary European History*, 15, 2 (2006), pp. 195–222

10   Cf. R. Eatwell, 'Reflections on fascism and religion', in *Totalitarian Movements and Political Religions*, 4 (2003), pp. 155–63; L. Klinkhammer, 'Il fascismo italiano tra religione di stato e liturgia politica' in V. Ferrone (ed.), *La chiesa cattolica e il totalitarismo. VIII giornata Luigi Firpo. Atti del convegno, Torino, 25–26 ottobre 2001*, Olschki, Florence 2004, pp. 185–203; M. Blinkhorn, 'Afterthoughts. Route maps and landscapes: historians, "fascist studies" and the study of fascism', in *Totalitarian Movements and Political Religions*, 5 (2004), pp. 507–26; R. Bosworth, *Mussolini's Italy. Life under the dictatorship 1915–1945*, Allen Lane, London 2005, pp. 3–8, 202–3, 296, 496; J. Pollard, '"Clerical fascism": context, overview and conclusion', in *Totalitarian Movements and Political Religions*, 8 (2007), pp. 433–46

11   For a good survey of the debates, see E. Gentile, 'Political religion: a concept and its critics – a critical survey', in *Totalitarian Movements and Political Religions*, 6 (2005), pp. 19–32

1: *The Fruits of Victory, 1919–20*

1   C. Duggan, *Francesco Crispi. From nation to nationalism*, Oxford University Press, Oxford 2002, pp. 495, 579, 619, 691

2   S. Sonnino, *Diario 1866–1912* (ed. B. Brown), vol. 1, Laterza, Bari 1972, p. 9 (17 May 1866)

3   G. Belardelli, L. Cafagna, E. Galli della Loggia and G. Sabbatucci, *Miti e storie dell'Italia unita*, Il Mulino, Bologna 1999, p. 109

4   Cf. G. Gaballo, *Ero, sono e sarò fascista. Un percorso attraverso il fondo archivistico di Angela Maria Guerra*, Le Mani, Recco 2001, p. 15

5   E. Lussu, *Marcia su Roma e dintorni. Fascismo visto da vicino*, Imprimerie S.F.I.E., Paris 1933, pp. 10–11

6   Archivio Diaristico Nazionale, Pieve Santo Stefano (ADN), DP/99, Carlo Ciseri, 'Diario 1915–84', October 1919

7 Ibid., 'marzo, 1920'

8 Ibid., 'agosto, 1920'

9 Cf. Duggan, *Francesco Crispi*, pp. 630, 678–9

10 Ruggiero Bonghi, 'L'ufficio del principe in uno stato libero', *Nuova antologia*, 16 January 1893, pp. 343–6, 351, 355

11 Sidney Sonnino ('Un deputato'), 'Torniamo allo Statuto', *Nuova antologia*, 1 January 1897, pp. 25–6

12 Duggan, *Francesco Crispi*, pp. 676–7

13 V. Zamagni, *Dalla periferia al centro. La seconda rinascita economica dell'Italia: 1861–1981*, Il Mulino, Bologna 1990, pp. 116, 121, 128–9

14 A. M. Banti, *Storia della borghesia italiana*, Donzelli, Rome 1996, p. 293

15 G. Amendola, *Carteggio. Vol. 1: 1897–1909*, ed. E. D'Auria, Laterza, Rome–Bari 1986, p. 87 (to Eva Kuhn, 6 June 1904)

16 'Gian Falco' (G. Papini), 'Campagna per il forzato risveglio' (*Leonardo*, 1906), in D. Frigessi (ed.), *La cultura italiana del '900 attraverso le riviste. Vol. 1: 'Leonardo', 'Hermes', 'Il Regno'*, Einaudi, Turin 1960, pp. 312, 314

17 G. Prezzolini, *La Voce 1908–1913. Cronaca, antologia e fortuna di una rivista*, Rusconi, Milan 1974, pp. 758 (11 August 1910), 761 (28 August 1910)

18 A. Asor Rosa, 'La cultura', in *Storia d'italia. Vol. 4: Dall'Unità ad oggi (2)*, Einaudi, Turin 1975, p. 1254 (underlined in the original)

19 G. Papini, 'Crispi', *Il Regno*, 29 May 1904

20 A. M. Banti, *Storia della borghesia italiana*, Donzelli, Rome 1996, p. 335

21 A. Frescura, *Diario di un imboscato*, Mursia, Milan 1999, p. 224

22 Asor Rosa, 'La cultura', p. 1407

23 G. D'Annunzio, 'La preghiera di Sernaglia', in G. D'Annunzio, *Versi d'amore e di gloria. Vol. 2: Laudi del cielo del mare della terra e degli eroi*, Mondadori, Verona 1952, pp. 1112–21

24 M. Macmillan, *Peacemakers. The Paris conference of 1919 and its attempt to end war*, John Murray, London 2002, p. 289

25 Duggan, *Francesco Crispi*, pp. 496–531, 551–68, 593–7

26 Macmillan, *Peacemakers*, pp. 120, 293

27 Ibid., p. 292

28 Ibid., p. 292

29 Ibid., pp. 308–9

30 Ibid., p. 306

31 Ibid., p. 311

32 M. Piazzesi, *Diario di uno squadrista toscano 1919–1922*, Bonacci, Rome 1980, pp. 53–4

33 Ciseri, 'Diario 1915–1984', 'agosto, 1920'

34 G. D'Annunzio, *Prose di ricerca, di lotta, di commando, di conquista, di tormento, d'indovinamento, di rinnovamento, di celebrazione, di rivendicazione,*

di liberazione, di favole, di giochi, di baleni, Vol. 1, Mondadori, Verona 1947, pp. 870–1, 878–80, 892–3

35 J. Woodhouse, *Gabriele D'Annunzio. Defiant archangel*, Oxford University Press, Oxford 1998, p. 318

36 Ibid., p. 327

37 Cf. M. Giampaoli, *1919*, Libreria del Littorio, Rome–Milan 1928, pp. 130–1

38 R. Farinacci, *Squadrismo. Dal mio diario della vigilia 1919–1922*, Edizioni Ardita, Rome 1933, p. 19

39 G. Giudice, *Benito Mussolini*, UTET, Turin 1969, pp. 281, 284

40 Mussolini, *Opera omnia*, vol. 13, pp. 154, 160

41 Ibid., p. 72

42 R. Bosworth, *Mussolini*, Arnold, London 2002, p. 133

43 Giudice, *Mussolini*, p. 295

44 Ibid., p. 293

45 M. Ledeen, *D'Annunzio a Fiume*, Laterza, Rome–Bari 1975, p. 88

46 E. Susmel, *La città di passione. Fiume negli anni 1914–1920*, Treves, Milan 1921, pp. 241–3

47 ADN, MG/03, Giovanni Bartoli, 'Episodi della mia vita militare', pp. 19–21

48 O. Sitwell, *Noble Essences or courteous revelations*, Macmillan, London 1950, pp. 118–19

49 Ibid., p. 123

50 P. Alatri, *Gabriele D'Annunzio*, UTET, Turin 1983, pp. 392–3

51 Bartoli, 'Episodi della mia vita militare', p. 21

2: From Rhetoric to Violence, 1920–22

1 V. Rabito, *Terra matta*, Einaudi, Turin 2007, pp. 46, 54, 62–3

2 E. Forcella and A. Monticone, *Plotone d'esecuzione. I processi della prima guerra mondiale*, Laterza, Rome–Bari 1968, pp. 434, 442

3 Cf. G. Procacci, *Soldati e prigionieri italiani nella grande guerra. Con una raccolta di lettere inedite*, Editori riuniti, Rome 1993, pp. 150–72

4 G. Rochat, 'La prigionia di guerra', in M. Isenghi (ed.), *I luoghi della memoria. Strutture ed eventi dell'italia unita*, Laterza, Rome–Bari 1997, p. 389

5 Forcella and Monticone, *Plotone d'esecuzione*, p. lviii

6 G. Fortunato, *Carteggio 1912/1922*, ed. E. Gentile, Laterza, Rome–Bari 1979, p. 248 (4 October 1915)

7 Ibid., pp. 268, 275–80, 282–3

8 Rabito, *Terra matta*, p. 137

9 Ibid.

10   Ibid., pp. 138–42, 144

11   G. Fortunato, *Dopo la guerra sovvertitrice*, Laterza, Bari 1921, pp. 47–8

12   Rabito, *Terra matta*, pp. 147–9

13   Ibid., pp. 143, 149

14   G. Lorenzoni, *Trasformazione e colonizzazione del latifondo siciliano*, Carlo Cya, Florence 1940, p. 42

15   Cf. S. Lupo, *Il fascismo. La politica in un regime totalitario*, Donzelli, Rome 2000, p. 62

16   G. Giolitti, *Memorie della mia vita*, vol. 2, Treves, Milan 1922, pp. 596–7

17   G. De Rosa, *Giolitti e il fascismo in alcune sue lettere inedite*, Edizioni di storia e letteratura, Rome 1957, p. 23

18   M. Piazzesi, *Diario di uno squadrista toscano 1919–1922*, Bonacci, Rome 1980, pp. 77, 80

19   I. Bonomi, *La politica italiana dopo Vittorio Veneto*, Einaudi, Turin 1953, p. 142

20   ADN, MP/94, Giulio Teoni, 'Gioie, dolori, entusiasmi, delusioni e consolazioni'

21   E. Gentile, *Storia del partito fascista 1919–1922. Movimento e milizia*, Laterza, Rome–Bari 1989, p. 153

22   Piazzesi, *Diario*, p. 165 (21 May 1921)

23   Ibid., p. 76 (15 June 1920)

24   J. Petersen, 'Elettorato e base sociale del fascismo italiano degli anni Venti', in *Studi storici*, 16 (3), July–September 1975, p. 659

25   R. Suzzi Valli, 'The myth of *squadrismo* in the fascist regime', in *Journal of Contemporary History*, 35 (2), 2000, pp. 135–6

26   Ibid., pp. 136–7

27   M. Franzinelli, *Squadristi. Protagonisti e tecniche della violenza fascista 1919–22*, Mondadori, Milan 2003, pp. 49–50

28   Lupo, *Il fascismo*, p. 68

29   Franzinelli, *Squadristi*, pp. 56–7

30   P. Dogliani, *Il fascismo degli italiani. Una storia sociale*, UTET, Turin 2008, p. 18

31   E. Lussu, *Marcia su Roma e dintorni. Fascismo visto da vicino*, Imprimerie S.F.I.E., Paris 1933, pp. 24–6

32   Franzinelli, *Squadristi*, pp. 46–7

33   Gentile, *Storia del partito fascista*, pp. 493–4

34   R. De Felice, *Mussolini il fascista (1). La conquista del potere 1921–1925*, Einaudi, Turin 1966, p. 35

35   Piazzesi, *Diario*, pp. 114–16, 164

36   Ibid., pp. 141, 166, 199–200

37   R. Farinacci, *Squadrismo. Dal mio diario della vigilia 1919–1922*, Edizioni Ardita, Rome 1933, pp. 90–1

38 Lupo, *Il fascismo*, p. 63

39 Mussolini, *Opera omnia*, vol. 16, pp. 445–6 (21 June 1921)

40 Gentile, *Storia del partito fascista*, p. 250

41 De Felice, *Mussolini il fascista (1)*, pp. 173–89

42 I. Balbo, *Diario 1922*, Mondadori, Milan 1932, p. 42

43 Piazzesi, *Diario*, p. 199

44 Ibid., p. 213

45 G. Bastianini, *Uomini cose fatti. Memorie di un ambasciatore*, Vitagliano, Milan 1959, p. 6

46 P. Orano, *Mussolini da vicino*, Pinciana, Rome 1928, pp. 57–8

47 G. Pini, *Filo diretto con Palazzo Venezia*, Cappelli, Bologna 1950, pp. 20, 23

48 M. Sarfatti, *Dux*, Mondadori, Milan 1926, p. 295

49 T. Nanni, *Benito Mussolini*, Libreria della Voce, Florence 1915, p. 18

50 Pini, *Filo diretto*, p. 20

51 U. Ojetti, *Cose viste 1921–1943*, Sansoni, Florence 1960, p. 17

52 G. Bottai, *Diario 1935–1944* (ed. G. B. Guerri), Rizzoli, Milan 2001, p. 71 (29 December 1935)

53 Fondazione Mondadori, Archivio Giuseppe Bottai, b. 48, f. 8, 4 October 1919

54 Ibid., 27 July 1920

55 Ibid., 25 March 1920

56 Ibid., b. 41, f. 10, 22 May 1924

57 G. Bottai, *Diario 1944–1948* (ed. G. B. Guerri), Rizzoli, Milan 1988, p. 316

58 Lupo, *Il fascismo*, p. 71

59 Ibid., p. 84; Lussu, *Marcia su Roma*, p. 183

60 De Felice, *Mussolini il fascista (1)*, pp. 6–7

61 Lupo, *Il fascismo*, pp. 94–8

62 Balbo, *Diario 1922*, pp. 18, 44

63 D. Grandi, *Il mio paese. Ricordi autobiografici* (ed. R. De Felice), Il Mulino, Bologna 1985, pp. 37, 115

64 Y. De Begnac, *Taccuini mussoliniani* (ed. F. Perfetti), Il Mulino, Bologna 1990, pp. 115, 198–9

65 G. Bottai, 'Disciplina', in *Critica fascista*, 15 July 1923

66 Piazzesi, *Diario*, p. 122 (6 March 1921)

67 De Begnac, *Taccuini*, p. 199

68 T. Cianetti, *Memorie dal carcere di Verona* (ed. R. De Felice), Rizzoli, Milan 1983, pp. 78–80

3: *Return to Order, 1922–24*

1   M. Franzinelli, *Squadristi. Protagonisti e tecniche della violenza fascista 1919–22*, Mondadori, Milan 2003, p. 113

2   G. De Rosa, *Giolitti e il fascismo in alcune sue lettere inedite*, Edizioni di storia e letteratura, Rome 1957, p.17 (to Camillo Prezzolini, 21 July 1922)

3   E. Gentile, *Storia del partito fascista 1919–1922. Movimento e milizia*, Laterza, Rome–Bari 1989, pp. 604–9

4   S. Lupo, *Il fascismo. La politica in un regime totalitario*, Donzelli, Rome 2000, pp. 100, 110

5   L. Russo, 'Conversazioni con Benedetto Croce', *Belfagor*, anno viii, 1 (31 January 1953), p. 7

6   J. Woodhouse, *Gabriele D'Annunzio. Defiant archangel*, Oxford University Press, Oxford 1998, pp. 361–4

7   G. Albanese, *La Marcia su Roma*, Laterza, Rome–Bari 2006, pp. 70–1

8   Mussolini, *Opera omnia*, vol. 18, p. 412 (20 September 1922)

9   Russo, 'Conversazioni con Benedetto Croce', p. 6

10 I. Balbo, *Diario 1922*, Mondadori, Milan 1932, pp. 195, 198–9, 212

11 Mussolini, *Opera omnia*, vol. 18, p. 454 (24 October 1922)

12 ADN, MP/97, Giulio Bianchi Bandinelli, 'Le confessioni di un nonagenario del Novecento', pp. 53, 56

13 ADN, MP/94, Giulio Teoni, 'Gioie, dolori, entusiasmi, delusioni e consolazioni'

14 Ibid.

15 A. Lyttelton, *The Seizure of Power. Fascism in Italy 1919–1929*, Weidenfeld and Nicolson, London 1973, pp. 86–7

16 Gentile, *Storia del partito fascista*, pp. 679–80

17 R. De Felice, *Mussolini il fascista (1). La conquista del potere 1921–1925*, Einaudi, Turin 1966, pp. 373–4

18 ADN, MG/91, L. N., 'Trittico di testimonianze lontane', pp. 80–2. At the request of the archive, I have not used the author's real name.

19 G. B. Guerri, *Bottai. Un fascista critico*, Feltrinelli, Milan 1976, pp. 46–7. Cf. L. Piccioni, *San Lorenzo. Un quartiere romano durante il fascismo*, Edizioni di storia e letteratura, Rome 1984, pp. 35–7

20 L. N., 'Trittico', pp. 82–4

21 Ibid., pp. 87–9

22 T. Cianetti, *Memorie dal carcere di Verona* (ed. R. De Felice), Rizzoli, Milan 1983, pp. 95–6

23 ADN, DP/96, A. P., 'Di sesso e giovinezza', letter to Gina, 29 October 1922. I have altered the author's name.

24   M. Piazzesi, *Diario di uno squadrista toscano 1919–1922*, Bonacci, Rome
      1980, pp. 256–7 (31 October 1922)

25   R. Farinacci, *Squadrismo. Dal mio diario della vigilia 1919–1922*, Edizioni
      Ardita, Rome 1933, p. 187

26   Mussolini, *Opera omnia*, vol. 19, pp. 17–23 (16 November 1922)

27   E. Lussu, *Marcia su Roma e dintorni. Fascismo visto da vicino*, Imprimerie
      S.F.I.E., Paris 1933, pp. 63–4

28   S. Lupo, *Il fascismo. La politica in un regime totalitario*, Donzelli, Rome
      2000, pp. 123–4

29   Lyttelton, *The Seizure of Power*, pp. 114–15

30   *Discorsi parlamentari di Antonio Salandra. Pubblicati per deliberazione della
      Camera dei Deputati*, vol. 3, Camera dei Deputati, Rome 1959, p. 1489
      (7 May 1921)

31   O. Dinale, *Quarant'anni di colloqui con lui*, Ciarrocca, Milan 1953, p. 94

32   Lupo, *Il fascismo*, p. 117

33   Lyttelton, *The Seizure of Power*, p. 104

34   De Felice, *Mussolini il fascista (1)*, pp. 431–6

35   Mussolini, *Opera omnia*, vol. 19, p. 49 (27 November 1922)

36   Ibid., p. 192 (30 March 1923)

37   Ibid., Vol. 20, p. 62 (28 October 1923)

38   Ibid., p. 72 (30 October 1923)

39   ADN, DP/91, S. B., 'Diario per sistemare la mia vita', 4 November 1922.
      I have altered the author's name.

40   Ibid., 19 January 1923

41   Ibid., 22 March 1923

42   Mussolini, *Opera omnia*, vol. 20, p. 62 (28 October 1923)

43   G. Salvemini, *Memorie e soliloqui. Diario 1922–1923* (ed. R. Pertici), Il
      Mulino, Bologna 2001, p. 327 (9 April 1923)

44   *Dove va il mondo? Inchiesta tra scrittori italiani con una conclusione di
      Arcangelo Ghisleri*, Libreria politica moderna, Rome 1923, pp. 67–8

45   R. Bosworth, *Mussolini's Italy. Life under the dictatorship 1915–1945*, Allen
      Lane, London 2005, pp. 121–2

46   C. Mori, *Con la mafia ai ferri corti*, Mondadori, Milan 1932, p. 128

47   *Il Giornale Fascista* (Trapani), 24 December 1922

48   ADN, MP/07, Bruno Palamenghi, 'Cinquant'anni della mia vita 1884–
      1934', pp. 574–5

49   M. Giampaoli, *1919*, Libreria del Littorio, Rome–Milan 1928, p. 134

50   E. Gentile, *Fascismo di pietra*, Laterza, Rome–Bari 2007, p. 199

51   De Felice, *Mussolini il fascista (1)*, p. 758

52   Mussolini, *Opera omnia*, vol. 19, p. 191 (30 March 1923), vol. 20, p. 289
      (29 May 1924), vol. 21, p. 221 (11 December 1924)

53 Ibid., vol. 20, pp. 63, 108 (28 October 1923, 16 November 1923)

54 D. Mack Smith, *Mussolini*, Granada, London 1983, pp. 69–71

55 Ibid., pp. 71–2

56 A. Berselli, *L'opinione pubblica inglese e l'avvento del fascismo (1919–1925)*, Franco Angeli, Milan 1971, pp. 106, 120–1

57 A. C. Jemolo, *Chiesa e stato in Italia. Dalla unificazione a Giovanni XXIII*, Einaudi, Turin 1965, p. 192

58 G. M. Trevelyan, *The historical causes of the present state of affairs in Italy. Sidney Ball memorial lecture, delivered before the University of Oxford 31 October 1923*, Oxford University Press, Oxford 1923, pp. 8, 12, 15–16

59 Ibid., pp. 17, 20

60 M. Gilbert, *Winston Churchill. Vol. V: 1922–1939*, Heinemann, London 1976, p. 226

61 Cf. P. Edwards, 'The Austen Chamberlain–Mussolini meetings', in *The Historical Journal*, vol. 14, no. 1 (1971), pp. 157–64

62 Berselli, *L'opinione pubblica inglese*, p. 129

63 J. Barros, *The Corfu Incident of 1923. Mussolini and the League of Nations*, Princeton University Press, Princeton 1965, pp. 20–79

64 Mussolini, *Opera omnia*, vol. 20, pp. 15–17 (9 September 1923); Mack Smith, *Mussolini*, p. 84

65 Mack Smith, *Mussolini*, p. 85

66 Mussolini, *Opera omnia*, vol. 20, p. 63 (28 October 1923)

67 Barros, *The Corfu Incident of 1923*, pp. 68–9

68 R. Bosworth, *Mussolini*, Arnold, London 2002, p. 188

69 Barros, *The Corfu Incident of 1923*, p. 93

70 ADN, DP/99, Carlo Ciseri, 'Diario 1915–84', August 1923, 28 October 1923

71 E. Gentile, *Il culto del littorio. La sacralizzazione della politica nell'Italia fascista*, Laterza, Rome–Bari 1993, pp. 276–7

72 A. De' Stefani, 'Vilfredo Pareto', in *Gerarchia*, 1923, p. 1189

73 A. Beltramelli, *L'uomo nuovo (Benito Mussolini)*, 2nd edition, Mondadori, Milan 1926, pp. 57, 145, 360

74 L. Santoro, *Roberto Farinacci e il partito nazionale fascista, 1923–1926*, Rubbettino, Soveria Mannelli 2008, p. 149

75 Ibid., p. 164; Lyttelton, *The Seizure of Power*, pp. 188–201

76 Cf. S. Lupo, *Il fascismo. La politica in un regime totalitario*, Donzelli, Rome 2000, pp. 156–66

77 L. Villari, *The Awakening of Italy. The fascista regeneration*, Methuen, London 1924, p. 185

78 Mussolini, *Opera omnia*, vol. 20, pp. 48, 64, 74 (24 October 1923, 28 October 1923, 30 October 1923)

79   Ibid., vol. 19, p. 259 (8 June 1923)

80   G. Amendola, 'Un anno dopo', *Il Mondo*, 2 November 1923, quoted in Lupo, *Il fascismo*, p. 19

81   Mussolini, *Opera omnia*, vol. 14, p. 193 (12 December 1919); Mack Smith, *Mussolini*, p. 52

82   D. Binchy, *Church and State in Fascist Italy*, Oxford University Press, Oxford 1970, pp. 78–9

83   M. Franzinelli, *Il clero del duce, il duce del clero. Il consenso ecclesiastico nelle lettere a Mussolini (1922–1945)*, Edizioni La Fiaccola, Ragusa 1998, pp. 21–4

84   *Ubi arcano dei consilio*, 23 December 1922. Text in http://www.vatican. va/holy_father/pius_xi/encyclicals/documents/hf_p-xi_enc_23121922_ ubi-arcano-dei-consilio_en.html

85   L. Bedeschi, *Don Minzoni. Il prete ucciso dai fascisti*, Bompiani, Milan 1973, pp. 28–9

86   Ibid., pp. 15, 100–1

4: The Man of Providence

1   A. Lyttelton, *The Seizure of Power. Fascism in Italy 1919–1929*, Weidenfeld and Nicolson, London 1973, pp. 141–5

2   Ibid., pp. 136–7

3   P. Nenni, *Sei anni di guerra civile*, Rizzoli, Milan 1945, pp. 174–8 (first published in French in 1930)

4   M. Canali, *Il delitto Matteotti. Affarismo e politica nel primo governo Mussolini*, Il Mulino, Bologna 1997, pp. 106–7, 161–73

5   S. Lupo, *Il fascismo. La politica in un regime totalitario*, Donzelli, Rome 2000, pp. 184–5

6   D. Mack Smith, *Mussolini*, Granada, London 1983, p. 91

7   R. Bosworth, *Mussolini*, Arnold, London 2002, p. 196

8   Ibid., p. 198

9   R. De Felice, *Mussolini il fascista (1). La conquista del potere 1921–1925*, Einaudi, Turin 1966, p. 645

10   Lyttelton, *The Seizure of Power*, p. 243

11   Mack Smith, *Mussolini*, p. 95; Mussolini, *Opera omnia*, vol. 21, p. 39 (2 August 1924)

12   T. Cianetti, *Memorie dal carcere di Verona* (ed. R. De Felice), Rizzoli, Milan 1983, pp. 113–14

13   Lyttelton, *The Seizure of Power*, pp. 257–8

14   Ibid., pp. 258, 263

15   Mussolini, *Opera omnia*, vol. 21, pp 236–40

16   De Felice, *Mussolini il fascista* (1), p. 723

17   N. D'Aroma, *Vent'anni insieme. Vittorio Emanuele e Mussolini*, Cappelli, Bologna 1957, p. 141

18   E. Lussu, *Marcia su Roma e dintorni. Fascismo visto da vicino*, Imprimerie S.F.I.E., Paris 1933, pp. 195–6

19   Cf. D. Grandi, *Il mio paese. Ricordi autobiografici*, Il Mulino, Bologna 1985, p. 263

20   Y. De Begnac, *Vita di Benito Mussolini. Vol. 1: Alla scuola della rivoluzione antica*, Mondadori, Milan 1936, pp. 319–20

21   G. Volpe, *Guerra, dopoguerra, fascismo*, La Nuova Italia, Venice 1928, pp. 270–1 (1 June 1921)

22   ADN, DP/00, Raffaella Valenti, 'Cronaca', 28 November 1925, 12 March 1926

23   Ibid., 22 May 1926

24   P. Dogliani, *Il fascismo degli italiani. Una storia sociale*, UTET, Turin 2008, pp. 144, 146

25   C. Gower Chapman, *Milocca. A Sicilian village*, Allen and Unwin, London 1973, pp. 11, 15, 19

26   Ibid., p. 20

27   Dogliani, *Il fascismo degli italiani*, pp. 225–6

28   Gower Chapman, *Milocca*, pp. 7–8

29   Ibid., p. 155

30   Ibid., pp. 217–18

31   Ibid., pp. 3–6

32   Ibid., p. 155

33   Ibid., pp. 52, 248–51

34   Ibid., p. 249

35   N. Valeri, *D'Annunzio davanti al fascismo: con documenti inediti*, Le Monnier, Florence 1963, p. 117

36   Bosworth, *Mussolini*, p. 202

37   C. Sforza, 'La libertà di stampa e gli insegnamenti della storia', in *Corriere della Sera*, 21 January 1925

38   Bosworth, *Mussolini*, p. 466

39   L. Santoro, *Roberto Farinacci e il partito nazionale fascista, 1921–1926*, Rubbettino, Soveria Mannelli 2008, p. 204

40   M. Sarfatti, *Dux*, Mondadori, Milan 1926, pp. 295, 298

41   Volpe, *Guerra, dopoguerra, fascismo*, p. 388 ('Ripensando al congresso fascista', in *Gerarchia*, August 1925)

42   A. Mussolini, 'L'uomo e la folla', *Il Popolo d'Italia*, 25 May 1926

43   'Santa Milizia', in *I Fasci Italiani all'Estero*, 2 May 1925, quoted in E. Gentile,

Il culto del littorio. La sacralizzazione della politica nell'Italia fascista, Laterza, Rome–Bari 1993, p. 109

44   M. Franzinelli, *Il clero del duce, il duce del clero. Il consenso ecclesiastico nelle lettere a Mussolini (1922–1945)*, Edizioni La Fiaccola, Ragusa 1998, pp. 31–2

45   *Corriere della Sera*, 19 November 1925

46   P. Mazzolari, *Diario 1916–1926* (ed. A. Bergamaschi), Edizioni Dehoniane, Bologna 1999, p. 536

47   Ibid., pp. 538–9

48   Ibid., pp. 539–40

49   Text at: http://www.vatican.va/holy_father/pius_xi/speeches/documents/hf_p-xi_spe_19251214_iam-annus_it.html Cf. A. C. Jemolo, *Chiesa e stato in Italia. Dalla unificazione a Giovanni XXIII*, Einaudi, Turin 1965, pp. 218–19

50   Franzinelli, *Il clero del duce*, p. 91

51   *Corriere della Sera*, 12 September 1926

52   D. Susmel (ed.), *Carteggio Arnaldo-Benito Mussolini*, La Fenice, Florence 1954, p. 40 (12 September 1926)

53   *Corriere della Sera*, 2 November 1926

54   A. Aquarone, *L'organizzazione dello stato totalitario*, Einaudi, Turin 1965, pp. 71–2

55   Lyttelton, *The Seizure of Power*, p. 298

56   Aquarone, *L'organizzazione dello stato totalitario*, pp. 386–92

57   Franzinelli, *Il clero del duce*, p. 54; D. A. Binchy, *Church and State in Fascist Italy*, Oxford University Press, Oxford 1970, pp. 140–1

58   ADN, DP/08, Andreina Del Panta, 'Piccolo giornale', 3 April 1927

59   P. Ardali, *San Francesco e Mussolini*, Paladino, Mantua 1926, p. 5

60   Del Panta, 'Piccolo giornale', 5 June 1927

61   Ibid., 25 October 1927

62   Ibid., 8 January 1928

5: *Purifying the Nation's Soul*

1   L. Federzoni, *Italia di ieri per la storia di domani*, Mondadori, Milan 1967, p. 13

2   G. De Frenzi (Luigi Federzoni), *Per l'italianità del 'Gardasee'*, Ricciardi editore, Naples 1909, pp. 5, 7, 54–5

3   P. Arcari, *La coscienza nazionale in Italia. Voci del tempo presente raccolte ed ordinate da Paolo Arcari*, Libreria editrice Milanese, Milan 1911, p. 82

4   A. Salandra, *Memorie politiche 1916–1925*, Garzanti, Milan 1951, p. 67

5   A. Vittoria, 'Luigi Federzoni', in *Dizionario biografico degli italiani*,
     vol. 45, Istituto della enciclopedia italiana, Rome 1995, p. 797

6   L. Federzoni, *1927. Diario di un ministro del fascismo* (ed. A. Macchi),
     Passigli, Florence 1993, p. 21 (1 January 1927)

7   *Il Giornale d'Italia*, 13 May 1925 ('Il paradosso dell'anti-libertà)

8   R. De Felice, *Mussolini il fascista (2): L'organizzazione dello stato fascista
     1925–1929*, Einaudi, Turin 1968, p. 177

9   Mussolini, *Opera omnia*, vol. 22, pp. 467–70 (5 January 1927)

10   Vittoria, 'Luigi Federzoni', p. 798

11   Federzoni, 1927, p. 28 (6 January 1927)

12   Ibid., pp. 25, 54, 90, 131

13   Reale Accademia d'Italia, statuto, art. 2. For the text and further
     information see http://www.lincei-celebrazioni.it/i1926i.html

14   Federzoni, 1927, pp. 91–2 (13 February 1927)

15   Ibid., pp. 34–5

16   O. Spengler, *The Decline of the West* (trans. from the German by
     C. Atkinson), Allen and Unwin, London 1932, vol. 2, pp. 415, 507

17   R. De Felice, *Mussolini il Duce (1). Gli anni del consenso 1929–1936*, Einaudi,
     Turin 1974, pp. 38–9

18   S. Lanaro, *Nazione e lavoro. Saggio sulla cultura borghese in Italia 1870–1925*,
     Marsilio, Venice 1979, pp. 44–58

19   A. Lyttelton, *The Seizure of Power. Fascism in Italy 1919–1929*, Weidenfeld
     and Nicolson, London 1973, p. 373

20   ADN, DV/88, Mario Carlotti, 'Giornale di bordo R. Nave "Conte di Cavour"'

21   *Cremona Nuova*, 22 December 1925, 30 December 1925, in L. Santoro,
     Roberto Farinacci e il partito nazionale fascista, 1923–1926, Rubbettino,
     Soveria Mannelli 2008, pp. 310, 318

22   M. Sarfatti, *Dux*, Mondadori, Milan 1926, p. 198

23   Mussolini, *Opera omnia*, vol. 22, p. 190

24   Cf. *Corriere della Sera*, 27 May 1927

25   Mussolini, *Opera omnia*, vol. 22, pp. 364–7

26   Ibid., p. 366

27   R. Meloni, 'L'episcopato umbro dallo stato liberale al fascismo', in
     A. Monticone (ed.), *Cattolici e fascisti in Umbria (1922–1945)*, Il Mulino,
     Bologna 1978, p. 157

28   C. Ipsen, *Dictating Demography. The problem of population in Fascist Italy*,
     Cambridge University Press, Cambridge 1996, p. 76–7

29   R. De Felice, *Mussolini il rivoluzionario. 1883–1920*, Einaudi, Turin 1965,
     p. 77 (1 October 1909)

30   Mussolini, *Opera omnia*, vol. 19, pp. 36, 50, 62, 93 (21 November 1922,
     27 November 1922, 11 December 1922, 6 January 1923)

31 Ibid., vol. 20, p. 284 (24 May 1924)

32 Ibid., vol. 21, p. 362 (22 June 1925)

33 Ibid., p. 426 (28 October 1925)

34 Ibid., p. 381 (17 August 1925)

35 Ibid., vol. 24, pp. 283–4 (27 October 1930)

36 Archivio dello stato, Pavia (ASP), Carte Mori (CM), b. 9, Giovanni Furolo to Mori, 23 August 1922

37 Ibid., CM, b. 1, Gaetano David to Mori, 9 March 1923

38 Ibid., Mori to Emanuele, 10 January 1923

39 C. Mori, *Tra le zagare oltre la foschia*, Carpigiani e Zipoli, Florence 1923, pp. 73, 122

40 Fondazione Gentile, Carteggio Giovanni Gentile, Gentile to Federzoni, 8 April 1925

41 C. Duggan, *Fascism and the Mafia*, Yale University Press, New Haven–London 1989, pp. 142, 158–63, 241–3

42 Ibid., pp. 161–2

43 Ibid., pp. 159–60

44 Ibid. pp. 174–5

45 Mussolini, *Opera omnia*, vol. 22, pp. 373–5

46 ASP, CM 21, typed report to 'Eccellenza' (1928)

47 Archivio Centrale dello Stato (ACS), Pubblica Sicurezza (PS), 1927, b. 157, copy of letter from Mariano Fazio forwarded to the Ministry of the Interior, 30 August 1927

48 Duggan, *Fascism and the Mafia*, pp. 183–4

49 Ibid., p. 184

50 Archivio dello Stato, Palermo, Questura di Palermo, letter from Commissario di PS, Bagheria, 21 May 1927

51 ASP, CM 21, typed report to 'Eccellenza' (1928)

52 ASP, CM 10, Mori to Suardo, 9 November 1927

53 'The war on the Mafia – a zealous prefect', *The Times*, 7 February 1928; *Il Giornale di Sicilia*, 11 February 1928; ASP, CM 9, Washburn Child, 1929

54 G. Caprì, 'Di Giorgio e Mori ai ferri corti', in *L'Osservatore politico letterario* (Milan), January 1977, pp. 43–8 (Di Giorgio to Mussolini, 19 March 1928)

55 Duggan, *Fascism and the Mafia*, pp. 249–50

56 ASP, CM 49, speech to I Congresso Regionale ANIF, 6 June 1926

57 *L'Ora* (Palermo), 13 October 1928

58 *Sicilia Nuova*, 6 April 1926, 3 July 1926, 11 December 1926; *Piff Paff*, 9 December 1927; *Il Giornale di Sicilia*, 15 May 1928, 26 November 1928; *L'Ora*, 23 July 1928, 8 October 1928

59 A. Cucco, *Il mio rogo* (unpublished MS), ch. 3, pp. 6–8. Cf. *Sicilia Nuova*, 6 April 1926

60 ASP, CM 17, undated speeches to 'agricoltori', 'fascisti' etc.

61 Ibid., CM 'Relazioni, pubblicazioni, studi e discorsi (8)', speech to fascists of Termini Imerese

62 Ibid., CM 16, undated speech to 'cittadini' (1927?)

63 Ibid.

64 *L'Ora*, 25 December 1928

65 'La rinascita siciliana, e la funzione sociale dell'autorità', *La Civiltà Cattolica*, 18 June 1927

66 ASP, CM 'Relazioni, pubblicazioni, studi e discorsi (8)', speech to the Lega Nazionale Antiblasfema, 21 October 1928

67 Ibid., speech to *podestà* and *segretari*, 28 February 1929; ASP, CM 17, speech to '*delegati podestarili ed ai presidenti delle sezioni combattenti delle borgate di Palermo*', 5 March 1929

68 *Il Giornale di Sicilia*, 22 March 1929

69 C. Gower Chapman, *Milocca. A Sicilian village*, Allen and Unwin, London 1973, p. 156

70 ASP, CM 'Relazioni, pubblicazioni, studi e discorsi (8)', rough notes on Di Giorgio, Cucco, Giunta, Rocco etc.

71 Atti parlamentari, Senato, Discussioni, 17 March 1930. Cf. Ibid., Camera dei Deputati, Discussioni, 6 March 1930 (Arpinati)

72 ASP, CM 12, Mori to Mondadori, 2 April 1933

73 De Felice, *Mussolini il Duce (1)*, p. 23 (27 July 1931)

74 Archivio Petacco, Avv. Comm. Giuseppe Sciarrino to Mori, 26 December 1931

75 Ibid., Filippo Agnello to Mori, 27 June 1932

76 Mussolini, *Opera omnia*, vol. 42, p. 53 , Mussolini to Albini, 23 June 1933

77 Atti parlamentari, Camera dei Deputati, Discussioni, 9 April 1932 (Romano)

78 ASP, CM 9, Giudice (name illegible) to Mori, 18 March 1930

79 S. Colarizi, *L'opinione degli italiani sotto il regime 1929–1943*, Laterza, Rome–Bari 2009, p. 159

80 A. Checco, 'Le campagne siciliane degli anni Venti', *Archivio storico per la Sicilia orientale*, fasc. 2–3, 1978, pp. 645–703

81 S. Laudani and P. Travagliante, 'Palermo e Catania: dinamica demografica e trasformazioni urbane (1880–1940)', *Storia urbana*, April–June 1984, p. 127

82 ACS, PNF, Situazione politica ed economica delle provincie, 12 (Palermo), report of 5 July 1938

83 P. Dogliani, *Il fascismo degli italiani. Una storia sociale*, UTET, Turin 2008, p. 151; V. Zamagni, *Dalla periferia al centro. La seconda rinascita economica dell'Italia: 1861–1981*, Il Mulino, Bologna 1990, pp. 393–4

84   The National Archives, FO 371 19549, James Dodds to Eric Drummond, 4 February 1935

85   Ibid., FO 371 18431, Eric Drummond to John Simon, 31 March 1934; ACS, PS, 1930–1, sez. II, b. 56, report from Albini, 21 April 1930; ACS, PNF, Situazione politica ed economica delle provincie, 12 (Palermo), report of 13 December 1939

86   Ipsen, *Dictating Demography*, pp. 84–5

87   Ibid., pp. 179–84

88   C. Petacci, *Mussolini segreto. Diari 1932–1938* (ed. M. Suttora), Rizzoli, Milan 2009, p. 424 (11 October 1938). Cf. Ibid., pp. 62, 110, 189, 254, 385–6

89   G. Ciano, *Diario 1937–1943* (ed. R. De Felice), Rizzoli, Milan 1980, p. 391 (29 January 1940)

90   Ibid., pp. 394, 444–5 (7 February 1940, 21 June 1940)

6: *Spaces for Dissent*

1   B. Croce, *Pagine sparse*, vol. 2, Laterza, Bari 1960, p. 495 (speech to a meeting of the Consiglio Nazionale del Partito Liberale, Rome, 28 June 1925)

2   B. Croce, *Taccuini di lavoro*, vol. 2 (1917–1926), Arte tipografica, Naples 1987, pp. 441–2 (6 October 1925)

3   Ibid., p. 453 (15 December 1925)

4   F. F. Rizi, *Benedetto Croce and Italian Fascism*, University of Toronto Press, Buffalo–London 2003, p. 104

5   B. Croce, *Epistolario. Scelta di lettere curata dall'autore 1914–1935*, vol. 1, Istituto italiano per gli studi storici, Naples 1967, pp. 126–7

6   Croce, *Taccuini*, vol. 2, p. 503 (1 November 1925)

7   Rizi, *Benedetto Croce*, pp. 114–16

8   Ibid., pp. 120–1

9   M. Canali, *Le spie del regime*, Il Mulino, Bologna 2004, pp. 60–1

10   Rizi, *Benedetto Croce*, pp. 125–7

11   R. De Felice, *Mussolini il fascista (2): L'organizzazione dello stato fascista 1925–1929*, Einaudi, Turin 1968, pp. 304–11

12   B. Croce, *Taccuini di lavoro*, vol. 3 (1927–1936), Arte tipografica, Naples 1987, pp. 51, 104 (6 December 1927, 15 November 1928)

13   B. Croce, *Nuove pagine sparse, vol. 1: vita – pensiero – letteratura*, 2nd edition, Laterza, Bari 1966, p. 324

14   Rizi, *Benedetto Croce*, pp. 148–9

15   Ibid., pp. 149–50, 174

16 G. Fortunato, *Carteggio 1927/1932* (ed. E. Gentile), Laterza, Rome–Bari 1981, p. 70 (17 October 1927)

17 Ibid., p. 90

18 Cf. G. Ansaldo, *L'antifascista riluttante. Memorie dal carcere e dal confino 1926–1927*, Il Mulino, Bologna 1992, p. 412

19 Cf. A. Grandi, *I giovani di Mussolini. Fascisti convinti, fascisti pentiti, antifascisti*, Baldini e Castoldi, Milan 2001.

20 P. Calamandrei, *Diario, vol. 1 (1939–41)* (ed. G. Agosti), pp. 10–11, 29 (9 April 1939, 4 May 1939)

21 C. Petacci, *Mussolini segreto. Diari 1932–1938* (ed. M. Suttora), Rizzoli, Milan 2009, p. 114 (12 December 1937)

22 R. Bosworth, *Mussolini*, Arnold, London 2002, p. 220

23 M. Franzinelli, *I tentacoli dell'Ovra. Agenti, collaboratori e vittime della polizia politica fascista*, Bollati Boringhieri, Turin 1999, p. 388

24 Canali, *Le spie del regime*, p. 303

25 Cf. G. De Luna, *Donne in oggetto. L'antifascismo nella società italiana 1922–1939*, Bollati Boringhieri, Turin 1995, pp. 17–28

26 Canali, *Le spie del regime*, pp. 80–1

27 ADN, DG/98, Perla Cacciaguerra, 'Vinceremo … Mah!!! Diario di guerra 4 ottobre 1943 – 4 maggio 1945', 5 June 1944

28 Canali, *Le spie del regime*, pp. 175–6

29 Ibid., p. 179

30 E. Rossi, *Una spia del regime*, Feltrinelli, Milan 1955, pp. 17–18

31 Canali, *Le spie del regime*, p. 155. Cf. G. Artero, *Costantino Lazzari. Vita di un socialista lombardo da Bertani a Lenin (1857–1927)*, http://www.stori axxisecolo.it/antifascismo/biografie%20antifascisti145.html

32 Canali, *Le spie del regime*, p. 153. Cf. Franzinelli, *I tentacoli dell'Ovra*, pp. 321–2

33 F. Cordova, *Il 'consenso' imperfetto. Quattro capitoli sul fascismo*, Rubbettino, Soveria Mannelli 2010, pp. 291–9

34 Ibid., pp. 300–2. Cf. P. Milza, *Mussolini*, Fayard, Paris 1999, pp. 73–4

35 Cordova, *Il 'consenso' imperfetto*, pp. 309–17

36 ADN, DP/94, G. E., 'Diario di una bambina degli anni 30', September 1928, 28 October 1929. At the request of the archive I have altered the author's name.

37 A. Cento Bull, *Capitalismo e fascismo di fronte alla crisi. Industria e società bergamasca 1923–1937*, Il Filo di Arianna, Bergamo 1983, pp. 145–6, 152–3, 160–2

38 ADN, DP/90, Angela Martina, 'Il mio diario 1933–47'

39 Ibid.

40 Ibid.

41 L. Passerini, *Torino operaia e fascismo. Una storia orale*, Laterza, Bari 1984, pp. 169–70

42 Ibid., p. 170

43 De Luna, *Donne in oggetto*, p. 17

44 ADN, MP/97, Giulio Bianchi Bandinelli, 'Le confessioni di un nonagenario del Novecento', pp. 56–123. Cf. R. Bianchi Bandinelli, *Dal diario di un borghese e altri scritti*, Mondadori, Milan 1948, p. 51

45 Bianchi Bandinelli, 'Le confessioni di un nonagenario del Novecento', pp. 123–4

46 Ibid., p. 117

47 Ibid.

48 A. M. Caredio Benayà, *Il ponte delle catene*, Artemide edizioni, Rome 2004, pp. 121–2

49 ADN, DP/85, Ettore Castiglioni, 'Diario di un alpinista', 10 June 1940

50 Ibid., 6 July 1940

51 M. Ferrari, *Storia di Ettore Castiglioni*, TEA, Milan 2010, p. 8

52 ADN, 'Diario di un ragazzo', undated, but spring 1942. The family wishes the authorship to remain anonymous. I have used Pietro Ambrosini as a pseudonym.

53 Ibid., 13 March 1937

54 Ibid., 12 December 1937

55 Ibid., 19 March 1939

56 Ibid., 13 March 1938, 12 December 1938

57 I. Silone, *Fontamara*, Mondadori, Milan 1949, pp. 163–6

58 Ibid., pp. 129–30

59 D. Biocca and M. Canali, *L'informatore. Silone, i comunisti e la polizia*, Luni, Milan 2000, p. 137 (letter to Emilia Bellone, 13 April 1930)

60 ADN, MP/95, Guido Morselli, 'I tre marescialli d'Italia', pp. 14, 19–20

61 Ibid., pp. 21–2, 32

62 Cordova, *Il 'consenso' imperfetto*, pp. 83–4, 173–4

63 S. Colarizi, *L'opinione degli italiani sotto il regime 1929–1943*, Laterza, Rome–Bari 2009, pp. 65–70, 139–52

64 Passerini, *Torino operaia*, p. 100

65 Ibid., pp. 98–9

66 S. Rossi, 'Io, cantastorie', in *Diario italiano. Memorie, diari, epistolari dell'Archivio di Pieve Santo Stefano. 13: 1945, l'anno della rivolta* (ed. S. Tutino), Giunti, Florence 1991, pp. 34–5

67 Passerini, *Torino operaia*, pp. 81–2

68 O. Gaspari, *L'emigrazione veneta nell'agro pontino durante il periodo fascista*, Morcelliana, Brescia 1985, pp. 63–5

69   R. Bosworth, *Mussolini's Italy. Life under the dictatorship 1915–1945*, Allen Lane, London 2005, pp. 334–6

70   Ibid.

71   C. Levi, *Cristo si è fermato a Eboli*, Mondadori, Milan 1977, p. 108

7: *Imparting Faith*

1   ADN, DP/92, Albina Chiodo, 'Anni di scuola'

2   G. Bini, 'Romanzi e realtà di maestri e maestre', in *Storia d'Italia. Annali 4: intellettuali e potere* (ed. C. Vivanti), Einaudi, Turin 1981, pp. 1204–5

3   S. Pivato, *Pane e grammatico. L'istruzione elementare in Romagna alla fine dell'800*, Franco Angeli, Milan 1983, p. 53

4   C. Gower Chapman, *Milocca. A Sicilian village*, Allen and Unwin, London 1973, p. 148

5   M. Barbagli, *Disoccupazione intellettuale e sistema scolastico in Italia (1859–1973)*, Il Mulino, Bologna 1974, pp. 196–7

6   L. Minio-Paluello, *Education in Fascist Italy*, Oxford University Press, Oxford 1946, p. 66

7   E. Codignola, *Il problema dell'educazione nazionale in Italia*, Vallecchi, Florence 1925, pp. 331–6

8   Mussolini, *Opera omnia*, vol. 20, p. 130 (13 December 1923)

9   T. Koon, *Believe, Obey, Fight. Political socialization in Fascist Italy, 1922–1943*, University of North Carolina Press, Chapel Hill 1985, p. 55

10   Mussolini, *Opera omnia*, vol. 22, p. 23 (5 December 1925)

11   Cf. M. Dei, *Colletto bianco, grembiule nero. Gli insegnanti elementari italiani tra l'inizio del secolo e il secondo dopoguerra*, Il Mulino, Bologna 1994, pp. 259, 271–6

12   Chiodo, 'Anni di scuola', 24 April 1927, 26 January 1928

13   Ibid., 12 April 1926, 23 November 1926, 29 February 1928

14   Ibid., 7 April 1926, 29 February 1928, 25 May 1928

15   Codignola, *Il problema dell'educazione nazionale in Italia*, pp. 225–6

16   N. Padellaro, *La scuola vivente*, Paravia, Turin 1930, pp. 10–12

17   P. Zunino, *L'ideologia del fascismo. Miti, credenze e valori nella stabilizzazione del regime*, Il Mulino, Bologna 1985, p. 231

18   R. Cantalupo, 'La classe dirigente e il suo Duce', *Gerarchia*, 1926, p. 9

19   M. Galfré, *Il regime degli editori. Libri, scuola e fascismo*, Laterza, Rome–Bari 2005, p. 85

20   Ibid., p. 83

21   S. Grana, *Mussolini spiegato ai bimbi. Facili conversazioni sull'opera del Duce*

di prima e dopo la Marcia su Roma rivolte ai piccoli e utili ai grandi, Sergio, Florence 1927, pp. 22, 94, 187

22   Dei, *Colletto bianco, grembiule nero*, pp. 259, 271–2

23   Ibid., p. 276

24   P. Gios, 'Il diario di Maria Teresa Rossetti: una giovane intellettuale tra fascismo e antifascismo', in A. Ventura (ed.), *Sulla crisi del regime fascista 1938–1943. La società italiana dal 'consenso' alla Resistenza*, Marsilio, Venice 1996, October 1926, 15 November 1926, December 1926, 23 March 1927

25   Z. Marazio, *Il mio fascismo. Storia di una donna*, Verdechiaro, Baiso 2005, p. 26

26   Ibid., pp. 28–33

27   Ibid., pp. 41–2

28   Ibid., pp. 42–3

29   Ibid., p. 57

30   ADN, DP/Adn2, Alberto Allocato, 'L'inverno', 28 October 1928, 9 December 1926

31   Galfré, *Il regime degli editori*, p. 22

32   Allocato, 'L'inverno' ('Un semplice italiano')

33   G. Aliberti, *La resa di Cavour. Il carattere nazionale italiano tra mito e cronaca, 1820–1976*, Le Monnier, Florence 2000, p. 149

34   E. Gentile, *Contro Cesare. Cristianesimo e totalitarismo nell'epoca dei fascismi*, Feltrinelli, Milan 2010, p. 175

35   Koon, *Believe, Obey, Fight*, pp. 93–7

36   Mussolini, *Opera omnia*, vol. 26, p. 259 (26 May 1934)

37   Koon, *Believe, Obey, Fight*, p. 97

38   R. Bosworth, *Mussolini's Italy. Life under the dictatorship 1915–1945*, Allen Lane, London 2005, p. 290

39   R. De Felice, *Mussolini il fascista (2): L'organizzazione dello stato fascista 1925–1929*, Einaudi, Turin 1968, pp. 399–402, 412–13

40   Gentile, *Contro Cesare*, p. 182 (25 March 1928, 28 March 1928)

41   Ibid., p. 183 (*Il Popolo d'Italia*, 29 March 1928)

42   De Felice, *Mussolini il fascista (2)*, p. 413

43   Archivio Segreto del Vaticano (ASV), AES, Italia, IV periodo, fasc. 401, Arturo Agosti, 26 August 1929

44   Ibid., fasc. 443, report on the funeral of Filippo Raimondo

45   Ibid., fasc. 401, copy of circular, 1929/30

46   Ibid., fasc. 401, report from Presidente, Giunta diocesana, Senigallia, 3 February 1930

47   Ibid., fasc. 101, promemoria, 17 December 1931

48   ASV, Archivio Nunziatura, Italia, fasc. 28, b. 114, letter of Bishop of Acireale, 23 April 1931

49 ASV, AES, Italia, IV periodo, fasc. III, letter of Giovanni Pizzocolo, 30 January 1930

50 Ibid., fasc. 113, reports on ONB camps, Rome, 1932

51 Ibid., fasc. 112, report on Umbria, 1931

52 Ibid., report, 1931

53 ADN, DP/99, Carlo Ciseri, 'Diario 1915–1984', 28 October 1923, 1928, 1929

54 M. Berezin, *Making the Fascist Self. The political culture of interwar Italy*, Cornell University Press, Ithaca and London 1997, pp. 202–3

55 A. Staderini, 'La "Marcia dei martiri": la traslazione nella cripta di Santa Croce dei caduti fascisti', in *Annali di storia di Firenze*, III (2008), http://www.dssg.unifi.it/SDF/annali2008.htm, p. 204

56 Berezin, *Making the Fascist Self*, p. 120 (*La Nazione*, 26 October 1934)

57 Staderini, 'La "Marcia dei martiri"', pp. 204–7

58 Ciseri, 'Diario 1915–1984', 27 October 1934

59 *Autobiografie di giovani del tempo fascista*, Quaderni di Humanitas, Morcelliana, Brescia 1947, pp. 15–16

60 Ibid., pp. 18–22

61 Ibid., pp. 19–25

62 A. Grandi, *I giovani di Mussolini. Fascisti convinti, fascisti pentiti, antifascisti*, Baldini e Castoldi, Milan 2001, p. 117. Cf. ibid., pp. 72, 80, 85; F. Gambetti, *Gli anni che scottano*, Mursia, Milan 1967, p. 135; Zunino, *L'ideologia del fascismo*, pp. 374–5

63 Gios, 'Il diario di Maria Teresa Rossetti: una giovane intellettuale tra fascismo e antifascismo', pp. 425–6 (1 February 1932)

64 Ibid., p. 426

65 Ibid., p. 426

66 Ibid., p. 427

67 Ibid., pp. 427–8

68 Ibid., p. 431 (5 May 1936)

69 Ibid., pp. 439–41 (10 September 1938)

70 Ibid., p. 434

71 Ibid., pp. 434–5

72 Ibid., pp. 446–9

73 ADN, MG/02, D. P., 'Memorie di vita militare (ed altro) 1940–1943', pp. 237, 263–6. I have altered the author's name.

74 Ibid., pp. 272–5

75 Ibid., pp. 275–8

76 Ibid., pp. 278–9

77 ADN, DP/99, Primo Boccaleri, 'Diario della mia vita e della mia missione in Dalmazia, 1941–1942'

78   Ibid., 3 December 1941, 7 December 1941

79   Ibid., 9 December 1941, 10 December 1941

80   Ibid., 11 December 1941

81   Ibid., 23 March 1942

82   Ibid., 21 April 1942, 9 May 1942

83   Ibid., 14 June 1942

84   Ibid.

85   Ibid., 17 June 1942

86   Estratto dal verbale delle deliberazioni della giunta comunale. Deliberazione n. 240, 30 September 2009, www.comune.novara. it/comune/delibere/giunta/002-GIUNTA-2009/043-GC30.09.2009/240-30.09.2009.pdf

8: *The Politics of Intimacy*

1   T. Mazzatosta and C. Volpi, *L'italietta fascista (lettere al potere 1936–1943)*, Cappelli, Bologna 1980, pp. 66, 72

2   Ibid., pp. 15–21

3   C. Petacci, *Verso il disastro. Mussolini in guerra. Diari 1939–40* (ed. M. Franzinelli), Rizzoli, Milan 2011, p. 46

4   C. Petacci, *Mussolini segreto. Diari 1932–1938* (ed. M. Suttora), Rizzoli, Milan 2009, p. 127

5   Petacci, *Verso il disastro*, p. 39

6   C. Delcroix, *Un uomo e un popolo*, Vallecchi, Florence 1928, p. 83

7   Petacci, *Mussolini segreto*, p. 236

8   Ibid., p. 319

9   Petacci, *Verso il disastro*, p. 44

10   Petacci, *Mussolini segreto*, pp. 60–1

11   Mazzatosta and Volpi, *L'italietta fascista*, p. 66. For another housewife who wrote obsessively to Mussolini and whose sanity was doubted by the staff in the Segretaria Particolare, see Archivio Centrale dello Stato (ACS), Segreteria Particolare del Duce (SPD), Carteggio Ordinario (CO), Sentimenti, b. 3095, Domenica Vecchio to Ciano, 5 July 1941

12   D. Baratieri, 'Sanity from a lunatic asylum: Ida Dalser's threat to Mussolini's image', forthcoming in S. Gundle, C. Duggan and G. Pieri (eds), *The Cult of the Duce. Mussolini and the Italians*, Manchester University Press, Manchester 2013 (unpublished MS)

13   Ibid.

14   Ibid.

15   Petacci, *Mussolini segreto*, p. 475

16 C. Alvaro, *Terra nuova. Prima cronaca dell'agro pontino*, Istituto fascista di cultura, Edizioni di novissima, Rome 1934, p. 54

17 G. Pini, *Filo diretto con Palazzo Venezia*, Cappelli, Bologna 1950, p. 103

18 P. Orano, *Mussolini da vicino*, Pinciana, Rome 1928, pp. 149–51

19 A. Grandi, *I giovani di Mussolini. Fascisti convinti, fascisti pentiti, antifascisti*, Baldini e Castoldi, Milan 2001, p. 315

20 Orano, *Mussolini da vicino*, pp. 107–8

21 O. Gaspari, *L'emigrazione veneta nell'agro pontino durante il periodo fascista*, Morcelliana, Brescia 1985, pp. 152–3

22 Ibid., p. 153

23 Ibid., pp. 154–5

24 Z. Marazio, *Il mio fascismo. Storia di una donna*, Verdechiaro, Baiso 2005, p. 39

25 ACS, SPD, CO, Sentimenti, b. 3095, Matilde and Luigi Vitale, 28 October 1941

26 Cf. Ibid., bb. 2831, 3088, 3090, 3095

27 S. Serenelli, 'A town for the cult of the Duce: Predappio as a site of pilgrimage', forthcoming in Gundle, Duggan and Pieri (eds), *The Cult of the Duce*

28 Ibid.

29 Ibid.

30 Ibid.

31 P. Willson, *Peasant Women and Politics in Fascist Italy. The 'massaie rurali'*, Routledge, London 2002, pp. 155–6

32 ACS, SPD, CO, Sentimenti, b. 2768

33 Ibid., bb. 2815, 2816

34 ADN, DP/90, Athe Gracci, 'Diario della mia vita (1938–47)', 18 April 1939

35 Ibid., 30 August 1939

36 B. Mussolini, *Pensieri pontini e sardi* (August 1943), in Mussolini, *Opera omnia*, vol. 34, p. 279

37 A. Mussolini, 'L'uomo e la folla' in *Il Popolo d'Italia*, 25 May 1926

38 G. Gamberini, 'Premesse autoritarie', in *Il Popolo d'Italia*, 23 July 1927

39 G. Pini, 'Divagazioni', *Critica fascista*, 1 December 1927, quoted in E. Gentile, *Il culto del littorio. La sacralizzazione della politica nell'Italia fascista*, Laterza, Rome–Bari 1993, p. 275

40 *Corriere della Sera*, 3 November 1936

41 Grandi, *I giovani di Mussolini*, p. 72

42 G. Bottai, *Diario 1935–1944* (ed. G. B. Guerri), Rizzoli, Milan 2001, p. 379 (19 May 1943)

43   R. Bosworth, 'Per necessità famigliare: hypocrisy and corruption in fascist Italy', *European History Quarterly*, vol. 30, no. 3 (2000), pp. 362–3, 368

44   A. Imbriani, *Gli italiani e il Duce. Il mito e l'immagine di Mussolini negli ultimi anni del fascismo (1938–1943)*, Liguori, Naples 1992, p. 114 (19 August 1932)

45   M. Di Figlia, *Farinacci. Il radicalismo fascista al potere*, Donzelli, Rome 2007, pp. 161–4, 184–97

46   R. Bosworth, 'Imitating Mussolini with advantages: the case of Edgardo Sulis', *European History Quarterly*, vol. 32, no. 4 (2002), pp. 523–4

47   Ibid., pp. 524–5

48   E. Sulis, *Imitazione di Mussolini*, Novecentesca, Milan 1934, pp. 10, 17–18, 27, 91, 111

49   Bosworth, 'Imitating Mussolini with advantages', pp. 525–7

50   Bottai, *Diario 1935–1944*, p. 246 (17 January 1941)

51   Ibid., p. 247 (20 January 1941)

52   Fondazione Mondadori, Archivio Bottai, b. 62, 273b, letter to wife, 6 March 1941

53   Bottai, *Diario 1935–1944*, p. 295 (4 January 1942)

54   Ibid., p. 71 (29 December 1935)

55   G. Ciano, *Diario 1937–1943* (ed. R. De Felice), Rizzoli, Milan 1980, p. 697 (8 February 1943)

56   T. Cianetti, *Memorie dal carcere di Verona* (ed. R. De Felice), Rizzoli, Milan 1983, pp. 136, 394

57   Ibid., p. 373

58   Ibid., p. xiv

59   V. Zamagni, *Dalla periferia al centro. La seconda rinascita economica dell'Italia: 1861–1981*, Il Mulino, Bologna 1990, pp. 324–30

60   C. T. Schmidt, *The Plough and the Sword. Labor, land, and property in fascist Italy*, Columbia University Press, New York 1938, p. 165

61   M. Clark, *Modern Italy 1871–1995*, Longman, London 1996, p. 267

62   R. De Felice, *Mussolini il Duce (1). Gli anni del consenso 1929–1936*, Einaudi, Turin 1974, p. 141

63   G. Toniolo, *L'economia dell'Italia fascista*, Laterza, Rome–Bari 1980, pp. 245–56, 337–42

64   G. Salvemini, *Under the Axe of Fascism*, Gollancz, London 1936, p. 10

65   S. Colarizi, *L'opinione degli italiani sotto il regime 1929–1943*, Laterza, Rome–Bari 2009, p. 134

66   Ibid., pp. 133–44

67   ACS, SPD, CO, Sentimenti, bb. 2757, 2760 etc.

68   V. Zaghi, *Lettere al Duce. I Polesani scrivono a Mussolini (1927–1941)*, Minelliana, Rovigo 2009, pp. 25–7, 80, 82, 94, 160, 171

69 Mazzatosta and Volpi, *L'italietta fascista*, pp. 31–2

70 Ibid., pp. 25–6

71 Zaghi, *Lettere al Duce*, p. 47

72 ACS, SPD, CO, Sentimenti, b. 2789, Collecroce di Nocera Umbra, 18 December 1938

73 Ibid., b. 2762, name not clear (initials and accompanying abstract sketch), 28 October 1940

74 Ibid., b. 2822, Maria Casanova, Parma, 14 March 1941

75 Ibid., letter from rice worker in Lentigione (name not clear), 10 May 1941

76 Ibid., b. 3090, Mariettina Guazzini, 10 July 1941

77 Mazzatosta and Volpi, *L'italietta fascista*, pp. 95, 100

78 ACS, SPD, CO, Sentimenti, b. 2847, Ersilia Reale, 12 November 1942

79 Ibid., b. 2822, Rosina Leto, 2 April 1941

80 B. Ceva, *5 anni di storia italiana 1940–1945. Da lettere e diari di caduti*, Edizioni di comunità, Milan 1964, p. 135 (Riccardo Beduschi, 9 January 1941)

81 Ibid., pp. 197–8 (Enrico Remondini)

82 ACS, SPD, CO, Sentimenti, b. 2823, Franco Oldrini, 18 May 1941

83 Ibid, b. 2793, Rosaria Celebre, 10 March 1936

9: *A Place in the Sun*

1   ADN, DP/Adn2, Albertina Roveda, 'Diario di Albertina', 1 January 1935

2   Mussolini, *Opera omnia*, vol. 20, p. 289 (29 May 1924)

3   A. Del Boca, *Gli italiani in Libia. Dal fascismo a Gheddafi*, Laterza, Rome–Bari 1988, p. 84

4   Roveda, 'Diario di Albertina', 15 October 1936

5   G. Rochat, *Le guerre italiane 1935–1943. Dall'impero d'Etiopia alla disfatta*, Einaudi, Turin 2005, pp. 15–19

6   Mussolini, *Opera omnia*, vol. 27, pp. 158–9 (2 October 1935)

7   Roveda, 'Diario di Albertina', 27 December 1935

8   G. Salvemini, 'Pio XI e la guerra etiopica', in *Opere di Gaetano Salvemini. 3: Scritti di politica estera*, vol. 3, Feltrinelli, Milan 1967, p. 754

9   ACS, SPD, CO, Sentimenti, b. 2806, Giuliano Di Domenico, 29 September 1935

10 Ibid., 'Giuseppina', Milan, 23 September 1935

11 Ibid., Giuseppe Grigoni, 2 October 1935

12 Ibid., 'G. B.', 23 September 1935, Silvio Iatosti (priest), 7 October 1935, Silvio Fasso (priest), 4 October 1935, 'Giuseppina', Milan, 23 September 1935

13   Ibid., 'Un fascista', undated (but late September 1935)

14   Ibid., 'Goliardi Bolognesi', early October 1935

15   R. Bosworth, *Mussolini's Italy. Life under the dictatorship 1915–1945*, Allen Lane, London 2005, pp. 385–6

16   F. Gambetti, *Gli anni che scottano*, Mursia, Milan 1967, p. 250. Cf. A. Lessona, *Memorie*, Edizioni Lessona, Rome 1963, pp. 143, 355; L. Federzoni, *Italia di ieri per la storia di domani*, Mondadori, Milan 1967, p. 138; R. Guariglia, *Ricordi 1922–1946*, Edizioni scientifiche italiane, Naples 1949, pp. 172–3

17   ADN, DP/99, Carlo Ciseri, 'Diario 1915–84', 3 October 1935

18   ADN, DG/99, Espedito Russo, 'Diario 1935–36', 3 October 1935

19   Ibid.

20   Rochat, *Le guerre italiane 1935–1943*, pp. 32–8

21   P. Terhoeven, *Oro alla patria. Donne, guerra e propaganda nella giornata della Fede fascista*, Il Mulino, Bologna 2006, p. 30

22   Ibid., p. 114

23   Ibid., p. 102

24   Ibid., pp. 99, 103, 115, 157

25   Ibid., p. 194

26   Ibid., pp. 172–5

27   Ibid., pp. 271–4

28   Bosworth, *Mussolini's Italy*, p. 369

29   P. Calamandrei, *Diario, vol. 1 (1939–41)* (ed. G. Agosti), La Nuova Italia, Florence 1982, p. 340

30   Rochat, *Le guerre italiane*, pp. 66–7; A. Del Boca, *Gli italiani in Africa orientale. La conquista dell'impero*, Laterza, Rome–Bari 1979, pp. 490–1

31   Ibid., p. 489

32   A. Del Boca, 'I crimini del colonialismo fascista', in id. (ed.), *Le guerre coloniali del fascismo*, Laterza, Rome–Bari 1991, p. 238

33   Baron Aloisi, *Journal (25 juillet 1932 – 14 juin 1936)*, Plon, Paris 1957, pp. 367–8

34   D. Mack Smith, *Le guerre del Duce*, Laterza, Rome–Bari 1976, p. 97

35   A. M. Caredio Benayà, *Il ponte delle catene*, Artemide edizioni, Rome 2004, pp. 234, 241–2

36   Fondazione Mondadori, Archivio Bottai, b. 62, f. 273a, letters to wife, 28 October 1935, 24 February 1936

37   G. Bottai, *Diario 1935–1944* (ed. G. B. Guerri), Rizzoli, Milan 2001, pp. 86 (3 February 1936), 102 (16 May 1936)

38   ADN, DG/96, Vasco Poggesi, 'Africa orientale italiana', 6 March 1935, 11 March 1935

39   Ibid., 25 April 1935, 5 July 1935, 10 July 1935, 11 July 1935, 6 December 1935

40   Ibid., 17 August 1935, 19 August 1935

41 Ibid., 6 December 1935

42 Ibid., 10 December 1935

43 S. Luzzatto (ed.), *La strada per Addis Abeba. Lettere di un camionista dall'Impero (1936–1941)*, Paravia, Milan 2000, p. 63 (7 May 1937)

44 Fondazione Mondadori, Archivio Bottai, b. 62, f. 273a, letters to wife, 16 October 1935, 19 October 1935, 18 January 1936, 21 February 1936, 24 February 1936

45 ADN, DG/98, Mario Saletti, 'Sono in ufficio soletto', 27 December 1935, 14 January 1936

46 Ibid., 13 January 1936

47 Ibid., 12 April 1936

48 ADN, DG/95, Manlio La Sorsa, 'Il mio viaggio in Africa', 30 January 1936

49 Ibid.

50 Ibid., 27–29 February 1936

51 Ibid., 20 March 1936

52 Ibid., 8 March 1936

53 Ibid., 5 April 1936

54 Ibid., 21 May 1936

55 Ibid., 8 August 1936, 30 August 1936, 8 September 1936

56 Ibid., 30 August 1936 (also undated, pp. 190–1)

57 Ibid., 28 July 1936

58 Ibid., 4 December 1936

59 Ibid., 8 May 1936

60 Ibid., 3 July 1936

61 Ibid., 27 October 1936

62 Z. Marazio, *Il mio fascismo. Storia di una donna*, Verdechiaro, Baiso 2005, p. 44–7

63 ADN, DG/86, Sandra Cironi, 'Diario di scuola media, 1935–1936'

64 ADN, DP/02, Roberto Cohen, 'Se trovi una donna', 14 September 1935, 19 September 1935, 8 November 1935

65 L. Ceci, '"Il Fascismo manda l'Italia in rovina." Le note inedite di monsignor Domenico Tardini (23 settembre – 13 dicembre 1935)', in *Rivista storica italiana*, 2008, fasc. 1, pp. 342–3 (1 December 1935)

66 P. Gios, 'Il diario di Maria Teresa Rossetti: una giovane intellettuale tra fascismo e antifascismo', in A. Ventura (ed.), *Sulla crisi del regime fascista 1938–1943. La società italiana dal 'consenso' alla Resistenza*, Marsilio, Venice 1996, p. 431 (5 May 1936)

67 Mussolini, *Opera omnia*, vol. 27, pp. 268–9

68 U. Ojetti, *Cose viste 1921–1943*, Sansoni, Florence 1960, pp. 1422–5

69 G. Volpe, *Storici e maestri*, Sansoni, Florence 1967, p. 471

70   R. Moseley, *Mussolini's Shadow. The double life of Count Galeazzo Ciano*, Yale University Press, New Haven and London 1999, p. 27

71   The full text of the speech can be found in the League of Nations Official Journal, Special Supplement 151, Records of the Sixteenth Ordinary Session of the Assembly, Plenary Meeting, 30 June 1936, pp. 22–5. Film footage of Haile Selassie's arrival in Geneva, the heckling by Italian journalists, and the start of the speech (which he delivered in his native Amharic) can be found at: http://www.criticalpast.com/video/65675029415_Haile-Selassie_League-of-Nations_16th-Assembly_leaves-railway-station

72   Del Boca, *Gli italiani in Africa orientale*, p. 711

73   *Carteggio D'Annunzio–Mussolini (1919–1938)* (eds R. De Felice and E. Mariano), Mondadori, Milan 1971, pp. 364, 376

74   E. Gentile, *Fascismo di pietra*, Laterza, Rome–Bari 2007, pp. 132–3 (16 May 1936)

75   R. Bosworth, *Mussolini*, Arnold, London 2002, p. 310

76   R. De Felice, *Mussolini il Duce (2). Lo stato totalitario 1936–1940*, Einaudi, Turin 1981, p. 265

77   C. Petacci, *Mussolini segreto. Diari 1932–1938* (ed. M. Suttora), Rizzoli, Milan 2009, p. 80 (4 November 1937)

78   Ibid., p. 492 (2 February 1934, 6 January 1936)

79   Ibid., p. 494

80   Ibid., pp. 495–6 (2 June 1936)

81   L. Greco, *Una storia italiana 1936–1946*, Adriano Gallina, Naples 1986, p. 32

82   Del Boca, *Gli italiani in Africa orientale*, pp. 717–20

83   Petacci, *Mussolini segreto*, p. 74 (27 October 1937)

10: *Defence of the Race*

1   C. Poggiali, *Diario AOI. 15 giugno 1936 – 4 ottobre 1937*, Longanesi, Milan 1971, p. 12

2   L. Preti, *Impero fascista, africani ed ebrei*, Mursia, Milan 1968, pp. 219–21

3   Poggiali, *Diario AOI*, pp. 18–20 (17–18 June 1936)

4   G. Bonsaver, *Censorship and Literature in Fascist Italy*, University of Toronto Press, Toronto 2007, pp. 95–9

5   R. Bosworth, *Mussolini's Italy. Life under the dictatorship 1915–1945*, Allen Lane, London 2005, p. 369

6   A. Lessona, *Memorie*, Edizioni Lessona, Rome 1963, p. 299 (Lessona to Graziani, 5 August 1936)

7   Poggiali, *Diario AOI*, pp. 35–6 (27 June 1936)

8   Bosworth, *Mussolini's Italy*, pp. 369, 414

9   Poggiali, *Diario AOI*, p. 38

10 Bosworth, *Mussolini's Italy*, p. 385

11 E. Ludwig, *Colloqui con Mussolini. Riproduzione delle bozze della prima edizione con le correzioni autografe del Duce*, Mondadori, Milan 1950, p. 71

12 Baron Aloisi, *Journal (25 juillet 1932 – 14 juin 1936)*, Plon, Paris 1957, p. 382 (8 May 1936)

13 C. Petacci, *Mussolini segreto. Diari 1932–1938* (ed. M. Suttora), Rizzoli, Milan 2009, pp. 282 (6 April 1938), 393 (4 August 1938)

14 Ibid., pp. 385–6 (17 July 1938)

15 Poggiali, *Diario AOI*, p. 127 (5 December 1936)

16 Ibid., pp. 90–1

17 R. Pankhurst, 'Come il popolo etiopico resistette all'occupazione', in A. Del Boca (ed.), *Le guerre coloniali del fascismo*, Laterza, Rome–Bari 1991, pp. 262–3

18 Poggiali, *Diario AOI*, pp. 182–3

19 G. Rochat, *Le guerre italiane 1935–1943. Dall'impero d'Etiopia alla disfatta*, Einaudi, Turin 2005, p. 83

20 Pankhurst, 'Come il popolo etiopico resistette all'occupazione', pp. 265–6

21 A. Del Boca, *Italiani brava gente?*, Neri Pozza, Vicenza 2005, pp. 217–21

22 A. Del Boca, *Gli italiani in Libia. Dal fascismo a Gheddafi*, Laterza, Rome–Bari 1988, p. 16

23 Pankhurst, 'Come il popolo etiopico resistette all'occupazione', pp. 269–70

24 L. Federzoni, *Italia di ieri per la storia di domani*, Mondadori, Milan 1967, p. 146

25 Pankhurst, 'Come il popolo etiopico resistette all'occupazione', pp. 277–8 (Arconvaldo Bonaccorsi, May 1940)

26 Preti, *Impero fascista, africani ed ebrei*, p. 221 (19 May 1939)

27 Poggiali, *Diario AOI*, p. 277 (19 September 1937)

28 Ibid., pp. 283–4 (3 October 1937)

29 S. Patriarca, *Italianità. La costruzione del carattere nazionale*, Laterza, Rome–Bari, 2010, p. 159

30 Petacci, *Mussolini segreto*, p. 265 (25 March 1938)

31 Preti, *Impero fascista, africani ed ebrei*, pp. 91–2 (25 October 1938)

32 F. Gambetti, *Gli anni che scottano*, Mursia, Milan 1967, p. 228

33 G. Pintor, *Doppio diario 1936–1943* (ed. M. Serri), Einaudi, Turin 1978, pp. 56, 58–9

34 A. Grandi, *I giovani di Mussolini. Fascisti convinti, fascisti pentiti, antifascisti*, Baldini e Castoldi, Milan 2001, p. 243

35   G. Silvano Spinetti, *Difesa di una generazione*, Edizioni Polilibraria, Rome 1948, pp. 131–166

36   ADN, DG/89, Paolino Ferrari, 'Proderit die ultionis', December 1938

37   Ibid., June 1939

38   Ibid., 1 November 1939

39   G. Ciano, *Diario 1937–1943* (ed. R. De Felice), Rizzoli, Milan 1980, p. 149 (18 June 1938)

40   Ferrari, 'Proderit die ultionis', December 1938, September 1939, 28 July 1940

41   Ibid., January 1940, 28 July 1940, 22 October 1940

42   Cf. ACS, SPD, CO, Sentimenti b. 2810, letters from soldiers in Spain to Mussolini

43   D. Mack Smith, *Mussolini*, Granada, London 1983, p. 250

44   Mussolini, *Opera omnia*, vol. 28, pp. 248–53

45   Ciano, *Diario*, p. 45 (14 October 1937). Cf. ibid., p. 70 (19 December 1937)

46   Mussolini, *Opera omnia*, vol. 29, pp. 75–7 (30 March 1938)

47   L. Gasparotto, *Diario di un deputato. Cinquant'anni di vita politica italiana*, Dall'Oglio, Milan 1945, pp. 280–2

48   R. J. Crum, 'Shaping the fascist "new man": Donatello's *St. George* and Mussolini's appropriated Renaissance of the Italian nation', in C. Lazzaro and R. J. Crum (eds), *Donatello among the Blackshirts: history and modernity in the visual culture of Fascist Italy*, Cornell University Press, Ithaca and London 2005, pp. 136–7

49   Mussolini, *Opera omnia*, vol. 29, pp. 188–9

50   Petacci, *Mussolini segreto*, p. 313 (7 May 1938)

51   R. Graziani, *Ho difeso la patria*, Garzanti, Milan 1948, pp. 167–8; *Processo Graziani. Vol. 1: L'autodifesa dell'ex maresciallo nel resoconto stenografico*, Ruffolo, Rome 1948, pp. 107–8

52   S. Colarizi, *L'opinione degli italiani sotto il regime 1929–1943*, Laterza, Rome–Bari 2009, pp. 258–60

53   Petacci, *Mussolini segreto*, pp. 314–16 (7 May 1938, 10 May 1938)

54   R. Bianchi Bandinelli, *Dal diario di un borghese e altri scritti*, Mondadori, Milan 1948, pp. 180–1, 190

55   Petacci, *Mussolini segreto*, p. 196 (6 February 1938)

56   Ibid., p. 327 (17 May 1938)

57   Ciano, *Diario*, p. 115 (20 March 1938)

58   Ibid., p. 156 (10 July 1938)

59   Preti, *Impero fascista, africani ed ebrei*, pp. 73–4

60   I. Montanelli, 'Dentro la guerra', *Civiltà fascista*, 3 (1), January 1936

61   I. Montanelli, *XX Battaglione eritreo. Il primo romanzo e le lettere inedite dal fronte africano* (ed. A. Del Boca), Rizzoli, Milan 2010, p. 149

62   Interview of Enzo Biagi with Indro Montanelli in 1982, broadcast on

programme RT-Era ieri, Rai 3, 13 October 2008

63   For an English translation of the manifesto, see J. T. Schnapp (ed.), *A Primer of Italian Fascism*, University of Nebraska Press, Lincoln 2000, pp. 173–5

64   Mussolini, *Opera omnia*, vol. 29, pp. 188–90

65   *Il Giornale d'Italia*, 9 November 1938; *Il Regime Fascista*, 15 November 1938

66   ASV, Archivio della Nunziatura Apostolica d'Italia, b. 9, fasc. 5, letter of Pope to Mussolini, 4 November 1938; letter of Pope to king, 5 November 1938 etc.

67   Ciano, *Diario*, p. 217 (29 November 1938)

68   *La Difesa della razza*, 20 October 1938, 20 January 1939, 5 February 1939

69   Bosworth, *Mussolini's Italy*, p. 419

70   Cf. *La menzogna della razza. Documenti e immagini del razzismo e dell'antisemitismo fascista* (ed. Centro Furio Jesi), Grafis, Bologna 1994

71   S. Duranti, *Lo spirito gregario. I gruppi universitari fascisti tra politica e propaganda (1930–1940)*, Donzelli, Rome 2008, pp. 313–22

72   P. Orano, *Gli ebrei in Italia*, Pinciana, Rome 1937, p. 67

73   A. Ventura, 'Sugli intellettuali di fronte al fascismo negli ultimi anni del regime', in id. (ed.), *Sulla crisi del regime fascista 1938–1943. La società italiana dal 'consenso' alla Resistenza*, Marsilio, Venice 1996, pp. 369–70

74   ACS, DGPS, Polizia politica, b. 219, fasc. 2, 5 January 1939 (Rome), 12 March 1939 (Milan) etc.

75   Ibid., 28 August 1938 (Rome), 4 January 1939 (Rome), 9 January 1939 (Milan), 26 January 1939 (Milan), 14 March 1939 (Cuneo) etc.

76   Ibid., 24 August 1941 (Venice)

77   Ibid., 17 August 1939 (Milan), 7 February 1940 (Milan), 26 July 1940 (Rome), 10 August 1940 (Rome) etc.

78   Ibid., 22 April 1940 (Rome)

79   Ibid., 30 November 1941 (Milan)

80   Ibid., 6 November 1941

81   Ibid., 16 September 1941 (Merano)

82   E. Collotti, *Il fascismo e gli ebrei. Le leggi razziali in Italia*, Laterza, Rome–Bari 2003, p. 84

83   P. Gios, 'Il diario di Maria Teresa Rossetti: una giovane intellettuale tra fascismo e antifascismo', in A. Ventura (ed.), *Sulla crisi del regime fascista 1938–1943. La società italiana dal 'consenso' alla Resistenza*, Marsilio, Venice 1996, pp. 434–5

84   Ciano, *Diario*, p. 193 (6 October 1938). Cf. G. B. Guerri, *Giuseppe Bottai. Un fascista critico*, Feltrinelli, Milan 1976, pp. 166–70

85   G. Bottai, *Diario 1935–1944* (ed. G. B. Guerri), Rizzoli, Milan 2001, p. 133 (8 September 1938)

86   P. Calamandrei, *Diario, vol. 1 (1939–41)* (ed. G. Agosti), La Nuova Italia, Florence 1982, p. 45 (2 June 1939)

87   Ibid., p. 12 (10 April 1939). Cf. ibid., pp. 10–11 (9 April 1939), 45–6 (2 June 1939)

88   Ibid., p. 12 (10 April 1939)

89   *Il Popolo d'Italia*, 10 January 1939 Cf. ASV, Archivio della nunziatura apostolica d'Italia, b. 9, fasc. 5

90   D. Vanelli, 'Basta con gli ebrei', in *Vent'anni* (Turin), 7 September 1940, quoted in Duranti, *Lo spirito gregario*, p. 345

91   Calamandrei, *Diario, vol. 1 (1939–41)*, p. 60 (6 August 1939)

92   ADN, MG/02, D. P., 'Memorie di vita militare (ed altro) 1940–1943', p. 36

93   ADN, DP/02, Roberto Cohen, 'Se trovi una donna', 10 December 1936, September 1938

94   ADN, MP/91, Samuele Varsano, 'Le mie memorie', pp. 156, 221

95   P. Frandini, *Ebreo, tu non esisti! Le vittime delle leggi razziali scrivono a Mussolini*, Manni, San Cesario di Lecce 2007, p. 17

96   Petacci, *Mussolini segreto*, pp. 407 (4 September 1938), 423–4 (11 October 1938)

97   A. Stille, *Benevolence and Betrayal. Five Italian Jewish families under fascism*, Vintage, London 1993, pp. 20, 52–3, 63

98   Ibid., pp. 73–89

99   C. Gutkind (ed.), *Mussolini e il suo fascismo*, Le Monnier, Florence 1927, pp. 19, 28, 30

100   Frandini, *Ebreo, tu non esisti!*, pp. 95–6 (Gutkind to Mussolini, 3 September 1938)

101   Ibid., p. 97

102   The National Archives, HO 214/14, letter of Laura Gutkind to Anthony Eden, 18 July 1940 and to Home Office, 21 March 1941; letter from Home Office, 25 March 1941. Archives, Royal Holloway, University of London, D349 (Curt Gutkind), letter of Miss Jebb to Home Secretary, 5 July 1940

11: *War*

1   C. Petacci, *Mussolini segreto. Diari 1932–1938* (ed. M. Suttora), Rizzoli, Milan 2009, pp. 59–60, 62, 80, 110, 149–50, 189, 269, 354, 439–40 etc.

2   G. Ciano, *Diario 1937–1943* (ed. R. De Felice), Rizzoli, Milan 1980, p. 70 (19 December 1937)

3   Ibid., p. 609 (10 April 1942)

4   Petacci, *Mussolini segreto*, pp. 124 (22 December 1937), 126 (24 December 1937), 300 (18 April 1938)

5   G. Rochat, *Le guerre italiane 1935–1943. Dall'impero d'Etiopia alla disfatta*, Einaudi, Turin 2005, p. 183

6   Ibid., pp. 216, 233–4

7   L. Federzoni, *Italia di ieri per la storia di domani*, Mondadori, Milan 1967, p. 166

8   G. Bottai, *Diario 1935–1944* (ed. G. B. Guerri), Rizzoli, Milan 2001, p. 147 (15 May 1939)

9   Ibid., p. 147 (29 April 1939)

10   Ciano, *Diario*, p. 290 (29 April 1939)

11   Petacci, *Mussolini segreto*, p. 384 (17 July 1938)

12   Ibid., p. 425 (11 October 1938)

13   Ciano, *Diario*, p. 140 (23 May 1938); D. Mack Smith, *Mussolini*, Granada, London 1983, p. 263. Cf. G. Fettarappa-Sandri, 'Idee sulla guerra', *Gerarchia*, 1939, p. 32

14   Ciano, *Diario*, pp. 33, 187 (3 September 1937, 29–30 September 1938)

15   G. Bastianini, *Uomini cose fatti. Memorie di un ambasciatore*, Vitagliano, Milan 1959, p. 49

16   Ibid.

17   Ciano, *Diario*, pp. 176–7, 184 (12 September 1938, 25 September 1938)

18   Mussolini, *Opera omnia*, vol. 29, p. 192

19   Mack Smith, *Mussolini*, p. 263

20   ACS, SPD CO, Sentimenti, b. 2815. Cf. D. Grandi, *Il mio paese. Ricordi autobiografici*, Il Mulino, Bologna 1985, p. 452

21   Petacci, *Mussolini segreto*, pp. 413–17

22   D. Mack Smith, *Le guerre del Duce*, Laterza, Rome–Bari 1976, pp. 218–23

23   Ciano, *Diario*, pp. 326–33

24   R. De Felice, *Mussolini il Duce (2). Lo stato totalitario 1936–1940*, Einaudi, Turin 1981, p. 670 (1 September 1939)

25   Ciano, *Diario*, p. 349 (18 September 1939)

26   F. Anfuso, *Roma Berlino Salò. 1936–1945*, Garzanti, Milan 1950, pp. 100–1

27   P. Gios, 'Il diario di Maria Teresa Rossetti: una giovane intellettuale tra fascismo e antifascismo', in A. Ventura (ed.), *Sulla crisi del regime fascista 1938–1943. La società italiana dal 'consenso' alla Resistenza*, Marsilio, Venice 1996, p. 441

28   Ibid., pp. 439–41

29   Ibid., pp. 441–2 (31 March 1939)

30   Ibid., p. 444

31   ACS, DGPS, Polizia politica, b. 220, report from Milan (28 December 1938)

32   Ibid., reports from Genoa (8 January 1939), Milan (28 December 1938), Rome (15 August 1939) etc.

33   Ibid., report from Milan (7 January 1939)

34   Ibid., reports from Rome (1 January 1939, 4 April 1939, 19 May 1939), Milan (29 June 1939)

35   Ibid., report from Rome (26 January 1939)

36　S. Colarizi, *L'opinione degli italiani sotto il regime 1929–1943*, Laterza, Rome–Bari 2009, p. 271 (Milan, 8 October 1938)

37　Ibid., pp. 271–2. Cf. ACS, DGPS, Polizia politica, b. 226, fasc. 2, reports on visits of Mussolini to Turin (May 1939) and Milan (July 1939)

38　ACS, DGPS, Polizia politica, b. 220, report from Naples, 12 August 1939

39　Ibid., report from Rome (27 January 1939)

40　Ibid., reports from Bologna (February–March 1939)

41　ACS, DGPS, Polizia politica, b. 226, fasc. 2, reports of 8 May 1939, 12 May 1939, 13 May 1939, 4 June 1939

42　Ibid., report of 14 May 1939

43　Ibid., reports of 12 May 1939, 13 May 1939, 16 May 1939, 29 May 1939, 4 June 1939. Cf. L. Passerini, *Torino operaia e fascismo. Una storia orale*, Laterza, Rome–Bari 1984, pp. 225–7

44　ACS, DGPS, Polizia politica, b. 226, fasc. 2, report of 25 May 1939 on visits to Cuneo, Airasca, Moretta etc.

45　C. Petacci, *Verso il disastro. Mussolini in guerra. Diari 1939–1940* (ed. M. Franzinelli), Rizzoli, Milan 2011, pp. 129–30 (21 May 1939)

46　A. Imbriani, *Gli italiani e il Duce. Il mito e l'immagine di Mussolini negli ultimi anni del fascismo (1938–1943)*, Liguori, Naples 1992, pp. 39–48

47　Ibid., pp. 33, 42; ACS, DGPS, Polizia politica, b. 220, reports from Rome (8 February 1939), Naples (27 August 1939, 29 August 1939), Cagliari (26 August 1939) etc.

48　Bottai, *Diario 1935–1944*, p. 153 (28 August 1939)

49　Petacci, *Verso il disastro*, p. 161 (4 July 1939)

50　ACS, DGPS, Polizia politica, b. 219, fasc. 3, reports from Venice (1 September 1939), Rome (13 September 1939, 19 September 1939) etc.; ibid., b. 220, reports from Rome (3 August 1939), Bologna (28 August 1939), Naples (29 August 1939) etc.; Imbriani, *Gli italiani e il Duce*, pp. 56–9

51　Ciano, *Diario*, pp. 327–8

52　Cf. Bottai, *Diario 1935–1944*, p. 155 (31 August 1939)

53　Petacci, *Verso il disastro*, pp. 174–5 (27 August 1939)

54　ACS, DGPS, Polizia politica, b. 228, fasc. 3, report from Bolzano (23 September 1939)

55　Ibid., fasc. 4, report from Brindisi (25 September)

56　Ibid., b. 219, fasc. 3, reports from Rome (27 September 1939, 28 December 1939 etc); ibid., b. 228, fasc. 4, reports from Brindisi (25 September 1939, 10 October 1939 etc)

57　Ibid., b. 219, fasc. 3, reports from Rome (13 September 1939, 19 September 1939, 22 February 1940, 10 March 1940); ibid., report on Lombard countryside (28 September 1939)

58 Ibid., reports from Rome (November–December 1939); ibid., fasc. 4, reports from Brindisi (October 1939); ibid., b. 229, fasc. 1, reports from Sardinia (February 1940, 12 May 1940)

59 ADN, 'Diario di un ragazzo', pp. 27–8 (25 November 1939)

60 Ibid., p. 30 (15 January 1940)

61 Ibid., p. 19 (15 April 1939)

62 P. Calamandrei, *Diario, vol. 1 (1939–41)* (ed. G. Agosti), La Nuova Italia, Florence 1982, pp. 93–4 (30 September 1939)

63 Ibid., pp. 64–5 (22 August 1939)

64 Ibid., p. 46 (4 June 1939)

65 Ibid., p. 81 (9 September 1939)

66 Ibid., pp. 86–7 (20 September 1939)

67 Ibid., p. 187 (15 June 1940)

68 *Autobiografie di giovani del tempo fascista*, Quaderni di Humanitatis, Morcelliana, Brescia 1947, pp. 15–16

69 Ibid., pp. 16–17

70 D. Marchesini, *La scuola dei gerarchi*, Feltrinelli, Milan 1976, p. 121

71 G. Spinetti, *Difesa di una generazione (scritti ed appunti)*, Polilibreria, Rome 1948, pp. 115–16

72 B. Ceva, *5 anni di storia italiana 1940–1945. Da lettere e diari di caduti*, Edizioni di comunità, Milan 1964, p. 189 (31 May 1938)

73 Ibid., pp. 189–90 (18 March 1939)

74 Ibid., p. 191 (16 May 1940)

75 Ibid., p. 192 (5 June 1940)

76 Ibid., p. 192 (18 December 1940)

77 Ciano, *Diario*, pp. 391, 418 (29 January 1940, 11 April 1940)

78 Ibid., pp. 389–90, 415 (23 January 1940, 2 April 1940)

79 Bottai, *Diario 1935–1944*, p. 184 (2 April 1940)

80 De Felice, *Mussolini il Duce (2)*, pp. 772–5

81 Petacci, *Verso il disastro*, pp. 313–14 (11 April 1940)

82 De Felice, *Mussolini il Duce (2)*, p. 794

83 P. Cavallo, *Italiani in guerra. Sentimenti e immagini dal 1940 al 1943*, Il Mulino, Bologna 1997, pp. 31–42; Colarizi, *L'opinione degli italiani*, pp. 334–9

84 Imbriani, *Gli italiani e il Duce*, pp. 84–5, 91

85 Petacci, *Verso il disastro*, pp. 324–5 (27 May 1940)

86 De Felice, *Mussolini il Duce (2)*, pp. 834–5

87 Mussolini, *Opera omnia*, vol. 29, pp. 403–5

88 ADN, MP/Adn, Elvira Menichini, '10 giugno 1940'

89 ADN, DP/07, Don Luigi Serravalle, 'Anniversario della mia ordinazione sacerdotale', 15 May 1940

90 Ibid., 10 June 1940

91   ADN, DP/90, Angela Martina, 'Il mio diario 1933–47', p. 46 (11 June 1940)
92   ADN, DG/05, Pasqualina Caruso, 'Vivere per raccontare', 10 June 1940, 15 June 1940
93   ADN, 'Diario di un ragazzo', 11 June 1940
94   Ibid., 11 June 1940
95   Ibid., 26 June 1940
96   Ciano, Diario, p. 444 (19 June 1940)
97   Rochat, Le guerre italiane, pp. 249–51
98   ACS, DGPS, Polizia politica, b. 228, reports of 13 June 1940 (Bolzano), 20 June 1940 (Brindisi); ibid., b. 299, report of 21 June 1940 (Cagliari) etc.; Colarizi, L'opinione degli italiani, pp. 339–40
99   ADN, DG/89, Paolino Ferrari, 'Proderit die ultionis', 10 June 1940, 16 June 1940
100 Petacci, Verso il disastro, p. 336 (21 June 1940)
101 Ibid., p. 353 (4 July 1940); Ciano, Diario, pp. 444–5, 455–8 (21 June 1940, 5 August 1940 etc.)
102 Mack Smith, Le guerre del Duce, pp. 306–7
103 M. Carazzolo, Più forte della paura. Diario di guerra e dopoguerra (1938–1947), Cierre edizioni, Sommacampagna 2007, pp. 49–50 (20 July 1940)
104 Ibid., p. 53 (29 October 1940)
105 Imbriani, Gli italiani e il Duce, pp. 86–93; Cavallo, Italiani in guerra, pp. 139–60
106 ACS, SPD, CO, Sentimenti, b. 2821, Paola Dotti, 28 June 1940

12: The Road to Disaster

1   G. Bottai, Diario 1935–1944 (ed. G. B. Guerri), Rizzoli, Milan 2001, p. 228 (24 October 1940)
2   R. Guariglia, Ricordi 1922–1946, Edizioni scientifiche italiane, Naples 1949, p. 478
3   D. Mack Smith, Mussolini, Granada, London 1983, pp. 228, 267
4   G. Bastianini, Uomini cose fatti. Memorie di un ambasciatore, Vitagliano, Milan 1959, pp. 257–8
5   P. Calamandrei, Diario, vol. 1 (1939–41) (ed. G. Agosti), La Nuova Italia, Florence 1982, p. 254 (30 October 1940)
6   Ibid., p. 369 (22 July 1941)
7   Ibid., pp. 267–8, 351–2 (8 December 1940, 24 May 1941)
8   Ibid., pp. 379–80
9   A. Imbriani, Gli italiani e il Duce. Il mito e l'immagine di Mussolini negli ultimi anni del fascismo (1938–1943), Liguori, Naples 1992, pp. 102–21

10 C. Petacci, *Verso il disastro. Mussolini in guerra. Diari 1939–1940* (ed. M. Franzinelli), Rizzoli, Milan 2011, pp. 400–1 (30 November 1940)

11 ADN, DG/01, Antonio Brunello, 'Nel ricordo dei caduti di Lekduschaj', p. 335

12 Ibid., 20 January 1941

13 Ibid., 26 March 1941

14 N. Revelli, *L'ultimo fronte. Lettere di soldati caduti o dispersi nella seconda guerra mondiale*, Einaudi, Turin 1971, p. 60

15 Ibid., p. 124 (19 March 1941)

16 ADN, DP/08, Osvaldo Cosci, 'Il diario della mia naia', 8 March 1941

17 Mussolini, *Opera omnia*, vol. 30, pp. 51, 54 (23 February 1941)

18 Imbriani, *Gli italiani e il Duce*, pp. 101–21

19 Ibid., p. 139

20 ACS, SPD, CO, Sentimenti, b. 2830, Merope Panizzi, 4 February 1941

21 Ibid., anonymous letter, Rome, 24 February 1941

22 Ibid., anonymous letter, 23 February 1941

23 Ibid., b. 2823, Antonio Barnabina Caracci, 23 March 1941

24 Ibid., b. 2830, Oreste Orlà, 27 January 1941

25 Ibid., Mario Ercolino, 26 January 1941

26 B. Ceva, *5 anni di storia italiana 1940–1945. Da lettere e diari di caduti*, Edizioni di comunità, Milan 1964, p. 197

27 Ibid., pp. 197–8

28 ADN, DG/90, Giuseppe Caronia, 'Fronte greco. Diario di guerra 1940–41', p. 18 (12 October 1940)

29 Ibid., pp. 28, 52 (22 October 1940; 12 November 1940 – summarising what he had written earlier in a letter to 'Vittorio')

30 Ibid., p. 52 (12 November 1940)

31 Ibid., p. 68 (1 December 1940)

32 Ibid., p. 125 (1 March 1941)

33 Ibid., pp. 123–4 (27 February 1940)

34 Fondazione Mondadori, Archivio Bottai, b. 62, 273b, letter to wife, 7 February 1941

35 Ibid., letter to wife, 29 March 1941

36 Ibid., letter to wife, 27 April 1941

37 Caronia, 'Fronte greco', pp. 123–4 (27 February 1941)

38 Ibid., p. 140 (2 April 1941)

39 Ibid.

40 Ibid., pp. 145–6 (9 April 1941)

41 *Autobiografie di giovani del tempo fascista*, Quaderni di Humanitas, Morcelliana, Brescia 1947, pp. 55, 61

42 Ibid., p. 68

43 Caronia, 'Fronte greco', p. 150 (14 April 1941)

44 M. Ceccarelli De Grada, *Giornale del tempo di guerra. 12 giugno 1940 – 7 maggio 1945*, Il Mulino, Bologna, pp. 85, 89–90 (28 April 1941, 17 May 1941, 26 May 1941)

45 Ibid., p. 15 (introduction: M. Mazzucco, 'I giorni della passione')

46 Ibid., p. 57 (12 December 1940)

47 Ibid., pp. 60, 69 (22 December 1940, 9 February 1941)

48 Ibid., p. 117 (8 November 1941)

49 Ibid. pp. 95–6 (22 June 1941, 24 June 1941)

50 Calamandrei, *Diario, vol. 1*, pp. 289–91, 311, 369 (22 January 1941, 2 March 1941, 22 July 1941)

51 Revelli, *L'ultimo fronte*, p. 372 (31 August 1942). Cf. ibid., pp. 223, 367, 370 etc.

52 Archivio della scrittura popolare, Museo storico, Trento, Ivo Manica, 'Raccolta di lettere scritte dal fratello Ivo disperso nella battaglia sul Don 1942', 10 January 1942, 10 March 1942

53 Ibid.

54 ADN, DG/04, Ottaviano Plet, 'La colossale tragedia', 29 July 1941

55 Ibid., 25 August 1941, 31 August 1941

56 Ibid., 28 October 1941, 29 December 1941

57 Archivio della scrittura popolare, Museo storico, Trento, Valerio Conzatti, 'Settembre 1941 fronte russo', September 1941

58 Ibid., December 1941

59 Cf. Revelli, *L'ultimo fronte*, pp. 223, 367, 370, 372

60 Ceva, *5 anni di storia italiana*, p. 112

61 Revelli, *L'ultimo fronte*, p. 249

62 ADN, DG/05, Giuseppe Armellino, 'Diario', 10 June 1942, 20 June 1942, 12 May 1943

63 ADN, DG/87, Riccardo Martini, 'Laggiù lontano nel deserto Marmarico', pp. 344–5

64 Ibid., pp. 51–2

65 Ibid., pp. 248–9

66 Ibid., pp. 344–5

67 Ibid., pp. 355, 420–8

68 Ibid., pp. 802–3

69 Imbriani, *Gli italiani e il Duce*, p. 147 (28 January 1942)

70 Ceccarelli De Grada, *Giornale del tempo di guerra*, p. 168 (19–20 September 1942)

71 Ibid., p. 170 (27 September 1942)

72 R. De Felice, *Mussolini l'alleato 1940–1945. 1: L'Italia in guerra 1940–1943. Vol. 2: Crisi e agonia del regime*, Einaudi, Turin 1990, p. 1149–50

73   Imbriani, *Gli italiani e il Duce*, pp. 195–8

74   Cf. ACS, SPD, CO, Sentimenti, bb. 2768, 2771, 2847 etc.

75   Imbriani, *Gli italiani e il Duce*, pp. 183–92

76   P. Cavallo, *Italiani in guerra. Sentimenti e immagini dal 1940 al 1943*, Il Mulino, Bologna 1997, pp. 228–33

77   P. Monelli, *Roma 1943*, Migliaresi, Rome 1945, p. 40

78   The transmission can be found at: http://www.felliniallaradio.it/index.php?page_id=16

79   ADN, 'Diario di un ragazzo', spring 1942, 15 November 1942

80   Ibid., 15 November 1942, 12 July 1943

13: *The Final Act*

1   ADN, DG/99, Aldo Bacci, 'Appunti di un P.O.W', pp. 3, 4, 6, 20 (22 July 1943, 24 July 1943, 25 June 1944)

2   Ibid., p. 25 (1 February 1945)

3   R. De Felice, *Mussolini l'alleato 1940–1945. 1: L'Italia in guerra 1940–1943. Vol. 2: Crisi e agonia del regime*, Einaudi, Turin 1990, pp. 1373–4

4   G. Bottai, *Diario 1935–1944* (ed. G. B. Guerri), Rizzoli, Milan 2001, p. 412 (24 July 1943)

5   Cf. I. Bonomi, *Diario di un anno (2 giugno 1943 – 10 giugno 1944)*, Garzanti, Milan 1947, pp. v–xiii, 3–7

6   P. Monelli, *Roma 1943*, Migliaresi, Rome 1945, p. 155

7   Ibid., pp. 155–6

8   A. Grandi, *I giovani di Mussolini. Fascisti convinti, fascisti pentiti, antifascisti*, Baldini e Castoldi, Milan 2001, pp. 345–6

9   ADN, DG/96, Dino Villani, 'Le strade di Milano', pp. 7–9 (26 July 1943)

10   P. Cavallo, *Italiani in guerra. Sentimenti e immagini dal 1940 al 1943*, Il Mulino, Bologna 1997, pp. 374–7

11   P. Calamandrei, *Diario, vol. 2 (1942–45)* (ed. G. Agosti), La Nuova Italia, Florence 1982, pp. 154–7

12   ADN, DP/Adn2, Bruna Talluri, 'Cronaca di una passione', 28 July 1943

13   M. Ceccarelli De Grada, *Giornale del tempo di guerra. 12 giugno 1940 – 7 maggio 1945*, Il Mulino, Bologna 2011, p. 218 (26 July 1943)

14   ADN, DP/03, Zelinda Marcucci, 'Il mio diario', 29 July 1943

15   ADN, DG/90, Aldo Carugati, 'Memorie di guerra e prigionia', 31 July 1943

16   ADN, 'Diario di un ragazzo', 27 July 1943

17   ADN, DP/99, Carlo Ciseri, 'Diario 1915–84', 26 July 1943, 4 August 1943

18 E. Artom, *Diari gennaio 1940 – febbraio 1944* (ed. P. De Benedetti and E. Ravenna), Centro di documentazione ebraica contemporanea, Milan 1966, p. 56 (28 July 1943)

19 E. Aga Rossi, *Una nazione allo sbando. L'armistizio italiano del settembre 1943 e le sue conseguenze*, Il Mulino, Bologna 2003, pp. 98–102

20 R. Guariglia, *Ricordi 1922–1946*, Edizioni scientifiche italiane, Naples 1949, p. 705

21 G. Rochat, *Le guerre italiane 1935–1943. Dall'impero d'Etiopia alla disfatta*, Einaudi, Turin 2005, pp. 427–30

22 Monelli, *Roma 1943*, pp. 236–9

23 Ibid., pp. 239–40

24 L. Raganella, *Senza sapere da che parte stanno. Ricordi dell'infanzia e 'diario' di Roma in guerra (1943–44)* (ed. L. Piccioni), Bulzoni, Rome 2000, p. 125

25 ADN, DG/03, Vittoria Cozzi, 'Diario', 8 September 1943

26 Ibid., 12 September 1943

27 Ibid.

28 Ibid., 13 September 1943

29 V. Vettori, *Giovanni Gentile*, Editrice italiana, Rome 1967, pp. 151–2

30 G. Gentile, 'Ripresa' in *La Nuova antologia*, 1 January 1944, pp. 3–4

31 B. Croce, *Scritti e discorsi politici (1943–1947)*, Vol. 1, Laterza, Bari 1963, pp. 223–4

32 M. Carazzolo, *Più forte della paura. Diario di guerra e dopoguerra (1938–1947)*, Cierre edizioni, Sommacampagna 2007, p. 101 (10 September 1943)

33 ADN, DP/00, Angelo Peroni, 'Diario di un anno di guerra', 28 July 1943, 29 July 1943, 12 August 1943, 29 August 1943, 9 September 1943

34 Ibid., 12 August 1943, 16 October 1943

35 ADN, DP/85, Ettore Castiglioni, 'Diario di un alpinista', 27 August 1943

36 Ibid., 9 September 1943

37 Ibid., 26 September 1943

38 N. Revelli, 'La ritirata di Russia', in M. Isnenghi (ed.), *I luoghi della memoria. Strutture ed eventi dell'Italia unita*, Laterza, Rome–Bari 1997, p. 374

39 G. Pirelli, *Un mondo che crolla. Lettere 1938–1943*, Rosellina Archinto, Milan 1990, pp. 206, 284

40 Ibid., pp. 45–51

41 R. Vivarelli, *La fine di una stagione. Memoria 1943–1945*, Il Mulino, Bologna, 2000, pp. 14–16

42 Ibid., pp. 18–26

43 ADN, 'Diario di un ragazzo', 10 October 1943, 12 November 1943

44 ADN, DP/95, Maricilla Piovanelli, 'Dio', 26 July 1943

45   ADN, DP/98, D. C., 'Parte Augusto per la visita militare', 8 September
     1943. At the request of the archive I have altered the author's name.
46   ADN, DG/92, Mariannina Pastore, 'Giorno 24', 10 September 1944
47   ADN, DP/03, Angelo Galiano, 'Dal mio diario, 1938–52', 15 March 1944
48   Ibid.
49   Ibid.
50   C. Alvaro, *Quasi una vita. Giornale di uno scrittore*, Bompiani, Milan 1959,
     pp. 341–3, 354.
51   N. Gallerano, 'L'arrivo degli Alleati', in M. Isnenghi (ed.), *I luoghi della
     memoria. Strutture ed eventi dell'Italia unita*, Laterza, Rome–Bari 1997, p. 460
52   P. Calamandrei, *Diario, vol. 2 (1942–45)* (ed. G. Agosti), La Nuova Italia,
     Florence 1982, vol. 2, pp. 259–60, 270 (12 November 1943, 4 December 1943)
53   C. Malaparte, *La pelle. Storia e racconto*, Aria d'Italia, Rome-Milan 1949,
     pp. 40–2
54   N. Lewis, *Naples '44. An intelligence officer in the Italian labyrinth*, Eland,
     London 1983, pp. 108–10
55   C. Di Pompeo, *Più della fame e più dei bombardamenti. Diario dell'occupazione
     di Roma*, Il Mulino, Bologna 2009, pp. 26, 36, 81, 115, 136–7
56   P. Chessa and B. Raggi, *L'ultima lettera di Benito. Mussolini e Petacci: amore
     e politica a Salò 1943–45*, Mondadori, Milan 2010, pp. 46–7 (diary entry for
     28 October 1943)
57   ADN, DG/07, Danilo Durando, 'Ohimè, gente, udite!', 30 June 1944,
     16 July 1944, 19 September 1944
58   Cf. C. Pavone, *Una guerra civile. Saggio storico sulla moralità nella resistenza*,
     Einaudi, Turin 1991, pp. 169–89
59   R. Battaglia, *Storia della resistenza italiana*, Einaudi, Turin 1964, p. 662
60   ADN, DG/88, Giovanni Collina Graziani, 'Faenza nel baratro dei suoi
     665 giorni', 8 September 1944 and *passim*
61   ADN, DG/91, Antonio Borghi, 'Diario di guerra (1943–1945)', 13 May
     1944, 19 October 1944
62   ADN, DP/07, Don Luigi Serravalle, 'Anniversario della mia ordinanza
     sacerdotale', 10 September 1943, 8 November 1943, 11 September 1943,
     26 April 1945
63   ADN, DG/90, Peppino Zangrando, 'Il ragazzo e la trota del Piave',
     p. 24, 29–30 (autumn 1944)
64   Ibid., pp. 28, 30, 33
65   Ibid. pp. 30, 49 (February 1945)
66   Ibid., p. 56 (March 1945)
67   A. Zanella, *L'ora di Dongo*, Rusconi, Milan 1993, pp. 502–3
68   ADN, DG/87, Antal Mazzotti, 'Sotto il tallone nazifascista', 2 March
     1944

69   Ibid., 26 April 1945, 6 May 1945
70   Ibid., 29 April 1945

Epilogue

1   Z. Marazio, *Il mio fascismo. Storia di una donna*, Verdechiaro, Baiso 2005, p. 229

2   L. Garibaldi, *Le soldatesse di Mussolini. Con il memoriale inedito di Piera Gatteschi Fondelli, Generale delle Ausiliarie della RSI*, Mursia, Milan 1995, p. 93

3   Marazio, *Il mio fascismo*, pp. 234–7

4   Ibid., p. 24

5   ADN, DP/99, Carlo Ciseri, 'Diario 1915–84', 23 December 1945

6   L. La Rovere, *L'eredità del fascismo. Gli intellettuali, i giovani e la transizione al postfascismo 1943–1948*, Bollati Boringhieri, Turin 2008, pp. 93–8

7   Ibid., p. 128

8   Ibid., pp. 103–9, 216

9   ADN, DP/Adn2, Bruna Talluri, 'Cronaca di una passione', 10 May 1945

10   Cf. S. Duranti, *Lo spirito gregario. I gruppi universitari fascisti tra politica e propaganda (1930–1940)*, Donzelli, Rome 2008, pp. 10–27

11   P. Ginsborg, *A History of Contemporary Italy. Society and politics 1943–1988*, Allen Lane, London 1990, p. 92

12   C. Pavone, 'La continuità dello Stato. Istituzioni e uomini', in *Italia 1945–48. Le origini della Repubblica*, Giappichelli, Turin 1974, p. 252

13   Ibid., pp. 249, 253

14   Cf. G. Parotto, *Sacra officina. La simbolica religiosa di Silvio Berlusconi*, Franco Angeli, Milan 2007, pp. 15–48

15   http://www.corriere.it/politica/11_dicembre_15/bossi-berlusconi_ae81d932-2723-11e1-853d-c141a33e4620.shtml; *La Repubblica*, 16 December 2011

16   S. Luzzatto, *Il corpo del duce. Un cadavere tra immaginazione, storia e memoria*, Einaudi, Turin 1998, pp. 208–12. Cf. M. Proli, 'Il profondo legame di Adone Zoli con Predappio e la Romagna', in G. Gambetta and S. Mirabella (eds), *Adone Zoli. Un padre della Repubblica*, Bononia University Press, Bologna 2010

17   Cf. R. Zoli and P. Moressa, *Caro Mussolini . . . 1957–2007: cinquant'anni di missive al Duce nella cripta di Predappio*, Raffaelli Editore, Rimini 2007, pp. 40–1. The impression given here is somewhat inflationary.

18   The extracts from the registers for 2005 are from Zoli and Moressa, *Caro Mussolini*. Those for 2006–2012 come directly from the registers

kept in the 'Centro Studi Romano Mussolini' in the Villa Carpena near Forlì. I am grateful to the archivist and owners of the Villa Carpena for permission to consult these registers.

Acknowledgements

The research for this book grew out of a four-year project funded by the Arts and Humanities Research Council: 'The cult of the Duce: Mussolini and the Italians 1918–2005'. I am deeply grateful to the AHRC for its support and to all those involved in the project for creating such a stimulating and friendly forum for research and debate: Professor Stephen Gundle, Dr Giuliana Pieri, Dr Simona Storchi, Dr Sofia Serenelli, Dr Eugene Pooley, Dr Alessandra Antola, Dr Vanessa Roghi, Professor Richard Bosworth. One strand of the project was a study of Mussolini's home town of Predappio in the interwar years: the mayor of Predappio, Giorgio Frassineti, was extraordinarily generous with his assistance and hospitality. A number of colleagues have very kindly read parts or all of the book and I would like to thank them warmly for their helpful comments: Professor Paul Corner, Professor Richard Bosworth, Professor David Forgacs, Professor Stephen Gundle, Dr Francesca Medioli. Will Sulkin at the Bodley Head has been a meticulous, supportive and enormously helpful editor. I am indebted to the staff at a number of archives for their assistance and advice: the Archivio Centrale dello Stato and the Archivio Segreto Vaticano in Rome, the Fondazione Arnoldo and Alberto Mondadori in Milan, and the Archivio della Scrittura Popolare in Trento. Small sections of this book have appeared previously in *The Force of Destiny. A History of Italy since 1796* (Allen Lane, London 2007). I am grateful to the publisher for permission to use them.

I would like to thank the staff of the Archivio Diaristico Nazionale in Pieve Santo Stefano for their help and above all Cristina Cangi for her tireless work in contacting the authors of diaries and memoirs or their families and helping to secure permission to make citations. I am immensely grateful to all those authors and families that generously gave permission to quote from their texts. In a few cases, on the advice of the archive, I have anonymised the diaries. Where this has happened, an indication has been provided in the notes.

The Archivio Diaristico was created in 1984 on the initiative of the distinguished journalist Saverio Tutino as a 'bank' for the memories of ordinary people. Over the years it has built up a collection of around 7,000 diaries, autobiographies and sets of letters of men, women and children from all parts of the country and every walk of life. In order to encourage the recording and depositing of personal memories it stages an annual prize, the Premio Pieve (renamed the Premio Pieve Saverio Tutino recently following the death of the archive's founder), which attracts an enormous amount of media attention. Several countries, including France, Spain, Germany and Belgium, have followed the example of Pieve Santo Stefano and created national repositories for autobiographies. In an age when personal memories are so easy to neglect given the exceptional demands and facility of communication in the present, the establishment of further such centres dedicated to preserving records of how ordinary people acted, felt and thought in different times and contexts would be hugely welcome. And the benefits might not just be for the study of the past. It may be impossible to prevent the world from periodically generating regimes that can perpetrate and justify immense suffering, but the diaries and letters of those who have been caught up in the emotional turmoil of extremism have the capacity to open doors into individual hearts and minds and provide material for sobering and hopefully salutary reflection.

To comment on this book, please go to:
http://blogs.reading.ac.uk/modern-italian-history/

Index